www.wadsworth.com

wadsworth.com is the World Wide Web site for Wadsworth Publishing Company and is your direct source to dozens of online resources.

At *wadsworth.com* you can find out about supplements, demonstration software, and student resources. You can also send e-mail to many of our authors and preview new publications and exciting new technologies.

wadsworth.com
Changing the way the world learns®

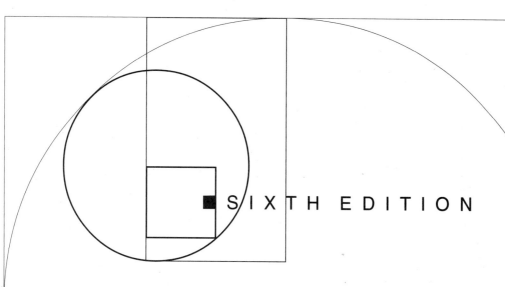

SIXTH EDITION

THEORIES OF HUMAN COMMUNICATION

Stephen W. Littlejohn

Albuquerque, New Mexico

Wadsworth Publishing Company
I(T)P® An International Thomson Publishing Company

Belmont, CA ■ Albany, NY ■ Boston ■ Cincinnati ■ Johannesburg
London ■ Madrid ■ Melbourne ■ Mexico City ■ New York
Pacific Grove, CA ■ Scottsdale, AZ ■ Singapore ■ Tokyo ■ Toronto

Executive Editor: *Deirdre Cavanaugh*
Assistant Editors: *Ryan E. Vesely, Megan Gilbert*
Editorial Assistant: *Matthew Lamm*
Marketing Manager: *Mike Dew*
Marketing Assistant: *Shannon Ryan*
Advertising Project Manager: *Tami Strang*
Project Editor: *Cathy Linberg*
Print Buyer: *Barbara Britton*
Permissions Editor: *Bob Kauser*
Production: *Anne Draus, Scratchgravel Publishing Services*

Designer: *John Edeen*
Copy Editor: *Jennifer Gordon*
Cover Designer: *Laurie Anderson*
Cover: *Wassily Kandinsky,* Circles in a Circle, *1923,*
    Philadelphia Museum of Art: The Louise and Walter
    Arensberg Collection
Compositor: *Scratchgravel Publishing Services*
Cover Printer: *Phoenix Color*
Printer: *R.R. Donnelley & Sons, Crawfordsville*

Printed in the United States of America
1   2   3   4   5   6   7   8   9   10

For more information, contact Wadsworth Publishing Company, 10 Davis Drive, Belmont, CA 94002,
or electronically at http://www.wadsworth.com

International Thomson Publishing Europe
Berkshire House
168-173 High Holborn
London WC1V 7AA, United Kingdom

Nelson ITP, Australia
102 Dodds Street
South Melbourne
Victoria 3205 Australia

Nelson Canada
1120 Birchmount Road
Scarborough, Ontario
Canada M1K 5G4

International Thomson Publishing Southern Africa
Building 18, Constantia Square
138 Sixteenth Road, P.O. Box 2459
Halfway House, 1685 South Africa

International Thomson Editores
Seneca 53
Colonia Polanco
11560 México D. F. México

International Thomson Publishing Asia
60 Albert Street
#15-01 Albert Complex
Singapore 189969

International Thomson Publishing Japan
Hirakawa-cho Kyowa Building, 3F
2-2-1 Hirakawa-cho, Chiyoda-ku
Tokyo 102 Japan

Library of Congress Cataloging-in-Publication Data

Littlejohn, Stephen W.
    Theories of human communication / Stephen W. Littlejohn. — 6th
ed.
        p.   cm.
    Includes bibliographical references and indexes.
    ISBN 0-534-54819-9 (alk. paper)
    1. Communication—Philosophy.   I. Title.
P90.L48   1998   1999
302.2'01—dc21   98-7919

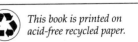

BRIEF CONTENTS

v

DETAILED CONTENTS

PREFACE

This sixth edition of *Theories of Human Communication* continues the tradition of providing a breadth of coverage, upper-level treatment, and balance. My assumption has always been that the study of communication theory at an advanced level requires students to have some facility with ideas, an appreciation for complexity, and general academic experience. Still, like the fifth edition, the preparation of the sixth included continued attention to matters of style and accessibility. I believe graduate students will still find the material "meaty," but undergraduates will find it somewhat more interesting and easier to understand. At the same time, however, much theoretical material is inherently difficult, and while improvement in composition is always possible, I am unwilling to sacrifice subtlety and complexity any more than necessary.

The primary purpose of this revision was to bring the material up to date. This edition includes no major reorganization or re-conceptualization, but adopting faculty will see significant updating of references and coverage over that of previous editions.

The essential features of previous editions have been retained. These include separate treatment of a wide variety of communication theories reflecting the diverse aspects of our field; research examples of many theories; extensive footnotes and bibliography; and Commentary and Critique sections in each chapter.

In each edition of *Theories of Human Communication,* I have written a new capstone chapter that presents a more personal reflection on the subject. In this edition, the new capstone chapter presents my thoughts on what it means to be a student of communication theory. This chapter could be read first or last, and in either case it will provide students with a personal context for the work they will do in this course.

Acknowledgments

I would like to thank the following reviewers of past editions. They are: Richard N. Armstrong, State University of New York, Brockport; Isabelle Bauman, University of Washington; David Brenders, Emerson College; Brant Burleson, Purdue University; Fred L. Casmir, Pepperdine University; Kernneth N.

Cissna, University of South Florida, Tampa; Forrest Conklin, University of Norther Iowa; John E. Crawford, Arizona State University, Tempe; Frank Dance, University of Denver; Loren Dickinson, Walla Walla College; William Donaghy, University of Wyoming; Valerie Downs, Cal State University, Northridge; William Eadie, Cal State University, Northridge; Robert Emmery, California State University, Fullerton; Mary Anne Fitzpatrick, University of Wisconsin, Madison; Kathryn French, Southern Illinois University–Carbondale; Lawrence Frey, Wayne State University; Blaine Goss, University of Oklahoma; Robert Goyer, Arizona State University; Jerold Hale, Miami University; Martha Haun, University of Houston; Dean Hewes, University of Minnesota; Mark Hickson, Mississippi State University; Edward Hinck, Central Michigan University; Randy Hirokawa, University of Iowa; Stephen King, San Diego State University; Devorah Lieberman, Portland State University; Roxanne Parrott, University of Georgia; Jay Rayburn, Florida State University; Rebecca Rubin, Cleveland State University; R. C. Ruechelle, California State College, Stanislaus; Susan Shimanoff, San Francisco State University; Craig Allen Smith, University of North Carolina, Greensboro; Roger Smitter, Albion College; John Sutterhoff, California State University, Chico; and Gordon Whiting, Brigham Young University.

I also thank the reviewers of this edition: Don Ellis, University of Hartford; Larry Haapanen, Lewis-Clark State College; Robert Harrison, Gallaudet University; Jim Hasenauer, California State University at Northridge; and Judith Yaross Lee, Ohio University.

I want to express special appreciation to my research assistant, Sheena Mahlotra, for her many hours of hard work on this edition.

Stephen W. Littlejohn

An Invaluable Aid to Your Study of Communication Theories

The author has prepared—with coauthor Roberta Gray—a student guide entitled *Learning and Using Communication Theories*. This insightful guide helps you achieve a better understanding of theory and its application. Following the organization of this textbook, the guide includes chapter outlines, learning objectives, ideas for theory application, and sample tests to help you prepare for exams.

THEORIES
OF HUMAN
COMMUNICATION

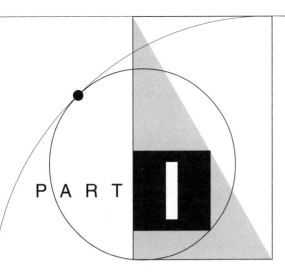

THE NATURE
OF INQUIRY
AND THEORY

PART I

COMMUNICATION THEORY AND SCHOLARSHIP

As long as people have wondered about the world, they have been intrigued by the mysteries of human nature. The most commonplace activities of our lives—the things we take for granted—become great puzzles when we try to understand them. Communication is intertwined with all of human life, and any study of human life must touch on this subject. Some scholars treat communication as central while others see it as more peripheral, but it is always there.

In this book, we treat communication as central to human life. Our guiding question is how scholars from various traditions have described and explained this universal human experience. This book illustrates the quest to understand human social interaction. Although this book does not complete the puzzle of communication, it does show how many of the pieces have been shaped and joined.

WHAT IS COMMUNICATION THEORY?

Any attempt to explain or represent an experience is a theory, an idea of how something happens. Everybody uses theories; we cannot live without them. Our theories guide us in understanding things and deciding how to act, and they change from time to time as we observe new things and acquire new perspectives. Our theories identify patterns of events so we know what to expect. They draw our attention to important aspects of everyday life. They help us decide what is important and what is not. And they enable us to predict what will happen next.

Communication professors often ask their students to explain communication, to say clearly what is happening when people interact and why. Of course, different people see different things, so you will always get different explanations. That is why there are so many theories of communication.

Although the word *theory* can be used to describe the educated guesswork of ordinary people living their everyday lives, a scholar uses the term more precisely. A scholar's work involves studying a particular kind of experience with a keen eye. A scholar's theory, which is based on systematic observation, is his or her best representation of the subject being studied. As you will see in the next chapter, theory building is not an easy task but requires a great deal of focused observation, hypothesizing, and revision.

The term *communication theory* can refer to a single theory, or it can be used to designate the collective wisdom found in the entire body of theories related to the communication process. Most courses titled "Communication Theory" cover a wide variety of approaches to the topic.

Much disagreement exists about what constitutes an adequate theory of communication. This textbook presents a wide variety of theories, discussed in terms of their assumptions, claims, strengths, and weaknesses. As you read through the book, you will make your own judgments about which theories are most helpful.

⬤ WHY STUDY COMMUNICATION THEORY?

Communication is one of the most pervasive, important, and complex aspects of human life. The ability to communicate on a higher level separates humans from other animals. Our daily lives are strongly affected by our own communication with others as well as by messages from people we don't even know, living and dead, from many parts of the world. Because communica-

tion is so vital to our lives, surely it deserves our careful attention.

Teachers sometimes provide students with a set of recipes for improving communication, but the communication process is too complicated to be approached in this way. Formulas may be useful in particular situations, but they inevitably fail as circumstances become complex. Theories are crucial because they permit us to make our way through what may be a rather difficult thicket.

Everybody tries to make sense of their own experience. We assign meaning to what is going on, both inside us and around us. Sometimes the meaning is shared, and sometimes it is not. Sometimes it is clear and other times vague or contradictory. By developing an understanding of a variety of theories of communication, we interpret events in more flexible, useful, and discriminating ways.

A colleague of mine used to say that the study of communication theory will help students see things they never saw before. One writer put it this way: "The paradigm observer is not the man who sees and reports what all normal observers see and report, but the man who sees in familiar objects what no one else has seen before."[1] This widening of perception, or unhitching of blinders, helps us transcend habits and become increasingly adaptable and flexible. To borrow some analogies from philosopher Thomas Kuhn, "Looking at a contour map, the student sees lines on paper, the cartographer a picture of a terrain. Looking at a bubble-chamber photograph, the student sees confused and broken lines, the physicist a record of familiar subnuclear events."[2] Theories, then, provide a set of useful tools for seeing new and useful things.

---

1   N. R. Hanson, *Patterns of Discovery* (Cambridge: Cambridge University Press, 1961), p. 30.
2   Thomas S. Kuhn, *The Structure of Scientific Revolutions* (Chicago: University of Chicago Press, 1970), p. 111.

THE ACADEMIC STUDY OF COMMUNICATION

Although communication has been studied since antiquity,[3] it became an especially important topic in the twentieth century. One author describes this development as a "revolutionary discovery," largely caused by the rise of communication technologies such as radio, television, telephone, satellites, and computer networking, along with industrialization, big business, and global politics.[4] Clearly, communication has assumed immense importance in our time.

Intense interest in the academic study of communication began after World War I, as advances in technology and literacy made communication a topic of concern.[5] The subject was further promoted by the popular twentieth-century philosophies of progressivism and pragmatism, which stimulated a desire to improve society through widespread social change.

Several developments led to this interest in communication. The political influence of public messages spurred considerable research on propaganda and public opinion. In the early part of this century, researchers began attitude and opinion studies to try to discover the extent to which public opinion could be influenced by the media.

During this same period, the social sciences were developing, and sociology and social psychology emerged as leaders in the study of communication. Much of the research in sociology in the 1930s investigated the ways in which communication affects individuals and communities. Popular research topics in social psychology included the effects of movies on children, propaganda and persuasion, and group dynamics.

Another research tradition in the early part of the century centered on education. Some areas of special emphasis were the use of radio in education, the teaching of basic communication skills like public speaking and group discussion, and the effects of various kinds of communication in the classroom.

The first half of the twentieth century was also dominated by commercial interests such as advertising. Much of the early research, even in universities, was driven by the desire of people in business to know more about communication for marketing purposes.

After World War II, the social sciences became fully recognized as legitimate disciplines, and the interest in psychological and social processes became intense. Persuasion and decision making in groups were central concerns, not only among researchers but in society in general. After World War II, then, communication studies became quite important.

The approaches to the study of communication, however, took different turns in Europe and the United States. In the United States, researchers tended to study communication quantitatively to try to achieve objectivity. Although the researchers were never in complete agreement on this objective ideal, quantitative methods were the standard for many years. European investigations, on the other hand, were influenced more by historical, cultural, and critical interests and were largely shaped by Marxism. Over the years, tension has grown between these two traditions, although considerable influence has flowed both ways as scientific procedures have developed a toehold in Europe and critical perspectives have been taken seriously in North America.

The study of communication as we understand it in the United States and in Europe is thoroughly Western. Virtually all the theories

3   See, for example, John Stewart, *Language as Articulate Contact* (Albany: SUNY Press, 1995), pp. 33–101; W. Barnett Pearce and Karen A. Foss, "The Historical Context of Communication as a Science," in *Human Communication: Theory and Research*, eds. G. L. Dahnke and G. W. Clatterbuck (Belmont, CA: Wadsworth, 1990), pp. 1–20; Nancy Harper, *Human Communication Theory: The History of a Paradigm* (Rochelle Park, NJ: Hayden, 1979).
4   W. Barnett Pearce, *Communication and the Human Condition* (Carbondale: Southern Illinois University Press, 1989).
5   This brief history is based on Jesse G. Delia, "Communication Research: A History," in *Handbook of Communication Science*, eds. C. R. Berger and S. H. Chaffee (Newbury Park, CA: Sage, 1987), pp. 20–98. See also the symposium, John Durham Peters (ed.), "Tangled Legacies," *Journal of Communication* 46 (1996): 85–147; Everett M. Rogers, *A History of Communication Study: A Biographical Approach* (New York: Free Press, 1994).

discussed in this book come from the Western academic tradition. Eastern ways of thinking, however, can also contribute to our understanding of communication. In a valuable and interesting treatment, Lawrence Kincaid contrasts a variety of Western and Eastern perspectives on communication theory.[6]

Kincaid notes a number of differences between Asian and Western perspectives.[7] For one, Eastern theories tend to focus on wholeness and unity, whereas Western perspectives are preoccupied with measuring parts and do not integrate these parts into a unified process.

Second, much Western theory is dominated by a vision of individualism. People are considered to be active in achieving personal aims. Most Eastern theories, on the other hand, view communication outcomes as unplanned and natural consequences of events. Even the many Western theories that share the Asian preoccupation with unintended events tend to be individualistic and highly cognitive, whereas most Eastern traditions stress emotional and spiritual convergence as communication outcomes.

A third difference deals with language and thought. Most Western theories are dominated by language. In the East, verbal symbols, especially speech, are downplayed and viewed with skepticism. Western-style thinking is also mistrusted in the Eastern tradition. What counts in many Asian philosophies is intuitive insight gained from direct experience. Such insight can be acquired by not intervening in natural events, which explains why silence is so important in Eastern communication.

Finally, relationships are conceptualized differently in the two traditions. In Western thought, relationships exist between two or more individuals. In many Eastern traditions, relationships are between social positions of role, status, and power.

Many universities and colleges now have departments of communication, speech communication, or mass communication, but the subject remains largely eclectic and multidisciplinary. The diversity of work in communication theory reflects the complexity of communication itself. Looking for the best theory of communication is not particularly useful since communication is more than one activity.

Each theory looks at the process from a different angle, and each provides insights of its own. Of course, all theories are not equally valid or useful, and an investigator will find particular theories more useful than others for certain kinds of work. We should therefore welcome rather than avoid a multitheoretical orientation.[8]

Still, the tendency to view communication from the narrow confines of specific academic disciplines is strong. Because fields are somewhat arbitrary, traditional disciplines do not necessarily provide the best method of packaging knowledge. Interdisciplinary cooperation is essential for a useful understanding of this subject.[9] University courses related to communication are found in many departments, just as the theories described in this book represent a wide range of fields. As Dean Barnlund observes, "While many disciplines have undoubtedly benefited from adopting a communication model, it is equally true that they, in turn, have added greatly to our understanding of human interaction."[10] Remember that when people tell you they are communication experts, they are saying little. Their primary interests may be in the sciences or the arts, mathematics or literature, biology or politics.[11]

---

6   D. Lawrence Kincaid, *Communication Theory: Eastern and Western Perspectives* (San Diego: Academic, 1987).

7   Kincaid, *Communication Theory*, pp. 331–353.

8   For an excellent case in favor of multiple approaches to communication, see John Waite Bowers and James J. Bradac, "Issues in Communication Theory: A Metatheoretical Analysis," in *Communication Yearbook 5*, ed. M. Burgoon (New Brunswick, NJ: Transaction, 1982), pp. 1–28.

9   For an exploration of the value of treating communication as an interdisciplinary study, see Thomas Streeter, "Introduction: For the Study of Communication and Against the Discipline of Communication," *Communication Theory* 5 (1995): 117–129; and David Sholle, "Resisting Disciplines: Repositioning Media Studies in the University," *Communication Theory* 5 (1995): 130–143.

10   Dean Barnlund, *Interpersonal Communication: Survey and Studies* (New York: Houghton Mifflin, 1968), p. v.

11   The multidisciplinary nature of the study of communication is examined in Stephen W. Littlejohn, "An Overview of the Contributions to Human Communication Theory from Other Disciplines," in *Human Communication Theory: Comparative Essays*, ed.

Researchers in most fields consider communication as a secondary process. For example, psychologists study individual behavior and view communication as a particular kind of behavior. Sociologists focus on society and social process, seeing communication as one of many social factors. Anthropologists are interested primarily in culture, and if they investigate communication, they treat it as an aspect of a broader theme. Do we conclude that communication is less significant than behavior, society, and culture? No, we do not.

In recent years many scholars have recognized that communication is central to all human experience and have emphasized it above other topics. Some of these scholars were trained in traditional disciplines, and others studied in academic departments of communication, speech communication, or mass communication. Regardless of their original academic homes, however, these scholars have formed the new field called communication.[12] This field is characterized by its focus on communication as the central topic and by its attention to the entire breadth of communication concerns. The work of such organizations as the International Communication Association and the National Communication Association, along with numerous journals devoted to the topic, typify what is happening in the field. Indeed, the young communication field is now producing fresh theories, many of which are covered in this textbook.

◖ DEFINING COMMUNICATION

Communication is difficult to define. The word is abstract and, like most terms, possesses numerous meanings.[13] Theodore Clevenger has noted that "the continuing problem in defining communication for scholarly or scientific purposes stems from the fact that the verb 'to communicate' is well established in the common lexicon and therefore is not easily captured for scientific use. Indeed, it is one of the most over-worked terms in the English language."[14] Scholars have made many attempts to define communication, but establishing a single definition has proved impossible and may not be very fruitful.

Frank Dance took a major step toward clarifying this muddy concept by outlining a number of basic elements used to distinguish communication.[15] He found three points of "critical conceptual differentiation" that form the basic dimensions of communication. The first dimension is *level of observation*, or abstractness. Some definitions are broad and inclusive; others are restrictive. For example, the definition of communication as "the process that links discontinuous parts of the living world to one another" is quite general.[16] On the other hand, communication as "the means of sending military messages, orders, etc., as by telephone, telegraph, radio, couriers," is restrictive.[17]

The second distinction is *intentionality*. Some definitions include only purposeful message sending and receiving; others do not impose this limitation. The following is an example of a definition that includes intention: "Those situations in which a source transmits a message to a receiver with conscious intent to affect the latter's

F. E. X. Dance (New York: Harper & Row, 1982), pp. 243–285; and W. Barnett Pearce, "Scientific Research Methods in Communication Studies and Their Implications for Theory and Research," in *Speech Communication in the 20th Century*, ed. T. W. Benson (Carbondale: Southern Illinois University Press, 1985), pp. 255–281.

12   For a recent discussion of the status of the communication field, see Tony Atwater, "Communication Theory and Research: The Quest for Credibility in the Social Sciences," in *An Integrated Approach to Communication Theory*, eds. M. B. Salwen and D. W. Stacks (Mahwah, NJ: Erlbaum, 1996), pp. 539–549; and Stanley A. Deetz, "Future of the Discipline: The Challenges, the Research, and the Social Contribution," in *Communication Yearbook 17*, ed. S. A. Deetz (Thousand Oaks, CA: Sage, 1994), pp. 565–600.

13   There are 126 definitions of communication listed in Frank E. X. Dance and Carl E. Larson, *The Functions of Human Communication: A Theoretical Approach* (New York: Holt, Rinehart & Winston, 1976), Appendix A.

14   Theodore Clevenger, Jr., "Can One Not Communicate? A Conflict of Models," *Communication Studies* 42 (1991): 351.

15   Frank E. X. Dance, "The 'Concept' of Communication," *Journal of Communication* 20 (1970): 201–210.

16   Jurgen Ruesch, "Technology and Social Communication," in *Communication Theory and Research*, ed. L. Thayer (Springfield, IL: Thomas, 1957), p. 462.

17   *The American College Dictionary* (New York: Random House, 1964), p. 244.

behaviors."[18] A definition that does not require intent is this one: "It is a process that makes common to two or several what was the monopoly of one or some."[19]

The third dimension is normative *judgment.* Some definitions include a statement of success or accuracy; other definitions do not contain such implicit judgments. The following definition, for example, presumes that communication is successful: "Communication is the verbal interchange of a thought or idea."[20] The assumption in this definition is that a thought or idea is successfully exchanged. Another definition, on the other hand, does not judge whether the outcome is successful or not: "Communication [is] the transmission of information."[21] Here information is *transmitted,* but it is not necessarily *received* or understood.

Debates on the definition of communication are perennial. Figure 1.1 shows nine behaviors that might be considered to be communication.[22] These nine behaviors hinge on how two questions are answered: (1) Must communication be intentional? (2) Must communication be received? The columns in the figure consist of intentional and unintentional behaviors, and the rows indicate whether the source behaviors were received.

In Figure 1.1, the first column is source behaviors that are unintentional. These are "symptomatic" because they could be read as a sign of some state in the communicator such as fatigue, nervousness, or anger. The second column denotes nonverbal behaviors that are intentionally sent to another person, such as waving to a friend or shrugging if you don't know the answer to a question. The third column includes intentional verbal, or language-oriented, acts, such as writing a letter, having a conversation, or giving a speech.

The three rows in Figure 1.1 represent whether the message is received. The first row is "not received," meaning that no one observes the source's actions or hears the message. How many times have you yawned or maybe even said, "I'm tired," but no one was there to see or hear it? The

second consists of incidental reception, in which someone sees something but it does not register consciously. You might say to a friend, "I'm tired," and your friend would realize that you had looked tired, though she had not paid attention to it at the time. The third row is paying conscious attention to the source's behaviors.

Now we have nine things that might possibly be considered communication:

1A. Nonperceived symptomatic behavior—you yawn, but no one sees it. (Most people agree that this is not communication. At least it is not *interpersonal* communication, but some might call it *intrapersonal* communication.)

1B. Incidentally perceived symptoms—you yawn, and your friend later realizes that you were tired even though she didn't pay any attention to it at the time.

1C. Symptoms attended to—you yawn, and your friend says, "Am I that boring?"

2A. Nonperceived nonverbal messages—you wave at a friend, but he doesn't see you.

2B. Incidental nonverbal messages—your friend later says, "I'm sorry I didn't wave back, but I was thinking about something else and didn't realize you had waved to me until after I turned the corner."

18   Gerald R. Miller, "On Defining Communication: Another Stab," *Journal of Communication* 16 (1966): 92.
19   Alex Gode, "What Is Communication?" *Journal of Communication* 9 (1959): 5.
20   John B. Hoben, "English Communication at Colgate Re-Examined," *Journal of Communication* 4 (1954): 77.
21   Bernard Berelson and Gary Steiner, *Human Behavior* (New York: Harcourt, Brace, and World, 1964), p. 254.
22   Michael T. Motley, "On Whether One Can (Not) Communicate: An Examination Via Traditional Communication Postulates," *Western Journal of Speech Communication* 54 (1990): 1–20; Janet Beavin Bavelas, "Behaving and Communicating: A Reply to Motley," *Western Journal of Speech Communication* 54 (1990): 593–602; Wayne A. Beach, "On (Not) Observing Behavior Interactionally," *Western Journal of Speech Communication* 54 (1990): 603–612; Michael T. Motley, "Communication as Interaction: A Reply to Beach and Bavelas," *Western Journal of Speech Communication* 54 (1990): 613–623; Peter A. Andersen, "When One Cannot Not Communicate: A Challenge to Motley's Traditional Communication Postulates," *Communication Studies* 42 (1991): 309–325; Michael T. Motley, "How One May Not Communicate: A Reply to Andersen," *Communication Studies* 42 (1991): 326–339; Clevenger, "Can One Not Communicate?"

	SOURCE BEHAVIOR		
RECEIVER BEHAVIOR	Unintentional Behavior (Symptoms)	Intentional Behavior	
		Nonverbal	Verbal
Not Received	1A Nonperceived symptomatic behavior	2A Nonperceived nonverbal messages	3A Nonperceived verbal messages
Received Incidentally	1B Incidentally perceived symptoms	2B Incidental nonverbal messages	3B Incidental verbal messages
Attended To	1C Symptoms attended to	2C Nonverbal messages attended to	3C Verbal messages attended to

FIGURE **1.1**

Communication-Related Behaviors

2C. Nonverbal messages attended to—you wave to a friend, and she waves back.

3A. Nonperceived verbal messages—you send a letter to a friend, but it gets lost in the mail.

3B. Incidental verbal messages—you lecture your daughter for having a messy room, and although she knows you are talking to her, she really isn't paying much attention.

3C. Verbal messages attended to—you give a speech to a group that is eager to hear what you have to say.

Which of the above acts are communication and which are not? At least three defensible positions can be taken. The first, espoused by Michael Motley, is that communication should be limited to messages that are intentionally directed at other persons and received by them.[23] Of the nine types of behavior, Motley would limit communication to those cells outlined in Figure 1.2(a). The second position, promoted by Peter Andersen, is that communication should include any behaviors that are meaningful to receivers in any way, whether intended or not.[24] These would include the cells outlined in Figure 1.2(b). Finally, Clevenger agrees with Motley that only intentionally sent messages that are received should count as communication but that intentionality is hard to determine. He suggests that communication behavior should include both intentional sending and receiving, which would include even more cells, as outlined in Figure 1.2(c).[25]

23   Motley, "On Whether One Can(Not) Communicate"; "Communication as Interaction"; "How One May Not Communicate."
24   Andersen, "When One Cannot Not Communicate."
25   Clevenger, "Can One Not Communicate?"

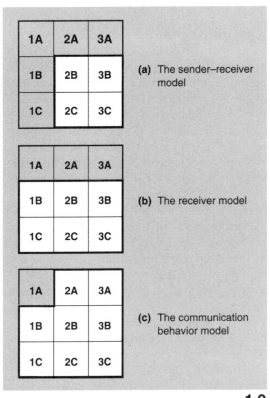

1A	2A	3A
1B	2B	3B
1C	2C	3C

(a) The sender–receiver model

1A	2A	3A
1B	2B	3B
1C	2C	3C

(b) The receiver model

1A	2A	3A
1B	2B	3B
1C	2C	3C

(c) The communication behavior model

FIGURE **1.2**

What Is Communication and What Is Not?

You can see that these three authors—and this is true of virtually all communication scholars—agree that intentional acts that are received do count as communication, but they disagree on what else might be considered communication.

These definitional issues are important, as Andersen reminds us: "While there is not a right or wrong perspective, choices regarding [definitions] are not trivial. These perspectives launch scholars down different theoretical trajectories, predispose them to ask distinct questions, and set them up to conduct different kinds of communication studies."[26] Different definitions have different functions and enable the theorist to do different things. A definition should be evaluated on the basis of how well it helps a scholar to accomplish the purposes of an investigation. Different sorts of investigations often require sepa-

rate, even contradictory, definitions of communication. Definitions, then, are tools that should be used flexibly. In this book we will look at theories that define communication in a variety of ways.

Dance's conclusion is relevant: "We are trying to make the concept of 'communication' do too much work for us."[27] He calls for a family of concepts; collectively, the theories included in the following chapters specify some of the members of this family.

⬤ THE PROCESS OF INQUIRY IN COMMUNICATION

Inquiry is the systematic study of experience that leads to understanding and knowledge. People engage in inquiry when they attempt to find out about something in an orderly way. It is not just one process, of course. Many modes can be used, but all are distinguished from common experience.

A Basic Model of Inquiry

All inquiry involves three stages.[28] The first is asking questions. Gerald Miller and Henry Nicholson believe that inquiry is "nothing more . . . than the process of asking interesting, significant questions . . . and providing disciplined, systematic answers to them."[29] Questions of *definition* call for concepts as answers, seeking to clarify what is observed or inferred (What is it? What will we call it?). Questions of *fact* ask about properties and relations in what is observed (What does it consist of? How does it relate to other things?). Questions of *value* probe aesthetic,

---

26   Andersen, "When One Cannot Not Communicate," p. 309.
27   Dance, "The 'Concept' of Communication," p. 210.
28   The process of inquiry is described in Gerald R. Miller and Henry Nicholson, *Communication Inquiry* (Reading, MA: Addison-Wesley, 1976).
29   Miller and Nicholson, *Communication Inquiry*, p. ix. See also, Don W. Stacks and Michael B. Salwen, "Integrating Theory and Research: Starting with Questions," in *An Integrated Approach to Communication Theory and Research*, eds. M. B. Salwen and D. W. Stacks (Mahwah, NJ: Erlbaum, 1996), pp. 3–14.

pragmatic, and ethical qualities of the observed (Is it beautiful? Is it effective? Is it good?).

The second stage of inquiry is *observation*. Here, the scholar looks for an answer. Methods of observation vary significantly from one tradition to another. Some scholars observe by examining records and artifacts, others by personal involvement, others by using instruments and controlled experiment, others by interviewing people. Whatever is used, the investigator employs some planned method for answering the questions.

The third stage of inquiry is *constructing answers*. Here, the scholar attempts to define, to describe and explain, to make judgments. This stage is usually referred to as *theory* and is the focus of this book.

People often think of the stages of inquiry as linear, occurring one step at a time—first questions, then observations, and finally answers. But inquiry does not proceed in this fashion. Each stage affects and is affected by the others. Observations often stimulate new questions, and theories are challenged by both observations and questions. Theories lead to new questions, and observations are determined in part by theories. Inquiry, then, is more like running around a circle than walking in a straight line. Figure 1.3 illustrates the interaction among the stages of inquiry.

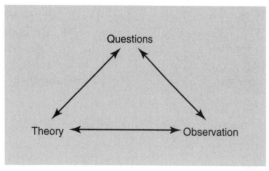

Questions

Theory ⟷ Observation

FIGURE **1.3**

The Stages of Inquiry

Types of Scholarship

The preceding section outlines the basic elements of inquiry, but it ignores important differences. Different types of inquiry ask different questions, use different methods of observation, and lead to different kinds of theory. Methods of inquiry can be grouped into three broad forms of scholarship: scientific, humanistic, and social scientific.[30] Although these forms of scholarship share the common elements discussed in the previous section, they also have major differences.[31]

Scientific Scholarship.   Science often is associated with objectivity. Is science really objective? If by objectivity you mean suspension of values, science definitely is not objective. However, if by objectivity you mean standardization, science is indeed objective, or, more accurately, it aims to be objective. The scientist attempts to look at the world in such a way that all other observers, trained the same way and using the same methods, would see the same thing. Replications of a study should yield identical results.

Standardization and replication are important in science because scientists assume that the world has observable form, and they view their task as seeing the world as it is. The world sits in wait of discovery, and the goal of science is to observe and explain the world as accurately as possible. Because there is no divinely revealed way to know how accurate one's observations are, the scientist must rely on agreement among observers. This is why objectivity and replicability are so important. If all trained observers report the same results, we feel confident that the object has been accurately observed. Because of the empha-

30   An excellent discussion of scholarship can be found in Ernest G. Bormann, *Theory and Research in the Communicative Arts* (New York: Holt, Rinehart & Winston, 1965). See also Nathan Glazer, "The Social Sciences in Liberal Education," in *The Philosophy of the Curriculum,* ed. S. Hook (Buffalo: Prometheus, 1975), pp. 145–158; James L. Jarrett, *The Humanities and Humanistic Education* (Reading, MA: Addison-Wesley, 1973); Gerald Holton, "Science, Science Teaching, and Rationality," in *The Philosophy of the Curriculum,* ed. S. Hook (Buffalo: Prometheus, 1975), pp. 101–108.
31   See, for example, C. P. Snow, *The Two Cultures and a Second Look* (Cambridge: Cambridge University Press, 1964).

sis on discovering a knowable world, scientific methods are especially well suited to problems of nature.

Humanistic Scholarship.   Whereas science is associated with objectivity, the humanities are associated with subjectivity. Science aims to standardize observation; the humanities seek creative individuality. If the aim of science is to reduce human differences in what is observed, the aim of the humanities is to understand individual subjective response.[32] Most humanists are more interested in individual cases than generalized theory.

Whereas science is an "out there" activity, the humanities stress the "in here." Science focuses on the discovered world; the humanities focus on the discovering person. Science seeks consensus; the humanities seek alternative interpretations. Humanists often are suspicious of the claim that there is an immutable world to be discovered, and they tend not to separate the knower from the known. The classical humanistic position is that who one is determines what one sees. Because of its emphasis on the subjective response, humanistic scholarship is especially well suited to problems of art, personal experience, and values.

Science and the humanities are not so far apart that they never come together. Almost any program of research and theory building includes some aspects of both scientific and humanistic scholarship. At times the scientist is a humanist, using intuition, creativity, interpretation, and insight. Ironically, the scientist must be subjective in creating the methods that will eventually lead to objective observation, making research design a creative process. In turn, at times the humanist must be scientific, seeking facts that enable experience to be understood. As we will see in the next section, the point where science leaves off and the humanities begin is not always clear.

The Special Case of the Social Sciences.   A third form of scholarship is the social sciences.

Although many social scientists see it as an extension of natural science, using methods borrowed from physics, social science is a world apart.[33] Paradoxically, it includes elements of both science and the humanities but is different from both.[34]

In seeking to observe and interpret patterns of human behavior, social scholars make human beings the object of study. To understand human behavior, the scholar must observe it. If behavioral patterns do in fact exist, then observation must be as objective as possible. In other words, the social scientist—like the natural scientist—must establish consensus on what is observed. Once the behavioral phenomena are accurately observed, they must be explained or interpreted.

Interpreting may be complicated by the fact that the object of observation, the human subject, is itself an active, knowing being. Unlike objects in the natural world, the human subject is capable of having knowledge, possessing values, making interpretations, and taking action. Can "scientific" explanation of human behavior take place without consideration of the "humanistic" knowledge of the observed person? This question is the central philosophical issue of social science and has provoked considerable concern and debate akin to an identity crisis.[35] In the

---

32   James A. Diefenbeck, *A Celebration of Subjective Thought* (Carbondale: Southern Illinois University Press, 1984).
33   See, for example, Charles R. Berger and Steven H. Chaffee (eds.), "The Study of Communication as a Science," in *Handbook of Communication Science* (Newbury Park, CA: Sage, 1987), pp. 15–19. For an interesting discussion of the scientific nature of communication research, see Glenn G. Sparks, W. James Potter, Roger Cooper, and Michel Dupagne, "Is Media Research Prescientific?" in *Communication Theory* 5 (1995): 273–289.
34   See, for example, Robert T. Craig, "Why Are There So Many Communication Theories?" *Journal of Communication* 43 (1993): 26–33; Hubert M. Blalock, *Basic Dilemmas in the Social Sciences* (Beverly Hills, CA: Sage, 1984), p. 15; Anthony Giddens, *Profiles and Critiques in Social Theory* (Berkeley: University of California Press, 1983), p. 133; Peter Winch, *The Idea of a Social Science and Its Relation to Philosophy* (London: Routledge & Kegan Paul, 1958).
35   See, for example, Klaus Krippendorff, "Conversation or Intellectual Imperialism in Comparing Communication (Theories)," *Communication Theory* 3 (1993): 252–266; Donald W. Fiske and Richard A. Shweder (eds.), "Introduction: Uneasy Social Science," in *Metatheory in Social Science: Pluralisms and Subjectivities* (Chicago: University of Chicago Press, 1986), pp. 1–18; Kenneth J. Gergen, *Toward Transformation in Social Knowledge* (New York: Springer-Verlag, 1982).

past, the majority of social scientists believed that scientific methods alone would suffice to uncover the mysteries of human experience, but today many realize that a strong humanistic element is also needed.

Communication as a Social Science.   Communication involves understanding how people behave in creating, exchanging, and interpreting messages. Consequently, communication inquiry combines both scientific and humanistic methods.[36] The theories covered in this book, as examples of social science, vary significantly in the extent to which they use scientific or humanistic elements. Traditionally, humanistic theories of communication have been referred to as rhetorical theory and scientific theories as communication theory. This distinction is not particularly useful. All theories we will discuss deal with human communication, and both humanistic and scientific theories are worthy of inclusion in our body of knowledge about human communication.

◖ ORGANIZING COMMUNICATION THEORY

One of the most daunting tasks facing a student of communication theory is how to organize this huge body of material, for it defies clear classification. No system of categories is perfectly appropriate for organizing this material, although several schemes could, with qualification, be used.

In this section we look at four ways of organizing communication theory: by genres, or philosophical approaches; by level; by the categories of core theory; and by the structure of the field.

Genres of Communication Theory

In this section, we look at a five-part model of communication theory that can help us see the similarities and differences among these schemes. These genres capture some important

philosophical similarities and differences among the communication theories now in vogue. They also parallel the current philosophies in the social sciences.

These categories are not pure, however, and you will detect similarities and overlaps among them.[37] Anderson calls such categories "conventionalized theory domains," or "theory families."[38]

Structural and Functional Theories.   This genre includes a broad group of loosely associated approaches to social science. Although the meanings of the terms *structuralism* and *functionalism* are imprecise, they generally designate the belief that social structures are real and function in ways that can be observed objectively.[39]

---

36   This position is developed in Thomas B. Farrell, "Beyond Science: Humanities Contributions to Communication Theory," in *Handbook of Communication Science*, eds. C. R. Berger and S. H. Chaffee (Newbury Park, CA: Sage, 1987), pp. 123–139.

37   Many typologies of scholarship have been developed. For a discussion of the problems involved in describing differences, see Stanley Deetz, "Describing Differences in Approaches to Organization Science," *Organization Science* 7 (1996): 191–207. See also Fred R. Dallmayr, *Language and Politics* (Notre Dame, IN: University of Notre Dame Press, 1984); Lawrence Grossberg, "Does Communication Theory Need Intersubjectivity? Toward an Immanent Philosophy of Interpersonal Relations," in *Communication Yearbook 6*, ed. M. Burgoon (Beverly Hills, CA: Sage, 1984), pp. 171–205; and John Stewart, "Speech and Human Being," *Quarterly Journal of Speech* 72 (1986): 55–73. These categories also approximate those of Gibson Winter, *Elements for a Social Ethic: Scientific and Ethical Perspectives on Social Process* (New York: Macmillan, 1966). Winter's scheme was later elaborated by Richard McKeon, "Gibson Winter's Elements for a Social Ethic: A Review," *Journal of Religion* 49 (1969): 77–84; and by Ted J. Smith III, "Diversity and Order in Communication Theory: The Uses of Philosophical Analysis," *Communication Quarterly* 36 (1988): 28–40. The above categories are also similar to the model by G. Burrell and G. Morgan, *Sociological Paradigms and Organizational Analysis* (London: Heinemann, 1979). For an elaboration of the Burrell and Morgan model, see Karl Erik Rosengren, "From Field to Frog Ponds," *Journal of Communication* 43 (1993): 6–17; and Karl Erik Rosengren, "Culture, Media, and Society: Agency and Structure, Continuity and Change," in *Media Effects and Beyond*, ed. Karl Erik Rosengren (London: Routledge, 1994), pp. 3–28.

38   James A. Anderson, *Communication Theory: Epistemological Foundations* (New York: Guilford, 1996), p. 9.

39   For an excellent discussion of structualism and functionalism, see Anthony Giddens, *Central Problems in Social Theory* (Berkeley: University of California Press, 1979). The distinction between structural and functional theory is clearly made by Paul E. Meehl, "What Social Scientists Don't Understand," in *Metatheory in Social Science: Pluralisms and Subjectivities*, eds. D. W. Fiske and R. A. Shweder (Chicago: University of Chicago Press, 1986), pp. 317–319. For a discussion of functionalism in communication studies, see Carl Patrick Burrowes, "From Functionalism to Cultural Studies: Manifest Ruptures and Latent Continuities," *Communication Theory* 6 (1996): 88–103.

For example, a communication researcher might assume that personal relationships are organized in particular ways, just as a house consists of materials combined according to a plan. Here the relationship is viewed as a social structure. The researcher would further assume that the relationship is not static, but that it has attributes such as bonding, dependency, power, trust, and so forth.

Structuralism and functionalism go back at least as far as Plato,[40] who believed that truth is ascertained through careful reflective thought, and Aristotle,[41] who believed that knowledge is obtained through observation and classification.

System theory (Chapter 3) is firmly planted in the structural-functional tradition.[42] Modern structuralism generally recognizes Emile Durkheim, who emphasized the concept of social structure, and Ferdinand de Saussure, founder of structural linguistics, as key figures.[43]

Although structuralism and functionalism are often considered in combination, they differ in emphasis. Structuralism, which is rooted in linguistics, stresses the organization of language and social systems. Functionalism, which is rooted in biology, stresses the ways organized systems work to sustain themselves. Systems consist of variables that are causally related to other variables in a network of relations. A change in one variable creates change in others. Putting these two approaches together results in the depiction of a system as a structure of elements with functional relations. For example, organizational communication researchers would see an organization as a system of related parts such as departments, rankings, climate, work activities, and products. These parts combine to produce certain effects such as communication accuracy and satisfaction.

Structural and functional theories share certain characteristics. First, they assume stability

over time, which is called *synchrony,* rather than assuming change, or *diachrony.* For example, researchers have found that higher status individuals in an organization will often violate the territory of lower status individuals, but that lower status individuals will rarely violate the territory of higher status employees.

A second feature of the structural-functional approach is its focus on the unintended consequences of action rather than purposeful outcomes. Structuralists mistrust concepts like "subjectivity" and "consciousness" and look for factors beyond the control and awareness of the persons involved. For this reason, such theories are sometimes called antihumanist. To return to the example of organizational communication, a structuralist would be more interested in features of the organization that are outside the awareness and control of workers, such as the naturally occurring networks that have evolved but were not planned.

Third, such theorists share a belief in independent reality. They subscribe to the discovery method discussed earlier in the chapter, in which knowledge is discovered through careful observation. How would we know, for example, that status and territorial violation are related? We know by figuring out how to measure status, how to observe territorial behavior, and how to correlate these two variables.

Fourth, the theories tend to separate language and symbols from the thoughts and objects being symbolized. This tendency is an example of *dualism* because it implies two distinct parts—the object and the symbol. The world exists in and of itself, and language is just a tool for representing what is already there. So when organizational theorists give names to aspects of an organization—such as hierarchy, status, and networks—they make a clear correspondence between the terms and what has been observed in research.

Dualism necessitates the fifth characteristic—the use of the correspondence theory of truth. The *correspondence theory* states that language must correspond with reality; symbols must accurately represent things. So, for example, we must be very careful that our terms are precise.

40 *Meno.*
41 *Prior Analytics; Posterior Analytics.*
42 G. W. F. Hegel, *Phenomenology of Spirit,* trans. A. V. Miller (Oxford: Oxford University Press, 1977).
43 Emile Durkheim, *The Division of Labor in Society* (London: Collier-Macmillan, 1964); Ferdinand de Saussure, *Course in General Linguistics* (London: Peter Owen, 1960).

We would want the terms *status* and *territorial violation* to be clear and unambiguous.

Structural and functional theorists see communication as a process in which individuals use language to convey meanings to others. The language and symbol systems used in communication have a life of their own apart from the people who employ these tools. Predictably then, structuralists judge good communication as accurate and clear and view communication competence as the accurate, precise, and skillful use of language and other symbols.

These ideas have been extremely influential in the field of communication and have set the tone for how many scholars in the United States view communication today. In recent years, however, communication theories of this genre have come under scrutiny, and other traditions have assumed equal importance.

Cognitive and Behavioral Theories.   Like its structural-functional cousin, this genre is a combination of two traditions that are not the same but share many characteristics. The primary difference between the two genres is in their focus and history. Structural and functional theories tend to focus on social and cultural structures, whereas cognitive and behavioral theories tend to focus on the individual.

Psychology is the primary source of the cognitive and behavioral theories of human life. Traditionally, psychological behaviorism has dealt with the connection between stimuli, or inputs, and behavioral responses, or outputs—the relationship, say, between rewards and learning. Cognitivism recognizes the stimulus–response link but takes it one step further by emphasizing the information processing that occurs between the two. The term *cognition* refers to thinking or mind, so cognitivism focuses on how people think. Until the mid-1960s or so, *behaviorism* was the favored term. Today, most psychologists and communication scholars of this tradition identify themselves as *cognitivists*.[44]

Cognitive research is "variable analytic" in that it attempts to outline the significant variables involved in human thought and show how

they work. Cognitive researchers are also interested in the link between thinking and behavior. A cognitive theory of communication, for example, might address the ways people evaluate such message features as credibility, organization, and argumentation, and it might predict the kinds of information that would have an impact on how people think.

Interactionist Theories.   The theories of this genre view social life as a process of interaction. In short, communication (interaction) is the vehicle by which we learn how to behave and what things mean.[45]

Interactionist theorists view communication as the glue of society. Society could not exist without it. Social structures such as organizations, groups, families, and institutions do not preexist; they are created and sustained by interaction. This genre is an important part of communication theory because it makes communication the most important force in social life.

Interactionist theorists regard social structures as products, not determinants, of interaction. Social structures do not enable communication to take place; rather, communication enables social structures to exist. For example, a family is shaped by the way its members communicate.

The focus is on how language is used to enact or create social structures and on how language and other symbol systems are reproduced, maintained, and changed through use. Meaning is not something objective to be transferred but is created by people in the act of communication. So, for example, how you see your parents is determined by years of communication between you and them and your discussions with many other people about your parents in particular and parenthood in general.

---

44   For a good general discussion of cognitivism, see John O. Greene, "Evaluating Cognitive Explanations of Communicative Phenomena," *Quarterly Journal of Speech* 70 (1984): 241–254.
45   Gün R. Semin and Kenneth J. Gergen, "Everyday Understanding in Science and Daily Life," in *Everyday Understanding: Social and Scientific Implications,* eds. Gün R. Semin and Kenneth J. Gergen (London: Sage, 1990), pp. 1–18. For a sampling of social approaches, see Wendy Leeds-Hurwitz, "Forum on Social Approaches to Communication," *Communication Theory* 2 (1992): 131–172; 329–356.

Interaction leads to and reinforces shared meaning and establishes conventions like rules, roles, and norms that enable further interaction to take place. Conventions, or standard meanings and actions, are worked out through interaction. Of course, meanings change from time to time, from situation to situation, and from one group to another. In the final analysis, then, interaction within actual groups is both the seat of tradition and the origin of change.

Because meanings and actions change from one situation to another, knowledge is situational, not universal. This brand of scholarship tends to describe the meanings and actions within particular social groups and cultures and does not usually predict particular outcomes based on a set of known laws.

For example, a social theory of organizational communication might show that organizational culture is achieved by storytelling and rituals. Because the stories and rituals in different organizations are not the same, organizations have very different cultures. This kind of theory could be used to trace the changes in an organization's culture over time as new generations of members come and go and new stories and rituals are developed.

Interpretive Theories. This genre includes theories that try to discover meaning in actions and texts, from ancient scrolls to the behavior of teenagers. The theories of this genre describe the process by which understanding occurs, making a sharp distinction between understanding and scientific explanation. The goal of interpretation is not to discover laws that govern events, but to uncover the ways people actually understand their own experience.[46]

Interpretive theorists celebrate subjectivism, or the preeminence of individual experience. They usually emphasize language as the center of experience, believing that language creates a world of meaning within which the person lives and through which all experience is understood.

Interpretive theorists describe the process whereby the active mind uncovers the meanings of experience in whatever form it may take.

Sometimes understanding involves interpretation of culture or of writings or artifacts of various kinds. These theorists tend to avoid prescriptive judgments about observed phenomena, and interpretations are often cast in tentative and relative terms.

A number of theories of communication are interpretive. These include theories of cultural interpretation, organizational culture, and textual interpretation (Chapter 10). One research tradition, for example, examines the communication practices of various cultures and attempts to understand what they mean to the members of those cultures. Interpretive and interactionist theories have a strong kinship based on their mutual concern for language and meaning and their use of interpretive methods.

Critical Theories. Critical theories consist of a loose confederation of ideas held together by a common interest in the quality of communication and human life. These theories focus especially on issues of inequality and oppression. Critical theorists do not merely observe; they also criticize. Most critical theorists are concerned with the conflict of interests in society and the ways communication perpetuates domination of one group over another. Many critical theories are based on Marxism, although most have gone well beyond original Marxist thought.[47]

An important branch of critical theory is feminist scholarship, which examines and questions the division of experience into masculine and feminine categories. Feminist scholars are also concerned with oppression and the distribution of power in society.[48]

Critical theories borrow heavily from most of the other genres. Although they reject cogniti-

---

46   For a good discussion of the interpretive approach, see Anderson, *Communication Theory*, pp. 24–28. See also Stewart, "Speech and Human Being."
47   For an overview of critical theory, see Mike R. Allen, "Critical and Traditional Science: Implications for Communication Research," *Western Journal of Communication* 57 (1993): 200–208.
48   See, for example, Karen A. Foss and Sonja K. Foss, "Incorporating the Feminist Perspective in Communication Scholarship: A Research Commentary," in *Doing Research on Women's Communication: Alternative Perspectives in Theory and Method*, eds. C. Spitzack and K. Carter (Norwood, NJ: Ablex, 1989), pp. 65–94.

vism, many of these theories are structuralist or even functionalist in orientation, because they are looking for the underlying social structures that affect class and gender relations in society.[49] This genre borrows from interactionist theories by acknowledging the importance of culture and the ways in which material practices, or everyday actions, reproduce and sometimes change culture. Critical theorists share with interpretive theorists the central concern for language and for the ways language affects experience. These theories also make heavy use of interpretive methods.

Important differences exist among these five genres in what is assumed about knowledge, reality, and values. Each genre has its own powers and limits. Each enables theorists to do some things and not others. The various schools of thought within each genre also have their own advantages and disadvantages, as do individual theories themselves.

Structural and functional theories specify general categories and relations among variables in systems of all types. Such theories are weak in revealing the tone and color of individual events and particular human experiences. For example, a functional theory of organizations could indicate the consequences of certain managerial styles for productivity, but it would not help you understand the feelings that individual workers might have about their supervisors and the stories they tell to help them cope with the job.

Cognitive theories describe and explain general aspects of thinking. Such theories tell us a lot about the psychology of individuals, but they say little about the dynamics of social groups. Cognitive theories are designed to show how people in general think, but they are not well suited to explain how action is accomplished jointly, between people. For example, a cognitive theory of message processing might tell how an individual weighs information in forming an attitude about a topic, but it cannot reveal the

ways meanings are created over time by interaction in groups or how attitudes are affected by cultural values.

Interactionist theories are designed to uncover social processes and to show how behavior is affected by group norms and rules. These theories also show how communication can change social conventions. Thus, the power of these theories is in describing and explaining interpersonal dynamics and relationships. They are good at expressing the ways people and groups change from situation to situation and from moment to moment, but they are weak at uncovering the structures of human life that exist across all situations. For example, an interactionist theory might show how your self-concept changes from one occasion to another, depending on the values and rules of the group with which you affiliate. The same theory, however, would not do a good job of helping you understand your enduring personality.

Interpretive theories are powerful for revealing the meanings of individual experiences, writings, and social structures, and critical theories stress values or interests for judging events, situations, and institutions. Such theories can be effective agents for change, which the other genres are not. At the same time, interpretive and critical theories are not suited for making scientific statements about the laws that govern human affairs. Thus, for example, a critical theory might help an observer analyze the speeches of a certain group and reveal how the discourse reflects the group's oppression in society at large. Such a theory would lead to certain conclusions about institutional changes needed to reduce or eliminate the oppression. On the other hand, the theory would not tell us much about the general process of persuasion and how it operates. Nor would it want to.

These genres are more than theory types. They also embody philosophical commitments and values and reflect the kind of work that different theorists believe is important.

Part II of this book is organized roughly around the five genres. Chapters 3, 4, and 5 provide a good look at structural-functionalism.

---

49   The rebirth of functionalism in critical cultural studies is explored in some detail by Burrowes, "From Functionalism to Cultural Studies."

Chapters 6 and 7 are cognitive in orientation, and Chapters 8 and 9 tend to be interactionist. Chapter 10 is interpretive, and Chapter 11 is critical.

Levels of Communication

Another way of classifying theories is by level, or context. Communication always occurs in context—in a setting or situation. The contexts of communication can be divided theoretically in a variety of useful ways. For example, you can divide the field vocationally into categories like health communication, business and professional communication, and instructional communication. You can distinguish between those settings in which communication is more or less involved with technologies and those in which it is not. Often intercultural communication is considered to be separate from intracultural communication.

The most common division in the field is by level—along the lines of interpersonal, group, organizational, and mass. Handbooks, textbooks, and college curricula often are divided into sections corresponding to these levels. In your communication major, for example, you will probably take courses in interpersonal communication, group communication, organizational communication, and mass communication.

Interpersonal communication deals with communication between people, usually in face-to-face, private settings. *Group communication* relates to the interaction of people in small groups, usually in decision-making settings. Group communication necessarily involves interpersonal interaction, and most of the theories of interpersonal communication apply also at the group level. *Organizational communication* occurs in large cooperative networks and includes virtually all aspects of both interpersonal and group communication. It encompasses topics such as the structure and function of organizations, human relations, communication and the process of organizing, and organizational culture. Finally, *mass communication* deals with public communication, usually mediated. Many aspects of interpersonal, group, and organiza-

tional communication are involved in the process of mass communication.

Unfortunately, however, organizing communication in this way reinforces the tendency to think of these communication levels as types that are different from one another. The levels merely offer a convenient way of organizing certain theories. The division of the field into these levels—especially the division between mass communication and the others—has been contested, and work has been done to bridge these two groups.[50]

The chapters in Part III are designed to address a central theoretical concern relevant to each level. Chapter 12 deals with relationships, which is a central concern of interpersonal communication. Chapter 13 deals with decision making as a key topic in group communication theory. Chapter 14 addresses communication and networks, and the focus of Chapter 15 is media. These chapters are not designed to cover all the mainstream theories of each level. In fact, you will find other theories relevant to these four levels throughout this book.

Developing Core Communication Theory

Many of the theories you will encounter in this book deal with special aspects of communication. As we saw in the previous section, some theories explain particular levels of communication, whereas others focus on general concepts and processes common to all communication. We can refer to general treatments as *core communication theory.*

Core theory is especially significant because it helps us understand communication in general.

---

50   See, for example, Kathleen K. Reardon and Emmeline G. dePillis, "Multichannel Leadership: Revisiting the False Dichotomy," in *An Integrated Approach to Communication Theory and Research*, eds. M. B. Salwen and D. W. Stacks (Mahwah, NJ: Erlbaum, 1996), pp. 399–407; John Durham Peters, "The Gaps of Which Communication Is Made," *Critical Studies in Mass Communication* 11 (1994): 117–140; Joseph N. Cappella (ed.), "Symposium on Mass and Interpersonal Communication," *Human Communication Research* 15 (1988): 236–318; Robert P. Hawkins, John M. Wiemann, and Suzanne Pingree (eds.), *Advancing Communication Science* (Newbury Park, CA: Sage, 1988).

Core theories provide insight into processes that operate whenever communication takes place. Special theories that deal with particular aspects or levels of communication may also clarify the core process. The following list illustrates the types of elements included in core communication theories.

First, core theories can tell us something about the *development of messages*. How do we create what we write, say, and express to others? What mental processes are involved? To what extent and in what ways are messages created in interaction with others? How does the process of message development differ from culture to culture, and what are the cultural mechanisms that enter into the message development process?

Second, core theories often address *interpretation and the generation of meaning*. How do humans understand messages, and how does meaning arise in interaction with other people? How does the mind process information and interpret experience? To what extent and in what ways are meaning and understanding products of culture?

Third, core theories sometimes discuss message structure. *Message structure* consists of the elements of messages in the form of writings, the spoken word, and nonverbal forms. How are messages put together, and how are they organized? In what ways does the organization of a message create meaning? How are communicators' messages in a dialogue organized, and how do the participants in a conversation mesh their talk?

The fourth element often addressed by core theories is *interactional dynamics*. This involves relationships and interdependency among communicators and the joint creation of discourse and meaning. It addresses the give and take, the production and reception, between parties in a communication transaction, whether those parties are individuals or groups.

Finally, core theories may also help us understand *institutional and societal dynamics*, or the ways power and resources are distributed in society, the ways culture is produced, and the interaction among segments of society.

No single theory can address all these elements, although when one or more elements are included in a theory, others may be implicated because of the relationship between elements. For example, a theory may focus on interactional dynamics while telling us something indirectly about how messages are organized. This happens because interactional dynamics and message structure are related to each other. Similarly, a theory that discusses message production may also say something about message reception, because they involve similar cognitive mechanisms in processing information.

As you study the various theories in this book, always look for the ways each might contribute to core theory. You will find that many of the theories in Part II address core concepts and processes directly and, as a group, explain a great deal about communication. Other theories in Part II and all those in Part III relate more to particular communication levels, but they too can provide core insights if you examine them closely.

The Intellectual Structure of the Communication Field

In a remarkable attempt to capture both the unity and diversity of the communication field, John Powers has created a model of the intellectual structure of the discipline that accommodates all of the genres, levels, and elements of core theory discussed in this chapter.[51]

Powers imagines the work of the field in four tiers that can be summarized as follows:

Tier 1—The content and form of messages

Tier 2—Communicators as
(a) Individuals
(b) Participants in social relationships
(c) Members of cultural communities

Tier 3—Levels of communication, including
(a) Public

---

51   John H. Powers, "On the Intellectual Structure of the Human Communication Discipline," *Communication Education* 44 (1995): 191–222.

(b) Small group

(c) Interpersonal

Tier 4—Contexts and situations in which communication occurs, such as health care, courts, organizations, religion, and many others.

This model can be used to organize virtually all of the work of the field, including theory, research, and practical application. For our purposes, it is yet another way—a very useful way—for understanding similarities and differences among theories of communication.

Indeed, the chapters in Parts II and III of this book conform pretty well to Powers's first three tiers. In Part II, Chapters 4 and 5 address message structures, Chapters 6 and 7 cover theories of the individual communicator, Chapters 8 and 9 focus mostly on social concerns, and Chapters 10 and 11 largely address cultural matters. Part III of this text looks at levels of communication similar to those in Powers's third tier. Because the material in the fourth tier is quite specific, it is beyond the scope of this book.

◖● SUMMARY

This chapter is important because it sets the stage for the entire book. Here, you learned about the nature of theory and inquiry and how communication has been studied. Remember that communication theory is not just a mental exercise. Although working with concepts can be rewarding in and of itself, understanding the process of communication by studying theories also provides insights that can make you a better, more adaptive communicator. Communication has assumed great importance in our times, and this is not going to change. Studying communication theory can make you a more informed member of society and can help you understand some of the problems you will face in many areas of your life. Communication theory is also empowering because it can suggest ideas about how to intervene or institute change.

It does not make sense for you to memorize a list of definitions of communication; you can certainly create enough of your own. But it is important to remember that definitions are created to focus attention on certain observations and experiences that are relevant at the moment. In theory building, definitions are skeletal x-rays of the central concerns of the theory builder. Having a single simple definition of communication would be nice, but in our field, this tidy state of affairs is not possible. The study of communication is too diverse, and multiple definitions are unavoidable, as are multiple theories.

In this chapter and the next, you begin to learn how people think as they create knowledge. This may be the most important learning of the entire book. The content of what we know about communication will change, but the basic approaches to knowledge will not. You will be able to use what you learn about communication for a time, but you will be able to use what you learn about inquiry and critical thinking for the rest of your life. If you go on professionally in communication or some other field in the social sciences, this overview of the theory-building process should be especially valuable.

Remember that there are a variety of ways to create knowledge, and each has its own powers and limits. You will develop preferences based on your own aptitudes and interests in scientific or humanistic methods, and you may even become proficient in moving from one way of knowing to another. Just keep in mind what these tools can and cannot do for you. Remember also that social processes such as communication can never be completely understood from the vantage point of any single way of knowing, and significant contributions have been made by a variety of discovery, interpretive, and critical methods.

One of the most important lessons in this chapter is that a theory is not just a simple exposition of fact or reality. Theories are based on certain assumptions about knowledge, values, and things, and theories therefore differ not only in content but also in form and philosophical perspective. Theoretical categories are useful for understanding similarities and differences among theories, but they are not pure types. Differences abound within each category, and you will even see that theories placed in one category may have some similarities with those placed in another. Theories can also be organized around levels, which can be useful, as long as you keep in mind the substantial overlap among levels.

CHAPTER 2

THEORY IN THE PROCESS OF INQUIRY

In the study of human communication, as in all branches of knowledge, it is appropriate, even compelling, to ask ourselves how we come to profess what we think we know. The question of truth, discovery, and inquiry is a particularly important place to begin this book because every theorist presented here has taken a stab at truth. This chapter discusses the special role of theory in the process of inquiry.

◖ THE NATURE OF THEORY

What is theory? Uses of the term range from Farmer Jones's theory about when his pullets will start laying eggs to Einstein's theory of relativity. People sometimes use the term to mean any unsubstantiated guess about something. Theory often is contrasted with "fact." Even among scientists, writers, and philosophers, the term *theory* is used in a variety of ways.

The purpose of this book is to represent a wide range of thought about the communication process. Therefore, the term *theory* is used in its broadest sense as any conceptual representation or explanation of a phenomenon.[1] Communication theories are attempts of various scholars to represent what is considered important in the process of communication. We can make three generalizations about theories.

First, all theories are abstractions. Theories of communication are not themselves the process being conceptualized. As a result, every theory is partial; every theory leaves something out. A theory focuses on certain things and ignores others. This truism is important because it reveals the basic inadequacy of any theory. No single theory will ever reveal the whole of truth.

Second, all theories must be viewed as constructions. Theories are created by people, not

---

1   See Steven H. Chaffee, "Thinking About Theory," in *An Integrated Approach to Communication Theory and Research,* eds. M. B. Salwen and D. W. Stacks (Mahwah, NJ: Erlbaum, 1996), pp. 15–32; Stephen W. Littlejohn, "Communication Theory," in *Encyclopedia of Rhetoric and Composition: Communication from Ancient Times to the Information Age,* ed. T. Enos (New York: Garland, 1996), pp. 117–121; Karl Erik Rosengren, "Substantive theories and Formal Models—Bourdieu Confronted," *European Journal of Communication* 10 (1995): 7–39.

ordained by God. Theories represent various ways observers see their environments, but theories themselves do not reflect reality.[2] Many readers and theorists forget this principle, and students often are trapped by the conception that reality can be seen in this or that theory. Abraham Kaplan writes, "The formation of a theory is not just the discovery of a hidden fact; the theory is a way of looking at the facts, of organizing and representing them. . . . A theory must somehow fit God's world, but in an important sense it creates a world of its own."[3] Stanley Deetz adds that "a theory is a way of seeing and thinking about the world. As such it is better seen as the 'lens' one uses in observation than as a 'mirror' of nature."[4]

Let us take an analogy from biology. Two observers using microscopes may see different things in an amoeba, depending on the observers' theoretical points of view. One observer sees a one-celled animal; the other sees an organism without cells. The first viewer stresses the properties of an amoeba that resemble all other cells—the wall, the nucleus, the cytoplasm. The second observer compares the amoeba to other whole animals, which have ingestion of food, excretion, reproduction, and mobility. Neither observer is wrong. Their theoretical frameworks simply stress different aspects of the observed object.[5] We will see this point again and again in the following chapters. Because theories are constructions, questioning a theory's usefulness is wiser than questioning its truthfulness.[6] This statement is not intended to imply that theories do not represent reality but that any given truth can be represented in a variety of ways, depending on the theorist's orientation.

The third generalization about theories is that they are intimately tied to action. How we think, our theories, guide how we act; and how we act, our practices, guide how we think. In the world of scholarship, formal theories and intellectual practices are inseparable.[7] James Anderson states the matter: "Theory . . . contains a set of instructions for reading the world and acting in it. . . . [It] speaks to the singular, overarching question of 'What do I believe to be true in living this

scholar's life?' No scholarship has greater importance than the authentic theory."[8]

This book is like an art gallery. As you stroll through the gallery, you do not question the truthfulness of various paintings or sculptures. You think some are more artistic, more appealing, or more useful for providing a particular perspective than others. You may even question the composition or representativeness of a piece of art, but on some level you can enjoy them all as different creations, each with its own values. Students sometimes complain that there are too many communication theories. If we instead compare theories to paintings in a gallery, we get a fuller and more complete appreciation and understanding of communication.

◖ BASIC ELEMENTS OF THEORY

Theories are composed of two elements—concepts and explanations. Let us consider each in turn.

Concepts in Theories

The first and most basic aspect of a theory is its concepts. Humans are by nature conceptual beings. Our entire symbolic world—everything

---

2   This idea is explored by Klaus Krippendorff, "Conversations or Intellectual Imperialism in Comparing Communication (Theories)," *Communication Theory* 3 (1993): 252–266; and W. Barnett Pearce, "On Comparing Theories: Treating Theories as Commensurate or Incommensurate," *Communication Theory* 2 (1991): 159–164.
3   Abraham Kaplan, *The Conduct of Inquiry* (San Francisco: Chandler, 1964), p. 309.
4   Stanley A. Deetz, *Democracy in an Age of Corporate Colonization: Developments in Communication and the Politics of Everyday Life* (Albany: SUNY Press, 1992), p. 66. The mirror analogy is developed and critiqued by Richard Rorty, *Philosophy and the Mirror of Nature* (Princeton, NJ: Princeton University Press, 1979).
5   Examples from N. R. Hanson, *Patterns of Discovery* (Cambridge, MA: Cambridge University Press, 1961), pp. 4–5.
6   This point is made also in Thomas L. Jacobsen, "Theories as Communications," *Communication Theory* 2 (1991): 145–150.
7   See James Anderson, *Communication Theory: Epistemological Foundations* (New York: Guilford, 1996), pp. 7–9.
8   Quoted in "Anderson Succeeds Ellis as *Communication Theory* Editor, Invites Papers," *ICA Newsletter* 24-1 (January 1996): 1.

known—is understood as concepts. Thomas Kuhn writes, "Neither scientists nor laymen learn to see the world piecemeal or item by item; . . . both scientists and laymen sort out whole areas together from the flux of experience."[9]

What is a concept then? A concept consists of grouping things and events into a category according to observed qualities. In our everyday world, some things are considered to be trees, some houses, some cars.

The communication theorist observes many variables in communication and classifies and labels them according to perceived patterns. A goal of theory, then, is to present useful concepts. An important part of conceptualizing is labeling. We identify our concepts by symbols, usually words, so that a set of terms is an integral part of any theory. Concepts and definitions cannot be separated. Together they tell us what the theorist is looking at and what is considered important. Consider an example from an elementary school classroom:

> The teacher presents four boxes. In each there is a picture—of a tree, cat, dog, and squirrel, respectively. The child is asked which one is different. A child worthy of second grade immediately picks the tree. The child knows not only how to divide plants from animals, but also that the plant/animal distinction is the preferred one to apply . . . [but] the choice is arbitrary and hardly a very interesting way to think about the problem. The squirrel as easily could have been picked if the child had distinguished on the basis of domesticity or things we bought at the store. Or the dog could have been picked because the cat, squirrel, and tree relate in a playful, interactive way. Or the child could have picked the cat since the other three are in the yard.[10]

Some theories stop at the concept level, providing only a list of concepts without explaining how they relate to one another. Such theories are known as *taxonomies*. Introductory communication textbooks often include basic taxonomies that list the "parts" of the communication process, such as source, message, receiver, feedback, and so forth. Theories that stop at the concept level are primitive because the goal of theory

building is to provide an understanding of how things work. Indeed, because taxonomies do not explain, many scholars believe that they are not really theories. The best theories, then, go beyond concepts to provide explanations—statements about how the variables relate to one another—showing how concepts are connected.

Explanation in Theories

Explanation is more than merely naming and defining variables; it identifies regularities in the relationships among those variables. Explanations account for an event by referring to what is going on within the event or between it and some other event. In simplest terms, explanation answers the question, Why? Explanation relies primarily on the principle of necessity.

An explanation designates some logical force among variables that makes particular outcomes "necessary." If x occurs, then y is necessary or probable: If children see a lot of television violence (x), they will develop violent tendencies (y). In the social sciences, necessity is rarely taken as absolute. Instead, we can say that one thing is "often" or "usually" associated with another, that there is a *probable* relationship: If children see a lot of television violence (x), they will probably (p) develop violent tendencies (y).

There are a variety of kinds of necessity and therefore a variety of kinds of explanation. Here we will look at three models for understanding explanation.

Causal and Practical Necessity. One simple but useful way to distinguish different forms of explanation is causal and practical necessity.[11]

9   Thomas S. Kuhn, *The Structure of Scientific Revolutions*, 2d ed. (Chicago: University of Chicago Press, 1970), p. 28.
10   Deetz, *Democracy*, pp. 71–72.
11   Based on P. Achinstein, *Laws and Explanation* (New York: Oxford University Press, 1971); see also Donald P. Cushman and W. Barnett Pearce, "Generality and Necessity in Three Types of Theory About Human Communication, with Special Attention to Rules Theory," *Human Communication Research* 3 (1977): 344–353. For an excellent discussion of explanation in the social sciences, see Paul F. Secord (ed.), *Explaining Human Behavior: Consciousness, Human Action, and Social Structure* (Beverly Hills, CA: Sage, 1982).

Causal necessity explains events in terms of cause–effect, where behavior is seen as an outcome of causal forces. *Practical necessity* explains events in terms of achieving a goal—intentional action designed to achieve a future state. Causal necessity explains behavior as a response, whereas practical necessity sees action as controllable. In causal necessity, the consequent event is determined by some antecedent event. In practical necessity, behavior is "necessary" because of a choice someone makes.

To better understand the difference between causal and practical necessity, consider how you might explain to a friend why you failed a test. If you said that you just aren't very good at this subject and had bad teachers in high school, you would be using causal necessity: My bad grade was caused by things I can't control. On the other hand, if you did quite well on the test, you would probably use practical necessity: I needed to increase my grade-point average and studied hard.

Kenneth Gergen and Mary Gergen add three more categories.[12] *Person-centered explanations* concentrate on factors inside the person, whereas *situation-centered explanations* involve primarily outside factors. Some situation-centered explanations focus on factors occurring before the action being explained, and some focus on those occurring after the action.

Laws, Rules, and Systems.   Traditionally in the field of communication, theories have been separated into three types, depending on their primary method of explanation. Law theories are believed to rely primarily on causal necessity because they make heavy use of cause–effect statements. Rules theories are said to rely more on practical necessity because they hold that people follow rules in order to achieve their intentions. In between these two types of theory lies the systems approach, which purportedly relies on logical chaining and centers on the logical relations among elements of a system that has both causal and practical necessity.

Doubt has been cast on the utility of this laws-rules-systems distinction.[13] The differences may not be as clear as suggested by its advocates. Systems and rules have much in common, and there are important differences in explanation within these categories. For example, rules theorists disagree among themselves as to how much power rules exert over people's actions, and system theorists equivocate about whether system relations are causal, practical, or both. Keep in mind that we are not discarding the terms *laws, rules,* and *systems,* because they can be a useful way to classify theories.

Mindscapes.   Explanations are really part of larger schemes or ideas about how things work. Magoroh Maruyama refers to these as *mindscapes.*[14] Although there are many mindscape types, Maruyama isolates four common ones:

1. *Nonreciprocal causal models.* Events are caused by simple overarching laws, and events do not influence one another. Once you discover the covering law or influence, you can predict how things will work. In the human sciences, all individual behavior is caused by the same set of factors. An example is the current movement in several sciences to explain human behavior as biologically and genetically determined.

2. *Independent-event models.* Events are fairly isolated from one another, act on their own, and have little dependence on one another. In social relations, this means that society is nothing more than many individuals acting independently. Everyone must stand up for themselves.

12   Kenneth J. Gergen and Mary M. Gergen, "Explaining Human Conduct: Form and Function," in *Explaining Human Behavior: Consciousness, Human Action, and Social Structure,* ed. P. F. Secord (Beverly Hills, CA: Sage, 1982), pp. 127–154.

13   This controversy is well summarized in Ernest Bormann, *Communication Theory* (New York: Holt, Rinehart & Winston), chap. 7. See also Charles R. Berger, "The Covering Law Perspective as a Theoretical Basis for the Study of Human Communication," *Communication Quarterly* 25 (1977): 7-18; Donald P. Cushman, "The Rules Perspective as a Theoretical Basis for the Study of Human Communication," *Communication Quarterly* 25 (1977): 30–45; Peter R. Monge, "The Systems Perspective as a Theoretical Basis for the Study of Human Communication," *Communication Quarterly* 25 (1977): 19–29. See also Ted Smith III, "Diversity and Order in Communication Theory: The Uses of Philosophical Analysis," *Communication Quarterly* 36 (1988): 28–40.

14   Michael T. Caley and Daiyo Sawada (eds.), *Mindscapes: The Epistemology of Magoroh Maruyama* (Amsterdam: Gordon and Breach, 1994).

3. *Homeostatic causal-loop models.* Events are parts of systems and therefore influence one another. There is a tendency for events to achieve balance and stability in the system. Many social and cultural theories are of this type. They hold that society is a fairly stable pattern of interaction among institutions, groups, communities, and individuals.

4. *Morphogenetic causal-loop models.* Events are parts of systems and influence one another, but these influences cause the system to grow and become more complex. People can draw on many resources and make choices to achieve positive change.

The Traditional Ideal of Theory

Traditional social science has been dominated by an approach to theory and research modeled on the experimental natural sciences.[15] Such methods are based on four processes: (1) developing questions, (2) forming hypotheses, (3) testing the hypotheses, and (4) formulating theory. This approach is known as the *hypothetico-deductive method,* in which theory is seen as a codification of hypotheses, findings, or both from a series of tests. This approach is based on the assumption that we can best understand complex things in terms of fine analysis of parts, which suggests the alternate label, the *variable-analytic tradition.*

Hypothesis testing is a painstakingly slow process in which theories are fine-tuned by numerous tests. The four processes—questioning, hypothesizing, testing, and theorizing—are repeated in an incremental building-block process. Figure 2.1 illustrates the hypothetico-deductive method.[16] This method is based on five major concepts: hypothesis, operationism, control and manipulation, covering laws, and prediction.

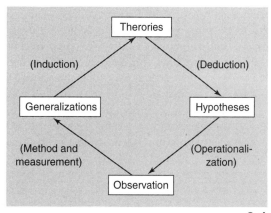

F I G U R E **2.1**

The Classical Ideal of Science

Reprinted with permission: Walter L. Wallace (ed.), *Sociological Theory: An Introduction* (New York: Aldine de Gruyter). Copyright © 1969 by Walter L. Wallace.

The first concept is *hypothesis,* which is a well-formed guess about a relationship between variables. It is based on intuition, personal experience, or, most desirably, previous research and theory. In fact, hypotheses often are based on an inductive process of generalizing from numerous observations.

A hypothesis must be testable; in other words, the variables brought together must be defined carefully so that any trained researcher could observe them in precisely the same way. Further, the relationship stated by the hypothesis must be framed so that potential rejection is possible. In other words, the hypothesis must be falsifiable. If it is not, any test will yield either a positive result or an equivocal one, and it will be impossible to discover whether the hypothesis is wrong. Hypothesis testing, then, is really a process of looking for exceptions.

Suppose, for example, that you think that people act on the basis of intrinsic rewards. In other words, they do things they find personally rewarding. Could you test this hypothesis? You could certainly find instances of people doing things because they liked to do them, but could you find instances of people doing things they did not like? Because virtually anything could be

15   See, for example, Steven H. Chaffee, "Thinking About Theory"; Michael J. Beatty, "Thinking Quantitatively," in *An Integrated Approach to Communication Theory and Research,* eds. M. B. Salwen and D. W. Stacks (Mahwah, NJ: Erlbaum, 1996), pp. 33–44; Myron W. Lustig, "Theorizing About Human Communication," *Communication Quarterly* 34 (1986): 451–459.
16   Figure 2.1 is adapted from Walter L. Wallace, *Sociological Theory: An Introduction* (Chicago: Aldine, 1969), p. ix.

intrinsically rewarding to someone, no action could be ruled out. This hypothesis is poorly stated because you could never disprove it. Some people may even do certain things because, in some perverse way, they find punishment itself rewarding.

Operationism is the principle that all variables in a hypothesis should be stated in ways that explain exactly how to observe them. Operational definitions are the most precise possible definitions because they tell you how the concept is to be observed. An operational definition of intelligence, for example, is the Stanford-Binet intelligence test. An operational definition of dominance might be a particular set of observer ratings on dominant versus submissive messages.

You could improve on your intrinsic reward hypothesis, then, by specifying more precisely what you mean. Something like the following might work: A person will repeat an action rated as highly rewarding on an intrinsic rewards test. Here, intrinsic reward is operationally defined as a rating on an intrinsic reward scale. You will notice that this wording makes the hypothesis falsifiable.

As you can see from this example, operationism relies on *measurement*, or the use of precise, usually numerical, indications. Measurement enables you to detect differences that might otherwise be hard to specify. For example, you might have subjects rate their activities on a 7-point scale, from highly unrewarding to highly rewarding. With this scale you could measure the difference between an activity that is moderately rewarding and one that is only mildly rewarding. You could also measure the difference between one person who found a particular activity highly rewarding and another who found the same activity unrewarding.

Measurement is evaluated in terms of two criteria—validity and reliability. *Validity* is the degree to which an observation measures what it is supposed to. How do we know, for example, that the subject's rating really measures reward? Perhaps the rating is influenced by some other hidden factor, or perhaps it reflects nothing in particular. Researchers have methods of estimating whether their measures are valid.

Reliability is the degree to which the construct is measured accurately, and it is most often estimated by consistency. If your bathroom scale gives you a different weight each day, even though you have not gained or lost weight, it is unreliable, just as an intelligence test giving a different result on separate occasions is also unreliable. If all items on a test are designed to measure the same thing, intelligence say, and they prove to be very inconsistent with one another, the test is said to be unreliable.

Clearly, validity and reliability are related to each other. Reliability is a necessary but not sufficient condition for validity. A measure cannot be valid if it is not first reliable.

Returning to your intrinsic rewards study, you must now determine whether your scale actually measures reward. You might do this, for example, by making sure that it is consistent with other known measures of the same thing. If you can show this, you can argue that the scale is valid. But you would still need to establish its reliability. You might do this by administering the test to the same group of people on two occasions to see that the responses were nearly the same.

The third concept of traditional science is *control and manipulation*. These factors are considered important because they are the only way causality can be ascertained. If one set of variables is held constant (control) and another set is systematically varied (manipulation), the researcher can detect the effect of the manipulated variables without worrying about whether other variables had hidden effects. Control and manipulation can be exercised directly, as in experiments, or through certain kinds of statistics.

Let's return to the intrinsic rewards hypothesis. Assume that you have refined your reward scale and found it valid and reliable. How would you then test your hypothesis? Would you give a list of activities to a group of subjects and have them rate each in terms of intrinsic reward? That would tell you how rewarding the subjects found each activity, but it would not tell you whether they would actually do the things they say are rewarding. You might consider having the subjects rate each item twice—once on reward value and once on how frequently they actually do it. That would give you an idea of the correlation between reward and activity, but it would not be sufficient to say that one caused the other.

To really test your hypothesis, you would need to set up an experiment in which you actually tested rewarding activities against unrewarding ones, to see if the former are repeated and the latter not. You might do this by having one group of people do a rewarding set of tasks such as tasting cookies and another an unrewarding one such as tasting raw vegetables to see if the first group eats more than the second.

The fourth concept is the *covering law*. The covering law is a theoretical statement of cause and effect relevant to a particular set of variables across situations. In traditional science, the covering law is believed to be significant because of its power in explaining events. Covering laws also enable the researcher to make predictions about future events.

Very few social scientists seek covering laws anymore. They realize that absolutely universal statements are unrealistic. Instead, investigators seek statistical relationships among variables, and their "laws" are probabilistic.[17] Instead of saying that reward leads to action, you would say that reward *usually* leads to action.

Prediction is the final concept of classical social science inquiry. Prediction is an important outcome of inquiry because it gives people power over their environment. If, for example, I can predict that certain behaviors will be repeated if they are rewarding, I may be able to control people's behavior by manipulating the reward value of the desired actions.

The Alternative Paradigm

The classical approach to research and theory explained above is firmly planted in the scientific tradition of "knowledge as discovery." As Chap-

ter 1 points out, however, the discovery method is often rejected by scholars in other traditions.[18] These critics sometimes refer to the classical ideal as "old paradigm" and their own work as "new paradigm."[19] (I prefer the less demeaning designations of "traditional" and "alternative.")

In the above section, we imagined that you were trying to test the relationship between action and rewards. Alternative-paradigm theorists would not appreciate your intrinsic-rewards hypothesis very much. They might find your idea interesting and even useful, but they would say that this is just one of many ways to understand a person's behavior, and they would find ludicrous your reduction of reward to a check on a scale. They might also say that your statement that rewards cause behavior is arbitrary and that the link could just as validly be stated in the opposite direction: Action is taken purposely to *create* rewards.

Robyn Penman has outlined five tenets of the alternative paradigm.[20] First, action is voluntary. Persons are in part self-moving, and you cannot predict behavior based on outside variables. If this is true, it would be hard to predict how people would behave based on rewards. For example, some people like raw vegetables better than cookies, or maybe they don't actually like vegetables more but prefer them because vegetables are healthier.

Second, knowledge is created socially. That means that communication theories themselves are created by communication, the very process

---

17 Robert Bostrom and Lewis Donohew, "The Case for Empiricism: Clarifying Fundamental Issues in Communication Theory," *Communication Monographs* 59 (1992): 109–129.
18 See, for example, Robyn Penman, "Good Theory and Good Practice: An Argument in Progress," *Communication Theory* 3 (1992): 234–250; and Klaus Krippendorff, "Conversation or Intellectual Imperialism in Comparing Communication (Theories)," *Communication Theory* 3 (1993): 252–266.
19 See, for example, Rom Harré and Paul F. Secord, *The Explanation of Social Behavior* (Totowa, NJ: Littlefield, Adams, 1979), pp. 19–25.
20 Penman, "Good Theory," based on Kenneth Gergen, *Toward Transformation in Social Knowledge* (New York: Springer-Verlag, 1982); see also, James A. Anderson, "Thinking Qualitatively," in *An Integrated Approach to Communication Theory and Research*, eds. M. B. Salwen and D. W. Stacks (Mahwah, NJ: Erlbaum, 1996), pp. 45–59.

they are designed to explain. There is no one-to-one relationship between the ideas in a theory and objective reality. So the intrinsic rewards hypothesis is a creation of the theorist, one of many ways of understanding behavior, not a mirror of the "real" reason people do things.

Third, theories are historical. They reflect the settings and times in which they are created, and as times change, so too will theories. Our culture in the United States is materialistic and individualistic. The entire system is predicated on the idea that people are motivated by rewards and punishments. It is no wonder, then, that an intrinsic rewards hypothesis would seem logical. In another era or in another culture, such an idea might not even come up. Stanley Deetz writes:

> All current theories will pass in time. It is not as if they are in error, at least little more or less so than those in the past. They were useful in handling different kinds of human problems, problems we might find ill-formed and even silly, as others will ours. What remains is the human attempt to produce theories that are useful in responding to our own issues. We are struggling to find interesting and useful ways of thinking and talking about our current situations and helping us build the future we want.[21]

Fourth, theories affect the "reality" they are covering. Theorists are not separate from the worlds they create, but are part of those worlds. If your intrinsic rewards hypothesis is believed, people will start treating others as reward driven. They will offer rewards when they want something done and withhold them when they do not. Pretty soon people will be operating in an environment created by the ideas of the theorist, and a kind of self-fulfilling prophecy may result.

Fifth, theories are value laden. They are never neutral. An alternative-paradigm critic would say that your hypothesis is rife with values. You chose to look at rewards because your attention was drawn to this particular variable above all other possible ones. You chose to look at individual behavior because you value the person over other possible units of analysis such as the group or culture. This priority is not inherently bad, but it does contain values; and you should

recognize your values, according to alternative-paradigm critics.

The tension between the traditional and alternative paradigms is considerable, and it is not trivial.[22] Later in this chapter, we discuss in greater detail the issues that divide these schools of thought.

⦿ THEORY DEVELOPMENT AND CHANGE

Although theory is an abstraction from reality, it is important to realize the relationship between the two. Theory is not purely abstract, without grounding in actual experience. Experience affects theory, and theory in turn affects one's conception of experience.

We formulate theory from experiences (including research). Good theory development, then, is a constant process of testing and formulating. For the traditionalist, this testing is a process of improving hypotheses about the "real" world. For the alternative-paradigm theorist, it is a process of fine-tuning interpretive frameworks for understanding the flow of events.

Theory development therefore always requires research. Research enables the specific investigation of facts considered significant, it allows one to test the theory's predictive power or interpretive utility, and it is a way of developing and articulating the theory further.[23]

How Theories Change

Theories may change in three ways. The first is *growth by extension*. Here, knowledge is expanded piece by piece, moving from an understanding of one bit of reality to an adjoining bit by adding new concepts to the old. For example, you might develop a theory of the use of insults

---

21   Deetz, *Democracy*, p. 77.
22   See, for example, the critique of the new paradigm by Bostrom and Donohew, "The Case for Empiricism."
23   Kuhn, *Structure*, pp. 25–27.

in conflict situations. Your theory would change by extension if you added ideas about how compliments and jokes also occur in conflict situations.

The second way, *growth by intension,* is the process of developing an increasingly precise understanding of an individual concept.[24] Your theory of insults in conflict would change by intension if you could elaborate more and more on the role of insults. Obviously, a theory can change by extension and intension at the same time. You might develop your conflict theory by elaborating on insults and adding other variables such as humor and avoidance.

The third way theories change is through *revolution.*[25] In his well-known book on scientific revolutions, Thomas Kuhn states that "normal science" is a process of developing theory with relative consensus among scientists on the basic nature of the things being explained. At some point an extraordinary case is discovered that runs counter to prevailing assumptions of the theory in use. At this point a crisis develops, leading to the development of an entirely new theoretical approach. The new theory (or set of theories) represents a different, competing way of looking at the world. For example, you might discover that conflict is something entirely different than previously understood, making the investigation of insults irrelevant or trivial.

Gradually, more and more members of the field accept the revolutionary theory, until it becomes the primary theoretical approach in a new normal science. In a scientific revolution, two paradigms are pitted against one another. The old paradigm represents normal science, and the new one represents the revised view. Paradigms are sets of concepts and variables that a group of scholars believe to be important to study, accompanied by a particular opinion of how these things operate. In normal science most scholars agree that certain things are important and should be studied. These scholars also share ideas about how to explain these things.

In a scientific revolution, the concepts and operations come to be understood in a radically dif-

ferent fashion, requiring redefinition of an entire field of knowledge. Previous areas of study may die, others may be born, and new weddings may occur. "What were ducks in the scientist's world before the revolution are rabbits afterwards. The man who saw the exterior of the box from above later sees its interior from below."[26] We can now see why critics of traditional social science are quick to call their approach "new paradigm" and why traditionalists dislike this label.

The Work of the Theorist

As we have seen, theories are not just things to be read and learned. They are constantly evolving works. Theories are like arguments in which advocates put forth claims believed worthy of consideration. This kind of work involves several tasks.[27]

At the heart of theory work, of course, is the hard application of acceptable methods, in which the subject matter is "subdued, unmasked, disciplined, and mastered by some superior approach, some set of terms, or a methodology."[28] Anderson describes the significance of this part of the work:

> The achievement of coherent meaning within an analytical frame is a celebratory occasion. This meaning is the medal of honor of the analytic work. It validates the effort. The achievement of this meaning is the evidence of the object and of the superiority of one's analysis over common sense. It is the instrumentality of the analysis, and, in the best of situations, allows an increasing number of others to pursue their goals.[29]

Many other kinds of related work are also necessary in making theory. One must establish *authority* to make theoretical claims through a complex process of establishing professional credibility over time within the discipline and the highly proficient use of acceptable forms of

24   Kaplan, *Conduct,* p. 305.
25   Kuhn, *Structure.*
26   Kuhn, *Structure,* p. 111.
27   Anderson, *Communication Theory,* pp. 127–153.
28   Anderson, *Communication Theory,* p. 141.
29   Anderson, *Communication Theory,* p. 141.

writing and presentation. One must argue successfully for the *significance* of the work, and one must present the work in a *voice* recognizable within the intellectual community and appropriate to the form of argument being used.

The scholar's work can be presented in a variety of forums, and part of the work of the theorist is to know what these are, where they are, and how to access them. Scholars work hard to develop a presentation appropriate for the forum selected, which means being reviewed by peers, accepting criticism, revising the work, and resubmitting it for publication.

⬤ THE FUNCTIONS OF THEORY

Nine important and overlapping functions of theory can be identified. The first function of theory is to *organize and summarize* knowledge. We do not see the world in bits of data, but organize and synthesize the world.[30] We seek patterns and try to discover connections. Theories are one way of accomplishing this organization of knowledge. An added benefit of this function is theory's contribution to accumulated knowledge. The student, practitioner, or scientist does not have to start all over with each investigation. Knowledge is organized into a body of theories, and the investigator begins a study with the organized knowledge of generations of previous scholars.

The second function is *focusing*. Theories, besides organizing data, focus attention on some variables and relationships and not on others. Thus, theories are like maps. From the overall surface, a map points out recreation spots, communities, picnic grounds, and shopping centers. To the persistent question, What will I look at? the theory points out areas for investigation.

Third, theories *clarify* what is observed. The clarification not only helps the observer understand relationships but also interpret specific events. Theories provide guideposts for interpreting, explaining, and understanding the complexity of human relations.

Fourth, theories offer an *observational* aid. Closely related to the focus function, the observational function points out not only *what* to observe but *how* to observe. Especially for theories that provide operational definitions, the theorist gives the most precise indication possible about what is meant by a particular concept. Thus, by following directions the reader is led to observe details elaborated by the theory.

The fifth function of theories, *prediction*, is one of the most widely discussed purposes of scientific inquiry. Many theories allow a theory builder to make predictions about outcomes and effects in the data. This ability to predict is important in applied areas such as persuasion and attitude change, psychotherapy, small-group dynamics, organizational communication, advertising, public relations, and mass media. Teachers work toward developing skills and abilities to improve communication competence. Various communication theories aid this process by helping us substitute well-founded predictions for good guesses.

The sixth theoretical function, the *heuristic function*, refers to the familiar axiom that a good theory generates research. The speculation forwarded in theories of communication often provides a guide about the direction the research will take and thus aids in furthering the investigation. This heuristic function of aiding discovery is vital to the growth of knowledge and is in a sense an outgrowth of each of the other functions of theory.

Seventh, theories serve an indispensable *communicative function*. Most investigators want and need to publish their observations and speculations for other interested persons.[31] Theory provides a way to do this and provides an open forum for discussion, debate, and criticism. Through the communication of numerous explanations of the things we study, comparison and theory improvement become possible.

---

30   This function is discussed in some detail by Charles R. Berger, "Evidence? For What?" *Western Journal of Communication* 58 (1994): 11–19.
31   The communicative function is addressed in Krippendorff, "Conversations."

The eighth function of theories is *control*. This function addresses values and enables the theorist to judge the effectiveness and propriety of certain behavior. Such theory is often referred to as *normative* in that it seeks to establish norms of performance. Much theory, of course, does not seek to fulfill this function at all, though many theorists now believe that all theory is value laden and control oriented, even when the theorist does not admit it.[32]

The final function of theory is the *generative function*. This is particularly relevant to the interpretive and critical traditions and alternative-paradigm social science. In short, it means using theory to challenge existing cultural life and to generate new ways of living—the use of theory to achieve change. Kenneth Gergen states the generative function in these terms: "The capacity to challenge the guiding assumptions of the culture, to raise fundamental questions regarding contemporary social life, to foster reconsideration of that which is 'taken for granted,' and thereby to generate fresh alternatives for social action."[33]

☉ PHILOSOPHICAL ISSUES IN THE STUDY OF COMMUNICATION

Philosophy studies the foundations of ideas. In this section we look at some significant questions about the assumptions of our theories. This subject is sometimes called *metatheory*.

Communication Metatheory

Metatheory, as the prefix *meta-* suggests, is a body of speculation on the nature of inquiry that is *above* or *over* the specific content of given theories. It addresses such questions as what should be observed, how observation should take place, and what form theory should take. It is theory about theory. Metatheoretical debates are a natural consequence of uncertainty over the status of knowledge in a field. Since the 1970s, metatheory has dominated the communication field. Communication scholars have come to question their methods and theories, precisely because of the problems of social science summarized in Chapter 1.[34]

Philosophical issues are complex but can be grouped into three major themes: epistemology (questions of knowledge), ontology (questions of existence), and axiology (questions of value).

Issues of Epistemology

Epistemology is the branch of philosophy that studies knowledge, or how people know what they claim to know. Any good discussion of inquiry and theory will inevitably come back to epistemological issues. Because of the diversity of disciplines involved in the study of communication and the resulting divergence of thought, epistemological issues are important in this field. The basic issues can be expressed as questions.[35]

To what extent can knowledge exist before experience? Many believe that all knowledge arises from experience. We observe the world and thereby come to know about it. Yet is there something in our basic nature that provides a kind of knowledge even before we experience the world? Many philosophers believe so. This kind of knowledge would consist of inherent mechanisms of thinking and perceiving. For example, strong evidence exists that children do not learn language entirely from hearing it spoken. Rather, they may acquire language by using innate models to test what they hear.

---

32   For a good recent exploration of normative theory, see Robert T. Craig and Karen Tracy, "Grounded Practical Theory: The Case of Intellectual Discussion," *Communication Theory* 5 (1995): 248–272.

33   Kenneth J. Gergen, *Toward Transformation*, p. 109.

34   For good discussions of metatheoretical issues, see Anderson, *Communication Theory*; Donald W. Fiske and Richard A. Shweder (eds.), *Metatheory in Social Science: Pluralisms and Subjectivities* (Chicago: University of Chicago Press, 1986); Mark R. Levy (ed.), "The Future of the Field," a special issue of *Journal of Communication* 43 (Summer 1993); Brenda Dervin, Lawrence Grossberg, Barbara O'Keefe, and Ellen Wartella (eds.), *Rethinking Communication: Paradigm Issues* (Newbury Park, CA: Sage, 1989).

35   This analysis is from Stephen W. Littlejohn, "Epistemology and the Study of Human Communication" (paper delivered at the Speech Communication Association, New York, November 1980). See also Stephen W. Littlejohn, "An Overview of Contributions to Human Communication Theory from Other Disciplines," in *Human Communication Theory: Comparative Essays*, ed. F. E. X. Dance (New York: Harper & Row, 1982), pp. 247–249. For another approach, see Anderson, *Communication Theory*, pp. 102–185.

To what extent can knowledge be certain? Is knowledge potentially certain, there for the taking by whoever can discover it? Is truth absolute, or is the knowable relative and changing? The debate over this issue has persisted for hundreds of years. Communication theorists vary in their assumptions about the certainty of truth. Those who take a universal stance will admit to errors in their theories, but they believe that these errors are merely a result of not yet having discovered the complete truth. Relativists would have us believe that knowledge will never be certain because universal reality simply does not exist.

By what process does knowledge arise? This question is extremely complex, and the debate on the issue lies at the heart of epistemology. To this point, Anatol Rapoport presents the following amusing anecdote about three baseball umpires:

> The first umpire, who was a "realist," remarked, "Some is strikes and some is balls, and I calls them as they is." Another, with less faith in the infallibility of the professional, countered with, "Some is strikes and some is balls, and I calls them as I sees them." But the wisest umpire said, "Some is strikes and some is balls, but they ain't nothing till I calls them."[36]

There are at least four positions on the issue. Mentalism, or *rationalism,* suggests that knowledge arises out of the sheer power of the human mind to know the truth. ("I call 'em as they are.") This position places ultimate faith in human reasoning to ascertain truth. *Empiricism* states that knowledge arises in perception. We experience the world and literally "see" what is going on. ("I call 'em as I see 'em.") *Constructivism* holds that people create knowledge in order to function pragmatically in the world and that they project themselves into what they experience. ("They ain't nothin' till I call 'em.") Constructivists believe that phenomena in the world can be fruitfully understood many different ways and that knowledge is what the person has made of the world. Finally, taking constructivism one step further, *social constructionism* teaches that knowledge is a product of symbolic interaction within social groups. In other words, reality is socially constructed and a product of group and cultural life. (So, our umpires might conclude in the end, "They're what we agree they are.")

Is knowledge best conceived in parts or wholes? Gestaltists teach that true knowledge consists of general, indivisible understandings. They believe that phenomena are highly interrelated and operate as a system. Analysts, on the other hand, believe that knowledge consists of understanding how parts operate separately.

To what extent is knowledge explicit? Many philosophers and scholars believe that you cannot know something unless you can state it. Knowledge is thus seen as explicit. Others claim that much of knowledge is hidden, that people operate on the basis of sensibilities that are not conscious and that they may be unable to express. Such knowledge is said to be *tacit.*[37]

The way scholars conduct inquiry and construct theories depends largely on their epistemological assumptions. Many basic positions arise from the issues just described. Numerous fine distinctions can be made among these positions, but two broad contrasting *worldviews* help crystallize the differences.[38]

Worldview I is based on empiricist and rationalist ideas. It treats reality as distinct from the human being, something that people discover outside themselves. It assumes a physical, knowable reality that is self-evident to the trained observer.[39]

---

36   Anatol Rapoport, "Strategy and Conscience," in *The Human Dialogue: Perspectives on Communication,* eds. F. Matson and A. Montagu (New York: Free Press, 1967), p. 95.

37   See Michael Polanyi, *Personal Knowledge* (London: Routledge & Kegan Paul, 1958).

38   This analysis is supported in part by several sources. See, for example, Anderson, *Communication Theory;* Georg H. von Wright, *Explanation and Understanding* (Ithaca, NY: Cornell University Press, 1971); and Joseph Houna, "Two Ideals of Scientific Theorizing," in *Communication Yearbook 5,* ed. M. Burgoon (New Brunswick, NJ: Transaction, 1982), pp. 29–48. Many other schemes have been devised to classify epistemological approaches. See, for example, Stephen Pepper, *World Hypotheses* (Berkeley: University of California Press, 1942); B. Aubrey Fisher, *Perspectives on Human Communication* (New York: Macmillan, 1978); Kenneth Williams, "Reflections on a Human Science of Communication," *Journal of Communication* 23 (1973): 239–250; Barry Brummett, "Some Implications of 'Process' or 'Intersubjectivity': Postmodern Rhetoric," *Philosophy and Rhetoric* 9 (1976): 21–51; Gerald Miller, "The Current Status of Theory and Research in Interpersonal Communication," *Human Communication Research* 4 (1978): 175.

39   Bostrom and Donohew, "The Case for Empiricism."

Discovery is important in this position; the world is waiting for the scientist to find it. Because knowledge is viewed as something acquired from outside oneself, Worldview I is often called the *received view*. Objectivity is all important, with investigators being required to define the exact operations to be used in observing events. Most mainstream physical science is Worldview I, and much behavioral and social science follows suit.

Worldview I aims to make lawful statements about phenomena, developing generalizations that hold true across situations and over time. Scholars in this tradition try to reveal how things appear and work. In so doing, the scholar is highly analytical, attempting to define each part and subpart of the object of interest. This is therefore the worldview behind the traditional ideal of theory in the social sciences.

Worldview II takes a different turn by relying heavily on constructivism and considering the world in process. In this view people take an active role in creating knowledge.[40] A world of things exists outside the person, but the individual can conceptualize these things in a variety of useful ways. Knowledge therefore arises not out of discovery but from interaction between knower and known. For this reason the perceptual and interpretive processes of individuals are important objects for study.

Worldview II attempts not to uncover universal laws but to describe the rich context in which individuals operate. It is humanistic in that it stresses the individual subjective response. Knowing is interpreting—an activity in which everybody is believed to engage. Many theories of communication take a Worldview II stance, which is based on the assumption that communication itself is a vital vehicle in the social construction of reality.[41] This is the stuff of the alternative paradigm discussed earlier in this chapter.

Issues of Ontology

Ontology is the branch of philosophy that deals with the nature of being, or more narrowly, the nature of the things we seek to know.[42] Actually,

epistemology and ontology go hand in hand because our ideas about knowledge depend in part on our ideas about reality. In the social sciences, ontology deals largely with the nature of human existence, and in communication ontology centers on the nature of human social interaction.

Ontological issues are important because the way a theorist conceptualizes communication depends in large measure on how the communicator is viewed. At least four issues are important.[43]

To what extent do humans make real choices? Although all investigators probably would agree that people perceive choice, there is a long-standing philosophical debate on whether real choice is possible. On one side of the issue are the determinists, who state that behavior is caused by a multitude of prior conditions and that humans are basically reactive and passive. On the other side of the debate are the pragmatists, who claim that people plan their behavior to meet future goals. This group sees people as decision-making, active beings who affect their own destinies. Middle positions also exist, suggesting either that people make choices within a restricted range or that some behavior is determined whereas other behavior is a matter of free will.

Is human behavior best understood in terms of states or traits?[44] States are temporary conditions

---

40   Krippendorff, "Conversations"; Penman, "Good Theory." See also Joanna Macy, *Mutual Causality in Buddhism and General System Theory* (Albany: SUNY Press, 1991), pp. 117–137.
41   See, for example, Peter Berger and Thomas Luckmann, *The Social Construction of Reality* (Garden City, NY: Doubleday, 1966); Alfred Schutz, *The Phenomenology of the Social World*, trans. George Walsh and Frederick Lehnert (Evanston, IL: Northwestern University Press, 1967); Kenneth Gergen, "The Social Constructionist Movement in Modern Psychology," *American Psychologist* 40 (March 1985): 266–275; Harré and Secord, *Explanation.*
42   For a discussion of ontology, see Alasdair MacIntyre, "Ontology," in *The Encyclopedia of Philosophy*, vol. 5, ed. P. Edwards (New York: Macmillan, 1967), pp. 542–543. For an excellent recent exploration of ontological issues in communication theory, see Anderson, *Communication Theory*, pp. 13–101.
43   For an ontological discussion of communication theory, see John Waite Bowers and James J. Bradac, "Issues in Communication Theory: A Metatheoretical Analysis," in *Communication Yearbook 5*, ed. Michael Burgoon (New Brunswick, NJ: Transaction, 1982), pp. 1–28.
44   This debate is summarized by Peter A. Andersen, "The Trait Debate: A Critical Examination of the Individual Differences Paradigm in the Communication Sciences," in *Progress in Communication Sciences*, eds. B. Dervin and M. J. Voigt (Norwood, NJ: Ablex, 1986).

affecting people. The state view argues that humans change and go through numerous states in the course of a day, year, or lifetime. The state view characterizes humans as dynamic. The trait view believes that people are mostly predictable because they display more or less consistent characteristics. People may change because their traits have changed, but traits do not change easily. Humans are basically static. Many social scientists, of course, believe that both traits and states characterize human behavior.

Is human experience primarily individual or social? Many social scientists view humans as individuals. Although these scholars understand that people are not in fact isolated from one another and that interaction is important, they understand behavior as individualistic. Their unit of analysis is the individual human psyche. Many other social scientists, however, focus on social life as the primary unit of analysis. These scholars believe that humans cannot be understood apart from their relationships with others in groups and cultures. This issue is especially important to communication scholars because of our focus on interaction.[45]

To what extent is communication contextualized? The question is whether behavior is governed by universal principles or whether it depends on situational factors. Some philosophers believe that human life and action are best understood by looking at universal factors; others believe that behavior is richly contextual and cannot be generalized beyond the immediate situation. The middle ground on this issue is that behavior is affected by both general and situational factors.

Although numerous ontological positions can be seen in communication theory, we can usefully group them into two basic contrasting stands: actional and nonactional. *Actional theory* assumes that individuals create meanings, have intentions, and make real choices. Theorists of the actional tradition are reluctant to seek universal laws because they assume that individual behavior is not governed entirely by prior events. Instead, they assume that people behave differently in different situations because rules change.

Nonactional theory assumes that behavior is basically determined by and responsive to biology and environment. Laws are usually viewed as appropriate in this tradition; active interpretation by the individual is downplayed.

Issues of Axiology

Axiology is the branch of philosophy studying values. For the communication scholar, three axiological issues are especially important.[46]

Can theory be value free? Classical science claims that theories and research are value free; scholarship is neutral, attempting to get the facts as they are. When a scientist's values impinge on his or her work, the result is bad science.[47] But there is a different position on this issue: that scholarship is free of substantive values but embodies such metavalues as the pursuit of truth, the importance of ideas and objectivity, and the value of science itself. Here, the contention is that science is not value free because the researcher's work is guided by an interest in certain ways of conducting inquiry.[48]

Taking yet another view, some contend that theory can never be value free, in method or in substance. Scientists choose what to study, and those choices are affected by personal as well as institutional values. Government and private organizational values determine what research is funded; political and economic ideologies both feed and are fed by particular ways of viewing the world embodied by different forms of theory and research.[49]

A substantial political argument on values in science is occurring. Traditional scientists claim that they are not responsible for the ways scientific knowledge is used, that it can be used for good or ill. Critics object that scientific knowl-

---

45   See, for example, Berger and Luckmann, *Social Construction;* Gergen, "Social Constructionist Movement."
46   For a good contemporary discussion of axiology, see Anderson, *Communication Theory,* pp. 186–199.
47   See, for example, Kaplan, *Conduct,* p. 372.
48   For a development of this position, see for example, Joli Jensen, "The Consequences of Vocabularies," *Journal of Communication* 43 (1993): 67–74.
49   See, for example, Brian Fay, *Social Theory and Political Practice* (London: Allen & Unwin, 1975); Penman, "Good Theory."

edge by its very nature is instrumentalist and control oriented and that it necessarily promotes power domination in society. Traditional communication knowledge, in this view, is an administrative tool of the power elite. The critics of science do not themselves claim to be above power, but they see themselves as making a choice in favor of a set of values that challenges domination in society rather than perpetuating it. This debate is discussed in more detail in Chapter 11.

To what extent does the practice of inquiry influence that which is studied? This second major value issue centers on the question of whether scholars intrude on and thereby affect the process being studied. The traditional scientific viewpoint is that scientists must observe carefully without interference, so that accuracy can be achieved. Critics doubt this is possible. Observation by its very nature distorts that which is being observed. Sometimes the distortion is great, sometimes small, but it is always there.

On a higher level, certain critics maintain that theory and knowledge themselves affect the course of human life.[50] This presents two potential problems. First, the scholar, by virtue of scholarly work, becomes an agent of change. That role must be actively understood and reckoned with. At the very least, the scholar must consider the ethical issues. Second, studying human life changes that life, so that what you believe you know at one time may not be true at another time. This second point has particularly profound epistemological implications.[51]

Finally, *to what extent should scholarship attempt to achieve social change?* Should scholars remain objective, or should they make conscious efforts to help society change in positive ways? Many believe that the proper role of the scholar is to produce knowledge: Let the technicians and politicians do what they will with it. Other scholars vociferously disagree: Responsible scholarship involves an obligation to promote positive change. Obviously, this second view is consistent with the critical approach to the development of knowledge.[52]

Overall then, two general positions reside in these axiological issues. First, *value-conscious*

scholarship recognizes the importance of values to research and theory and makes a concerted effort to direct those values in positive ways. What those directions should be, of course, is a matter of debate. Second, *value-neutral scholarship* believes that science is aloof from values and not a great concern.

◖ HOW TO EVALUATE A COMMUNICATION THEORY

As you encounter theories of communication, you will need a basis for judging one against another. The following is a list of criteria that can be applied to the evaluation of many theories.[53] Remember that no theory is perfect. All have limitations, and the following criteria are therefore ideals.

Theoretical Scope

A theory's scope is its comprehensiveness or inclusiveness. Theoretical scope relies on the *principle of generality,* or the idea that a theory's explanation must be sufficiently general to cover a range of events beyond a single observation.[54]

---

50   See, for example, Fay, *Social Theory;* Gergen, *Toward Transformation,* pp. 21–34; Penman, "Good Theory."

51   This issue is explored by Sheila McNamee, "Research as Social Intervention: A Research Methodology for the New Epistemology" (paper presented at the Fifth International Conference on Culture and Communication, Philadelphia, October 1988).

52   See, for example, Cees J. Hamelink, "Emancipation or Domestication: Toward a Utopian Science of Communication," *Journal of Communication* 33 (1983): 74–79.

53   Evaluation is discussed in greater depth in Penman, "Good Theory"; Bross, *Design,* pp. 161–177; Karl W. Deutsch, "On Communication Models in the Social Sciences," *Public Opinion Quarterly* 16 (1952): pp. 362–363; Calvin S. Hall and Gardner Lindzey, *Theories of Personality* (New York: Wiley, 1970), chap. 1; Kaplan, *Conduct,* pp. 312–322; Kuhn, *Structure,* pp. 100–101, 152-156. For an excellent illustration of how a critic might use these criteria, see the theoretical critiques of interpersonal deception theory: James B. Stiff, "Theoretical Approaches to the Study of Deceptive Communication: Comments on Interpersonal Deception Theory," *Communication Theory* 6 (1996): 289–296; Bella M. DePaulo, Matthew E. Ansfield, and Kathy L. Bell, "Theories About Deception and Paradigms for Studying It: A Critical Appraisal of Buller and Burgoon's Interpersonal Deception Theory and Research," *Communication Theory* 6 (1996): 297–311.

54   Achinstein, *Laws;* Cushman and Pearce, "Generality." See also Stuart Sigman, "Do Social Approaches to Interpersonal Communication Constitute a Contribution to Communication Theory," *Communication Theory* 2 (1992): 347–356.

When an explanation is a mere speculation about a single event, it is not a theoretical explanation. On the other hand, explanations that go beyond a single instance to cover a range of events are theoretical.

The scope of a theory is critical. Stanley Deetz writes that "Few theories are failures in regard to specific situations, and all theories ultimately fail if applied far enough outside of the specific conditions for which they were developed. Theories thus differ more in the sizes of their domains and the realistic nature of their parameters than in correctness."[55]

Two types of generality exist. The first is the coverage of a broad domain. Theories that meet the test of generality in this way deal with many phenomena. A communication theory that meets this test would explain a variety of communication-related behaviors. This has been one of the appeals of system theory (Chapter 3), for example, which explains an incredibly wide spectrum of events.

A theory need not cover a large number of phenomena to be judged as good, however. Indeed, many fine theories are narrow in coverage. Such theories possess the second type of generality: They deal with a narrow range of events, but their explanations of these events apply to a large number of situations. Such theories are said to be powerful. Certain theories of relationship breakups (Chapter 12) illustrate this type of generality. They only cover one topic, but they are powerful because they explain many instances of relationship dissolution.

Appropriateness

Are the theory's epistemological, ontological, and axiological assumptions appropriate for the theoretical questions addressed and the research methods used? In the last chapter, we discussed the fact that different genres of theory allow scholars to do different kinds of things. One criterion by which theories can be evaluated is whether their claims are consistent with their assumptions. If you assume that people make choices and plan actions to accomplish goals, it would be inappropriate to predict behavior on the basis of causal events. If you assume that the most important things affecting behavior are unconscious, it would be inappropriate to report survey data in which subjects were asked why they did certain things. If you believe that theory should be value free, it would be inappropriate to base your definition of communication on some standard of effectiveness.

In a way, then, appropriateness is a kind of logical consistency between theories and assumptions. For example, some writers from the cognitive tradition state that people actively process information and make plans to accomplish personal goals. Yet theories produced by these researchers often make lawlike statements about universal behaviors, which, if true, would leave little room for purposeful action.

Heuristic Value

Will the theory generate new ideas for research and additional theory? Heuristics was discussed in some detail earlier in the chapter, and we mentioned the importance of heuristic value. One example among many is Robert Bales's interaction process theory (Chapter 13), which has spawned much research and further theorizing about group communication. Even Bales's critics find his ideas useful as springboards to develop new concepts.

Validity

Generally speaking, validity is the truth value of a theory. Of course, we must be careful to understand that "truth" is not intended to mean absolute, inerrant fact. Rather, there may be a variety of "truth values" in an experience. Validity as a criterion of theory has at least three meanings.[56]

One kind of validity is that of *value*, or worth. This kind of validity is importance or utility, whether the theory has value. It is the primary

---

55   Deetz, *Democracy,* p. 69.
56   This analysis adapted from David Brinberg and Joseph E. McGrath, *Validity and the Research Process* (Beverly Hills, CA: Sage, 1985).

form of validity in interpretive and critical theories. Stanley Deetz writes: "The problem with most theories is not that they are wrong or lacking in confirming experiences but that they are irrelevant or misdirect observation, that is, they do not help make the observations that are important to meeting critical goals and needs."[57]

The second kind of validity is that of *correspondence,* or fit. Here the question is whether the concepts and relations specified by the theory can actually be observed. Classical science assumes that one and only one representation will fit, whereas interpretive sciences believe that a number of theories may fit simultaneously. In the latter case, we judge between those theories on the basis of the first kind of validity—utility or value.

The third kind of validity is *generalizability,* which refers to the extent to which the tenets of the theory apply across situations. This is the classical definition of validity and applies almost exclusively to traditional, discovery-oriented, lawlike theories.

Parsimony

The test of parsimony involves *logical simplicity.* If two theories are equally valid, the one with the simplest logical explanation is said to be the best. For example, although classical information theory (Chapter 3) can be faulted on other grounds, it is highly parsimonious. A few core assumptions and premises lead logically to a variety of claims about channels, signals, messages, and transmission.

Openness

Finally, theories can be judged according to their *openness.* This criterion is especially important in the alternative paradigm. It means that a theory is open to other possibilities.[58] It is tentative, contextual, and qualified. The theorist recognizes that his or her construction is a way of looking rather than a reproduction of reality. It admits to diversity and invites dialogue with other perspectives. It acknowledges its own incompleteness.

◗ SUMMARY

In this chapter you have learned about the study of communication, the nature of theory, and the various forms that theory building can take. You have also learned what theories can do for us and how to evaluate a communication theory.

Theories are constructions: They are created by human interpreters just as all discourse is created. Theories cannot be taken as truth because they are abstractions, and different scholars will see different things in the same observation. Therefore, the constructions employed to understand communication are extremely diverse. They vary not only in what is covered but also in their form and style, and a good deal of disagreement exists about what constitutes a legitimate theory. This forces us to take a rather broad view of theory as any conceptual representation of communication. This broad coverage should be seen as an opportunity, rather than an obstacle, because it will help us explore a wide variety of representations and styles. It will let us see examples of a whole range of ways of depicting knowledge. Although a theory course in certain narrower fields may be like a tour of a Renaissance portrait gallery, ours is like a tour of the full museum with numerous types and forms of art.

Regardless of their differences, however, all theories are basically composed of concepts, or labeled categories, used to classify observations. Many theories also have explanations, which tell us why communication works as it does. Several models of explanation are discussed in this chapter, but what is most important to remember is that all rely on some form of necessity or logical relations among concepts. The logic employed by the theory creates a kind of "force" that makes one statement follow naturally from another.

---

57 Deetz, *Democracy,* p. 67.
58 This point is developed in some detail by Penman, "Good Theory."

Traditionally, you have learned, theory is hypothetical and deductive. In other words, the theory is built on hypotheses and research. A researcher suggests a relationship, tests that relationship, and revises hypotheses on the basis of the research. Theory building in this traditional view is incremental and grows on the basis of repeated hypothesis testing.

Not all theories follow this traditional norm, however, because scholars debate a number of metatheoretical issues affecting the development of communication theory. The assumptions a researcher makes about knowledge, reality, and value determine his or her methods, the form of theoretical statements, and the ways norms and values are treated.

Whatever their form, theories constantly change and develop. Often they grow incrementally, as envisioned in traditional science, by extension from one bit of knowledge to the next. Here, the theory becomes more and more extensive as it grows in coverage. Often, however, theories change in another way, by intension, so that they delve deeper into the subject at hand. More and more detail about the subject is revealed within the theory. The third form of change is revolution, in which the old theory is dumped and a new conceptualization emerges.

As you examine the theories in the following pages, consider the ways in which they meet a variety of functions. How do they organize our knowledge about communication? What elements of the communication process do they focus our attention on? What do they clarify? How do they tell us to observe communication events? Do they enable us to make any predictions? What new research questions do they suggest, and what holes do they leave unfilled? How have scholars used these theories to communicate with one another about their ideas? And what ideas do these theories generate that can improve social life?

As you look closely at each theory, you will find some that appeal to you and others that do not. You will find some very helpful in your personal quest for understanding, and you will find others that are less so. As you evaluate these theories, think about their scope: How much do they tell us? Think about the appropriateness of their claims: Are they logically consistent? Think about their heuristic value: Do they suggest ideas for further research? And their parsimony: Are they simple but elegant? Finally, how open are the theories you encounter?

Now take a deep breath and plunge in.

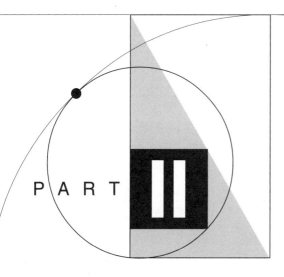

TOPICS IN COMMUNICATION THEORY

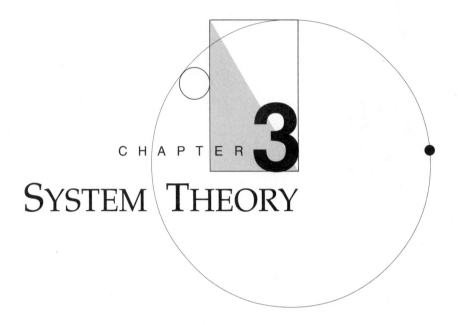

CHAPTER 3

SYSTEM THEORY

One of the most general theoretical approaches to communication is system theory. System theory and two related fields, cybernetics and information theory, offer broad perspectives on how the world operates. System theory deals with the interaction among elements of a larger process, cybernetics deals with control and regulation in systems, and information theory focuses on the measurement and transmission of signals. This group of theories can help us understand a wide variety of physical, biological, social, and behavioral processes.[1]

The roots of system thinking began at least as far back as the nineteenth century with the theory of Georg Hegel. Hegel viewed the world as being in process and controlled by a tension between opposites. For example, a cold war between two superpowers would be followed historically by an antithesis such as the collapse of one of the superpowers and a new world order. The tension experienced between these opposites—the struggle between the forces of the old and new world orders in our example—would be resolved through a synthesis of the two, such as the creation of a plethora of new nation-states

and ethnic strife. The synthesis itself becomes a new position, only to be thrown off balance again by a new antithesis, beginning the process all over. Hegel explained historical development in terms of this dynamic process, called *dialectic*.[2]

Karl Marx quickly applied Hegel's thinking to the distribution of power in society, using it to unite labor in opposition to capitalism (see Chapter 11).[3] Charles Darwin, too, relied on the idea that species evolve and adapt to pressures from outside. However, he explained the process differently than did Hegel and Marx. For Darwin, change is brought about by adaptations and accommodations.[4]

---

1   For excellent discussions of general system theory and other system approaches, see Chang-Gen Bahg, "Major Systems Theories Throughout the World," *Behavioral Science* 35 (1990): 79–107.
2   See, for example, Walter Kaufmann (ed.), *Hegel: Texts and Commentary* (Garden City, NY: Anchor, 1966).
3   See, for example, Anthony Giddens, *Profiles and Critiques in Social Theory* (Berkeley: University of California Press, 1982), especially chaps. 8 and 9.
4   Marjorie Grene, *The Knower and the Known* (Berkeley: University of California Press, 1974), chap. 7. For a more detailed treatment of the influence of Darwin on communication study, see Everett M. Rogers, *A History of Communication Study: A Biographical Approach* (New York: Free Press, 1994), pp. 41–64.

Although system theory is a product of Western intellectual history, it has similarities to certain Eastern philosophies as well. As a group, Eastern philosophies stress patterns and wholes, which are the centerpieces of system theory. Too, system theory and Eastern philosophies avoid simple linear causal reasoning and focus instead on the ways in which many considerations affect one another.[5]

System theory as we know it today was probably best codified by Ludwig von Bertalanffy, a biologist, who established the field of study known as *general system theory*. GST is a broad, multidisciplinary approach to knowledge.[6] Basically, this version of system theory uses system principles to show how things in many different fields are quite similar to one another.[7] For example, the processes that govern economic growth, biological development, and social movements might be viewed in similar terms.

◖ FUNDAMENTAL SYSTEM CONCEPTS

What are these qualities that seem to characterize so many different kinds of things? First, let's define a system and then look at the system's qualities.

What Is a System?

Any system can be said to consist of four things.[8] The first is *objects*—the parts, elements, or variables within the system. These may be physical or abstract or both, depending on the nature of the system. Second, a system consists of *attributes*—the qualities or properties of the system and its objects. Third, a system has *internal relationships* among its objects. This characteristic is a crucial aspect, and we will take a closer look at internal relationships throughout this chapter.[9] Fourth, systems also possess an *environment*. They do not exist in a vacuum but are affected by their surroundings. A *system*, then, is a set of things that affect one another within an environment and form a larger pattern that is different from any of the parts.

One of the most common distinctions is between closed and open systems.[10] A *closed system* has no interchange with its environment. It moves toward internal chaos, disintegration, and death. The closed system model most often applies to physical systems like stars, which do not have life-sustaining qualities. An *open system* receives matter and energy from its environment and passes matter and energy to its environment. The open system is oriented toward life and growth.

A family is an excellent example of an open system.[11] The members of a family are the "objects," and their characteristics are attributes. The family system is formed by the interaction among the members. Families also exist in a social and cultural environment, and the family and its environment influence each other. Family members are not isolated, and their relationships must be taken into account to fully understand the family as a unit.

System Qualities

Biological, psychological, and sociocultural systems possess certain common characteristics. You will notice that the following qualities are

5   See, for example, Joanna Macy, *Mutual Causality in Buddhism and General System Theory* (Albany: SUNY Press, 1991); and Todd Evan Pressman, "A Synthesis of Systems Inquiry and the Eastern Mode of Inquiry," *System Research* 9 (1992): 46–63.

6   For a biographical sketch of Bertalanffy, see "Ludwig von Bertalanffy," *General Systems* 17 (1972): 219–228. For a good general summary of GST, see Macy, *Mutual Causality*, pp. 69–89.

7   For an example of formalized GST, see Masanao Toda and Emir H. Shuford, "Logic of Systems: Introduction to a Formal Theory of Structure," *General Systems* 10 (1965): 3–27.

8   A. D. Hall and R. E. Fagen, "Definition of a System," in *Modern Systems Research for the Behavioral Scientist*, ed. W. Buckley (Chicago: Aldine, 1968), pp. 81–92.

9   Walter Buckley (ed.), "Society as a Complex Adaptive System," in *Modern Systems Research for the Behavioral Scientist* (Chicago: Aldine, 1968), pp. 490–513.

10   Hall and Fagen, "Definition"; Anatol Rapoport, "Foreword," in *Modern Systems Research for the Behavorial Scientist*, ed. W. Buckley (Chicago: Aldine, 1968), pp. xiii–xxv. For an excellent short description of open versus closed systems, see Ludwig von Bertalanffy, *General Systems Theory: Foundations, Development, Applications* (New York: Braziller, 1968).

11   Considerable research has been done over the years on family communication. See, for example, Arthur P. Bochner and Eric M. Eisenberg, "Family Process: System Perspectives," in *Handbook of Communication Science*, eds. C. R. Berger and S. H. Chaffee (Newbury Park, CA: Sage, 1987), pp. 540–563.

not mutually exclusive, but each relates in some way to all the others.[12]

Wholeness and Interdependence.   A system is a unique whole.[13] It involves a pattern of relationships that is different from any other system. As the saying goes, the whole is more than the sum of its parts. To understand this idea, examine for a moment the opposite view of *physical summativity*, in which a "whole" is merely a collection of parts with no interaction among them, like a box of stones. But a system is the product of the forces or interactions among the parts. A group of people standing in a row at a bus stop is not much of a system, but a group of people sitting around a table discussing a problem certainly is.

A system is a whole because its parts relate to one another and cannot be understood separately. Any part of the system is always constrained by its dependence on other object parts, and this pattern of interdependence organizes the system itself.[14]

Interdependence is easily illustrated in families. A family is a system of interacting individuals, and each member is influenced by the actions of the others. Although each person has some freedom, no one is completely free because of family bonds. The behaviors of a family are patterned and structured, somewhat predictable. What one family member does or says follows from other family behaviors and leads to further behaviors. Because interdependence is the most important characteristic of systems, it is worth exploring in some detail here.

The interdependence among the variables of a system is *correlations*.[15] In a correlation, two or more variables change together. In a family, for example, anger and yelling might be correlated. Correlations are rarely pure or perfect but are a matter of degree. Some associations are very strong, others quite weak. In a complex system, many variables interrelate with one another in a web of influences that vary in strength. For example, anger, loudness, frustration, withdrawal, and remorse might be tied together in a family. But variables can be related to one another in different ways.

One variable sometimes causes change in another one. For example, use of power by one family member may cause another to give in. Here, power is directly correlated causally with compliance. Traditionally, causality is considered one-way: variable A affects variable B. In systems, however, causality often runs both ways, such that variable A and variable B influence each other.

Take nagging and withdrawing, for example. As the father nags, the son withdraws, and as the son withdraws, the father nags. Each affects the other. Actual causation in communication is difficult to confirm, although establishing how the participants in a system *perceive* the causes is often useful. For example, the father may perceive that the son's withdrawal causes him to nag, whereas the son perceives that the father's nagging causes him to withdraw.

Variables also may be associated indirectly. In such a relationship, the two variables are correlated but do not cause each other directly; they are both caused by a third variable. For example, performance in school and in doing housework could be connected. Children who get their jobs done at home also seem to do well in school, and children who do not do very well at school are also remiss in getting house chores done. If this correlation were discovered, the researcher might uncover a third variable—perhaps the amount of time parents spend with children. Spending more time with children may bring about greater cooperation at home and school.

A more complex form of indirect relationship occurs in a chain of influence. Variable A causes B, which causes C, which causes D, which causes E, which causes A, in a causal ring.

For example, a father's dominance could cause the mother to withdraw, which causes the

---

12   Bahg, "Major System Theories."
13   Rapoport, "Foreword"; Hall and Fagen, "Definition."
14   For a sophisticated discussion of the various ways in which people can think about interdependence in systems, see Magoroh Maruyama's theory of mindscapes, summarized in Michael T. Caley and Daiyo Sawada (eds.), *Mindscapes: The Epistemology of Magoroh Maruyama* (Amsterdam: Gordon and Breach, 1994).
15   Bahg, "Major System Theories," p. 104.

child to get depressed, which prevents her from going to school, which creates problems with the teacher. The teacher calls the parents, and the father gets mad. In his domineering style, he tells the mother to get the kid to school, and she withdraws.

Complex systems consist of a network of relationships. A variable is related not just to one other variable but to a potentially large number of other variables, to the point that it becomes difficult to study. Researchers deal with this problem by taking the system apart and examining relationships one at a time. There are several ways of doing this; these methods together are known as *multivariate analysis.*[16]

An example is multiple regression analysis, in which one variable—the *dependent variable*—is correlated with several other *independent variables.* An equation is used to reveal the strength of the correlation between the dependent variable and the group of independent variables. In a family, for example, you might discover that adolescent rebellion (the dependent variable) is predicted by three independent variables: parental authoritarianism, strength of peer group, and age.

Hierarchy. Systems tend to be embedded within one another. In other words, one system is part of a larger system.[17] Arthur Koestler expresses this idea in the following tale:

> There were once two Swiss watchmakers named Bios and Mekhos, who made very fine and expensive watches. Their names may sound a little strange, but their fathers had a smattering of Greek and were fond of riddles. Although their watches were in equal demand, Bios prospered, while Mekhos just struggled along; in the end he had to close his shop and take a job as a mechanic with Bios. The people in the town argued for a long time over the reasons for this development and each had a different theory to offer, until the true explanation leaked out and proved to be both simple and surprising.
>
> The watches they made consisted of about one thousand parts each, but the two rivals had used different methods to put them together. Mekhos had assembled his watches bit by bit—

rather like making a mosaic floor out of small coloured stones. Thus each time when he was disturbed in his work and had to put down a partly assembled watch, it fell to pieces and he had to start again from scratch.

> Bios, on the other hand, had designed a method of making watches by constructing, for a start, sub-assemblies of about ten components, each of which held together as an independent unit. Ten of these sub-assemblies could then be fitted together into a sub-system of a higher order; and ten of these sub-systems constituted the whole watch. . . .
>
> Now it is easy to show mathematically that if a watch consists of a thousand bits, and if some disturbance occurs at an average of once in every hundred assembling operations—then Mekhos will take four thousand times longer to assemble a watch than Bios. Instead of a single day, it will take him eleven years. And if for mechanical bits, we substitute amino acids, protein molecules, organelles, and so on, the ratio between time-scales becomes astronomical; some calculations indicate that the whole life-time of the earth would be insufficient for producing even an amoeba—unless he [Mekhos] becomes converted to Bios' method and proceeds·hierarchically, from simple sub-assemblies to more complex ones.[18]

A system, then, is a series of levels of increasing complexity. The larger system of which a system is a part is called the *suprasystem,* and the smaller system contained within a system is called the *subsystem.* Figure 3.1 illustrates the idea of system hierarchy with a tree model.

Families illustrate hierarchy very well. The suprasystem is the extended family, which itself is part of the larger system of society. Several nuclear family units are part of the extended family, and each family unit may have subsystems such as spouses, children, and parent–child units.

Koestler calls system hierarchy the *Janus effect:*

---

16   See, for example, Peter R. Monge and Joseph N. Cappella, *Multivariate Techniques in Human Communication Research* (New York: Academic, 1980).

17   For excellent discussions of hierarchy, see Arthur Koestler, *The Ghost in the Machine* (New York: Macmillan, 1967); W. Ross Ashby, "Principles of the Self-Organizing System," in *Principles of Self-Organization,* eds. H. von Foerster and G. Zopf (New York: Pergamon, 1962), pp. 255–278.

18   Koestler, *Ghost,* pp. 45–47.

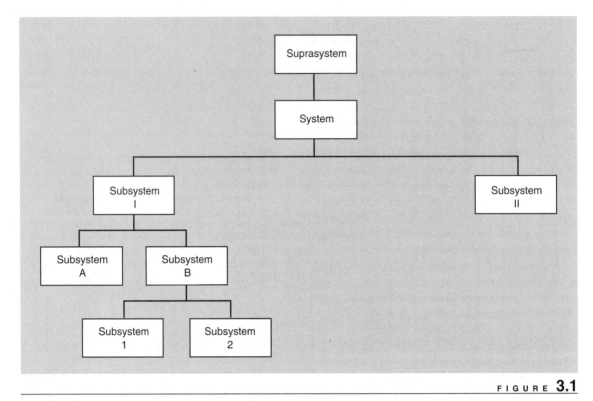

FIGURE **3.1**

System Hierarchy

The members of a hierarchy, like the Roman god Janus, all have two faces looking in opposite directions: the face turned toward the subordinate levels is that of a self-contained whole; the face turned upward toward the apex, that of a dependent part. One is the face of the master, the other the face of the servant.[19]

The natural question at this point is where a system ends and its environment begins. Because systems are part of other systems, boundaries are arbitrary and can only be established by the observer. We can take a very broad view by observing a number of systems that interact with one another in a large suprasystem, or we can take a narrower view by observing a smaller subsystem where the larger system is the environment. For example, you could look at a large extended family (a suprasystem) or two siblings in a nuclear family (a subsystem).

Self-Regulation and Control. Many systems are goal-oriented, and such systems regulate their behavior to achieve certain aims. The parts of a system must behave in certain ways and must respond to feedback. Families illustrate this. A family can have a variety of control mechanisms. For example, it may rely on one dominant member for making decisions and providing guidance. This person monitors the family and asserts control as necessary whenever signs (feedback) of deviation from family standards are detected. Other families may handle control very differently, as is the case for those families with strict role divisions that permit members to exert control over certain kinds of decisions and not others. We'll take a closer look at this aspect of systems in the section on cybernetics.

Interchange with the Environment. Remember that open systems interact with their environment. They take in and let out matter and energy,

19   Koestler, *Ghost*, p. 48.

having *inputs* and *outputs*.[20] For example, parents must adjust constantly to their children's relationships outside the family and deal with influences from friends, teachers, and television.

Balance. Balance, sometimes referred to as *homeostasis,* is self-maintenance.[21] The system must somehow detect when it is off kilter and make adjustments to get back on track. Deviation and change do occur and can be tolerated by a system, but only for so long. Eventually, the system will fall apart if it does not maintain itself.

The need for balance explains why families seem to struggle so hard to keep things on an even keel. For example, why do parents keep nagging children to behave? Why do couples who are having serious marital difficulties frequently try to get back together? From a system perspective, these efforts are natural attempts to maintain homeostasis. Indeed, many families have trouble maintaining balance in a complex social environment and do not survive. Often uncomfortable patterns such as anger and blame become part of the family system itself, and these patterns get repeated over and over in the system's attempt to maintain itself. You can see from this example that balance is not necessarily a comfortable state of affairs.

Change and Adaptability. Because it exists in a dynamic environment, a system must be adaptable.[22] Paradoxically, to survive a system must have balance, but it must also change. Complex systems sometimes have to change structurally to adapt to the environment, and that kind of change means getting off balance for a time. Advanced systems actually reorganize themselves to adjust to environmental pressures. The technical term for system change is *morphogenesis.*

To continue our example, families do change. As members age and develop, as new members come and old members leave, and as the family faces new challenges from the environment, it must adapt.

Equifinality. Finality is the goal achievement or task accomplishment of a system. *Equifinality* means that a particular final state may be accom-

plished in different ways and from different starting points. The adaptable system can achieve that goal under a variety of environmental conditions. The system is capable of processing inputs in different ways to produce its output.[23] If one pathway fails, another one can take its place. If one process gets cut off, another process steps in. Smart parents, for example, know that children's behavior can be affected by a variety of techniques, that family decision making can occur in more than one way, and that children learn several methods for securing the compliance of the adults in their world.

We have seen in this section that systems are dynamic wholes in which parts relate to one another in complex patterns of interaction. Something happens in a system to make it more than the sum of its parts. What is the currency of system interactions? What is the medium by which system influences occur? We turn now to a kindred field that attempts to answer these questions—information theory.

◖ INFORMATION THEORY

Information theory, which grew out of the boom in the telecommunications industry after World War II, is the area of study most concerned with communication in systems. *Information theory* involves the quantitative study of signals. It has practical applications in the electronic sciences that design transmitters, receivers, and codes to facilitate efficient handling of information. It has also been used widely in the behavioral and social sciences.[24]

Information theory developed from investigations in physics, engineering, and mathematics, which were concerned with the organization of

---

20   Gordon Allport, "The Open System in Personality Theory," in *Modern Systems Research for the Behavioral Scientist,* ed. W. Buckley (Chicago: Aldine, 1968), pp. 343–350; Hall and Fagen, "Definition."
21   Ashby, "Principles."
22   Hall and Fagen, "Definition"; Buckley, "Adaptive System"; Koestler, *Ghost.*
23   Von Bertalanffy, *General Systems Theory,* chap. 3.
24   Several brief histories of the movement are available. See, for example, Rogers, *A History,* pp. 411–444.

events. Claude Shannon, a telecommunications engineer at Bell Telephone Laboratories, synthesized the early work in information theory. His book with Warren Weaver, *The Mathematical Theory of Communication*, is now a classic.[25]

Basic Concepts

Information can be understood by starting with entropy, a related concept borrowed from thermodynamics. *Entropy* is randomness, or lack of organization in a situation. A totally entropic situation is unpredictable. Because most of the situations we are confronted with are partially and not completely predictable, entropy is a variable. If dark clouds come over the sky, you could predict rain, and you might be right or wrong. Because weather is an organized system, predictions are never certain. You cannot predict rain conclusively. The entropy existing in the situation causes some uncertainty. In short, the more entropy, the less organization and predictability.

What does this have to do with information? *Information* is a measure of the uncertainty, or entropy, in a situation. The greater the uncertainty, the more the information. When a situation is completely predictable, no information is present. This is a condition known as *negentropy*.

This definition of information is confusing because most people associate information with certainty or knowledge. As used by the information theorist, however, the concept does not refer to meaning but only refers to the quantification of stimuli or signals.

On closer examination, this idea of information is not as nonsensical as it first appears, if you consider information as the number of signals required to reduce completely the uncertainty in the situation. For example, your friend is about to flip a coin. Will it land heads up or

tails up? You are uncertain; you cannot predict. This uncertainty will be eliminated by seeing the result of the flip. Now suppose that you have received a tip that your friend's coin is two-headed. The flip is fixed, resulting in no uncertainty and no information. In other words, you could not receive any more signals that would help you predict any better than you already can. In short, a situation with which you are completely familiar has no new information for you.

There is yet a third way to understand this concept. Information can be thought of as the number of choices, or alternatives, available to a person in predicting an outcome. In a complex situation with many possible outcomes, more information is available than in a simple situation with few outcomes. In other words, a person would need more facts to predict the outcome of a complex situation than to predict the outcome of a simple one. For example, there is more information in a two-dice toss than in the toss of a single die and more information in a single-die toss than in a coin flip. Because information is a function of the number of alternatives, it reflects the degree of freedom in making choices within a situation. The more information in a situation, the more choices you can make within that situation.

Language and Information

Many messages consist of a series of stimuli received sequentially, or one at a time. In written language, for example, one letter follows another, and words flow one at a time. Information theory can be applied to this kind of situation. If the letters in a sentence were arranged randomly, you could never predict what letter might follow any other letter. Decoding would be difficult because of the great amount of information in the message. But letters (or sounds in speech) are not organized randomly. There are various predictable patterns. These patterns make decoding easier because there is less information, or greater predictability. For example, in English an adjective has a high probability of being followed by a noun. A *q* is always followed by a *u*

25   Claude Shannon and Warren Weaver, *The Mathematical Theory of Communication* (Urbana: University of Illinois Press, 1949). Two sources were particularly helpful in the preparation of this section: Allan R. Broadhurst and Donald K. Darnell, "An Introduction to Cybernetics and Information Theory," *Quarterly Journal of Speech* 51 (1965): 442–453; Klaus Krippendorff, "Information Theory," in *Communication and Behavior*, eds. G. Hanneman and W. McEwen (Reading, MA: Addison-Wesley, 1975), pp. 351–389.

in English. Thus, the overall arrangement of a sentence is patterned and partially predictable. This is called *redundancy.*

On the other hand, a sentence does contain some uncertainty because you can never predict with complete accuracy. If you could, there would be no freedom of choice. Once the first letter was written, all the other letters would follow automatically. Language is blessed with moderate redundancy, allowing ease of decoding with freedom of encoding.

Language information is an example of a *Markov process,* in which certain things follow other things in a chain. A Markov process is a series of events, one happening after another in time, such that the occurrence of one element in the chain establishes a probability that another particular element will follow. Language is an example of a Markov process. Many other phenomena follow the same pattern, for example, a workday consists of a series of somewhat predictable tasks and driving from one city to another requires following a sequence of turns.

Markov processes like language must be discussed in terms of *average* redundancy because the actual amount varies from point to point in the chain. For example, the average redundancy in English is about 50 percent.

Information Transmission

Information theory is not concerned with the meaning of messages, only with their transmission and reception. This is particularly important in electronic communication, where signals are transmitted along a line or through a medium.

The basic model of transmission developed by Shannon and Weaver is shown in Figure 3.2.[26] In this model the *source* formulates or selects a *message,* consisting of signs to be transmitted. The *transmitter* converts the message into a set of *signals* that are sent over a *channel* to a *receiver.* The receiver converts the signals into a message. This model can be applied to a variety of situations. A television message is a good example in

the electronic arena: The producers, directors, and announcers are the source; the message is transmitted by airwaves (channel) to the TV set, which converts electromagnetic waves back into a visual impression for the viewer.

In interpersonal communication the speaker's brain is the source, the vocal system the transmitter, and the air medium the channel. The listener's ear is the receiver, and the listener's brain the destination. The final element in this model, *noise,* is any disturbance in the channel that distorts or otherwise masks the signal.

Whether the message is coded into regular language, electronic signals, or some other verbal or nonverbal code, the problem of transmission is the same: to reconstruct the message accurately at the destination, as any television viewer with a snowy screen can testify.

Now you can begin to see the role of redundancy in a message. Redundancy compensates for noise. As noise distorts, masks, or replaces signals, redundancy allows the receiver to correct or fill in missing or distorted data. For example, suppose you receive from a friend a letter that has been smeared by rain. The first sentences might look like this: "How - - - yo-? I a-fine." Or perhaps because of static, a sentence of radio news comes across as, "The Pres- - - -ed States has - clared. . . ." You can make some sense out of these distorted sentences because of the predictability or redundancy in the language.

Another factor limiting accurate transmission is channel capacity. *Channel capacity* is usually defined in terms of the maximum amount of information that can be transmitted over a channel in a given time period (per millisecond, perhaps). The actual amount of information in the channel is *throughput.* If throughput exceeds channel capacity, distortion will occur or transmission will slow down, as when you set your amplifier too high, beyond the capacity of the speakers.

If you do much Web surfing, you know firsthand the limitations of channel capacity. You may be frustrated downloading a file with a 28.8 modem because you have a channel capacity problem. One answer is to increase the size of the channel by going to a 33.3 or higher modem. On

---

26   Shannon and Weaver, *Mathematical Theory,* p. 5.

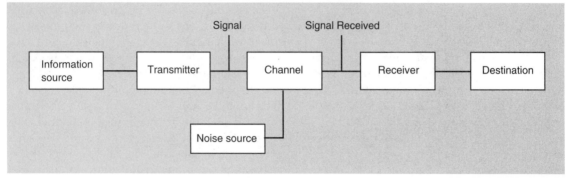

FIGURE **3.2**

Shannon and Weaver's Model of Communication

From *Mathematical Theory of Communication* by Claude Shannon and Warren Weaver. Copyright © 1949 by the Board of Trustees of the University of Illinois. Reprinted by permission of the University of Illinois Press.

Sunday mornings, you can zoom from one site on the Web to another pretty quickly, but by Sunday evening, the Internet is like mud—thick and slow. What's the difference? Not channel capacity, but throughput demand. Hardly anyone is on the Web on Sunday morning, but by evening, everyone wants to get on.

What, then, is necessary for efficient transmission? Efficient transmission involves coding at a maximum rate that will not exceed channel capacity. It also means using a code with sufficient redundancy to compensate for the amount of noise present in the channel. Too much redundancy means transmission will be inefficient; too little means it will be inaccurate.

◖ CYBERNETICS

Cybernetics is the study of regulation and control in systems.[27] An important feature of open systems, as we saw earlier, is that they are regulated, seek goals, and are purposeful. This is the subject of cybernetics.

Feedback Processes

Cybernetics deals with the ways a system gauges its effect and makes necessary adjustments. The simplest cybernetic device consists of a sensor, a comparator, and an activator. The *sensor* provides *feedback* to the *comparator*, which determines whether the machine is deviating from its established norm. The comparator then provides guidance to the *activator*, which produces an output that affects the environment in some way. This fundamental process of output-feedback-adjustment is the basis of cybernetics.

Feedback mechanisms vary in complexity, as Figure 3.3 illustrates.[28] The most basic distinction is between active and passive behavior. *Active behavior* comes from the system itself, whereas *passive behavior* results strictly from outside stimulation. Scratching an itch is passive behavior, but waving to a friend is active. Active behavior can be further divided into purposeless, or random, and purposeful behavior. *Purposeful behavior* is

27   Rollo Handy and Paul Kurtz, "A Current Appraisal of the Behavioral Sciences: Communication Theory," *American Behavioral Scientist* 7 (6, 1964): 99–104. Supplementary information is found in Gordon Pask, *An Approach to Cybernetics* (New York: Harper & Row, 1961); G. T. Guilbaud, *What Is Cybernetics?* (New York: Grove, 1959). For a historical review, see Norbert Wiener, *Cybernetics or Control and Communication in the Animal and the Machine* (Cambridge, MA: MIT Press, 1961), pp. 1–29. See also Rogers, *A History*, pp. 386–410. For a cybernetic approach to communication, see D. J. Crowley, *Understanding Communication: The Signifying Web* (New York: Gordon and Breach, 1982), especially chap. 1.
28   Arturo Rosenblueth, Norbert Wiener, and Julian Bigelow, "Behavior, Purpose, and Teleology," *Philosophy of Science* 10 (1943): 18–24 [reprinted in *Modern Systems Research for the Behavioral Scientist,* ed. W. Buckley (Chicago: Aldine, 1968), pp. 221–225].

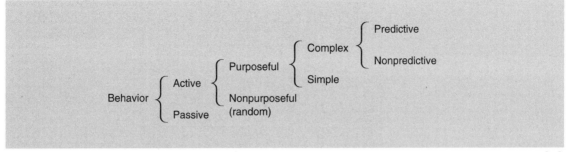

FIGURE **3.3**

Model of Cybernetic Complexity

From *Philosophy of Science*, "Behavior, Purpose, and Teleology," by Arturo Rosenblueth, Norbert Weiner, and Julian Bigelow. Copyright © 1943 by the Williams & Wilkins Co. Reprinted by permission of the publisher.

directed toward an objective or aim, whereas *random behavior* is not. Rubbing one's face or moving a hand may be just a random action, but when done to express an idea or emphasize a point, the action is clearly purposeful.

All purposeful behavior requires feedback, which varies in complexity, as indicated in the model, and purposeful behavior may be further subdivided into complex and simple types.[29] In *simple systems* the organism responds to feedback only by turning on or off. A thermostat is a perfect example of a simple feedback mechanism. *Complex systems,* however, use positive and negative feedback to adjust and adapt during the action itself. Complex systems may be predictive or nonpredictive. *Predictive behavior* is based on anticipated position or response rather than actual position or response. A good quarterback passes the football to the spot where the receiver will be, not to where the receiver is at the moment. Often, the quarterback even releases the ball before the receiver turns to look for it.

A simple feedback model is represented in Figure 3.4. In the figure, B is an energy source directing outputs to C. A is the control mechanism responding to feedback from C. Depending on the complexity of the system and the nature of the output, the control mechanism itself is restricted in the kind of control it can exert. Figure 3.5 illustrates some possible situations.[30]

The first model in Figure 3.5 demonstrates a situation where the signal itself is modified, in this case amplified, by A. A high-pitched squeal from a loudspeaker is an example. The next model illustrates a simple switch such as a thermostat or circuit breaker. The third model illustrates selection control in which A chooses a channel or position on the basis of criteria. In a guided missile, for example, the guidance system may specify turning in one direction or another, based on feedback from the target.

A regulated system must possess certain control guidelines. The control center must "know" what environmental conditions to respond to and how. It must possess a sensitivity to aspects of the environment that are critical to its goal seeking.[31]

Feedback can be classified as positive or negative, depending on the way the system responds to it. *Negative feedback* is an error message indicating deviation, and the system adjusts by reducing or counteracting the deviation. The most important type of feedback in homeostasis is negative feedback because it maintains a steady state.

---

29   I have changed the original nomenclature here to avoid confusion and inconsistency with previous usage in this chapter. The authors' intent is unchanged.
30   Adapted from Guilbaud, *Cybernetics.*
31   Walter Buckley, *Sociology and Modern Systems Theory* (Englewood Cliffs, NJ: Prentice-Hall, 1967), pp. 52–53.

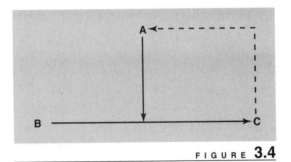

FIGURE **3.4**

A Simple Feedback Model

A system can also respond by amplifying or maintaining deviation, in which case the feedback is *positive*. This kind of interaction is important in morphogenesis, or system growth such as learning. The inflationary cycle in economics is an example of positive feedback effects. Whether in mechanical or human systems, the response to negative feedback is "cut back, slow down, discontinue." Response to positive feedback is "increase, maintain, keep going."

Figure 3.6 illustrates three system states. The first is a steady state, the second a growth state, and the third a change state. A *steady state* involves the use of negative feedback to keep the system on track. Negative feedback signals deviate from the standard, and the system adjusts in order to return to the line. Notice that the system is always moving; it is constantly changing, but it never gets too far from the desired state because of negative feedback. For example, a manager may want to maintain a supportive relationship with all her subordinates. She continually tries to be supportive, and when employees are feeling unsupported, she detects the dissatisfaction and tries harder to make them feel included. This manager may waver from time to time but, because of negative feedback, maintains support most of the time.

The second state is *growth*. Here as the system deviates, positive feedback maintains the deviation, and the result is farther and farther movement from the original state. The system accelerates some behavior, and if this continues indefinitely, the system will disintegrate.

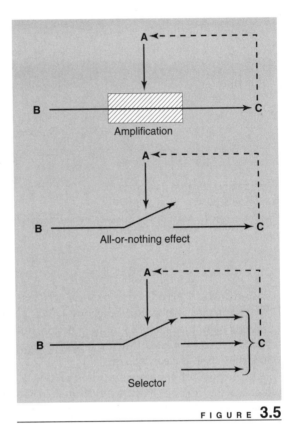

FIGURE **3.5**

Illustrative Control Models

Relational spirals are an example. A relational spiral occurs when partners increase the intensity of their responses to each other. Imagine, for example, that a woman goes out with friends without telling her boyfriend, and when he discovers this, he gets irritated. She thinks that his irritation is unjustified and decides to go out with her friends again. Now he gets even more upset, and she goes out again just to make the point that she has the right to do so. In time, she is going out very frequently with her friends, and he is exploding in anger and jealousy. Here, each partner's actions are taken as positive feedback, creating even more deviation from the original state. If the spiral does not stop, the relationship will not survive. Notice that "positive" feedback does not mean "good" feedback; indeed, it may be very bad. And negative feedback

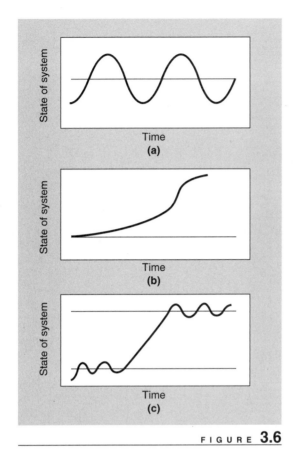

FIGURE **3.6**

**Three Feedback States: (a) Steady State,
(b) Growth State, and (c) Change State**

is not necessarily bad, because it is needed by the system to maintain balance.

The third state is *change*. Here, the system moves from one state to another state. It requires both negative and positive feedback. Positive feedback gets the system moving in a new direction, but negative feedback comes into play at some level to return the system to balance. The ability of systems to maintain balance and yet continue to adapt and renew themselves is a remarkable feature of both natural and human systems.[32]

Let's return to our example of the supportive manager. As sometimes happens, too much support causes the suppression of productive conflict and the stifling of needed change. Assume that

our manager begins to get feedback saying that her department is not productive enough. She responds by criticizing her employees' work habits and in the process becomes less supportive. At some point the workers' productivity increases, and she reduces her criticism. At this point the system has moved to a new state of somewhat less supportiveness and a bit more scrutiny.

Complex Networks

Our discussion of feedback thus far has given the impression that a system responds as a unit to feedback from the outside. This impression is realistic only for the simplest systems such as a heater and thermostat. As a series of hierarchically ordered subsystems, advanced systems are more complex. A subsystem at any moment may be part of the larger system or part of the environment.[33] Further, we know that subsystems respond to one another. As a result we must expand the concept of feedback in complex systems. In a complex system, a series of feedback loops exist within and among subsystems, forming *networks*. At some points the feedback loops are positive, at other points negative. But always, consistent with the basic feedback principle, system output returns as feedback input. No matter how complicated the network, one always comes back to the beginning.

A simple illustration of a system network is the example of urbanization in Figure 3.7.[34] In this figure the pluses (+) represent positive relationships and the minuses (–) negative ones. In a positive relationship, variables increase or decrease together. In a negative relationship, as one increases, the other decreases. For example, as the number of people in the city (P) increases, modernization also increases. With increased

32   For an excellent discussion of the paradox of stability and change in systems, see Margaret Wheatley, "Change, Stability, and Renewal: The Paradoxes of Self-Organizing Systems," in *Leadership and the New Science: Learning About Organization from an Orderly Universe* (San Francisco: Berrett-Kochler, 1992), pp. 75–99.

33   Magoroh Maruyama, "The Second Cybernetics: Deviation-Amplifying Mutual Causal Processes," *American Scientist* 51 (1963): 164–179. See also, Caley and Sawada, *Mindscapes,* pp. 99–109.

34   Maruyama, "The Second Cybernetics," p. 311.

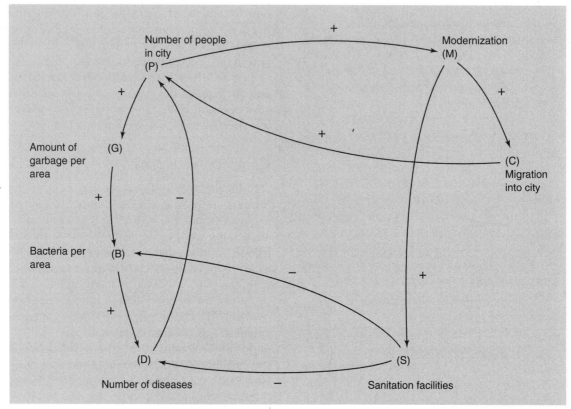

FIGURE **3.7**

A Simplified Feedback Network

From *American Scientist*, "The Second Cybernetics," by Magoroh Maruyama. Copyright © 1963. Reprinted by permission of the publisher.

modernization comes increased migration, which in turn further increases the population. This relationship is an example of a positive feedback loop. A negative relationship is illustrated by the effect of the number of diseases (D) on population (P).

As our discussion to this point implies, cybernetics is a central process in systems, for it explains such qualities as wholeness (a portion of a system cannot be understood apart from its loops among subsystems), interdependence (subsystems are constrained by mutual feedback), self-regulation (a system maintains balance and changes by responding appropriately to positive and negative feedback), and interchange with the environment (inputs and outputs create feedback loops).

Although these cybernetic concepts originated in the fields of physiology, engineering, and mathematics, they have tremendous implications in the behavioral and social sciences.[35] As Norbert Wiener, the founder of cybernetics, states, "This principle in control applies not merely to the Panama locks, but to states, armies, and individual human beings. . . . This matter of social feedback is of very great sociological and anthropological interest."[36]

Indeed, cybernetics is a way of thinking. Emphasizing circular reasoning, cybernetics chal-

35   See Karl Deutsch, "Toward a Cybernetic Model of Man and Society," in *Modern Systems Research for the Behavioral Scientist,* ed. W. Buckley (Chicago: Aldine, 1968), pp. 387–400.
36   Norbert Wiener, *The Human Use of Human Beings: Cybernetics in Society* (Boston: Houghton Mifflin, 1954), pp. 49–50.

lenges the very idea that one thing causes another in a linear fashion. It calls our attention to the ways in which things impact one another in a circular way.[37] What goes around comes around. In its more recent forms, cybernetics claims that observers can never see how a system works by standing outside the system itself because the observer is always on some level engaged cybernetically with the system being observed. Let's see how this is so.

Second-Order Cybernetics

Whenever you observe a system, you affect and are affected by the system.[38] The term *second-order cybernetics* was coined by Heinz von Foerster to capture this idea. Second-order cybernetics is sometimes called the "cybernetics of the observing system," because it shows how observation itself is a cybernetic mechanism with feedback loops between the observer and observed.

It is also called the "cybernetics of knowing" because it shows that knowledge is a product of feedback loops between the knower and the known.[39] What we observe in a system is determined in part by the categories and methods of observation, which in turn are affected by what is seen. This circle is a cybernetic system, and observers cannot escape it.

The ideas of second-order cybernetics have been developed by a closely knit group of thinkers, including von Foerster himself, Gregory Bateson, Humberto Maturana, and Francisco Varela.[40]

Second-order cybernetics is revolutionary in system theory because it says that objective observation and knowledge are not possible. Traditional system theory and cybernetics treat systems as objectively observable, but in second-order cybernetics, the observed system both affects and is affected by the observer. This idea has powerful implications not only for system theory but for the philosophy of knowing as well (see Chapter 2). Von Foerster puts the matter in these terms:

One may see this fundamental epistemological change if one considers oneself first to be an independent observer who watches the world go by; or if one considers oneself to be a participant actor in the drama of mutual interaction, of the give and take in the circularity of human relations.[41]

This theory seems strange at first because we human beings feel separate from what we observe. This impression is a result of *autopoiesis*, or the tendency of a living system to distinguish itself from other systems and to act in ways that maintain a sense of autonomy or separateness.[42] Yet the structural relationships within a system limit the distinctions that the system can make. In other words, what we see in another system is very much determined by our own makeup and history, including past interactions with other people.

At the same time, when we observe another system, we are affected by the structure and history of that system. In second-order cybernetics, this is called *structural coupling*. Here two systems can have mutual effects. They coordinate their actions, and they can evolve together. This is true in the natural world as well as in human relations.

The cybernetics of observation becomes quite interesting when the observed system is the observer's own environment. People make this kind of observation all the time. For example, if

---

37 See, for example, Klaus Krippendorff, "Cybernetics," in *International Encyclopedia of Communications,* eds. Erik Barnouw et al. (New York: Oxford University Press, 1989), vol. 1, pp. 443–446; Søren Brier, "Forward," *Cybernetics and Human Knowing: A Journal of Second Order Cybernetics and Cyber-Semantics* 1 (1992). (http://www.db.dk/dbaa/sbr/vol1/v1-1for.htm).

38 Heinz von Foerster, *Observing Systems: Selected Papers of Heinz von Foerster* (Seaside, CA: Intersystems Publications, 1981). For information about von Foerster, his ideas, and his life, see Francisco Varela, "Heinz von Foerster, the Scientist, the Man: Prologue to the Interview," *SEHR* 4(2). (http://shr.stanford.edu/shreview/4-2/text/varela.html); Stefano Franchi, Güven Güzeldere, and Eric Minch, "Interview: Heinz von Foerster," *SEHR* 4(2). (http://shr.stanford.edu/shreview/4-2/text/interviewconf.html).

39 Rodney E. Donaldson, "Cybernetics and Human Knowing: One Possible Prolegomenon," *Cybernetics and Human Knowing* 1 (1992): 1–4; Brier, "Forward."

40 Chief among their works are Gregory Bateson, *Steps to an Ecology of Mind* (New York: Ballantine, 1972); Humberto Maturana and Francisco Varela, *The Tree of Knowledge: The Biological Roots of Human Understanding* (Boston: Shambhala, 1992).

41 Heinz von Foerster, "Ethics and Second-Order Cybernetics," *SEHR* 4(2): 4. (http://shr.stanford.edu/shreview/4-2/text/foerster.html).

42 Randall Whitaker, "Overview of Autopoietic Theory." (http://www.acm.org/signois/auto/ATReview.html#Background).

you try to explain how brains work, you must account for how your own brain is working right now as you explain how brains work. Your observation of the system must include an observation of the observation itself! Another example is observing a group of which you are a member. You cannot do this completely if you do not take into account your own behavior (including your observing) as a member of the group.

Family system therapy has made good use of second-order cybernetics and illustrates how it works.[43] Old-style system theorists would say that the therapist can work as an outsider by observing, diagnosing, and prescribing, but second-order cybernetics denies this. When the therapist meets a family, the therapist (herself a system) observes and interacts with the family (another system). The therapist and the family constitute a cybernetic system of feedback loops, in which each affects the other in a new system.

Therefore, the therapist must realize that the therapeutic relationship itself is a system, and the therapist should look at this bigger system too. In other words, the therapist is part of the system being observed. Therapy is a series of *interactions* and is viewed in this tradition as an organic, step-by-step process that can shift from one direction to another. Although the therapist and family hope that the result will be healthier, happier relationships, the precise outcome cannot be predicted or prescribed in advance. The idea is to affect the patterns of interaction in the system in such a way that the family itself comes to discover new ways of changing its system in a positive way.

Human beings always have choices in how they act within a larger cybernetic system. As a part of many systems that have interacted with many other systems, people have a tremendous repertoire of ways to respond to feedback. A fundamental principle of autopoiesis is that the system can act in many ways to maintain its identity as a system.

This means that when you observe another system, you can frame your observations in a variety of ways, and when you respond to what you see, you can act in a variety of creative ways.

As an observer, then, you can assume some personal responsibility for how the framework with which you observe may affect the system, how your responses may change the system, and how your observations of the system may change you.

Ecologists use this kind of reasoning. They understand that a redwood forest, say, can be understood in a variety of ways and that how we understand the forest will affect how we act toward it, which in turn will change us and the natural and social environments in which we live.

Because observers never work in isolation and are part of many systems, the second-order cybernetic process can be quite complex. How we observe a given system, what we see when we observe, and the ways in which we engage a system are produced by a history of interaction with many groups of people over a lifetime. Observation and engagement of any system then is a *social* process. Second-order cybernetics, therefore, is related to theories of *social constructionism* (Chapter 9), with both placing interaction and communication at the center of knowing.[44]

◖ DYNAMIC SOCIAL IMPACT THEORY: A SYSTEM THEORY OF COMMUNICATION

System theory has had a major influence on the study of human communication. Although it would be impossible to mention all the lines of work that reflect system influences, several of these appear in the following chapters. In this section, we will look at a very general theory that illustrates clearly how system theory can be applied to communication.

---

43   For a good discussion of applications of system theory in family therapy, see Janet Yerby, "Family Systems Theory Reconsidered: Integrating Social Construction Theory and Dialectical Process," *Communication Theory* 5 (1995): 339–365.
44   Yerby, "Family System Theory."

Dynamic social impact theory (DSIT) has been developed by Bibb Latané and his colleagues.[45] The theory imagines society as a giant communication system consisting of numerous cultural subsystems, which include individuals interacting with one another. Because the most basic elements of the system are individuals, let's begin there.

DSIT adopts the widely held axiom that individuals are different in many ways. They have different ideas, beliefs, attitudes, and behaviors. But individuals also share many characteristics with others, and they tend to group together into clusters of like-minded people. Indeed, cultures are large groupings of individuals who share common ideologies and practices. DSIT attempts to explain, in system terms, how these commonalities develop and how cultures form.

Individuals are not isolated. They interact with one another in social spaces. *Social spaces* are the "areas" in which people meet, communicate, and influence one another. Latané has found that social space is largely a physical space, constrained by actual physical distance among individuals. Other things being equal, on average you will be more influenced by people close to you than by individuals far away. Physical distance, however, is not the only aspect of social space. For many reasons, we do not interact equally with everyone in proximity. Various social arrangements, such as race and class, keep people from interacting even though they may live and work quite close to one another.

Another factor influencing social space are various media of communication that enable people to communicate at a distance, including telephone, e-mail, and mass media. Imagine all of the people you are most likely to communicate with. Most of them live and work close to you, but some may be at a distance. You all occupy a common social space and are likely to influence one another in various ways.

To help understand how dynamic social impact works, imagine your university as a social world. Let's say you are a graduate student in the communication department. With whom are you most likely to communicate? Probably with other members of the communication department and especially those with whom you have regular contact. You are less likely to communicate with medical students or staff members in the grounds maintenance department. You could therefore predict that you will share more attributes with other members of the communication department than with people from other, more distant groups.

In time, as you interact more and more with communication department members, you will begin to influence one another and think alike in certain ways. You will share knowledge, and attitudes will begin to converge. After a while, you might even begin to identify a communication department culture, a way of thinking and doing things common to the department. Even within the department, there will be certain subgroups. For example, a small group of graduate students may get together socially, maybe even going out for drinks every Friday afternoon.

This group clustering phenomenon is caused by mutual influence among individuals who share a common social space. The shared characteristics of a group change dynamically with new contacts and interactions.

Clearly, this grouping phenomenon is not random. Influence among individuals varies along three dimensions. The first is the *strength* of influence of various individuals in the social space. The second is *immediacy,* or closeness between people, or openness of channels between persons. The third is the *number* of people in the social space. If you have many people, a large number of whom are influential, drawn together to communicate, the grouping tendency will be very high. If there are fewer people, few influential people, and little opportunity to talk, grouping will be less likely.

One thing is clear: Individuals in contact with one another will not remain random,

---

45   Bibb Latané, "Dynamic Social Impact: Robust Predictions from Simple Theory," in *Modelling and Simulation in the Social Sciences from the Philosophy of Science Point of View,* eds. R. Hegselmann, U. Mueller, and K. G. Troitzsch (Dordrecht, Netherlands: Kluwer Theory and Decision Library, 1996), pp. 287–310; see the symposium on DSIT, Edward L. Fink, "Dynamic Social Impact Theory and the Study of Human Communication," *Journal of Communication* 46 (1996): 4–77.

unconnected nodes but will organize themselves cybernetically into a dynamic structure of groups with common characteristics. You can see how the organization of the system perpetuates itself: Groups form by proximity in the social space, but those groups in turn give additional structure to the social space, which in a circular way affects the possible patterns of influence within the space itself.

This self-organizing tendency explains the formation of minority groups. Over time the influence of the majority is considerable because of sheer numbers, leading to a preponderance of beliefs being shared by most of the people within the social space. Yet, ironically, continued communication within a minority group bolsters its shared beliefs and practices, shielding it from the majority view. This is a cybernetic mechanism that ensures diversity within the larger system.

Imagine that upon entering the graduate program, you find that the students and faculty differ in their attitudes toward qualitative and quantitative research methods. At first there is no real grouping of individuals into two camps, but over time groups begin to develop. Because of the strong influence of certain members of the department and relatively close relations among some, a majority view favoring quantitative research develops. More and more students come to affiliate with the quantitative group. At the same time, however, a minority qualitative group emerges and reinforces its own view by continual communication among themselves.

An interesting thing happens when groupings like this occur. Once a group is formed, its interaction brings about additional influence and even more convergence on issues that are not logically related to the topics that brought the group together in the first place. For example, suppose that certain members of the quantitative group smoke, and because of their frequent interaction with one another, others start to smoke too. Perhaps the unique interaction patterns in the qualitative group do not lead to this outcome. You would observe, then, that the quantitative group tend to be smokers, whereas the qualitative group are not. Quantitative methods and smoking become correlated, even though there is no

logical connection between these, and such correlations give further structure to the system.

If the individuals within a social space had equal contact with one another, you would expect that divergent views would slowly converge to the center, making everyone in the social space the same and not extreme in any way. Eventually, you might predict, everyone in the department would come to favor quantitative methods. We know, of course, that this is rarely the case, for the system tends to maintain diversity. This is because interaction is never entirely random, and influence is never entirely linear. Nonlinearity in the system is therefore very important for maintaining system change and diversity. Let's see how.

Especially on important issues, people do not just keep changing incrementally over time. They cling to their ideas and practices for quite a while until a "tipping point" is reached and a shift occurs—the straw that broke the camel's back. Once the pressure to change outweighs the pressure to stay the same, a major shift may occur.

The more important the issue and the more involved the individual is with the issue, the less linear change seems to be. In fact, in the face of increasing social pressure, you can actually become more extreme in the views you hold. From our example above, the quantitative and qualitative groups may become quite polarized, creating even more diversity than before.

You can see positive and negative feedback loops at work here. Negative feedback loops tend to cancel out diversity and lead to convergence, whereas positive feedback loops tend to create diversity and lead to divergence. Imagine society as a huge system of interacting individuals in which many such loops continually bring about both social order and diversity.

COMMENTARY AND CRITIQUE

System theory has been a popular and influential tradition in communication. Because it is a complex set of variables that relate to one another, communication seems to be a natural topic for the application of system principles. System theory can be useful for understanding communication in general as well as instances of communication occurring in everyday life.

System theory also shows us concretely how functionalism works (Chapter 1). Functional approaches to theory examine the links, influences, and associations among the parts of a system, and many of the ideas presented in this chapter demonstrate how this is done.

In the abstract, fundamental system principles may seem esoteric, but when you see them in actual operation, they make sense. The most important system principle is wholeness and interdependence. What really makes a system work is the interaction among its parts. Even system qualities such as self-regulation and interchange with the environment are basically extensions of the interdependence principle.

Interdependence is a cybernetic process, because system parts influence and control one another. Although the simple feedback loop is basic to cybernetics, most complex systems—certainly all human systems—make use of entire networks of influence.

System ideas have been criticized on several fronts, although their supporters remain undaunted.[46] Six major issues have emerged:

1. Does the generality of system theory provide the advantage of integration or the disadvantage of ambiguity?
2. Does the theory's openness provide flexibility in application or confusing equivocality?
3. Is system theory merely a philosophical perspective, or does it provide useful explanations?
4. Has system theory generated useful research?
5. Is the system paradigm an arbitrary convention, or does it reflect reality in nature?
6. Does system theory help to simplify, or does it make things more complicated than they really are?

The first issue clearly relates to theoretical scope. From the beginning, supporters have claimed that system theory provides a common vocabulary to integrate the sciences and that it establishes useful logics that can be fruitfully applied to a broad range of topics. Others, however, claim that system theory merely confuses. If it is everything, it is really nothing. If all phenomena follow the same system principles, we have no basis for understanding how one thing is different from anything else.

Along the same line, some critics point out that system theory cannot have its cake and eat it too. Either it must remain a general framework without explaining real-world events, or it must abandon general integration in favor of making substantive claims. Jesse Delia expresses this concern:

> General System Theory manifests a fundamental ambiguity in that at points it seems to present a substantive perspective making specific theoretical claims and at other points to present a general abstract language devoid of specific theoretical substance for the unification of alternative theoretical views.[47]

The second issue is this: Does the theory's openness provide flexibility of thought or confusing equivocality? Detractors claim that the theory embodies what Delia calls "a fancy form of the fallacy of equivocation." In other words, by permitting a variety of applications in different domains, it cannot prevent inconsistencies among these applications. Two theories using system principles may even contradict each other. Where, then, Delia asks, is the supposed unity brought about by system theory? This problem is exacerbated by the fact that system theories can employ various logics, which are not necessarily consistent with one another.[48]

Chang-Gen Bahg points out that "system theory" as a label is confusing.[49] There are actu-

---

46   For arguments supporting system theory, see especially Ludwig von Bertalanffy, "General Systems Theory: A Critical Review," *General Systems* 7 (1962): 1–20; Buckley, *Sociology*; Peter Monge, "The Systems Perspective as a Theoretical Basis for the Study of Human Communication," *Communication Quarterly* 25 (1977): 19–29; B. Aubrey Fisher, *Perspectives on Human Communication* (New York: Macmillan, 1978).
47   Jesse Delia, "Alternative Perspectives for the Study of Human Communication: Critique and Response," *Communication Quarterly* 25 (1977): 51. See also Edgan Taschjan, "The Entropy of Complex Dynamic Systems," *Behavioral Science* 19 (1975): 3.
48   Delia, "Alternative Perspectives," pp. 51–52.
49   Bahg, "Major Systems Theories."

ally a variety of system theories with different names. Bahg discusses twenty-one different system theory traditions. To make matters worse, different system theories sometimes use the same name. "System theory" means different things in different parts of the world.

Particularly confusing among system theories are their different epistemologies, or ways of understanding events. Some are very mechanical and imply a world that works like a machine. Others, like second-order cybernetics, see systems as socially constructed (see Chapter 9).[50]

Supporters answer that openness is one of the main advantages of system theory. It provides not a single tool but a variety of related tools to use in many useful ways. That a set of common ideas such as wholeness and interdependence has been used in so many different ways shows the rich potential of the system enterprise.[51]

Apropos of the third issue, some critics question whether the system approach is a theory at all, claiming that it has no explanatory power. Although it gives us a perspective or way of conceptualizing, it provides little basis for understanding why things occur as they do. B. Aubrey Fisher agrees:

> These principles are quite abstract (that is to say, general). Consequently, they can be applied in numerous ways by differing theorists with equally different results. In fact, system "theory" is probably a misnomer. . . . In short, system theory is a loosely organized and highly abstract set of principles, which serve to direct our thinking but which are subject to numerous interpretations.[52]

System advocates would agree with this assessment of general system theory but point out that any given system theory of communication could itself be highly explanatory. Even if system principles are useful, however, their application to real problems may distract observers from significant problems ignored by system principles. Family system therapy is such a case, according to H. Russell Searight and William Merkel, who write: "By focusing almost solely upon interpersonal interactions as sources of clinical problems, family therapy has neglected intrapersonal factors such as central nervous system dysfunction.

This neglect has created unnecessary barriers to treating problems such as attention deficit disorder, learning disabilities, and panic disorder."[53]

Searight and Merkel extend this point further by suggesting that family system theory is culturally inappropriate in the United States. This country is typically an individualistic culture, and problems are understood largely in individualistic terms. There seems to be a split, then, between family system therapy and the culture at large. Searight and Merkel do not reject system therapy, but they judge it as overly closed to other important approaches and hope that future refinements will take into account insights from different theories.

The fourth critical issue questions system theory's heuristic value or its ability to generate research. According to Donald Cushman, "Systems is a perspective which has produced more staunch advocates than theoretical empirical research."[54] Again, critics return to the extreme generality of the approach as the basis of their criticism. They claim that the theory simply does not suggest substantive questions for investigation.

In contrast, advocates claim that the fresh perspective provided by system theory suggests new ways of looking at old problems and thus is highly heuristic. Wayne Beach points out, for example, that a great deal of fruitful research followed Aubrey Fisher and Leonard Hawes's 1971 article on small-group systems.[55] Today a system approach is often assumed in communication theory. It is taken for granted in much of the work of the field without being labeled as such.

---

50   Yerby, "Family System Theory."
51   See, for example, Bahg, "Major Systems Theories."
52   Fisher, *Perspectives*, p. 196. See also von Bertalanffy, "Critical Review."
53   H. Russell Searight and William T. Merkel, "Systems Theory and Its Discontents: Clinical and Ethical Issues," *The American Journal of Family Therapy* 19 (1991): 19–31.
54   Donald Cushman, "The Rules Perspective as a Theoretical Basis for the Study of Human Communication," *Communication Quarterly* 25 (1977): 30–45.
55   B. Aubrey Fisher and Leonard C. Hawes, "An Interact System Model: Generating a Grounded Theory of Small Groups," *Quarterly Journal of Speech* 57 (1971): 444–453. See also Wayne Beach, "Stocktaking Open-Systems Research and Theory: A Critique and Proposals for Action" (paper presented at the annual conference of the Western Speech Communication Association, Phoenix, November 1977).

The fifth issue relates to the validity of system theory. Critics question whether system theory was developed to reflect what really happens in nature or to represent a useful convention for conceptualizing complex processes. In fact, system advocates themselves take different positions on this issue. Critics place system theory in a dilemma. If the theory attempts to describe phenomena as they really are, it is invalid. It posits similarities among events that are not really there. If, on the other hand, the theory provides merely a useful vocabulary, attributed similarities among events are only semantic and essentially useless for understanding those events. As Delia points out: "[Events] have different referents; they require different explanations; calling them the same thing . . . does not make them the same."[56] Bertalanffy calls this objection the "So what?" argument.[57]

The final issue of system theory is parsimony. Adherents claim the world is so complex that a sensible framework such as system theory is necessary to sort out the elements of world processes. Critics generally doubt that events are that complex. They claim that system theory overcomplicates events that are essentially simple. Charles Berger states the case against overcomplication:

> In the behavioral sciences . . . we may be the victims of what I call irrelevant variety. Irrelevant variety is generated by the presence of attributes in a situation which have little to do with the phenomenon we are studying but which give the impression that what we are studying is very complex. . . . Merely because persons differ along a larger number of physical, psychological, and social dimensions, does not mean that all of these differences will make a difference in terms of the phenomena we are studying. . . . It is probably the case that relatively few variables ultimately can account for most of the action.[58]

And yet, system theory *can* be a parsimonious approach, as dynamic social impact theory so well illustrates.

These six criticisms of general system theory are probably fair. However, actual system theories of communication must be evaluated on their own merit. The many theories of communication that make use of system principles are specific and help us understand concrete experiences, as we can see from the examples earlier in this chapter. You will also notice that these theories tend to be consistent and mutually supportive. Because of system influences, a common vocabulary makes these theories coherent and useful as a group.

The coherence among system theories of communication does not invalidate the criticism that general system theory can be applied in inconsistent ways, but at least in the study of communication, we find instances of consistent application in which system principles clarify rather than obscure. Further, although general system theory is not very explanatory, various applications of system theory can be quite explanatory, as DSIT well illustrates.

No survey of communication is complete without at least touching on information theory. Although this theory has been influential in a variety of ways, these days the concepts of information theory are often considered arcane in human communication studies. The subject is much more relevant to communication technology and engineering. If you are technically minded, enjoy mathematics, and tinker with electronics or broadcasting equipment, you will appreciate information theory and see its relevance. At the same time, however, if you like analogies and looking at human experience by applying physical concepts, you will see the relevance of information theory as a metaphor.

It is not surprising that most students of human communication today find information theory difficult to apply and less relevant than many of the other theories you will encounter in this book. The most directly applicable topic from information theory as presented in this chapter is Shannon and Weaver's model of transmission, which has been immensely popular,

56 Delia, "Alternative Perspectives," p. 51.
57 Von Bertalanffy, "Critical Review."
58 Charles Berger, "The Covering Law Perspective as a Theoretical Basis for the Study of Human Communication," *Communication Quarterly* 75 (1977): 7–18. See also Gerald R. Miller, "The Pervasiveness and Marvelous Complexity of Human Communication: A Note of Skepticism" (keynote address delivered at the Fourth Annual Conference in Communication, California State University, Fresno, May 1977). See also Beach, "Stocktaking."

although somewhat simplistic, in teaching the basic elements of communication for nearly a half century.

Although it is indispensable for developing advanced electronic communication devices, some of the original information theorists, system theorists, and other scholars looked to information theory for answers it could not provide. Shannon and Weaver hoped to use the theory as an overarching model for all human and machine communication. However, even Colin Cherry, whose famous 1957 treatise on communication was based largely on information theory, argued later that "the language of physical science is inadequate for discussion of what is essentially human about human communication."[59]

Most criticism of information theory relates to the standard of appropriateness.[60] The philosophical assumptions of the theory are not considered appropriate for understanding many aspects of human communication. Roger Conant captures the essence of the argument:

> When Shannon's theory first appeared it provoked a lot of optimism, not only in the telephone company for which it had clear technical applications, but also among biologists, psychologists, and the like who hoped it would illuminate the ways in which cells, animals, people, and perhaps even societies use information. Although the theory has been put to use in these ways, the results have not been spectacular at all. . . . Shannon's theory provides practically no help in understanding everyday communication.[61]

Many critics have centered on the ill-advised use of the term *information* as a symptom of this problem. Because the usage of the term is at such odds with popular meanings of *information*, much confusion has resulted. Ironically, information theory is not at all about information as we commonly understand it. One critic has suggested that the approach be retitled the "theory of signal transmission."[62] Because the term *information* as used by these theorists is so difficult to apply to human communication, other scholars have developed new definitions of the term that have caused even more befuddlement.[63] Of course, terminological confusion is only a symp-

tom of the problems involved in stretching the concept to fit alien domains. Three such problems have been cited frequently in the literature.

The first is that information theory is designed as a measurement tool based on statistical procedures. Human messages in their full complexity are not easily broken down into observable, measurable signals. Although the phonetic structure of language is amenable to analysis, when you add vocal cues, not to mention body language, information measurement becomes virtually useless. Also, many of the codes used in human communication are continuous, not discrete; that is, they do not consist of off-on signals. Such codes are difficult to fit into the mathematical paradigm.

A second problem of applying information theory to human communication is that the theory downplays meaning. Even if we could predict the amount of information received by a listener, we would know nothing of the degree of shared understanding among the communicators or the impact of the message on them.

Finally, information theory does not deal with the contextual or personal factors affecting an individual's channel capacity. For example, learning, which improves one's ability to comprehend certain types of messages and ultimately one's capacity to receive signals, is left untouched in classical theory.

System theory, cybernetics, and information theory provide an excellent backdrop for many theories of communication. Let us turn our attention now to some of the specific topics of communication theory.

---

59   Colin Cherry, *On Human Communication*, 3d ed. (Cambridge, MA: MIT Press, 1978), p. ix.
60   Criticism of information theory can be found in many sources, including the following, on which my summary relies: Anatol Rapoport, "The Promise and Pitfalls of Information Theory," *Behavioral Science* 1 (1956): 303–309 [reprinted in *Modern Systems Research for the Behavioral Scientist*, ed. W. Buckley (Chicago: Aldine, 1968), pp. 137–142]. See also Handy and Kurtz, "Current Appraisal"; Roger C. Conant, "A Vector Theory of Information," in *Communication Yearbook 3*, ed. D. Nimmo (New Brunswick, NJ: Transaction, 1979), pp. 177–196.
61   Conant, "Vector Theory," p. 178.
62   Yehoshua Bar-Hillel, "Concluding Review," in *Information Theory in Psychology*, ed. H. Quastler (Glencoe, IL: Free Press, 1955), p. 3.
63   See, for example, Krippendorff, "Information Theory."

THEORIES OF SIGNS AND LANGUAGE

In the previous chapter, we looked at system theory, one general way of understanding human communication. Beginning with Chapter 4, we look now at specific aspects of communication itself. John Powers, in a wide-ranging integration of the various strands of the communication discipline, suggests that the field can be divided into a series of tiers, the most central of which is *messages*.[1] Messages, according to Powers, have three structural elements—signs and symbols, language, and discourse. As a central aspect of communication, then, message structures are an appropriate topic to cover early in this book. Accordingly, in Chapter 4 we will look at some theories of signs, symbols, and language, and in Chapter 5, we will move on to discourse structures. Signs are the basis of all communication. In these two chapters, we will explore the importance of signs and symbols to human life and the often elaborate ways they are used.

A *sign* designates something other than itself, and *meaning* is the link between an object or idea and a sign. These basic concepts tie together an amazingly broad set of theories dealing with symbols, language, discourse, and nonverbal behaviors—theories that explain how signs are related to their meanings and how signs are organized. In general, the study of signs is referred to as *semiotics*.[2]

● SEMIOTICS

The first modern theory of signs was developed by the nineteenth-century philosopher and logician Charles Saunders Peirce, founder of modern semiotics.[3] Peirce defined *semiosis* as a

1   John H. Powers, "On the Intellectual Structure of the Human Communication Discipline," *Communication Education* 4 (1995): 191–222.
2   For a good overview, see Wendy Leeds-Hurwitz, *Semiotics and Communication: Signs, Codes, Cultures* (Hillsdale, NJ: Erlbaum, 1993). See also Kaja Silverman, *The Subject of Semiotics* (New York: Oxford University Press, 1983); and Arthur Asa Berger, *Signs in Contemporary Culture: An Introduction to Semiotics* (Salem, WI: Sheffield, 1989).
3   Charles Saunders Peirce, *Charles S. Peirce: Selected Writings*, ed. P. O. Wiener (New York: Dover, 1958). See also, for example, John Stewart, *Language as Articulate Contact: Toward a Post-Semiotic Philosophy of Communication* (Albany: SUNY Press, 1995), pp. 76–81; Christopher Hookway, *Peirce* (London: Routledge & Kegan Paul, 1985); Max H. Fisch, *Peirce, Semiotic, and Pragmatism* (Bloomington: Indiana University Press, 1986); Thomas A. Goudge, *The Thought of Peirce* (Toronto: University of Toronto Press, 1950); John R. Lyne, "Rhetoric and Semiotic in C. S. Peirce," *Quarterly Journal of Speech* 66 (1980): 155–168.

relationship among a sign, an object, and a meaning. The sign represents the object, or referent, in the mind of an interpreter. Peirce referred to the representation of an object by a sign as the *interpretant*. For example, the word *dog* is associated in your mind with a certain animal. The word is not the animal, but the association you make (the interpretant) links the two. All three elements are required in an irreducible triad in order for signs to operate. This three-part relationship is clearly depicted in a well-known model created by C. K. Ogden and I. A. Richards, shown in Figure 4.1.[4]

An informative illustration of semiosis is the study of generic pronouns by Wendy Martyna.[5] Traditionally in English, the pronoun *he* has been used to designate both males and females when a singular pronoun is required, as in the sentence, "When a teacher returns tests, he usually discusses them with the class." Martyna was interested in finding out what generic pronouns people would actually use in such situations and their meanings for these pronouns. Forty students at Stanford completed a series of sentences requiring the use of a generic pronoun. Some of the sentences referred to people traditionally thought of as male ("Before a judge can give a final ruling, he must weigh the evidence"). Some referred to people traditionally considered female ("After a nurse has completed training, she goes to work"). And some were neutral ("When a person loses money, he is apt to feel bad").

The researcher found that the participants usually used a pronoun that was consistent with sex stereotypes. In the neutral sentences, the masculine was most often used, although some participants deliberately suggested role reversals by switching the pronouns, and others tried to avoid sexism by using a combination, as in *he or she*. Women were less likely to use the masculine generic than men.

After the participants completed the sentences, the researcher asked them what image they had when they completed a sentence. Most often, they imagined a man in male-stereotyped sentences and a woman in female-stereotyped ones. In neutral sentences, the image was almost exclusively male.

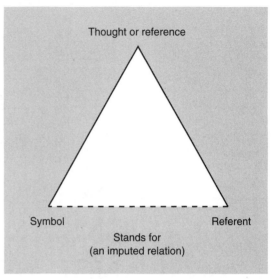

FIGURE **4.1**

Ogden and Richards's Meaning Triangle

From *The Meaning of Meaning*, by C. K. Ogden and I. A. Richards. Copyright © 1923. Reprinted by permission of Harcourt Brace Jovanovich and Routledge & Kegan Paul.

This study clearly illustrates that the sign, in this case a pronoun, is connected to its referent through the mind of the user. Meaning thus depends on the image or thought of the person in relation to the sign and the object being signified. Many semiotic theorists have elaborated and expanded this basic idea. Here, we will discuss three of the best known—Charles Morris, Susanne Langer, and Umberto Eco.

Morris on Signs, Behavior, and Interaction

Charles Morris is a well-known philosopher who wrote for many years about signs and values.[6] For Morris, a sign is a stimulus that elicits a

4   C. K. Ogden and I. A. Richards, *The Meaning of Meaning* (London: Kegan, Paul, Trench, Trubner, 1923).
5   Wendy Martyna, "What Does 'He' Mean?" *Journal of Communication* 28 (1978): 131–138.
6   Morris's classic work on signs is *Signs, Language, and Behavior* (New York: Braziller, 1946). A shorter version can be found in "Foundations of the Theory of Signs," in *International Encyclopedia of Unified Science*, vol. 1, part 1 (Chicago: University of Chicago Press, 1955), p. 84. A unified theory of signs and values is developed in *Signification and Significance* (Cambridge, MA: MIT Press, 1964).

readiness to respond. In a Latin-influenced vocabulary, he defines the *interpreter* as the organism that takes a stimulus as a sign, the *interpretant* as a disposition to respond in a certain way because of the sign, the *denotatum* as anything designated by the sign that enables the organism to respond appropriately, and the *significatum* as the conditions making the response possible.

Let's take a look at some simple examples. In classical conditioning, a dog is taught to respond to a buzzer as a sign of food. When the conditioned buzzer is sounded, the dog salivates in preparation for food. Here, the buzzer is a sign, and the dog is the interpreter. The dog's readiness for food is the interpretant, and because the food itself will enable the dog to fulfill the goal, the food is the denotatum. The edible quality of the food is the significatum.

Suppose, in a second example, that a father says to his child, "Let's go get some toys." The word *toys* is the sign, the child is the interpreter, her disposition to go to the toy box is the interpretant, the presence of the toys in the box is the denotatum, and the fact that they can be played with is the significatum.

These terms establish the basic elements of Morris's system of semiotics. More important, however, is the role of signs, and on this subject Morris has much to say. People and animals, even machines perhaps, use signs in three ways, which means that a sign has three values, or factors. These are the designative, the appraisive, and the prescriptive.

The *designative* aspect of signs directs the interpreter to specific objects or particular types of denotata. In other words, the sign is used to designate something. The *appraisive* aspect of a sign orients the interpreter to particular qualities of the denoted object, which enables one to appraise or evaluate the object. The *prescriptive* aspect directs one to respond to the object in certain ways. In other words, signs prescribe a range of ways in which the interpreter can behave toward the designated object or idea.

In the dog food example above, the designative factor directs the dog to food. The dog may even come to expect a certain kind of food. The appraisive factor tells the dog that the food is good, and the prescriptive factor compels the dog to eat it.

One of the most important systems of signs for people is language. In language, signs consist of sound groupings that have meaning. Sounds are combined into phrases, clauses, and sentences, which designate objects. Morris refers to simple linguistic signs as *ascriptors*, because they signify something about an object or idea. The sentence "The boy is happy" is an ascriptor designating boy and signifying happiness.

Like any sign, ascriptors can be designative, appraisive, or prescriptive. For example, a physician might say, "Here is an ointment that will stop your itching. Rub it in three times a day." "Here is an ointment" designates the object, "that will stop your itching" is an appraisal of the value of the object, and "Rub it in three times a day" is an obvious prescription.

Morris wrote about semiotics for at least thirty years. During this time his theory became increasingly sophisticated. His early ideas discussed above are basic and somewhat limited, but they do help us understand the nature of signs. Morris's later expanded theory is a much fuller, more human conception.

The expanded theory is influenced by system theory (Chapter 3) and symbolic interactionism (Chapter 8) among others. Specifically, Morris shows that all human action involves signs and meaning in various intriguing ways. Any act consists of three stages—perception, manipulation, and consummation.[7] In *perception* the person becomes aware of a sign. In the *manipulation* stage, the person interprets the sign and decides how to respond to it. Then the act is *consummated* by an actual response.

The designative value of signs predominates in the perceptual stage, the prescriptive value predominates in manipulation, and the appraisive marks consummation. So our itchy patient becomes aware of the medication because of the doctor's mentioning it in a perceptual stage, decides to try it in the manipulation

---

7   George Herbert Mead, *Mind, Self, and Society* (Chicago: University of Chicago Press, 1934). See also Chapter 8.

TABLE **4.1**

Stages of Action in Relation to Dimensions of Signifying and Value

Stages of Action	Dimensions of Signifying	Dimensions of Value
Perceptual	Designative	Detachment
Manipulatory	Prescriptive	Dominance
Consummatory	Appraisive	Dependence

SOURCE: From *Signification and Significance* by Charles Morris (Cambridge, MA: MIT Press, 1964).

stage because of the physician's prescription, and actually applies the ointment in the consummation stage because of the doctor's appraisal of the effectiveness of the medicine.

Morris's most important innovation is his application of signs to the study of values. Morris shows how values stress different things and how they relate to signs. Certain values stress dependence, others emphasize detachment, and still others relate to dominance.

As we recall from system theory, a system influences and is influenced by other systems. When one system is being affected by another, it is said to be *dependent* on the other system. When it is affecting another system, it is *dominant* over that other system. A state of *detachment* exists when a system is more or less autonomous. Detachment, then, corresponds to perception and the designative mode of signification. Dominance corresponds to the manipulation and prescriptive factors, and dependence corresponds to consummation and appraisive values. Table 4.1 summarizes these relationships.[8]

Suppose, for example, that you are watching television one evening, and you see a new commercial for some product you do not currently use. Viewing the commercial represents the perceptual stage of the act. Here you are detached, simply taking it in. After seeing the commercial, however, you may spend some time thinking about it, considering what was meant by some of the statements in the advertisement, perhaps determining the relevance of the product for your-

self. This stage is manipulation. Here you are dominating by thinking over the information and making your decision to buy or not to buy. The third stage would occur in actually purchasing the new product (consummation). Here you allow yourself to become "dependent" on the product, at least temporarily.

At each point in this process, signs are used. In the first stage, the product is identified, and various aspects are designated. In the manipulation stage, you are deciding how to act toward the product (whether or not to buy), thus using primarily prescriptive signs. Finally, in consummation you discover and signify to yourself your like or dislike for the product.

All of our examples so far feature a single individual, but groups can act too. Putting on a party, having a class, arranging a car pool, managing an automobile dealership, and conducting an orchestra are just a few examples. When you think about it, very few acts are strictly individual. Group acts, called *social acts,* go through the same stages as individual ones, but in a group you can divide the labor. Because of role specialization, some people may be primarily responsible for perceptual aspects of the act, others for manipulation, and still others for consummation.

In addition, a given individual may show a preference for certain aspects of individual and social acts. This preference—expressed in terms of detachment, dominance, or dependence—represents the person's values.

A value may be individual or social. Social values deal with a person's relationship to others, and individual values deal with his or her

8   Morris, *Signification,* p. 22.

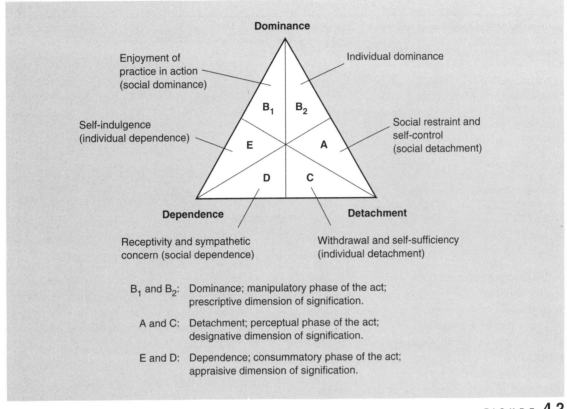

B₁ and B₂: Dominance; manipulatory phase of the act; prescriptive dimension of signification.

A and C: Detachment; perceptual phase of the act; designative dimension of signification.

E and D: Dependence; consummatory phase of the act; appraisive dimension of signification.

FIGURE **4.2**

Model of the Relation of Values, Signs, and the Act

From *Signification and Significance* by Charles Morris. (Cambridge, MA: MIT Press, 1964).

personal preferences. Morris identifies five value clusters, including social restraint and self-control, enjoyment of practice in action, withdrawal and self-sufficiency, receptivity and sympathetic concern, and self-indulgence. Figure 4.2 shows the relationship of these factors to the three-point model of the act developed earlier.[9]

Morris's most enduring contribution is his designation of three fields of sign theory. The first field is *semantics,* or the study of how signs relate to things. Here we are interested in what a sign is taken to designate, the relationship between the world of signs and the world of things. The second is *syntactics,* or the study of how signs relate to other signs. This field examines grammar and system structure and points to the

ways signs are organized into larger sign systems. Finally, in the field of *pragmatics* we are interested in the actual use of codes in everyday life, including the effects of signs on human behavior and the ways people mold signs and meanings in their actual interaction.

Donald Ellis has done an especially fine job of showing the importance of each of these areas, and he has developed syntactics and pragmatics in some detail.[10] Ellis points out that human beings operate with both a syntactic code and a pragmatic code.

9   Morris, *Signification,* p. 26.
10   Donald G. Ellis, "Syntactic and Pragmatic Codes in Communication," *Communication Theory* 2 (1992): 1–23.

TABLE **4.2**

Summary of Syntactic and Pragmatic Codes

Feature	Pragmatic Code	Syntactic Code
Meaning	In person, assumed	In text
Comprehension	Coherence: Link language to experience	Cohesion: Internal lexical ties
Reasoning	Subjective, organic	Logic
Structure	Implicit	Explicit
Context	High context	Low context
Fragmentation–Integration	Fragmented	Integrated
Involved–Detached	Involved	Detached
Level of Planning	Unplanned	Planned
Oral–Literate	Oral-like	Literate-like

Syntactic codes consist of a generalizable set of features that enable people to communicate in a wide variety of situations. People cannot always rely on situational meanings, and syntactic codes are necessary to enable persons who do not share common experience to communicate. Consequently, syntactic codes are more internally complete and formal. People understand syntactic codes because they know the rules of the grammar and denotations of terms, not because they share a lot of specialized knowledge. Legal writing used for wills and contracts is a good example; it aims to remove ambiguity and leave as little as possible up to the imagination of the communicators.

Pragmatic codes tend to be used in everyday speech and rely on the practical knowledge of particular groups within given situations. Pragmatic codes can only be understood because of the shared knowledge of those involved in the situation. As an example, consider the following terms: *got it done, chop shop, custom studio, artist, ink, clean spots, fade, boutique, nice work*. You know all of these words, but not in the same way as members of the tattoo subculture. Ellis uses this example to illustrate a very specific pragmatic code. For example, the word *clean* as used by this group is not intended to be the opposite of *dirty* but designates a place on the skin not yet tattooed.

Most talk and writing have both syntactic and pragmatic code features, and differences between messages are generally a matter of degree. Table 4.2 lists the various features of these two aspects of coding.[11]

Langer's Theory of Symbols

A prominent and useful theory of language is that of Susanne Langer, whose *Philosophy in a New Key* has received considerable attention by students of symbolism.[12] Langer considers symbolism to be the central concern of philosophy, a topic that underlies all human knowing and understanding. According to Langer, all animal life is dominated by feeling, but human feeling is affected by conception and symbols—and language.

Langer makes a distinction between signs and symbols. She uses the term *sign* in a more restricted sense than Morris to mean a stimulus that signals the presence of something else. A sign corresponds closely to the actual signified object. In this sense clouds may be a sign of rain,

---

11   Ellis, "Syntactic and Pragmatic," adapted from p. 18.
12   Susanne Langer, *Philosophy in a New Key* (Cambridge, MA: Harvard University Press, 1942). See also *Mind: An Essay on Human Feeling*, 3 vols. (Baltimore: Johns Hopkins University Press, 1967, 1972, 1982). A good secondary source is Stewart, *Language as Articulate Contact*, pp. 92–101.

laughter a sign of happiness, and a red light a sign of cross traffic. A *symbol* is more complex: "Symbols are not proxy of their objects, but are *vehicles for the conception of objects.*"[13] Symbols allow a person to think about something apart from its immediate presence. In other words a symbol is "an instrument of thought."[14]

Not only do people have a capacity to use symbols, but they possess a basic need for symbols, and symbol-making is a continuous process tantamount to eating and sleeping. Much human behavior can be explained in terms of meeting the symbolic need.

Like Peirce and Morris, Langer sees meaning as the complex relation among the symbol, the object, and the person. As she puts it, "If there is not at least one thing meant and one mind for which it is meant, then there is not a complete meaning."[15] Thus, we have both a logical and psychological sense of meaning—the logical being the relation between the symbol and referent and the psychological the relation between the symbol and the person.

The real significance of language, however, is not in individual words, but in *discourse.* Words name things, but "before terms are built into propositions, they assert nothing, preclude nothing . . . say nothing."[16] By tying words together into sentences, people create *propositions,* which are complex symbols that present a picture of something. The word *dog* brings up a conception, but its combination with other words provides a unified picture: The little brown dog is nestled against my foot. Because language possesses this rich potential for combination and organization, it truly makes us human. Through language we communicate, we think, and we feel.

How, then, do symbols work? Any symbol, including a proposition, communicates a *concept,* a general idea, pattern, or form. The concept is a meaning shared among communicators, but each communicator also will have a private image or meaning that fills in the details of the common picture. This private image is the person's *conception.*

Meaning therefore consists of the individual's private conception and the common concept shared with others. For example, Vincent van Gogh's paintings are filled with symbols with both common and private meanings. The common meanings in these paintings are accessible to anybody who views them; they are the generally recognized images in the scene. The private meanings are those of van Gogh himself and others who have studied the artist.[17]

For instance, his painting *Open Bible* is a view of a large open Bible sitting next to a candle. Next to the Bible is a small copy of a novel, Emile Zola's *The Joy of Living.* For the common viewer, these images are just objects, but for the artist, these images have very particular private meanings. As a whole the painting symbolizes the life and death of the artist's father. Van Gogh's father, a minister, is symbolized by the open Bible. His death is symbolized by the candle, which casts a light on a passage from Isaiah about the suffering servant. The title of the smaller book symbolizes the elder van Gogh's life.

Van Gogh discussed the symbolism of his work in a letter to his brother:

I want to paint men and women with that something of the eternal which the halo used to symbolize, and which we seek to convey by the actual radiance and vibration of our coloring.

. . . I am always in the hope of being able to express the love of two lovers by a wedding of two complementary colors, their mingling and their opposition, the mysterious vibration of kindred tones. To express the thought of a brow by the radiance of a light tone against a somber background. To express hope by some star, the eagerness of a soul by a sunset radiance.[18]

Langer's vocabulary includes three additional terms: signification, denotation, and connotation. *Signification* is the meaning of a sign, or a simple stimulus announcing the presence of some object. Signification is a simple one-to-one

13 Langer, *Philosophy in a New Key,* p. 61.
14 Langer, *Philosophy in a New Key,* p. 63.
15 Langer, *Philosophy in a New Key,* p. 56.
16 Langer, *Philosophy in a New Key,* p. 67.
17 A semiotic analysis of van Gogh's work was done by Mark Roskill, "'Public' and 'Private' Meanings: The Paintings of van Gogh," *Journal of Communication* 29 (1979): 157–169.
18 Quoted in Roskill, "'Public' and 'Private' Meanings," p. 157.

relationship between sign and object, as between a stop sign and cross traffic.

Denotation is the relation of the symbol to its object. For example, the denotation of the symbol *dog* may be your image of a little brown puppy at your feet. This relationship between the word and the puppy occurs only in your mind through your idea of the animal. Even when the puppy is not present, you can think of it because of the relationship between the symbol and idea.

The *connotation* of a symbol is the direct relationship between the symbol and the conception. Connotation includes all of one's personal feelings and associations attached to a symbol. Here you are less concerned with the object (a puppy) associated with the symbol than with your own private orientation to that object—many happy childhood memories, for example.

Langer notes that humans possess a built-in tendency to *abstract*. Abstraction is a process of forming a general idea from a variety of concrete experiences. It is a process of leaving out details in conceiving of objects, events, or situations in ever more general terms. For example, the word *dog* may have a specific connotation, but this conception is incomplete; it always leaves something out. The more abstract the symbol, the sketchier the conception: A *dog* is a *mammal*, which is an *animal*; an animal is a *living thing*, which is an *object*. Each successive term in this series leaves out more details and is therefore more abstract than the previous term.

So far we have emphasized Langer's ideas about language, which she calls *discursive symbolism*. However, she also admits the importance of nondiscursive, or *presentational*, symbols. Some of the most important human experiences are emotional and are best communicated through forms such as worship, art, and music.

Eco's Semiotics

In this section we describe the work of Italian semiotician Umberto Eco, who has produced one of the most comprehensive and contemporary theories of signs.[19] Eco's theory is important be-

cause it integrates earlier semiotic theories and advances semiotic thinking to a new level.

Eco believes that semiotics should include both a "theory of codes" and a "theory of sign production." Theories of codes, like those of Morris and Langer, must come to grips with the structure of language and other signs, but theories of sign production are necessary to explain the ways signs are actually used in social and cultural interaction. Eco presents ideas about the stability of signs as well as their variation.

The process of representing things by signs is *signification* or *semiosis*, a four-part system:

1. conditions or objects in the world
2. signs
3. a repertoire of responses
4. a set of correspondence rules between signs and objects and between signs and responses

Eco uses the example of a dam in which a set of sensors activates a series of lights to tell an operator the height of the water level. A white light might mean that the water level is below normal, and the dam should be shut to let the water build up. If an amber light is lit, the water level is normal, and nothing should be done. If, however, the red light is lit, the water level is too high, and the operator must open the dam to let some out.

The water levels are the worldly conditions, the lights are the signs, and the actions that an operator can take are the responses. Notice how the signs cannot function without a set of correspondence rules. The rules tell the operator what water level each light represents and what should be done.

The system of objects, signs, and response possibilities constitutes an s-code, or *code system*. The *s-code* is a structure in and of itself apart from its actual use and can be studied as such, as in the case of the simple light system at the dam. However, a code system as actually employed by real people requires that we look at the human

---

19   Eco's primary semiotic works include *A Theory of Semiotics* (Bloomington: Indiana University Press, 1976); and *Semiotics and the Philosophy of Language* (Bloomington: Indiana University Press, 1984).

factor. When we do that, we are switching our focus from the s-code to the code.

A *code* is a set of correspondence rules used by a person or group. Any s-code can be adapted time and time again as people create a variety of codes for different purposes. Different colored lights might be substituted at the dam. At certain times, it might be okay to let the dam overflow, and at other times the engineers may decide to let it drop without refilling.

The formal grammar of a language is an s-code; it is a structure that can be studied apart from its actual use. As we will see later in the chapter, linguists do this all the time. The way people adapt and use the grammar in everyday life, however, is rich with human variation. Eco discusses four ways in which people use signs. First, there is *recognition*, in which a person sees a sign as an expression of something tangible. A doctor's recognition of symptoms and a detective's use of clues are examples. Second, there is *ostension,* in which a person points to an example to represent something. For example, you might hold up an empty soda can to signal a friend to buy you a soda at the store. Third, *replica* is the use of arbitrary signs in combination with other signs. The use of language, certain gestures, emblems, musical notes, and so forth are replicas. Finally, there is *invention,* or proposing a new way to organize a code. Art is a good example of invention.

A *sign function* is the association of a sign with its referent according to a rule (red light—too full). The sign function is the relationship between the sign and the signified, between an expression and a content. It is tempting to think of the content as an existing thing or a referent; however, Eco is careful to point out that the content is never the thing itself but a cultural conception of the thing. He designates a sign with slashes, as in /dog/, and the actual object with double slashes, as in //dog//.

The content of the sign function, however, is designated <dog>, which is a concept of "dogness." For certain North Americans, the concept is one of being a pet, while for certain Southeast Asians, it is one of being food. Sometimes the referent simply does not exist, as in the case of fantasies like mermaids, lies, and jokes. In the example of the dam, the real content of the sign function is not the water level per se but one's meanings for the water level—for example, <safe>, <danger>, and <flood>.

Codes are organized sets of rules that relate to and define one another. Signs as expressions can be broken down into further expressions and contents, and contents, too, can be subdivided in this way. So the expression /red light/ has the subcode of /flood/, which means <danger>. The content <high water> can also be broken down into a subcode of /open valve/ with a meaning of <let water out>. In fact, code systems are completely defined in terms of their internal relations. *All sign functions are defined ultimately in terms of other sign functions.*

Eco defines *denotation* as a simple sign–content relation. *Connotation* is a sign that is related to a content via one or more other sign functions. For example, the sign function /dog/—<dog> is a denotation; a connotation would be /dog/—<stinky>, which is derived from a more complicated link: <dog>—/hairy/—/smells/—<stinky>.

Any system of contents, signs, and responses can be related to one another in innumerable ways. Any sign can have many possible contents or sign functions. Complex combinations of sign functions are often used to elaborate an idea or feeling, which Eco calls text, message, or discourse. Because of the possibility of multiple meanings, then, communication always involves interpretation, which is the use of sign functions to translate and explain other sign functions.

To continue this analysis, an *interpretant* is the relationship between one sign function and another; it is the means by which people understand and interpret language. For example, I might ask you, "What is a /fire/?" You would then answer, "/Fire/ is <burning>." "What," I then ask, "is /burning/?" "/Burning/ is <hot>." Children in the process of learning codes drive parents crazy by their interminable search for interpretants. Eco shows how dictionaries are simple catalogs of interpretants, one sign being related to another. Human interpretation, however, is more similar to the working of an encyclopedia than a dictionary because of the nearly infinite number of possible sign functions that are related to one another in a complex web of actual and possible relations. Remember, interpretants are not facts or truths but cultural conceptions that establish the representational meaning of signs.

In sum, then, codes establish what correspondence rules are in force in a particular context. These codes are established by convention within cultural groups. Meanings are therefore cultural units. Not only is meaning cultural, but cultures are semiotic.

◖ THE STRUCTURE OF LANGUAGE

The study of language has been heavily influenced by semiotics and vice versa.[20] The modern founder of structural linguistics was Ferdinand de Saussure, who along with figures such as Peirce, Ogden, Morris, Langer, and Eco made substantial contributions to the structural tradition in communication early in this century. Later, significant questions arose concerning the ways language is actually produced, understood, and acquired, leading to newer cognitive approaches. We will review both the classical structural and cognitive theories briefly in the following pages.

Classical Foundations

Saussure taught that signs, including language, are arbitrary.[21] He noted that different languages use different words for the same thing and that there is usually no physical connection between a word and its referent. Therefore, signs are conventions governed by rules. Not only does this assumption support the idea that language is a structure, but it also reinforces the general idea that language and reality are separate. Saussure,

then, saw language as a structured system representing reality. He believed that linguistic researchers must pay attention to language forms, such as speech sounds, words, and grammar. Although language structure is arbitrary, language *use* is not at all arbitrary, because it requires established conventions. You cannot choose any word you wish, nor can you rearrange grammar at a whim.

Language described in structural terms, then, is strictly a system of formal relations without substance. The key to understanding the structure of the system is *difference.* The elements and relations embedded in language are distinguished by their differences. One sound differs from another (like *p* and *b*); one word differs from another (like *pat* and *bat*); one grammatical form differs from another (like *has run* and *will run*). This system of differences constitutes the structure of the language. Both in spoken and written language, distinctions among signified objects in the world are identified by corresponding distinctions among linguistic signs. No linguistic unit has significance in and of itself; only in contrast with other linguistic units does a particular structure acquire meaning.

Saussure believed that all a person knows of the world is determined by language. Unlike other semioticians, then, Saussure does not see signs as referential. Signs do not *designate* objects but *constitute* them. There can be no object apart from the signs used to designate it. In this regard, Saussure's work set the stage for much

---

20   Leeds-Hurwitz, *Semiotics and Communication*, p. 13. For good brief overviews of the study of language, see Scott Jacobs, "Language and Interpersonal Communication," in *Handbook of Interpersonal Communication*, eds. Mark L. Knapp and Gerald R. Miller (Thousand Oaks, CA: Sage, 1994), pp. 199–228; Irwin Weiser, "Linguistics," in *Encyclopedia of Rhetoric and Composition*, ed. Theresa Enos (New York: Garland, 1996), pp. 386–391; David Graddol, Jenny Cheshire, and Joan Swann, *Descriptive Language* (Buckingham, England: Open University Press, 1994), pp. 65–101; Adrian Akmajian, Richard A. Demers, Ann K. Farmer, and Robert M. Harnish, *An Introduction to Language and Communication* (Cambridge, MA: MIT Press, 1994), pp. 123–192.
21   Ferdinand de Saussure's primary work on this subject is *Course in General Linguistics* (London: Peter Owen, 1960). Excellent secondary sources include Stewart, *Language as Articulate Contact*, pp. 81–87; Anthony Giddens, *Central Problems in Social Theory: Action, Structure, and Contradiction in Social Analysis* (Berkeley: University of California Press, 1979); and Fred Dallmayr, *Language and Politics* (Notre Dame, IN: University of Notre Dame Press, 1984).

twentieth-century thought not only in structural linguistics but also interactionist theory (Chapters 8 and 9) and interpretive and critical theories (Chapters 10 and 11).[22]

Saussure made an important distinction between formal language, which he called *langue,* and the actual use of language in communication, which he referred to as *parole.* These two terms correspond to language and speech. Language (langue) is a formal system that can be analyzed apart from its use in everyday life. Speech (parole) is the actual use of language to accomplish purposes. Language is not created by users, but speech is. Indeed, speech makes use of language, but it is less regular and more variable than the formal system of language from which it derives. In other words, when you speak you are using language, but you are also adapting it to enable you to achieve goals.

Linguistics, to Saussure, is the study of langue, not parole: "Taken as a whole, speech [parole] is many-sided and heterogeneous; straddling several areas simultaneously . . . we cannot put it into any category of human facts, for we cannot discover its unity. Language [langue], on the contrary, is a self-contained whole and a principle of classification."[23]

One difference between langue and parole, according to Saussure, is stability. Language is characterized by *synchrony,* meaning that it changes very little over time. Speech, on the other hand, is characterized by *diachrony,* meaning that it changes constantly from situation to situation.

Because of its constant flux, some believe that speech is not particularly suitable for scientific study, which is why linguistics must take a language-oriented, synchronic focus. The point here is not that language never changes, only that language form cannot be understood unless a synchronic perspective is adopted.

As we will see in Chapters 8 and 9, however, the distinction between language and speech, and that between synchrony and diachrony, is sharply criticized by theorists from other traditions. We return to the topic of language in Chapter 5 where we explore in more detail theories of how language functions in discourse, or speech.

Structural Linguistics

Let us turn now to a more detailed discussion of language structure itself. Influenced by the work of Saussure, theorists developed the standard model of sentence structure between about 1930 and 1950.[24] Basically, this model breaks down a sentence into components in hierarchical fashion. Sounds and sound groups combine to form word roots and word parts, which in turn combine to form words, then phrases. Phrases are put together to make clauses or sentences. Thus, language can be analyzed on various levels, roughly corresponding to sounds, words, and phrases.

The first level of analysis involves the study of *phonetics,* or speech sound. A particular speech sound is a *phone.* Phones that sound very similar are grouped into a sound family called *phoneme,* which is the basic building block of any language. Any dialect of a language contains a number of phonemes, which are combined according to rules to produce *morphemes,* the smallest meaningful linguistic unit. Words are combined according to the rules of grammar to form *phrases,* which are linked together into *clauses* and *sentences.*

This structural approach provides an orderly classification of language parts, and segments are sequenced in a sentence-building process. At each level of analysis is a set of classes (for example, phonemes or morphemes) that can be observed in the native language. Sentences are always built up from the bottom of the hierarchy, so that succeeding levels depend on the formation of lower levels. This scheme is known as phrase-structure grammar, a set of rules called *syntax.* Phrase-structure grammar consists of

---

22   See Art Berman, *From the New Criticism to Deconstruction* (Urbana: University of Illinois Press, 1988), pp. 114–143.
23   de Saussure, *Course,* p. 9.
24   The major writings of this period include Leonard Bloomfield, *Language* (New York: Holt, Rinehart & Winston, 1933); Charles Fries, *The Structure of English* (New York: Harcourt, Brace & World, 1952); Zellig Harris, *Structural Linguistics* (Chicago: University of Chicago Press, 1951). An excellent summary and critique of this period can be found in J. A. Fodor, T. G. Bever, and M. F. Garrett, *The Psychology of Language: An Introduction to Psycholinguistics and Generative Grammar* (New York: McGraw-Hill, 1974).

rewrite rules that "re-write" the sentence or other unit into its parts.

For example, a sentence can be broken down according to the following rewrite rule:

sentence = noun phrase (NP) + verb phrase (VP)

The verb phrase can be broken down further according to the following rewrite rule:

VP = verb (V) + noun phrase (NP)

This process continues until all units of the sentence are accounted for. Phrase structures are often illustrated by a tree diagram, as shown in Figure 4.3.

Although this approach provides a useful description of the structure of language, it fails to explain how people produce and understand language. This latter question, far more central to communication than language structure, has captured the attention of psycholinguists and sociolinguists since about 1950.

We know that people must possess an intuitive knowledge of their language in order to produce meaningful, grammatical speech. What is the nature of this knowledge? How is it acquired? How is it used? The literature that has emerged from this work is extensive, controversial, and at times highly technical.

Old-fashioned phrase-structure grammar is no longer believed to be adequate by itself to explain the generation of sentences.[25] The primary objection to classical linguistics is that although it is useful as a descriptive tool, it is powerless to explain how language is generated. For example, phrase-structure grammar would analyze the following two sentences exactly the same way, even though their syntactic meanings are different.[26]

John is easy to please.

John is eager to please.

These sentences have entirely different syntactic meanings. In the first sentence, John is the object of the infinitive *to please*. In the second John is the noun phrase of the sentence. Regular phrase structure provides no way to explain

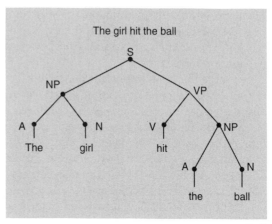

The girl hit the ball

FIGURE **4.3**

A Simple Tree Diagram

these different grammatical meanings by examining the sentences themselves.

Problems like this lead to a series of questions that traditional phrase-structure grammar cannot answer:

- How can a speaker produce an infinite number of novel sentences from just a few rules?
- By what cognitive process are sentences generated and understood?
- How is syntactic ambiguity to be accounted for?
- How is language acquired?

To answer questions such as these, linguists developed generative grammar.[27]

25   For an explanation and critique of finite-state and phrase-structure grammar, see Noam Chomsky, "Three Models for the Description of Language," *Transactions on Information Theory* IT-2 (1956): 113–124; and Jerry Fodor, James Jenkins, and Sol Saporta, "Psycholinguistics and Communication Theory," in *Human Communication Theory*, ed. F. E. X. Dance (New York: Holt, Rinehart & Winston, 1967), pp. 160–201.
26   Examples from Gilbert Harmon, *On Noam Chomsky: Critical Essays* (Garden City, NY: Anchor, 1974), p. 5.
27   For a brief overview of generative grammar, see Jacobs, "Language and Interpersonal Communication"; and Thomas Wasow, "Grammar," in *International Encyclopedia of Communications*, vol. 2, eds. Erik Barnouw et al., (New York: Oxford University Press, 1989), pp. 234–238; Graddol, Cheshire, and Swann, *Descriptive Language*, pp. 85–89.

Generative Grammar

Noam Chomsky is the primary force behind generative grammar. As a young linguist in the 1950s, Chomsky parted company with the classical theorists to develop an approach that since has become the mainstay of contemporary linguistics.[28] Like any theoretical tradition, generative grammar now has several positions within it, although the tradition as a whole is built on a cluster of essential ideas.

First, generative grammar rests on the assumption that sentence generation is central to sentence structure. The form of a sentence cannot be separated from the process by which it is generated. Old-style linguistics was powerful in *describing* the structure of a sentence, but it did not explain how sentences are actually produced by the speaker. Further, there is the suspicion that the surface structure of a sentence may actually mislead us about how sentences are really structured within the mind.

Second, the objective of generative grammar is to isolate a set of rules that explains how any sentence could be generated. Inventing a new rule for each construction is not workable because the brain cannot operate by an infinite set of rules, though people can produce and understand an infinite number. An adequate grammar must explain this paradox. The answer lies in a relatively small number of rules that can be used over and over again to produce novel sentences.

The third essential feature of generative grammar is the transformation. (In fact, generative grammar is also named *transformational grammar*.) At some point the surface structure of a sentence must have been transformed from some other deeper form, and generative grammar seeks to explain this transformation process.

In treating the study of mind as a natural science, Chomsky believes that principles of language and mind are universal and can be discovered by scientists. He is analytical in approach and seeks inherent mechanisms of mind. However, he also sees the individual as creative, so he promotes the idea that knowledge arises from a projection of innate categories onto the world of actual experience.[29] In short, Chomsky is a champion of rationalism, a point of view that until the past decade or two has not been popular in this century.[30]

Generative grammar is highly technical, and we will not cover it in detail here.[31]

Language is a fascinating and important subject, but the signs used in communication are certainly not limited to the linguistic. Much of the nuance of meaning is communicated nonverbally.

◖ THEORIES OF NONVERBAL COMMUNICATION

Scholars disagree about what nonverbal communication is, as Randall Harrison points out:

> The term "nonverbal communication" has been applied to a bewildering array of events. Everything from the territoriality of animals to the protocol of diplomats. From facial expression to muscle twitches. From inner, but inexpressible, feelings to outdoor public monuments. From the message of massage to the persuasion of a punch. From dance and drama to music and mime. From the flow of affect to the flow of traffic. From extrasensory perception to the economic policies of international power blocks. From fashion and fad to architecture and analog computer. From the smell of roses to the taste of steak. From Freudian symbol to astrological sign. From the rhetoric of violence to the rhetoric of topless dancers.[32]

---

28   For a list of Chomsky's works, see the Bibliography.
29   Chomsky discusses features of his epistemology in *Rules and Representations* (New York: Columbia University Press, 1980).
30   The philosopher most associated with rationalism is René Descartes (seventeenth century). See *Meditations on First Philosophy*, trans. Laurence J. LaFleur (Indianapolis, IN: Bobbs-Merrill, 1960).
31   For a brief summary, see previous editions of this book: Stephen W. Littlejohn, *Theories of Human Communication*, 5th ed. (Belmont, CA: Wadsworth, 1996), pp. 75–77; 4th ed. (Belmont, CA: Wadsworth, 1992), pp. 74–77. See also Jacobs, "Language and Interpersonal Communication"; and Wasnow, "Grammar."
32   Randall Harrison, *Beyond Words: An Introduction to Nonverbal Communication* (Englewood Cliffs, NJ: Prentice-Hall, 1974), pp. 24–25. Conceptual issues are discussed in Judee K. Burgoon, "Nonverbal Signals," in *Handbook of Interpersonal Communication*, eds. Mark

As the above quotation shows, there is little agreement on what counts as nonverbal communication. To make this question even more challenging, research on nonverbal behavior is extensive and comes from many fields.[33] For these reasons, classifying and organizing this material is difficult. Various topics relevant to nonverbal communication are covered later in the book; for now, let's concentrate on structural approaches to nonverbal coding.

Burgoon characterizes nonverbal code systems as possessing several structural properties. First, nonverbal codes tend to be *analogic* rather than digital. Whereas digital signals are discrete, like numbers and letters, analogic signals are continuous, forming a spectrum or range, like sound volume and the brightness of light. Therefore, nonverbal signals like facial expression and vocal intonation cannot simply be classed into one category or another—like loud or soft, bright or dim—but are gradations.

A second feature found in some, but not all, nonverbal codes is *iconicity*, or resemblance. Iconic codes resemble the thing being symbolized (like depicting the shape of something with your hands). Third, certain nonverbal codes seem to elicit *universal meaning*. This is especially the case with such signals as threats and emotional displays, which may be biologically determined. Fourth, nonverbal codes enable the *simultaneous transmission* of several messages. With the face, body, voice, and other signals, several different messages can be sent at once. Fifth, nonverbal signals often evoke an *automatic response* without thinking. An example would be stepping on the brake at a red light. Sixth, nonverbal signals are often emitted quite *spontaneously*, as when you let off nervous energy.

We can use Morris's three dimensions of semantics, syntactics, and pragmatics, defined earlier in the chapter, to characterize nonverbal forms (as well as language). *Semantics* refers to the meanings of a sign. For example, two fingers held up behind someone's head is a way of calling him a "devil." *Syntactics* refers to the ways signs are organized into systems with other signs. One might, for example, hold up two fin-

gers behind someone's head, laugh, and say "Joke's on you!" Here a gesture, a vocal sign (laughing), facial expressions, and language combine to create an overall meaning. *Pragmatics* refers to the effects or behaviors elicited by a sign or group of signs, as when the "devil" sign is taken as a joke rather than an insult.

The meanings attached to both verbal and nonverbal forms are context-bound, or determined in part by the situation in which they are produced. Both language and nonverbal forms allow communicators to combine relatively few signs into an almost limitless variety of complex expressions of meaning.

Nonverbal code systems are often classed according to the type of activity used in the code. Burgoon suggests seven types: kinesics (bodily activity); vocalics, or paralanguage (voice); physical appearance; haptics (touch); proxemics (space); chronemics (time); and artifacts (objects).[34]

As examples, we will look at three well-established theories of kinesics and proxemics.

Birdwhistell on Kinesics

Ray Birdwhistell is considered the originator of kinesics.[35] An anthropologist interested in language, Birdwhistell uses linguistics as a model for his kinesic work. In fact, kinesics is popularly referred to as "body language." Let us look at the foundational ideas of Birdwhistell's theory.

In *Kinesics and Context* Birdwhistell lists seven assumptions on which he bases his theory:[36]

1. All body movements have potential meaning in communicative contexts. Somebody can always assign meaning to any bodily activity.

L. Knapp and Gerald R. Miller (Thousand Oaks, CA: Sage, 1994), pp. 229–285; see also Mark Knapp and Judith Hall, *Nonverbal Communication in Human Interaction* (New York: Holt, Rinehart & Winston, 1992).
33   For a broad overview of research, see Burgoon, "Nonverbal Signals."
34   Burgoon, "Nonverbal Signals," p. 232.
35   Birdwhistell's major works include *Introduction to Kinesics* (Louisville, KY: University of Louisville Press, 1952); *Kinesics and Context* (Philadelphia: University of Pennsylvania Press, 1970).
36   Birdwhistell, *Kinesics and Context*, pp. 183–184.

2. Behavior can be analyzed because it is organized, and this organization can be subjected to systematic analysis.

3. Although bodily activity has biological limitations, the use of bodily motion in interaction is considered to be a part of the social system. Different groups will therefore use gestures differently.

4. People are influenced by the visible bodily activity of others.

5. The ways in which bodily activity functions in communication can be investigated.

6. The meanings discovered in research on kinesics result from the behavior being studied as well as the methods used for research.

7. A person's use of bodily activity will have idiosyncratic features but will also be part of a larger social system shared with others.

Birdwhistell's work is based largely on the perceived similarities between bodily activity and language, which has been called the *linguistic-kinesic analogy.*

> This original study of gestures gave the first indication that kinesic structure is parallel to language structure. By the study of gestures in context, it became clear that the kinesic system has forms which are astonishingly like words in language. The discovery in turn led to the investigation of the components of these forms and to the discovery of the larger complexes of which they were components. . . . It has become clear that there are body behaviors which function like significant sounds, that combine into simple or relatively complex units like words, which are combined into much longer stretches of structured behavior like sentences or even paragraphs.[37]

The similarity of hierarchical structure in kinesics to that of linguistics is striking, and the problem of the kinesicist is similar to that of the linguist: "Kinesics is concerned with abstracting from the continuous muscular shifts which are characteristics of living physiological systems those groupings of movement which are of significance to the communicational process and thus to the interactional systems of particular social groups."[38]

Out of the thousands of perceptible bodily motions produced in a short period of time, certain of these emerge as important in communication. Such movements are called kines. A *kine* is a range of motions or positions seen as a single motion or position. A perceptible movement of the eyelid or a turn of the hand would be an example of a kine. What is defined as a kine in one cultural group may not be in another.

Kines are further grouped into *kinemes,* elements that have distinct meanings. Like the phoneme in linguistics, the kineme is a group of relatively interchangeable kines. For example, up to twenty-three different positions (kines) of the eyelids can be discerned, but they can be grouped into about four kinemes. Kinemes, like phonemes, occur in context. A complex combination of kinemes throughout the body such as a wink, a smile, and a wave of the hand is called a *kinemorph.*

Ekman and Friesen on Kinesics

For many years Paul Ekman and Wallace Friesen collaborated on research that led to an excellent general model of kinesic behavior, concentrating their work on the face and hands.[39] Their goal was ambitious: "Our aim has been to increase understanding of the individual, his feelings, mood, personality, and attitudes, and to increase understanding of any given interpersonal interaction, the nature of the relationship, the status or quality of communication, what impressions are formed, and what is revealed about interpersonal style or skill."[40]

These authors analyzed nonverbal activity three ways: by origin, by coding, and by usage.

---

37 Birdwhistell, *Kinesics and Context*, p. 80.
38 Birdwhistell, *Kinesics and Context*, p. 192.
39 Ekman and Friesen's major works include "Nonverbal Behavior in Psychotherapy Research," in *Research in Psychotherapy,* vol. 3, ed. J. Shlien (Washington, DC: American Psychological Association, 1968), pp. 179–216; "The Repertoire of Nonverbal Behavior: Categories, Origins, Usage, and Coding," *Semiotica* 1 (1969): 49–98; *Emotion in the Human Face: Guidelines for Research and an Integration of Findings* (New York: Pergamon, 1972); *Unmasking the Face* (Englewood Cliffs, NJ: Prentice-Hall, 1975).
40 Paul Ekman and Wallace Friesen, "Hand Movements," *Journal of Communication* 22 (1972): 353.

Origin is the source of an act. A nonverbal behavior may be *innate* (built into the nervous system), *species-constant* (universal behavior required for survival), or *variant* across cultures, groups, and individuals. As examples, one could speculate that eyebrow raising as a sign of surprise is innate, that marking territory is species-constant, and that shaking the head back and forth to indicate no is culture-specific.

Coding is the relationship of the act to its meaning. An act may be *arbitrary,* with no meaning inherent in the sign itself. By convention in our culture, for example, we agree that head nodding is an indication of yes, but this coding is purely arbitrary. Other nonverbal signs are *iconic* and resemble the thing being signified. For instance, we often draw pictures in the air or position our hands to illustrate what we are talking about. The third category of coding is *intrinsic*. Intrinsically coded cues contain their meaning within them and are themselves part of what is being signified. Crying is an example of intrinsic coding. Crying is a sign of emotion, but it is also part of the emotion itself.

The third way to analyze a behavior is by *usage*. Usage also includes the degree to which a nonverbal behavior is intended to convey information. A *communicative act* is used deliberately to convey meaning. *Interactive acts* actually influence the behavior of the other participants. An act is both communicative and interactive if it is intentional and influential. For example, if you deliberately wave to a friend as a sign of greeting and the friend waves back, your cue is communicative and interactive. Some behaviors are not intended to be communicative but nevertheless provide information for the perceiver. Such acts are said to be *informative.* On a day when you are feeling less than friendly, you may duck into a hallway to avoid meeting an acquaintance coming your way. If the other person sees the avoidance, your behavior has been informative even though you did not intend to communicate.

All nonverbal behavior is one of five types, depending on origin, coding, and usage. The first type is the *emblem.* Emblems have a verbal translation of a rather precise meaning. They are normally used in a deliberate fashion to communicate a particular message. The victory "V" and the black power fist are examples. The origin of emblems is cultural learning, and emblems may be either arbitrary or iconic.

Illustrators are the second kind of nonverbal cues. Illustrators are used to depict what is being said verbally. They are intentional, though we may not always be directly aware of them. They include eight types:

> *batons*—movements that accent or emphasize
>
> *ideographs*—"sketching" the direction of a thought
>
> *deictic movements*—pointing
>
> *spatial movements*—depicting or outlining space
>
> *rhythmic movements*—pacing motions
>
> *kinetographs*—depicting physical actions
>
> *pictographs*—drawing a picture in the air
>
> *emblematic movements*—illustrating a verbal statement

These types can be combined, since some motions are combinations of types. Illustrators are informative or communicative in use and occasionally may be interactive. They are learned.

The third type of nonverbal behavior is the *adaptor,* which serves to facilitate release of bodily tension. Examples are hand wringing, head scratching, or foot jiggling. *Self-adaptors* are directed to one's own body. They include scratching, stroking, grooming, squeezing. *Alter-adaptors,* like slapping someone on the back, are directed to another's body. *Object-adaptors,* such as twisting a paper clip, are directed at things. In any case, adaptors can be iconic or intrinsic. Rarely are they intentional, and one is usually not aware of one's own adaptive behaviors. Although they are rarely communicative, they are sometimes interactive and often informative.

Regulators, the fourth type of behavior, are used to control or coordinate interaction. For example, we use eye contact to signal speaking and

TABLE **4.3**

Characteristics of Nonverbal Behavior

Behavior	Origin	Coding	Usage
Emblems	Learned	Arbitrary or iconic	Communicative
Illustrators	Learned	Iconic	Informative Communicative Interactive
Adaptors	Innate Species-constant Variant	Iconic or intrinsic	Informative Interactive
Regulators	Learning	Intrinsic or iconic	Interactive
Affect displays	Innate Species-constant Variant	Intrinsic	Informative Interactive

listening roles in a conversation. Regulators are primarily interactive. They are coded intrinsically or iconically, and their origin is cultural learning.

The final category of behavior is the *affect display*. These behaviors, which may be in part innate, involve the display of feelings and emotions. The face is a particularly rich source for affect display, although other parts of the body also may be involved. Affect displays are intrinsically coded. They are rarely communicative, often interactive, and always informative. These types of nonverbal behaviors are summarized in Table 4.3.

Hall on Proxemics

Edward Hall shares the view of other communication theorists that communication occurs through multiple channels.[41] Just as language varies from culture to culture, so do nonverbal behaviors. Specifically, *proxemics* refers to the use of space in communication: "the study of how man unconsciously structures microspace—the distance between men in conduct of daily transactions, the organization of space in his houses

and buildings, and ultimately the layout of his towns."[42]

According to Hall, the way space is used in interaction is very much a cultural matter. Different senses are important to different cultures. In some countries, such as the United States, sight and hearing predominate; in other places, such as Arab cultures, smell is also important. Some cultures rely on touching more than others. In general, the predominant senses of a culture partially determine the way in which space is used within that culture.

Proxemics also vary because cultural definitions of the self are different. People in most Western cultures learn to identify the self through the skin and clothes. Arabs, however, place the self deeper in the middle of the body. For these reasons, then, the people of a particular culture arrange their space in certain ways.

Hall defines three basic types of space. *Fixed-feature space* consists of unmovable things such

41   Edward Hall's major works include *The Silent Language* (Greenwich, CO: Fawcett, 1959); "A System for the Notation of Proxemic Behavior," *American Anthropologist* 65 (1963): 1003–1026: and *The Hidden Dimension* (New York: Random House, 1966).
42   Hall, "A System for Notation," p. 1003.

as walls and rooms. *Semifixed-feature space* includes movable objects like furniture. *Informal space* is the personal territory around the body that travels with a person, which determines the interpersonal distance between persons. Anglo-American culture, for example, uses four discernible distances: intimate (0 to 18 inches), personal (1 to 4 feet), social (4 to 12 feet), and public (over 12 feet).

When people are engaged in conversation, eight factors may be involved in how they use their space:

1. *Posture-sex factors*: These include the sex of the participant and the basic position (standing, sitting, lying).
2. *Sociofugal-sociopetal axis*: The word *sociofugal* means discouragement of interaction and *sociopetal* implies encouragement. Axis is the angle of the shoulders relative to the other person. The speakers may be facing each other, may be back to back, or may be positioned toward any other angle in the radius. Thus, some angles, like face to face, encourage interaction, while others, like back to back discourage it.
3. *Kinesthetic factors*: This is the closeness of the individuals in terms of touchability. Individuals may be in physical contact or within close distance, they may be outside body contact distance, or they may be positioned anywhere in between these extremes. This factor also includes the positioning of body parts as well as which parts are touching.
4. *Touching behavior*: People may be involved in caressing and holding, feeling, prolonged holding, pressing against, spot touching, accidental brushing, or no contact.
5. *Visual code*: This category includes the manner of eye contact ranging from direct (eye-to-eye) to no contact.
6. *Thermal code*: This element involves the perceived heat from the other communicator.
7. *Olfactory code*: This factor includes the kind and degree of odor perceived in the conversation.
8. *Voice loudness*: The loudness of speech can affect interpersonal space.

◖ COMMENTARY AND CRITIQUE

The study of signs and language is an important core of communication theory. It not only provides a way of looking at communication but also has had a powerful impact on almost all perspectives now employed in communication theory. At the heart of semiosis is the basic notion of the triad of meaning. Although various theorists have defined the elements of the triad somewhat differently or have stressed different aspects of it, this triad constitutes the heart of semiotic thinking.

Semiotic thinking has gone through a variety of versions. Peirce was primarily responsible for developing the idea of the sign-referent-interpretation unit, and others have built on this basic notion. Saussure applied semiotics to language, whereas Birdwhistell, Hall, and others emphasized nonlanguage forms.

Saussure's idea of difference has been a key concept in our understanding of language, but it applies equally well to all sign systems. Signs do not have a life of their own as independent markers. They assume significance only by virtue of the difference among signs. Semiotics, then, always makes distinctions.

For Morris, signification is a behavioral phenomenon, and a sign is understood in terms of how it predisposes people and animals to respond in certain ways. Much of human life, including meaning, action, interaction, and values, constitutes behavioral semiotic processes for Morris. If Morris's semiotics is behavioristic, Langer's is cognitive and emotive. For Langer, meaning consists of feeling and conception. For Langer symbols are tools of thought.

Morris's threefold division of semiotics into semantics, syntactics, and pragmatics has been especially useful in understanding the structural tradition. Many semioticians, including Morris, Langer, and Eco, have been preoccupied with the semantic dimension, in which the sign brings an idea, feeling, or conception into the mind of the person.

Syntactics, or the relationship among signs, has dominated the study of language and nonverbal communication. Saussure's idea of difference is especially important because it captures that character of signs making organization possible. Individual signs differ, making it possible to distinguish one from another; and organizational patterns differ as well, causing any grammatical structure to imply a meaning different from that implied by other structures.

Pragmatics is the study of how signs make a difference in people's lives. It is the study of the practical effects of signs. In a general sense, many communication theories are pragmatic because they deal with the outcomes or effects of communication. We begin looking at some pragmatic elements in the next chapter, and we will encounter them again at various points in this book.

Classical semiotics, which today may seem self-evident and simplistic to anyone with a modicum of background in language or communication, laid the foundation for more sophisticated linguistic and communication theories in the twentieth century.

Leeds-Hurwitz shows that because semiotics studies relationships within a complex network of things, it is at the heart of a number of broad communication concerns.[43] The semiotician may begin with individual signs, but the function of a sign can only be known by its connection with other signs in complex codes, and indeed even culture, with all that this broad concept entails, is viewed by some as a system of connected codes. Eco himself wrote: "Every act of communication to or between human beings—or any other intelligent biological or mechanical apparatus—presupposes a signification system as its necessary condition."[44] Thomas Sebeok added: "The subject matter of semiotics, it is often credited, is the exchange of any messages whatsoever, in a word, *communication*. . . . Semiotics is therefore classifiable as that pivotal branch of an integrated science of communication."[45]

Although the ideas covered in this chapter have a certain intuitive appeal, they have been criticized.[46] Most critics agree that language is certainly conventional, but its arbitrariness is more in question. Arbitrariness makes sense only if one accepts that language and speech are separate and that signs are separate from their referents.

Visual signs create special problems in this regard. Most people live constantly in a world of images, and with the electronic media, especially video, imagery becomes increasingly important as central signs in our culture. Yet, visual images do not quite fit the semiotic norm of representation. Surely, images can be understood as representing things, but they are not arbitrary or separate from what is represented. Images resonate with deep levels of actual experience in a way that arbitrary signs do not.[47]

Because visual codes are more open in their potential meanings, their interpretation is ultimately subjective and more connected to the internal perceptual and cognitive processes of the viewer than to conventional restricted representations. This is not to say that a person's meaning for an image is entirely individual. Visual means can and are affected by social learning too, but perceiving visual images is not the same as understanding language. Images require pattern recognition, organization, and discrimination, not just representational connections. Thus the meanings of visual images are a product of both individualized and social perception and knowledge.[48]

In a recent critique of semiotics, John Stewart challenges five commitments of semiotic theory.[49] The first is the *two worlds* commitment, the idea that signs and objects are separate with one representing the other. The second commitment is *atomism*, or the practice of analyzing sign

43   Leeds-Hurwitz, *Semiotics and Communication,* pp. 3–21.
44   Eco, *A Theory of Semiotics,* p. 9.
45   Thomas Sebeok, "The Doctrine of Sign," in *Frontiers in Semiotics,* eds. J. Deely, B. Williams, and F. E. Kruse (Bloomington: Indiana University Press, 1986), p. 36.
46   For a critique of structuralism, see Giddens, *Central Problems.*
47   Harry Redner, *A New Science of Representation: Towards an Integrated Theory of Representation in Science, Politics, and Art* (Boulder, CO; Westview, 1994).
48   Sandra E. Moriarty, "Abduction: A Theory of Visual Interpretation," *Communication Theory* 6 (1996): 167–187.
49   John Stewart, "The Symbol Model vs. Language as Constitutive Articulate Contact," in *Beyond the Symbol Model: Reflections on the Representational Nature of Language,* ed. John Stewart (Albany: SUNY Press, 1996), pp. 9–63; Stewart, *Language as Articulate Contact.* A similar argument is made by Pierre Bourdieu, *Language and Symbol Power* (Cambridge, MA: Harvard University Press, 1991).

systems, including language, by breaking them into small parts. The third commitment is *representation*, the belief that signs represent things other than themselves. Next, there is the *system* commitment, which leads to the depiction of signs in objective systems that can be examined and understood from outside. Finally, Stewart critiques the *tool* assumption, or the idea that signs and language are a way of transmitting thoughts and ideas from one place to another.

Stewart does not claim that all language and semiotic scholars explicitly accept these claims. Indeed, as we have seen in this chapter, several make attempts to expand semiotics beyond the simplistic word-thing relationship. Stewart's concern is the baggage that the vocabulary of "sign" and "symbol" bring with it. Once you use these terms, you are led to adopt the five commitments, even if tacitly, which may belie or distort the more complex vision held by the theorist.

Stewart's primary objection to the five commitments is that they just do not work out in practice. When you try to apply them to ongoing social interaction, you run into serious obstacles. Take the words *so, and, about,* and *sure* as examples. What do these represent? Certainly not objects. You might say they represent states of some kind or ideas, but states and ideas can only be represented by other words. In these cases, meaning is established not by the sign-object relationship, but by the sign-sign relationship; and the latter is determined by how the signs are used by communicators, not by any structural feature of the signs themselves.

Even the task of breaking down sign systems like language into units is problematic. Take a stop sign as an example. What, exactly, is the sign here? Is it the letter *S,* the word *STOP,* the shape of the sign, where it is placed on the road? Or some combination of these? The same difficulty is encountered in trying to analyze language. If you listen to language the way it is actually spoken, phonemes, morphemes, and grammatical rules become distorted and broken. The speech is still understandable, but not as neatly analyzed as formal linguistics leads us to believe.

Stewart shares the belief of many critics that the use of signs establishes and constructs the very thing those signs are said to represent. Even Saussure acknowledged that for all practical purposes our knowledge of the world is completely determined by language. These critics also believe that language and communication cannot be separated in the way that Saussure does with his langue-parole distinction because speech and other communicative forms are the mechanisms by which language and signs are created, maintained, and changed.[50] Later semioticians like Eco acknowledge this difficulty. At the same time, certain interactionists and interpretive scholars (Chapters 8, 9, and 10) attack the problem head-on by focusing on the uses of language and nonverbal forms in actual interaction rather than on the structure of the sign system itself.

As an alternative to semiotics, Stewart proposes that language is "constitutive articulate contact." Language is constitutive because its use *constitutes* or constructs the categories by which we understand the world, and it is *articulate contact* because our social worlds are made by human beings using language when they come into contact with one another. Language is a medium in which things get worked out through dialogue.

Donald Ellis takes yet another position on meaning.[51] He would agree with Stewart that signs are not simple representations of real objects, but in order for communication to occur, we must have an assumption of meaning. The system of relations among signs must allow communicators to find real meaning, or communication could not take place. We must share a sense of coherence in messages, or no amount of understanding will be possible, and we must assume that when we make use of the rules of language, large numbers of people who know those rules will be able to understand the meaning we intend.

---

50   This idea is more fully explored in Chapters 8 and 9 of this textbook and is elaborated by Robert Hodge and Gunther Kress, *Social Semiotics* (Ithaca, NY: Cornell University Press, 1988).
51   Donald G. Ellis, "Fixing Communicative Meaning: A Coherentist Theory," *Communication Research* 22 (1995): 515–544.

This does not mean that everyone will react the same way to a message or even think the same thoughts. Different people will connect meanings to one another in many different ways, but a basic coherent meaning is still necessary for understanding to occur.

Chomskian linguistics has been described as a true Kuhnian revolution (see Chapter 2). It is generally praised as providing answers to questions that classical and behaviorist linguistics could not handle. Its major strengths are usually seen as its parsimony and explanatory power. However, language is one of our most difficult intellectual puzzles, and even generative grammar has its weaknesses. Basically, generative grammar has been criticized on two fronts—its scope and its validity.

Two problems of scope warrant discussion here. First, generative grammar generally ignores or downplays semantics. Primarily, it is a theory of grammar, of syntax; problems of individual lexical units and their meanings are ignored as unimportant. Second, critics are bothered by the failure of generative grammarians to consider problems of language as used in everyday life. Generative grammar treats language as an abstraction, claiming that an understanding of the anomalies of language use is unimportant to an understanding of language itself.

Generative grammar makes a sharp distinction between language *competence* and language *performance*. The former is knowledge of grammar; the latter is language use. Staying within the tradition of structural linguistics, generative grammarians steadfastly maintain that performance is not a linguistic concern and are not very interested in how language is used in social interaction. The theory therefore does not account for local and cultural variations of language, nor does it account for the commonly observed phenomenon of ungrammatical speech.

Much of the criticism of generative grammar questions its validity. A good deal of disagreement exists within the generative movement itself about the locus of meaning. Where in the process of sentence generation is meaning established? Chomsky has shown that meaningfulness cannot reside strictly at the surface level, yet deep analysis by itself may not be adequate for the establishment of meaning.

Transformational theory's validity problems result from the difficulty of observing generative processes. Linguists must rely on inferences made from observing spoken sentences. Classical linguistics failed to make this inferential leap from observed behavior to hidden processes, and thus it fell short. As a result of its strong reliance on inference, generative theory operates primarily from logical force (see Chapter 2), relying mostly on the strength of the logical connections among inferences. It also relies heavily on reasoning from "residues." In other words, alternative explanations are attacked and shown to be inadequate. What cannot be disproved—the residue—is taken as the best explanation. Linguistic writings are filled with demonstrations of how a given explanation will not work in explaining a particular construction. The use of inference, logical necessity, and residues in the development of generative theory is not inherently weak, however, for it is the only available method for developing theory in the absence of direct observation.

The work on nonverbal communication has been important because it shows that communication consists of many types of signs. At the same time, by emphasizing the nonverbal, most of these theories distract us from the holistic nature of the communication code. Indeed, the analytical nature of both linguistics and nonverbal research belies the complexity of the communication process.[52] This problem is the *fallacy of analysis*. Leeds-Hurwitz describes the problem in these terms: "[Nonverbal codes] are separated only temporarily by analysts in order to make research easier. But we as analysts have gone perhaps too far in our efforts to make research easy, forgetting to ever recombine the separate elements again. To

---

52 For a discussion of the limitations of nonverbal communication theories, see Judee Burgoon and Thomas Saine, *The Unspoken Dialogue: An Introduction to Nonverbal Communication* (Boston: Houghton Mifflin, 1978), chap. 2; and Mark Knapp, John Wiemann, and John Daly, "Nonverbal Communication: Issues and Appraisal," *Human Communication Research* 4 (1978): 271–280.

me, the purpose of studying nonverbal communication is to aid the understanding of social interaction as a whole."[53]

Ironically, as nonverbal communication research separates language from other behavior, much of it has relied heavily on a linguistic analogy. In other words, nonverbal codes are believed by some to be organized essentially the same way as language. This belief is not surprising because of the common semiotic heritage of the two lines of research. As the early semioticians so clearly spelled out, the syntax or organization among signs is the most important constituent of meaning. Saussure applied this idea to language, and theorists like Birdwhistell adopted linguistic ideas about syntax to nonlinguistic signs.

---

53   Leeds-Hurwitz, *Semiotics and Communication*, p. xvii.

This problem is the *fallacy of the linguistic analogy*. Although some superficial similarities may be observed between language and bodily behavior, more differences than similarities exist. Language is presented sequentially and involves discrete signs; nonverbal codes are not presented in a sequential manner and usually do not consist of discrete behaviors. Although language is organized hierarchically, no good evidence shows that nonverbal acts are organized in this way. Language tends to be used consciously, and nonverbal signs are often displayed unconsciously.

One of the limits of most of the theories in this chapter is that they focus on the smallest units of meaning and low-level organizations of signs. The true richness of communication occurs at a higher level, when signs are combined into complex messages. We turn to this concern in Chapter 5 in our discussion of discourse.

C H A P T E R **5**

THEORIES OF DISCOURSE

In the previous chapter, we discussed language and coding. We saw there that communication can take place with the use of single signs or a combination of signs. Usually communication involves much more than simple utterances and actions. Most communication, from the mundane to the elaborate, consists of complex acts that form messages, or *discourse.*

In his study of the intellectual structure of the communication discipline, John Powers identified *messages* as central to the communication process.[1] He noted that messages have three structural properties: (1) relatively independent signs and symbols, (2) language as a formal code, and (3) relatively interconnected discourse structures.

In the previous chapter, we explored several theories in the first two categories—signs and language. In this chapter, we look to theories in the third category—discourse. This involves using signs and language in a coherent and integrated way to make a statement or achieve a goal.

Discourse analysis enables us to look closely at how messages are organized, used, and under-

stood. The structure of discourse will change depending on what you want to accomplish. The process of discourse analysis enables us to examine the various ways in which accomplishments are achieved through messages.[2]

Although writing and even nonverbal behavior can be considered discourse, most discourse analysis concentrates on naturally occurring talk. There are several strands of discourse analysis, sharing a common set of concerns.[3]

Scott Jacobs outlines three types of problems tackled by discourse analysis.[4] The first is the *problem of meaning.* How do people understand

---

1   John Powers, "On the Intellectual Structure of the Human Communication Discipline," *Communication Education* 44 (1995): 191–222.
2   Scott Jacobs, "Language and Interpersonal Communication," in *Handbook of Interpersonal Communication,* eds. Mark L. Knapp and Gerald R. Miller (Thousand Oaks, CA: Sage, 1994), pp. 199–228; see also Donald G. Ellis and William A. Donohue (eds.), *Contemporary Issues in Language and Discourse Processes* (Hillsdale, NJ: Erlbaum, 1986).
3   For a brief discussion of the various uses of the term *discourse analysis,* see Jonathan Potter and Margaret Wetherell, *Discourse and Social Psychology: Beyond Attitudes and Behavior* (London: Sage, 1987), pp. 6–7.
4   Jacobs, "Language and Interpersonal Communication."

messages? What information is embedded in the structure of a statement that enables another person to know that, for example, "Is Sybil there?" means that you want to talk to her on the telephone, or "You sure are hot" means you think the other person is on a winning streak?

The second challenge of discourse analysis is *the problem of action,* or knowing how to get something done through talk. What kinds of choices do we have when we want to do something like make a request or greet someone? How does a person decide how to say something, and how can he or she know the difference between an appropriate and an inappropriate way of putting something into words?

The *problem of coherence,* the third question of discourse analysis, involves figuring out how to make patterns of talk sensible and logical. In a conversation, for example, there is a back-and-forth flow among participants. How do they string words together rationally? What principles are used to connect one statement with another in a way that everyone understands? If you look at a transcript of a conversation carefully, you often find that it seems disjointed; yet, the communicators made sense of what they were saying as they went along. How did they do this?

Because we understand, act, and have coherent conversations intuitively, these questions may seem mundane; but these questions are challenging when you really try to answer them systematically. Several theories have been proposed to explain meaning and action in discourse. Most of these theories are based on the concept of rules, so we begin there.

◖ RULE THEORY

The rules tradition has had a major impact on the field of communication. The idea that people operate by rules in language, discourse, and social action has become widely accepted.[5] Susan Shimanoff summarizes the point:

> In order for communication to exist, or continue, two or more interacting individuals must share rules for using symbols. Not only must they have rules for individual symbols, but they

must also agree on such matters as how to take turns at speaking, how to be polite or how to insult, to greet, and so forth. If every symbol user manipulated symbols at random, the result would be chaos rather than communication.[6]

Despite its diversity, the rule approach is held together by certain common assumptions.[7] The *action principle* states that although some human behavior is mechanical, our most important behaviors are actively initiated by the individual. People choose courses of action to achieve their goals. Because most rule theorists agree that actions are intentional, they see behavior as rule-governed rather than law-governed.

As we saw in Chapter 1, however, some social scientists do not subscribe to the action principle, believing instead that behavior is mostly governed by causal laws. Even rule theorists will tell you certain rules are so deeply embedded in language that we follow them automatically in an almost causal way. By definition, to speak the language is to follow its rules. Some discourse analysis also uses rules in this highly programmed way, and when this is the case, the distinction between rules and laws becomes fuzzy indeed.

Another basic assumption of most rules theories is that social behavior is structured and organized. Certain behaviors recur in similar situations, although social interaction patterns vary from one to another. Discourse patterns, then, are organized, but organization is highly situational. Thus, most of these theories emphasize the relationship between the way people act and

---

5   Susan B. Shimanoff, *Communication Rules: Theory and Research* (Beverly Hills, CA: Sage, 1980), pp. 31–88, lists some of the major scholars who have studied rules as well as a variety of definitions and explanations of rules.

6   Shimanoff, *Communication Rules,* pp. 31–32.

7   The similarities and differences among rule theories are discussed in such sources as Donald P. Cushman, "The Rules Perspective as a Theoretical Basis for the Study of Human Communication," *Communication Quarterly* 25 (1977): 30–45; W. Barnett Pearce, "Rules Theories of Communication: Varieties, Limitations, and Potentials" (paper presented at the meeting of the Speech Communication Association, New York, 1980); Stuart J. Sigman, "On Communication Rules from a Social Perspective," *Human Communication Research* 7 (1980): 37–51; Shimanoff, *Communication Rules;* and Donald Cushman, "The Rules Approach to Communication Theory: A Philosophical and Operational Perspective," in *Communication Theory: Eastern and Western Perspectives,* ed. D. L. Kincaid (San Diego, CA: Academic Press, 1987), pp. 223–234.

the situation in which the action occurs. In fact, rules scholars criticize law-governed theories precisely because of their perceived failure to reflect such variation.

Rules allow us to organize social interaction. Rules affect the options available in a given situation, yet because rules are situational, they explain why people behave differently at various times and places.

Approaches to Rules

There are three general approaches to rules—the rule-following approach, the rule-governed approach, and the rule-using approach.[8]

Rule-Following Approach.   In this view rules are seen simply as observed behavioral regularities. A recurring pattern is said to happen "as a rule." Barnett Pearce calls such rules weak laws because they are cast in the form of a statement of what is expected to happen. This approach does not explain why particular patterns happen, but only lists predictable behaviors. Many linguistic and discourse theories are of this type, suggesting that speakers unconsciously follow rules of grammar and discourse with a high degree of regularity.

Rule-Governed Approach.   Here, rules are considered to be beliefs about what should or should not be done to achieve your objective. The rule-governed approach attempts to uncover communicators' intentions and to define the socially acceptable ways goals are accomplished. For example, if you want to join in a conversation at a party, you would approach the group but not speak until recognized nonverbally. Breaking in too quickly would be a rule violation that could ruffle a few feathers. The rule-governed approach presumes that people know the rules and have the power to follow or violate them. It also assumes that people usually act consciously, intentionally, and rationally.

Because you use speech in a variety of ways to achieve your objectives, you know how to do so effectively and appropriately. When you want to greet a person, make a request, object to what

someone is doing, or bond with a friend, you employ the rules. You are free to choose your goals, but once having done so, you must employ certain rules to achieve them.

Rule-Using Approach.   This final approach to rules imagines social life to be more complex than do the other two approaches. The actor is confronted with a variety of rules for accomplishing various intentions. The actor chooses which rules to use in carrying out an intention. People are rule critics and choose to follow some rules and discard others. This approach thereby provides a basis for evaluating what choices people make in social situations and even allows for people to create new options.

Rule using also helps us understand communication competence by revealing how well a person sorts through the set of objectives and rules to plan a strategy. In a highly homogeneous situation, such as joining a cocktail party conversation, the rules are few and simple. Here, the rule-governed approach is sufficient to explain what occurs, but in complex situations like preparing for a speech, organizing a meeting, or writing a letter, the rule-using approach is preferable.

To get a better idea of how rules might be used in producing and understanding discourse, let's look now at speech act theory.

Speech-Act Theory

Ludwig Wittgenstein, a German philosopher, began a line of thought called *ordinary language philosophy*.[9] He taught that the meaning of language depends on its actual use. Language, as used in

---

8   Pearce, "Rules Theories." See also Joan Ganz, *Rules: A Systematic Study* (Paris: Mouton, 1971).
9   Wittgenstein's best-known early work was *Tractatus Logico-Philosophicus* (London: Routledge & Kegan Paul, 1922); his later work, which forms the foundation for ordinary language philosophy, is *Philosophical Investigations* (Oxford: Basil Blackwell, 1953). See also the excellent summary by David Silverman and Brian Torode, *The Material Word: Some Theories of Language and Its Limits* (London: Routledge & Kegan Paul, 1980); Richard Buttney, "The Ascription of Meaning: A Wittgensteinian Perspective," *Quarterly Journal of Speech* 72 (1986): 261–273; and Allan Janik and Stephen Toulmin, *Wittgenstein's Vienna* (New York: Simon & Schuster, 1973).

ordinary life, is a *language game* because it consists of rules. In other words, people follow rules to accomplish things with language. When you give and obey orders, ask and answer questions, and describe events, you are engaged in language games. Like ordinary games such as chess and poker, each language game has a different set of rules.

Later J. L. Austin referred to the practical use of language as speech acts.[10] Speech-act theory, then, is built on the foundation laid by Wittgenstein and Austin.[11] Today Austin's protégé John Searle is most often associated with the theory.

In this theory, the *speech act* is the basic unit of language used to express meaning, an utterance that expresses an intention. Normally, the speech act is a sentence, but it can be a word or phrase as long as it follows the rules necessary to accomplish the intention, or to play the language game.

When one speaks, one performs an act. The act may be stating, questioning, commanding, promising, or a number of other possibilities. Speech, then, is not just used to designate something; it actually does something. That is why it is called speech *act*. Consequently, speech-act theory does not stress the individual referents of symbols but the intent of the act as a whole. If a speech act is successful, the recipient will understand the speaker's intention.

If you make a promise, you are communicating an intention about something you will do in the future, but more important, you are expecting the other communicator to realize from what you have said what your intention is. If you say,

"I promise to pay you back," you assume the other person knows the meaning of the words. But knowing the words is not enough; knowing what you intend to accomplish by using the words is vital.

Whenever you make a statement like "I will pay you back," you are performing at least three and maybe four acts. The first is an *utterance act,* or the simple pronunciation of the words. Second, you are performing a *propositional act* because you are saying something you believe to be true. Third, and most important from a speech-act perspective, you are performing an *illocutionary act* designed to fulfill an intention. (In this example you are making a promise, and it is important to communication that your listener understand this intention.) Finally, you may be performing a *perlocutionary act,* designed to have an actual effect on the other person's behavior. (Maybe you are trying to get him to loan you some money.)

Because the difference between illocution and perlocution is sometimes hard to grasp, let's pursue it a little further. An illocution is an act in which the speaker's primary concern is that the listener understand the intention—to make a promise, a request, or whatever. A perlocution is an act in which the speaker expects the listener not only to understand but to act in a particular way because of that understanding. If I say, "I am thirsty," with the intention of having you understand that I need something to drink, I am performing an illocutionary act. I may also want you to bring me a glass of water. This is called an indirect request, and it is both illocutionary and perlocutionary.

Now let's look at the distinction between propositional acts and illocutionary acts in more detail. The proposition can be understood as one aspect of the content of a statement. It designates some quality or association of an object, situation, or event. "The cake is good," "Salt is harmful to the body," "Her name is Karen" are all examples of propositions. Propositions can be evaluated in terms of their truth value.

In speech-act theory, however, truth and logic are not considered central. Rather, the question is

---

10   J. L. Austin, *How to Do Things with Words* (Cambridge, MA: Harvard University Press, 1962); *Philosophy of Language* (Englewood Cliffs, NJ: Prentice-Hall, 1964). For a general summary of Austin's ideas, see also Potter and Wetherell, *Discourse and Social Psychology,* pp. 14–18.

11   John Searle, *Speech Acts: An Essay in the Philosophy of Language* (Cambridge: Cambridge University Press, 1969); "Human Communication Theory and the Philosophy of Language: Some Remarks," in *Human Communication Theory,* ed. F. E. X. Dance (New York: Holt, Rinehart & Winston, 1967), pp. 116–129. Good secondary sources include John Stewart, "Concepts of Language and Meaning: A Comparative Study," *Quarterly Journal of Speech* 58 (1972): 123–133; Paul N. Campbell, "A Rhetorical View of Locutionary, Illocutionary, and Perlocutionary Acts," *Quarterly Journal of Speech* 59 (1973): 284–296; Robert Gaines, "Doing by Saying: Toward a Theory of Perlocution," *Quarterly Journal of Speech* 65 (1979): 207–217.

what a speaker intends to do by uttering a proposition. Hence, for Searle, propositions must always be viewed as part of a larger context—the illocution. Searle would be interested in acts such as the following: I *ask* whether the cake is good; I *warn* you that salt is harmful to the body; I *state* that her name is Karen. What the speaker is doing with the proposition is the speech act— in these examples, to ask, to warn, and to state. The meaning of a speech act is its *illocutionary force.* You might, for example, state the proposition "The cake is good" ironically to mean just the opposite: This cake is the worst I ever ate. Here what appears to be a simple proposition has the illocutionary force of an insult.

Searle states fundamentally that "speaking a language is engaging in a rule-governed form of behavior."[12] Two types of rules are important— constitutive and regulative. *Constitutive rules* actually create games; that is, the game is created, or "constituted," by its rules. For example, football as a game exists only by virtue of its rules. The rules make up the game. When you observe people following a certain set of rules, you know the game of football is being played. These rules therefore tell you what to interpret as football, as opposed to baseball or soccer.

In speech acts constitutive rules tell you what to interpret as a promise, as opposed to a request or a command. One's intention is largely understood by another person because of the constitutive rules; they tell others what to count as a particular kind of act.

For example, how do you know a promise when you hear one? Promising involves five basic rules. First, it must include a sentence indicating the speaker will do some future act. Second, the utterance can only be made if the listener would rather that the speaker do the act than not do it. Third, a statement is a promise only when it would not otherwise be obvious to the speaker and hearer that the act would be done in the normal course of events. Fourth, the speaker must intend to do the act. Finally, a promise involves

the establishment of an obligation for the speaker to do the act. These five rules "constitute" a sufficient set of conditions for an act to count as a promise.

Any illocutionary act must have a basic set of constitutive rules. The *propositional content rule* specifies some condition of the referenced object. In a promise, for example, the speaker must state that a future act will be done, to repay a debt perhaps. *Preparatory rules* involve the presumed preconditions in the speaker and hearer necessary for the act to take place. For example, in a promise the utterance has no meaning unless the hearer would rather the future act be done than not be done. In our illustration, the hearer wants to get repaid. The *sincerity rule* requires the speaker to mean what is said. You must truly intend to repay the debt for the statement to count as a promise. The *essential rule* states that the act is indeed taken by the hearer and speaker to represent what it appears to be on the face. In other words the promise establishes a contractual obligation between speaker and hearer.

These constitutive rule types are believed to apply to a wide variety of illocutionary acts, such as requesting, asserting, questioning, thanking, advising, warning, greeting, and congratulating.

The second kind of rule is regulative. *Regulative rules* provide guidelines for acting within a game. The behaviors are known and available before being used in the act, and they tell us how to use speech to accomplish a particular intention. For example, if I want something, I make a request. When I request something of you, you are obligated either to grant the request or to turn it down.

Speech acts are not successful when their illocutionary force is not understood, and they can be evaluated in terms of the degree to which they employ the rules. Whereas propositions are evaluated in terms of truth or *validity,* speech acts, then, are evaluated in terms of *felicity,* or the degree to which the conditions of the act are met.

Although many speech acts are direct and involve the use of an explicit statement of intent, other speech acts are indirect. For example, in requesting that his family come to the table, a

---

12 Searle, *Speech Acts,* p. 22.

father might say, "Is anybody hungry?" On the face this appears to be a question, but in actuality it is an indirect request.

Searle outlines five types of illocutionary acts. The first he calls *assertives*. An assertive is a statement that commits the speaker to advocate the truth of a proposition. It includes such acts as stating, affirming, concluding, and believing. The second are *directives*, illocutions that attempt to get the listener to do something. They are commands, requests, pleadings, prayers, entreaties, invitations, and so forth. *Commissives*, the third type, commit the speaker to a future act. They consist of such things as promising, vowing, pledging, contracting, and guaranteeing. The fourth, *expressives*, are acts that communicate some aspect of the speaker's psychological state, such as thanking, congratulating, apologizing, condoling, and welcoming. Finally, a *declaration* is designed to create a proposition that, by its very assertion, makes it so. Examples include appointing, marrying, firing, and resigning. To illustrate, you are not married until an authorized person actually says the words, "I *pronounce* you husband and wife."

Speech-act theory identifies what it takes to make a successful statement, to have an intention understood. But speech acts are rarely isolated; they are usually part of ongoing conversations. How we organize conversations is a fascinating and important question in communication theory.

☙ CONVERSATION ANALYSIS

One of the most interesting and popular lines of work in communication is conversation analysis.[13] This is part of a branch of sociology called *ethnomethodology*, which is the detailed study of how people organize their everyday lives.[14] It involves a set of methods for looking carefully at the ways people work together to create social organization.

A conversation, like any aspect of social life, is viewed as a social achievement because it requires that we get certain things done cooperatively through talk.[15] Conversation analysis attempts to discover in detail exactly what those achievements are. The primary concern of conversation analysis is *sequential organization*, or the ways speakers organize their talk, turn by turn.

Of utmost importance in conversation analysis is the assumption that conversations are stable and orderly. Even when they appear sloppy on the surface, there is an underlying organization to all coherent talk, and the participants themselves actually create it as they go along. The analyst works inductively by first examining the details of actual conversations— many conversations—and then generalizing possible principles by which the participants themselves organized their own talk.

As an example, consider the simple task of telling a story. When you tell a story, it may appear that you just say it, but your story is really a joint achievement accomplished by you and your listeners. Although you probably take an extended turn, your story is made possible by the cooperation of others in carefully organized turns. First, you have to get the floor by offering to tell a story, and others acknowledge and permit you to do so. During the story itself, listeners may take various types of turns to recognize and reinforce the story, indicate understanding, give you further permission to continue talking, direct or affect the story in some way, or correct or repair something you said. All of this requires work and organization on the part of everyone.[16]

---

13   This section deals with conversation in the discourse analysis tradition, emphasizing the verbal structure of conversational texts. There is also a tradition that studies the management of conversations in a broader sense, including the nonverbal elements. See Joseph N. Cappella, "The Management of Conversations," in *Handbook of Interpersonal Communication*, eds. M. L. Knapp and G. R. Miller (Beverly Hills, CA: Sage, 1985), pp. 393–439.
14   Ethnomethodology is most often associated with its originator, sociologist Harold Garfinkel; see his *Studies in Ethnomethodology* (Englewood Cliffs, NJ: Prentice-Hall, 1967). For a brief description of this tradition, see Potter and Wetherell, *Discourse and Social Psychology*, pp. 18–23. See also Graham Button (ed.), *Ethnomethodology and the Human Sciences* (Cambridge: Cambridge University Press, 1991).
15   For detailed discussions of conversation analysis, see George Psathas, *Conversation Analysis: The Study of Talk-in-Interaction* (Thousand Oaks, CA: Sage, 1995); Anna-Brita Stenström, *An Introduction to Spoken Interaction* (London: Longman, 1994); Robert Nofsinger, *Everyday Conversation* (Newbury Park, CA: Sage, 1991).
16   Jenny Mandelbaum, "Interpersonal Activities in Conversational Storytelling," *Western Journal of Speech Communication* 53 (1989): 114–126.

Conversation analysis is concerned with a variety of issues.[17] First, it deals with what speakers need to know to have a conversation—knowing the rules of conversation. The features of a conversation such as turn taking, silences and gaps, and overlaps have been of special interest. Conversation analysis is also concerned with rule violation and the ways people prevent and repair errors in talk.

Certainly the most popular, and perhaps the most significant, aspect of conversation analysis is *conversational coherence*.[18] Simply defined, coherence is connectedness and meaningfulness in conversation. A coherent conversation seems well structured and sensible to the participants. Coherence is normally taken for granted, yet the production of coherence is complex and not altogether understood.

Conversational Maxims

A good place to begin the topic of coherence is the theory of H. Paul Grice.[19] Grice proposed a set of very general assumptions to which all conversationalists must subscribe in order to be perceived as competent. The first and most general is the *cooperative principle,* which reads: One's contribution must be appropriate. Cooperation here does not necessarily mean expression of agreement, but it does mean that one is willing to contribute something in line with the purpose of the conversation. More specifically, cooperation is achieved by following four maxims.

Grice's first is the *quantity maxim*: One's contribution should provide sufficient, but not too much, information. You violate the quantity maxim when your comments are too brief or too verbose. The second is the *quality maxim*: One's contribution should be truthful. You violate the quality maxim when you deliberately lie or communicate in a way that does not reflect an honest intention. The third is the *relevancy maxim*: Comments must be pertinent. You violate this maxim when you make an irrelevant comment. The fourth maxim is the *manner maxim*: Do not be obscure, ambiguous, or disorganized.

You are probably thinking by now that these maxims seem absurdly simple and obvious, but the associated question of how speakers actually use them and how they handle apparent violations is far more complicated and interesting. Of course, the cooperative principle and maxims are often violated, sometimes on purpose, but what makes them so important is that they are never violated without disrupting the flow of conversation or affecting the perceptions of others in the conversation. In other words, violations are a problem communicators must deal with cooperatively.

When a maxim appears to be violated, communicators wonder what is going on. We manage these violations by making certain interpretations, called *conversational implicatures*, that help us understand what is being implied or implicated by the apparent violation. To assume that the violator is living up to the cooperative principle, the listener must attribute some additional meaning that will make the speaker's contribution seem to conform to the principle. In fact, when you deliberately violate a maxim, you assume that your listener will understand that you really do intend to be cooperative. If, for example, you say, "It is raining cats and dogs," you are technically violating the quality maxim, but others know that you are speaking metaphorically. This is an example of conversational implicature.

Conversational implicature allows you to use all kinds of interesting, indirect statements to achieve your purposes, without being judged incompetent. In fact, competence itself requires the effective use of implicature. Without it our conversations would be dull, predictable, and lifeless.

One of the most common types of violation is to say something indirectly. Indirect communication is important for a variety of social and personal reasons such as politeness. If, for example, someone asks you how much your car cost, you

---

17   These issues are outlined in Margaret L. McLaughlin, *Conversation: How Talk Is Organized* (Beverly Hills, CA: Sage, 1984).
18   See Robert T. Craig and Karen Tracy (eds.), *Conversational Coherence: Form, Structure, and Strategy* (Beverly Hills, CA: Sage, 1983).
19   H. Paul Grice, "Logic and Conversation," in *Syntax and Semantics,* vol. 3, eds. P. Cole and J. Morgan (New York: Academic, 1975), pp. 41–58.

might say, "Oh, quite a bit." Now, on the surface, that violates the maxim of quantity and appears uncooperative, but competent conversationalists will realize that this is really an indirect statement meaning, "It's none of your business."

The study of conversational implicature is really the study of the rules people use to justify violations of other rules; and these implicatures are very important for the overall management of conversations.

Another way that you manage the cooperative principle is to give clues that you are violating a maxim while still intending to be cooperative. Such clues are called *licenses for violations* because they enable you to violate a maxim without objection. For example, you could say, "I might be exaggerating a little, but . . . " Or you might end a statement by prompting, " . . . if you know what I mean." Using phrases and qualifications such as these is a way of asking for a license to violate one or more of the maxims.

Here's a portion of a typical conversation:

Kay: How did you and your husband meet?
Betty: Well, that's a long story.
Kay: Okay, I'm not going anywhere, let's hear it.

When Betty says, "It's a long story," she is seeking Kay's permission to violate the quantity maxim.[20]

Conversational Coherence

Coherence involves the question of how communicators create clear meaning. How do you know what is appropriate or inappropriate for keeping a conversation well organized? A variety of theories have been proposed.[21] Some of these use *local* principles, and other theories use *global* ones.

Using Local Principles: The Sequencing Approach. The idea behind the sequencing approach is that a conversation consists of a series of rule-governed speech acts, and coherence is achieved by making sure that each act is an appropriate response to the previous act. For ex-

ample, the question, "Hi, how are you?" is normally followed by, "Fine, how are you?"

Sequencing approaches focus on the *adjacency pair*, which is two speech acts in a row. The *first-pair part* (FPP) is the first utterance, and the *second-pair part* (SPP) is the following utterance. By this approach, a conversation is coherent if proper rules of sequencing are consistently used between the FPP and the SPP.

Perhaps the most influential sequencing model is that of Harvey Sacks, Emanuel Schegloff, and Gail Jefferson.[22] This is basically a turn-taking theory, which stipulates that the next turn in a conversation must be a proper response to complete a particular adjacency-pair type. For instance, a question is to be followed by an answer, a greeting by another greeting, an offer by an acceptance, a request by an acceptance or a rejection. A number of adjacency-pair types have been discussed in the literature: assertion-assent/dissent, question-answer, summons-answer, greeting-greeting, closing-closing, request-grant/denial, insult-response, apology-acceptance/refusal, compliment-acceptance/rejection, threat-response, challenge-response, accusation-denial/confession, and boast-appreciation/derision.

The completion of one speech act signals a turn for another speaker, who is obligated to respond according to appropriate rules. The speaker may designate who the next speaker is to be, or another speaker can appropriately take a turn, as long as a proper response is given. Failing a response, the speaker may continue talking.

Further, adjacency pairs include a *preference for agreement*. In other words, the SPP is normally expected to agree with the FPP. For example, a statement is normally followed by an agreement ("Don't you just love the sun?" "Sure do.") and a

---

20   Examples of violations are from Susan Swan Mura, "Licensing Violations: Legitimate Violations of Grice's Conversational Principle," in *Conversational Coherence: Form, Structure, and Strategy*, eds. R. T. Craig and K. Tracy (Beverly Hills, CA: Sage, 1983), pp. 101–115.
21   For a summary of some of the approaches, see Craig and Tracy, *Conversational Coherence*.
22   Harvey Sacks, Emanuel Schegloff, and Gail Jefferson, "A Simplest Systematics for the Organization of Turn Taking for Conversation," *Language* 50 (1974): 696–735.

request is followed by an acceptance ("Can I borrow your sunscreen?" "Sure."). This does not mean that people always agree, but disagreement calls for special action in the form of an account, excuse, or argument.

Of course, conversations are usually more complex than the simple adjacency-pair concept implies. For example, you might use a presequence or an insertion. A *presequence* is an adjacency pair whose meaning depends on another series of acts that has not yet been uttered. Here, the initial FPP is an invitation for a subsequent one:

FPP: Have you washed your hands? (presequence)
SPP: No, why?
FPP: 'Cause dinner's ready.
SPP: Okay, I'll do it.

The speaker here intends to make a request, but it cannot be understood as such without including the presequence question.

An *insertion* is an adjacency pair that is between the two parts of another pair and is subordinate to the main pair. Such insertions are necessary to clarify the intention of the initial FPP. Here is an example:

FPP_1:   Would you like to go out sometime?
FPP_2:   With you? (insertion)
SPP_2:   Yeah, me.
SPP_1:   Oh, okay.

Such a move is also an example of an *expansion*, which means that a subsequent speaker expands the sequence to include additional or subsidiary intentions. An expansion is involved whenever a segment of talk that could theoretically be accomplished in one turn, like a greeting, compliment, or request, is played out over several turns. This system enables us to parse, or separate, a conversation into parts. Table 5.1 shows an example.

The adjacency-pair idea has been quite useful and applies to many conversations, but conversation analysts now generally agree that coherence

---

TABLE **5.1**

A Conversational Sequence

Greeting-greeting		FPP	Hi.
	FPP	SPP	Hi. Great dress.
Compliment-acceptance			
	SPP	FPP	Thanks. My mom bought it for me this weekend.
Assertion-assent			
	FPP	SPP	Yeah, it looks great on you.
Compliment-rejection			
	SPP		Well, not that great really.
		FPP	How's Terry?
Question-answer			
		SPP	He's okay, getting better and better.
		FPP	Will he be out of the hospital soon?
Question-answer			
	FPP	SPP	In about three days, I think.
Assertion-assent			
	SPP		Great.
		FPP	Well, I gotta go.
Closing-closing			
		SPP	Yeah, me too. See ya.

cannot be explained strictly by local rules such as these. It is easy to identify sequences that are obviously clear to the communicators but have adjacent statements that do not make sense out of context. In the next section, we look at how these more complicated situations are handled.

Using Global Principles: The Inferential-Strategic Approach.   The pragmatic, or rational, approach to conversational coherence assumes that conversations are practical acts that achieve goals. Achieving the goal of a conversation requires that the participants reason their way through it. "If I want such and such, I have to do thus and so." Thus the coherence of a conversation depends on the reasoning process of the communicators. They make decisions about what to say and how to achieve their intentions, and coherence is really judged in accordance with this overall reasoning. If the sequence of acts appears rational in relation to agreed-on goals, it is judged coherent.

This theory, most often associated with Sally Jackson and Scott Jacobs, definitely uses a global approach.[23] These scholars use the game analogy to explain how conversation works. The game itself is controlled by a set of rules, which players must know. The players have objectives in the game, and they use the rules of the game to achieve those objectives. The game is coherent because the appropriate use of rules accomplishes rational objectives. So players must have two kinds of knowledge: They must know the rules of the game and what constitutes rational play within the parameters of the rules.

For example, in playing Monopoly you are expected to accumulate properties and cash by purchasing property, houses, and hotels, and you must do this according to rules. In Monopoly your moves are not judged rational or coherent based on whether they are consistent with

the moves that came before or after but on whether they are consistent with the overall objectives of the game.

Conversations can be complicated because, like a game, they are played with other people. One person's moves must mesh with those of other players, and this requires agreement on purpose and some reciprocity of perspective. Utterances have a force that obliges a hearer to understand the speaker's intent, and the speaker must meet certain felicity conditions in order for understanding to occur. Communicators respond not to each individual speech act but to the overall intentions of others. The coherence of a conversation is not judged by adjacency pairs, but by the unfolding plan of the game.

Jackson and Jacobs stipulate two kinds of rules necessary for such coherence. *Validity rules* establish the conditions necessary for an act to be judged as a sincere move in a plan to achieve a goal. *Reason rules*, Jackson and Jacob's second type, require the speaker to adjust statements to the beliefs and perspectives of the other participants. This does not mean that speakers say only what listeners want to hear but that they frame their statements in a way that makes logical sense within the perspective of what the other person thinks is going on. For example, if you are talking with a friend about how you did on an exam, you might think it a bit odd if he just blurted out, "I want pizza for dinner." You would wonder what that has to do with anything.

Basically, then, these rules help communicators set up a logical system so that a conversation will feel coherent. Remember that these rules may be violated, and coherence is not always achieved. Communicators may also disagree about whether a sequence meets the required conditions of validity and reason, and such disagreement is often the basis for conflict. Ultimately, because conversations are practical, goal-oriented acts, communicators must constantly judge whether the interaction is leading toward the desired goal and, if it is not, whether and what kinds of adjustments must be made in the conversational moves. This fact makes conversa-

23   Scott Jacobs, "Language," in *Handbook of Interpersonal Communication*, eds. M. L. Knapp and G. R. Miller (Beverly Hills, CA: Sage, 1985), pp. 330–335; also see Scott Jacobs and Sally Jackson, "Speech Act Structure in Conversation: Rational Aspects of Pragmatic Coherence," in *Conversational Coherence: Form, Structure, and Strategy*, eds. R. T. Craig and K. Tracy (Beverly Hills, CA: Sage, 1983), pp. 47–66.

tion a dynamic process of back-and-forth practical reasoning.

Donald Ellis proposes a *coherentist theory of meaning* to explain this process further.[24] Understanding discourse is a pragmatic act in which communicators use shared meanings to achieve coherence. Communication is possible only because communicators possess shared meanings. Three characteristics of discourse make understanding possible.

The first characteristic is *intelligibility*. Discourse is intelligible if it contains or points to evidence that enables communicators to make inferences about its meaning. A father may ask his son, "Is that your coat on the floor?" The son correctly reasons that this is a request or command for him to pick up the coat. Both father and son have experience in similar situations that make it possible for them to share this meaning. The coat on the floor, the timing of the father's question, and the use of similar questions in the past are evidence that the boy can use to draw this conclusion.

The second characteristic is *organization*. Statements are part of larger organized systems of linguistic structures. You cannot assign any meaning you want to a sentence, but a statement's meaning is limited, and competent communicators know what the possible range of meanings are. This quality of discourse makes rational talk possible.

Jackson and Jacobs's analogy of the game is useful here. The rules of the game tell us what moves mean and how to respond rationally within the system of permissible moves. In the game of making requests, communicators know that questions can be taken as a form of request, so the father's question may be understood as a statement about what his son should do. Indeed, within this situation, it probably should be understood in this way.

And this fact leads to Ellis's third characteristic of discourse—*verification*. In the stream of a conversation, one's statements can verify, or confirm, the meaning of other statements. When the son in our example replies, "Yeah, I'll pick it up." He is verifying the command issued by the father. Thus, participants use the give and take of their conversation to test meaning and reason their way to an agreed-upon conclusion.

Using global principles does not negate the value of local principles. Indeed, adjacency-pair coherence is a special case of a rational action. The FPP invites the listener to join into a kind of microplan for achieving a goal, and the SPP is coherent if it joins into that plan. A greeting invites the listener to make contact, and a returned greeting fulfills a kind of greeting contract. Responses to an FPP may simply and directly cooperate, may indirectly cooperate, may approximate agreement, or may attempt to extend, change, or refuse the goal set up by the first utterance. Over a sequence of utterances, communicators actually negotiate a goal-achievement plan. Jackson and Jacobs call this *the transformation of belief/want contexts*. Communicators ask themselves mentally, What do we want to accomplish here and what logical moves are required by each of us to accomplish this? The conversation will be coherent if agreement is achieved and the actions seem appropriate for achieving the goals.

To see more concretely how these ideas can be applied, let's look at Jackson and Jacobs's applications of their theory to requests.[25] Actually, requests are among the most studied of all speech acts, and their theory provides an excellent extension and modification of a whole line of research.

You can handle requests in a variety of ways. Your actions can range from very direct to indirect to irrelevant. The clearer and more direct a request and the clearer and more direct the response, the more coherent the request sequence. This is because directness supports clarity and relevance. Therefore, if I say, "Please pass the butter," my goal is clear and your response,

24   Donald G. Ellis, "Fixing Communicative Meaning: A Coherentist Theory," *Communication Research* 22 (1995): 515–544.
25   Scott Jacobs and Sally Jackson, "Strategy and Structure in Conversational Influence Attempts," *Communication Monographs* 50 (1983): 285–304; Sally Jackson and Scott Jacobs, "Conversational Relevance: Three Experiments on Pragmatic Connectedness in Conversation," in *Communication Yearbook 10*, ed. M. McLaughlin (Newbury Park, CA: Sage, 1987), pp. 323–347.

"Sure," is obviously relevant. On the other hand, if I say, "My toast is dry," my goal of getting you to pass the butter is less clear, and your response, "You should turn the toaster down a little," just frustrates me.

Jackson and Jacobs provide a list of utterance types that may be taken as a request, ranging from direct to irrelevant. "Please pass the butter" is an absolutely direct request. An indirect request would be less clear: "My toast is dry." A hint is even less direct: "Some people at this table have something I sure would like."

There are also utterances commonly found in conversations that function as prerequests. These set up the listener for a request in the future. An example is, "Could I interrupt to ask for something?"

Once a request or prerequest is made, a listener can respond in a variety of direct or indirect ways. If the communicator recognizes the intent of a request, he or she can clarify things by responding directly. An example would be an *anticipatory move*, in which the listener recognizes the hidden or indirect request and grants it immediately ("My toast is sure dry." "Here, have some butter."). Such moves provide coherence because they are oriented to the apparent goals of the other communicator. Responses that misinterpret the speaker's statement are less coherent, as in the case of someone who takes an innocent statement to be a request that was never intended as such.

A fruitful line of theory that illustrates the inferential-strategic approach is conversational argument, the topic of the following section.

Conversational Argument

The study of conversational argument is another major application of the rational/pragmatic model explained above, and it illustrates that model very well.[26] This area of study treats arguments as conversations, showing how they follow rational coherence rules. Specifically, conversational argument allows people to manage disagreement. Managing disagreement, like any of the structural features of talk, is a rule-governed, cooperative achievement.

There can be a number of levels of disagreement in conversation. In the typical case, both parties openly disagree and state reasons for their positions. More typically, however, the disagreement is less open. Because of the preference for agreement, the goal of conversational argument is to achieve agreement. Each turn must be a rational move toward bringing agreement about, and the coherence of an argument is largely judged in terms of the rationality of moves in achieving this objective. Thus, conversational argument is a method of managing disagreement so that it is minimized and so that agreement is achieved as quickly as possible.

There are basically two kinds of arguments. *Argument*$_1$ involves *making* an argument, or stating a case by giving reasons. One makes an argument by presenting a case or supporting one's position with reasons, as in "Mary is arguing that smoking is bad for her son's health." *Argument*$_2$ is *having* an argument, or exchanging objections, as in "Mary and her son are arguing about smoking." People can make an argument without having one, but they cannot easily have an argument without making one.[27]

Here is an example of a typical argument:

George: Well, I better get this grass cut.
Harry: Yeah, me too.
George: Can I borrow your mower?
Harry: Well, I really need it myself.
George: I'll return it right away.
Harry: Last time you kept it two weeks.
George: No, I'll return it.
Harry: Last spring you kept it a month.
George: Gosh, Harry, I really will get it back to you today.

---

26   The best recent statement of the theory of conversational argument is Frans H. van Eemeren, Rob Grootendorst, Sally Jackson, and Scott Jacobs, *Reconstructing Argumentative Discourse* (Tuscaloosa: University of Alabama Press, 1993). See also Frans H. van Eemeren and Rob Grootendorst, *Argumentation, Communication, and Fallacies: A Pragma-Dialectical Perspective* (Hillsdale, NJ: Erlbaum, 1992); Douglas N. Walton, *Plausible Argument in Everyday Conversation* (Albany: SUNY Press, 1992); Scott Jacobs and Sally Jackson, "Building a Model of Conversational Argument," in *Rethinking Communication: Paradigm Exemplars*, vol. 2, eds. B. Dervin, L. Grossberg, B. J. O'Keefe, and E. Wartella (Newbury Park, CA: Sage, 1989), pp. 153–171.

27   This distinction was originally made by Daniel J. O'Keefe, "Two Concepts of Argument," *Journal of the American Forensic Association* 13 (1977): 121–128.

Here, George makes a request and a promise. The argument (argument₂) ensues because Harry does not grant the request as would normally be expected and he challenges George's promise. In objecting, Harry makes an argument (argument₁) by saying that George has not been reliable in the past, and George comes back by supporting his intent to return the item.

Like all conversations, arguments have a certain order and rationality that may or may not be apparent on the surface. For the participants the argument will probably seem coherent because of the cooperative principle, which, in the case of arguments, requires the communicators to cooperate in creating a dispute-resolving episode.

This is ironic because arguments do not sound very cooperative, but you cannot have an argument unless both parties cooperate in doing so. Notice that the following somewhat comical conversation is not a very coherent argument because one party refuses to cooperate:

Katie: You never turn your reports in on time, Sara.

Sara: I know, I really like taking my time on things.

Katie: But this infuriates me!

Sara: Just what I really like, a good emotional reaction.

Katie: Stop it. I want to know why you are falling down on the job.

Sara: I sure do enjoy being the center of attention. This is great!

Arguers are essentially agreeing to use certain kinds of speech acts and to meet certain goals, and in the above conversation, Sara refuses to participate in the game.

Just as promises and requests have their own requirements, so do arguments. To have an argument, you must put forth an opinion that you do not expect the other person initially to accept. In conversational argument theory this is called a *standpoint.* You have to support the standpoint with certain assertions that you expect will not be immediately apparent to the other person. And, of course, you are not cooperating in "having an argument" if you do not at least initially believe your own standpoints and assertions.

There are many forms an argument can take, but there is one idealized form that most arguments approximate. This consists of four stages necessary for a complete argument to take place—opening, confrontation, argumentation, and concluding. These should not be considered the "steps" of an argument because they rarely occur in this order. Instead, you should think of these as aspects or parts of an argument. When they are all present, the communicators are said to be participating in a *critical discussion.*

The *confrontation* stage identifies the disagreement. The *opening stage* establishes agreement on how the dispute will be handled. The *argumentation* stage includes an exchange of competing positions. The *concluding stage* establishes resolution or continued disagreement.

These stages are characterized by certain kinds of speech acts, as outlined in Table 5.2.[28] In general the idealized model is like a code of conduct for having an argument. People will come as close to it as they can within the constraints of the situation. The idealized model is a measuring stick by which actual arguments can be compared and evaluated.

◖ COMMENTARY AND CRITIQUE

No discussion of language or communication is complete without addressing discourse, or message units larger than sentences that are part of ongoing communication, including talk, written texts, and even nonverbal forms. Although language and other symbol systems are the building blocks of communication, discourse is the product of communication itself.

Discourse as a part of everyday life is governed by rules, and much has been written about this topic. Rules are guidelines for action, and they say how language is used at every level—semantic, syntactic, and pragmatic. In other words, communicators use rules to determine how a sentence should be uttered, what words

28   Van Eemeren, Grootendorst, Jackson, and Jacobs, *Reconstructing,* p. 31.

TABLE **5.2**

Distribution of Speech-Act Types Across Functional Stages in Discussion

Stage in Discussion	Speech-Act Type
Confrontation	
1.1	expressing standpoint (assertive)
1.2	accepting or not accepting standpoint (commissive)
Opening	
2.1	challenging to defend standpoint (directive)
2.2	accepting challenge to defend standpoint (commissive)
2.3	deciding to start discussion; agreeing on discussion rules (commissive)
Argumentation	
3.1	advancing argumentation (assertive)
3.2	accepting or not accepting argumentation (commissive)
3.3	requesting further argumentation (directive)
3.4	advancing further argumentation (assertive)
Concluding	
4.1	establishing the result (assertive)
4.2	accepting or withholding acceptance of standpoint (commissive)
4.3	upholding or retracting standpoint (assertive)
(Any stage)	
5.1	requesting usage declarative (directive)
5.2	defining, precizating [sic], amplifying, and so on (usage declarative)

mean, and how to use language in ongoing communication. In this chapter we have seen how rules are used in the production of speech acts and in conversations.

The rule concept has been popular in communication studies because it acknowledges that people can make choices while still behaving somewhat predictably. Still, rule theory has had its share of critics. Criticism of rule theory has centered around two issues: conceptual coherence and explanatory power. Even its adherents admit that the rule tradition lacks unity and coherence. Jesse Delia verbalizes this objection in strong terms:

> The terrain covered by notions of "rules," then, is broad, grossly diffuse, and imprecisely articulated. And the real problem for any position purporting to be a general rules perspective is that the meaning of "rule" does not remain constant either within or across these domains. The "rules" territory taken as a whole is, in fact, little short of chaotic. At the least, it is clear that there is no unifying conception of the rule construct, of the domain of phenomena to which the construct has reference, of whether rules have generative power in producing and directing behavior . . . or of the proper way to give an account of some domain of phenomena utilizing the construct. The idea of "rules" as a general construct represents only a diffuse notion devoid of specific theoretical substance.[29]

The theories we have covered illustrate this lack of coherence. Linguistic rules are bound to an inherent structure of language and as such pretty much determine how sentences are generated and understood. As described by Searle, speech acts also are regulated by strict rules. Wittgenstein, on the other hand, considers the rules of language games to be malleable and changeable, much as in the rule-using tradition. The original conversation-analysis work, especially that governed by adjacency sequencing, used rules in the narrower, more restrictive sense; but Jackson and Jacobs in their global, rational approach see rules as something that communicators negotiate in the conversation itself.

The second issue related to rule theory involves its explanatory power. Critics generally believe that rule approaches cannot be explanatory as long as they fail to develop general principles that cut across contexts. To identify the rules in operation within a particular context is

29   Jesse Delia, "Alternative Perspectives for the Study of Human Communication: Critique and Response," *Communication Quarterly* 25 (1977): 54.

not sufficient to explain communication. Charles Berger believes that "at some point one must go beyond the description of 'what the rules are' and ask why some rules are selected over others . . . [and] what social forces produced the kinds of conventions and appropriate modes of behavior we now observe."[30] Berger's view is that a covering law approach is necessary to explain events, and rule theories are nothing more than covering laws in disguise.

Most rule advocates do not go along with this argument. Shimanoff points out that most rule explanations, in contrast to law explanations, are practical, or reason giving. Behaviors are explained in terms of their practical impact on creating desired outcomes. Although universal explanations are not desirable, and perhaps not even possible, rule theories should seek reason-giving explanations that cover relatively broad classes of situations, even to the point of allowing for prediction.[31]

The appropriate question here is not whether rule theories are explanatory but what kind of explanation the critic believes is necessary. Clearly, Berger and Shimanoff disagree on the level of generality necessary for adequate explanation. We must also keep in mind that different rule theories possess different levels of explanatory power.

Recall from Chapter 2 that explanation is made possible by principles of necessity and generality. Pearce discusses rule approaches in terms of these criteria.[32] Rule-following approaches tend not to be explanatory because they merely describe recurring behavior without indicating any form of necessity. Rule-governed approaches explain in terms of practical necessity, although their generality is somewhat limited. Pearce believes that the rule-using approach has the highest potential for explanatory power in terms of both practical and logical necessity and generality.

An important application of rule theory has been ordinary language philosophy and speech-act theory, which are among the most productive and useful creations of contemporary philosophy and social science. The power of these theories is in their use of intent to explain discourse. When we communicate we not only convey content, referential meaning, or our own version of truth but also an intent to do something with the words we use. This idea expresses so clearly how people use language to act or to accomplish objectives.

Still, speech-act theory has influenced a number of other theoretical lines of work, including conversation analysis. As researchers have worked with the concept of speech acts and applied it to various contexts, they have brought a number of weaknesses to light.

Critics generally agree that intentions are an important aspect of meaning, that speech constitutes a form of action, and that speech acts are governed by rules, but they argue that the conceptual categories of speech-act theory are vague or meaningless. Austin's threefold distinction among locutionary, illocutionary, and perlocutionary acts has been severely criticized from this standpoint, prompting one critic to state: "And now Austin has, in my judgment, erected a structure that is in imminent danger of collapse."[33]

Critics question the utility of locution as a concept, if the utterance of a locution automatically constitutes an illocution, as Austin claims it does. The distinction between illocutionary and perlocutionary acts is equally unclear to many readers, who point out that even if one could observe the difference between these concepts, it is doubtful that they constitute a useful distinction for guiding our understanding of speech acts. It would perhaps be more fruitful to recognize that any given speech act may be fulfilling a variety of intents and may be taken in a variety of different ways by different listeners.[34]

---

30   Charles R. Berger, "The Covering Law Perspective as a Theoretical Basis for the Study of Human Communication," *Communication Quarterly* 25 (1977): 12.
31   Shimanoff, *Communication Rules*, pp. 217–234.
32   Pearce, "Rules Theories."
33   Campbell, "A Rhetorical View," p. 287.
34   This point is made by John Lyne, "Speech Acts in a Semiotic Frame," *Communication Quarterly* 29 (1981): 202–208; and by Robert Trapp, "The Role of Disagreement in Interactional Argument," *Journal of the American Forensic Association* 23 (1986): 23–41.

The distinction between regulative and constitutive rules is equally fuzzy.[35] The problem here is that once any act becomes standardized, as in the case of almost all illocutionary acts, rules no longer are constitutive in the sense of creating new acts. Rules that regulate can be taken as constitutive, and rules that constitute an act also regulate.

Another application of rule theory, and one also heavily influenced by speech acts, is conversation analysis, the ethnomethodological study of ways actors cooperate in organizing interaction. It involves the careful examination of the details of actual conversations in an attempt to discover how people accomplish tasks and solve problems together.

Basically, conversation is a cooperative endeavor. People must play the game by the same rules or they would never know what was going on. For cooperation to occur, participants make certain assumptions about the other person, that he or she is conversing in good faith with the intent to speak in accordance with the rules. Even blatant violations of conversational rules are interpreted through implicature as being cooperative. Indeed, the combination of basic rules of cooperation such as appropriate quantity of talk, truthfulness, relevance, and organization with the flexibility permitted by conversational implicature makes it possible for humans to enact an infinite number of often creative expansions of talk to meet a whole array of intentions.

Perhaps the most important aspect of conversation analysis is the discovery of ways conversations are made coherent. This is also one of the most problematic aspects of the field. Originally, conversation analysts explained coherence strictly in terms of local rules, or the ways adjacent pairs of turns were consistent with one another. Most analysts now agree, however, that strictly local, adjacency explanations are inadequate.[36]

This weakness has given rise to more global explanations of coherence. Perhaps the most interesting of these is the rational model of Jackson and Jacobs. In this more humanistic explanation, communicators understand what is going on within a broader context than the simple sequence of acts at a given moment. They use conversation to negotiate plans, and the overall conversation itself comes to be rational. Acts that appear unrelated to one another when examined locally become consistent when you understand the broader context in which they appear.

A significant application of the rational approach is Jackson and Jacobs's work on conversational argument, which looks at the ways communicators manage disagreements in conversations. It examines the ways speakers and listeners have an argument and the ways they make arguments in conversations. The distinction between *making* an argument and *having* one is important and captures two dimensions of conversations—the individual speech act and the organization of interactions.

One major objection to conversation analysis is that it works entirely within the confines of the discourse itself. The researcher makes observations and inferences entirely on the basis of the text, without reference to outside factors or even the opinions of the participants themselves. The researcher relies solely on his or her own intuitions as a member of the culture in analyzing the discourse.[37] Although this procedure has merits, it is insensitive to the problem of possible multiple interpretations of speech acts. The participants in a conversation may not understand what is going on in the same way as the researcher thinks they do. Kathy Kellermann and Carra Sleight have written that coherence is not in the text but is in the cognitive system of the perceiver.[38] Although cues may be presented in the discourse, the actual coherence itself results from the application of a knowledge structure in the mind of the communicator to the discourse.

35   Shimanoff, *Communication Rules*, pp. 84–85. For additional critique, see McLaughlin, *Conversation*, pp. 63–68.
36   Jacobs, "Language."
37   This process is discussed in some depth by Wayne Beach, "Orienting to the Phenomenon," in *Communication Yearbook 13*, ed. James Anderson (Newbury Park, CA: Sage, 1990), pp. 216–244.
38   Kathy Kellermann and Carra Sleight, "Coherence: A Meaningful Adhesive for Discourse," in *Communication Yearbook 12*, ed. James Anderson (Newbury Park, CA: Sage, 1989), pp. 95–129.

This view is supported by Teun A. van Dijk. Van Dijk adds another level of analysis, however, in suggesting that cognition and societal power structures are linked through discourse.[39] Certain ideologies of domination and control are expressed through discourse and thereby come to affect the thinking of both the oppressor and oppressed in society. In turn, these thoughts, held in cognition, affect how we talk, or discourse, which in turn reproduces societal power arrangements and oppression. For van Dijk, you cannot separate societal structures, discourse structures, and cognitive structures.

A related issue is whether conversational organization is correlated without other outside factors such as characteristics of the communicators or social situation. Without going outside the discourse itself, the researcher cannot know whether such associations exist. Most conversation analysts agree that they are not concerned with these kinds of issues and leave such questions to others who do not use conversation-analysis methods.

A natural tension exists between discourse analysis and poststructural approaches to texts. Discourse analysts of every variety assume that the meaning and function of talk can be uncovered by careful examination of the structure of the text. Poststructuralists deny this assumption out of hand.

Poststructural theorists do not see discourse as a strategic method of accomplishing individual objectives. Poststructuralism is most generally understood as a reaction against structural theories of language and discourse, including most of the theories discussed in Chapters 4 and 5.

Most poststructuralists reject the idea that discourse is primarily a tool of communication. It may be considered so by communicators, but in fact it functions in far more profound ways that defy the traditional methods of discourse analysis discussed in this chapter. The three best-known poststructuralists are Jacques Derrida, Jacques Lacan, and Michel Foucault. Their ideas differ substantially from one another, and, in fact, calling poststructuralism theoretical at all is stretching the truth. If anything, it is probably

antitheoretical because of its rejection of the truth claims of discourse, including theories themselves.[40]

Jacques Derrida rejects absolutely the idea that language means anything definite.[41] He believes that there are always alternative meanings in a text and that any proposed meaning is only one alternative. Derrida's method of *deconstruction* is designed to take meaning apart and show that texts cannot be understood as expressions of particular meanings or truths.

Jacques Lacan, a student of Freud, deals with the effects of discourse on the self.[42] He shows how, at an early age, when the child is beginning to see the self as a unified being, language shapes some ideas about the self and represses others. The self is thus nothing in and of itself but is a product of discourse.

Foucault takes a somewhat different approach and denies that communicators create and use discourse to meet their goals.[43] The structure of

39   Teun A. van Dijk, "Discourse Semantics and Ideology," *Discourse and Society* 6 (1995): 243–289; Teun A. van Dijk, "Principles of Critical Discourse Analysis," *Discourse and Society* 4 (1993): 249–283; Teun A. van Dijk, *Communicating Racism: Ethnic Prejudice in Thought and Talk* (Newbury Park, CA: Sage, 1987).

40   For an excellent discussion of poststructuralism, see Art Berman, *From the New Criticism to Deconstruction: The Reception of Structuralism and Post-Structuralism* (Urbana: University of Illinois Press, 1988). A briefer treatment is Robert Young (ed.), "Post-Structuralism: An Introduction," in *Untying the Text: A Post-Structuralist Reader* (Boston: Routledge & Kegan Paul, 1981), pp. 1–28.

41   Derrida's chief work is *Of Grammatology*, trans. G. Spivak (Baltimore: Johns Hopkins University Press, 1976). For a brief overview, see the third edition of this book, *Theories of Human Communication* (Belmont, CA: Wadsworth, 1989), pp. 58–60. A more thorough treatment is that of Berman, *From the New Criticism*, pp. 199–222. See also Anthony Giddens, *Central Problems in Social Theory: Action, Structure, and Contradiction in Social Analysis* (Berkeley: University of California Press, 1979), pp. 28–48.

42   See Jacques Lacan, *The Four Fundamental Concepts of Psycho-Analysis*, trans. A. Sheridan (New York: Norton, 1981). See also Berman, *From the New Criticism*, pp. 185–194.

43   Foucault's primary works on this subject include *The Archaeology of Knowledge*, trans. A. M. Sheridan Smith (New York: Pantheon, 1972); *The Order of Things: An Archaeology of the Human Sciences* (New York: Pantheon, 1970); and *Power/Knowledge: Selected Interviews and Other Writings 1927–1977*, trans. Colin Gordon and others, ed. Colin Gordon (New York: Pantheon, 1980). For an excellent short summary, see Sonja K. Foss, Karen A. Foss, and Robert Trapp, *Contemporary Perspectives on Rhetoric* (Prospect Heights, IL: Waveland, 1991). See also Carole Blair, "The Statement: Foundation of Foucault's Historical Criticism," *Western Journal of Speech Communication* 51 (1987): 364–383; Sonja K. Foss and Ann Gill, "Michel Foucault's Theory of Rhetoric as Epistemic," *Western Journal of Speech Communication* 51 (1987): 384–402; Nancy Fraser, *Unruly Practices: Power, Discourse, and Gender in Contemporary Social Theory* (Minneapolis: University of Minnesota Press, 1989), pp. 17–68.

discourse and how it is used are determined, not by communicators, but historical and social processes in which certain forms of discourse are made necessary by power structures prevalent during the period. In Foucault's theory, discourse forms the very structure of knowledge in an era. The rules embedded in discourse dictate how we do what we do, and speakers are merely taking roles established in the discursive formation. For Foucault, as one poststructuralist, the text precedes the talk in the sense that language has both knowledge and action embedded in it and predetermines how actors will respond in their use of speech.

Donald Ellis, a defender of language and discourse theory, attacks poststructuralism head-on:

> Little could be more contrary to a theory of communication than principles that emerge from poststructuralism and the critical theory that it spawns. Human beings are language-using and message-producing animals, and theories of human communication engage us in understanding how messages are interpreted, evaluated, understood, and produced. A theory of communication must position itself away from poststructuralists who "de-form" language, and move closer to a theory of communication based on intentionality where meaning is "in-formed" by how language is directed toward objects and processes in the world.[44]

In the next two chapters, we move to a set of theories that deal with communicators apart from discourse. We will examine the cognitive structures and processes that affect discourse production and processing.

---

44   Donald G. Ellis, "Post-Structuralism and Language: Non-Sense," *Communication Monographs* 58 (1991): 213–224.

6

THEORIES OF
MESSAGE
PRODUCTION

Communication is a message-centered process that relies on information, and many communication theories have been developed to address these concerns. We discuss theories of message production in this chapter and those of message reception in the following one. We separate these theories in this book for purposes of organization, but the cognition involved in both is frequently part of the same general process.

The theories discussed in Chapters 6 and 7 center on the individual. Most of these theories acknowledge the social nature of communication, but they do not use social explanations. Rather, these theories view message production and reception as psychological matters, focusing on individual traits, states, and processes.[1]

The theories of message production and reception use three types of psychological explana-tions: trait explanations, state explanations, and process explanations. *Trait explanations* focus on relatively static characteristics of individuals and the ways these characteristics are associated with other traits and variables—the relationship be-tween particular personality types and certain sorts of messages. These theories predict that when you have a certain personality trait, you will tend to communicate in certain ways. For example, people with argumentative personali-ties like to debate.

State explanations focus on states of mind that persons experience for a period of time. Unlike traits, states are relatively unstable and transi-tory. Here we are interested in how certain states affect the sending and receiving of messages. For instance, when you are highly ego-involved in a topic, you are more likely to be cautious in evalu-ating arguments against your position.

Trait and state explanations can be used in concert with one another. Behavior is only par-tially determined by traits, and a researcher might try to determine which behaviors are traitlike and which are statelike. The way you ac-tually communicate is probably the product of

---

1   For a discussion of the significance of this line of theory, see John H. Powers, "On the Intellectual Structure of the Human Communication Discipline," *Communication Education* 44 (1995): 191–222; Howard Giles and Richard L. Street, Jr., "Communicator Characteristics and Behavior," in *Handbook of Interpersonal Communication*, eds. Mark L. Knapp and Gerald R. Miller, (Thousand Oaks, CA: Sage, 1994), pp. 103–161.

both. Perhaps the most commonly held belief among psychology researchers today is that your behavior is determined by a combination of traits and situational factors. How you communicate at any given moment depends on your traits as an individual and the situation in which you find yourself.[2]

The third approach found in theories of message production and reception is *process explanation*. Here, we are interested in how you actually send and receive messages. Process explanations attempt to capture the mechanisms of your mind. They focus on the ways information is acquired and organized, how memory is used, how you decide how to act, and a host of other similar concerns. Trait and state approaches are not incompatible with process explanations, and these may be combined.

Several of the process theories covered here are cognitive in orientation. The *cognitive tradition* concentrates on the mental processes that mediate between inputs and outputs, between stimulus and response.[3] Cognitive theories assume you have purposes and make choices, and these theories deal with the mental processes that make your actions possible. Cognitive theories focus on the content, structure, and process of your mind.

The content of the cognitive system consists of the information—thoughts, attitudes, and concepts—that you use to understand your experiences and plan your actions. The structure of the system consists of how you organize the content of your thoughts within your memory banks and the process, or operations, you use to manage this content—how you actually change it and use it on a daily basis. We'll take a closer look at content and process of cognition in the following chapter.

● TRAITS AND SITUATIONS

Numerous traits have been studied in communication research, and we cannot cover them all here.[4] In this section we concentrate on several prominent ones and conclude with an interesting situational theory.

Communication Apprehension

Many people are afraid of communication. Since about 1970 there has been much research on the problem of *communication apprehension* and related concepts. Perhaps the best developed of these programs is that of James McCroskey and his colleagues, who have discovered that fear of communicating is a serious practical problem for many people.[5]

Communication apprehension (CA) can be a trait or a state. *Traitlike CA* is an enduring tendency to be apprehensive about communication in a variety of settings, and individuals who suffer from this kind of fear may avoid all sorts of oral communication. In contrast, some people are afraid of only certain kinds of communication like public speaking but may exhibit little fear of other types of communication. Such fear is called *generalized-context CA*. Still others are afraid of communicating with certain specific people or groups like the homeless, a situational form called *person–group CA*.

Almost everybody suffers from time to time from communication apprehension as a state. There are times, such as giving a speech, when the threat is high or the situation is nerve-racking, and you will feel afraid, but normal anxiety does not mean that you have a *trait* of high communication anxiety.

Communication apprehension is a variable, ranging from low to high. Normal apprehension is not a problem, but pathological CA, in which an individual suffers high traitlike fear of com-

---

2   For a discussion of situational factors in communication, see Lynn C. Miller, Michael J. Cody, and Margaret L. McLaughlin, "Situations and Goals as Fundamental Constructs in Interpersonal Communication Research," in *Handbook of Interpersonal Communication*, 2nd ed., ed. Mark L. Knapp (Thousand Oaks, CA: Sage, 1994), pp. 162–197.
3   For an introduction to cognitive process, see Patricia G. Devine, David L. Hamilton, and Thomas M. Ostrom, *Social Cognition: Impact on Social Psychology* (San Diego: Academic, 1994), pp. 2–13; John O. Greene, "Evaluating Cognitive Explanations of Communicative Phenomena," *Quarterly Journal of Speech* 70 (1984): 241–254.
4   For an overview of several traits studied by communication researchers, see Giles and Street, "Communicator Characteristics."
5   This work is summarized in James C. McCroskey, "The Communication Apprehension Perspective," in *Avoiding Communication: Shyness, Reticence, and Communication Apprehension*, eds. J. A. Daly and J. C. McCroskey (Beverly Hills, CA: Sage, 1984), pp. 13–38.

munication, certainly is. Abnormally high CA creates serious personal problems, including extreme discomfort and avoidance of communication to the point of preventing productive and happy participation in society.

For example, McCroskey and others have found that CA has a serious effect on students at school.[6] Students high in CA score lower on the ACT aptitude test, and they tend to have lower grade-point averages than do less apprehensive students. Highly apprehensive students have special difficulty in small classes because of the expectations for students to talk. These students also have difficulty with individualized instruction because they have to interact one on one with the instructor, which frightens them. Highly apprehensive students tend to do best in large lecture classes, where they can hide in the crowd.

McCroskey is now convinced that the cause of high trait CA is biological.[7] CA is highly correlated with neuroticism and introversion, two apparently biological personality traits. These traits have been shown to be determined primarily by genetics, which strongly suggests that CA, too, is a genetic trait. This is a retreat from the generally accepted thesis held by many CA researchers, including McCroskey himself at an earlier time, that fear of communication is learned. From a biological perspective, here is how communication apprehension seems to work:

The limbic system of the brain controls emotion, and our emotional differences often relate to these brain differences. The more sensitive your limbic system, the more anxiety you may experience. Stimuli in the environment are processed through a part of your brain known as the *behavioral inhibition system* (BIS). Negative stimuli cause an arousal of the BIS, which in turn activates your limbic system. When your BIS is stimulated, you tend to pay more attention to threats. Thus, people who have an overactive BIS will be more prone to anxiety and fear than individuals with a less activated one.

In communication apprehension, something has to happen to cause communication to be viewed as a very aversive stimulus. This involves yet another part of your brain, the *behavioral activation system* (BAS). Because it is associated with rewards, this system seems to stimulate motivation and brings about action. Even apprehensive persons are at least occasionally motivated to communicate because of perceived rewards. For example, you might go ahead and give a presentation in a speech class because you want a high grade. In this case the BAS would enable you to do something potentially fearful.

The problem for highly apprehensive individuals is that they will experience extreme fear in the process of giving the speech, making the overall experience quite unpleasant. They will remember this and continue to associate the communication experience with negative stimuli.

The biological approach is quite new in communication studies, and it will be interesting to see the course of this direction in the future.

Rhetorical Sensitivity

Rhetorical sensitivity—the tendency to adapt messages to audiences—was discovered by Roderick Hart and his colleagues.[8] These theorists found that effective communication arises from sensitivity and care in adjusting what you say to a listener or audience.

Hart contrasts three general types of communicators.[9] *Noble selves* stick to their personal ideals without variation and without adapting or adjusting to others. *Rhetorical reflectors* are

6   James C. McCroskey, "Classroom Consequences of Communication Apprehension," *Communication Education* 26 (1977): 27–33.
7   James C. McCroskey and Michael J. Beatty, "Communication Apprehension," in *Personality and Communication: Trait Perspectives* (New York: Hampton, in press); Michael J. Beatty and James C. McCroskey, "Interpersonal Communication as Temperamental Expression," in *Personality and Communication: Trait Perspectives* (New York: Hampton, in press); Michael J. Beatty and James C. McCroskey, "Communication Apprehension as Temperamental Expression: Toward the Development of a Communibiological Theory of Communication Inhibition" (Paper presented at the Western Communication Association, Monterey, CA, February 1997).
8   Roderick P. Hart and Don M. Burks, "Rhetorical Sensitivity and Social Interaction," *Speech Monographs* 39 (1972): 75–91; Roderick P. Hart, Robert E. Carlson, and William F. Eadie, "Attitudes Toward Communication and the Assessment of Rhetorical Sensitivity," *Communication Monographs* 47 (1980): 1–22. See also Steven A. Ward, Dale L. Bluman, and Arthur Dauria, "Rhetorical Sensitivity Recast: Theoretical Assumptions of an Informal Interpersonal Rhetoric," *Communication Quarterly* 30 (1982): 189–195.
9   This part of the theory is based on the work of Donald Darnell and Wayne Brockriede, *Persons Communicating* (Englewood Cliffs, NJ: Prentice-Hall, 1976).

individuals who, at the opposite extreme, mold themselves to others' wishes, without following personal scruples. *Rhetorically sensitive* individuals, as a third type, moderate these extremes.

Rhetorical sensitivity embodies concern for self, concern for others, and a situational attitude. For Hart, this type is clearly superior to the other two. It leads to more effective understanding and acceptance of ideas. Rhetorically sensitive people accept personal complexity, understanding that each individual is a composite of many selves. You are not the same person in a professor's office as you are at a party with your friends, and you will communicate differently in these two situations if you are rhetorically adaptive.

Rhetorically adaptive individuals avoid rigidity in communicating with others, and they attempt to balance self-interests with the interests of others. These people try to adjust what they say to the level, mood, and beliefs of the other person. They do not forsake their own values, but they realize that they can communicate those values in a variety of ways. Rhetorically sensitive people are aware of the appropriateness of communicating or not communicating particular ideas in different situations. An idea can be expressed in many ways and can be adapted to the audience to be effective.

To better understand the rhetorically sensitive person in contrast with the noble self and rhetorical reflector, Hart and his colleagues created a questionnaire called RHETSEN and administered it to over 3,000 students at 49 universities.[10] In this study the researchers found substantial variation. Most people have varying degrees of all three types with one predominate type.

The variation among people seems to be associated with a variety of factors, including philosophical, economic, geographic, and cultural differences. Certain groups such as families and ethnic groups may teach and reinforce the values of particular types. For example, noble selves tend to be politically liberal, young, Jewish, and competitive. Rhetorical reflectors tend to be conservative, midwestern churchgoers, and they are older than the average noble self. Rhetorical sensitivity seems to be a white middle-class trait

found especially among groups that are politically independent, do not attend church, and have few ethnic ties.

Hart also administered RHETSEN to a group of about 500 nurses and found very similar patterns.[11] For example, nurses under the age of 35 were more rhetorically sensitive than the average, and those over 55 were more rhetorically reflective. The nurses with more education were more rhetorically sensitive than those with less education. Registered nurses tended to have more of the noble self than other types of nurses, and aides and licensed practical nurses tended to exhibit rhetorical reflector behaviors.

Communicator Style

The idea of rhetorical sensitivity suggests that individuals have a predominant manner or style in which they communicate. *Communicator style*, investigated by Robert Norton and his colleagues, is based on the idea that we communicate on two levels.[12] Not only do we give information, but we also present that information in a certain form that tells others how to understand and how to respond to a message.

For example, you might tell a friend about an experience but signal at the same time that your message is to be taken with authority, with disinterest, with humor, or with any number of different attitudes. Norton believes that these signals function as a "style message" by "signaling how a literal (primary) message should be taken, filtered, interpreted, or understood."[13]

Style messages may be delivered before, during, or after the primary message. Norton further believes that the tendency to expect style messages is so strong that if faced with ambiguous or contradictory messages, people look for style cues that will inform them of how the message is to be taken. For example, a comment that could be taken either seriously or jokingly will be inter-

---

10   Hart, Carlson, and Eadie, "Attitudes," p. 19.
11   Hart, Carlson, and Eadie, "Attitudes," p. 19.
12   Robert Norton, *Communicator Style: Theory, Applications, and Measures* (Beverly Hills, CA: Sage, 1983).
13   Norton, *Communicator Style*, p. 31.

preted in accordance with what the receiver believes to be the style of the speaker.

Over time, as you gain experience interacting with another person, you will repeat various styles. For instance, you might be viewed repeatedly as gruff, laid-back, whimsical, serious, and so on. Norton's thesis is that characteristics repeatedly associated with your communication constitute your dominant style.

Styles, of course, are not totally individual, since cultures affect how people behave and how they perceive others, as in the case of Hispanic "machismo" or Japanese "reserve."

Although your style is your predominant way of communicating, it is not the only way you communicate, and in fact your style can be multifaceted and include several different types.

There are numerous possible styles. Each style is a combination of certain variables. Norton has found nine variables that can enter into your overall style, including dominance, dramatic behavior, contentiousness, animation, impression leaving, relaxation, attentiveness, openness, and friendliness. Considerable overlap exists among these variables. For example, dramatic behavior and animation seem to go together, as do attentiveness and friendliness. Dominance and contentiousness also fit together.

Aggression

Aggression, or the application of pressure on another person, is commonly observed in communication. Dominick Infante and his colleagues have been responsible for developing this concept in the communication literature.[14] These authors note that aggression can be constructive when it aims to improve communication or enhance a relationship, or it can be destructive when it causes dissatisfaction or harms the relationship in some way.

Aggression consists of four traits—assertiveness, argumentativeness, hostility, and verbal aggressiveness. The first two are positive traits, and the second pair are negative. *Assertiveness* involves putting your rights forward without hampering other individuals' rights. As a trait, it is the tendency to act forthrightly in your own best interest. It may involve such practices as asserting leadership, initiating conversations, defending your rights in social situations, and resisting pressure from others to conform.

Argumentativeness is the tendency to engage in conversations about controversial topics, to support your own point of view, and to refute opposing beliefs. Infante believes that argumentativeness can improve learning, help people see others' points of view, enhance credibility, and build communication skill. Argumentative individuals are by definition assertive, although not all assertive people are argumentative.

Hostility is the tendency to display anger. It is important to note that one can be assertive, even argumentative, without anger. Unlike assertiveness and argumentativeness, then, hostility involves irritability, negativism, resentment, and suspicion. It is clearly a negative trait.

Verbal aggressiveness is often, though not always, associated with hostility. It is the attempt to hurt someone, not physically, but emotionally. Whereas arguments attack ideas and beliefs, verbal aggression attacks the ego or self-concept. Whereas arguments are reasoned, verbal aggressiveness includes such tactics as insults, profanity, threats, and emotional outbursts. It results in anger, embarrassment, hurt feelings, and other negative reactions.

It is important to understand that verbal aggressiveness and hostility are not the same thing as argumentativeness. In fact, Infante believes that when you are unable to argue constructively, you may lash out with verbal aggressiveness, especially if you are a hostile person. Knowing how to argue properly may be a solution to otherwise hurtful aggressive tendencies.

As a case in point, Infante and two colleagues studied husbands and wives in violent relationships and discovered that violent marriages are

---

14 For a summary of this work, see Dominick A. Infante and Andrew S. Rancer, "Argumentativeness and Verbal Aggressiveness: A Review of Recent Theory and Research," in *Communication Yearbook 19*, ed. Brant R. Burleson (Thousand Oaks, CA: Sage, 1996), pp. 319–352; Dominic A. Infante, Andrew S. Rancer, and Deanna F. Womack, *Building Communication Theory* (Prospect Heights, IL: Waveland, 1993), pp. 162–168.

characterized by higher verbal aggressiveness and lower argumentativeness than are nonviolent ones.[15] It seems that many nonviolent spouses deal with their problems by arguing constructively, whereas violent spouses may be unable to solve their differences in this way.

Keep in mind that these four traits are variables. In other words, people differ in their predispositions to be assertive, argumentative, hostile, or verbally aggressive. Some people often behave in one or more of these ways, and others seldom do. However, Infante is quick to point out that these traits do not always determine your behavior. Highly aggressive people do not always aggress, and individuals who have little aggressiveness sometimes do act assertively, argumentatively, or even hostilely. Thus, these traits can also be states that are affected by the situation. For example, highly argumentative people will often refrain from arguing if they perceive that they cannot win or that winning may not be important, and highly hostile people will sometimes refrain from being hostile toward authority figures.

Equivocation Theory

The manner in which you communicate is only partially determined by traits. Indeed, your state of mind and communication behavior are very much affected by external factors, especially your perception of the situation.[16]

An interesting theory of situational influence is Janet Beavin Bavelas's theory of *equivocal communication*.[17] Some messages are deliberately unclear, not direct or straightforward. Most people use equivocal communication from time to time, to protect other peoples' feelings and to escape from the unpleasant consequences of clarity. What do you say when a friend asks for your opinion of a hideous dress? You equivocate: "That's an interesting print. I've never seen it before."

According to these theorists, all communication consists of a simple four-part process: (1) I, (2) am saying something, (3) to you, (4) in this situation. When you are clear and direct, all four of these parts are clearly expressed, but when you equivocate, you are ambiguous about one or more of them. Sometimes you may be unclear about what *you* really think, making the *I* equivocal. Sometimes you may be unclear about the statement itself, making the *something said* equivocal. Sometimes you may be unclear about whom you are addressing, making the *to you* equivocal, and sometimes you may be unclear about the time or place, making the *situation* equivocal.

Departing from the cognitive, psychological orientation of most of the theories in this chapter, Bavelas and her colleagues believe that equivocal behavior is *entirely* a result of the situation. And they are quite clear about when people use equivocal messages: You use this strategy in avoidance-avoidance situations.

An *avoidance-avoidance situation* is a conflict in which all of the apparent alternatives have negative consequences. At times like this, you don't know what to do because all of the options are bad, like staying on the 10th floor of a burning building or jumping out the window! In communication, such a situation exists when any clear message would be undesirable. For example, if a student sitting next to you who just presented a terrible report in class whispers, "How did I do?" any clear answer would be undesirable. If you say, "Great!" you are lying, but if you say, "Terrible," you risk hurting the student's feelings. The solution is to equivocate: "You didn't seem nervous at all."

The Bavelas group has found this response to avoidance-avoidance situations many times in their studies. For instance, the student-report situation was presented to subjects in a variety of experiments. In one, they were asked which statement from a list they would most likely use in response. In another, they were asked to write a note to the other student, and in a third version

15   Dominick A. Infante, Teresa A. Chandler, and Jill E. Rudd, "Test of an Argumentative Skill Deficiency Model of Interspousal Violence," *Communication Monographs* 56 (1989): 163–177.
16   Miller, Cody, and McLaughlin, "Situations and Goals."
17   Janet Beavin Bavelas, Alex Black, Nicole Chovil, and Jennifer Mullett, *Equivocal Communication* (Newbury Park, CA: Sage, 1990).

of the experiment, subjects were actually asked to talk to the other student on the telephone. In each case, subjects who were told that the other student had done a poor job equivocated in their responses more than did subjects who were told that the other student had done a splendid job.

This line of work shows that the situation can have a powerful effect on communication behavior, irrespective of individual tendencies and traits. What it does not tell us is the process by which people come to decide why and how to send particular types of messages. We turn to this topic next.

◖ PROCESS THEORIES

Unlike trait theories, *process theories* attempt to explain the mechanism by which communicators produce messages, or as we will see in the following chapter, how they process information in the reception of messages. Here we will look at theories related to several processes—accommodating, assembling and planning, constructing, and gaining compliance.

Accommodation

If you observe interaction closely, you will notice that speakers frequently adjust their behaviors to one another. Researchers have also noticed this and have studied it in a variety of ways.[18] One of the best-developed theories related to interpersonal adjustment, called *accommodation theory*, was formulated by Howard Giles and his colleagues.[19]

Several researchers have confirmed the common observation that communicators often seem to mimic one another's behavior. For example, two speakers may adjust their accents to sound more alike, may begin to speak at the same speed, or may use mirrorlike gestures. Sometimes speakers do just the opposite and actually exaggerate their differences.

The process of *convergence,* or coming together, and *divergence,* or moving apart, is the subject of speech accommodation theory. Accommodation has been seen in almost all imaginable communication behaviors, including accent, rate, loudness, vocabulary, grammar, voice, gestures, and other features. Convergence or divergence can be *mutual,* in which case both communicators come together or go apart, or it can be *nonmutual,* in which one person converges to or diverges from the other. Convergence can also be *partial* or *complete.* For example, you might speak somewhat faster so that you are a little closer to another person's speech rate, or you might go all the way and speak just as fast as this person does.

Although accommodation may be done consciously, it is usually out of awareness. The use of accommodation is similar to any number of other functional but subconscious processes that are scripted, or enacted without having to attend to all the details of each behavior. You are probably more aware of divergence than convergence.

Accommodation researchers have found that accommodation can be important in communication. It can lead to social identity and bonding or disapproval and distance. For instance, convergence often happens in situations in which you seek the approval of others. This can occur in groups that are already alike in certain ways because such groups consist of similar individuals who already can coordinate their actions. The result of convergence can be increased attractiveness, predictability, intelligibility, and mutual involvement.

When you converge, you rely on your perception of the other person's speech qualities. Often you are correct in this perception, but sometimes you can be wrong, which will lead to negative results. For example, people sometimes converge

---

18   For a summary of this work, see Judee K. Burgoon, Leesa Dillman, and Lesa A. Stern, "Adaptation in Dyadic Interaction: Defining and Operationalizing Patterns of Reciprocity and Compensation," *Communication Theory* 3 (1993): 295–316.

19   One of the most recent and complete expositions of this theory is Howard Giles, Justine Coupland, and Nikolas Coupland, "Accommodation Theory: Communication, Context, and Consequence," in *Contexts of Accommodation: Developments in Applied Sociolinguistics,* eds. Howard Giles, Justine Coupland, and Nikolas Coupland (Cambridge: Cambridge University Press, 1991), pp. 1–68. See also Howard Giles, Anthony Mulac, James J. Bradac, and Patricia Johnson, "Speech Accommodation Theory: The First Decade and Beyond," in *Communication Yearbook 10,* ed. M. L. McLaughlin (Newbury Park, CA: Sage, 1987), pp. 13–48.

not with the other person's actual speech but with a stereotype, such as when a nurse speaks to an elderly patient using "baby talk" or when someone speaks loudly and slowly to a blind person.

Observing how people evaluate the convergence of others is interesting. Typically, some convergence is appreciated. You tend to respond favorably to someone who makes an attempt to speak in your style. But you will probably dislike too much convergence, especially if you think it is inappropriate. People tend to appreciate convergence from others that is accurate, well intended, and appropriate in the situation.

How you evaluate convergence depends in part on why you think others are copying you, or their motive. Studies have shown that when listeners perceive that the speaker is intentionally speaking in a style close to their own, they will tend to like it, but when convergence is seen as out of the speaker's control, it may be distasteful to the other party. Almost certainly, any convergence move that is seen as inappropriate in the situation or done out of ill will would be evaluated negatively. This would include, for example, mocking, teasing, insensitivity to social norms, or inflexibility.

Of course, you do not always match the behavior of others in order to seek their approval. Often higher-status speakers will slow their speech or use simpler vocabulary when talking with a person who has lower status to increase understanding. In contrast, lower-status communicators will sometimes upgrade their speech to match the higher-status person because they want that person's approval.

Accommodation often seems to be associated with power. For example, in New York City where blacks are viewed as having more power than Puerto Ricans, the latter converge more to the accent of the former. In organizations, subordinates have been observed to converge with superiors more often than the opposite.

Although the rewards of speech convergence can be substantial, so are the costs. Convergence requires effort, and it may mean the loss of personal identity. Sometimes it is even viewed as abnormal and may be frowned on.

Instead of converging, you sometimes maintain your own style or actually move in the opposite direction. You may work to maintain your own style when you want to reinforce your identity. This would be the case, for example, among members of an ethnic group with a strong accent, who work to perpetuate the accent in the face of threats from homogenizing influences of a dominant culture. Divergence often functions to accentuate in-group identity vis-à-vis members of an out-group.

Sometimes members of a group will accentuate their speech characteristics in a strange community to elicit sympathy from the host group. This is a kind of "self-handicapping" method that frees speakers from responsibility for violation of certain social norms with which they may not be familiar. Sometimes, too, speakers will diverge from the style of other speakers in order to affect the others' behavior in some way. Teachers may deliberately talk over the heads of students in order to "challenge" the students to learn. You might speak extra slowly when talking with a very fast speaker in order to get him or her to slow down.

Cognitive Message Preparation

Cognition helps us organize knowledge in order to act appropriately in given situations, including communication. What cognitive processes determine how we communicate? Here we look at two theories that address this question—action-assembly theory and planning theory.

Action-Assembly Theory. This work has been developed by John Greene to explain communicative action.[20] Action-assembly theory examines the ways you organize your knowledge and use it in communication.

---

20   John O. Greene and Deanna Geddes, "An Action Assembly Perspective on Social Skill," *Communication Theory* 3 (1993): 26–49; John O. Greene, "Action-Assembly Theory: Metatheoretical Commitments, Theoretical Propositions, and Empirical Applications," in *Rethinking Communication: Paradigm Exemplars*, eds. B. Dervin, L. Grossberg, B. J. O'Keefe, and E. Wartella (Newbury Park, CA: Sage, 1989), pp. 117–128; "A Cognitive Approach to Human Communication: An Action Assembly Theory," *Communication Monographs* 51 (1984): 289–306.

According to this theory, you have *content knowledge* and *procedural knowledge.* You know *about* things, and you know *how to do* things. Your procedural knowledge consists of an awareness of the consequences of various actions in the different situations you face. This overall procedural knowledge consists of a large number of "procedural records," each of which is composed of knowledge about an action, its outcomes, and the situations in which it is appropriate. You will behave effectively on future occasions, because you remember what happened when you behaved that way before.

For example, how do you know how to introduce yourself to another person at a party? From experience and watching others do it, you have knowledge of various ways. These memories tell you not only how to introduce yourself but also the possible outcomes and the situations in which each method should be used. You would probably introduce yourself differently to a person you have never met than to someone you have already met. You have formal and informal styles of introducing yourself. You have methods you use when you really want to get to know someone and other methods when you don't.

Thus, acting involves "assembling" appropriate possible actions. Out of all the actions in your procedural memory, you must select the most appropriate ones. How do you do this? You select an action sequence when the conditions match those of a similar occasion.

A number of outcomes may be desired, including achieving an objective with another person, expressing information, managing conversations, producing intelligible speech, and other results. When introducing yourself, for example, you may want to meet the other person, make yourself look good, and have a good time, all in one set of actions. You essentially assemble the procedures necessary to accomplish these objectives, and the resulting "plan" is called the *output representation.* The term *plan* is in quotation marks in the previous sentence because you do not always lay it out carefully in advance, although you often do plan consciously.

We often use preorganized sets of behavior, called *unitized assemblies,* that are already as-sembled and ready for action. This kind of routine is efficient because it requires little time and effort. You don't have to think much about what to do because the whole sequence is already there in your memory. Greeting rituals are a good example of unitized assemblies. Unfortunately, as we all know, people sometimes use such a routine inappropriately when it would have been better to take parts of it and assemble them in a different way.

The most abstract level in the hierarchy is the *interactional representation,* or a sense of the overall objective to be achieved by the action within the communication itself, such as making an introduction. Next is *ideational representation,* or the ideas to be expressed in the course of achieving the interactional objectives. The third level is the *utterance representation,* which includes the appropriate language. Finally, the *sensorimotor representation* helps us activate the proper neural commands to produce the message, which may include use of the speech mechanism. This same set of representations is used in all communication actions, even the most complex ones such as giving a speech, managing a conflict, or writing a book.

Thus, the cognitive system must coordinate rather different levels of behavior in a single action, requiring knowledge of how to speak (sensorimotor), language (utterances), appropriate content (knowledge), and the larger goal-oriented interactional behavior. As you act, all of these levels come together in a coordinated action.

In the process of composing this paragraph, for example, my cognitive system had to integrate into a coherent action at least four levels of representation: typing (sensorimotor), sentence structure (language), knowledge of action-assembly theory, and general strategy for communicating the theory clearly. All were stored in my procedural memory and were selected from a variety of possible ways to write the paragraph.

It is clear, then, that no single action can stand by itself. Every action implicates other actions in one way or another. To introduce yourself, you have to use a variety of actions from moving your vocal chords to using certain words and gestures. To write a paragraph, you must combine a variety of actions from coordinating knowledge to using language to writing or typing. Actions, then, are integrated into a hierarchy of knowledge. Each piece of knowledge in the overall routine is a representation of something that needs to be done. Thus, once you decide on a higher-order goal, such as making an introduction, other lower-level routines are suggested.

This idea of a hierarchy of action is useful because it explains why we do not have to access our entire memory every time we want to do something. Once one action is decided on, the other actions required to do it are already limited. You may still have some choice, but in most cases you can make those choices quickly.

The action-assembly process is complex and not always successful. To do something well requires not only knowledge and motivation, but the ability to retrieve and organize the necessary actions efficiently and quickly. If you make a mistake or have trouble doing something, even when you have the correct knowledge and motivation, it means you are not able to put together the best routine for any of the following reasons: You are not practiced in doing it, you are unable to pay attention to important aspects of the situation, you are relying too much on unitized routines, or other problems are occurring in the action-assembly process.

Action assembly takes time and effort. Thinking is work. The more complex the assembly task, the more time and effort it takes. Introducing yourself is usually not as difficult as giving a speech. Even though communicators seem to respond to a situation immediately without effort, research shows that every response does take time, if only a fraction of a second, and that more complex tasks take more time than simple ones. You know from your own experience that you think through and struggle with communicating in unfamiliar situations. This difficulty in processing information in communication can be seen in people's pausing and dysfluency patterns. When people take a long time to say something, pause and stutter, or generally seem confused, they may be having difficulty in inte-

grating procedural knowledge and formulating an action. When people respond quickly and fluently, they are demonstrating that the task is relatively easy for them in this situation.

Planning Theory.   Here we look at a similar theory, produced by Charles Berger, to explain the process that individuals go through in planning their behavior, specifically their communication behavior.[21] The study of planning is a centerpiece of cognitive science, and psychologists have given the subject considerable thought and research. Linking cognitive planning with communication behavior, however, has not received as much attention, and Berger hopes to close this gap by his own research and theory.

This link is especially important because communication is so obviously involved in our conscious attempts to achieve goals. If you want to do well in a class, you probably talk to other students, friends, and even the professor to find out what might be done. Your assignments will be carefully crafted to meet requirements, and you will think quite consciously about what to do and how to do it.

Among the many goals we try to achieve every day, from meeting dietary needs to getting where we want to go, *social goals* are especially important. Because we are social creatures, other people are important in our lives, and we aim to influence them in a variety of ways. We can achieve many types of goals by communicating in particular ways, but communication is absolutely central in meeting social goals. Understanding something about how we plan to meet such goals, then, is an important research aim.

Studying goal behavior is no easy task. For one thing, goals tend to be complex. Goals seem to be arranged in hierarchies, and achieving certain goals first makes it possible to achieve other ones. For example, you may find another person attractive and want to get to know this person, but you will probably have to accomplish quite a

---

21   Charles R. Berger, *Planning Strategic Interaction: Attaining Goals Through Communicative Action* (Mahwah, NJ: Erlbaum, 1997).

few subgoals first, such as finding a way to start a conversation with this person.

Many of our goals are actually part of the planning process itself. These *metagoals* guide the plans we make. For example, we usually want to do planning in the easiest way possible, making efficiency an important metagoal. (That's why we don't re-invent the wheel every time we take a drive.) We want to behave in socially appropriate ways, so social appropriateness is another metagoal. Another metagoal is politeness, for whatever else we might want to accomplish in our communication, we often aim to be polite.

What, then, is a plan? Berger writes that plans are "hierarchical cognitive representations of goal-directed action sequences."[22] In other words, plans are mental images of the steps one will go through to meet a goal. They are hierarchical because certain actions are necessary to set things up so that other actions will work. Planning, then, is the process of thinking up these action plans.

Because we want our planning to be efficient, we often rely on *canned plans* we have used before. These are stored in *long-term memory,* and we rely on them whenever possible. You have started so many conversations in your life, you know how to do it without thinking; you rely on the same methods you have used over and over again.

Often canned plans don't work, or are foiled in some way. Or the goal is new and complicated and requires fresh thinking. Let's say you need a substantial loan and think you can get the money from a close relative, say your aunt. You have never done this before and don't know exactly how to approach it. Here you must put a new plan together in your *working memory.* The working memory is a place where you can use parts of old plans, knowledge, and creative thinking to come up with a way to approach the problem.

The strength of the goal seems to influence how complex our plans tend to be. If you really want something very badly, you will probably work pretty hard and come up with a fairly

elaborate plan. If you really need the loan, you will probably work out the plan quite carefully. Of course, the complexity of your plan will also depend on how much knowledge you have about loans and about your aunt as well as your knowledge about persuasion. Berger refers to information about the topic (for example, loans and relatives) as *specific domain knowledge* and information about how to communicate (for example, persuading people) as *general domain knowledge.* The theory predicts that the more you know (specific and general), the more complex your plan will be. Obviously, then, if you have a lot of motivation and knowledge, you will create more complex plans, and if your motivation and knowledge are low, your plan will probably be underdeveloped.

Naturally, however, there are limits on how complicated a plan can be. In interpersonal communication, this is especially so because of the metagoals of efficiency and social appropriateness. You can't do just anything you want because of the effort it would take and because some actions are not socially appropriate. For example, you probably would not make up a 100-point plan to get money from your aunt because that would take too much effort, and you certainly would not include the socially unacceptable strategy of insulting her to secure the loan.

What happens if your attempt to achieve a goal is thwarted? If the goal is important, you will probably persist, but it is unlikely that you will continue to use the same strategy over and over. There are two things you might consider. One course of action is to try different specific actions, which Berger calls *low-level plan hierarchy alterations,* or you could adjust more general actions (*abstract alterations*).

People tend to make lower-level adjustments first. For example, say you decide to broach the subject of the loan by just mentioning that your tuition is due. Suppose that your aunt replies, "Boy, I bet you're glad you had such a high-paying job last summer!" You don't get the reaction you expected, and you will probably try a different message, something like, "Right, and that did help, but my books were so expensive and

---

22   Berger, *Planning Strategic Interaction,* p. 25.

my apartment rent is out of sight." This is an example of a low-level alteration.

Sometimes, though, the situation calls for alteration of a higher level of strategy. For example, if your aunt were to say, "Yes, money can sure be a problem. My assets are all tied up in a big investment deal right now, and I am also having a little cash flow problem myself," you would probably reconsider what you were trying to accomplish. Instead of asking for the loan now, you might change your goal a little and decide to wait a few weeks.

Berger's theory suggests that whether you make low- or high-level adjustments depends largely on how motivated you are to achieve the goal. If the goal is very important, you will tend to make higher-level adjustments, and you will do so sooner than if your motivation is low.

Planning and goal achievement are very much tied into our emotions. We are not robots, and if our goals are thwarted, we tend to react negatively. On the other hand, if our plans go well, we often feel uplifted. The negative feelings we experience when we fail to meet a goal depend on how important the goal is. They also are determined in part by how hard we have worked to achieve the goal and how close to the goal we actually got. If you worked really hard to get the loan from your aunt, and she led you on so you were pretty optimistic about getting it, you would be really upset if the final answer was, "Sorry, but no."

Berger has said that social appropriateness is an important metagoal. We normally act in socially appropriate ways, but there are exceptions. Because of the negative emotions we often feel when goals are thwarted, we often act in socially unacceptable ways when this happens. This is especially true if our goals are repeatedly thwarted and if the thwarted goals are quite important to us. Something else will happen at times like this too: We keep trying to get to the goal, but out of desperation, we tend to use simpler and simpler plans.

Even if we try to maintain a complex plan, we may falter and have trouble invoking it. The ease with which we follow a plan is called *action fluidity*, and people find that they sometimes have

great fluidity and sometimes not. The more complex a plan and the more emotional we get, the less fluid our actions become.

For example, in an experiment conducted by Berger and his colleagues, subjects were asked to present arguments supporting their position on a controversial campus issue to another person.[23] Some of the subjects were given no time to plan their arguments, others were given some planning time, and others were given planning time and invited to prepare contingency plans as well.

The person to whom the subjects gave their argument was actually a confederate of the experimenter instructed to resist their arguments and thereby frustrate the subjects. The experimenters then counted the number of disruptions in the subjects' speech as a measure of fluidity. The subjects who were given an opportunity to develop alternative plans were less fluid in general than those who were not. This result was probably caused by the fact that this group had more complex plans.

There may be many variables affecting how easily one can put a plan into effect. One of these is the degree of complexity that an individual can handle in his or her thinking. The following theory, constructivism, addresses this concern.

Constructivism

Constructivism, a theory developed by Jesse Delia and his colleagues, has had immense impact on the field of communication.[24] The theory

23   Charles R. Berger, Susan H. Karol, and Jerry M. Jordan, "When a Lot of Knowledge Is a Dangerous Thing: The Debilitating Effects of Plan Complexity on Verbal Fluency," *Human Communication Research* 16 (1989): 91–119.

24   For a summary of the theory and its various tributaries and applications, see John Gastil, "An Appraisal and Revision of the Constructivist Research Program," in *Communication Yearbook 18*, ed. Brant Burleson (Thousand Oaks, CA: Sage, 1995), pp. 83–104. See also Brant R. Burleson, "The Constructivist Approach to Person-Centered Communication: Analysis of a Research Exemplar," in *Rethinking Communication: Paradigm Exemplars*, eds. B. Dervin, L. Grossberg, B. J. O'Keefe, and E. Wartella (Newbury Park, CA: Sage, 1989), pp. 29–46; Jesse G. Delia, "Interpersonal Cognition, Message Goals, and Organization of Communication: Recent Constructivist Research," in *Communication Theory: Eastern and Western Perspectives*, ed. D. L. Kincaid (San Diego, CA: Academic, 1987), pp. 255–274; Jesse G. Delia, Barbara J. O'Keefe, and Daniel J. O'Keefe, "The Constructivist Approach to Communication," in *Human Communication Theory: Comparative Essays*, ed. F. E. X. Dance (New York: Harper & Row, 1982), pp. 147–191.

says that individuals interpret and act according to conceptual categories of the mind. Reality does not present itself in raw form, but must be filtered through the person's own way of seeing things.

Constructivism is based partially on George Kelly's theory of personal constructs, which proposes that persons understand experience by grouping events according to similarities and distinguishing between things by their differences.[25] Perceived differences are not natural, but determined sets of opposites within the individual's cognitive system. Opposite pairs like tall-short, hot-cold, and black-white, used to understand events and things, are called *personal constructs.* Hence the name of Kelly's theory: personal construct theory.

An individual's cognitive system consists of numerous such distinctions. By classifying an experience into categories, the individual gives it meaning. So, for example, you might see your mother as tall and your father as short, coffee as hot and milk as cold, your favorite jacket as black and a favorite hat as white.

Constructs are organized into interpretive schemes, which identify something and place the object in a category. With interpretive schemes, we make sense out of an event by placing it in a larger category. Interpretive schemes develop as you mature, according to the *orthogenetic principle,* by moving from relative simplicity and generality to relative complexity and specificity.[26] Thus, very young children have simple construct systems, while most adults have much more sophisticated ones. When you were young, for example, you might have placed all people into two types, big and little. Now, on the other hand, you have an immense number of constructs with which to distinguish among different people.

Constructivism recognizes that constructs have social origins and are learned through interaction with other people. Consequently, culture seems especially significant in determining the meanings of events. Culture can influence the way communication goals are defined, how goals should be achieved, as well as the types of constructs employed in the cognitive schema.[27]

Although it acknowledges the impact of social interaction and culture on the cognitive system, constructivism deals primarily with individual differences in construct complexity and strategies used in communication.

Individuals with highly developed interpretive schemes make more discriminations than those who see the world simplistically. Although the construct system develops throughout childhood and adolescence, even adults differ widely in their cognitive complexity. Also, different parts of your construct system differ in complexity, so that you might have elaborate thoughts about music but simple ideas about international relations.

Because cognitive complexity plays an important role in communication, this concept is a mainstay of constructivism.[28] Complexity or simplicity in the system is a function of the relative number of constructs and the degree of distinctions you can make. An individual varies in cognitive complexity across topics and over time. The number of constructs you use is called *cognitive differentiation.* Cognitively sophisticated people can make more distinctions than can cognitively uncomplicated people. That is why many of us go to a tax accountant every year.

Delia and his colleagues have shown that messages vary according to complexity. Simple messages attack only one goal, more complex messages separate goals and deal with each in turn, and the most sophisticated messages actually

25 George Kelly, *The Psychology of Personal Constructs* (New York: North, 1955).
26 H. Werner, "The Concept of Development from a Comparative and Organismic Point of View," in *The Concept of Development,* ed. D. B. Harris (Minneapolis: University of Minnesota Press, 1957).
27 For a discussion of the effects of culture on the cognitive system, see James L. Applegate and Howard E. Sypher, "A Constructivist Theory of Communication and Culture," in *Theories in Intercultural Communication,* eds. Y. Y. Kim and W. B. Gudykunst (Newbury Park, CA: Sage, 1988), pp. 41–65.
28 The idea of cognitive complexity was originally developed by Walter H. Crockett, "Cognitive Complexity and Impression Formation," in *Progress in Experimental Personality Research,* vol. 2, ed. B. A. Maher (New York: Academic, 1965), pp. 47–90. See also Harold M. Schroder, Michael S. Driver, and Siegfried Streufert, *Human Information Processing: Individuals and Groups Functioning in Complex Social Situations* (New York: Holt, Rinehart & Winston, 1967).

integrate several goals in one message.[29] We often attempt to accomplish more than one thing by a single action, and our messages vary in the extent to which they can achieve multiple, sometimes conflicting, objectives simultaneously. Cognitive differentiation thus affects how complex messages can be.

Further, the simplest persuasive messages only address your own goals without considering the other person's needs, whereas more adaptive, complex persuasive messages are designed to meet your needs and the needs of the other person.

For example, if you want to get a person to change his or her behavior, to stop smoking perhaps, you might want to do it in a way that would help the other person save face. This would require you to achieve at least two objectives in the same message: deliver a nonsmoking message and protect the other person's ego. Simple messages cannot do this, but more complex messages can be employed precisely for this purpose. Constructivists have found that one's tendency to help the other person save face is directly related to his or her cognitive complexity.

Interpersonal constructs are especially important because they guide how we understand other people. Individuals differ in the complexity with which they view others. If you are cognitively simple, you will tend to stereotype other people, whereas if you have more cognitive differentiation, you will make more subtle and sensitive distinctions.

The research on this topic has shown that cognitive complexity generally leads to greater understanding of others' perspectives and better ability to frame messages in terms understandable to others. This ability, called *perspective taking*, seems to lead to more sophisticated arguments and appeals.[30] Adjusting one's communication to others is referred to as *person-centered communication*, and people vary in their use of person-centered messages.

Compliance gaining is one of several types of communication that have been studied from a person-centered perspective.[31] Persuasive messages range from the least to the most person-centered. On the simplest level, for example, one could attempt to achieve the single objective of compliance by commanding or threatening. On a more complex level, one might also try to help a person understand why compliance is necessary by offering reasons for complying. On an even higher level of complexity, a communicator could try to elicit sympathy by building empathy or insight into the situation. As one's messages become more complex, they necessarily involve more goals and are more person-centered.

Comforting messages have also been studied from a constructivist perspective. People try to provide social support to others in a variety of ways, and some of these methods are more sophisticated than others. Research on comforting messages generally supports the view that cognitively complex individuals produce more sophisticated messages than less complex individuals, that sophisticated messages are more person-centered than less sophisticated ones, and that more sophisticated messages are more effective in eliciting comfort than less sophisticated ones.[32]

As an example of person-centered communication, consider the study of Susan Kline and Janet Ceropski on doctor–patient communication.[33] This study involved forty-six medical students, who completed a variety of tests, partici-

---

29   Multiple goal achievement is developed in detail by Barbara J. O'Keefe and Gregory J. Shepherd, "The Pursuit of Multiple Objectives in Face-to-Face Persuasive Interactions: Effects of Construct Differentiation on Message Organization," *Communication Monographs* 54 (1987): 396–419.

30   This literature is reviewed by Claudia Hale, "Cognitive Complexity-Simplicity as a Determinant of Communication Effectiveness," *Communication Monographs* 47 (1980): 304–311.

31   See, for example, Jesse G. Delia, Susan L. Kline, and Brant R. Burleson, "The Development of Persuasive Communication Strategies in Kindergartners Through Twelfth-Graders," *Communication Monographs* 46 (1979): 241–256; James L. Applegate, "The Impact of Construct System Development on Communication and Impression Formation in Persuasive Messages," *Communication Monographs* 49 (1982): 277–289.

32   Brant R. Burleson, "Comforting Messages: Significance, Approaches, and Effects," in *Communication of Social Support: Messages, Interactions, Relationships, and Community*, eds. Brant R. Burleson, Terrance L. Albrecht, and Irwin G. Sarason (Thousand Oaks, CA: Sage, 1994), pp. 3–28.

33   Susan L. Kline and Janet M. Ceropski, "Person-Centered Communication in Medical Practice," in *Emergent Issues in Human Decision Making*, eds. G. M. Phillips and J. T. Wood (Carbondale: Southern Illinois University Press, 1984), pp. 120–141.

pated in videotaped interviews with patients, and wrote statements on what they thought the purpose of medical interviews to be.

The interviews were carefully examined by the researchers and classified according to how person-centered they were. The person-centered messages used by the medical students were found to be more complex than messages that were not person-centered. The researchers found that about 40 percent of the medical students were person-centered in persuading patients. These individuals explained why compliance was necessary and took patients' feelings into consideration. About 50 percent of the subjects used person-centered communication in dealing with distress by acknowledging rather than denying patients' feelings, helping patients understand their discomfort, and giving advice on how to relieve the distress. Finally, about 70 percent of those studied used person-centered communication in gathering information. Their questions were more detailed, and they gave patients more leeway in telling their story.

This research confirms that those who use person-centered strategies have more complex cognitive schemas for understanding other people and are better able to take the perspective of others and to have empathy for others.

Recently, however, Barbara O'Keefe has suggested that different message strategies may involve more than mere differences in construct differentiation.[34] People may actually employ different *message design logics,* or conceptions of what communication itself is.

O'Keefe outlines three possible message design logics that range from least person-centered to most person-centered. The *expressive logic* sees communication as a mode of self-expression for communicating feelings and thoughts. Its messages are open and reactive in nature, with little attention given to the needs or desires of others. An example of a message resulting from this logic would be an angry response to a friend who forgot to get tickets to a concert:

Now we are not going to get our tickets. I was counting on getting to go to this concert. This is my favorite group and I really really wanted to hear them. I have been thinking about this for weeks. Nothing I really want to do ever works out. I am going to be mad at you for a long time about this.[35]

The *conventional logic* sees communication as a game to be played by rules. Here communication is a means of self-expression that proceeds according to accepted rules and norms. It tends to be polite and appropriate. A response to the ticket situation using conventional logic might go like this:

It was your responsibility to pick up the tickets. Everyone decided what job they would do in organizing this evening, and that was the job you picked. So you will just have to figure out some way to get them yourself, even if you have to pay a taxi to deliver them.[36]

The *rhetorical logic* views communication as a way of changing the rules through negotiation. Messages designed with this logic tend to be flexible, insightful, and person-centered. Following is an example of how the ticket situation might be handled by someone who uses the rhetorical logic:

Gee, I'm sorry you have been so pressed. This really has put us in a pickle. I know what you can do. Bob has to go right by the ticket office on his way home from work. Call the ticket office and charge the tickets on your Master Card. Then call Bob and see if he can stop and pick up the tickets. Or maybe he could just pick you up and run you by the ticket office.[37]

Compliance Gaining

Gaining the compliance of another person is one of the most common uses of communication. It involves trying to get other people to do what you want them to do, or to stop doing something you don't like. Compliance-gaining messages are among the most researched areas in the field. A number of approaches have been taken to this

34   Barbara J. O'Keefe, "The Logic of Message Design: Individual Differences in Reasoning About Communication," *Communication Monographs* 55 (1988): 80–103.
35   O'Keefe, "Logic," p. 100.
36   O'Keefe, "Logic," p. 102.
37   O'Keefe, "Logic," p. 103.

topic, far too many to cover in this brief treatment.[38] Here, we will look at three of the most influential.

Marwell and Schmitt. The prolific research program on compliance-gaining strategies in the communication field received its impetus from the groundbreaking studies of Gerald Marwell and David Schmitt.[39] These researchers isolated sixteen strategies commonly used in gaining the compliance of other people, as outlined in Table 6.1.

Marwell and Schmitt use an exchange-theory approach: Compliance is an exchange for something else supplied by the compliance seeker. If you do what I want, I will give you something in return—esteem, approval, money, relief from obligations, good feelings, and other things. The exchange approach, which is frequently used in social theory, rests on the assumption that people basically act to gain something from others in exchange for something else. This model is inherently power-oriented. In other words, you can gain the compliance of others if you have sufficient resources to give them what they want. The power dimension of compliance gaining is discussed in more detail later in this section.

One of the most important theoretical questions about compliance-gaining tactics has been how to reduce the list of all possible tactics to a manageable set of general strategies or dimensions. A long list of how people persuade others does not tell you much more than you already know. A shorter list would crystallize the tactics into essential qualities, functions, goals, or some other set of dimensions that would help explain

---

For some recent reviews of this work, see James B. Stiff, *Persuasive Communication* (New York: Guilford, 1994), pp. 199–211; David R. Seibold, James G. Cantrill, and Renee A. Meyers, "Communication and Interpersonal Influence," in *Handbook of Interpersonal Communication*, 2nd ed., eds. Mark L. Knapp and Gerald R. Miller (Thousand Oaks, CA: Sage, 1994), pp. 542–588; Michael G. Garko, "Perspectives on and Conceptualizations of Compliance and Compliance-Gaining," *Communication Quarterly* 38 (1990): 138–157; Gerald R. Miller, "Persuasion," in *Handbook of Communication Science*, eds. C. R. Berger and S. H. Chaffee (Newbury Park, CA: Sage, 1987), pp. 446–483.

39 Gerald Marwell and David R. Schmitt, "Dimensions of Compliance-Gaining Strategies: A Dimensional Analysis," *Sociometry* 30 (1967): 350–364.

TABLE **6.1**

Marwell and Schmitt's Compliance-Gaining Strategies

1. *Promising* Promising a reward for compliance
2. *Threatening* Indicating that punishment will be applied for noncompliance
3. *Showing expertise about positive outcomes* Showing how good things will happen to those who comply
4. *Showing expertise about negative outcomes* Showing how bad things will happen to those who do not comply
5. *Liking* Displaying friendliness
6. *Pregiving* Giving a reward before asking for compliance
7. *Applying aversive stimulation* Applying punishment until compliance is received
8. *Calling in a debt* Saying the person owes something for past favors
9. *Making moral appeals* Describing compliance as the morally right thing to do
10. *Attributing positive feelings* Telling the other person how good he or she will feel if there is compliance
11. *Attributing negative feelings* Telling the other person how bad he or she will feel if there is noncompliance
12. *Positive altercasting* Associating compliance with people with good qualities
13. *Negative altercasting* Associating noncompliance with people with bad qualities
14. *Seeking altruistic compliance* Seeking compliance simply as a favor
15. *Showing positive esteem* Saying that the person will be liked by others more if he or she complies
16. *Showing negative esteem* Saying that the person will be liked less by others if he or she does not comply

---

what people are actually accomplishing when they try to persuade other people.

In an attempt to create such a set of principles, Marwell and Schmitt asked subjects to apply the sixteen items to various compliance-gaining situations, and from these data the items were analyzed. Five general strategies, or clusters of tactics, emerged. These included *rewarding* (for example, promising), *punishing* (for instance, threatening), *expertise* (as in displaying knowledge of rewards), *impersonal commitments* (examples would include moral appeals), and *personal commitments* (such as debts).

Another, more complicated way to classify compliance-gaining strategies was done by Schenck-Hamlin, Wiseman, and Georgacarakos.

Schenck-Hamlin, Wiseman, and Georgacarakos. Concerned about the lack of a theoretical basis for taxonomies such as Marwell and Schmitt's, William Schenck-Hamlin, Richard Wiseman, and G. N. Georgacarakos developed a scheme based on strategies that subjects indicated they actually used.[40]

Specifically, four elements are isolated in this model. The first is the degree to which the persuader reveals the compliance-gaining goals. In other words, does the communicator make his or her objective known? Some strategies are straightforward and *direct,* others are *indirect,* and still others are *misleading.* You might, for example, ask your roommate directly to turn off the stereo because you have to study. Or you might go about it indirectly by hinting that you need some peace and quiet. Or you might be downright deceptive and tell your roommate that the neighbors had complained about the noise.

The second element of compliance gaining is whether the strategy is based on *sanctions* such as rewards and punishments or on *reasons* and *explanations.* For example, you might tell your roommate that if she does not turn off the stereo, you will be noisy when she wants to study, a threat that constitutes a negative sanction. Other strategies are based on explanation and reasons. For instance, you might tell your roommate how hard it is for you to study when there is a lot of noise.

The third element of compliance gaining is whether the rationale for the required action is stated or implied. A simple request implies a reason but does not state it, whereas an explanation actually provides the rationale. This is the difference between simply saying, "Please turn off the stereo," versus, "Could you turn off the stereo 'cause I have a hard time studying around noise."

The fourth element of compliance gaining has to do with who controls the situation. In the case of a threat or promise, for example, the *persuader* controls the outcome. In the case of a guilt appeal, the control is in the hands of the *other person.* When you suggest that your roommate will feel guilty if she does not turn off the stereo, you are relying on a state of affairs that she herself controls.

Table 6.2 summarizes these elements and their associated compliance-gaining tactics. Table 6.3 gives some examples of each tactic.

Wheeless, Barraclough, and Stewart. One of the most comprehensive analyses of the compliance-gaining literature is that of Lawrence Wheeless, Robert Barraclough, and Robert Stewart, who review and integrate the variety of compliance-gaining schemes.[41] These researchers believe that compliance-gaining messages are best classified according to the kinds of power employed by communicators when attempting to gain the compliance of another individual. Power is access to influential resources. It is a result of interpersonal perception, since people have as much power as others perceive that they have.

The Wheeless group isolated three general types of power. The first is the perceived ability *to manipulate the consequences* of a certain course of action. Parents often use this kind of power when punishing and rewarding their children. If you tell your children that you will buy them new boots if they stay indoors out of the rain, you are using this source of power.

The second kind of power is the perceived ability to determine one's *relational position* with the other person. Here the powerful person can identify certain elements of the relationship that

40   William J. Schenck-Hamlin, Richard L. Wiseman, and G. N. Georgacarakos, "A Model of Properties of Compliance-Gaining Strategies," *Communication Quarterly* 30 (1982): 92–100; Richard L. Wiseman and William Schenck-Hamlin, "A Multidimensional Scaling Validation of an Inductively-Derived Set of Compliance-Gaining Strategies," *Communication Monographs* 48 (1981): 251–270.
41   Lawrence R. Wheeless, Robert Barraclough, and Robert Stewart, "Compliance-Gaining and Power in Persuasion," in *Communication Yearbook 7,* ed. R. N. Bostrom (Beverly Hills, CA: Sage, 1983), pp. 105–145.

TABLE **6.2**

Definitions of the Strategies

I. Sanction Strategies
   A. Reward Appeals
      1. Rewards are controlled by the actor.
         a. *Ingratiation:* Actor's preferred [*sic*] goods, sentiments, or services precede the request for compliance. They range from subtle verbal or nonverbal positive reinforcement to more blatant formulas of "apple polishing" or "brown-nosing." Manipulations in behavior include gift giving, supportive listening, love and affection, or favor-doing. Form: Present reward from actor implies compliance.
         b. *Promise:* Actor's proffered [*sic*] goods, sentiments, or services are promised the target in exchange for compliance. This may include a bribe or trade. A variant is compromise, in which gains and losses are perceived in relative terms, so that both actor and target give in order to receive. Sometimes compromise is called trading-off, log-rolling, or finding a "middle-of-the-road" solution. Form: Compliance implies future reward from actor.
         c. *Debt:* Actor recalls obligations owed him or her as a way of inducing the target to comply. Past debts may be as tangible as favors or loans, or as general as the catch-all "After all I've done for you . . ." Form: Past reward from actor implies compliance.
      2. Rewards are controlled by the target.
         Esteem: Target's compliance will result in automatic increase of self-worth. Actor's appeal promises this increase in areas of target's power, success, status, moral/ethical standing, attention and affection of others, competence, ability to handle failure and uncertainty well, and/or attempts to aspire. "Everyone loves a winner" is the fundamental basis for appeal. "Just think how good you will feel if you would do this." Form: Compliance implies future reward because of target's action.
      3. Rewards are controlled by circumstance.
         Allurement: Target's reward arises from persons or conditions other than the actor. The target's compliance could result in a *circumstance* in which other people become satisfied, pleased, or happy. These positive attitudes will be beneficial to the target. "You'll always have their respect" is an example. Form: Compliance implies future reward because of the action of forces other than the actor or target.
   B. Punishment Appeals
      1. Punishments are controlled by the actor.
         a. *Aversive stimulation:* Actor continuously punishes target, making cessation contingent on compliance. Pouting, sulking, crying, acting angry, whining, "the silent treatment," and ridicule would all be examples of aversive stimulation. Form: Non-compliance implies present punishment.
         b. *Threat:* Actor's proposed actions will have negative consequences for the target if he or she does not comply. Black-mailing or the suggestion of firing, violence, or breaking off a friendship would all be examples of threats. Form: Non-compliance implies future punishment.
      2. Punishments are controlled by the target.
         Guilt: Target's failure to comply will result in automatic decrease of self-worth. Areas of inadequacy might include professional ineptness, social irresponsibility, or ethical/moral transgressions. Form: Non-compliance implies future punishment because of target's action.
      3. Punishments are controlled by circumstance.
         Warning: Target's punishment arises from persons or conditions other than the actor. The target's non-compliance could lead to a *circumstance* in which other people become embarrassed, offended, or hurt. Resulting negative attitudes from those people will have harmful consequences for the target. "You'll make the boss unhappy" and "What will the neighbors say" are examples. Form: Non-compliance implies future punishment because of the action of forces other than the actor or target.

II. Altruism Strategies
   Altruism: Actor requests the target to engage in behavior designed to benefit the actor rather than the target. Asking the target for help is typical. Intensity of the appeal may be manipulated by making the target feel unselfish, generous, self-sacrificing, heroic, or helpful. "It would help me if you would do this," and "Do a favor for me" exemplify the direct approach of the altruistic strategy. Two variants are sympathy ("I am in big trouble, so help me.") and empathy ("You would ask for help if you were me."). Form: Comply for my sake.

(continued on next page)

Definitions of the Strategies *(continued)*

III. Argument Strategies
   A. Response controlled by the Rationale, and Rationale *not* revealed by the actor.
       Direct request: The actor simply asks the target to comply. The motivation or inducement for complying is not provided by the actor, but must be inferred by the target. In some cases the actor's message appears to offer as little influence as possible, so that the target is given the maximum latitude of choice. "I I were you, I would . . ." and "Why don't you think about . . ." are instances of direct request. In other cases the strategy takes on a form where the actor demands the target's compliance. Examples would be "I want you to do this" and "Do this." Form: You (might) comply.
   B. Response controlled by the Rationale, and Rationale revealed by the actor.
       Explanation: One of several reasons are advanced for believing or doing something. A reason may include the following: (1) credibility, "I know from experience." Form: The reason for complying is my trustworthiness, integrity, exemplary action, or expertise; (2) reference to a value system, "It's in the best interests to . . ." Form: Since we value this, you should comply; (3) inference from empirical evidence, "Everything points to the logic of this step." Form: The reason for complying is based on the following evidence.
   C. Response controlled by Rationale; situational context revealed by actor.
       Hinting: Actor represents the situational context in such a way that the target is lead [*sic*] to conclude the desired action or response. Rather than directly requesting the desired response, the actor might say, "It sure is hot in here," rather than directly asking the target to turn down the heat. Form: Given this context, target should infer desired response.

IV. Circumvention Strategies
   Deceit: Actor gains target's compliance by intentionally *misrepresenting* the characteristics or consequences of the desired response. "It's easy," when in fact it is neither simple nor easy. "By doing this, you'll be handsomely rewarded," but the actor does not have the ability to give that reward. Form: Given false rationale or reward, compliance is requested.

Persuasive Messages for the Stereo Situation

1. *Ingratiation:* I would be nice and polite to my roommate, then ask her to turn off the stereo.
2. *Promise:* I would promise to do a favor for my roommate if she will turn off the stereo now.
3. *Debt:* I would recall past favors I've done and say my roommate owes me a few hours of quiet.
4. *Esteem:* I would tell my roommate that it would be very thoughtful of her to turn off the stereo.
5. *Allurement:* I would tell my roommate that our apartment will be a more comfortable place for us to study if the stereo is turned off.
6. *Aversive Stimulation:* I would act irritated toward my roommate until she turns off the stereo.
7. *Threat:* I would tell my roommate to turn off the stereo now or I will not cooperate when she wants to study.
8. *Guilt:* I would tell my roommate that it was inconsiderate of her to play the stereo while I'm trying to study.
9. *Warning:* I would tell my roommate that our neighbors will complain if she does not turn off the stereo.
10. *Altruism:* I would ask my roommate to turn off the stereo for my sake.
11. *Direct Request:* I would simply ask my roommate to turn off the stereo.
12. *Explanation:* I would explain to my roommate that the stereo's volume is too loud to study by.
13. *Hinting:* I would drop subtle hints about how hard it is to study.
14. *Deceit:* I would lie, implying that our neighbors had complained about the loud stereo.

will bring about compliance. For example, if your boyfriend or girlfriend thinks you are not all that committed to the relationship, you may be able to get a lot of cooperation because he or she may be afraid you will want to leave the relationship.

The third type of power involves the perceived ability to *define values* or *obligations* or both. Here one person has the credibility to tell the other what norms of behavior are accepted or necessary. Returning a favor is a good example of this. Behaving kindly is another. Being sensitive to others' needs is still another example. In each case, one communicator defines what is right and good, and the other person complies by behaving in accordance with this standard.

In a compliance-gaining situation, then, one assesses his or her power and chooses tactics that invoke that power. Wheeless lists a number of tactics associated with the three classes of power. For example, the ability to affect another person's expectations and consequences may lead you to use tactics like promises, threats, and warnings. The ability to manipulate the relationship may lead you to choose such tactics as saying you like the other person, attributing positive or negative esteem, making emotional appeals, flattering, and so on. The third category of power—defining values and obligations—may lead you to use moral appeals, debt, guilt, and other similar techniques.

◖ COMMENTARY AND CRITIQUE

Although message production can be understood from a variety of perspectives—including social, interpretive, and critical, all discussed in some detail later in this book—the predominant approach in the United States has been individual and cognitive. Some of these theories focus on the traits of individuals and how they are correlated with various message behaviors, others deal with the effects of the situation on message behavior, and still others concentrate on the actual processes of producing messages.

Although these theories have many differences, they share a common concern for behavior and the generative mechanisms that produce it. These concerns are not new. Indeed, the individualistic and cognitive traditions have dominated the human sciences throughout the twentieth century.

The individualistic approach is common in the study of communication and in the behavioral and social sciences at large. This is understandable within our cultural milieu.[42] Western thought since the eighteenth-century Enlightenment has been dominated by the individual. The autonomous person is the primary unit of analysis in much Western thinking.[43] The psychological view sees persons as entities with characteristics that lead them to behave in independent ways. It sees the single human mind as the locus for processing and understanding information and generating messages. It is hardly surprising, then, that psychological explanations have been so appealing to many communication scholars.

Yet the individualistic approach by no means exhausts the ways communication and other social processes can be understood. Ironically, the defining feature of communication is that it happens between people, so communication cannot be explained solely from the perspective of the individual mind.[44] Even certain researchers in the cognitive tradition are now acknowledging this difficulty. Vincent Waldron and Donald J. Cegala recently wrote:

> Although cognition is typically treated as an individual-level variable in communication

42   John W. Lannamann, "Deconstructing the Person and Changing the Subject of Interpersonal Studies," *Communication Theory* 2 (1992): 139–148; "Interpersonal Communication Research as Ideological Practice," *Communication Theory* 1 (1991): 179–203.

43   See, for example, Robert N. Bellah and others, *Habits of the Heart* (Berkeley: University of California Press, 1985); Alistair MacIntyre, *After Virtue* (Notre Dame, IN: University of Notre Dame Press, 1984); Floyd W. Matson, *The Idea of Man* (New York: Delacorte, 1976). A critique of the assumptions of the individual mind is presented in Rom Harré, "Language Games and Texts of Identity," in *Texts of Identity*, eds. J. Shotter and K. Gergen (London: Sage, 1989), pp. 20–35.

44   John Shotter and Kenneth J. Gergen, "Social Construction: Knowledge, Self, Others, and Continuing the Conversation," in *Communication Yearbook 17*, ed. Stanley Deetz (Thousand Oaks, CA: Sage, 1994), pp. 3–33; Giles and Street, "Communicator Characteristics."

research, a systems perspective suggests extending our views about cognition beyond the individual. For example, conversation, particularly between friends or intimates, both reflects and creates the cognitive interdependence of the partners.[45]

Psychological theorists respond to this criticism in three ways. One is to acknowledge the social nature of communication but to argue that social explanations by themselves are also inadequate. Communication in this view is both social and individual. The individual is involved in the process and must be studied. Focusing on the individual does not negate the value of social theories, but it does provide a vital link in our overall understanding of communication.[46]

The second answer to the criticism is to refute it directly. Although communication involves people acting together in some fashion, everything that happens in this process is filtered through and generated by the separate minds of the individuals involved. Although the outcome of communication may be social in nature, its ultimate genesis is individual, making psychological explanations crucial.[47]

The third answer is to expand cognitive process research to include interdependence. In discussing her research plans, Sally Planalp has written that "the first line of research that I plan to pursue deals with mutual knowledge in interpersonal communication. Mutual knowledge is knowledge that conversation partners share, know they share, and rely on in communicating with one another."[48]

Psychological theories of communication concentrate on traits, states, and processes. Trait theories deal with dispositions of individuals and the correlates of these dispositions. State theories look at the interaction between traits and situations. Process theories attempt to explain the mechanism employed. Although most theories of message production and processing focus on one or more of these types of explanation, few deal strictly with only one. For example, the theory of communication apprehension deals with the state of apprehension in its various forms, only one of which is traitlike.

Trait theories of communication abound.[49] Not only have "communication traits" been developed, but much research has made use of other related traits such as self-monitoring, self-esteem, and dogmatism. Here, we only present a few of the more prominent trait theories, including communication apprehension, communicator style, aggressiveness, and rhetorical sensitivity. In this chapter constructivism is treated as a process theory, although it makes heavy use of the trait of cognitive complexity.

Most of these theories have proved interesting and useful, but like most theories that concentrate on traits, they do not go far enough in explaining the link between traits and actions. Dean Hewes and Sally Planalp make this point in strong terms:

> Predispositions do not explain much. Whenever trait theorists have been pressed to explain why a trait works, they have been forced to look for the mechanisms *behind* that trait, mechanisms outside the realm of predispositions that almost always involve processes of interpretation and production of behavior or adaptation. Trait approaches, when successful, *do* warn us that something about individuals is the locus of causality for social action, but by oversimplifying explanations of individuals' capabilities they do not take us far enough. They tell us *that* individuals are important in the study of human communication but not *how* or *why*.[50]

Trait theories, although they do not ignore the situation, certainly downplay it. If a trait is stable across contexts, then by definition it will usually override situational factors. The entire idea of

---

45   Vincent R. Waldron and Donald J. Cegala, "Assessing Conversational Cognition: Levels of Cognitive Theory and Associated Methodological Requirements," *Human Communication Research* 18 (1992): 606.

46   For an example of this response, see Dean E. Hewes and Sally Planalp, "The Individual's Place in Communication Science," in *Handbook of Communication Science*, eds. C. R. Berger and S. H. Chaffee (Newbury Park, CA: Sage, 1987), pp. 146–183.

47   For an example of this point of view, see Greene, "Action-Assembly Theory."

48   Sally Planalp, "Communication, Cognition, and Emotion," *Communication Monographs* 60 (1993): 3–4.

49   For a discussion and critique of the trait tradition, see Gün R. Semin, "Everyday Assumptions, Language, and Personality," in *Everyday Understanding: Social and Scientific Implications*, eds. Gün R. Semin and Kenneth J. Gergen (London: Sage, 1990), pp. 151–175.

50   Hewes and Planalp, "Individual's Place."

testing for a trait is predicated on this assumption. And yet much research, such as that of Cody and McLaughlin and of Bavelas, shows that people do behave differently in different situations. A natural theoretical tension exists between trait explanations and situational ones. A challenge for both trait and situational theories is to deal with this tension more directly.[51]

One answer to this dilemma is to combine trait and situational explanations, suggesting that a certain amount of variation is caused by situational factors and another portion of variation by traits. This solution is inherently problematic, however, because of the assumption of stability in trait measurement. Trait instruments are designed and tested to capture stability, and correlating such a measure with other measures of situational difference is methodologically and conceptually inconsistent.

Trait theories are designed to identify qualities in persons. This is a semantic process, for the theorist must label the qualities believed to exist. Thus, like all theoretical concepts, traits are constructed by the theorist. Indeed, some sophisticated data analysis will be required to verify the fit of the hypothesized trait to research subjects' actual behaviors and perceptions, but ultimately a name is attached and an abstraction is reified.

This process of construction can lead to problems. One is clarity and distinctiveness of traits. For example, what is the difference between communication apprehension, shyness, reticence, neuroticism, introversion, and avoidance? Are these the same trait or similar ones, or are they conceptually different? Among communication apprehension researchers, little agreement exists on the overall dimensions that bind this cluster of variables.[52] Even more confusion results from the advent of the biological approach to CA, which correlates this trait with very basic brain functions, leading to the conclusions that communication apprehension may be no different from any fear-based reaction.

Confusion can easily result from labeling. For instance, Infante divides aggression into four categories of traits—assertiveness, argumentativeness, hostility, and verbal aggressiveness. Here, the general term *aggression* is used to label both positive and negative traits, but *verbal aggressiveness* labels only a negative trait. How, then, can assertive and argumentative behaviors, which are largely verbal, be positive? This may sound like a word game, but it illustrates the kinds of semantic difficulties that trait labeling can involve.

A second problem created by trait construction is the endless number of traits that can be and are "discovered." Virtually any tendency can be defined as a trait. According to trait theory, a person is not only a bundle of traits but a very large bundle at that. How can we say in any given situation which traits predominate over others, and, indeed, how can any trait predominate over another if traits are stable across contexts?

The key question for evaluating trait theories, then, is not whether the traits actually exist but how useful are they in communication scholarship, teaching, and intervention? What are the limits of the utility of trait definition? We know, for example, that communication apprehension has been a useful concept for communication teachers who must deal with a practical difficulty that many students face in communication classes.

The third problem resulting from the constructed nature of traits is their value orientation. Trait theories often originate in an attempt to identify individuals who have particular positive or negative communication qualities. This is certainly the case with at least three of the theories discussed in this chapter—communication apprehension, rhetorical sensitivity, and aggressiveness. Other trait theories end up making value judgments by virtue of the correlations discovered in research. The results of research on

51   These issues are explored by Peter A. Anderson, "The Trait Debate: A Critical Examination of the Individual Differences Paradigm in the Communication Sciences," in *Progress in Communication Sciences*, eds. B. Dervin and M. J. Voigt (Norwood, NJ: Ablex, 1986).
52   A critique of this line of work can be found in Gerald R. Miller, "Some (Moderately) Apprehensive Thoughts on Avoiding Communication," in *Avoiding Communication: Shyness, Reticence, and Communication Apprehension*, eds. J. A. Daly and J. C. McCroskey (Beverly Hills, CA: Sage, 1984), pp. 237–246.

communicator style and cognitive complexity have been applied, at least implicitly, in this way.

Consequently, trait definitions are often value laden. This feature makes such theories normative, or prescriptive, in orientation. For example, we learn from the theories in this chapter that it is better to be low in communication apprehension than to be high; it is better to be rhetorically adaptive than to be a noble self; it is better to be argumentative and assertive than to be hostile and verbally aggressive; it is better to have more construct differentiation than less; and it is probably better to have a dramatic style than a nondramatic one (at least if you are a teacher).

Normative theories have a place and can serve positive functions in the study of communication. Indeed, some argue that all theories are at least implicitly value laden and ideological, as we will see in Chapter 11. A potential problem occurs when one confuses the researcher's value concept with an objective trait. The way traits are described and measured will often lead the reader to believe that something in the person is being discovered objectively, when in fact the researcher has carefully designed a test to find instances of thoughts, behaviors, and feelings that exemplify the theorist's own positive and negative values.

This state of affairs can create theoretical difficulties. What, for example, do we do with people who display a negative trait? Because traits are defined as stable predispositions, do we merely condemn and avoid these individuals, or do we reform them? If people can change their traits—and most trait theorists would at least entertain the possibility—perhaps the trait is merely a state. Then the important theoretical questions deal with how, when, and under what conditions people behave one way as opposed to another.

The theory of rhetorical sensitivity makes an excellent case in point. This theory arose as a reaction to the humanistic movement of the 1960s and 1970s, which was dominated by what Hart and his colleagues came to call the noble self. Hart and Burks clearly advocate rhetorical sensitivity over other possible responses. The theory treats rhetorical sensitivity as a trait, im-

plying that individuals may exercise little choice over whether they are noble selves, rhetorical reflectors, or rhetorically sensitive individuals, yet the very idea of rhetorical sensitivity implies change and choice. Indeed, the original formulation arose from a desire to help people become more effective communicators. There is a definite change in the tone of reporting used by Hart and his associates between the early articles and the later ones. The original response to humanistic psychology was pejorative in tone, whereas the later research report on the RHETSEN scale was stated in the vocabulary of objective realism.

Is rhetorical sensitivity a trait or is it a desired state? The theory is unclear on this question. If rhetorical sensitivity is a trait, RHETSEN tells us who is good and who is bad at communication according to the authors' ideology of effectiveness. A particular danger of this theory is that it identifies rhetorical sensitivity (a valued trait) and its foils (devalued traits) with certain groups of people of particular religions, geographic locations, cultural identities, and occupational affiliations. Does this mean that certain classes and groups of people are better communicators than others?

An alternative to trait theories are situational ones. Here the emphasis is shifted from the psyche of the communicator to the effects of the situation on his or her behavior. Bavelas and her colleagues are very strong in stating that the situation is everything, at least in equivocal communication. This conclusion is fraught with the same error of simplism possessed by trait theories. Some of Bavelas's subjects did not respond as predicted, even though most did. Any methodologist could tell you that some of this variance could be attributed to personality traits of individual subjects, but Bavelas did not measure that.

It seems that neither a strictly trait nor situational explanation is adequate. Both are necessary, since behavior is usually a product of both traits and situations. People with a particular trait will not always behave consistently with that trait because the situation differs. And not everyone will respond the same way within a situation because they do have individual differences.[53]

Process theories are designed in part to overcome many of the problems encountered by trait and state theories. Three kinds of process theories are encountered in this chapter. One, illustrated by compliance-gaining research, consists of observing behavioral regularities. These theories describe what people do—in this case, what messages they use to gain compliance. Often such theories deduce the implicit strategic choices people are making on the basis of an analysis of message types. The work of Schenck-Hamlin and his colleagues illustrates this move by showing that people choose between direct, indirect, and deceptive options; that they choose between sanctions and arguments; and that they decide whether to use messages that maintain or abdicate control in some way. The Wheeless group makes the same kind of move with power, indicating what power choices people have available to them.

By inferring strategic choice from behavior, both theories are "cognitive" in a weak sense. The problem here is that you can never be sure, based on an external analysis of behavior, what actual cognitive mechanisms are in operation. Just because someone makes a promise, for example, does not mean that the individual has strategically chosen to be direct, to use sanctions, and to maintain control over the consequences of interaction. In fact, some entirely different set of dimensions may have been operating in the person's mind.

Classifying message strategies is especially problematic, as the work on compliance-gaining strategies illustrates. In a severe critique of this work, Kathy Kellermann and Tim Cole point out that the classification schemes used in this research have been entirely inadequate, that they are incomplete, unclear, and even invalid.[54] Daniel O'Keefe is sufficiently concerned about this problem that he calls for the abandonment of the strategy concept altogether.[55] Instead, he believes, we should look at the features of

compliance-gaining discourse, without trying to attribute strategy.

Seibold and his colleagues believe that the difficulty of compliance-gaining research is overreliance on the *strategic choice model*. They suggest instead a *goal limitation model*, in which a communicator's choices are constrained by his or her goals within the situation.[56] Under the former model, communicators were viewed as strategy machines that defined an influence goal and made a decision about how to achieve it. Under the more recent model, communicators do have goals, but they may be multiple and vague. The actual strategic choices people make rely on some combination of programmed habit and situational constraints. People will vary in what they believe to be effective and appropriate and the logics they use in constructing messages. Rather than listing strategies, then, these authors suggest that our time would be better spent understanding the cognitive and situational constraints on message choices.

Another type of process theory goes one step further to correlate message choices with other behaviors and traits. Speech accommodation theory and constructivism are examples. The former looks at the relationship between accommodation and a variety of social functions, and the latter associates cognitive complexity with message production. Unlike theories of the first type, these actually measure some states of mind or perceptions in some way and correlate them with observed messages or communication behaviors. In fact, the associations observed between message choices and other variables can be taken as evidence that the proposed cognitive

53   Various problems related to the simplicity of this theory are discussed by Eric Eisenberg, "Equivocal Communication" [book review], *Communication Theory* 1 (1991): 351–354.

54   Kathy Kellermann and Tim Cole, "Classifying Compliance Gaining Messages: Taxonomic Disorder and Strategic Confusion," *Communication Theory* 4 (1994): 3–60. See also the entire special issue of *Communication Theory* 4, no. 1 (February 1994). See also Charles R. Berger, *Planning Strategic Interaction*, pp. 3–6.

55   Daniel J. O'Keefe, "From Strategy-Based to Feature-Based Analyses of Compliance Gaining Message Classification and Production," *Communication Theory* 4 (1994): 61–69.

56   Seibold, Cantrill, and Meyers, "Communication and Interpersonal Influence."

mechanism is valid. Indeed, constructivism has done this again and again by correlating perspective taking with cognitive complexity.

Constructivism does posit a cognitive structure behind message selection. People make distinctions by applying cognitive constructs to what is perceived. As differentiation becomes increasingly complex, more differences can be seen, and more sophisticated messages can be constructed. In a critique of this representation, Gastil points out that the actual cognitive process by which distinctions are made, goals established, and messages constructed is fuzzy.[57] How is information actually processed in this system? What is the nature of memory, and how are cognitive constructs held and retrieved from memory? Finally, how are strategic choices actually made?

The third kind of process theory attempts to provide just such an explanation by describing the cognitive mechanism that generates actions. Action-assembly theory is an example. This kind of problem is difficult to study. The behaviorists were correct in asserting that cognitive processes cannot be observed directly. Indeed, one reason why so much trait research has been done is that it is relatively easy in comparison to cognitive process research.

All cognitive research involves indirect observation and a great deal of inference. The theorist posits certain cognitive mechanisms and looks for evidence in actual behavior. Action-assembly research, for example, looks for differences in the amount of time it takes to process information in difficult versus simple tasks. Because the action-assembly process takes time, these differences are taken as evidence of the existence of the proposed mechanism. The problem is that such evidence indicates only that the proposed model *could be* operating, not that it *is* operating. Many other cognitive models might lead to the same behavioral differences.[58]

Clearly, process theory is difficult. It is hard enough to substantiate the existence and nature of a single process, but communication is probably driven by multiple simultaneous processes. Many researchers are becoming aware that current process theories are inadequate, as Austin Babrow points out: "Emerging views are sensitizing researchers to issues that have often been glossed over: (a) Communication involves multiple, substantively distinct processes; (b) these processes may be redundant, complementary, or contradictory; and (c) processes may mediate or moderate other processes."[59]

Accommodation is a good example of the difficulty of the single-process view. According to this theory, accommodation may consist of one of just two processes, convergence or divergence. Burgoon and her colleagues point out that this distinction may be too simple and that more care needs to be taken in establishing which of several processes may be occurring, singly or in combination, when convergence or divergence takes place.[60]

The coverage of this chapter is admittedly limited. This chapter is the first in a two-chapter set on theories of message production, reception, and processing. As such, it tells only part of the story of how people process information to generate and understand messages. Although it is necessary to divide this material in some way in order to study it, these chapters should be read in concert with each other. Together, they present a variety of interrelated theories on the role of the individual in communication. To complete the picture, we turn now to theories of message processing and communication outcomes.

---

57   Gastil, "An Appraisal."
58   Confirming cognitive processes by research is difficult. This problem is discussed in some detail by Waldron and Cegala, "Assessing Conversational Cognition."
59   Austin Babrow, "The Advent of Multiple-Process Theories of Communication," *Journal of Communication* 43 (1993): 110.
60   Burgoon, Dillman, and Stern, "Adaptation."

C H A P T E R **7**

THEORIES OF MESSAGE RECEPTION AND PROCESSING

This is the second chapter in a two-part series on theories of message production and processing. In Chapter 6 we dealt with theories explaining how messages are produced. Here we concentrate on how they are received. The main question of the theories in this chapter is how human beings come to understand, organize, and use the information contained in messages. The amount of theorizing on this topic is vast, and we can only touch on it here.[1] This chapter includes some classic treatments of the subject of message processing as well as some recent extensions.

Most of the theories in this chapter are firmly in the cognitive tradition, which was described in Chapter 1. Briefly, cognition is the study of thinking, or information processing. In an excellent recent review, Thomas Ostrom and his colleagues outline three broad dimensions of the cognitive system—codes, structures, and processes.[2]

Cognitive codes are the basic elements of information that are kept in memory and manipulated in various ways when we think. The precise nature of these codes are in dispute; we likely have several types of codes operating at the same time. Some coding possibilities include linguistic propositions, visual images, event memories, action sequences, and emotions.

The second dimension is *cognitive structures*, or ways of organizing codes. It is clear that single things such as words, sentences, or images are not independent units. We organize them in some way. Again, cognitive psychologists disagree about exactly how this is done, but several theories have been proposed. One common explanation, for example, is that codes are grouped into categories that differ from one another. For example, "trees" would probably be in a different category from "fish." Another approach is that the elements of cognition are linked to one another by associative pathways or links in complex networks. For example, you might associate

---

1   For a brief summary of the message tradition in communication studies, see Klaus Krippendorff, "The Past of Communication's Hoped-for Future," *Journal of Communication* 43 (1993): 34–44.

2   Thomas M. Ostrom, John J. Skowronski, and Andrezej Nowak, "The Cognitive Foundation of Attitudes: It's a Wonderful Construct," in *Social Cognition: Impact on Social Psychology*, eds. Patricia G. Devine, David L. Hamilton, and Thomas M. Ostrom (San Diego: Academic, 1994), pp. 196–258.

"trees" with the color "green." A more elaborate version of this theory is the structured network approach, in which associative networks are embedded in larger networks in a hierarchical fashion, something like the hypertext of the World Wide Web.

The third dimension of cognition is *cognitive processes,* or operations. What happens to what and when? Again, various theories have been proposed. One is the spreading-activation approach, which suggests that something in the environment activates or stimulates a node in the cognitive network, and this activation spreads out and excites other nodes that then come into play. An example is action assembly, discussed in Chapter 6, which states that people assemble "instructions" from memory in hierarchical fashion to accomplish a task.

The chapter is divided into three interrelated segments. The first deals with processes of *interpretation,* or understanding, and meaning. The theories summarized here define meaning and show how it develops, how the content of messages and intentions of communicators are understood, and how the causes of behavior are assessed.

The second section deals with *information organization.* These theories tell us how information is integrated into the cognitive system and how it affects attitudes, how we think about information that relates to our attitudes, and how consistency is used as an organizing principle.

The third section of the chapter relates to the process of *making judgments.* These theories deal with how information is compared to what we already know and expect, deviations from expectations, and how the value of information is assessed. As you probably already suspect, this is a rather technical and complicated body of theory. Let's get started.

◖◗ MESSAGE INTERPRETATION

Interpretation is one term for how we understand our experience. Chapter 10 presents a number of theories of interpretation from a textual and

philosophical perspective, but in this chapter we approach the subject psychologically, emphasizing three aspects. The first aspect is the meanings assigned to concepts. The second aspect deals with understanding communicators' intentions. The third has to do with understanding the causes of behavior.

Osgood on Meaning

Charles Osgood, a well-known researcher of the 1960s, developed one of the most influential theories of meaning. In those days, psychology was dominated by behaviorism, but cognitive approaches were just beginning to get popular, and his theory actually has a foot in both traditions. Osgood's theory, then, deals with the ways in which meanings are learned and how they relate to thinking and behavior.[3] This theory was immensely influential and is now considered a classic. Although it is not as popular today, it is still useful and a good place to begin thinking about the topics of this chapter. Let's begin with a simple example and see how Osgood would work with it.

What associations do you have for the word *flight?* Perhaps you see flight as a gentle, floating, pleasant experience, or maybe you see it as rough, dangerous, and frightening. Whatever your associations, these are your *connotations* for the term. Osgood's theory attempts to explain what these connotations consist of and where they come from.

The learning theory used by Osgood begins with the assumption that individuals respond to stimuli in the environment, forming a stimulus–response relationship. He believes that this basic S–R association is responsible for the establishment of meaning, which is an internal, mental response to a stimulus. When you see an airplane, for example, an internal association will appear in your mind, and this association constitutes your meanings for the concepts of airplanes and flight.

---

3   Charles Osgood, "On Understanding and Creating Sentences," *American Psychologist* 18 (1963): 735–751.

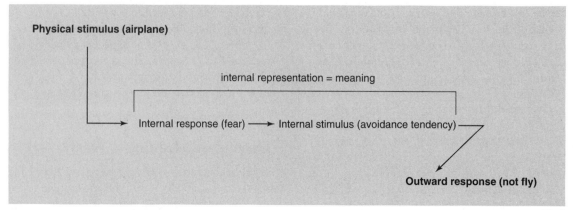

Physical stimulus (airplane)

internal representation = meaning

Internal response (fear) ⟶ Internal stimulus (avoidance tendency)

Outward response (not fly)

FIGURE **7.1**

Meaning as Internal Representation

Your actual association between the stimulus and response is somewhat more complicated than the above example implies. Outwardly, you see a physical stimulus (the plane), and you have a behavioral response (not to board). This response is mediated by internal representations in your mind, which is your meaning lying between the outward stimulus (airplane) and your response (not getting on). The outward stimulus leads to an internal meaning, which leads to an outward response.

The internal meaning itself can be broken down into two parts, an internal response and an internal stimulus. The whole chain, then, consists of the following: (1) physical stimulus → (2) internal response → (3) internal stimulus → (4) outward response. A person who is afraid of flying, for example, has an internal response (fear) to the airplane, and this fear leads to an avoidance tendency, which is an internal stimulus for the outward response of not boarding the plane. Figure 7.1 illustrates this.

In addition to physical objects, we also have meanings for the signs of those objects, such as words and gestures. In other words, when the sign is paired with the meaning, that sign comes to elicit the same or a similar response. This is why the mere mention of flying frightens some people. Even if they are not actually scared at the mention of an airplane, they will tell you that they would prefer not to fly because they know what their actual response would be.

Meaning, because it is internal and unique to the person's own experience with the natural stimulus, is said to be *connotative*. If you are afraid of spiders, a spider elicits an escape response. When the word *spider* is associated with the object as it might have been when you were a small child, a portion of your response (fear) becomes associated with the word itself. This internal meaning mediates your response to the word, even when the actual object is not present.[4]

Most meanings are not learned as a result of direct experience with the natural stimulus but are learned by an association between one sign and another, a process that can occur in the abstract out of physical contact with the original stimulus. Here the meaning of one concept "rubs off" by association with another. To continue our example, imagine that as a child you had already established internal responses to the words *spider, big,* and *hairy*. Let's say you listened to a story about a tarantula, characterized as a "big, hairy spider." Through association you would now have a meaning for the new word *tarantula*, which may also carry some mixture of the con-

4   Charles Osgood, "The Nature of Measurement of Meaning," in *The Semantic Differential Technique*, eds. J. Snider and C. Osgood (Chicago: Aldine, 1969), pp. 9–10.

notations earlier attached to the other words because of its association with these words. If you associated *spider* with *fear,* *big* with *dangerous,* and *hairy* with feeling *creepy,* then you might well react to a real or imagined tarantula by running away. The examples of the fear of flying and the fear of spiders are negative, but all meanings—including positive and neutral ones—are learned the same way.

One of Osgood's major contributions is his work on the measurement of meaning. This method of measuring meaning, the *semantic differential,* assumes that one's meanings can be expressed by the use of adjectives.[5] The method begins by finding a set of adjectives that could be used to express your connotations for any stimulus, including a sign. These adjectives are set against one another as opposites, such as good-bad, high-low, slow-fast. You are given a topic, word, or other sign and are asked to indicate on a 7-point scale how you associate the sign with the adjective pairs. A scale looks like this:

$$\text{good } \_\_:\_\_:\_\_:\_\_:\_\_:\_\_:\_\_ \text{ bad}$$

The subject places a check mark on any space between these adjectives to indicate the degree of good or bad associated with the stimulus. The subject may fill out as many as fifty such scales for each stimulus, each with a different set of bipolar adjectives. For example, you might be presented with a word like *airplane* or *spider* and asked to fill out this set of scales.

Osgood then uses a statistical technique called factor analysis to find your basic dimensions of meaning. His findings in this research have led to the theory of *semantic space.*[6] Your meaning for any sign is said to be located in a metaphorical space of three major dimensions: evaluation, activity, and potency. A given sign, perhaps a word or concept, elicits a reaction in the person, consisting of a sense of *evaluation* (good or bad), *activity* (active or inactive), and *potency* (strong or weak). Your connotative meaning will lie somewhere in this hypothetical space, depending on your responses on the three factors. Figure 7.2 illustrates the semantic space.

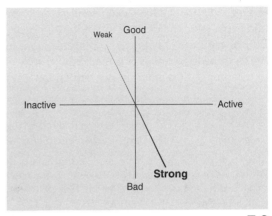

F I G U R E **7.2**

Three-Dimensional Semantic Space

Airplane, for example, might be viewed as good, active, and potent. Or it might be seen as bad, active, and potent. A *spider* might be perceived as bad, passive, and potent, or perhaps good, active, and weak.

Osgood and others have done semantic differential research on a variety of types of concepts, including words, music, art, and even sonar sounds.[7] In addition, they have done research across a wide range of cultures. Osgood believes that the three factors of meaning—evaluation, activity, and potency—apply across all people and all concepts.[8] If these dimensions are universal as Osgood believes they are, he has significantly advanced our understanding of meaning. This claim is controversial, however, and we examine it more carefully in the concluding section of this chapter.

---

5   Osgood, "Nature."
6   Osgood has hypothesized that bipolarity is the basic factor in all language and human thought. See Charles Osgood and Meredith Richards, "From Yang and Yin to *and* or *but,*" *Language* 49 (1973): 380–412.
7   A sampling of studies illustrating the applications can be found in James Snider and Charles Osgood (eds.), *The Semantic Differential Technique* (Chicago: Aldine, 1969). This work also includes an atlas of approximately 550 concepts and their semantic profiles.
8   This point of view is expressed in Charles Osgood, "Semantic Differential Technique in the Comparative Study of Cultures," in *The Semantic Differential Technique,* eds. J. Snider and C. Osgood (Chicago: Aldine, 1969), pp. 303–323; and *Cross Cultural Universals of Affective Meaning* (Urbana: University of Illinois Press, 1975).

Osgood's theory has been useful to describe and explain the meaning of individual concepts. But concepts are only part of communication. In the next theory, we look at a more complex level of meaning—the communicator's intention.

Relevance Theory

Relevance theory by Dan Sperber and Deirdre Wilson attempts to explain how listeners come to understand speakers' intentions.[9] Two approaches have been used to tackle this problem, the coding model and the inferential model.

The *coding model*, as explained in Chapter 4, is most often associated with semiotics, suggesting that words and other symbols convey meaning. Osgood's theory is consistent with this model. The *inference model* suggests that meaning is not simply transferred but must be inferred by communicators from evidence in the message. Sperber and Wilson believe both models are useful because communication occurs in both ways. Sophisticated human communication, however, cannot be explained entirely from a coding perspective, making the inferential approach essential.

In the coding model, meaning is a simple association between a symbol or stimulus and a referent, but in human communication meaning is more complex, for it involves the intentions of the communicators. People produce messages not merely to represent referents but to achieve purposes. In communication, the chief problem for the sender is to get his or her intention across, and the chief problem for the receiver is to understand that intention accurately. The receiver can interpret intentions only by making inferences, and people can understand each other only from the perspective of their own knowledge because one can never be sure what the other person knows.

A simple example illustrates the role of inference in understanding messages. Suppose that a friend tells you the weather is nice today. With

coding you can easily understand the literal meaning of the sentence, but why did the speaker tell you this? Unless your friend is explicit about the intention, you will have to make an inference.

A communicator will always have two levels of intent. The *informative intention* is the desire to have the listener become aware of something, and the *communicative intention* is to have that person realize the purpose of the statement. In the example above, your friend obviously wants you to become aware of the good weather, but she also wants you to know that she intends to inform you of this, or perhaps she even wants you to be aware of another less obvious intent. How, then, do you actually go about figuring out the informative intention?

Context is the key for inferring an intention. Your context is your assumptions. The chief problem here is that different people have different assumptions and therefore operate in different contexts. In other words, people live in different cognitive environments. Your *cognitive environment* consists of all facts (or believed facts) that you rely on.

Human cognition is designed to be efficient. In other words, it is designed to reach certain goals with the least possible effort. New information is considered relevant when it can be combined with what you already know to make an inference. When you combine new information with old information in this way, the new information is said to affect the context by strengthening existing assumptions, leading to the abandonment of former assumptions, or adding new ones. By definition, then, relevant information has greater impact on the cognitive environment than does irrelevant information.

Suppose your friend told you recently that she would like to go on a picnic. When she later tells you that the weather is good, you can put these two statements together and infer that her intention is to get you to invite her on a picnic. The new information about the weather has had a contextual effect and is therefore relevant.

Relevance is obviously a matter of degree. It depends on the size of the contextual effect and

---

9   Dan Sperber and Deirdre Wilson, *Relevance: Communication and Cognition* (Cambridge, MA: Harvard University Press, 1986).

the amount of cognitive effort required to process the information. To be efficient, people try to get the most effect for the least amount of processing effort. When this is successfully done, they have maximized the relevance of the information.

Thus, when you communicate, you try to modify the cognitive environment of the other person and affect his or her assumptions. The changes you make in this person's cognitive environment may be concrete, as in a factual claim, or vague, like a feeling or impression.

Because of the need for efficiency, you cannot use your entire cognitive environment as the context for understanding the message because it would be too demanding. Even if you could remember all of it at once, the effort required would be tremendous and very inefficient. Imagine how hard it would be to interpret a message if you had to use everything you knew to understand it.

Therefore, you select a smaller context in which to understand the other communicator's intentions. You do this first by narrowing down the information in your immediate memory to the things most relevant at this particular time and place. Then you select a context that will maximize the relevance of the information in the message. In other words, you ask yourself, "From what is available to me right now, what do I need to assume to make sense of this message with the least amount of effort?" Now, the speaker will help you with this. Here is how.

Speakers know that they have two primary tasks—to get your attention and to present a message that is potentially relevant. Thus, relevance itself is always a major goal of the communicator. The speaker always presents you with a *guarantee of relevance.* You can assume when people talk to you that they think what they have to say is relevant to your assumptions in some way. This is the *presumption of relevance* on your part. The speaker then gives you evidence or signs of the relevance of the message, and you look for those signs.

Now, as a listener you have only to hypothesize various intentions by testing any possible intention that occurs to you with the relevancy

principle. So you ask, "Can this possible intention be relevant to me based on the chosen context?" If not, it probably is not the intention of the speaker. The first hypothesized intention that works will be assumed to be the correct one. In some cases, you may immediately see that more than one intention could work, and if that happens, you will experience the message as ambiguous.

For example, if in addition to saying that she wanted to go on a picnic, your friend also mentioned that she would like your help with the yard work, you would have two assumptions as part of the context for interpreting her subsequent weather report. You hypothesize almost simultaneously that you could go on a picnic or stay home and work in the yard. Suddenly, your friend's intention is ambiguous. In this case, you would probably resolve the ambiguity by asking her what she wants to do.

Language is especially useful in communicating intent. It is so much more explicit than nonverbal signs and contains its own rules of meaning. Language therefore provides direct evidence of what the communicator is trying to do. The problem with language is that it is often used indirectly, so that what is said is not what is meant. Here the listener must infer an appropriate *implicature,* or implied intent. Recall from Chapter 5 that conversations are peppered with such implied intent and that, to be competent in conversations, you must have the ability to use implicature.

Again, the principle of relevance is used here to determine the actual intent of the speaker. If the direct statement does not seem relevant, you will naturally explore implied intentions that will turn out to be relevant. Actually, unless she just wants you to know that it is a nice day, your friend's statement about the weather probably does involve an implicature of some sort. Surely, you think, she is not just commenting on the weather. What is her real intent? You determine that by figuring out how the weather comment is relevant to you at that moment.

In this section we have dealt with understanding intent. Of course, this is not all that is going on in receiving messages. Another kind of interpretation involves attributing the causes of behavior.

Attribution Theory

Attribution theory deals with the ways people infer the causes of behavior. Unlike scientific psychology, which attempts to ascertain the actual causes of behavior, "naive psychology," as attribution theory is sometimes called, centers on the *perceived* causes of behavior by ordinary people in everyday life. It explains the processes by which you come to understand your own behavior and that of others.

Fritz Heider, founder of attribution theory, outlines several kinds of causal attributions that people commonly make.[10] These include situational causes (being affected by the environment), personal effects (influencing things personally), ability (being able to do something), effort (trying to do something), desire (wanting to do it), sentiment (feeling like it), belonging (going along with something), obligation (feeling you ought to), and permission (being permitted to).

There is not a one-to-one relationship between the observed behavior and the cause. A variety of behaviors may be perceived as stemming from a single cause, or, conversely, one behavior may be thought to arise from several causes. When you are communicating, then, you often need to resolve such ambiguities.

For example, let's say you are the supervisor in a small company. You notice that one of your employees seems particularly industrious all of a sudden. You will probably want to figure out why. You might think that this person is being forced to work hard, which would be an attribution to the environment. Or you might think that he is angling for a raise. Or maybe he is ingratiating himself to you. Or maybe he is bored and needs to keep himself busy.

Naturally, people make use of this context to help them determine the cause of the behavior. So in assessing your employee's hard work, you also can get additional information by observing him at work repeatedly over time. And you can observe when he works hard and when he does not.

Causal perception is mediated variables in your own psychological makeup. One of these is your meanings. You always assign meaning to what you observe, and these are crucial to what you "see." Meanings help you integrate your perceptions and organize your observations into patterns that help you make sense of the world. Because of a need for consistency, you define things in such a way that helps you make sense of them, so that your attributions become integrated and consistent. For example, if you think that you have a great company, you may have a tendency to attribute your employee's hard work to loyalty.

The way you resolve ambiguities and establish a consistent pattern may be different from the way other people do so. Heider calls individual patterns of perception *perceptual styles*. He recognizes that any state of affairs may give rise to a number of interpretations, each of which seems true to the person involved.

One of the most interesting attributions occurs when you perceive that someone did something on purpose. If you think that someone did something on purpose, you are recognizing two underlying attributes, ability and motivation. Suppose, for example, that an associate of yours fails to show up for a meeting. You figure that she could not make it or didn't try. If she wasn't able, something might have been wrong with her (such as illness), or something else might have prevented her appearance (for example, a flat tire). If she did not try, she either didn't want to (an attribution of intent) or was too lazy (an attribution of exertion).

Now you can see what happens in interpersonal perception. In this instance you will infer the causes of your associate's behavior according to your overall experience, your meanings, the situational factors, and your own perceptual style.

Another interesting kind of attribution happens when you think that you "ought" to do something. An obligation is seen as an impersonal, objective demand. It can have a tremen-

---

10   Fritz Heider, *The Psychology of Interpersonal Relations* (New York: Wiley, 1958).

dous sense of validity because most people would agree with it. For example, you might say, "You ought to go to the dentist," or "I ought to report the theft." But "oughts" do not necessarily correspond with values. Perhaps you dread going to the dentist even though you think you should. Because people want to be consistent, they will balance their obligations and values:

> There exists a tendency to be in harmony with the requirements of the objective order. Thus the situation is balanced if one likes to do what one ought to do, if one likes and enjoys the entities one believes are valuable, if happiness and goodness go together, if p [perceiver] admires the person he likes and likes the person with whom he shares values, if what ought to be conforms with what really is, etc.[11]

Heider's theory was highly influential. We will not take the space here to discuss the many other attribution theories, but let's look at an extended example of how attribution works in everyday life. Brant Burleson tape-recorded a conversation between two teaching assistants about a student.[12] In this conversation one teacher, Don, complains to his colleague Bob that one of his students failed an exam three times. Don is very concerned and explores the reasons for the student's failure.

Don and Bob first explore the possibility that the test was too hard, but Don says that the test was not changed and that no one else failed it. They also establish that the student's behavior was consistent over time. Thus, they were able to rule out test difficulty as a cause. They then conclude that the failure must be something about the student herself. Either she did not have the ability or she wasn't trying. She completed all assignments and took the test three times, so she appeared to be trying. By deduction, then, they conclude that she just does not have the ability to pass the test. In the end Don says that he will ask her to drop the class because he doesn't think she can pass the course.

In this example, it looks like Don and Bob are being very logical and systematic in trying to determine the student's problem, but one of the most common research findings is that people are often illogical and biased in their attributions. People are not always objective when making causal inferences about themselves and other people. Rather than weighing all factors, people seem to make quick judgments based on available cues and emotional factors. Research also shows that people's prior judgments are hard to dislodge, no matter how compelling the evidence. Thus, once you make an attribution, you are apt to stick with it.

Yet there is a persistent assumption in attribution theory that people are logical and systematic. How do we reconcile these research findings? Several researchers have adopted the position that people can process information in both logical and nonlogical ways, depending on the circumstances such as motivation. If motivation to promote the self is high, as when we need to save face, there is probably a tendency to be biased in favor of self-serving, situational attributions. If you really want to make a positive impression on your date, you will probably attribute the fact that you are late to something you couldn't control, like having too much to do. On the other hand, when a person is motivated to control the situation, there will probably be a bias toward attributions of personal responsibility. So you might respond to your boss's compliment about a job well done that you worked really hard on it.

One of the most persistent findings in attribution research is the *fundamental attribution error.* This is the tendency to attribute the cause of events to personal qualities. It is a feeling that people are personally responsible for what happens to them. In general, we seem to be insensitive to many circumstantial factors that cause events, overlooking things that may not be the person's fault.

This tendency, however, is reduced when we are evaluating our own responsibility. In other words, we tend to blame other people for what happens to them, but blame the situation for what happens to us. If your roommate fails a test, you are apt to claim that he did not study

---

11 Heider, *Psychology,* p. 233.
12 Brant R. Burleson, "Attribution Schemes and Causal Inference in Natural Conversations," in *Contemporary Issues in Language and Discourse Processes,* eds. D. G. Ellis and W. A. Donohue (Hillsdale, NJ: Erlbaum, 1986), pp. 63–86.

hard enough, but if you fail the test, you will probably say that the test was too hard.

The literature on attribution theory is vast.[13] We do not have the space here to summarize all of this, but let's look at one illustrative study. Alan Sillars conducted a landmark study on the effects of attribution in conflict resolution among college roommates. This research shows how attribution can affect communication in everyday life.[14] Sillars conducted two studies. In the first, he asked college students to write about a conflict they had had with their roommates, and in the second study, he actually videotaped roommates discussing problems such as irritability, boyfriend or girlfriend problems, and disagreements about music. He then looked for three types of conflict strategies, including passive methods such as avoidance or submission; competitive strategies such as requests, demands, and threats; and cooperative strategies such as problem solving. He found that the roommates' attributions very much affected the kinds of strategies they employed in managing their conflicts.

If, for example, the students saw their roommates as cooperative, they were more likely to use a cooperative strategy. Attributing self-blame led to the use of cooperative strategies, whereas attributing blame to the other person led to competitive ones. The attribution of certain negative personality traits to the other person also seemed to prevent the use of cooperation. In addition, Sillars found that, because of the fundamental attribution error, both partners tended to blame the other for the conflict and saw themselves as merely responding to it.

Interpretation is an important aspect of message receiving. Once a message is understood, its information must be organized in some way. Let's turn to this issue next.

◖ INFORMATION ORGANIZATION

In this section we will deal with the ways you organize and manage information and how information affects your cognitive system. Several of the theories in this chapter deal with *attitudes*. Attitude and attitude change have been popular subjects in communication research and theory for fifty years.[15] Originally, attitudes were studied as a kind of "mental" behavior that is learned and shaped largely as other behaviors are. In more recent years, however, attitude theory has taken a distinct cognitive turn. Attitudes are viewed as elements of the cognitive system that you hold in your memory and access when you respond to various situations.[16]

Information-Integration Theory

The information-integration approach centers on the ways people accumulate and organize information about some person, object, situation, or idea and form attitudes. An *attitude* is a predisposition to act in a positive or negative way toward some object. The information-integration approach is one of the most popular models of the nature of attitudes and attitude change.[17]

According to this theory, all information has the potential of affecting your attitudes, but two variables are important in how attitudes are

13   For a recent summary, see Eliot R. Smith, "Social Cognition Contributions to Attribution Theory and Research," in *Social Cognition: Impact on Social Psychology,* eds. Patricia G. Devine, David L. Hamilton, and Thomas M. Ostrom (San Diego, CA: Academic, 1994), pp. 77–108. See also David R. Seibold and Brian H. Spitzberg, "Attribution Theory and Research: Formalization, Review, and Implications for Communication," in *Progress in Communication Sciences,* vol. 3, eds. B. Dervin and M. J. Voigt (Norwood, NJ: Ablex, 1981), pp. 85–125; Alan L. Sillars, "Attribution and Communication," in *Social Cognition and Communication,* eds. M. E. Roloff and C. R. Berger (Beverly Hills, CA: Sage, 1982), pp. 73–106.

14   Alan L. Sillars, "Attributions and Communication in Roommate Conflicts," *Communication Monographs* 47 (1980): 180–200; "The Sequential and Distributional Structure of Conflict Interaction as a Function of Attributions Concerning the Locus of Responsibility and Stability of Conflict," in *Communication Yearbook 4,* ed. D. Nimmo (New Brunswick, NJ: Transaction, 1980), pp. 217–236.

15   For a good discussion of attitude theory and its importance, see Ostrom, Skowronski, and Nowak, "The Cognitive Foundation of Attitudes"; James Price Dillard, "Persuasion Past and Present: Attitudes Aren't What They Used to Be," *Communication Monographs* 60 (1993): 90–97.

16   David R. Roskos-Ewoldsen, "Attitude Accessibility and Persuasion: Review and a Transactive Model," in *Communication Yearbook 20,* ed. Brant Burleson (Thousand Oaks, CA: Sage, 1997), pp. 185–225; Ostrom, Skowronski, and Nowak, "The Cognitive Foundation of Attitudes."

17   Contributors include Norman H. Anderson, "Integration Theory and Attitude Change," *Psychological Review* 78 (1971): 171–206; Martin Fishbein and Icek Ajzen, *Belief, Attitude, Intention, and Behavior* (Reading, MA: Addison-Wesley, 1975); Robert S. Wyer, *Cognitive Organization and Change* (Hillsdale, NJ: Erlbaum, 1974).

changed. The first is valence, or direction. *Valence* refers to whether information supports your beliefs or refutes them. When information supports your beliefs and attitudes, it has "positive" valence. When it does not, it has "negative" valence. If you favor term limits for elected officials, a statement opposing term limits would be negative and one supporting them would be positive.

The second variable that affects the impact of information is the *weight* you assign to the information. Weight is a function of credibility. If you think the information is probably true, you will assign a higher weight to it; if not, you will assign a lower weight.

So valence affects *how* information influences your attitudes, and weight affects *how much* it does so. When the weight of information is low, the information will have little effect, no matter what its valence. Suppose that you have two friends, one who strongly favors legalized euthanasia and another who strongly opposes it. Suppose that a television documentary airs a report that legalized mercy killing has been badly abused in other countries. How will this information affect your friends' attitudes toward the issue?

Let's begin with your first friend, who favors legalization. If he assigns little weight to the news report, this information will not affect his attitude much one way or the other. On the other hand, if he decides that the information is true, he will assign a high weight to it, and it will affect his attitude. The combination of a high weight and a negative valence will change his attitude to be less in favor.

Now let's look at your second friend, who opposes legalized euthanasia. Again, if she assigns low weight to the information, it will have little effect, but if she believes this information and assigns high weight to it, it will make her even more opposed to legalization than she originally was. Why? Because the combination of high weight and positive valence reinforces her opinion.

An attitude is considered to be an accumulation of information about an object, person, situation, or experience. Attitude change occurs because new information adds to the attitude or

because it changes one's judgments about the weight or valence of other information. Any one piece of information usually does not have too much influence on an attitude because the attitude consists of a number of things that could counteract the new information.

You would not expect your friends to completely reverse their attitudes because they have other beliefs that enter the picture. Your friend who favors legalized euthanasia does so for a number of reasons, and he may not be very worried about abuse. Even though the television program persuades him that mercy killing has been abused in certain other countries, he might say that abuse can be prevented by good regulations. Let's now look at extensions on this theory that help explain why attitudes do not change easily.

One of the best-known and respected information-integration theorists is Martin Fishbein.[18] Fishbein highlights the complex nature of attitudes in what is known as *expectancy-value theory*.

According to Fishbein, there are two kinds of belief. The first is *belief in* a thing. When you believe in something, you would say that this thing exists. Your second kind of belief, *belief about*, is your sense of the probability that a particular relationship exists between two things. For example, you might *believe in* the existence of pain and suffering late in life. You may also have a *belief about* pain and suffering, that people want to die so that they can avoid it.

Attitudes differ from beliefs because they are evaluative. Attitudes are correlated with beliefs and lead you to behave a certain way toward the attitude object. So the two beliefs mentioned above would probably lead you to vote in favor of a ballot proposition that would legalize euthanasia.

Fishbein sees attitudes as organized together, as general attitudes are predicted from specific ones in a summative fashion. So a general positive attitude toward euthanasia would consist of

---

18   Fishbein has published several articles on this topic. See the Bibliography. For an excellent secondary source, see David T. Burhans, "The Attitude-Behavior Discrepancy Problem: Revisited," *Quarterly Journal of Speech* 57 (1971): 418–428. For more recent treatments, see Fishbein and Ajzen, *Belief;* Daniel J. O'Keefe, *Persuasion: Theory and Research* (Newbury Park, CA: Sage, 1990), pp. 45–60.

TABLE **7.1**

A Simplified Example of an Attitude Hierarchy According to Fishbein Model

Attitude object (*o*) → jogging		*N* = 6 (number of beliefs in system)
Associated concepts (x_i)	Probability of association (B_i)	Evaluation (a_i)
x_1 Cardiovascular health	B_1 Jogging promotes cardiovascular vigor.	a_1 Cardiovascular vigor is good.
x_2 Disease	B_2 Jogging reduces the chance of disease.	a_2 Disease is bad.
x_3 Obesity	B_3 Jogging reduces weight.	a_3 Being overweight is bad.
x_4 Mental health	B_4 Jogging promotes peace of mind.	a_4 Letting off mental tensions is good.
x_5 Friendship	B_5 Jogging introduces a person to new friends.	a_5 Friendship is important.
x_6 Physique	B_6 Jogging builds better bodies.	a_6 A beautiful body is appealing.

other attitudes—about life, death, individual rights, and pain and suffering. The relationship between beliefs and attitudes is represented algebraically as follows:[19]

$$A_o = \sum_i^N B_i a_i$$

where

A_o = attitude toward object o

B_i = strength of belief *i* about *o*; that is, the probability or improbability that *o* is associated with some other concept *x*

a_i = evaluative aspect of *B*; that is, the evaluation of *x*

N = number of beliefs about *o*

(Read the formula as follows: An attitude toward an object equals the sum of each belief about that object times its evaluation.)

The distinctive feature of Fishbein's formula is that it stresses the fact that attitudes are a function of a complex combination of beliefs and evaluations. The example in Table 7.1 helps

clarify this model. This table describes a hypothetical attitude toward jogging. Here, jogging is associated with beliefs about six concepts—cardiovascular health, disease, obesity, mental health, friendship, and physique. Each of these concepts is associated with a belief, and each belief has either positive or negative valence. In this example, when you add up all the beliefs times the evaluations, you end up with a very positive attitude about jogging.

According to this theory, attitude change can occur from three sources. First, information can alter the believability, or weight, of particular beliefs. The two friends mentioned above might learn, for example, that the report on the abuse of euthanasia is erroneous. Second, information can change the valence of a belief. For instance, your friends might learn that these "abuses" were technical and legal and not self-serving in any way, making the information seem positive rather than negative. Finally, information can add new beliefs to the attitude structure. So, for example, your friends might learn that euthanasia was actually requested in the vast majority of cases.

This theory suggests some of the ways information affects the cognitive system, but how do the resultant attitudes affect behavior? This is a more complicated issue. In the *theory of reasoned action*, Icek Ajzen and Martin Fishbein argue that

---

19   Martin Fishbein (ed.), "A Behavior Theory Approach to the Relations Between Beliefs About an Object and the Attitude Toward the Object," in *Readings in Attitude Theory and Measurement* (New York: Wiley, 1967), p. 394.

behavior results in part from intentions, a complex outcome of attitudes.[20]

Specifically, your intention to behave in a certain way is determined by your attitude toward the behavior and a set of beliefs about how other people would like you to behave. Consider your progress in college as an example. Do you plan to continue until you get your degree or drop out for a while? The answer to this question depends on your attitude toward school and what you think other people want you to do. Each factor—your attitude and others' opinions—is weighted according to its importance. Sometimes your attitude is most important, sometimes others' opinions are most important, and sometimes they are more or less equal in weight. The formula is as follows:

$$BI = A_B w_1 + (SN)w_2$$

where

BI = behavioral intention
A_B = attitude toward the behavior
SN = subjective norm (what others think)
w_1 = weight of attitude
w_2 = weight of subjective norm

(Read the formula as follows: Your intention to do something equals your attitude toward the behavior times the strength of that attitude plus what others think times the strength of their opinion.)

Now let us return to the example of your intention regarding college. If you have developed a poor attitude toward school and your friends are encouraging you to drop out for a semester to work, that is probably what you will do. On the other hand, if your friends are encouraging you to stick it out and their opinions are very important to you, you will probably stay despite your negative attitude. If your friends' opinions don't matter that much, your attitude will win out, and your intention will be to get a job.

The preceding formula predicts your behavioral *intention,* but it does not necessarily predict the *actual behavior.* This is because you do not always behave in accordance with your intentions. We know that people are notorious for going against their own best intentions. Sometimes, for example, people cannot do what they want because they are not able to. Smokers may want to stop smoking but cannot because they are addicted. You might want to drop out of school, but your parents' threat to cut off your support might prevent you from doing so.

One of the most powerful factors in how you organize information is consistency. Let us turn now to some theories that address the principle of consistency.

Consistency Theories

Undoubtedly, one of the largest bodies of work related to attitude, attitude change, and persuasion is consistency theory. All consistency theories begin with the same premise: People are more comfortable with consistency than inconsistency. Consistency, then, is a primary organizing principle in cognitive processing, and attitude change can result from information that disrupts this balance.

Although the vocabulary and concepts of these theories differ, the basic assumption of consistency is present in all of them. In system language (Chapter 3), people seek homeostasis; persons are open systems that aim to achieve self-maintenance and balance.

In the remainder of this section, two theories of cognitive consistency are summarized. These were chosen because of their prominence in the field and their relatively complete explanations. The first is Leon Festinger's theory of cognitive dissonance, and the second is Milton Rokeach's theory of attitudes, beliefs, and values.

The Theory of Cognitive Dissonance. Leon Festinger's theory of cognitive dissonance is one of the most important theories in the history of social psychology. Over the years it has produced

20   Fishbein and Ajzen, *Belief;* Icek Ajzen and Martin Fishbein, *Understanding Attitudes and Predicting Social Behavior* (Englewood Cliffs, NJ: Prentice-Hall, 1980). See also James B. Stiff, *Persuasive Communication* (New York: Guilford, 1994), pp. 51–57.

a prodigious quantity of research and volumes of criticism, interpretation, and extrapolation.[21]

Festinger teaches that any two cognitive elements, including attitudes, perceptions, knowledge, and behaviors, will have one of three kinds of relationships. The first of these is null, or *irrelevant*; the second is consistent, or *consonant*; and the third is inconsistent, or *dissonant*. Dissonance occurs when one element would not be expected to follow from the other. If you think that smoking is harmful to your health, you would probably not smoke. What is consonant or dissonant for one person, however, may not be for another, so we must always ask what is consistent or inconsistent within a person's own psychological system.

Two overriding premises govern dissonance theory. The first is that dissonance produces tension or stress that creates pressure to change. Second, when dissonance is present, the individual will not only attempt to reduce it but will also avoid situations in which additional dissonance might be produced. The greater the dissonance, the greater the need to reduce it. For example, the more inconsistent your smoking is with your knowledge of its negative effects, the greater the pressure you will feel.

Dissonance itself is a result of two other variables—the importance of the cognitive elements and the number of elements involved in the dissonant relation. In other words, if you have several things that are inconsistent and if they are important to you, you will experience greater dissonance. If health is not important to you, knowledge that smoking is bad for your health is probably not going to affect your actual smoking behavior.

How do you deal with your cognitive dissonance? Festinger imagined a number of methods. First, you might change one or more of the cognitive elements, a behavior or an attitude perhaps. For example, as a smoker, you might stop smoking, or you might stop believing that it is harmful to health. Second, new elements might be added to one side of the tension or the other. For instance, you might switch to chewing tobacco. Third, you might come to see the elements

as less important than they used to be. For example, you might decide that health isn't as important as state of mind. Fourth, you might seek consonant information such as evidence for the benefits of smoking by reading tobacco company studies. Fifth, you might reduce dissonance by distorting or misinterpreting the information involved. This could happen if you decided that although smoking is a health risk, it is not as harmful as the weight you would gain if you stopped smoking. No matter which of these methods you employed, it would reduce your dissonance and make you feel better about your attitudes, beliefs, and actions.

Much of the theory and research on cognitive dissonance has centered around the various situations in which dissonance is likely to result. These include such situations as decision making, forced compliance, initiation, social support, and effort.

Decision making has received a great deal of research attention. Salespeople label the dissonance that occurs after buying something "buyer's remorse." In 1970 an interesting study was published about automobile buying.[22] Often, while waiting for delivery of a car, a customer will cancel the purchase because of *postdecisional dissonance*, or buyer's remorse. In this study, a group of automobile customers were called twice during the period between signing the contract and actual delivery to reassure them about their purchase. Members of a control group were not called. As expected, significantly more of those who were not called canceled the order (about twice as many).

The amount of dissonance one experiences as a result of a decision depends on four variables, the first of which is the importance of the decision. Certain decisions, such as that to skip breakfast, may be unimportant and produce

---

21   Leon Festinger, *A Theory of Cognitive Dissonance* (Stanford, CA: Stanford University Press, 1957). Many short reviews of dissonance theory are available. See, for example, Stiff, *Persuasive Communication,* pp. 68–75; O'Keefe, *Persuasion.*
22   J. H. Donnelly and J. M. Ivancevich, "Post-purchase Reinforcement and Back-Out Behavior," *Journal of Marketing Research* 7 (1970): 399–400.

little dissonance, but buying a car can result in a great deal of dissonance.

The second variable is the attractiveness of the chosen alternative. Other things being equal, the less attractive the chosen alternative, the greater the dissonance. You will probably suffer more dissonance from buying an ugly car than a pretty one.

Third, the greater the perceived attractiveness of the unchosen alternative, the more the felt dissonance. If you wish you had saved your money to go to Europe instead of buying a car, you will suffer dissonance.

Finally, the greater the degree of similarity or overlap between the alternatives, the less the dissonance. If you are debating between two similar cars, making a decision in favor of one will not result in much dissonance, but if you are deciding between buying a car and going to Europe, you might have quite a bit.

Another situation in which dissonance is apt to result is forced compliance, or being induced to do or say something contrary to your beliefs or values. This situation usually occurs when a reward is involved for complying or a punishment for not complying. Dissonance theory predicts that the less the pressure to conform, the greater the dissonance. If you were asked to do something you didn't like doing but you were paid quite a bit for doing it, you would not feel as much dissonance as if you were paid very little.

For example, after completing a boring task, subjects in a well-known experiment were "bribed" to tell other subjects that the task would be fun.[23] Some of these participants were paid $1 to lie, and the others were paid $20. As expected, because they experienced more dissonance, the $1 liars tended to change their opinion of the task to actually believe it was fun, whereas the $20 liars tended to maintain their belief that the task was dull.

The less external justification (such as reward or punishment), the more you must focus on the internal inconsistency within yourself. This is why, according to the dissonance theorist, "soft" social pressures can be so powerful: They can cause a great deal of dissonance. It also explains why you might stay in a high-paying job you dislike. The high pay can be used as a justification for doing so.

Dissonance theory also makes several other predictions. The theory predicts, for example, that the more difficult one's initiation into a group, the greater commitment one will develop. The more social support one receives from friends on an idea or action, the greater the pressure to believe in that idea or action. The greater the amount of effort one puts into a task, the more one will rationalize the value of that task. Have you ever put a lot of work into an assignment you hadn't looked forward to, only to discover after completing it that you liked it after all?

Rokeach: Attitudes, Beliefs, and Values. One of the most comprehensive theories on attitude and change is that of Milton Rokeach. He has developed an extensive explanation of human behavior based on beliefs, attitudes, and values.[24] His theory builds on earlier work and provides some interesting and valuable extensions.

Rokeach believes that each person has a highly organized system of beliefs, attitudes, and values, which guides behavior. *Beliefs* are the hundreds of thousands of statements that we make about self and the world. Beliefs can be general or specific, and they are arranged within the system in terms of their centrality or importance to the ego. At the center of the belief system are those well-established, relatively unchangeable beliefs that form the core of the belief system. At the periphery of the system lie numerous insignificant beliefs that can change easily. Believing that your parents have a good marriage is probably pretty central, since it impacts a lot of other things you assume to be true. Believing that you need a haircut, on the other hand, is peripheral.

23   Leon Festinger and James M. Carlsmith, "Cognitive Consequences of Forced Compliance," *Journal of Abnormal and Social Psychology* 58 (1959): 203–210.

24   Milton Rokeach, *Beliefs, Attitudes, and Values: A Theory of Organization and Change* (San Francisco: Jossey-Bass, 1969); *The Nature of Human Values* (New York: Free Press, 1973).

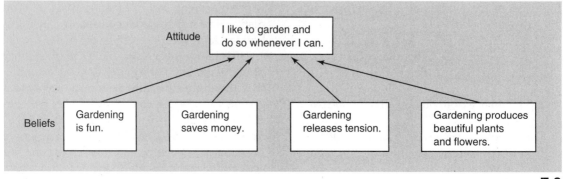

Attitude — I like to garden and do so whenever I can.

Beliefs — Gardening is fun. | Gardening saves money. | Gardening releases tension. | Gardening produces beautiful plants and flowers.

FIGURE **7.3**

A Simple Example of the Belief Structure of an Attitude

The more central a belief, the more resistant it is to change and the more impact such change will have on the overall system. In other words, if one of your central beliefs changes, expect rather profound changes in how you think about many things. This is why children are so shaken when parents they assumed to have a great marriage separate.

Attitudes are groups of beliefs that are organized around a focal object and predispose a person to behave in a particular way toward that object. You have hundreds of thousands of beliefs and probably thousands of attitudes, each consisting of a number of beliefs about the attitude object. Figure 7.3 illustrates, in overly simple form, the organization of an attitude.

Rokeach believes attitudes are of two important kinds that must always be viewed together. These are *attitude toward object* and *attitude toward situation*. One's behavior in a particular situation is a function of these two in combination. If you do not behave in a given situation consistently with your attitudes toward certain things, it is probably because your attitude toward the situation prevents it. An example of this kind of inconsistency is eating foods you do not like when they are served to you as a guest. The point here is that behavior is a complex function of a variety of sets of attitudes, and the system consists of many beliefs ranging in their centrality.

Rokeach believes that of the three concepts in explaining human behavior, values are the most

important. *Values* are specific types of beliefs that are central in the system and act as life guides. Values are of two kinds. *Instrumental values*—such as hard work and loyalty—are guidelines for living on which we base our daily behavior. *Terminal values* are the ultimate aims of life toward which we work; examples include wealth and happiness.

Another component in the belief-attitude-value system that assumes great overall importance is your *self-concept,* your beliefs about yourself. It is your answer to the question, Who am I? Self-concept is particularly important to the system because self-regard is a primary motivation supported by all other elements of the cognitive system.[25] Thus, while beliefs, attitudes, and values comprise the components of your system, self-concept provides its guiding goal or purpose.

Rokeach is basically a consistency theorist. He includes a number of significant hypotheses about attitudes, beliefs, and values, but he concludes that people are guided by a need for consistency and that inconsistency creates a pressure to change. Rokeach has broadened his explana-

---

25   Richard E. Petty and John T. Cacioppo, *Communication and Persuasion: Central and Peripheral Routes to Attitude Change* (New York: Springer-Verlag, 1986). For brief summaries, see Stiff, *Persuasive Communication*, pp. 179–191; and O'Keefe, *Persuasion*, pp. 95–116. For an additional explanation and refutation of critiques, see Richard E. Petty and others, "Conceptual and Methodological Issues in the Elaboration Likelihood Model of Persuasion: A Reply to the Michigan State Critics," *Communication Theory* 3 (1993): 336–362.

tion of consistency far beyond the other theories of this tradition. Taking the total system into consideration, he sees consistency as extremely complex. Rokeach calls his work a comprehensive theory of change.

Rokeach believes that the most important inconsistencies in a person's psychological system are those involving cognitions about the self. Only when inconsistencies involve the self-conception will there be significant, lasting change. The reason for this is that such contradictions increase self-dissatisfaction. Because maintenance of self-regard is the overall aim of the psychological system, it is natural that this should be so.

Thus far we have discussed the interpretation and organization of information. One of the outcomes of information processing is judgment. The theories in the following section address this point.

◉ JUDGMENT PROCESSES

The theories in this section deal with the ways individuals make judgments in communication—judgments of arguments, nonverbal behavior, belief claims, and attitudes.

Elaboration Likelihood Theory

Social psychologists Richard Petty and John Cacioppo developed elaboration likelihood theory as a general summation of insights from many other attitude-change theories. It has become one of the most popular persuasion theories today.

According to this theory, you evaluate information in various ways. Sometimes you evaluate messages in an elaborate way, using critical thinking, and sometimes you do so in a simpler, less critical manner. Sometimes you are thoughtful about arguments, and other times you are not. *Elaboration likelihood* is the probability of critical evaluation of arguments, and it can range from little to great. The likelihood of elaboration

depends on the way a person processes the message. There are two: the central and peripheral routes. Elaboration, or critical thinking, occurs in the *central route* and nonelaboration, or the lack of critical thinking, in the *peripheral* one. Thus, when you process information through the central route, you actively think about and weigh it against what you already know. When you process information through the peripheral route, you are much less critical.

When you use the central route, you consider arguments carefully, and if your attitude changes, it is apt to be relatively enduring and will probably affect how you actually behave. On the other hand, if you use the peripheral route, any resulting change is probably temporary and may have less effect on how you act. Keep in mind, however, that because elaboration likelihood is a variable, you will probably use both routes somewhat, depending on the degree of personal relevance.

Your critical thinking depends on two general factors—motivation and ability. When you are highly motivated, you are likely to use central processing, and when motivation is low, peripheral processing is more likely. For example, if you are a typical college student, you would pay more attention to the campus newspaper's arguments for and against fee increases than you would to its arguments for and against installing new roofing on the student center.

Motivation consists of at least three things. The first is involvement, or the personal relevance of the topic. The more important the topic, the more likely that you will think critically about the issues involved. The second factor in motivation is diversity of argument. You will tend to think more about arguments that come from a variety of sources. The reason for this is that when you hear several people talking about an issue, you cannot make snap judgments very easily. Other things being equal, then, where multiple sources and multiple arguments are involved, receivers tend to process the information centrally.

The third factor in motivation is one's personal tendency to enjoy critical thinking. People who enjoy mulling over arguments will probably use more central processing than those who do not.

No matter how motivated you are, however, you cannot use central processing unless you have the ability to do so. Most students would be more critical of a speech on fashion trends than one on quarks and electrons.

Figure 7.4 illustrates the central and peripheral processing.[26] According to this figure, if you are not motivated and do not have the ability to process the message, you will be monitoring peripheral cues. If you are motivated and can process the message, you will compare the information in the message with what you already know. If that knowledge is insufficient to make these kinds of judgments, you'll go the peripheral route.

When processing information in the central route, you will carefully consider the arguments. What might persuade you under these conditions? Certainly the degree to which the message matches your previous attitude would have an effect here. Messages that are more favorable to your view would probably be evaluated more positively than those that are not. On the other hand, the strength of the argument certainly plays a role because in central processing you are thinking critically. You identify good and bad arguments, and you tend to be influenced more by good ones.

In peripheral processing, you do not look closely at the strength of the argument. Indeed, you make judgments quickly about whether to believe what you hear or read on the basis of simple cues. For example, when source credibility is high, the message may be believed. Also, you tend to believe people you like. The number of arguments can also be a cue in that you may rely on the sheer number of arguments to determine whether to accept a message. In most peripheral processing, many types of cues are used.

The following experiment is an example of how central and peripheral processing work. In the experiment, 145 students were asked to evaluate audiotaped arguments in favor of instituting comprehensive examinations for seniors at their college.[27] Two versions were used, one with strong arguments and the other with weak ones. Half of the students were told that the examination could go into effect the following year, but the other half were led to believe that the change would not occur for ten years. Obviously, the first group would find the message more personally relevant than the second group and would therefore be more motivated to scrutinize the arguments carefully. It was expected that these students would be less susceptible to peripheral cues.

To test this hypothesis, the researchers told half of the high-relevance group and half of the low-relevance group that the tape was based on a report from a high school class, and the other half of these groups was told that it was based on a report of the Carnegie Commission. Thus, the first group was presented with a low-source credibility cue, whereas the other group was presented with a high-credibility cue.

As expected, the students who heard the highly relevant message were motivated to pay careful attention to the quality of the arguments and were more influenced by the arguments than were the students who heard the less relevant message. Those students who heard the less relevant message were more influenced by credibility as a peripheral cue than were the other students. Petty, Cacioppo, and their colleagues have done a number of similar studies with the same results.

The lesson from this theory might seem to be that you should always be critical in evaluating messages, but, practically speaking, you cannot always attend carefully to every message. Some combination of central and peripheral processing is always to be expected. Most of the time, you are influenced by both. Even when motivation and ability are low, you might still be influenced somewhat by strong arguments, and even when you are processing in the central route, other less critical factors can also affect your attitudes.

26 Petty and Cacioppo, *Communication*, p. 4.
27 Richard E. Petty, John T. Cacioppo, and R. Goldman, "Personal Involvement as a Determinant of Argument-Based Persuasion," *Journal of Personality and Social Psychology* 41 (1981): 847–855.

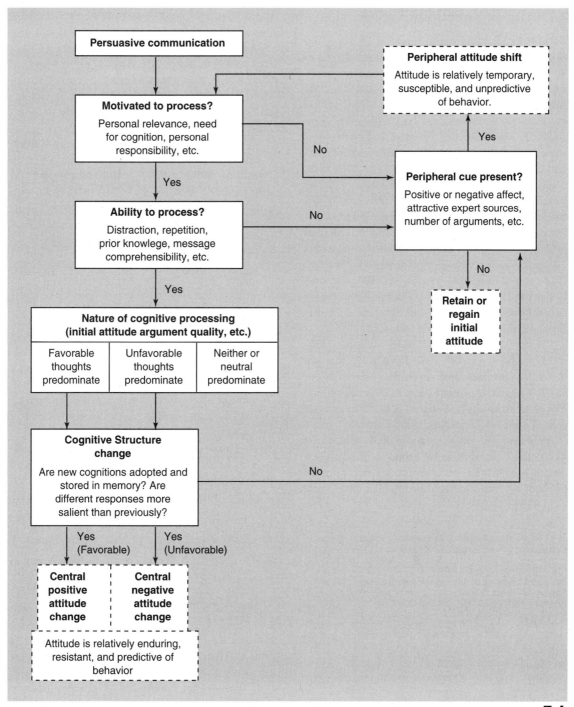

FIGURE **7.4**

Schematic Depiction of the Two Routes to Persuasion

From *Communication and Persuasion: Central and Peripheral Routes to Attitude Change* by Richard E. Petty and John T. Cacioppo. © 1986 by Springer-Verlag. Reprinted by permission of the publisher.

Expectancy Violations Theory

People usually behave according to accepted norms, but this is not always the case. How do you respond when people violate your expectations? This interesting question has been the subject of various theories.[28] Here, we look at one particularly promising approach developed on the basis of a number of research studies by communication researcher Judee Burgoon and her colleagues.[29]

According to this theory, we have expectations about the behavior of another person based on social norms as well as our previous experience with the other person and the situation in which the behavior occurs. These expectations can involve virtually any nonverbal behavior, including, for example, eye contact, distance, and body angle. (Actually, we probably have expectations for verbal behavior as well, but this theory does not address this subject.)

The common assumption is that when expectancies are met, the other person's behaviors are judged as positive, and when they are violated, the behaviors are judged as negative; however, Burgoon has found that this is not always the case. Violations are often judged favorably.

Whether judged as good or bad, violations cause the perceiver to be aroused. If someone stands too close to you or too far away, if another person's eye contact is abnormal, or if an individual violates some other set of expectations, you will feel differently. This arousal is not necessarily negative. In fact, in some cases it might feel pleasant, especially when the other person seems to like you. Sometimes, however, violations can make you feel uncomfortable. Apparently, we learn to have expectations and to detect violations early in life, even in infancy.

What seems to happen is that your attention is drawn to behavior that would otherwise go unnoticed. When your expectations are met, you don't notice the behavior, but when they are violated, you become distracted by it. This distraction may be what causes you to get aroused. And this leads you to evaluate the other person's behavior.

Imagine, for example, that you have just been introduced to an attractive person. In getting to know each other, you talk about everything from the weather to family. Suddenly you become aware that this person is standing unusually close to you. You try to back off, but the other person continues to move in. Your first tendency will be to interpret this behavior, then evaluate it. You might interpret the behavior as a "come on." If you like this person, this will be good, but if you don't, it will be bad.

An important variable in the evaluation process is *reward valence*, or the degree to which you find the interaction rewarding. A conversation might be rewarding, for example, because it will lead to a positive outcome. On the other hand, valence might be negative because it entails more costs than benefits. One of the reasons sexual harassment can be such a problem is that it is a negative behavior in what may be an otherwise rewarding setting, such as a job situation.

Figure 7.5 illustrates the violation–evaluation process. The figure shows that expectations arise from one's perception of the communicator's characteristics, the state of the relationship, and the context in which the behavior occurs.

Violations accentuate the judgments made in this process. Here the reward valence of the other communicator is especially strong: Violations cause arousal, which in turn accentuate evaluation of communication with the other person and

28   See, for example, Joseph N. Cappella, "The Management of Conversational Interaction in Adults and Infants," in *Handbook of Interpersonal Communication,* eds. Mark L. Knapp and Gerald R. Miller (Thousand Oaks, CA: Sage, 1994), pp. 406–407; Peter A. Andersen, "Nonverbal Immediacy in Interpersonal Communication," in *Multichannel Integrations of Nonverbal Behavior,* eds. A. W. Siegman and S. Feldstein (Hillsdale, NJ: Erlbaum, 1985), pp. 1–36; Joseph N. Cappella and John O. Greene, "A Discrepancy-Arousal Explanation of Mutual Influence in Expressive Behavior for Adult-Adult and Infant-Adult Interaction," *Communication Monographs* 49 (1982): 89–114; M. L. Patterson, *Nonverbal Behavior: A Functional Perspective* (New York: Springer-Verlag, 1983).
29   Judee K. Burgoon and Jerold L. Hale, "Nonverbal Expectancy Violations: Model Elaboration and Application," *Communication Monographs* 55 (1988): 58–79. For brief summaries see also Beth A. LePoire, "Two Contrasting Explanations of Involvement Violations: Expectancy Violations Theory Versus Discrepancy Arousal Theory," *Human Communication Research* 20 (1994): 560–591; Judee K. Burgoon, "Nonverbal Signals," in *Handbook of Interpersonal Communication,* eds. Mark L. Knapp and Gerald R. Miller (Thousand Oaks, CA: Sage, 1994), pp. 253–255.

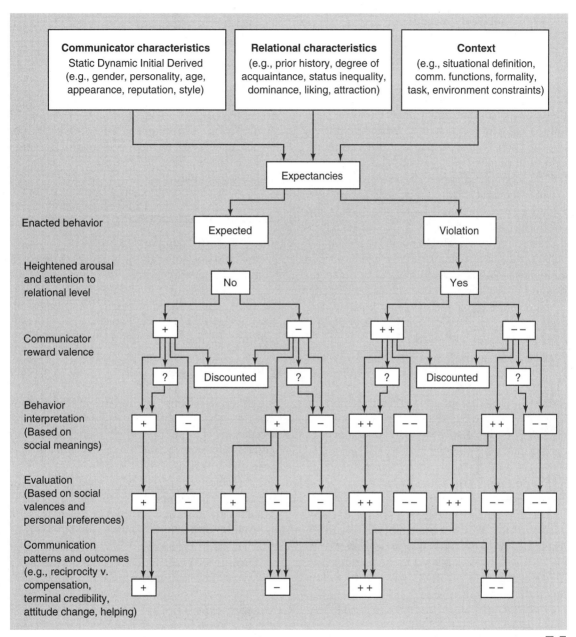

FIGURE **7.5**

Nonverbal Expectancy Violation Model

NOTE: For simplicity, communicator reward valence, behavior interpretation, and behavior evaluation valence have been dichotomized into positive and negative but should be understood to represent continua. Double pluses and minuses denote greater magnitude of effect.

From Judee K. Burgoon and Jerold L. Hale, "Nonverbal Expectancy Violations: Model Elaboration and Application," *Communication Monographs* 55 (1988): 64. Reprinted by permission of Speech Communication Association and the authors.

the meaning of the message. If the exchange is valued and the behavior has a positive meaning, a positive outcome will result.

Figure 7.5 includes other possibilities as well. The meaning of the behavior may be ambiguous, and one is not sure what to make of it. This theory predicts that ambiguous behavior by a valued communicator will be taken as positive, but such behavior by an unrewarding communicator will be taken as negative. Again, this effect will be accentuated in cases of a violation.

An interesting study of eye gaze shows how violations can affect judgments of behavior and communication outcomes.[30] The researchers trained four confederates to manipulate their eye behavior to effect seemingly natural violations in an interview. About 150 students in an organizational communication course volunteered to participate in the study as part of an interviewing assignment. They took the role of an employment interviewer, and each interviewed one of the confederates. In preparation for half of the interviews, the subjects were given a high-status résumé, and the other half were given a low-status one. The first group was set up to find the interview rewarding, whereas the other would obviously find it less so. Some interviewers got a confederate who gave them normal eye contact, some got a person who gave them no eye contact, and some got a confederate who gave above-normal eye contact.

The experiment aimed to test the effects of eye-gaze violations in high- and low-reward interactions. After the interview, each subject completed a set of scales related to the credibility of the applicant, how likely they would be to hire this individual, how attracted they were to this person, and other aspects of the relationship that developed between them in the interview.

The results of this experiment showed that the failure to have eye contact with the interviewer definitely hurt the applicants' images whether they were high or low status. A higher-than-normal level of eye gaze was also found to be a violation, but it was interpreted somewhat differently between the two conditions. High-status applicants with nearly constant eye contact were judged more favorably than were low-status applicants with constant eye contact.

One of the most interesting judgments we make about the behavior of others is their honesty. Over the past twenty years or so, there has been a great deal of research on deception and deception detection. As a natural extension of their work on expectancy violation, David Buller and Judee Burgoon have pulled much of this work together in a newly developing theory of interpersonal deception.

Interpersonal Deception Theory

Buller and Burgoon see deception and its detection as part of an ongoing interaction between communicators involving a back-and-forth process.[31] The deceiver may experience a certain amount of apprehension about being detected, and the receiver may experience a certain amount of suspicion about being deceived. These "internal" thoughts can often be seen in "outward" behavior. This being so, receivers look for signs of lying, and liars look for signs of suspicion. Over time, in this back-and-forth process, the sender may come to perceive that the deception was successful or not, and the receiver may come to see that the suspicion was warranted or not.

Deception apprehension and suspicion can come out in strategically controlled behaviors, but they are more apt to show up in nonstrategic behaviors, which the communicators do not control. This is a process called *leakage*. You might be suspicious that you are being lied to because of behaviors that the other person is not aware of, and if you are trying to deceive another person, you may experience apprehension based on the fact that the receiver could detect it through some behavior you are not controlling. For example, you might have perfect control of your voice and face, but your feet and hands give you away.

---

30   Judee K. Burgoon, "Communicative Effects of Gaze Behavior: A Test of Two Contrasting Explanations," *Human Communication Research* 12 (1986): 495–524.
31   David B. Buller and Judee K. Burgoon, "Interpersonal Deception Theory," *Communication Theory* 6 (1996): 203–242.

As we learned above, communicators' expectations are significant anchors with which to judge behavior. So expectations play a definite role in deception situations. When receivers' expectations are violated, their suspicions may be aroused. Likewise, when senders' expectations are violated, their deception apprehension may also be aroused.

Many factors affect this ongoing process—for example, the degree to which the communicators can actually interact fully. This variable is called *interactivity*. Talking face to face is more interactive than talking on the telephone, which in turn is more interactive than communicating by e-mail or letter. Interactivity can increase immediacy, or the degree of psychological closeness between the communicators. When we have high immediacy, we pay close attention to a variety of live cues. We may stand closer, look more attentively at what is going on, and generally avail ourselves of a richer set of actions. You might predict that the more "access" communicators have to one another's behavior, the more cognitive "data" they have to assess one another's intentions or suspicions, and sometimes this may be true. Yet research seems to indicate that the opposite can also happen. Immediacy and relational closeness can cause you to feel more engaged with others and less suspicious.

Also when we are relationally close, we have a degree of familiarity between us. When we are quite familiar with one another, we have certain biases or expectations about what we are going to see. A *truth bias* makes us less inclined to see deception. In a positive relationship, communicators more or less assume that they are telling one another the truth. Under these conditions, we will not be very suspicious about lying and may not pay close attention to behavioral deception cues. On the other hand, a *lie bias* may accentuate our suspicions and lead us to think people are lying when they may not be.

Our ability to deceive or detect deception is also affected by *conversational demand,* or the amount of "stuff" we have to do when we are communicating. If several things are going on at once or if the communication is complex and involves numerous goals, we cannot pay as close attention to everything as we would if the situational demands were light.

Familiarity also increases the amount of information we have about one another—both our histories and ways of behaving. So in some situations, familiarity may make it harder to lie and easier to detect lying.

Two other factors that affect the deception-detection process are the level of motivation to lie or to detect lying and the skill in deception and deception detection. Where motivation is high, our desire to deceive may override our apprehension about being caught. At the same time, if the receiver knows that our motivation is high, his or her suspicions will be increased. Some people are more skilled at deceiving than others because they have a larger range of behaviors they can perform. This could be counteracted, however, by the other person's ability to detect deception.

Remember, however, that communicators engage in both strategic and nonstrategic behaviors. When we lie, we typically exert a great deal of control over how we manage information, behavior, and image (all strategic behavior); but at the same time, we also display more nonstrategic cues that could be detected by others, depending on their motivation and skill. In highly interactive situations—those in which we are fully engaged with one another—we often dampen our use of nonstrategic behaviors, which in some situations could make it harder to detect the deception.

The purpose of deception also seems to enter the formula. Senders deceiving for personal gain may have a harder time hiding it than senders who deceive for more altruistic purposes. Of course, the results of deceptive behavior depend in part on how motivated the receiver is to detect it. If the receiver is suspicious and the lying matters, he or she will probably put quite a bit of effort into detecting the lie.

Deception and its detection involve a constant process of making judgments about the behaviors of others. One of the most powerful theories of how such judgment occurs is social judgment theory, to which we now turn.

Social Judgment Theory

Social judgment theory, the work of psychologist Muzafer Sherif and his associates, deals with the way people make judgments about messages.[32] This theory is based on early psychophysical research, in which persons were tested on their ability to judge physical stimuli such as the weight of an object or the brightness of a light. Using this work as an analogy, Sherif investigated the ways individuals judge messages, and he learned that many principles of psychophysics hold for social judgment as well.

Research shows that people make judgments on the basis of anchors, or reference points. Suppose that you were asked to judge the relative weight of five objects. On what would you base your judgment? If the experimenter handed you a weight and told you it was 10 pounds, you would first feel the reference weight and then judge the weight of the other objects based on the feeling of the first one. The known weight would act as an "anchor," influencing your perception of the others.

To demonstrate this idea of anchors, try a simple experiment. Take three bowls. Fill the first with hot water, the second with cold water, the third with tepid water. Put one hand in the hot water and the other in the cold water. After a few moments, place both hands in the third bowl. Your perceptions of the temperature of this water will be different for each hand because each hand had a different anchor, or reference.

Sherif reasons that similar processes operate in judging communication messages. In social perception anchors are internal and based on past experience. The internal anchor, or reference point, is always present and influences the way a person responds to messages. The more impor-

tant the issue is to one's ego, the stronger the anchor will influence what is understood.

In a social judgment experiment, you would be given a large number of statements about some issue. You then would be asked to sort them into groups according to their similarity. You could use as many groups as you wished. Then you would put the piles in order from positive to negative. Next you would indicate which piles of statements are acceptable to you personally, which are not acceptable, and which are neutral. (This is called a Q-sort.)

The first group forms your *latitude of acceptance,* the statements you can agree with; the second your *latitude of rejection,* those you cannot agree with; and the third your *latitude of noncommitment.* This research procedure is just a systematic way of simulating what happens in everyday life. On any issue, there will usually be a range of statements, pro or con, that you are willing to tolerate, and there will also be a range that you reject totally.

A person's latitudes of acceptance and rejection are influenced by a key variable—ego involvement. *Ego involvement* is the degree of personal relevance of an issue. It is the degree to which one's attitude toward something affects the self-concept, or the importance assigned to the issue.

For example, you may have read much about the depletion of the ozone layer and have come to believe that this is a serious problem. If you have not yet experienced any personal difficulties because of this problem, it may be unimportant to you, because your ego involvement is low. On the other hand, if you have already been treated for skin cancer, the issue would be considerably more ego involving.

Ego involvement makes a great deal of difference in how you respond to messages related to a topic. Although you probably have a more extreme opinion on those topics with which you are ego-involved, this is not always the case. You could have a quite moderate opinion and still be ego-involved.

What does social judgment say about communication? First, we know from Sherif's work that

32   The first major work in this area was Muzafer Sherif and Carl I. Hovland, *Social Judgment* (New Haven, CT: Yale University Press, 1961). See also Muzafer Sherif, Carolyn Sherif, and Roger Nebergall, *Attitude and Attitude Change: The Social Judgment-Involvement Approach* (Philadelphia: Saunders, 1965). For a brief overview of the theory, see Muzafer Sherif, *Social Interaction—Process and Products* (Chicago: Aldine, 1967), chaps. 16–18. Several secondary sources are also available; see, for example, Stiff, *Persuasive Communication,* pp. 138–142; Leonard Martin and Abraham Tesser (eds.), *The Construction of Social Judgments* (Hillsdale, NJ: Erlbaum, 1992); O'Keefe, *Persuasion,* pp. 29–44.

individuals judge the favorability of a message based on their own internal anchors and ego involvement. However, this judgment process can involve distortion. On a given issue, such as the ozone hole, a person may distort the message by contrast or assimilation. The *contrast effect* occurs when individuals judge a message to be farther from their own point of view than it actually is, and the *assimilation effect* occurs when persons judge the message to be closer to their own point of view than it actually is.

Basically, when a message is relatively close to one's own position, that message will be assimilated, whereas more distant messages will be contrasted. These assimilation and contrast effects are heightened by ego involvement. So, for example, if you believe strongly that industry should be regulated to stop chlorofluorocarbon (CFC) emissions, a moderately favorable statement might seem like a strong positive statement because of the assimilation effect, whereas a slightly unfavorable statement might be perceived to be strongly opposed to regulation because of the contrast effect. If you were highly ego-involved in the issue, this effect would be even greater.

The second area in which social judgment theory aids our understanding of communication is attitude change. Social judgment theory makes the following predictions:

First, messages falling within the latitude of acceptance facilitate attitude change. An argument in favor of a position within the range of acceptance will be somewhat more persuasive than an argument outside of this range. If you think that no CFC emissions should be allowed, you might be persuaded by a message advocating that some CFC emissions be permitted, provided this position is within your latitude of acceptance.

Second, if you judge a message to lie within the latitude of rejection, attitude change will be reduced or nonexistent. In fact, a *boomerang effect* may occur in which the discrepant message actually increases your position on the issue. Thus your positive attitude toward CFC regulation would probably not be changed by a message ad-

vocating no regulation, assuming it was in your latitude of rejection. In fact, such a message might even make you more firmly favor regulation.

Third, within the latitude of acceptance and noncommitment, the more discrepant the message from your own stand, the greater the expected attitude change. However, once the message hits the latitude of rejection, change will not be expected. A statement farther from your own attitude will probably bring about more change than one that is not very far from your position.

Finally, the greater your ego involvement in the issue, the larger the latitude of rejection, the smaller the latitude of noncommitment, and thus the less the expected attitude change. Highly ego-involved persons are hard to persuade. They tend to reject a wider range of statements than people who are not highly ego-involved, and rejected messages are not effective. So if you were highly ego-involved in the ozone-depletion problem, you would have a large latitude of rejection and would be persuaded by very few statements divergent from your own.

To illustrate how social judgment works, consider an interesting experiment done by a group of researchers shortly after Oklahoma passed a prohibition law in the 1950s.[33] The researchers recruited a number of people who were deeply involved in the issue on one side or the other and several who were moderate and not very involved in the issue. They found that those who were highly ego-involved and extreme in their opinions had much wider latitudes of rejection than did moderates, and the moderate subjects had much wider latitudes of noncommitment than did those who held extreme opinions. Interestingly, when presented with the same moderate message, the extreme "drys" judged it to be much more toward the nonprohibition side than did other subjects, and the "wets" judged it to be much more toward the prohibition side than the other subjects. In other words, both extreme groups had a contrast effect. Generally, the

---

33   Carl I. Hovland, O. J. Harvey, and Muzafer Sherif, "Assimilation and Contrast Effects in Reactions to Communication and Attitude Change," *Journal of Abnormal and Social Psychology* 55 (1957): 244–252.

attitude change experienced by the moderates after hearing a message on the issue was about twice as much as the attitude change experienced by those who were highly involved in the issue.

▌◖ COMMENTARY AND CRITIQUE

The theories discussed in this chapter explain how people process information. For the most part, these are receiver-oriented theories, which is not to suggest that they are divorced from message production. Indeed, message production and reception are two sides of the same coin and cannot be separated in actual practice, as interpersonal deception theory illustrates.

Still, these theories show us that communication depends on how messages are understood and judged. All these theories tell us in one form or another what message receivers do and how they do it. As a group, the theories address three interrelated accomplishments—interpreting, organizing, and judging.

The first of these accomplishments is interpretation. We assign meaning to concepts, we try to figure out intentions, and we attribute causes. The second accomplishment is organization, in which new information is integrated into a system of existing beliefs and attitudes. Finally, people constantly make judgments on the basis of information. We sometimes evaluate arguments carefully, and sometimes we attend to less central aspects of the message or source. As part of the judgment process, we evaluate nonverbal behaviors, argument claims, and attitude statements.

Although the theories in this chapter are organized around these three elements of information processing, each tells us something about all three accomplishments outlined above. Indeed, interpretation, organization, and judgment are basically different aspects of the same process.

The theories in this chapter share a number of ideas about how people process information.

Four general processes are suggested by the theories in this chapter. The first is *assigning meaning*. Osgood's theory of meaning shows us how individual concepts are interpreted on the basis of evaluation, potency, and activity. Relevance theory states that relevance is the key to interpreting intentions, and attribution theory addresses the causal nature of meaning. Even the nonverbal expectancy violations model shows that interpretation is a vital part of how nonverbal behaviors are judged.

Another mechanism that permits information processing is *reasoning*, or inference making. Reasoning enters into interpretation, organization, and judgment in a variety of ways. Several theories in this chapter address this concern. For example, relevance theory shows how communicators use messages to infer intentions, and attribution theory also reveals the reasoning process that people use to assess causes.

Several of the theories in this chapter also address the process of *comparing ideas*. This is the central idea of social judgment theory, and a number of other theories also provide insights into this process. Consistency theory and information-integration theory are examples. Consistency theories show us how new information is compared with the other elements of cognition and how inconsistency is handled. Information-integration theory shows us that various pieces of information are weighed in terms of their overall effects within the cognitive system.

Finally, several of these theories deal with processes of *change*. Information-integration theory shows how change occurs as a result of newly integrated information. Consistency theory shows how imbalance leads to change. Social judgment theory shows how change results from the perception of attitude statements. Elaboration likelihood theory shows the relative effects of central and peripheral processing on attitude change.

Virtually all theories in the chapter follow the rational person model to some extent. As a group these theories share the idea that people think through problems and situations rationally and objectively. There are exceptions, of course. For example, some adherents to attribution theory have made the point that people are often inaccurate and irrational in their judgments. Social judgment theory indicates that people often distort information, and elaboration likelihood theory says that people weigh evidence and evaluate arguments only part of the time. Virtually all theorists in this chapter, however, admit to the possibility of rational decision making, and few would deny that people try to be rational and objective.

The rational person model makes a clear assumption about the nature of human thought. Humans are conceived as independent, rational, choice-making beings. This view is deeply embedded in Western philosophy and is part of many Western cultural views. Many other cultures, however, would find this description of people strange. Like all theory, then, these approaches are definitely products of a particular worldview.[34]

This is a worldview that explains human experience in terms of individual cognition. It is a view that assumes a universal cognitive mechanism behind most action. The point of the experiments, measurements, hypotheses, and theories of message processing is to discover these underlying mechanisms. Many theories in this chapter exemplify this type of thinking directly; others are more specific in explaining certain types of behaviors.

Most of these theories posit certain principles, operations, or mechanisms that drive human thought and action. Other theories such as expectancy violation and attribution address particular types of thought and action. By extrapolation, all the latter theories also tell us indirectly something about general mechanisms as well.

Given their overall aim, then, the chief strengths of all these theories are their parsimony and intuitive appeal. Most explain a great deal with only a few key variables. Osgood narrows all of connotative meaning down to three dimensions. Sperber and Wilson show how relevance lies at the heart of interpretation. Fishbein and Ajzen show how a vast array of thought and behavior can be explained by a simple integrative mechanism. Festinger and even Rokeach reduce cognitive organization to a single principle of consistency. And so it goes. These theories are appealing because they truly help us understand rather esoteric processes normally baffling to the average person. One of the reasons cognitive explanations are so popular is the common "aha" response they produce.

Cognitive consistency theories are a good example of this strength. These theories have had a major impact on our thinking about attitude and attitude change. A mainstay of social psychology for many years, cognitive consistency is appealing because of its parsimony and heuristic value. For a twenty-year period, it stimulated a great deal of research. The popularity of consistency theory is understandable, given the goal of this field to discover a few important variables that would predict social behavior. Consistency theories do just that. They isolate certain elements of cognition and show how manipulations among these variables can predict a person's feelings, thoughts, or actions. They also appeal to the scientist's sense of logic, providing an explanation for behavior that makes intuitive sense. At one time consistency theories were so well accepted that debates centered not on whether people respond to dissonance but on ways to improve the precision of predictions based on these theories.

At the same time, however, there are serious hazards in this kind of theorizing. Two concerns are relevant here. First, there is the nagging question of universality: Are cognitive processes really universal, and if not, how wide a scope do these processes cover? Osgood's three "universal" dimensions of meaning offer a good example of the problem. Although many cognitive researchers admit the usefulness of semantic differential technique for measuring connotative meaning, they question the view that the factors of meaning—evaluation, potency, and activity—are invariant and universal across situations,

34   John W. Lannamann, "Deconstructing the Person and Changing the Subject of Interpersonal Studies," *Communication Theory* 2 (1992): 139–148; "Interpersonal Communication: Research as Ideological Practice," *Communication Theory* 1 (1991): 179–203.

concepts, and cultures. Although these factors have shown up in an amazingly diverse set of studies, they do not always appear; to suggest that they are universal is an overgeneralization. What appears as universal may in fact not be so.

Another problem in trying to discover cognitive universals is the mistaken idea that if one's hypothesized mechanism fits the data, it alone can explain the data, when any number of hypothesized mechanisms may explain what is going on. How, then, do we choose from among competing explanations? This is a difficult problem. The theory of cognitive dissonance, as an example, has been criticized for precisely this problem.[35]

The second concern related to the reduction of complex processes to a parsimonious set of predictors is oversimplification. The elaboration likelihood model (ELM), for example, has been criticized for leaving out important variables. Its predictions have not always been verified by research, and some believe that a more elaborate theory is necessary to explain the discrepancy.[36] Some researchers have reached a similar conclusion about expectancy-value theory.[37]

Of course, virtually all the theories in this chapter could be criticized for oversimplification. Most, for example, suggest that information is integrated or organized in a relatively consistent, rational fashion when we all know from our own experience that information processing is often problematic.

This point is the theme of Austin Babrow's emerging theory of *problematic integration*, which deals with the ways communication creates inconsistent, contradictory cognitions.[38] In opposition to consistency theory, which says that information is used to reduce inconsistency, Babrow shows how it often increases it. Ironically, we also use communication to cope with these sorts of problems, and the more we do so, the more difficult integration can become. Communication can make what we want inconsistent with what we expect, it can cause ambiguity, it can bring about ambivalence, and it can even make what we want or expect impossible. And reducing or eliminating these discrepancies is rarely easy and often impossible.

Cognitive processes do not present themselves in self-defined form. Despite the scientific leanings of many researchers, cognitive processes do not lie in wait of discovery, but must be defined by the theorist. Inquiry into information processing involves inferring underlying processes from observed behavior and naming the variables believed to be operating. As we have seen in the history of the social sciences, there is no end to the number of constructs that can be created and named. Theoretical definitions are abstract and partial, which always leaves room for additional constructing, naming, and defining. This state of affairs leads to the natural question of whether real structures of mind can ever be "discovered."[39]

In this chapter we have encountered a wide variety of constructs, which have been given a host of interesting names: dissonance, elaboration, attitude, expectancy, relevance, attribution, ego involvement, and more. The mere fact that these concepts vie for our attention as competing explanations of thought and action demonstrates the challenge of explaining cognition and action.

---

35   Natalia P. Chapanis and Alphonse Chapanis, "Cognitive Dissonance: Five Years Later," *Psychological Bulletin* 61 (1964): 21.

36   For a set of detailed critiques of elaboration likelihood theory, see Mark A. Hamilton, John E. Hunter, and Franklin J. Boster, "The Elaboration Likelihood Model as a Theory of Attitude Formation: A Mathematical Analysis," *Communication Theory* 8 (1993): 50–64; Paul Mongeau and James B. Stiff, "Specifying Causal Relationships in the Elaboration Likelihood Model," *Communication Theory* 8 (1993): 65–72; Mike Allen and Rodney Reynolds, "The Elaboration Likelihood Model and the Sleeper Effect: An Assessment of Attitude Change over Time," *Communication Theory* 8 (1993): 73–82.

37   Michael Burgoon, Deborah A. Newton, and Thomas S. Birk, "A Theory of Belief, Attitude, Intention, and Behavior Extended to the Domain of Corrective Advertising," in *Communication Yearbook 15*, ed. Stanley A. Deetz (Newbury Park, CA: Sage, 1992), pp. 263–286.

38   Austin Babrow, "Communication and Problematic Integration: Understanding Diverging Probability and Value, Ambiguity, Ambivalence, and Impossibility," *Communication Theory* 2 (1992): 95–130.

39   This point is explored in some detail by Kenneth J. Gergen and Gün R. Semin, "Everyday Understanding in Science and Daily Life," in *Everyday Understanding: Social and Scientific Implications*, eds. Gün R. Semin and Kenneth J. Gergen (London: Sage, 1990), pp. 1–18.

There are a variety of responses to this state of affairs. One is competition: Which theory will win? This response is problematic because of the impossibility of falsifying all but one explanation. Another response is integration: How can the theories be combined? This response is appealing because it recognizes the utility of all theories, but it is a pretext, resulting in a loss of parsimony and failure to discover cognitive universals. A third response is flexibility: How can each theory be used appropriately for certain purposes without denying the utility of the others? This approach has the benefit of enabling us to see more than could be viewed from the confines of a single theory, but it can only be done after abandoning the attempt to find a parsimonious, central mechanism of thought and action.

The creation and definition of constructs can lead to a self-fulfilling prophecy on the part of the theorist. In other words, once a set of constructs is found to fit, even if only partially, there is a strong tendency to see the same things no matter where you look. Osgood always "saw" evaluation, potency, and activity in his factor-analysis results.

Social judgment theory is a good example of how researcher biases affect the interpretation of results. In many of their experiments, researchers compared individuals who were highly ego-involved with people less involved and concluded that the differences were due to their level of involvement. Actually, these groups of people could have been different for other reasons as well, which would invalidate the interpretation offered by social judgment theory.[40]

Like the interpretation of any research results, social judgment theorists had to make certain assumptions in their interpretations. The theory assumes, for example, that there is a sequential, causal mechanism whereby judgment as a cognitive activity precedes attitude change, and social judgment research was unable to prove this assumption.

Looked at objectively, the results of many experiments on cognitive processes are less clear than the author believes them to be. For instance, most of the negative criticism of information-integration theory relates to the validity of measurement. Although the idea that attitudes consist of accumulated and weighted beliefs is generally accepted, much doubt exists that one can measure the overall accumulated weight and value of a belief system with any degree of validity. In the natural setting, a researcher would first have to isolate beliefs contributing to an attitude, measure them accurately, and factor out the influence of other elements of the system. Because this process is difficult or impossible to do, most research in this tradition is artificial, hypothetical, and controlled. This problem thus casts doubt on the external validity of the claims. A related problem is that disagreement exists about the way one accumulates information to form an attitude. The research evidence is equivocal on this point and casts doubt on the validity of the approach.[41] Research on ELM has also been criticized for lack of validity.[42]

The basic standard for any predictive theory is that it should be stated in such a way that contradictory evidence could prove the theory wrong in its predictions. In other words, the theory must be falsifiable. A chief complaint about dissonance theory, for example, is that it can be used to explain various, contradictory results and cannot be proved wrong, which creates a situation wherein the dissonance theorist wins no matter how an experiment comes out. If attitude change results from the manipulations, one can argue that the change was caused by dissonance; if attitude change does not occur, one can say that dissonance did not exist.

Furthermore, dissonance is such a general concept that it can take any number of forms.

---

40   This point is made by O'Keefe, *Persuasion*. For a thorough critique of social judgment theory, see Martin and Tesser, *Construction*.
41   For a review of the issues in this dispute, see Mary John Smith, *Persuasion and Human Action: A Review and Critique of Social Influence Theories* (Belmont, CA: Wadsworth, 1982), pp. 245–248; and O'Keefe, *Persuasion*, pp. 55–59.
42   Hamilton, Hunter, and Boster, "The Elaboration Likelihood Model."

Thus, the experimenter can claim that a particular result was caused by one kind of dissonance but that an entirely different result was produced by another kind of dissonance. This circular reasoning results because dissonance researchers do not measure dissonance per se but infer dissonance from behavior. Indeed, there is some question about whether dissonance is directly observable at all. This is the case with virtually all cognitive processes.

All these objections to theories of message processing are "easy punches." They belie the intelligence and hard work that has gone into the development of these theories. In Chapter 2, we noted that no theory has a direct line to truth. Theories are based on guess, inference, and creativity, and that is the best we can do. Whether or not you believe in universal processes of mind, the theories presented in this chapter and others like them provide insights that are intriguing and useful in our attempt to understand communication.

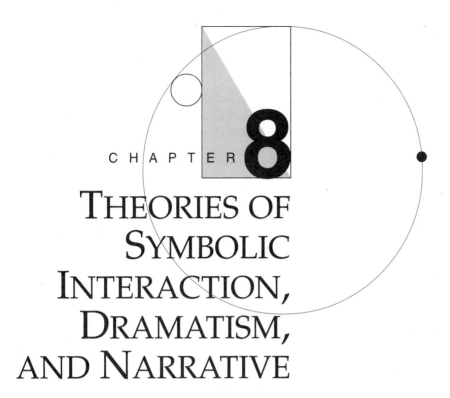

8

THEORIES OF SYMBOLIC INTERACTION, DRAMATISM, AND NARRATIVE

The theories discussed in Chapters 8 and 9 take quite a turn from the cognitive theories discussed in the previous two chapters. For the scholars in the interactional tradition, communication and meaning are unabashedly social, and cognitive explanations are seen as secondary at best.[1] For these theorists, meaning is created and sustained by interaction in the social group. Interaction establishes, maintains, and changes certain conventions—roles, norms, rules, and meanings—within a social group or culture, and these conventions in turn define the reality of the culture itself.

We discuss this group of theories in two chapters. This chapter covers the foundational literature in symbolic interactionism and closely related ideas on dramatism and narrative. Chapter 9 examines theories of the social construction of reality, rules, and culture. There is also an affinity between this genre and some of the interpretive theories addressed in Chapter 10.

◖ SYMBOLIC INTERACTIONISM

Symbolic interactionism is characterized by certain ideas about communication and society. Barbara Ballis Bal summarizes these:[2]

1. People make decisions and act in accordance with their subjective understandings of the situations in which they find themselves.

---

1 For an overview of social approaches, see Wendy Leeds-Hurwitz (ed.), *Social Approaches to Communication* (New York: Guilford, 1995). See also the forum on social approaches in *Communication Theory*, vol. 2 (May 1992): 131–177; and vol. 2 (November 1992): 329–356.
2 Barbara Ballis Lal, "Symbolic Interaction Theories," *American Behavioral Scientist* 38 (1995): 421–441. See also Joel M. Charon, *Symbolic Interactionism: An Introduction, an Interpretation, an Integration* (Englewood Cliffs, NJ: Prentice-Hall, 1992); Larry T. Reynolds, Interactionism: Exposition and Critique (Dix Hills, NY: General Hall, 1990); Jerome G. Manis and Bernard N. Meltzer (eds.), *Symbolic Interaction* (Boston: Allyn & Bacon, 1978). For continuing coverage of SI, see the ongoing editions of the journal *Studies in Symbolic Interaction*.

2. Social life consists of interaction processes rather than structures and is therefore constantly changing.
3. People understand their experience through the meanings found in the symbols of their primary groups, and language is an essential part of social life.
4. The world is made up of social objects that are named and have socially determined meanings.
5. People's actions are based on their interpretations, in which the relevant objects and actions in the situation are taken into account and defined.
6. One's self is a significant object and like all social objects is defined through social interaction with others.

According to symbolic interactionism, then, you are always attempting to achieve goals by interacting with other people. Your experience is shaped by the meanings that are created by using symbols when communicating in groups.

Early interactionism was divided into two schools.[3] The Chicago School, led primarily by Herbert Blumer, continued the work of George Herbert Mead. Blumer believed above all that the study of humans could not be conducted in the same manner as the study of things. Researchers should try to empathize with the subject, enter his or her experience, and attempt to understand the value of each person. Blumer and his followers avoided quantitative and scientific approaches and stressed life histories, autobiographies, case studies, diaries, letters, and nondirective interviews. Blumer particularly emphasized the importance of participant observation in the study of communication. Further, the Chicago tradition saw people as creative, innovative, and free to define each situation in unpredictable ways. Self and society were viewed as process, not structure; to freeze the process would be to lose the essence of social relationships.

The second tradition, the Iowa School, took a more scientific approach. Manford Kuhn and

Carl Couch, its leaders, believed that interactionist concepts could be operationalized. Although Kuhn accepted the basic tenets of symbolic interactionism, he argued that objective methods are more fruitful than the "soft" methods employed by Blumer. As we will see later in the chapter, Kuhn was responsible for a well-known measurement technique called the Twenty Statements Test.[4]

The basic ideas of these early schools of interaction live on today and have been adopted by many social scientists. Yet symbolic interactionism has changed significantly since its early years, as Gary Fine suggests.[5] It has expanded by adopting insights from other theoretical areas and has increasingly contributed to the work of other areas of social science.

Today, according to Fine, symbolic interactionism has incorporated the study of how groups coordinate their actions, how emotions are understood and controlled, how reality is constructed, how self is created, how large social structures get established, and how public policy can be influenced.

In this chapter we concentrate on classical symbolic interactionism, the basic ideas of the movement, and the theoretical extensions most recognized in the communication field—those of Erving Goffman and Kenneth Burke. We begin here with the Chicago School and the work of Mead and Blumer.

The Chicago School

George Herbert Mead is usually viewed as the primary originator of the movement, and his work certainly forms the core of the Chicago

---

3   Bernard N. Meltzer and John W. Petras, "The Chicago and Iowa Schools of Symbolic Interactionism," in *Human Nature and Collective Behavior*, ed. T. Shibutani (Englewood Cliffs, NJ: Prentice-Hall, 1970).
4   Meltzer and Petras, "Chicago and Iowa Schools."
5   Gary Alan Fine, "The Sad Demise, Mysterious Disappearance, and Glorious Triumph of Symbolic Interactionism, *Annual Review of Sociology* 19 (1993): 61–87.

School.[6] Herbert Blumer, Mead's foremost apostle, invented the term *symbolic interactionism,* an expression Mead himself never used. Blumer refers to this label as "a somewhat barbaric neologism that I coined in an offhand way. . . . The term somehow caught on."[7]

The three cardinal concepts in Mead's theory, captured in the title of his best-known work, are society, self, and mind. These categories are different aspects of the same general process, the *social act.* The social act is an umbrella concept under which nearly all other psychological and social processes fall. The act is a complete unit of conduct that cannot be analyzed into specific subparts. An act may be short and simple, such as tying a shoe, or it may be long and complicated like the fulfillment of a life plan. Acts relate to one another and are built up throughout a lifetime. Acts begin with an impulse; they involve perception and assignment of meaning, mental rehearsal, weighing of alternatives, and consummation.

In its most basic form, a social act involves a three-part relationship: an initial gesture from one individual, a response to that gesture by another, and a result. The result is the communicators' meaning for the act. Meaning does not reside solely in any one of these things but in the triadic relationship of all three.[8]

In a holdup, for example, the robber indicates to the victim what is intended. The victim responds by giving money or belongings, and in the initial gesture and response, the defined result (a holdup) has occurred. Even individual acts, such as a solitary walk, are interactional because they are based on gestures and responses that occurred many times in the past and continue in the mind of the individual. One never takes a walk by oneself without relying on meanings and actions learned in social interaction with others.

The *joint action* of a group of people, such as marriage, trade, war, or church worship, consists of an *interlinkage* of smaller interactions. Blumer notes that in an advanced society the largest portion of group action consists of highly recurrent, stable patterns that possess common and estab-

lished meanings for their participants. Because of the frequency of such patterns and the stability of their meanings, scholars have tended to treat them as structures, forgetting their origins in interaction. Blumer warns us not to forget that new situations present problems requiring adjustment and redefinition.

Even in highly repetitious group patterns, nothing is permanent. Each case must begin anew with individual action. No matter how solid a group action appears to be, it is still rooted in individual human choices: "It is the social process in group life that creates and upholds the rules, not the rules that create and uphold group life."[9]

Interlinkages may be pervasive, extended, and connected through complicated networks. Distant actors may be interlinked ultimately in diverse ways, but contrary to popular thinking, "a network or an institution does not function automatically because of some inner dynamics or system requirements: it functions because people at different points do something, and what they do is a result of how they define the situation in which they are called on to act."[10]

With this idea of social acts in mind, then, let us look more closely at the first facet of Meadian

---

6   Mead's primary work in symbolic interactionism is *Mind, Self, and Society* (Chicago: University of Chicago Press, 1934). For a general discussion of the history, influence, and methods of the Chicago School, see Jesse G. Delia, "Communication Research: A History," in *Handbook of Communication Science,* eds. C. R. Berger and S. H. Chaffee (Newbury Park, CA: Sage, 1987), pp. 30–37. For outstanding secondary sources on Mead and the Chicago School, see Everett M. Rogers, *A History of Communication Study: A Biographical Approach* (New York: Free Press, 1994), pp. 137–202; Bernard N. Meltzer, "Mead's Social Psychology," in *Symbolic Interaction,* eds. J. G. Manis and B. N. Meltzer (Boston: Allyn & Bacon, 1972), pp. 4–22; Charles Morris, "George H. Mead as Social Psychologist and Social Philosopher" (Introduction), in *Mind, Self, and Society;* and C. David Johnson and J. Stephen Picou, "The Foundations of Symbolic Interactionism Reconsidered," in *Micro-Sociological Theory: Perspectives on Sociological Theory,* vol. 2, eds. H. J. Helle and S. N. Eisenstadt (Beverly Hills, CA: Sage, 1985), pp. 54–70.
7   Herbert Blumer, *Symbolic Interactionism: Perspective and Method* (Englewood Cliffs, NJ: Prentice-Hall, 1969), p. 1.
8   Wayne Woodward, "Triadic Communication as Transactional Participation," *Critical Studies in Mass Communication* 13 (1996): 155–174.
9   Blumer, *Symbolic Interactionism,* p. 19.
10   Blumer, *Symbolic Interactionism,* p. 19.

analysis—society. *Society,* or group life, consists of the cooperative behaviors of society's members. Human cooperation requires that we understand others' intentions, which also entails figuring out what you and others will do in the future. Thus, cooperation consists of "reading" other people's actions and intentions and responding in an appropriate way.

Meaning is an important outcome of communication. Your meanings are the result of interaction with others. So, for example, although you may never have heard of a "toilet telephone," prison inmates know it well; they have learned that they can communicate by listening to voices traveling through the sewer pipes in the prison.

Further, we use meanings when we interpret the happenings around us. Interpretation is like an internal conversation: "The actor selects, checks, suspends, regroups, and transforms the meanings in light of the situation in which he is placed and the direction of his actions."[11]

Clearly, we could not communicate without sharing the meaning of the symbols we use. Mead calls a gesture with shared meaning a *significant symbol.* Society is made possible by significant symbols. Because of the ability to vocalize symbols, we literally can hear ourselves and thus can respond to the self as others respond to us. We can imagine what it is like to receive our own messages, and we can empathize with the listener and take the listener's role, mentally completing the other's response. Society, then, consists of a network of social interactions in which participants assign meaning to their own and others' actions by the use of symbols.[12] Even the various institutions of society are built up by the interactions of people involved in those institutions.

Consider the court system in the United States as an example. The courts are nothing more than the interactions among judges, juries, attorneys, witnesses, clerks, reporters, and others who use language to interact with one another. *Court* has no meaning apart from the interpretations of the actions of those involved in it. The same can be said for school, church, government, industry, and any other segment of society.

This interplay between responding to others and responding to self is an important concept in Mead's theory, and it provides a good transition to his second concept—the *self.*[13] You have a self because you can respond to yourself as an object. You sometimes react favorably to yourself and feel pride, happiness, and encouragement. You sometimes become angry or disgusted with yourself. The primary way you come to see yourself as others see you is through *role taking* or assuming the perspective of others, and this is what leads you to have a self-concept.

Another term for self-concept is *generalized other,* a kind of composite perspective from which you see yourself. The generalized other is your overall perception of the way others see you. You have learned this self-picture from years of symbolic interaction with other people in your life. *Significant others,* the people closest to you, are especially important because their reactions have been very influential in your life.

Consider, for example, the self-image of adolescents. As a result of their interactions with significant others such as parents, siblings, and peers, teenagers come to view themselves as they think others have viewed them. They come to take on the persona that has been reflected to them in their many interactions with other people. As they behave in ways that affirm this image, it is strengthened, and others respond accordingly in a cyclical fashion. So, for example, if a young person feels socially inept, he or she may withdraw, further reinforcing the image of being inadequate.

The self has two facets, each serving an essential function. The *I* is the impulsive, unorganized, undirected, unpredictable part of you. The *me* is the generalized other, made up of the organized and consistent patterns shared with others. Ev-

---

11   Blumer, *Symbolic Interactionism,* p. 5.
12   For a thoughtful discussion of the social nature of symbols, see Wendy Leeds-Hurwitz, "A Social Account of Symbols," in *Beyond the Symbol Model: Reflections on the Representational Nature of Language,* ed. John Stewart (Albany: SUNY Press, 1996), pp. 257–278.
13   For a probing discussion of self within this tradition, see Norbert Wiley, *The Semiotic Self* (Chicago: University of Chicago Press, 1994).

ery act begins with an impulse from the *I* and quickly becomes controlled by the *me.* The *I* is the driving force in action, whereas the *me* provides direction and guidance. Mead used the concept of *me* to explain your socially acceptable and adaptive behavior and the *I* to explain your creative, unpredictable impulses.

For example, many people will deliberately change their life's situation in order to alter their own self-concept. Here, the *I* moves the person to change in ways that the *me* would not permit. Such a change might have occurred, for example, when you went to college. Many high school students decide that they will use college to establish a new *me* by associating with a new group of significant others and by establishing a new generalized other. This is what people mean when they say that they got a new start.

Your ability to use significant symbols to respond to yourself makes thinking possible. Thinking is Mead's third concept, which he calls *mind.* The mind is not a thing, but a process. It is nothing more than interacting with yourself. This ability, which develops along with the self, is crucial to human life, for it is part of every act. *Minding* involves hesitating (postponing overt action) while you interpret the situation. Here you think through the situation and plan future actions. You imagine various outcomes and select and test possible alternatives.

People possess significant symbols that allow them to name objects. You always define an object in terms of how you might act toward it. A seascape is a seascape when you value looking at it. A glass of lemonade is a drink when you conceive of drinking it (or not drinking it). Objects become the objects they are through the individual's symbolic minding process; when the individual envisions new or different actions toward an object, the object is changed.

For Blumer, objects are of three types—physical (things), social (people), and abstract (ideas). People define objects differently, depending on how they act toward those objects. A police officer may mean one thing to the residents of an inner-city ghetto and something else to the inhabitants of a posh residential area; the different

interactions among the residents of these two vastly different communities will determine different meanings.

A fascinating study of marijuana use by Howard Becker illustrates the concept of social object very well.[14] Becker found that users learn at least three things through interaction with other users. The first is to smoke the drug properly. Virtually everyone Becker talked to said that they had trouble getting high at first until others showed them how to do it. Second, smokers must learn to define the sensation produced by the drug as a "high." In other words, the individual learns to discriminate the effects of marijuana and to associate these with smoking. Becker claims that this association does not happen automatically and must be learned through social interaction with other users. In fact, some experienced users reported that novices were absolutely stoned and didn't know it until they were taught to identify the feeling. Finally, users must learn to define the effects as pleasant and desirable. Again, this is not automatic; many beginners do not find the effects pleasant at all until they are told that they should consider them so.

Here, we see that marijuana is a social object. Its meanings are created in the process of interaction. How people think about the drug (mind) is determined by those meanings, and the assumptions of the group (society) are also a product of interaction. Although Becker does not report information about self-concept specifically, it is easy to see that part of the self may also be defined in terms of interactions in the marijuana-smoking community.

The Iowa School

Manford Kuhn and his students, although maintaining basic interactionist principles, take two new steps not previously seen in the old-line theory. The first is to make the concept of self more concrete; the second, which makes the first possible, is the use of quantitative research. In

---

14   Howard Becker, "Becoming a Marihuana User," *American Journal of Sociology* 59 (1953): 235–242.

this latter area, the Iowa and Chicago schools part company. Blumer strongly criticizes the trend in the behavioral sciences to operationalize; Kuhn makes a point to do just that! As a result Kuhn's work moves more toward microscopic analysis than does the traditional Chicago approach.[15]

Kuhn's theoretical premises are consistent with Mead's thought. Kuhn conceives of the basis of all action as symbolic interaction. The child is socialized through interaction with others in the society into which he or she is born. The person has meaning for and thereby deals with objects in the environment through social interaction. To Kuhn, the naming of an object is important, for naming is a way of conveying the object's meaning. Kuhn agrees with his Chicago colleagues that the individual is not a passive reactor but an active planner. He reinforces the view that individuals undertake self-conversations as part of the process of acting. Kuhn also stresses the importance of language in thinking and communicating.

Like Mead and Blumer, Kuhn discusses the importance of objects in the actor's world. The *object* can be any aspect of the person's reality: a thing, a quality, an event, or a state of affairs. The only requirement for something to become an object is that the person name it, represent it symbolically. Reality for people is the totality of their social objects, which are always socially defined.

A second concept important to Kuhn is the *plan of action*, a person's total behavior pattern toward a given object. *Attitudes*, or verbal statements that indicate the values toward which action will be directed, guide the plan. Because attitudes are verbal statements, they too can be observed and measured. Going to college involves a plan of action, actually a host of plans, guided by a set of attitudes about what you want to get out of college. You might be guided, for ex-

ample, by positive attitudes toward money, career, and personal success.

A third concept important to Kuhn is the *orientational other*, someone who has been particularly influential in a person's life. This term is essentially synonymous with *significant other*, as used by Mead. These individuals possess four qualities. First, they are people to whom the individual is emotionally and psychologically committed. Second, they are the ones who provide the person with general vocabulary, central concepts, and categories. Third, they provide the individual with the basic distinction between self and others, including one's perceived role differentiation. Fourth, the orientational others' communications continually sustain the individual's self-concept. Orientational others may be in the present or past; they may be present or absent. The important idea behind the concept is that the individual comes to see the world through interaction with particular other persons who have touched one's life in important ways.

Finally, we come to Kuhn's most important concept—the *self*. Kuhn's theory and method revolve around self, and it is in this area that Kuhn most dramatically extends symbolic interactionist thinking. The self-conception, the individual's plans of action toward the self, consists of one's identities, interests and aversions, goals, ideologies, and self-evaluations. Such self-conceptions are anchoring attitudes, for they act as one's most common frame of reference for judging other objects. All subsequent plans of action stem primarily from the self-concept.

Kuhn is responsible for a technique known as the *Twenty Statements Self-Attitudes Test* (TST) for measuring various aspects of the self. If you were to take the TST, you would be confronted with twenty blank spaces preceded by the following simple instructions:

There are twenty numbered blanks on the page below. Please write twenty answers to the simple question, "Who am I?" in the blanks. Just give twenty different answers to this question. Answer as if you were giving the answers to yourself, not to somebody else. Write the answers in the order that they occur to you.

---

15 Like many of the interactionists, Kuhn never published a truly unified work. The closest may be C. A. Hickman and Manford Kuhn, *Individuals, Groups, and Economic Behavior* (New York: Holt, Rinehart & Winston, 1956). See also Charles Tucker, "Some Methodological Problems of Kuhn's Self Theory," *Sociological Quarterly* 7 (1966): 345–358.

Don't worry about logic or "importance." Go along fairly fast, for time is limited.[16]

There are a number of ways to analyze the responses from this test, each tapping a different aspect of the self. Two of these are the ordering variable and the locus variable. The *ordering variable* is the relative salience of identifications the individual possesses. It is observable in the order of statements listed on the form. For example, if the person lists "Baptist" a great deal higher than "father," the researcher may conclude that the person identifies more readily with religious affiliation than with family affiliation. The *locus variable* is the extent to which the subject in a general way tends to identify with consensual groupings such as "American" rather than idiosyncratic, subjective qualities such as "strong."

In scoring the self-attitude test, you can place statements in one of two categories. A statement is *consensual* if it consists of a discrete group or class identification, such as student, woman, husband, Baptist, from Chicago, premedical student, daughter, oldest child, engineering student. Other statements are not descriptions of commonly agreed-on categories. Examples of *subconsensual* responses are happy, bored, pretty, good student, too heavy, good wife, interesting. The number of statements in the consensual group is the individual's locus score.

Symbolic interactionism has certainly been an influential force in social theories of communication. We turn now to several related theories.

DRAMATISM AND NARRATIVE

Dramatism and narrative are two closely associated movements that fit well under the interactionist umbrella. Theories of dramatism and narrative deal with stories, which are one of the most important ways people use symbols and create meaning. *Dramatism* is distinguished by its heavy reliance on a theatrical metaphor, and *narrative* is characterized by its use of story sequence.

The dramaturgical movement is closely aligned with symbolic interactionism and has been heavily influenced by it. The dramaturgists see people as actors on a metaphorical stage playing out roles. Bruce Gronbeck sketches the basic idea of dramatism, as shown in Figure 8.1.[17] Here action is seen as performance, or the use of symbols to present a story or script to interpreters. In the process of performance, meanings and actions are produced within a scene, or sociocultural context.

Several theorists might be termed *dramaturgical,* but dramaturgical theory lacks the unity required to be called a school. This section reviews the work of two very different dramaturgical theories—the landmark symbol theory of Kenneth Burke and the influential role theory of Erving Goffman.

An increasingly popular approach to communication is the narrative paradigm, which is akin to dramatism and consistent with the tenets of symbolic interactionism. Narrative theories focus on the ways people structure reality by telling stories. The story is not only a way of organizing a message but is also a common, some say universal, format for structuring interaction itself.[18] Howard Kamler expresses the importance of stories in this passage:

> Any communication is a sharing of stories. Most stories seem to cry out to be shared. And getting shared is perhaps the most profound function of stories. Stories are the stuff of communication. And the sharing of them is what transforms persons into communal beings. In trading our stories back and forth for inspection, agreement, disagreement, we are involved in the activity of making ourselves members of a community. Public story trade is at the heart of the social miracle about persons.[19]

---

16   Tucker, "Some Methodological Problems," p. 308.
17   Adapted from Bruce E. Gronbeck, "Dramaturgical Theory and Criticism: The State of the Art (or Science?)," *Western Journal of Speech Communication* 44 (1980): 317.
18   Narrative is a popular topic in literature and in communication. See, for example, W. J. T. Mitchell (ed.), *On Narrative* (Chicago: University of Chicago Press, 1980); Howard Kamler, *Communication: Sharing Our Stories of Experience* (Seattle: Psychological Press, 1983); Didier Coste, *Narrative as Communication* (Minneapolis: University of Minnesota Press, 1989).
19   Kamler, *Communication,* p. 49.

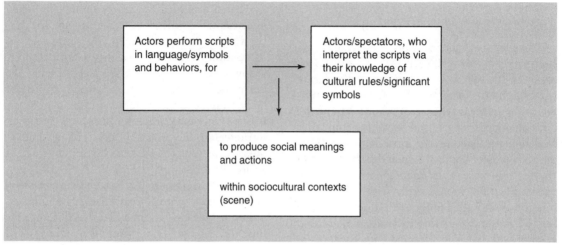

FIGURE **8.1**

Dramaturgical Model of Society

In this chapter we look at two theories of narrative. The first, Ernest Bormann's convergence theory, originated in small-group communication theory and has been expanded to cover a great deal more. The second, Walter Fisher's narrative theory, points to the function of stories in all communication.

Dramatistic and narrative theories are difficult to separate. Both deal with the meanings assigned to characters playing roles in a sequence of events. For this reason, the dramatistic and narrative theories are grouped together in this book.

The Dramatism of Burke

Kenneth Burke has written widely in many areas, including creative writing, literary and rhetorical criticism, social psychology, and linguistic analysis. Burke's concepts are not derived directly from the work of Mead and the other early sociologists, but his work is highly consistent with the other approaches presented in this chapter.

Burke is no doubt a giant among symbol theorists.[20] He has written over a period of fifty years, and his theory is the most comprehensive of all the interactionist theories. One follower

wrote, "It may be said without exaggeration that anyone writing today on communication, however 'original' he may be, is echoing something said by Burke."[21] Burke published a number of books, from 1931 to 1989.[22] A number of scholars have provided written interpretations of Burke's ideas.[23] In surveying Burke's communication theory, we will begin with a summary of his concept of action; then we will turn to his central ideas on symbols, language, and communication; and finally we will sketch Burke's method.

20   See, for example, Bernard L. Brock, "Evolution of Kenneth Burke's Criticism and Philosophy of Language," in *Kenneth Burke and Contemporary European Thought: Rhetoric in Transition*, ed. Bernard L. Brock (Tuscaloosa: The University of Alabama Press, 1995), pp. 1–33; Herbert W. Simons and Trevor Melia (eds.), *The Legacy of Kenneth Burke* (Madison: University of Wisconsin Press, 1989). Although in the communication field, Burke is most often considered a symbol theorist, he is also a major social critic. For a discussion of this aspect of his work, see Omar Swartz, *Conducting Socially Responsible Research* (Thousand Oaks, CA: Sage, 1997), pp. 68–90.
21   Hugh Duncan, "Communication in Society," *Arts in Society* 3 (1964): 105.
22   For a list of Burke's works, see the Bibliography.
23   For a comprehensive overview on Kenneth Burke, see William Rueckert (ed.), *Critical Responses to Kenneth Burke* (Minneapolis: University of Minnesota Press, 1969). For brief summaries, see Brock, "Evolution"; John F. Cragan and Donald C. Shields, *Symbolic Theories in Applied Communication Research: Bormann, Burke, and Fisher* (Cresskill, NJ: Hampton, 1995), pp. 61–81; Sonja K. Foss, Karen A. Foss, and Robert Trapp, *Contemporary Perspectives on Rhetoric* (Prospect Heights, IL: Waveland, 1991), pp. 169–208.

Burke sees the act as the basic concept in dramatism. His view of human action is consistent with that of Mead, Blumer, and Kuhn. Specifically, Burke distinguishes between action and motion. *Action* consists of purposeful, voluntary behaviors; *motions* are nonpurposeful, nonmeaningful ones. Objects and animals possess motion, but only human beings have action.

Burke views the individual as a biological and neurological being, distinguished by symbol-using behavior, the ability to act. People are symbol-creating, symbol-using, and symbol-misusing animals. They create symbols to name things and situations; they use symbols for communication; and they often abuse symbols by misusing them to their disadvantage.

Burke's view of symbols is broad, including an array of linguistic and nonverbal elements as well. Especially intriguing for Burke is the notion that a person can symbolize symbols. One can talk about speech and can write about words. History itself is a process of writing about what people have already spoken and written in the course of events.

People filter reality through a symbolic screen. Reality is mediated through symbols. Burke agrees with Mead that language functions as the vehicle for action. Because of the social need for people to cooperate in their actions, language shapes behavior.

Language, as seen by Burke, is always emotionally loaded. No word can be neutral. As a result, your attitudes, judgments, and feelings invariably appear in the language you use. Language is by nature selective and abstract, focusing attention on particular aspects of reality at the expense of other aspects. Language is economical, but it is also ambiguous.

An overriding consideration for all of Burke's work is his concept of guilt. The term *guilt* is Burke's all-purpose word for any feeling of tension within a person—anxiety, embarrassment, self-hatred, disgust, and so forth. For Burke, guilt is a condition caused by symbol use. He identifies three related sources of guilt, the first of which is *the negative*. Through language people moralize. They construct myriad rules and pro-

scriptions. These rules are never entirely consistent, and in following one rule, you necessarily are breaking another, creating guilt. Religions, professions, organizations, families, and communities all have implicit rules about how to behave. We learn these throughout life and therefore judge almost any action as good or bad.

The second reason for guilt is the *principle of perfection*. People are sensitive to their failings. Humans can imagine (through language) a state of perfection. Then, by their very nature, they spend their lives striving for whatever degree of this perfection they set for themselves. Guilt arises as a result of the discrepancy between the real and the ideal. Many peace activists are motivated by this kind of guilt. For example, a speaker at a rally may say that war is a barbaric and inappropriate method of resolving conflict in the twentieth century. This speaker can imagine a world without war and is motivated to speak out because of the principle of perfection.

A third reason for guilt is the *principle of hierarchy*. In seeking order, people structure society in social pyramids or hierarchies (social ratings, social orderings), which is done with symbols. Competitions and divisions result among classes and groups in the hierarchy, and guilt results. The ethnic strife in the former Yugoslavia is a perfect example.

For Burke, guilt is the primary motive behind all action and communication. We communicate to purge our guilt. In describing communication, Burke uses several nearly synonymous terms: persuasion, identification, consubstantiality, communication, and rhetoric. Let us see how these concepts are integrated in his theory.

First, *consubstantiality:* Any object has an essence, or substance. *Substance* is the general nature, or essence, of a thing. People have substance too, and each person has a separate substance; however, the substances of any two persons always overlap to some extent. The overlap is never total, making perfect communication impossible. Whatever communication occurs between individuals is a direct function of their shared, or common, substance, called consubstantiality.

When you and a friend are relaxing next to the swimming pool on a warm summer morning, you communicate with each other in a free and easy manner because you share meanings for the language in use. You are, so to speak, consubstantial. On the other hand, when you ask a question of a harried busboy in a Swiss restaurant, you may feel frustration because of your lack of shared meaning with this individual. To combine Mead and Burke, a significant symbol is one that allows for shared meaning through consubstantiality.

Another important term in Burke's theory is identification. As generally conceived, *identification* is similar to consubstantiality. The opposite of identification is *division*, or separateness. Division and the guilt it produces are the primary motives for communication. Through communication, identification is increased. In a spiraling fashion as identification increases, shared meaning increases, thereby improving understanding. Identification thus can be a means to persuasion and effective communication, or it can be an end in itself. Identification can be conscious or unconscious, planned or accidental.

Three overlapping sources of identification exist among people. *Material identification* results from goods, possessions, and things, like owning the same kind of car or having similar tastes in clothes. *Idealistic identification* results from shared ideas, attitudes, feelings, and values, such as being a member of the same church or political party. *Formal identification* results from the arrangement, form, or organization of an event in which both parties participate. If two people who are introduced shake hands, the conventional form of handshaking causes some identification to take place.

Identification is not an either-or occurrence but a matter of degree. Some consubstantiality will always be present merely by virtue of the shared humanness of any two persons. Identification can be great or small, and it can be increased or decreased by the actions of the communicators. Second, although any two persons will always experience some identification and some division, communication is more successful when identification is greater than division.

People of lower strata in a hierarchy often identify with persons at the top of the hierarchy, despite tremendous apparent division. This kind of identification can be seen, for example, in the mass following of a charismatic leader. Why does this happen? First, individuals perceive in others an embodiment of the perfection for which they themselves strive. Second, the mystery surrounding the charismatic person simultaneously tends to hide the division that exists. This phenomenon can be called *identification through mystification*.

Because it is so important to successful communication, people adopt certain *strategies* of identification when they interact with others. Since identification can occur in an almost unlimited number of ways, Burke does not attempt to outline all available strategies but suggests that in analyzing a rhetorical event, you should try to figure out what strategies the communicators are using.

Burke's most basic method for analyzing events is the *dramatistic pentad*. Pentad, meaning a group of five, is an analytical framework for the most efficient study of any act. The first part of the pentad is the *act*, what is done by the actor. It is a view of what the actor played, what was accomplished. The second part is the *scene*, the situation or setting in which the act was accomplished. It includes a view of the physical setting and the cultural and social milieu in which the act was carried out. The third component is the *agent*, the actor, including all that is known about the individual. The agent's substance reaches all aspects of his or her being, history, personality, demeanor, and any other contributing factors. The *agency*, the fourth component, is the means, or vehicle, the agent uses in carrying out the act. Agency may include channels of communication, devices, institutions, strategies, or messages. Fifth, the *purpose* is the reason for the act— the rhetorical goal, the hoped-for effect or result of the act.

For example, in writing a paper for your communication theory course, you, the agent, gather information and present it to the instructor (the act). Your course, your university, your library, your desk and room, the social atmosphere of your school constitute the scene; the format of the paper itself is the agency. You have a variety of purposes, including, in all likelihood, getting a good grade.

David Ling shows how Burke's pentad can be used to understand a communication event.[24] In 1969 Edward Kennedy, a senator from Massachusetts, was involved in an automobile accident with an aide, Mary Jo Kopechne, in which he accidentally drove a car off a bridge into a pond. Kennedy escaped, but Kopechne drowned. In a remarkable address to the people of Massachusetts about a week later, he explained what happened and attempted to regain the support of the people. Ling writes that Kennedy wanted to achieve two things—to minimize his own responsibility for the accident and to make the people responsible for whether or not he would continue in office.

Kennedy's appeal on the first point describes himself (agent) as a helpless victim of the events leading to the death of the young woman (scene). He explains his own failure to report the accident (act) as a consequence of his confusion and injuries. Kennedy's depiction makes him out to be a victim of a tragic situation. Later in his speech, Kennedy essentially offered to resign if the citizens wanted him to. Here, the scene shifted to the public reaction to the accident, the agent became the people of Massachusetts, the act was their decision as to whether he should resign, the agency would be a statement of resignation, and the purpose would be to remove him from office. Ling believes this was a very effective speech. The reaction was overwhelmingly positive, and Kennedy continued in office.

Goffman's Social Approach

Erving Goffman is one of the best-known sociologists of the twentieth century.[25] As a symbolic interactionist of the dramaturgical tradition, Goffman analyzes human behavior with a theatrical metaphor, in which the ordinary setting is a stage and people are actors who use performances to make an impression on the audience.

Let's begin by looking at Goffman's basic framework.[26] He begins with the assumption that the person must somehow make sense of events encountered in everyday life. Your interpretation of a situation is your *definition of the situation.*

In any typical situation, people tend to ask the mental question, "What is going on here?" Their answer constitutes a definition of the situation. Often the first definition is not adequate and a rereading may be necessary, as in the case of a practical joke, a mistake, or a misunderstanding. Rereading is important because we are often deceptive with one another.

One's definition of a situation can be divided into strips and frames. A *strip* is a sequence of activity such as opening the refrigerator door, removing the milk, pouring it into a glass, drinking it, and putting the glass into the dishwasher. A *frame* is a basic organizational pattern used to define the strip. The strip of activities listed above, for example, would probably be framed as "getting a snack."

Frame analysis thus consists of examining the ways experience is organized for the individual. The frame allows the person to identify and understand otherwise meaningless events, giving meaning to the ongoing activities of life. A natural framework is an unguided event of nature with which the individual must cope such as a windstorm. A social framework, on the other hand, is seen as controllable, guided by some intelligence, such as planning a meal. These two types of frameworks relate to one another because social beings act on and are in turn influenced by the natural order.

Frameworks, then, are the models we use to understand our experience, the ways we see

---

24   David A. Ling, "A Pentadic Analysis of Senator Edward Kennedy's Address to the People of Massachusetts, July 25, 1969," *Central States Speech Journal* 21 (1970): 81–86.
25   See the Bibliography for a listing of Goffman's works.
26   Erving Goffman, *Frame Analysis: An Essay on the Organization of Experience* (Cambridge, MA: Harvard University Press, 1974). See also Jef Verhoeven, "Goffman's Frame Analysis and Modern Micro-Sociological Paradigms," in *Micro-Sociological Theory: Perspectives on Sociological Theory*, vol. 2, eds. H. J. Helle and S. N. Eisenstadt (Beverly Hills, CA: Sage, 1985), pp. 71–100; Stuart J. Sigman, *A Perspective on Social Communication* (Lexington, MA: Lexington, 1987), pp. 41–56; Spencer Cahill, "Erving Goffman," in *Symbolic Interactionism: An Introduction, an Interpretation, an Integration*, ed. Joel M. Charon (Englewood Cliffs, NJ: Prentice-Hall, 1992), pp. 185–200.

things as fitting together into some coherent whole. A *primary framework* is a basic organizational unit such as conversing, eating, and dressing, but primary frames can be transformed or altered into *secondary frameworks*. Here the basic organizational principles of a primary frame are used to meet different ends. A game, for example, is a secondary framework modeled after the primary framework of a fight or competition. A large portion of our frameworks are not primary at all, though they are modeled after primary ones. Examples include plays, deceptions, experiments, and other fabrications. Ordinary life is filled with secondary frameworks.

Communication activities, like all activities, are viewed in the context of frame analysis. A *face engagement,* or *encounter,* occurs when people interact with one another in a focused way.[27] In a face engagement, you have a single focus of attention and a perceived mutual activity. In unfocused interaction in a public place, you acknowledge the presence of another person without paying much attention. This happens, for example, when you are standing in line at a bus stop. In such an unfocused situation, you may be accessible for an encounter that could begin when another passenger strikes up a conversation. Once an engagement begins, a mutual contract exists to continue the engagement to some kind of termination. Face engagements are both verbal and nonverbal, and the cues exhibited are important in signifying the nature of the relationship as well as a mutual definition of the situation.

People in face engagements take turns presenting dramas to one another. Storytelling, or recounting past events, impresses the listener by dramatic portrayal:

> I am suggesting that often what talkers undertake to do is not to provide information to a recipient but to present dramas to an audience. Indeed, it seems that we spend most of our time not engaged in giving information but in giving shows. And observe, this theatricality is not based on mere displays of feelings or faked exhibitions of spontaneity or anything else by way of the huffing and puffing we might derogate by calling theatrical. The parallel between

stage and conversation is much, much deeper than that. The point is that ordinarily when an individual says something, he is not saying it as a bold statement of fact on his own behalf. He is recounting. He is running through a strip of already determined events for the engagement of his listeners.[28]

In engaging others, you present a particular character to the audience. Like a stage actor, you present a character in a particular role, and your audience normally accepts the characterization.[29] Goffman believes that the self is literally determined by these dramatizations. Here is how he explains the self:

> A correctly staged and performed scene leads the audience to impute a self to a performed character, but this imputation—this self—is a product of a scene that comes off, and is not a cause of it. The self, then, as a performed character, is not an organic thing that has a specific location, whose fundamental fate is to be born, to mature, and to die; it is a dramatic effect arising diffusely from a scene that is presented, and the characteristic issue, the crucial concern, is whether it will be credited or discredited.[30]

You have only to think about the many situations in which you project a certain image of yourself. It is doubtful that you behave the same way with your best friend as you do with your parents, and it is unlikely that the self you present to a professor is the same one you present at a party. In most of the situations in which you participate, you decide on a role and enact it.

In attempting to define a situation, you go through a two-part process—first, you get information about the other people in the situation and, second, you give information about yourself. This process of exchanging information en-

---

27   On the nature of face-to-face interaction, see Erving Goffman, *Encounters: Two Studies in the Sociology of Interaction* (Indianapolis, IN: Bobbs-Merrill, 1961); *Behavior in Public Places* (New York: Free Press, 1963); *Interaction Ritual: Essays on Face-to-Face Behavior* (Garden City, NY: Doubleday, 1967); and *Relations in Public* (New York: Basic, 1971).
28   Goffman, *Frame*, p. 508.
29   The best sources on self-presentation are Erving Goffman, *The Presentation of Self in Everyday Life* (Garden City, NY: Doubleday, 1959); and *Relations in Public*.
30   Goffman, *Presentation*, pp. 252–253.

ables people to know what is expected of them. Usually, this exchange occurs indirectly through observing the behavior of others and structuring your own behavior to elicit impressions in others. *Self-presentation* is very much a matter of *impression management:*

> He may wish them to think highly of him, or to think that he thinks highly of them, or to perceive how in fact he feels toward them or to obtain no clear-cut impression; he may wish to insure sufficient harmony so that the interaction can be sustained, or to defraud, get rid of, confuse, mislead, antagonize, or insult them.[31]

Predicaments are especially interesting. Suppose you get blamed for something. You can respond in a number of ways—you can give excuses, justifications, apologies, and more. For example, in making an excuse, you might say that you didn't mean to do it, that you did not realize what would happen, or that you couldn't help it. Justifications include appeals to a higher authority, self-defense, loyalty, or some other set of values.[32]

Because all participants in a situation project images, an overall definition of the situation emerges. This general definition is normally rather unified. Once the definition is set, moral pressure is created to maintain it by suppressing contradictions and doubts. A person may add to the projections but never contradict the image initially set. The very organization of society is based on this principle.

Bormann's Convergence Theory

Convergence theory, often known as *fantasy-theme analysis,* is based on Robert Bales's research on small-group communication discussed later in Chapter 13.[33] Bales found that at moments of tension, groups will often become dramatic and share stories, or *fantasy themes,* to reduce the stress. Ernest Bormann applied this idea to rhetorical action in society at large.[34] Much of individuals' images of reality consists of narratives of how things are believed to be. These stories are created in symbolic interaction within small groups, and they are chained out from person to person and group to group.

Fantasy themes are part of larger dramas that are longer, more complicated stories called rhetorical visions. A *rhetorical vision* is essentially a view of how things have been, are, or will be. Rhetorical visions structure our sense of reality in areas that we cannot experience directly but can only know by symbolic reproduction. Consequently, such visions give us an image of things in the past, in the future, or in faraway places; in large measure these visions form the assumptions on which a group's knowledge is based.

In the corporate world, for example, plans are almost always designed to generate profit. In a limited marketplace, not all competitors will be profitable, so you would expect corporate planners to live in a world filled with competition-oriented rhetorical visions, and they would tell stories that express this vision.

Fantasy themes, and even the larger rhetorical visions, consist of dramatis personae (characters), a plot line, a scene, and sanctioning agents. The *characters* can be heroes, villains, and other supporting players. The *plot* line is the action or development of the story. The *scene* is the setting, including location, properties, and sociocultural milieu. Finally, the *sanctioning agent* is a source that legitimizes the story. This source may be an authority who lends credibility to the story or authorizes its telling, a common belief in God or

31 Goffman, *Presentation,* p. 3.
32 For a well-developed discussion of impression management in predicaments, see J. T. Tedeschi and M. Reiss, "Verbal Strategies in Impression Management," in *The Psychology of Ordinary Explanations of Social Behavior,* ed. C. Antaki (New York: Academic, 1981), pp. 271–309.
33 Robert F. Bales, *Personality and Interpersonal Behavior* (New York: Holt, Rinehart & Winston, 1970).
34 Bormann's major works on fantasy-theme analysis are *Communication Theory* (New York: Holt, Rinehart & Winston, 1980), pp. 184–190; *The Force of Fantasy: Restoring the American Dream* (Carbondale: Southern Illinois University Press, 1985); "Fantasy and Rhetorical Vision: The Rhetorical Criticism of Social Reality," *Quarterly Journal of Speech* 58 (1972): 396–407; and "Fantasy and Rhetorical Vision: Ten Years Later," *Quarterly Journal of Speech* 68 (1982): 288–305; Ernest G. Bormann, John F. Cragan, and Donald C. Shields, "An Expansion of the Rhetorical Vision Component of the Symbolic Convergence Theory: The Cold War Paradigm Case," *Communication Monographs* 63 (1996): 1–28. See also John F. Cragan and Donald C. Shields, *Applied Communication Research: A Dramatistic Approach* (Prospect Heights, IL: Waveland, 1981); John F. Cragan and Donald C. Shields, *Symbolic Theories,* pp. 29–48.

another sanctioning ideal like justice or democracy, or a situation or event that makes telling the story seem appropriate.

Imagine a group of executives gathering for a high-level meeting. Just before the meeting gets going, at the beginning, and at various points during the meeting, members will share experiences and stories—fantasy themes—that bring the group together. Some of these will be stories heard again and again. Each will have a cast of characters, a plot, a scene, and sanctioning agents. In many cases the sanctioning agent will be the company itself.

Rhetorical visions are never told in their entirety but are built up piecemeal by sharing associated fantasy themes. To grasp the entire vision, one must attend to the fantasy themes because these comprise the content of conversation in groups of people when the vision is being created and chained out. You can recognize a fantasy theme because it is repeated again and again. In fact, some themes are so frequently discussed and so well known within a particular group or community that the members no longer tell the whole episode, but abbreviate it by presenting just a "trigger" or *in-cue*. This is precisely what happens with an inside joke. An executive might say, for example, "Yeah, that's just like the *Frasier* episode!" and everyone will laugh, knowing just what she is referring to. Fantasy themes that develop to this point of familiarity are known as *fantasy types*—stock situations told over and over within a group.

As people come to share fantasy themes, the resulting rhetorical vision pulls them together and gives them a sense of identification with a shared reality. In this process, people converge or come to hold a common image as they share their fantasy themes. In fact, shared rhetorical visions—and especially the use of fantasy types—can be taken as evidence that convergence has occurred.

As rhetorical visions get established through the sharing of fantasy themes within a limited group, they fulfill a *consciousness-creating* function. They make people more aware of a certain way of seeing things. This happens because the

elements of rhetorical visions at this stage are novel and have explanatory power, and yet they can also attract attention and build consciousness because they imitate former ways of seeing things that look familiar.

Once consciousness is created among early adherents to a rhetorical vision, the consciousness can be disseminated, as more and more people are converted through *consciousness-raising* communication. There seems to be a critical mass of adherence at which widespread dissemination of the rhetorical vision takes place. After this happens, the rhetorical vision begins to fulfill a *consciousness-sustaining* function. Here the fantasy themes serve to maintain commitment.

Clearly, fantasy themes are an important ingredient in persuasion. Public communicators—in speeches, articles, books, films, and other media—often tap into the audience's predominant fantasy themes. Public communication can also add to or modify the rhetorical vision by amplifying, changing, or adding fantasy themes.

Karen Foss and Stephen Littlejohn's critique of *The Day After*—a television movie about a nuclear war that played in 1983 at the height of public concern over the nuclear arms buildup—shows how this process works.[35] These researchers asked about eighty people to write descriptions of what they thought a nuclear war would be like. They then compared these personal statements with the fantasy themes in the film and discovered a close association between the two.

The film was watched by a huge television audience, and it appears that it was effective in using a rhetorical vision shared with that audience. Foss and Littlejohn believe that the deep structure of the vision is irony, which consists primarily of the inconsistency of being both a detached observer and an involved participant in the nuclear-attack drama. This kind of irony is typical of the visions presented by films because films draw you in as a participant, but they also rely on you to be an observing and detached audience.

---

35   Karen A. Foss and Stephen W. Littlejohn, "*The Day After*: Rhetorical Vision in an Ironic Frame," *Critical Studies in Mass Communication* 3 (1986): 317–336.

Fisher's Theory of Narrative

Perhaps the most comprehensive narrative theory in the communication field is that of Walter Fisher.[36] Fisher believes that human rationality in all its forms is based essentially on narrative. Consequently, communication in all its forms can be understood as narrative.

Traditionally, narration, or storytelling, has been viewed as a different genre from argumentation. Arguments were viewed as rational, whereas stories were viewed as nonrational. Argument has been viewed customarily as a set of premises and conclusions based on specialized rules.

In disagreement with this traditional view, Fisher believes that narrative also involves rationality. Narrative can incorporate traditional rationality, but it goes beyond this to include other forms of rationality not often recognized. In other words, reasoning is more diverse than either technical or rhetorical argument recognizes, and the narrative paradigm encompasses a broader variety of types of rationality. Fisher summarizes:

> [In narrative] no form of discourse is privileged over others because its form is predominantly argumentative. No matter how strictly a case is argued—scientifically, philosophically, or legally—it will always be a story, an interpretation of some aspect of the world that is historically and culturally grounded and shaped by human personality.[37]

Persuasion occurs when people see good reasons for adopting a point of view. Good reasons can be presented in the form of traditional reasoning, or they can be presented in other ways. In the narrative paradigm, positive values constitute good reasons to accept a claim, no matter what form is used to express it. For example, if you want to persuade a friend to attend an animal rights rally, you might outline a number of reasons why animals need to be protected. If your friend accepts the values in the argument, he will probably go to the rally. Many people, however, are not persuaded by formal arguments like this one, so as an alternative, you might choose to tell the story of the abuse of beagles in a research lab. Again, if your friend accepts the values in the story, he will probably decide to go along. For many people the story would be more powerful than a list of reasons presented in traditional style.

What is narration? For Fisher, narration is more than traditional fictional stories and includes any verbal or nonverbal account that has a sequence of events to which listeners assign meaning. The narrative paradigm *describes* what people do when they communicate; it does not *dictate* what they should do, as does traditional argument learned in debate courses.

This does not mean all stories are equally effective. Some stories are better than others, and people do not need special knowledge or skill to tell the difference. Two criteria are used to establish the quality of a narrative—coherence and fidelity. *Coherence* is the degree to which a story makes sense, the extent to which it has meaning. Coherence is measured by the organization and structure of the story: A coherent story is well told. Coherence involves three kinds of consistency. The first is internal consistency, which Fisher calls *argumentative coherence* or *structural coherence*. This is the degree to which the parts of the story "hang together." The second type is external consistency, which Fisher calls *material coherence*, the congruence between this story and other stories, the degree to which the story seems complete in terms of the events previously learned from other sources. Finally, *characterological coherence* has to do with the believability of the characters in the story, both the narrators and the actors. What kind of choices do these characters make, and what kind of values do they espouse?

You know the difference between a well-told story and one that is confusing. You can tell when a story makes sense, when it is organized

---

36 Walter R. Fisher, *Human Communication as Narration: Toward a Philosophy of Reason, Value, and Action* (Columbia: University of South Carolina Press, 1987); see also "Narration, Reason, and Community," in *Writing the Social Text: Poetics and Politics in Social Science Discourse*, ed. Richard Harvey Brown (New York: Aldine, 1992), pp. 199–218; John F. Cragan and Donald C. Shields, *Symbolic Theories*, pp. 91–106.

37 Fisher, *Human Communication*, p. 49.

in a way that makes you pay attention and appreciate the art in the telling. But coherence is not everything. Indeed, a well-told story may still fail to persuade. It must also have fidelity.

Fidelity is the truthfulness or reliability of the story. A story has fidelity if it seems to ring true to the listener. A story with fidelity presents a "logic of good reasons," or a set of values that are taken as good reasons by the listener. Here, one judges five aspects of the narrative. First, the story is a tale of values. Second, these values are appropriate for the moral of the story, the decisions being made by characters, or the thesis communicated by the discourse. Third, the values are perceived to have positive consequences in the lives of people. Fourth, the values in the story are consistent with people's own experience. Fifth, the values are part of an ideal vision for human conduct.

Fisher uses Jonathan Shell's book *The Fate of the Earth* as an example. This book about the nuclear-weapons buildup was widely read in the early 1980s. It argued that the weapons race must stop and be reversed. Fisher states that the book was highly respected because it met the standards of coherence and fidelity. In other words, it was a well-told story that rang true to many people. It included a set of values that seemed especially relevant at that point in the history of the world. Experts refuted the book on technical grounds, but these technical arguments did not have the fidelity necessary to win public sentiment.

Because it is universal, narrative is liberating and empowering. It does not limit argumentation to those who have special skill or knowledge because everyone intuitively knows how to use and evaluate narrative. Unlike traditional argument, then, narrative is an egalitarian form. The lawyer arguing in court with traditional logic uses a kind of narrative, just as does a grandmother telling her grandchild about life during the Great Depression.

The general public will tend to evaluate arguments of all types in terms of narrative forms, making the narrative criteria of coherence and fidelity more effective in winning adherents than traditional logical criteria. This is the case because in its appeal to all the faculties, including reason, emotion, sensation, imagination, and values, narration more nearly captures the experience of the average person than does formal discourse, which is designed to appeal to a narrow range of specialized rationality. In addition, narrative ability is cultural knowledge and does not have to be learned in logic classes and law school. Finally, narration creates an identification among people and appeals to the public on an indirect, subconscious level.

For these reasons, narrative is especially powerful in public moral argument. A public moral argument deals with basic questions of good and bad, life and death, ideas about personhood, and how to live a life. It is aimed at all of society, not at small groups or individual communities. Some of the chief public moral arguments of our own time relate to abortion, the right to life, and reproductive choice; war and peace; women's rights; public education; church and state; and many others. Fisher believes that in public moral arguments, the rules of good narrative will win out over the rules of traditional argument. When expert argument is pitted against common narrative, the rhetoric of the experts will fail because it will not stand up to the coherence and fidelity expected by the public.

◖ COMMENTARY AND CRITIQUE

The theories in this chapter see communication as the thread with which the fabric of society is held together. A culture's reality is defined in terms of its meanings, which arise from interaction within social groups. Individuals' meanings for words and symbols, objects, stories, and roles are determined by the ways symbols are used to define objects and people in actual communication situations. Action, then, is a product of the meanings that arise from interaction. Figure 8.2 summarizes the basic interactional process.[38]

Social institutions are nothing more than grand networks of interaction in which common meanings are generated. The self as an object is

---

38   Charon, *Symbolic Interactionism*, p. 49.

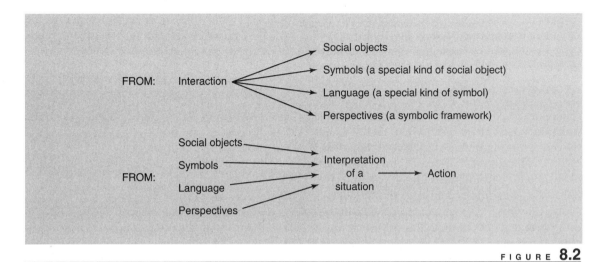

FIGURE **8.2**

Interaction to Action

especially important; the self, too, is defined in terms of symbols and meanings derived from one's interaction with other people.

As people interact in society, they perform in ways that make social life much like a drama. They act within scenes, make presentations, represent characters, and tell stories. These communication activities create, sustain, and change the very nature of reality in a group or culture.

Although many specific objections have been raised against symbolic interactionism, most can be combined into four major criticisms.[39] First, symbolic interactionism is said to be nonempirical. That is, one cannot readily translate its concepts into observable, researchable units. Second, it is said to be overly restrictive in the variables it takes into account. Critics have charged that it ignores crucial psychological variables on one end and societal variables on the other. Third, it uses concepts in an inexact, inconsistent way. Fourth, it takes a naively cooperative view of meaning. Let us look at each of these objections more closely.

The first major criticism of symbolic interactionism has broad implications. Despite Blumer's protests to the contrary, critics maintain that in actual practice the researcher does not know what to look for in observing interactionist concepts in real life. This problem seems to stem

from the vague, intuitive claims of early interactionists. What is mind, for example? How can this concept be observed? We already have noted Kuhn's failure to operationalize interactionist concepts without giving up his assumptions about the process nature of behavior. Most basically, this criticism questions the appropriateness of symbolic interactionism to lead to a more complete understanding of everyday behavior. As such, critics believe it to be more social philosophy than theory.

John Lofland's criticism is especially biting. He claims that interactionists participate in three main activities: "doctrinaire reiteration of the master's teachings, . . . [making] slightly more specific the general imagery, . . . [and connecting] descriptive case studies and interactionism."[40]

39   For reviews of specific objections to symbolic interactionism, see Michael A. Katovich and William A. Reese III, "Postmodern Thought in Symbolic Interaction: Reconstructing Social Inquiry in Light of Late-Modern Concerns," *The Sociological Quarterly* 34 (1993): 391–411. Gil Richard Musolf, "Structure, Institutions, Power, and Ideology: New Directions Within Symbolic Interactionism," *The Sociological Quarterly* 33 (1992): 171–189; Jerome G. Manis and Bernard N. Meltzer (eds.), "Appraisals of Symbolic Interactionism," *Symbolic Interaction* (Boston: Allyn & Bacon, 1978), pp. 393–440; Bernard N. Meltzer, John Petras, and Larry Reynolds, *Symbolic Interactionism: Genesis, Varieties, and Criticism* (London: Routledge & Kegan Paul, 1975); Reynolds, *Interactionism*, pp. 129–180.
40   John Lofland, "Interactionist Imagery and Analytic Interruptus," in *Human Nature and Collective Behavior*, ed. T. Shibutani (Englewood Cliffs, NJ: Prentice-Hall, 1970), p. 37.

As a result of this alleged failure, symbolic inter-actionism is not thought to be adequately heuristic, generating few testable hypotheses and little research.

Carl Couch, a leading proponent (and house critic) of the movement, points out that interactionists do engage in research but that their observations do not cast light on the theory's key concepts, making revision and elaboration difficult. Couch believes this circumstance need not be so, and his newer Iowa tradition has emerged out of a need for interactionists to do "serious sociological work."[41] Given some of the more recent work done in the area, this criticism, once valid, no longer holds. It is probably a more valid critique of early interactionism.

The second major criticism is that interactionism has either ignored or downplayed important explanatory variables. Critics say it leaves out the emotions of the individual on one end and societal organization on the other. These arguments as a whole make the case that interactionism is overly restrictive in scope. To cover as much of social life as it believes it does, interactionism must take into account social structures as well as individual feelings. Again, however, if we turn to the many theories associated with interactionist thinking, whether they go by the name symbolic interactionism or not, we find that a much wider range of concepts is included. In Chapter 9, for example, we will encounter the work of theorists who deal with such concerns as the social construction of emotions, values, and morality. We will look at the process of making accounts and enacting social life. All these topics have been well researched and are included in the interactionist tradition broadly conceived.[42]

The alleged failure of symbolic interactionism to deal with social organization is a major concern. Social organization or structure removes individual prerogative, a highly valued idea in old-style interactionism. Social structure is normally a matter of power, since some groups seem to have more influence in defining a situation than do others, but interactionists have been loath to admit this power inequality. However, the concept of power can be investigated from an interactionist perspective, and several research programs have begun to look at power.[43] Again, current interactionists have taken this criticism seriously and have done a great deal of work to show the relevance of symbolic interactionism (SI) to social structure and the production of power. Much of this work has been by merging SI with cultural studies, a critical research tradition discussed in Chapter 11.[44]

The third general criticism of symbolic interactionism is that its concepts are not used consistently. As a result such concepts as *I, me, self, role*, and others are vague. However, we must keep in mind that symbolic interactionism is not a unified theory. Rather, it is a general framework, and as we have seen, it has different versions. Therefore, although this is a valid criticism of early interactionism, it is not a fair picture of the movement today.

One inconsistency that persists in most versions of symbolic interactionism involves the problem of determinism. Most mainstream interactionists clearly teach that individuals and groups have the capacity to seek goals, to define situations in new ways, and to change. Yet the idea of the social genesis of meaning creates a kind of determinism. In other words, if the group creates meaning through interaction, the individual has little choice but to see the world in predetermined ways. Mead tried to handle this difficulty with the concept of the *I*, but this is a vague, mystical, and ill-defined concept.

41   Carl Couch, "Symbolic Interaction and Generic Sociological Principles" (paper presented at the Symposium on Symbolic Interaction, Boston, 1979).

42   Actually, much has been done in this area. See, for example, Thomas J. Scheff, *Microsociology: Discourse, Emotion, and Social Structure* (Chicago: University of Chicago Press, 1990); for a summary of work on emotion, see Bernard N. Meltzer and Nancy J. Herman, "Epilogue: Human Emotions, Social Structure, and Symbolic Interactionism," in *Interactionism: Exposition and Critique*, ed. Larry T. Reynolds (Dix Hills, NY: General Hall, 1990), pp. 181–225.

43   This line of work is discussed in Peter M. Hall, "Structuring Symbolic Interaction: Communication and Power," in *Communication Yearbook 4*, ed. D. Nimmo (New Brunswick, NJ: Transaction, 1980), pp. 49–60.

44   For a summary of this work, see Musolf, "Structure, Institutions, Power, and Ideology"; and Norman K. Denzin, *Symbolic Interactionism and Cultural Studies: The Politics of Interpretation* (Oxford: Blackwell, 1992); Michal M. McCall and Howard S. Becker, *Symbolic Interaction and Cultural Studies* (Chicago: University of Chicago Press, 1990); Meltzer and Herman, "Epilogue."

The question that plagues interactionism today is how people can act in accord with personal goals yet be affected by meanings that have been established through a history of interaction. Perhaps the most serious and credible answer to this problem has been forwarded by Anthony Giddens, who shows how action results in unintended consequences that return to constrain future action.[45] Many believe that Giddens has successfully reconciled structural, deterministic approaches with interactionist ones in a unified theory of social life. Giddens's theory is covered in more detail in Chapter 13.

The fourth objection to symbolic interactionism is its naive reliance on a basically cooperative view of meaning and self.[46] The problem here is that in classical symbolic interactionism, meanings, including the concept of the self, just sort of emerge effortlessly from interaction, and social life is essentially a cooperative endeavor. Yet critical theorists show that powerful groups often reflect views of certain persons in ways that are harmful and demeaning. How we see ourselves is not always defined by these negative views, and in fact, people often define themselves by opposing what others say about them. In other words, our conceptions of self often emerge from conflict and manipulation, not cooperation.

Indeed, theorists like Goffman say that people often manipulate situations in a variety of ways to present views of self that may be in opposition to customary ways of seeing things. This is possible because no one image of self emerges from a lifetime of interaction. Because we can define the self in so many ways, we can define ourselves in a variety of antithetical ways.

This view has not been lost on interactionists. In fact, interactionists themselves have done much to broaden the view of self, meaning, and action in social life.

The critical response to dramatism and narrative has been copious and spirited, and it is not possible to review all of these viewpoints.[47] Gronbeck summarizes the critique against dramaturgy.[48] Dramatism is not a unified theory. It still remains basically an "interest group" or coa-

lition of theories that share a metaphor rather than any particular set of theoretical terms or principles. The theories chosen for this chapter illustrate this lack of coherence in the movement.

Burke's is the grandest and perhaps the most elaborate of the four theories covered here. This breadth and complexity has elicited both praise and blame. Some believe that it has opened vistas of great import; others believe that Burke's lack of focus has led to interminable confusion, if not exhaustion. For example, John Stewart addresses Burke's apparent confusion in regard to the symbol model.[49]

Stewart's thesis is that we cannot separate symbols from things, but that reality itself may by the use of language in everyday communication. According to Stewart, Burke is ambivalent on this issue. He seems to acknowledge the importance of language in the construction of reality, yet his works are filled with the idea that symbols somehow represent a world apart. This is an interesting point because Burke has been so often identified with symbolic interactionism, which itself opposes the very symbol model that Stewart finds indefensible.

As another recent example, James Chesebro has argued that Burke's system is overly limited and needs revision to remain fresh in today's multicultural thinking.[50] Specifically, he worries

---

45 See, for example, Anthony Giddens, *New Rules of Sociological Method* (New York: Basic, 1976).
46 This view is explored in some depth by Katovich and Reese, "Postmodern Thought."
47 For a summary of criticisms of Burke, see Foss, Foss, and Trapp, *Contemporary Perspectives*, pp. 199–203. For criticism of Goffman, see Stephen W. Littlejohn, *Theories of Human Communication*, 2nd ed. (Belmont, CA: Wadsworth, 1983), pp. 180–181; and Randall Collins, "Erving Goffman and the Development of Modern Social Theory," in *The View from Goffman*, ed. J. Ditton (New York: St. Martin's, 1980), pp. 170–209. For criticism of Bormann, see Bormann, "Fantasy and Rhetorical Vision: Ten Years Later," and G. P. Mohrmann, "An Essay on Fantasy Theme Criticism," *Quarterly Journal of Speech* 68 (1982): 109–132. A critique and response to Fisher's work are Robert C. Rowland, "On Limiting the Narrative Paradigm: Three Case Studies," *Communication Monographs* 56 (1989): 39–54; and Walter R. Fisher, "Clarifying the Narrative Paradigm," *Communication Monographs* 56 (1989): 55–58.
48 Gronbeck, "Dramaturgical Theory."
49 John Stewart, *Language as Articulate Contact* (Albany: SUNY Press, 1995), pp. 197–228.
50 James W. Chesebro, "Extending the Burkeian System: A Response to Tompkins and Cheney," *Quarterly Journal of Speech* 80 (1994): 83–90.

that Burke offers a rather single-minded model for viewing human knowledge, a model that is inappropriately reliant on language and inappropriate for many cultures.

Of the four theories covered here, Goffman's ideas are perhaps least theoretical in that they are scattered and hard to assemble into a single rubric. His numerous writings are insightful and interesting but hard to integrate. He rarely uses the same vocabulary twice and, until the end of his career, seemed more interested in pointing out idiosyncratic observations than in making a general statement. Fortunately, his final work *Frame Analysis* provides an overall scheme that can be used to integrate a lifetime of work.

Bormann's theory is perhaps the most clearly focused of the dramaturgical and narrative theories presented in this chapter. It, too, has received both praise and blame. Bormann and his associates also put a good deal of work into clarifying and elaborating the vocabulary of fantasy-theme analysis. Bormann's work—and that of his critics and adherents—fulfills one of Gronbeck's suggestions: that the field of communication elaborate, clarify, and develop the concepts and terms of narrative.

The narrative paradigm has been useful. Indeed, telling stories and sharing rhetorical visions is a common, perhaps universal, human activity. The function of stories in communication and persuasion is therefore a significant area of study. Both Bormann and Fisher advance our knowledge of narrative by suggesting some of the elements of this dimension of communica-

tion. Both have proved useful in the actual examination of discourse.

Considerable controversy still exists about the place of narrative in communication. Critiques of symbolic convergence theory, for example, have been wide ranging. The theory has been criticized for failure to clarify basic assumptions; the inappropriateness of applying a small-group phenomenon to public, mass audiences; overreliance on the subjective observations of the researcher rather than the categories of the theory; and the theory's lack of a fresh perspective. These objections, of course, have not gone unanswered, and Bormann and his colleagues have responded that much of this criticism is polemical and unsubstantiated.[51]

Fisher's narrative paradigm has been criticized in similar ways. Robert Rowland, for example, has suggested that although narrative is a powerful dimension of much communication, it cannot be said to characterize all communication.[52] Fisher answers that his brand of narrative indeed underlies all communication and is especially important in persuasion.[53] For Fisher, narrative is more a dimension than a type of communication.

In the following chapter, we extend this discussion by pursuing the social construction of reality and cultural variations of meaning.

---

51   Ernest G. Bormann, John F. Cragan, and Donald C. Shields, "In Defense of Symbolic Convergence Theory: A Look at the Theory and Its Criticisms After Two Decades," *Communication Theory* 4 (1994): 259–294.
52   Rowland, "On Limiting the Narrative Paradigm."
53   Fisher, "Clarifying the Narrative Paradigm."

CHAPTER 9

THEORIES OF SOCIAL AND CULTURAL REALITY

Interactionist approaches to communication theory address the ways our understandings, meanings, norms, roles, and rules are worked out interactively in communication.[1] In the previous chapter, we looked at some foundational work in this area. We continue this discussion here by exploring the interactional worlds in which people live. This work as a group can be called the social approach to communication.[2] We begin our tour of this material with theories of the *social construction of reality*, an important intellectual tradition of our century.

THE SOCIAL CONSTRUCTION OF REALITY

The idea of the "social construction of reality" was expressed by philosopher Alfred Schutz in these words:

> The world of my daily life is by no means my private world but is from the outset an

intersubjective one, shared with my fellow men, experienced and interpreted by others: in brief, it is a world common to all of us. The unique biographical situation in which I find myself within the world at any moment of my existence is only to a very small extent of my own making.[3]

Our meanings and understandings, in short, arise from our communication with others, a notion of reality deeply embedded in sociological thought. Its best-known proponents are Peter

---

1   Much of this theory is based on the work of American pragmatism, especially the work of Dewey and Mead. For a philosophical discussion, see Vernon Cronen and Peter Lang, "Language and Action: Wittgenstein and Dewey in the Practice of Therapy and Consultation," *Human Systems: The Journal of Systemic Consultation and Management* 5 (1994): 5–43. For a discussion of the ideas of Wittgenstein in regard to the social construction of meaning, see John Shotter, "Before Theory and After Representationalism: Understanding Meaning 'From Within' a Dialogue Process," in *Beyond the Symbol Model: Reflections on the Representational Nature of Language*, ed. John Stewart (Albany: SUNY Press, 1996), pp. 103–134.
2   For a good general discussion of this school of thought, see Wendy Leeds-Hurwitz (ed.), *Social Approaches to Communication* (New York: Guilford, 1995). See also the forum "Social Approaches to Interpersonal Communication," *Communication Theory* 2 (1992): 131–172, 329–359.
3   Alfred Schutz, *On Phenomenology and Social Relations* (Chicago: University of Chicago Press, 1970), p. 163.

Berger and Thomas Luckmann in their treatise *The Social Construction of Reality.*[4] With the impetus from symbolic interactionism and the foundations of the work of Schutz and Berger and Luckmann, the social construction of reality has become a respectable and popular idea in the social sciences. Kenneth Gergen has labeled it the *social constructionist movement.*[5]

The basic idea of social construction can be illustrated in an interesting classroom exercise. Each student produces an object. The objects are put on a table in front of the class, and someone is then asked to sort them. This is easy to do. One might, for example, put wooden articles in one group, metal ones in another, cloth in another, and plastic in a fourth pile. Another student is then asked to sort the objects again. Someone else is asked to do it a third time. The objects are sorted again and again, each time in a different way. They might be sorted by size, use, color, number of parts, things you would or would not give a child, or things that could be used as a weapon and things that could not.

There is a seemingly endless number of ways to understand each object. You can see that our language gives us labels that we use to distinguish objects in our world.[6] How we understand objects and how we behave toward them depend in large measure on the social reality in force.

Like all movements, social constructionism is not entirely consistent and has various versions.[7] Most, however, share a set of assumptions. Robyn Penman summarizes these as follows:[8]

1. *Communicative action is voluntary.* Like the symbolic interactionists, most constructionists see that communicators make choices. This does not mean that people have free choice. Indeed, the social environment does constrain what can be and is done. Within a social group, people have the latitude to act in a variety of ways, but they are also prevented by meanings, moral orders, roles, and rules from unbridled action.
2. *Knowledge is a social product.* Knowledge is not something that is discovered objectively but is "achieved" through interaction with others in particular times and places. Language and

how it is used are particularly powerful in determining meanings and influencing action.

3. *Knowledge is contextual.* Our meanings for events derive from interaction in particular times and places, in a particular social milieu. Our understandings of events change as times change, and each of us understands our experience in a variety of ways, depending on the context in which we are working.
4. *Theories create worlds.* Theories, and scholarly and research activity in general, are not objective tools for the discovery of truth, but contribute to the creation of knowledge. Scholarship, which itself is a social activity, has an effect on what is being observed and how experience is understood.
5. *Scholarship is value laden.* What we "see" in an investigation, or what we explain in a theory of communication, is always affected by the values embedded in the approach used.

Traditionally, communication has been treated as a category different from other categories. Some things were considered to be commu-

---

4   Peter L. Berger and Thomas Luckmann, *The Social Construction of Reality: A Treatise in the Sociology of Knowledge* (New York: Doubleday, 1966).
5   Kenneth J. Gergen, "The Social Constructionist Movement in Modern Psychology," *American Psychologist* 40 (1985): 266–275; see also *Toward Transformation in Social Knowledge* (New York: Springer-Verlag, 1982). See also the special section on social constructionism in, Stanley Deetz (ed.), *Communication Yearbook 17* (Thousand Oaks, CA: Sage, 1994), pp. 3–300; Vivien Burr, *Introduction to Social Constructionism* (London: Routledge, 1995).
6   For a thorough discussion of the role of language in the construction of reality, see John Stewart, *Language as Articulate Contact: Toward a Post-Semiotic Philosophy of Communication* (Albany: SUNY Press, 1995). For a brief version, see John Stewart, "The Symbol Model vs. Language as Constitutive Articulate Contact," in *Beyond the Symbol Model: Reflections on the Representational Nature of Language,* ed. John Stewart (Albany: SUNY Press, 1996), pp. 9–68.
7   For a good description of the intellectual traditions and various versions of constructionism, see W. Barnett Pearce, "A Sailing Guide for Social Constructionists," in *Social Approaches to Communication,* ed. Wendy Leeds-Hurwitz (New York: Guilford, 1995), pp. 88–113; Klaus Krippendorff, "The Past of Communication's Hoped-for Future," *Journal of Communication* 43 (1993): 34–44; W. Barnett Pearce, "A 'Camper's Guide' to Constructionisms," *Human Systems: The Journal of Systemic Consultation and Management* 3 (1992): 139–161.
8   Robyn Penman, "Good Theory and Good Practice: An Argument in Progress," *Communication Theory* 2 (1992): 234–250. For another account, see John Shotter and Kenneth J. Gergen, "Social Construction: Knowledge, Self, Others, and Continuing the Conversation," in *Communication Yearbook 17,* ed. Stanley Deetz (Thousand Oaks, CA: Sage, 1994), pp. 3–33.

nication, and some things were not. *Communication* is not the same thing as *houses, horses,* and *hoops.* It is different from *eating, earning,* and *eloping.* Indeed, the field of communication is usually seen as distinct from other disciplines like physics, forestry, and geography.

With the advent of social constructionism, however, we can view communication differently—as a "perspective" rather than a "subject matter."[9] Because communication is the process by which all reality is constructed, it is involved in all things and separate from none. If we view communication as a perspective, we can no longer make the distinction between "communication" and "noncommunication," though we might distinguish between "the communication perspective" and "other perspectives."

What then is the *communication perspective?* W. Barnett Pearce has developed this idea in some depth in his book *Communication and the Human Condition.*[10] According to Pearce, a perspective is a way of looking at or thinking about something, and he sets out to establish *how* one would look at or think about things from the communication perspective.

In brief, whenever you look at something in terms of how it is constructed in interaction among people, you are taking a communication perspective, an idea firmly planted in the social constructionist tradition. For example, architecture is a form of expression in which designers, builders, and users make a certain social world. The cultures of the world differ substantially in how they express their values and beliefs through the kinds of buildings and homes they make. Clothing is another example. We use clothing to "say" things about ourselves. Even something as mundane as the lowly sidewalk makes a statement. Is the sidewalk wide and spacious, narrow and crowded, or cluttered with market carts and booths? How do people use sidewalks, and how do they evolve within a city?

Virtually any aspect of human experience can be viewed from the perspective of how it is made and used in the social construction of reality. Figure 9.1 from Pearce's book shows what we look at and think about when we are using the communication perspective.[11]

The term *resources,* at the top of the figure, is used to designate all of the building blocks we work with in life. Resources include ideas, values, stories, symbols, meanings, institutions, and anything else used to build a reality. These are shared with others and constructed jointly through interaction in society. *Practices,* the term at the bottom of the figure, designates what is done or performed. Practices are behaviors, actions, and forms of expression.

The point of Figure 9.1 is that resources and practices are tightly connected and cannot really be separated. Resources are constructed in practice, and practice is shaped by resources. This is the recursive loop of resources and practices, shown by the outer arrows.

In the inner loops, we see that resources and practices are connected through persons, which refers to persons-in-interaction-with-one-another. When people interact, they construct new resources or reaffirm old ones, and the interaction among people is itself shaped by resources.

The communication perspective, then, is a way of thinking about experience in which this resource–practice loop is observed, studied, and taken into account. You can illustrate this idea to yourself by thinking of any experience that is important to you. Let's say, for example, that you love skiing. How would you look at this sport from the communication perspective?

Skiing is a social world, a world of places, times of the year, equipment, abilities, habits, terms, attitudes, skills, and methods. People approach skiing with a host of resources, including ideas about what it is, views about the best equipment to use and places to go, how to get there, and how to organize the ski day. But these are not isolated pieces of knowledge; they are constantly reinforced by action. What you "know" about skiing and what you "do" about it are tightly connected. And it is always social, affected by interaction with others. When you realize this and

9   Stanley Deetz, "Future of the Discipline: The Challenges, the Research, and the Social Contribution," in *Communication Yearbook 17,* ed. Stanley Deetz (Thousand Oaks, CA: Sage, 1994), pp. 565–600.
10   W. Barnett Pearce, *Communication and the Human Condition* (Carbondale: Southern Illinois University Press, 1989).
11   Pearce, *Communication and the Human Condition,* p. 24.

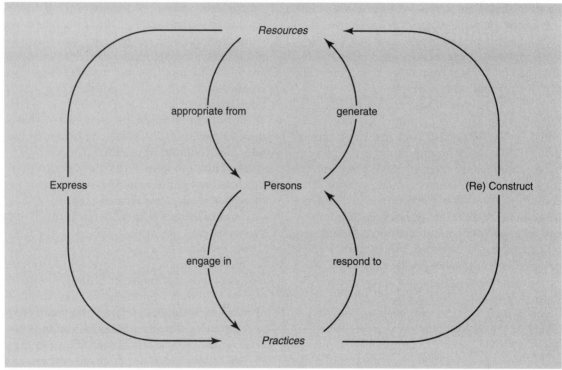

FIGURE **9.1**

The Communication Perspective

begin to take it seriously, you are using the communication perspective.

Even the "hard sciences" can be understood from the communication perspective. Any object in the natural world, from atoms to elk, is always understood from within a social world. Scientists jointly invent ways of looking at natural objects; together they create a vocabulary or set of terms to use: They attend conferences and share ideas; they write articles and books read by others; they share and debate the values of studying certain things and set priorities about what is most important to study; they debate the validity of one another's findings; and they appeal to outside agencies and the general public for support. All of these social practices shape the scientists' way of understanding the objects of their study. So even rocks, rockets, and red tides can be viewed from the communication perspective.

One of the most interesting "objects" of meaning in human life is the self, a topic to which we now turn.

The Social Construction of Self

Among contemporary social scientists who have made constructionist assumptions central to their work is Rom Harré. Recognizing that self is both individual and social, Harré emphasizes the ways individuals account for and explain their own behavior in particular episodes.

Harré and his colleague Paul Secord are responsible for *ethogeny*—the study of how people understand their actions within a predictable sequence of acts, called *episodes*.[12] An episode is an

12   Rom Harré and Paul Secord, *The Explanation of Social Behavior* (Totowa, NJ: Littlefield, Adams, 1972).

event with a beginning and an end that all participants would identify as such. Having dinner, making a speech, holding a commencement ceremony, having an argument, driving to work, and negotiating an agreement are episodes. Ethogeny involves the meaning of the episode and how participants understand the various acts in it. Further, the ordinary language that people use to describe and explain an episode reflects their meaning for it.

The social group or community, through interaction, creates "theories" to explain their experience of reality.[13] A group's theory characterizes an episode and predicts the logical outcome of actions within it. These "theories" are *structured templates* of the course of action anticipated in the episode. For example, two people who say they are "in love" have a theory of what love is and how it should be acted out, which becomes evident when the lovers are required to describe, explain, or account for their actions.

The meanings attached to the events of an episode give rise to rules that guide the participants' actions within the episode. Participants know how to act because of the rules in force at a particular moment. For instance, our hypothetical couple may engage in the episode of "making love," which consists of a series of acts with a beginning and an end, which have meaning and an anticipated course. The episode of making love will be different for other couples, who have their own definitions of what it means to make love and the action sequence required. The concept of rules is especially important in constructionist thought; we'll return to this subject later in the chapter.

The concept of *self*, which is so important in symbolic interactionism (Chapter 8), has been the chief concern of Harré in most of his theoretical work.[14] Harré says that like any other experience, the self is structured by a personal theory. That is, you learn to understand yourself by employing a theory that defines it. This may seem odd, but there is an important difference between a "self" and a "person."

For Harré, the *person* is a publicly visible being that is characterized by certain attributes and characteristics established within a culture or social group. For example, people in most European American cultures are viewed as autonomous beings that make choices to achieve goals. Not all cultures view people in this way.

The *self*, in contrast to the person, is your private notion of your own unity as a person. Personhood is *public*, whereas the self, though you may share it with others, is ultimately *private*. The character of persons is governed by your culture's theory of personhood; your self is governed by your theory of your own being as one member of the culture.

Personal being is thus two-sided, consisting of a social being (person) and a personal being (self). For example, many traditional cultures conceptualize the person as the embodiment of a role (such as mother, father, priest, worker). People in general are seen as manifestations of these roles. A single person, on the other hand, will assign a particular nature, feeling, and character to the self, as an individual within a role: "I am the father of Zuk and a field-worker. I am a good father and worker."

Your self theory is learned through a history of interaction with other people. All our thoughts, intentions, and emotions are cast in terms learned through social interaction. The range of possible "selves" is highly variable from one culture to another because the social realities of cultures are different from one to another.

For instance, most Western industrialized cultures stress theories of self that emphasize whole, undivided, and independent persons. The Javanese, in contrast, see themselves as being two independent parts—an inside of feelings and an outside of observed behaviors. Moroccans have yet another theory of self, as embodiments of places and situations, and their identities are always tied to these situations.[15]

---

13   Rom Harré, *Social Being: A Theory for Social Psychology* (Totowa, NJ: Rowman & Littlefield, 1979).

14   Harré, *Social Being;* see also *Personal Being: A Theory for Individual Psychology* (Cambridge, MA: Harvard University Press, 1984).

15   Clifford Geertz, *Local Knowledge: Further Essays in Interpretive Anthropology* (New York: Basic, 1983), p. 60.

The self consists of a set of elements that can be viewed spatially along three dimensions. The first dimension is *display*—whether an aspect of the self is displayed publicly or remains private. For example, you might define "emotions" as private and "personality" as public. In other cultures, "emotions" might be defined as quite public.

The second dimension is *realization,* or source—the degree to which some feature of the self is believed to come from within the individual or a group. Elements of a self that are believed to come from the person are *individually realized,* whereas those elements believed to derive from the person's relationship to the group are *collectively realized.* For instance, a self theory might treat "purpose" as individually realized because it seems to be something that individuals have on their own. On the other hand, "co-operation" may be collectively realized because it seems to be something that one can only do as a member of a group.

The third dimension—*agency*—is the degree of active power attributed to the self. *Active* elements (like "speaking" or "driving") are contrasted with *passive* elements (like "listening" or "riding"). One person's self may differ from another's because the various aspects of self such as emotion, personality, purpose, and cooperation are defined differently within the three-dimensional scheme. For example, people of Anglo-Saxon descent tend to treat emotions as privately displayed, individually realized, and passive. In other words, they feel that emotions just happen to them and are within them. Many southern Europeans on the other hand see emotions as public, collective, and active. In other words, they believe that emotions are something they create as a group and display together.

All self theories have three elements in common. First, they all contain a sense of *self-consciousness.* This means that one thinks of oneself as an object. When you think about yourself or talk about yourself, you are displaying consciousness of yourself. There are, then, two senses of the word *I*—the self that "knows" and the self that is "known about." Consider the fol-

lowing statement: "I_1 know that I_2 am afraid." I_1 reflects the sense of being aware, and I_2 reflects the sense of being the object of fear.

An important part of our conception of self is the consistency with which we define and practice I_1 and I_2. Harré calls this the *double singularity principle.*[16] A group's idea of self must treat each *I* as a consistent unity. You must possess a continual awareness of yourself as a unified being, and if you don't, you will be judged "abnormal" or "mentally ill." In other words, you must always see yourself as you. You must also have a sense of coherence or consistency among your various self attributions, making coherent sense out of your experience. The failure to do so will create a problem for you and others. Hypocrisy, for example, is seen as an incoherent and immoral state of saying one thing and doing another.

The first aspect of self, then, is self-consciousness. The other two aspects are *agency* and *autobiography.* The self is always seen as having certain powers to do things. People see themselves as agents, capable of having intentions and actions. *Autobiography* is a sense of having a history and a future. Your agency is evident whenever you plan something, and your autobiography is apparent whenever you tell someone about yourself.

Harré uses the Eskimo as an example of the construction of self.[17] The Eskimo self is viewed in a network of relations with others. An Eskimo may have private feelings, but these are generally considered unimportant. Important matters related to self are usually defined in terms of relationships with others. In English we would say, "I hear him." The Eskimo equivalent would be something like, "He is making a sound with reference to me." Both positive and negative emotions are considered public displays rather than private feelings.

Visitors sometimes observe that Eskimos tend to display emotions as a group. For example,

---

16   Rom Harré, "Is There Still a Problem About the Self?" in *Communication Yearbook 17,* ed. Stanley Deetz (Thousand Oaks, CA: Sage, 1994), pp. 55–73.
17   Harré, *Personal Being,* p. 87.

they all laugh together or they all cry together. Most Eskimo virtues are social in that they are necessary for the preservation of the community as a whole. Eskimo art illustrates this quality as well. Eskimos do not have a concept for individual creativity but believe they are merely releasing something already present in the material. When they carve a log, for example, the resulting figure is seen as being revealed by the log and not something created by the carver.

The Social Construction of Emotion

We usually do not think of emotions as "constructed," yet they can be considered so. Harré suggests that emotions are constructed concepts, like any other aspect of human experience, because they are determined by the local language and moral orders of the culture or social group.[18]

One of the scholars best known for work on the social construction of emotions is James Averill.[19] According to Averill, emotions are belief systems that guide one's definition of the situation. As such, emotions consist of internalized social norms and rules governing feelings. These norms and rules tell us how to define and respond to emotions. Emotions do have a physiological component, but identifying and labeling bodily feelings are learned socially within a culture. In other words, the ability to make sense of emotions is socially constructed.

Averill calls emotions *syndromes*, which are clusters or sets of responses that go together. No single response is sufficient by itself to define an emotion, but all must be viewed together. Emotional syndromes are socially constructed because people learn through interaction what particular clusters of behavior should be taken to mean and how to perform a particular emotion. Emotions are acted out in specific ways, and we learn these "roles" from communication. What does grief look like? It looks different in various societies. People must learn how to recognize and carry out the role of the grieving person, or the angry person, or the jealous person.

Each experience of an emotion has an *object*, which is where the emotion is directed, and each emotion has a limited range of possible objects. When you are angry, you are angry at someone. When you are envious, you have envy about some achievement or possession. When you grieve, you grieve some loss. As Averill points out, you cannot be proud of the stars because pride is something reserved for accomplishment. You may say that you "love" your new car, but you cannot really be "in love" with it. Nor can you say that someone's angry attack on you makes you feel jealous.

How an emotion is labeled, what it is called, is instrumental in how the emotion is experienced. You may have very different meanings for the same physiological response depending on whether you call it "anger" or "fear." You experience an emotion one way when you call it "jealousy" and quite another when you call it "loneliness." We have rules for what anger, fear, jealousy, and loneliness are, and we have rules for how to respond to these feelings, rules constructed in social interaction throughout a lifetime.

Four kinds of rules govern emotions. *Rules of appraisal* tell you what an emotion is, where it is directed, and whether it is positive or negative. *Rules of behavior* tell you how to respond to the feeling—whether to hide it, to express it in private, or to vent it publicly. *Rules of prognosis* define the progression and course of the emotion. How long should it last, what are its different stages, how does it begin, and how does it end? *Rules of attribution* dictate how an emotion should be explained or justified. What do you tell others about it? How do you express it publicly?

If you were angry at another person, your rules of appraisal would tell you what you were

18   Rom Harré (ed.), "An Outline of the Social Constructionist Viewpoint," in *The Social Construction of Emotions* (New York: Blackwell, 1986), pp. 2–14.
19   Among Averill's most pertinent writings in this line of work are "A Constructivist View of Emotion," in *Theories of Emotion*, eds. K. Plutchik and H. Kellerman (New York: Academic, 1980), pp. 305–339; "On the Paucity of Positive Emotions," in *Assessment and Modification of Emotional Behavior*, eds. K. R. Blankstein, P. Pliner, and J. Polivy (New York: Plenum, 1980), pp. 7–45; *Anger and Aggression: An Essay on Emotion* (New York: Springer-Verlag, 1982); "The Acquisition of Emotions During Adulthood," in *The Social Construction of Emotions*, ed. Rom Harré (New York: Blackwell, 1986), pp. 98–119.

feeling and who the target of the feeling was. These rules would also define whether that anger was positive (like righteous indignation) or negative (rage). Behavior rules would guide your behavior, including how to express the anger, whether to lash out or remain quiet, whether to aggress or retreat. Prognosis rules would guide how long the anger episode should last and the different phases through which it might pass. Finally, the rules of attribution would help you explain the anger ("She was acting like a jerk and made me mad").

Thus, emotions are not just things in themselves. They are defined and handled according to what has been learned in social interaction with other people. We learn emotional rules in childhood and throughout life. Averill is clear that people can and do change emotionally. When you enter a new life situation, you are exposed to new ways of understanding emotion, and your feelings, their expression, and the ways you manage those emotions change.

Averill conducted an interesting study in which he isolated over five hundred terms for various emotions, a list that was representative of emotional terms in the English language.[20] His subjects then rated these terms on a number of dimensions, including evaluation (for example, pleasant-unpleasant). He found that far more emotional terms were evaluated as negative (such as anger, jealousy) than positive (for instance, joy, happiness). This is an interesting puzzle: Why do negative emotions outweigh positive ones by about two to one?

The answer is that emotions do not come prepackaged as positive or negative, but we define them that way based on our social constructions. In Averill's sample, positive outcomes tend to be action-oriented, whereas negative results tend to be seen as beyond one's control. So, for example, courage is the result of one's brave actions, whereas jealousy is the consequence of an unfortunate situation.

Further, emotions in general tend to be viewed in our society as beyond control, something that just happens to us. So it is logical that positive outcomes are defined less as emotions

and more as actions, whereas negative outcomes are more often seen as emotions, which leads to the idea that emotional terms are more often negative than positive. In other cultures the outcome might be quite different.

For example, the Ifaluk of Micronesia have an emotion called *song*, or justifiable anger.[21] Actually, the Ifaluk experience several forms of anger, including that which accompanies sickness, that which builds up slowly from several bothersome irritations, that which is experienced when relatives do not live up to expectations, and that which is caused by personal misfortune. Clearly, in this culture, anger is not just anger; the various types are sharply distinguished, and *song*, or righteous indignation, is the only form approved of.

Further, justifiable anger among the Ifaluk occurs in a highly predictable pattern. A rule must be violated, and someone must point out that this occurred. The person who witnessed the violation must condemn the act, and the one who did it must react to this condemnation with fear, promising not to do it again.

Accounts in Social Construction

One of the ways people construct social realities is by making accounts, or explaining and justifying their behavior.[22] For example, if you forgot your mother's birthday, you would have some explaining to do. You might say that you were busy at school and forgot, which reinforces the idea that being productive is good; or that you lost your calendar, which suggests that record

20 Averill, "On the Paucity of Positive Emotions."
21 Catherine Lutz, "Morality, Domination, and Understandings of 'Justifiable Anger' Among the Ifaluk," in *Everyday Understanding: Social and Scientific Implications,* eds. Gün R. Semin and Kenneth J. Gergen (London: Sage, 1990), pp. 204–226.
22 For a classification of accounts, see Margaret L. McLaughlin, Michael J. Cody, and Nancy E. Rosenstein, "Account Sequences in Conversations Between Strangers," *Communication Monographs* 50 (1983): 102–125; Margaret L. McLaughlin, Michael J. Cody, and H. Dan O'Hair, "The Management of Failure Events: Some Contextual Determinants of Accounting Behavior," *Human Communication Research* 9 (1983): 208–224. For a longer, more diverse treatment, see Margaret L. McLaughlin, Michael J. Cody, and Stephen Read (eds.), *Explaining One's Self to Others: Reason-Giving in a Social Context* (Hillsdale, NJ: Erlbaum, 1992).

keeping is important; or that you have no excuse and are sorry, which says that family relationships should not be ignored. No matter what you say, you are reconstructing some aspect of the social reality in force at the time you make the account.

John Shotter provides a useful extension of constructionist thinking into the subjects of responsibility and morality.[23] Shotter believes that human experience cannot be separated from communication. Our speech both reflects and creates our experience of reality. Central to this link between communication and experience is the process of making accounts.

In everyday conversation the "I" cannot be separated from the "you," because the speaker (I) and the listener (you) go back and forth. So in a conversation, people are making demands on one another. They are telling others how to behave and what to think, and the morality of everyday life is constructed in this process.[24]

Communicators believe they have the power to act, yet they may feel somewhat constrained by rules of action. Rules may be followed or broken, but people are at least expected to explain their actions on the basis of rules or exceptions to those rules. Because of the presence of rules and our personal powers to follow or break them, we must think through and plan our actions, and these plans are largely framed in light of what we would have to say to explain what we did. Think about it: When you undertake an action, you often consider ahead of time what you would say if you had to explain that action to others. In other words, potential accounts actually help shape your actions before they occur.

Like other constructionists Shotter believes that people are constantly assigning meaning to and making sense of their experiences. The meanings assigned to an event are closely tied to the language used to account for the event in communication among participants. Richard Buttny suggests that in any kind of failure event the participants have an interest in controlling the meaning for that event.[25] Accounts serve precisely this function. They are a way of accomplishing goals, such as saving face and preserving relationships. Buttny says that accounts essentially reframe events by creating a context in which to interpret those events.

Buttny presents the example of a student–teacher conference about a speech assignment.[26] The teacher confronts the student on a poor performance, and the student offers an excuse: "It was a bad day, I just, ah, blew a math test before it, so I didn't really feel like speaking." Here, the student is trying to create the context of a bad day, in which it is okay to do poorly. By giving an account, the student attempts to control the meaning of the situation.

Shotter shows that the relationship between communication (talking and making accounts) and the experience of reality constitutes a loop: Communication determines how reality is experienced, and the experience of reality affects communication. Figure 9.2 illustrates this relationship.[27]

Let's return to the birthday example. Birthdays are an ordinary activity in most Western cultures, and we have a number of forms of talk relevant to this event, including certain kinds of accounts. The standard birthday card that apologizes in an amusing way for forgetting a birthday or being late is a good example of institutionalized accounting. These forms of talk in turn contribute to certain ideas we have about the importance of individuals and their lives. They also address our cultural theories of personal responsibility and interpersonal relations. (You better remember Mom's birthday, or she will think you don't care about her.) When you acknowledge a person's birthday, you are reinforcing the idea that individuals are important in our society, which is certainly an important part of our culture's theory of personhood. Those theories in

23   John Shotter, *Social Accountability and Selfhood* (Oxford: Blackwell, 1984).
24   This argument is developed in John Shotter, "Social Accountability and the Social Construction of 'You,'" in *Texts of Identity*, eds. J. Shotter and K. J. Gergen (London: Sage, 1989), pp. 133–151.
25   Richard Buttny, "Accounts as a Reconstruction of an Event's Context," *Communication Monographs* 52 (1985): 57–77. See also "Sequence and Structure in Accounts Episodes," *Communication Quarterly* 35 (1987): 67–83.
26   Buttny, "Accounts."
27   Shotter, *Social Accountability*, p. 140.

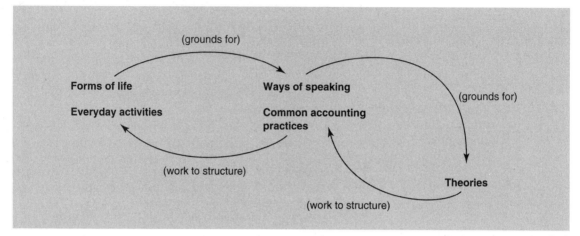

FIGURE **9.2**

Communication–Experience Loop

Adapted from *Social Accountability and Selfhood* by John Shotter. Copyright © 1984 by Basil Blackwell Publishers. Reprinted by permission of the publisher.

turn affect how we talk, including the forms of speech used in birthday celebrations.

Much like Harré, Shotter believes that the individual and the society are inseparable. Persons are not independent: "Attention is not concentrated upon the supposed relation between people's 'outer' behavior and their 'inner' workings, for it is not focused upon individuals at all, but upon the relations between people."[28] The overall milieu is essentially a moral world of rights, duties, privileges, and obligations. The moral framework of human experience is expressed in and through communication: "To preserve their autonomy, people must be able to account, not only for their actions, but also for themselves, i.e. who and what they are."[29]

RULES AND SOCIAL ACTION

Rules are an important part of social and cultural reality. Not only are they formed in the process of interaction, but they also govern interaction itself. We discussed rules at some length in Chapter 5. There, rules were defined as guidelines for action and meaning. Let's continue this discussion of rules.

Shimanoff's Rule-Governing Approach

Susan Shimanoff surveyed the literature on rules and formulated an overview that incorporates what she judges to be the best thinking in the field.[30] Her work is integrative and critically analyzes the divergent literature. Shimanoff defines a rule as "a followable prescription that indicates what behavior is obligated, preferred, or prohibited in certain contexts."[31] This definition incorporates the following four elements.

1. *Rules must be followable.* Actors can choose whether to follow or violate a rule. If a person has no choice in a course of action, then a "rule" is not being "followed." The laws of nature are not "followed" because there is no choice. Similarly, you are not following a rule by running out of a burning building. On the other hand, rules must deal with the possible. One cannot follow an impossible rule such as visiting your parents every weekend when they live 500 miles away.

28   Shotter, *Social Accountability*, p. 94.
29   Shotter, *Social Accountability*, p. 152.
30   Susan B. Shimanoff, *Communication Rules: Theory and Research* (Beverly Hills, CA: Sage, 1980).
31   Shimanoff, *Communication Rules*, p. 57.

2. *Rules are prescriptive.* By this Shimanoff means that a course of action is called for and that the failure to abide by the rule can be criticized. Prescriptions may state what is obligated, preferred, or prohibited, and negative evaluation may ensue if the rule is not followed. For this reason, behaviors that are permitted, but not preferred or required, are not governed by rules. For example, telling a joke may be permissible in certain situations, but you do not have to tell a joke.

3. *Rules are contextual.* A rule must do more than govern a single event, and it cannot be so broad that it governs everything. For example, if you decide on a whim to pick up a hitchhiker, you would not be following a rule because this is an isolated act that you have never done before. On the other hand, if you frequently pick up hitchhikers and you are expected to, you probably are following a rule. If you try to be kind to people in all your dealings, kindness would not be considered rule-governed because it always applies. On the other hand, if you are kind to people in need, you are following a rule: When someone is in need, be kind.

4. *Rules specify appropriate behavior.* They tell us what to do or not do, not how to think, feel, or interpret. For example, a rule may require you to apologize, but it cannot require you to feel sorry.

Shimanoff believes that the "if-then" format is best for stating a rule: "If . . . , then one (must, must not, should) . . ." The "if" clause specifies the context, and the "then" clause specifies the behavior. Consider the following examples:

If one is not the owner or guest of the owner, then one is prohibited from being in the land marked off by this sign.

If one is playing bridge and is the dealer, then one must bid first.

If one is wearing a hat and is entering a church, then one must remove his/her hat.

If one is playing chess and one's chess pieces are white, then one must move his/her piece first.[32]

To verify a rule theory, a researcher must be able to observe rules in operation in everyday interaction. If Shimanoff's rule model is accurate, you will be able to apply her criteria to any episode and identify the rules in force. Sometimes this is easy because the rules are explicit. In these situations rules are announced on a sign or in a game-rules book. Most often, identifying rules is more difficult because they are implicit, and they must be inferred from the behavior of the participants. Shimanoff shows how to do this.

Rules can be found by examining behavior in terms of three criteria:

1. Is the behavior controllable (to assess the degree to which the underlying rule is followable)?
2. Is the behavior criticizable (to assess whether the underlying rule is prescriptive)?
3. Is the behavior contextual (to assess whether people behave differently in various situations)?

If you can answer yes to all three, you have found a rule. Applying these criteria is not necessarily easy. Consider how difficult it would be to determine whether an action is criticized. We know that rule behavior is open to evaluation and that compliance may be praised while violation may be punished. Overt *sanctions* are easiest to identify in observing interactions because they involve verbal or nonverbal rewards and punishments. Sanctions may range from simple frowns or smiles to a stern lecture about rule violation. Besides noting sanctions, observers can also look for *repairs.* Here, a rule violator will behave in a way that reveals that a rule was violated. Apologizing is an example. In the absence of overt sanctions or repairs, the observer can simply ask participants whether a given behavior was appropriate or not.

People use rules in a variety of ways. Figure 9.3 identifies eight types of rule-related behavior.[33] Four of these are rule conforming, and four are rule deviating. Let us go through these in pairs, beginning at the center of the figure.

32 Shimanoff, *Communication Rules,* p. 79.
33 Shimanoff, *Communication Rules,* p. 127.

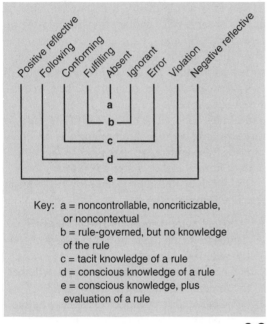

Key: a = noncontrollable, noncriticizable,
     or noncontextual
     b = rule-governed, but no knowledge
       of the rule
     c = tacit knowledge of a rule
     d = conscious knowledge of a rule
     e = conscious knowledge, plus
       evaluation of a rule

FIGURE **9.3**

Rule-Related Behavior

From *Communication Rules: Theory and Research* by Susan B. Shimanoff. Copyright © 1980 by Sage Publications. Reprinted by permission of the publisher.

Rule-fulfilling and *rule-ignorant behaviors* involve acting without knowing the rule. For example, there is an old rule that men should open doors for women. Imagine a little boy who naively opens a door for a woman. He is unaware that he has followed a rule, but the woman might respond by saying, "What a gentleman you are." This behavior is rule fulfilling because the boy didn't know what he was doing. Had the boy failed to open the door in ignorance (rule-ignorant behavior), the woman might have whispered to the boy's parents, "You need to teach your child good manners."

Conforming and *error behaviors* definitely are governed by rules, although the individual is not conscious of it at the time the rule is followed or not followed. Men often unconsciously open doors for women, and frequently they fail to do so, not out of ignorance but because they are not thinking about it at the moment. The first in-

stance is an example of conforming behavior, the second of error behavior.

Rule-following behavior is conscious compliance with the rule. To pursue our example, rule following would apply when a man intentionally steps ahead of a woman and opens a door. *Rule violation,* on the other hand, is intentional violation of the rule. For instance, a man may be tired and simply may not feel like opening the door for his companion.

Reflective behavior involves *positive reflection* or *negative reflection* (following or violating). The women's movement has brought many social rules into question. A man may consciously choose not to open the door for a woman, precisely because of his evaluation of what the gesture implies about gender roles. Or a woman may take the initiative to open a door first. A traditional man may make a point to open the door because, on reflection, he believes that the rule is a good one.

As an example of how rules operate, consider Shimanoff's study of marital communication.[34] To explore communication rules between husbands and wives, Shimanoff asked twenty couples to tape-record an hour's worth of their conversations. She interviewed the couples and analyzed their conversations to determine how husbands and wives express emotions to each other. Several types of emotional expressions were explored in this study.

Shimanoff found a strong tendency to express feelings in ways that help the spouse save face and not hurt one another's feelings. She therefore posited the following rules: (1) "When speaking with one's spouse, one should disclose face-honoring, face-compensating, and pleasant face-neutral emotions more frequently than face-threatening emotions"; (2) "When speaking with one's spouse, one should disclose unpleasant face-neutral emotions more often than hostile emotions towards one's spouse or regrets for transgressions against absent others."[35] Now,

---

34 Susan B. Shimanoff, "Rules Governing the Verbal Expression of Emotions Between Married Couples," *Western Journal of Speech Communication* 49 (1985): 147–165.
35 Shimanoff, *Communication Rules,* pp. 159–160.

these are not laws because they are sometimes violated. As we all know, husbands and wives do sometimes express their feelings in face-threatening ways, but as rules these guidelines help couples know how to express emotions in certain ways.

Coordinated Management of Meaning

The theory of the coordinated management of meaning (CMM), developed by Barnett Pearce, Vernon Cronen, and their colleagues, is the most comprehensive rule theory of communication.[36] The theory integrates work from system theory (Chapter 3), symbolic interactionism (Chapter 8), ethogeny (Chapter 9), speech acts (Chapter 5), and relational communication (Chapter 12).

Like all rule theories, CMM states that people interpret and act on the basis of rules. Individuals within any social situation first want to understand what is going on and apply rules to figure things out. They then act on the basis of their understandings, employing rules to decide what kind of action is appropriate.

There are two types of rules. *Constitutive rules* are essentially *rules of meaning*, used by communicators to interpret or understand an event or message. *Regulative rules* are essentially *rules of action*, used to determine how to respond or behave.

For example, if a friend says something to you, you decipher the meaning of the message. You interpret it; you figure out what it means. Usually this is a simple and almost unconscious

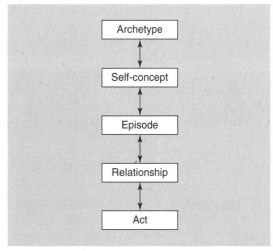

FIGURE **9.4**

Hierarchy of Contexts

Adapted from *Communication, Action, and Meaning* by W. Barnett Pearce and Vernon Cronen. Copyright © 1980 by Praeger Publishers. Reprinted by permission of the authors.

experience because your interpretation rules are immediately available and simple. Sometimes, however, interpretation is more difficult, and you may have to dig for appropriate rules of understanding. Once you feel you know what was said, you then respond in some way, and your action rules help you decide what to say in response. All communicators in an interaction are going through the same process of trying to mesh with one another.

Rules of meaning and action are always chosen within a context. The *context* is the frame of reference for interpreting an action, and your responses will differ from one context to another. One context is always embedded within another. In other words, each context is itself part of a bigger context. Figure 9.4 illustrates this idea.

Here, four typical contexts are depicted. The *relationship context* includes mutual expectations among members of a group. The *episode context* is an event. The *self-concept context* is one's sense of personal definition. Finally, the *archetype context* is an image of general truth. As an example, you might interpret your daughter's snippy remark as an insult within the context of your negative

36   W. Barnett Pearce and Vernon Cronen, *Communication, Action, and Meaning* (New York: Praeger, 1980); Vernon Cronen, Victoria Chen, and W. Barnett Pearce, "Coordinated Management of Meaning: A Critical Theory," in *Theories in Intercultural Communication*, eds. Y. Y. Kim and W. B. Gudykunst (Newbury Park, CA: Sage, 1988), pp. 66–98; Vernon Cronen, W. Barnett Pearce, and Linda Harris, "The Coordinated Management of Meaning," in *Comparative Human Communication Theory*, ed. F. E. X. Dance (New York: Harper & Row, 1982); W. Barnett Pearce, "The Coordinated Management of Meaning: A Rules Based Theory of Interpersonal Communication," in *Explorations in Interpersonal Communication*, ed. G. R. Miller (Beverly Hills, CA: Sage, 1976), pp. 17–36; Vernon Cronen, W. Barnett Pearce, and Linda Harris, "The Logic of the Coordinated Management of Meaning," *Communication Education* 28 (1979): 22–38.

relationship. The relationship, in turn, might be judged as negative in terms of the episode of an argument, which you view as typical given your self-concept as a headstrong person.

The order of contexts shown in Figure 9.4 is not universal and often shifts. Sometimes, for example, self is understood within the context of the relationship, but on other occasions the relationship is understood in reference to the self. Also, although the contexts listed in Figure 9.4 are representative and common, they by no means exhaust the possible contexts within which interpretations and actions are made. Humans have the ability to create a number of contexts for interpretation and action.

Any event or action being interpreted is known as a *text*. In the example above, the snippy comment is the "text," and your relationship is the "context." Often text and context form a loop (Figure 9.5), such that each is used from time to time to interpret the other.[37] This situation is called *reflexivity* because each context reflects the other. So, for example, your meaning for the snippy comment is affected by your relationship with your daughter, and your relationship is in turn affected by the comment. Reflexivity always enters the context hierarchy at some point because the hierarchy cannot keep going up forever. At some point the ladder of contexts must come to an end and start coming down again.

When the rules of meaning are consistent throughout the loop, the loop is said to be *charmed*, or self-confirming. The example of the link between your daughter's insult and relationship is a charmed loop; each confirms the other. Often, however, the rules of interpretation change from one point in the loop to another, causing a paradox, or *strange loop*, in which each

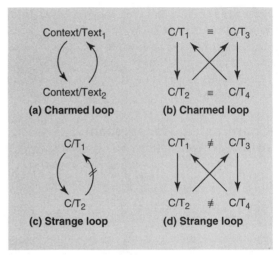

FIGURE 9.5

Text-Context Loop Patterns

Adapted from "Between Text and Context: Toward a Rhetoric of Contextual Reconstruction" by Robert J. Branham and W. Barnett Pearce, in *Quarterly Journal of Speech* 71 (1985): 23, 25. Reprinted by permission of the authors and publisher.

context disconfirms the other. This would happen, for example, if you felt that you had a good relationship, but it included lots of insulting comments. Here the relationship would not confirm the insults, and the insults would not confirm the relationship. The result would be confusion.

The strange loop of the alcoholic is illustrated in Figure 9.6. Notice here the alcoholic is confused about control. Within the context of the self as a controlled drinker, drinking is accepted as okay, but within the context of the episode of drinking, the self is defined as out of control, making drinking not okay. If you follow the loop in Figure 9.6, you see what many alcoholics go through. First, they drink and come to see themselves as out of control. Then they stop drinking, now believing they are in control, so that they can begin drinking again.

Pearce and Cronen use a set of symbols to demonstrate how rules operate. Three are important here:

$\overline{\qquad\qquad}\rceil$ = in the context of

$\longrightarrow$ = counts as

$\supset$ = if, then

---

37   Loops are discussed in Vernon E. Cronen, Kenneth M. Johnson, and John W. Lannamann, "Paradoxes, Double Binds, and Reflexive Loops: An Alternative Theoretical Perspective," *Family Process* 20 (1982): 91–112; and Robert J. Branham and W. Barnett Pearce, "Between Text and Context: Toward a Rhetoric of Contextual Reconstruction," *Quarterly Journal of Speech* 71 (1985): 19–36. For an interesting recent extrapolation and extension of this idea, see James R. Taylor, Francois Cooren, Nicole Giroux, and Daniel Robichaud, "The Communicational Basis of Organization: Between the Conversation and the Text," *Communication Theory* 6 (1996): 1–39.

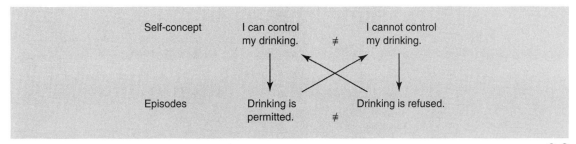

FIGURE **9.6**

The Alcoholic's Paradox

Adapted from "Between Text and Context: Toward a Rhetoric of Contextual Reconstruction" by Robert J. Branham and W. Barnett Pearce, in *Quarterly Journal of Speech* 71 (1985): 26. Reprinted by permission of the authors and publisher.

The first symbol denotes the context of an act, the second applies to a meaning rule, and the third is used to stipulate an action rule. Consider the following examples:

$$\overline{\text{insult} \xrightarrow{\quad\text{play}\quad} \text{joke}}$$

In the context of play, an insult is to be taken as a joke. *Meaning rule:* An insult counts as a joke.

$$\overline{\text{insult} \xrightarrow{\quad\text{conflict}\quad} \text{put-down}}$$

In the context of conflict, an insult is to be taken as a put-down. *Meaning rule:* An insult counts as a put-down.

$$\overline{\text{husband insults wife's family} \supset \text{wife cries}}$$
argument

In the context of an argument, when the husband insults the wife's family, she cries. *Action rule:* An insult leads to crying.

$$\overline{\left[\begin{array}{ll}\text{husband insults} & \supset \text{wife playfully} \\ \text{wife's family} & \text{hits husband}\end{array}\right] \longrightarrow \text{fun}}$$
playful banter

In play it is considered fun for the wife to "hit" the husband after he insults her family. *Action rule:* Wife should respond to husband's insult by "hitting" him. *Meaning rule:* This sequence of events is to be taken as fun.

Rules tell us what interpretations and actions are logical or appropriate in a given situation. This sense is called *logical force.* Because people behave in a manner consistent with their rules, rules provide a logical force for acting in certain ways.

Four types of logical force operate in communication. The first is *prefigurative,* or *causal force,* an antecedent-to-act linkage in which you perceive that you are being "pressured" to behave in certain ways because of prior conditions. If you think that you are being caused to do something, prefigurative force is at play. For example, you might tell someone that you are in school because your parents made you go.

Practical force is an act-to-consequent linkage in which you behave in a certain way to achieve a future condition. So, for example, you might believe you are in college because you want to get a better job than you could get with only a high school education.

The third type of logical force is contextual. *Contextual force* is a pressure from the context. Here, you believe that the action or interpretation is a natural part of the context. Within the context of your self-concept, for example, you might feel that going to college is just necessary, just part of who you are.

Finally, *implicative force* is a pressure to transform or change the context in some way. Here, you act to create a new context or to change an

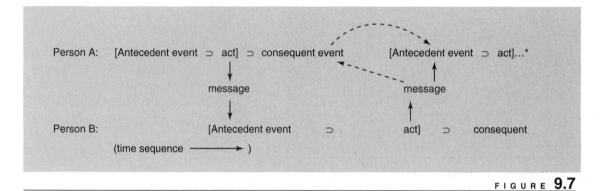

FIGURE **9.7**

Coordination Process

*Solid arrows denote constitutive rules. Broken arrows denote the coorientational state of comparing the subsequent message to the anticipated consequent event in anticipation of the next act. From *Communication, Action, and Meaning* by W. Barnett Pearce and Vernon Cronen. Copyright © 1980 by Praeger Publishers. Reprinted by permission of the authors.

existing one. Implicative force might come into play, for example, if your family did not value college and never encouraged its children to go on to school. You might take it on yourself to change this situation, to create a new family definition, to make the family proud of one of its members for getting a degree. In this kind of situation, you would actually be trying to change the context of family expectations.

In modern society a person is part of many systems, each with its own set of meaning and action rules. The rules are learned through interaction in social groups. Over time, individuals internalize many of these rules and draw on them to guide their actions. The basic problem of communication is that when an individual enters an interaction, that person has no way of knowing precisely what rules the other participants will be using. The primary task in all communication, then, is to achieve and then sustain some form of coordination.

Coordination involves meshing one's actions with those of another to the point of feeling that the sequence of actions is logical or appropriate. The communicators in an exchange need not interpret the events the same way, but each must feel, from within his or her own system of rules, that what is happening makes sense.

Figure 9.7 shows how coordination operates.[38] Person A acts in a certain way, and person B takes

this as a message. Person B uses meaning rules to interpret the message. Person A's act thus becomes an antecedent event to which person B responds, based on B's action rules. B's act is in turn interpreted by A as a message from the standpoint of A's meaning rules, and B's act becomes the consequent to A's initial move. If A and B are operating with substantially different rule structures, they will quickly discover that one person's behavior does not represent the consequent intended, and they will readjust their rules until some level of coordination is achieved.

Consider the simple example of a child trying to get back a ball after accidentally throwing it through a neighbor's window.[39] The adult begins with the following rule structure:

- *Meaning rule:* If I say, "Is this ball yours?" in a stern fashion, this act will be taken as anger, a demand for a confession, and a threat.
- *Action rule:* My act, taken as anger, will elicit crying and apologies. I, in turn, will become less angry and will give back the ball.

The child, on the other hand, has a different set of rules:

---

38   Pearce and Cronen, *Communication*, p. 174.
39   This example is adapted from Pearce and Cronen, *Communication*, pp. 162–164. Originally, the example was developed in K. T. Alvy, "The Development of Listener-Adapted Communication in Grade-School Children from Different Social Class Backgrounds," *Genetic Psychology Monographs* 87 (1973): 33–104.

- *Meaning rule:* When the neighbor says, "Is this your ball?" he is asking for information. My statement, "Give it back," will be taken as a request.
- *Action rule:* When the neighbor requests information, I will respond with a factual answer, "Yes, it is." I will say, "Give it back," and he will give it back.

Now observe the actual conversation:

Neighbor: Is this your ball?
Child: Yes, it is. Give it back.

Obviously, the neighbor did not get the expected response and will interpret the child's remark as impudence rather than the simple request intended by the child. At this point the interaction is not coordinated. Now the neighbor must adjust the action rule by trying a different approach:

Neighbor: Give it back? This ball went through my window. Do you know that?

If the child has a sufficiently complex rule structure to provide options, he may adjust so that a successful outcome can be achieved. If not, coordination may not be achieved. Consider:

Unsatisfactory outcome:
Child: Give my ball back. I'll tell Daddy if you don't give it back.
Neighbor: Get out of my yard, kid!

Successful outcome (coordination achieved):
Child: I'm sorry. I didn't mean to do it, and I will be careful in the future.
Neighbor: Okay. Here's your ball.

An important contribution of CMM is the idea that people can have perfectly satisfactory coordination without understanding one another. In other words, communicators can organize their actions in ways that seem logical to all parties, yet they understand what is going on in a variety of different ways. For example, a speaker and audience may coordinate very well. The speaker is dynamic and effusive, and the audience responds enthusiastically. The speaker thinks she is educating and persuading the audience, but the audience is merely entertained and forgets the point of the message within hours. Here, both sides are satisfied, and each thinks what happened was appropriate; yet what the speaker thought was happening did not happen.

As an example of coordination without understanding, Uma Narula and Barnett Pearce studied the communication patterns of development, or economic improvement, in India.[40] The Indian government has had such a program for many years, with legislation, direct action, and communication as its cornerstone. The communication aspect of the program was designed to make the people more aware of their problems and get them involved in local improvement projects. The result was that they became very aware of problems and the potential for improvement but they did not become involved in their own development. This is a case of coordination without understanding.

The rules used by the population to interpret and respond to the development campaigns were different from those of the government. The government intended to have the people become directly involved in development projects of their own. The people saw the direct action of the government as the answer and expected the government to do it all. This led to a pattern of "passive involvement," in which the population became increasingly critical of the government for not solving their problems for them. The government thought its communication program had been a failure, when in fact it had been very successful. The government did not realize that its own direct action was also taken by the population as a message—the message that problems could be solved by the government alone.

ⓒ Language and Culture

So far in this chapter, it should be apparent that language and culture are vital aspects of social life. In the final section of this chapter, we

---

40   Uma Narula and W. Barnett Pearce, *Development as Communication: A Perspective on India* (Carbondale: Southern Illinois University Press, 1986).

examine some prominent theories of culture and language and their link to one another.[41] In addition to the theories presented in this section, this subject is also taken up in Chapter 10.

The study of language and culture is known as *sociolinguistics,* a broad term covering any study of language that makes significant use of social data, or, conversely, any study of social life that makes use of linguistic data.

Sociolinguistics contrasts sharply with the structural approaches covered in Chapter 4, which view language as separate from communication. Today, most students of language believe that language is affected by both intrinsic structural properties and sociocultural factors.[42]

We turn now to two important theoretical contributions to language and culture, both classic theories of this genre.

Linguistic Relativity

The *Sapir-Whorf hypothesis,* otherwise known as the theory of linguistic relativity, is based on the work of Edward Sapir and his protégé Benjamin Lee Whorf.[43] Whorf is best known for his fieldwork in linguistics, and his analysis of the Hopi language is particularly well known. In his research Whorf discovered that fundamental syntactic differences are present among language groups. The Whorfian hypothesis of linguistic relativity simply states that the structure of a culture's language determines the behavior and habits of thinking in that culture. In the words of Sapir,

> Human beings do not live in the objective world alone, nor alone in the world of social activity as ordinarily understood, but are very much at the mercy of the particular language which has become the medium of expression for their society. . . . The fact of the matter is that the "real world" is to a large extent unconsciously built up on the language habits of the group. . . . We see and hear and otherwise experience very largely as we do because the language habits of our community predispose certain choices of interpretation.[44]

This hypothesis suggests that our thought processes and the way we see the world are shaped by the grammatical structure of the language. As one writer reacted, "All one's life one has been tricked . . . by the structure of language into a certain way of perceiving reality."[45]

Whorf spent much of his life investigating the relationship of language and behavior. His work with the Hopi illustrates the relativity hypothesis. Like all cultural groups, the Hopi possess a reality, which represents their view of the world at large. One area of Whorf's extensive analysis of Hopi thought is the analysis of time. Whereas many cultures refer to points in time (such as seasons) as nouns, the Hopi conceive of time as a passage or process. Thus, the Hopi language never objectifies time. The Hopi would not refer to summer as "in the summer." Instead, the Hopi would refer to the passing or coming of a phase that is never here and now but always moving, accumulating. In our culture three tenses indicate locations or places in a spatial analogy: past, present, and future. Hopi verbs have no tense in the same sense. Instead, their verb forms relate to duration and order. In the Standard Average European (SAE) languages, including English, we visualize time as a line. The Hopi conception is more complex, as illustrated in the following example.[46]

Suppose a speaker reports that a man is running: "He is running." The Hopi would use the word *wari,* which is a statement of *running as a fact.* The same word would be used for a report of past running: "He ran." For the Hopi, the statement of fact is what is important, not whether the event is presently occurring or happened in the past. If, however, the Hopi speaker wishes to report *running from memory* (the hearer

---

41   For a discussion of the role of culture in the communication field, see John H. Powers, "On the Intellectual Structure of the Human Communication Discipline," *Communication Education* 44 (1995): 191–222.

42   Gillian Sankoff, *The Social Life of Language* (Philadelphia: University of Pennsylvania Press, 1980), p. xvii.

43   Edward Sapir, *Language: An Introduction to the Study of Speech* (New York: Harcourt, Brace & World, 1921); Benjamin L. Whorf, *Language, Thought, and Reality* (New York: Wiley, 1956). In the Whorf book, the following articles are most helpful: John B. Carroll, "Introduction," pp. 1–34; "The Relation of Habitual Thought and Behavior to Language," pp. 134–159; "Language, Mind, and Reality," pp. 246–270.

44   Quoted in Whorf, *Language, Thought, and Reality,* p. 134.

45   Carroll (in Whorf's *Language, Thought, and Reality*), "Introduction," p. 27.

46   Adapted from Whorf, *Language, Thought, and Reality,* p. 213.

did not actually see it), a different form would be used, *era wari*. The English sentence "He will run" would translate *warikni*, which communicates *running as expectation*. Again, it is not the location in past, present, or future that is important to the Hopi but whether it is observed fact, recalled fact, or expectation. Another English form, "He runs [on the track team]," would translate *warikngwe*. This latter Hopi form again refers to *running as a condition*.

As a result of these linguistic differences, Hopi and SAE cultures will think about, perceive, and behave toward time differently. For example, the Hopi tend to engage in lengthy preparing activities. Experiences (getting prepared) tend to accumulate as time "gets later." The emphasis is on the accumulated experience during the course of time, not on time as a point or location. In SAE cultures, with their spatial treatment of time, experiences are not accumulated in the same sense. Elaborate and lengthy preparations are not often found. The custom in SAE cultures is to record events such that what happened in the past is objectified. Whorf summarizes this view: "Concepts of 'time' and 'matter' are not given in substantially the same form by experience to all men but depend upon the nature of the language or languages through the use of which they have been developed."[47]

Notice that the theory of linguistic relativity is different from the social constructionist theories discussed earlier in the chapter. In social constructionism people are believed to create their realities in the process of interaction, whereas Whorf and Sapir teach that reality is already embedded in the language and therefore comes preformed. Both theories deal with cultural reality, but they approach the topic in opposite ways.

Elaborated and Restricted Codes

One of the most important sociolinguistic theories is that of Basil Bernstein on elaborated and restricted codes.[48] This theory shows how the structure of the language employed in everyday talk reflects and shapes the assumptions of a social group. Bernstein is especially interested in social class and the ways the class system creates different types of language and is maintained by language.

The basic assumption of this theory is that the relationships established in a social group affect the type of speech used by the group. At the same time, the structure of the speech used by a group makes different things relevant or significant. This happens because different groups have different priorities, and language emerges from what is required to maintain relationships within the group. In other words, people learn their place in the world by virtue of the language codes they employ.

For example, in one family where a strict authoritarian control system is used, children learn that they must respond to simple commands. In this kind of family, persuasive appeals would be not only irrelevant but counterproductive. For Bernstein, role and language go hand in hand. The kinds of roles that children learn are reinforced by the kind of language employed in the community, especially the family. The term *code* refers to a set of organizing principles behind the language employed by members of a social group. Two children who both speak English might employ very different codes because their talk is different.

Bernstein's theory centers on two codes—elaborated and restricted. *Elaborated codes* provide a wide range of different ways to say something. These allow speakers to make their ideas and intentions explicit. Because they are more complex, elaborated codes require more planning, explaining why speakers may pause more and appear to be thinking as they talk. *Restricted codes* have a narrower range of options, and it is easier to predict what form they will take. These codes do not allow speakers to expand on or elaborate very much on what they mean.

Restricted codes are appropriate in groups in which there is a strongly shared set of assumptions and little need to elaborate on what is meant. Elaborated codes are appropriate in groups in which perspectives are not shared.

---

47 Whorf, *Language, Thought, and Reality,* p. 158.
48 Basil Bernstein, *Class, Codes, and Control: Theoretical Studies Toward a Sociology of Language* (London: Routledge & Kegan Paul, 1971).

Here, people are required to expand on what they mean. Restricted codes are oriented toward social categories, for which everybody has the same meaning, whereas elaborated codes are oriented toward individualized categories that others might not share.

For example, in some groups everybody knows the difference between masculine and feminine, and people are clearly identified in a male or female role. Everybody knows the place of a woman and a man, a girl and a boy. You can assume what people think and feel based on their gender identification, and there is little need to explore individual differences. In other groups, however, gender is not as useful because there is not a common understanding of what masculine and feminine mean. You can see that it would take more words to explore what is appropriate behavior for the individual child than it would to tell a girl to go to the kitchen and help her mother.

Thus, elaborated codes are used by speakers who value individuality above group identification. Because the intent of the speakers cannot be inferred from their role, they have to be able to express themselves individually in some detail. Bernstein offers the example of a couple that has just come out of a movie and stops by to visit with friends. There, they discuss the film at some length. The other couple has not seen it but can understand their friends' ideas about the film anyway:

> An hour is spent in the complex moral, political, aesthetic subtleties of the film and its place in the contemporary scene. . . . The meanings now have to be made public to others who have not seen the film. The speech shows careful editing, at both the grammatical and lexical levels. It is no longer contextualized. The meanings are explicit, elaborated and individualized. . . . The experience of the listeners cannot be taken for granted. Thus each member of the group is on his own as he offers his interpretation.[49]

A primary difference between the types of groups that use these two codes is their degree of openness. A *closed-role system* is one that reduces the number of alternatives for the participants. Roles are set, and people are viewed in terms of those roles. This understanding of who people are and how they should behave forms the basis of a common knowledge within the group. Because of this shared meaning in the group, an elaborated language is not necessary and therefore not cultured or learned.

An *open-role system* is one that expands the number of alternatives for individuals in the group. Roles are not categorical and simple; they are individualized and negotiated; they are fluid and change. Thus, there may be little shared understanding of a person's identity within an open system, and an elaborated code is necessary for communication to take place in this system.

Two major factors contribute to the development of an elaborated or restricted code within a system. The first is the nature of the major socializing agencies within the system, including the family, peer group, school, and work. Where the structure of these groups is well defined in terms of fixed roles, a restricted code is likely to develop. Where the structure of these groups is less well defined and has fluid roles, an elaborated code is more likely to be created.

The second major factor is values. Pluralistic societies that value individuality promote elaborated codes, whereas narrower societies promote restricted ones.

You can now see how codes are so strongly associated with social class. Bernstein says that members of the middle class use both types of systems. They may, for example, be exposed to rather open roles at home but somewhat closed ones in the workplace. Or peer groups may use closed roles, whereas the school employs open ones.

Members of the working class, however, are less likely to use elaborated codes. For working-class individuals, both the values and the role systems reinforce restricted codes, which leads Bernstein to write,

> Without a shadow of a doubt the most formative influence upon the procedures of socialization, from a sociological viewpoint, is social

---

49   Bernstein, *Class, Codes, and Control*, p. 177.

class. The class structure influences work and educational roles and brings families into a special relationship with each other and deeply penetrates the structure of life experiences within the family. . . . I shall go on to argue that the deep structure of communication itself is affected, but not in any final or irrevocable way.[50]

In a well-known study, Bernstein tape-recorded young men from the working class and the middle class in England talking about capital punishment.[51] He analyzed samples of this speech and found interesting class differences. Even when the data were controlled for intelligence, the working-class speakers used longer phrases, shorter words, and less pausing than middle-class speakers. With an elaborated code, the middle-class boys needed more planning time, which explains their shorter phrases and longer pauses.

Many other differences found in this study illustrate elaborated and restricted codes. For example, middle-class speakers used "I think" significantly more than did working-class speakers. Working-class speakers made greater use of short phrases at the end of sentences to confirm the other person's common understanding; these included expressions like "isn't it?" "you know," and "wouldn't he?" Middle-class speakers had longer, more complex verb phrases, more passive verbs, more uncommon adverbs and adjectives. And middle-class speakers made more use of the personal pronoun *I*.

Elaborated codes are empowering because they enable speakers to adapt to a wide range of audiences and appeal to widely different types of persons. On the other hand, elaborated codes can be alienating because, as Bernstein writes, they separate "feeling from thought, self from other, private belief from role obligation."[52]

Although he acknowledges the limitations of restricted talk, Bernstein does not devalue it: "Let it be said immediately that a restricted code gives access to a vast potential of meanings, of delicacy, subtlety and diversity of cultural forms, to a unique aesthetic the basis of which in condensed symbols may influence the form of the imagining."[53] However, Bernstein also notes that

those in power in society often do devalue this type of speech, which further perpetuates the class system.

The family is especially important in the development of code. Two types of families correspond to the two types of codes. *Position families* have a clear and formally determined role structure. They often have a closed communication system and use restricted codes. Such families tend to have sharp boundaries in their use of space and in their conception of objects and persons. They define objects and people in terms of their position.

Person-centered families determine roles on the basis of individuals' personal orientations rather than formally defined divisions. They tend to use open communication and elaborated codes. Roles and relations within these families tend to be unstable and constantly in negotiation. These families do not maintain sharp boundaries in their use of space or in their ideas about people and things.

Although a family may have a variety of means of exerting control and regulating behavior, there seems to be a predominant or preferred method employed, depending on the type of family. Some families prefer an *imperative mode* of regulation, which is based on command and authority. In this type of family, when Dad says, "Shut up," you do. This is preferred in hierarchical families in which certain members are defined as in control according to the role structure. This kind of control is delivered with a restricted code.

Other families prefer *positional appeals,* based on role-related norms. Here, control is exerted by relying on commonly understood norms associated with each role. Examples of this kind of appeal are "You are old enough to know better," or "Boys don't play with dolls." This kind of control can be expressed with restricted or elaborated codes, depending on the degree of differentiation in the system.

---

50 Bernstein, *Class, Codes, and Control*, p. 175.
51 Bernstein, *Class, Codes, and Control*, pp. 76–117.
52 Bernstein, *Class, Codes, and Control*, p. 186.
53 Bernstein, *Class, Codes, and Control*, p. 186.

Finally, *personal appeals* are based on individualized characteristics and individualized rules, and these appeals often consist of giving reasons for why a person should or should not do something. Again, the code employed can be restricted or elaborated, depending on the degree of shared understanding in the family.

◖● COMMENTARY AND CRITIQUE

For the most part, this chapter fills in the blanks left by symbolic interactionism in Chapter 8. We see here the many ways in which people construct reality through communication. The idea of social constructionism has won widespread favor because of its intuitive appeal. All theories in this chapter see a close relationship between language and reality. All show that the language used in a culture shapes the reality in which that culture lives.

We see from these theories that all aspects of reality are socially constructed, including, for example, the self and emotions. We have looked at the ways common forms of talk such as accounts contribute to the construction of reality within a social group or culture. Rules are an important part of a social reality, and they provide guidance for the communication that affects our sense of reality.

An important question deals with the role of interaction in this reality-constructing system. Symbolic interactionism assumes that language is an outcome of interaction. The social constructionists use the same assumption as the basis for the idea that reality is constructed through communication.

Sapir and Whorf, on the other hand, assume that language precedes interaction and that our interaction patterns are a result, not a cause, of language structure. In a remarkable review of the literatures on language learning, language differences, bilingualism, and sensori-neuroscience, Thomas Steinfatt concluded that although the Whorfian hypothesis cannot be tested, the evidence for it is weak.[54]

One can, of course, take a stand in the middle and suggest that both the language-thought and thought-language connections are true. Interaction does shape language, but language in turn shapes interaction.[55] Most constructionists today would probably agree with this position.

Bernstein's work illustrates this idea very well. The type of interaction in the family and other socializing institutions determines the sort of language learned, but language in turn reinforces the interaction patterns that led to it in the first place. We will return to the issue of the primacy of language versus interaction in Chapter 10 in our examination of phenomenology and textual interpretation.

Although the social constructionist thesis is appealing, there is also strong resistance to this idea from some quarters. Social constructionism remains controversial because it conflicts with the commonsense notion that reality is objective and independent, an idea deeply rooted in Western thought. Many social researchers and philosophers of science strongly believe that we use language to communicate about the objects in the world and that those objects exist in a particular form prior to any communication about them.

Although it seems patently obvious to constructionists that human experience is formed largely in and through culture, many sociobehavioral scientists have not adopted this assumption at all. Much social science still rests on the assumption that the human experience is largely universal, owing to a common biological inheritance and common cognitive structure. Noam Chomsky (Chapter 4), for example, has taught that language structures are universal and that cultural differences in languages are merely superficial. Further, he believes that certain language universals are innate and that lan-

---

54   Thomas M. Steinfatt, "Linguistic Relativity," in *Language, Communication, and Culture: Current Directions*, eds. Stella Ting-Toomey and Felipe Korzenny (Newbury Park, CA: Sage, 1989), pp. 35–75.
55   This intermediate position is given weight by the influential theory of structuration, attributed most notably to Anthony Giddens. See, for example, *Profiles and Critiques in Social Theory* (Berkeley: University of California Press, 1982), chaps. 1–3.

guage is acquired by an interaction between experience and wired-in structures. Charles Osgood (Chapter 7) has come to the conclusion that the dimensions of meaning are universal, which is antithetical to social constructionism.

If these structuralists are right, cultural relativists are barking up the wrong tree. We should not be looking for richly different language and meaning experiences; instead, we should discover the common universals that provide an explanatory basis for human behavior across the board. This is a debate that will not die, and we encounter it again at other points throughout this text.

Donald Ellis recently posed a series of thoughtful challenges to social constructionism. Ellis believes that communication cannot proceed without assuming that we live in a world of *a priori* realism. We must assume that we are all talking about the same thing, or communication cannot take place. This argument is based on two principles—semantic realism and coherentism.

Semantic realism is the idea that words have standard meanings. When you say something to someone, you assume that this person will share your meanings. You essentially enter a contract with your listener that says, "We agree to use a standard set of meanings." Further, these meanings are very stable. Although it is true that meanings change, communication could not occur if they did not remain essentially the same. Otherwise you could not read a nineteenth-century novel and understand it.

Semantic realism is not quite the same thing as scientific realism. The latter assumes that the structure of reality exists apart from humans' understandings of it, a proposition thoroughly rejected by constructionists. Semantic realism, on the other hand, says that meaning itself is real. These two—semantic and scientific reality—are related because we can only assume real meaning if we can also assume objective reality too. We need the structure of the world to give structure to meaning. This leads to Ellis's second principle.

The *coherentist principle* states that from a strictly pragmatic perspective meanings must be verifiable in experience. We can only assume se-

mantic realism by relating it to our perceptual experience. A table is a table because we can see and touch it. This does not mean that the table "really exists," only that we can assume it does because of a common experience of "tableness." There may be no giant map in heaven to verify reality, but we can trust our own experience to verify that what we say relates to something beyond what we say.

Ellis is not implying here that everyone always understands one another perfectly or that errors do not occur. But we have an ideal and clear sense of reality that gives us confidence that we can at least aim for understanding and rationality in our communications with others.

Social constructionists do not deny the facticity of objects in the world. If you are standing in the way of a locomotive, do not deny that it is real![56] The issue is not whether the locomotive exists apart from human construction, but how it is seen, what it is, and how it relates to other objects in the person's experience. A locomotive is not in and of itself a locomotive but is created by human beings within a vast and rich context of social meanings, and the oncoming locomotive can never be viewed as meaningful apart from social interaction. The same is true of the death and dismemberment that might occur if you did stand in front of the train. The meaning of injury and death as a result of an accident involving machinery would have vastly different meanings from one culture to another.

A serious question, however, remains: If reality is indeed socially constructed, how can we produce generalizable knowledge? If communication is context-bound, how is theory possible?[57] Acknowledging the attractiveness of social approaches, Joseph Cappella expresses the

---

56   The locomotive example is used by Richard A. Cherwitz and James W. Hikins, *Communication and Knowledge: An Investigation of Rhetorical Epistemology* (Columbia: University of South Carolina Press, 1986), p. 19. Cherwitz and Hikins advance an argument against constructionism similar to that of Ellis.
57   See, for example, Robert Bostrom and Lewis Donohew, "The Case for Empiricism: Clarifying Fundamental Issues in Communication Theory," *Communication Monographs* 59 (1992): 109–129; Stuart J. Sigman, "Do Social Approaches to Interpersonal Communication Constitute a Contribution to Communication Theory?" *Communication Theory* 2 (1992): 347–356.

pragmatic difficulty of this kind of scholarship in this question: "In short, when competing knowledge claims are generated, how will they be adjudicated?"[58] The answer to this critique is to fall back on the basic position of the movement. Good communication theory should not attempt to achieve a standard set of criteria. Instead, it should be judged in terms of its utility and its potential for enriching human experience.[59]

A related set of theories in this chapter are rule theories, which further add to our understanding of social and cultural reality. The rule concept is appealing because it explains a mechanism by which people understand reality. As pointed out in Chapter 5, however, the rule concept is not particularly coherent because different theories use different definitions of rules. For example, Shimanoff is firm in stating that a rule must deal with overt behavior. She believes that the concept should not apply to interpretation, whereas Pearce and Cronen apply rules not only to overt behavior but also to internal meanings.

This lack of consistency in the use of rules has led to some confusion. For instance, David Brenders in criticizing CMM relies on ideas from the rule-following tradition to show that Pearce and Cronen have blurred distinctions about meaning that Austin, Searle, and others (Chapter 5) thought important.[60] In their response, Cronen, Pearce, and Changsheng argue that the ideas about meaning implied by this tradition are not appropriate for understanding communication as the process by which people shape their very experience.[61] If communication is used as a tool to relay meanings, as Brenders suggests, the rules are followed to accomplish this task. If, on the other hand, communication is the process by which meaning itself is constructed, as Pearce and Cronen assert, rules themselves are part of the socially constructed reality, and rule-following approaches are not very useful.

Brenders's critique and the CMM response take us full circle back to the basic issue surrounding social constructionism: Is communication a tool for communicating accurately about the world, or is it the means by which the world itself is determined? I do not expect this controversy to be settled anytime soon.[62]

---

58 Joseph Cappella, "Remaking Communication Inquiry," in *Rethinking Communication: Paradigm Issues,* eds. Brenda Dervin, Lawrence Grossberg, Barbara O'Keefe, and Ellen Wartella (Newbury Park, CA: Sage, 1989), p. 142.
59 Penman, "Good Theory."
60 David A. Brenders, "Fallacies in the Coordinated Management of Meaning: A Philosophy of Language Critique of the Hierarchical Organization of Coherent Conversation and Related Theory," *Quarterly Journal of Speech* 73 (1987): 329–348.
61 Vernon E. Cronen, W. Barnett Pearce, and Xi Changsheng, "The Meaning of 'Meaning' in the CMM Analysis of Communication: A Comparison of Two Traditions," *Research on Language and Social Interaction* 23 (1989–1990): 1–40.
62 This issue is discussed by Sigman, "Social Approaches."

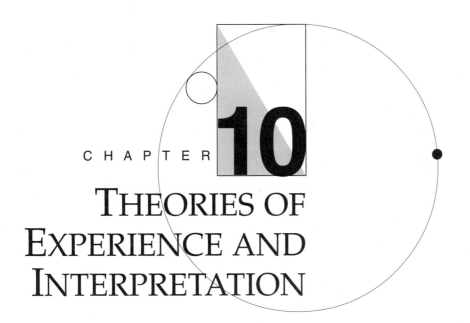

CHAPTER **10**

THEORIES OF
EXPERIENCE AND
INTERPRETATION

The field of communication explores a variety of human experiences. The theories in this chapter tell us about the nature of conscious experience and the role of communication in it. Specifically, we will explore two traditions, phenomenology and hermeneutics.[1]

The central assumption of most theories in this chapter is that people actively interpret their experience by assigning meaning to what they see. As you read this book, for example, you attend to it consciously, you interpret it, you actively assign meaning to what you are reading.

Interpretation, sometimes known by the German term *Verstehen* (understanding), is the active process of assigning meaning to something you observe, like a text, an act, or a situation—any experience, really. Because a message or other act could mean a variety of things, meaning cannot be simply "discovered." Interpretation, by definition, is an active, disciplined process of the mind, a creative act of searching for possible meanings.

◖ PHENOMENOLOGY

Phenomenology is the study of the knowledge that comes from consciousness, or the way you come to understand objects and events by consciously experiencing them. It looks at objects and events from your perspective as a perceiver. A *phenomenon* is the appearance of an object, event, or condition in your perception. Maurice Merleau-Ponty, a theorist of this tradition, expresses this point of view as follows: "All my knowledge of the world, even my scientific knowledge, is gained from my own particular point of view, or from some experience of the world without which the symbols of science would be meaningless."[2]

---

1 For a good recent overview of these areas, see James A. Anderson, *Communication Theory: Epistemological Foundations* (New York: Guilford, 1996).
2 Maurice Merleau-Ponty, *The Phenomenology of Perception*, trans. C. Smith (London: Routledge & Kegan Paul, 1974), p. viii. For an excellent general discussion of phenomenology, see

199

This approach is a striking departure from scientific methods that assume the existence of a reality that people cannot know in their ordinary experience. Phenomenology makes actual lived experience the basic data of reality. "Phenomenology means letting things become manifest as what they are, without forcing our own categories on them."[3] An "objective" scientist hypothesizes a particular structure and then looks to see if it is there; a phenomenologist never hypothesizes, but carefully examines actual lived experience to see what it looks like. If you want to know what love is, you would not ask the psychologists; you would tap into your own experience of love.

Stanley Deetz summarizes three basic principles of phenomenology.[4] First, knowledge is conscious. Knowledge is not inferred from experience but is found directly in conscious experience. Second, the meaning of a thing consists of the potential of that thing in one's life. In other words, how you relate to an object determines its meaning for you. A set of keys, for example, becomes a paperweight when you see that it could be used that way. The third assumption is that language is the vehicle of meaning. We experience the world through the language used to define and express that world. We know keys because of their associated labels: "lock," "open," "metal," "weight," and so forth.

In this section we will look at three groups of phenomenological theories—classical, social, and hermeneutic.

Classical Phenomenology

Edmund Husserl is usually considered the founder of modern phenomenology.[5] Husserl, who wrote during the first half of the twentieth century, attempted to develop a method for ascertaining truth through focused consciousness. For Husserl, no conceptual scheme outside of actual direct experience is adequate for uncovering truth; rather, the conscious experience of the individual must be the route for discovering reality. Only through conscious attention can truth be known. In other words, we can know the

things of the world by carefully examining them in an unbiased way.

Husserl believed that in everyday life (*Lebenswelt*) you experience things in a kind of *natural attitude* that is affected by all kinds of beliefs and prejudices. This natural way of living does not have sufficient discipline to permit true knowledge. To learn about a topic phenomenologically, you must bracket out the distractions of ordinary life. The term *bracket* is especially useful because it suggests that we do not get rid of ordinary beliefs but that we just put them off (in brackets) temporarily during a phenomenological investigation.

The term Husserl used to describe this process is *phenomenological reduction*, or *epoché*, which is the careful and systematic elimination of any subjective factors entering into one's pure experience of a thing.[6] In reduction, you bracket subjective factors—including history, biases, and interests—to eliminate these distorting elements and concentrate on the object of interest. One's pure consciousness of the object reveals its true essence, and disciplined observers will agree on what it is if they carefully attend to their awareness of it.

Once an event is successfully reduced in this way, a second, *transcendental*, reduction can be made. This reduction brackets experience itself, leading to a true understanding of what Husserl called the *transcendental ego*, or pure state of con-

also Michael J. Hyde, "Transcendental Philosophy and Human Communication," in *Interpersonal Communication*, ed. J. J. Pilotta (Washington, DC: Center for Advanced Research in Phenomenology, 1982), pp. 15–34.

3   Richard E. Palmer, *Hermeneutics: Interpretation Theory in Schleiermacher, Dilthey, Heidegger, and Gadamer* (Evanston, IL: Northwestern University Press, 1969), p. 128.

4   Stanley Deetz, "Words Without Things: Toward a Social Phenomenology of Language," *Quarterly Journal of Speech* 59 (1973): 40–51.

5   Edmund Husserl, *Ideas: General Introduction to Pure Phenomenology*, trans. W. R. B. Gibson (New York: Collier, 1962); *Phenomenology and the Crisis of Philosophy*, trans. Q. Lauer (New York: Harper & Row, 1965). For a brief summary of Husserl's ideas, see Zygmunt Bauman, *Hermeneutics and Social Science* (New York: Columbia University Press, 1978).

6   Reduction is clearly explained and illustrated by Amedeo Giorgi, "Phenomenology, Psychological Science, and Common Sense," in *Everyday Understanding: Social and Scientific Implications*, eds. Gün R. Semin and Kenneth J. Gergen (London: Sage, 1990), pp. 64–82.

sciousness. Social life, which leads to one's beliefs, attitudes, and values, can, like any other object or event, be bracketed and reduced. Doing so reveals the true essence of the human mind. Transcendental reduction is a psychological endeavor designed to uncover the nature of human thought. If I can attend to what I am doing when I am aware, I gain insight into what it means to have consciousness.

Now let's look at an example of a phenomenological reduction. In this example a psychologist wanted to know more about the topic of learning. He interviewed a restaurant manager about an event in which the manager learned something. The manager described how he learned about the inadequacies of employees. The psychologist then conducted a reduction of this interview to distill the essence of learning as expressed by the manager.

The following is the interview itself:

Researcher: What did you find out?
Manager: I learned about these girls [waitresses]. Last night with the snow and all, the young crowd came here. This place was packed and business was great. Then I realized the girls were cheating. We must have cooked hundreds of hamburgers, but when I went over the slips only a few people had paid for hamburgers. The girls gave their friends all this food and only wrote them a slip for a coke or a cup of coffee. This has been going on for months. Last night I caught them. I really didn't know what to do. I felt like I wanted to hit them; then I felt like crying because of all my hard work trying to make a go of it here. I learned that after all these months these girls don't have any respect for me. . . . I also found out that they don't give a

damn about their jobs. So I fire them, what do they care! All they are concerned about is getting a date for Friday night and giving away my food. . . .

Researcher: How was it that you learned all this last night?
Manager: I don't know. I guess I was watching more than usual and I knew we had sold lots of hamburgers. I watched and listened to these kids. If I had stayed blind to this whole thing much longer, they would have walked off with the store. I was just too trusting and I wanted to be their friend. That doesn't work—you can't be the friend and the boss. You can't run a restaurant without respect. No sir, old Harry isn't going to be fooled any longer.[7]

This passage reflects the natural attitude of the restaurant manager. His expression of anger and frustration about his employees is a natural *description*, the first step in a phenomenological analysis. In using a phenomenological method, the psychologist had to bracket everything in his own experience that could distract him from the essence of this event. The psychologist who analyzed the above passage describes how he applied phenomenology:

Now, even though I am a psychologist, I am required by phenomenology to put out of play all my psychological "knowledge about" learning. Thus I do not think about reinforcement, learning curves, sign-Gestalt theory, or any other concept or specific study of which I am aware. I also acknowledge that I have performed many phenomenological psychological analyses of learning similar to this one before, but I also must not let those analyses influence this one. . . . The point for the issue at hand is that one must really get into the

---

7   Example taken from Giorgi, "Phenomenology," p. 66.

description or phenomenon under study in an experiential way.[8]

The psychologist also points out that he must bracket out all his personal experience with learning, restaurants, employees, or anything else that could bias his understanding of this subject's own conscious experience. The resulting reduction leads to the following description:

> Learning is awareness of the necessity to reorganize a personal project based upon the discrepancy between the implicit assumptions brought to a situation vital for the continuance of the project and the perception and understanding of the actions of others in terms of the project in the same situation. It is also manifested in S's [subject's] discovery of the fact that he is prereflexively and ambiguously living out two conflicting roles with respect to the others involved in the project and in the ability of S to circumvent the difficulty by imagining he can choose to live out the project in terms of the preferred role in an unambiguous way.[9]

This passage states the results of the phenomenological reduction. It is the essence of learning as embodied in the experience of the manager and as interpreted by the phenomenologist. We now see more clearly that a reduction basically reduces a natural description to the essence of the experience behind it.

Husserl believed that phenomena have true essences that are revealed in conscious experience. In other words, people can successfully understand the true nature of things by bracketing out their own history and ideas. This is an idealistic notion, and it is controversial. Few phenomenologists today believe this. Because of the importance of language, communication, and social life to the conscious experience of people, most phenomenologists acknowledge our inability to divorce ourselves from these facts of life. We turn now to the work of two significant phenomenologists of the social tradition.

Social Phenomenology

Social phenomenology examines social relations, especially the use of language, in ordinary life. This school of thought acknowledges that our experience is inherently social and that consciousness cannot be divorced from language.

Maurice Merleau-Ponty was greatly influenced by Husserl, but he strongly rejected Husserl's idealism.[10] For Merleau-Ponty, the human being is an indivisible *body-subject,* a unified physical-mental being that creates meaning in the world. As a subject or knower, a person has a relationship to things in the world: Human life is both affected by the world and in turn defines and assigns meaning to the world. Merleau-Ponty is opposed to realism because things do not exist in and of themselves. People give meaning to the things in the world, but there is no human experience outside the world. Thus, the human *body-subject* and the world of things and events exist in a give and take, or dialogic, relationship, each affecting the other.

Communication is the vehicle by which you assign meaning to experience. Your thoughts result from speech because meaning itself is created by your speech. Merleau-Ponty makes a distinction between the use of speech to create meaning, which he calls the *speaking word,* and speech used to convey meaning to others, which is the *spoken word.* This distinction captures the fact that people both assign meaning and receive meaning. This distinction is similar to that of Saussure (Chapter 4) between *parole* (speech) and *langue* (language). When we communicate we may work out new ways of seeing the world through social interaction, or the "speaking word." At the same time, we have access to a whole range of understandings as part of the language, or "spoken word," available to us in everyday life.

It should be clear, then, why Merleau-Ponty rejects Husserl's idea of essence. Things do not

---

8   Giorgi, "Phenomenology," p. 73.
9   Giorgi, "Phenomenology," p. 67.
10   Merleau-Ponty's most important work is *Phenomenology of Perception* (New York: Humanities Press, 1962), original published in 1945 in Paris. See also Richard L. Lanigan, *Phenomenology of Communication: Merleau-Ponty's Thematics in Communicology and Semiology* (Pittsburgh, PA: Duquesne University Press, 1988); Remy C. Kwant, *The Phenomenological Philosophy of Merleau-Ponty* (Pittsburgh, PA: Duquesne University Press, 1963); Samuel B. Mallin, *Merleau-Ponty's Philosophy* (New Haven, CT: Yale University Press, 1979); Wayne Froman, *Merleau-Ponty: Language and the Act of Speech* (Lewisburg, PA: Bucknell University Press, 1982). Many other secondary sources are available.

have essences that can become apparent through perception. Rather, the meanings of things are always created by the subject through speech. The language you use at a particular time attaches certain meanings to the object of your experience, but those meanings are temporary and can change. For Merleau-Ponty, reduction to the "essence" is impossible.

How, then, does Merleau-Ponty conduct his phenomenology? He too calls for reduction of experience, but not to the true essence of a reality outside of the perceiver. Rather, we reduce experience to the meaning of the object as reflected in language.

Bracketing must still be used. Here you bracket any categories that could be distracting. In the case of the restaurant manager, for example, the reduction does not tell us about "learning" as an independent topic, but it tells us about the meaning of learning in the life of the manager based on the language used in its description. Remember, for Merleau-Ponty, you cannot separate the person from the world. Thus, the phenomenologist in this tradition concentrates not only on the thing itself but also on the language used to describe the thing and the meanings reflected in this language.

This brand of phenomenology assumes that people who share a language also share meanings. The analyst is therefore interested not in the subject's private meanings but in the public meanings available to everybody in the common language.

To illustrate phenomenology in this tradition, Richard Lanigan has his students go through three exercises.[11] In the first they explore their own experience by writing a description of an important event in their life that involves some kind of moral or social learning. Next, the students look for particular words and phrases that reveal the meaning of the event. They then interpret this language and write a brief statement that captures the meaning of the event based on the language of the original description.

In the second exercise, the students interview another person on the topic of body image and obesity. They go through the same process—first,

by analyzing the audiotaped interviews and looking for important revealing words and phrases; second, by extracting the meaning from that language; and third, by writing a statement that distills the subject's meanings into a few words.

In the third exercise, the students conduct another audiotaped interview in which they ask the subject a number of questions about his or her life. The same reductive procedure is then used to discover the meanings guiding the individual's life.

A contemporary of Merleau-Ponty was Alfred Schutz.[12] Schutz applies phenomenology to social life, investigating social events from the perspective of those actually participating in them. In everyday life you make three fundamental assumptions. First, you assume that reality is constant—that the world will remain as it appears. Second, you assume that your own experience of the world is valid. Ultimately, you will believe that what you see is accurate. Third, you see yourself as having the power to act and accomplish things, to affect the world.

The work of Schutz is important to communication theory because, like that of Merleau-Ponty, it makes communication central to the experience of individuals. Our world depends on what we learn from others in our social and cultural communities. This knowledge is always part of a historical situation, and people in various times and places experience the world differently. Reality is socially constructed within the group, which is why no universal reality can be found. As one commentator puts it, "The world, when filtered through my biographical situation, becomes 'my' world."[13]

11   Richard L. Lanigan, "Life History Interviews: A Teaching and Research Model for Semiotic Phenomenology," in *Phenomenology of Communication*, pp. 144–154.
12   Alfred Schutz, *The Phenomenology of the Social World*, trans. G. Walsh and F. Lehnert (Evanston, IL: Northwestern University Press, 1967); original published in 1932. For a clear summary of Schutz's ideas, see Robert A. Gorman, *The Dual Vision: Alfred Schutz and the Myth of Phenomenological Social Science* (London: Routledge & Kegan Paul, 1977). See also Richard Lanigan, "A Treasure House of Preconstituted Types: Alfred Schutz on Communicology," in *Phenomenology of Communication*, pp. 203–222.
13   Gorman, *Vision*, p. 38.

What is real for us depends on the categories employed within our culture. These categories are generalizations, which Schutz calls *typifications*. They are typical trees, typical children, typical love, typical greetings, ad infinitum; and trees, children, love, greetings, and everything else will vary from one social situation to another. Within a given social group, then, you understand other people and objects by placing them within a generalized category that "typifies" them.

Language and other signs consist of typifying categories. You interpret signs on the basis of the categories you share with others, and your communication can only be successful to the extent that you have shared meanings within social groups and communities.

Of course, typifications differ from group to group, from culture to culture, and from time to time. How, then, can we study social life at all? What can ever be known? Schutz's solution is to explore only the typifications of particular cultures and groups, not universal categories. General truths about human experience cannot be found, but specific truths of individual historical groups can be discovered. With this thesis Schutz takes us a long way from Husserl.

For Schutz, social knowledge consists of formulas or *social recipes*, typical, well-understood ways of doing things in particular situations. They enable you to classify things according to some kind of mutually understood logic, to solve problems, to take roles, to communicate, and to behave properly in different situations. Conducting negotiations, getting married, worshipping, raising children, selling goods, and most other social activities proceed according to these recipes.

We can now see a clear progression of ideas among the chief phenomenologists. Husserl believed that you can understand events in and of themselves by reducing perception to its pure state. Merleau-Ponty rejected this idea and wrote that all you can achieve is a sense of the meaning of events in the lives of subjects. Merleau-Ponty concentrated on public meaning, or that which is common to all subjects by virtue of their shared

language. Schutz takes this thinking one step further by denying the importance of common knowledge. For him, meaning is particular and peculiar to individual groups.

As social phenomenology, Schutz's philosophy provides backing for the social constructionist movement discussed in Chapter 9. It is an important part of the philosophy of social relativism prevalent in much communication theory today. It also makes us aware of the many ways in which human communities differ and the meanings that different people bring to an encounter. His ideas have had an impact on theories of cultural interpretation, which will be discussed later in the chapter.

Hermeneutic Phenomenology

The chief critic of classical phenomenology is the philosopher Martin Heidegger.[14] For Heidegger, phenomenology and hermeneutics merge in *hermeneutic phenomenology,* or *philosophical hermeneutics.* Heidegger denies the ability to reach truth through any kind of reduction. Instead, what is most important in human life is the natural experience that inevitably occurs by merely existing in the world. His philosophy has been called the *hermeneutic of Dasein,* which means "interpretation of being."

For Heidegger, the reality of something is not known by careful analysis or reduction but by natural experience, which is created by the use of language in everyday life. What is real is what is experienced through the natural use of language in context: "Words and language are not wrappings in which things are packed for the commerce of those who write and speak. It is in words and language that things first come into being and are."[15]

---

14 Martin Heidegger, *Being and Time,* trans. J. Macquarrie and E. Robinson (New York: Harper & Row, 1962); *On the Way to Language,* trans. P. Hertz (New York: Harper & Row, 1971); *An Introduction to Metaphysics,* trans. R. Manheim (New Haven, CT: Yale University Press, 1959). For secondary treatments, see Bauman, *Hermeneutics,* pp. 148–171; Palmer, *Hermeneutics,* pp. 124–161; Deetz, "Words"; John Stewart, "One Philosophical Dimension of Social Approaches to Interpersonal Communication," *Communication Theory* 2 (1992): 337–347.
15 Heidegger, *Introduction,* p. 13.

Hans-Georg Gadamer is today's leading proponent of philosophical hermeneutics.[16] A protégé of Heidegger, Gadamer is primarily interested in how understanding is possible in human experience. For Gadamer, individuals do not stand apart from things in order to analyze and interpret them; instead, we interpret naturally as part of our everyday existence. We cannot be human without interpreting. That means that our experience and the world we interpret are so closely intertwined that they are virtually the same thing.

The central tenet of Gadamer's theory is that one always understands experience from the perspective of presuppositions, or assumptions. Our tradition gives us a way of understanding things, and we cannot divorce ourselves from that tradition. Observation, reason, and understanding are never objectively pure; they are colored by history and our experience with other people.

Further, history is not to be separated from the present. We are always simultaneously part of the past, in the present, and anticipating the future. In other words, the past operates on us now in the present and affects our conceptions of what is yet to come. At the same time, our present notions of reality affect how we view the past.

These ideas do not deny change. Over time we become distanced from the events of the past. Our way of seeing things in the present time creates a temporal distance from an object of the past such that artifacts have both a strangeness and a familiarity. If you look at your grandmother's old dress from a dusty trunk in the attic, it will look somewhat familiar, but strange at the same time.

We understand an artifact because of what we have learned from history, which is a residue of highly relevant, but essential, meaning. For example, you recognize your grandmother's dress because of its "dressness" learned by viewing old pictures and reading and hearing about old-time fashion. Even though the dress might be very old, you still recognize buttons, lace, and other features that make this a dress.

In some ways, then, interpretation of historical events and objects, including written texts, is enhanced by historical distance. You can understand the Gettysburg Address because the essential meaning of the words lives on. Gadamer would agree that understanding a text involves looking at the enduring meanings of that text within a tradition and apart from the original communicators' intentions. Texts therefore become contemporaneous and speak to us in our own time.

The Gettysburg Address was originally a piece of spoken discourse designed to achieve a certain effect during the Civil War. Once spoken, however, the text lived on as an object of its own, rife with internal meaning. Unessential details—that it was written on the back of an envelope on the train by a tall, lanky president—drop away as the text itself reveals its meanings to us in our own time.

The meaning we get from a text, then, is a result of a "dialogue" between our own present-day meanings and those embedded in the language of the text. You do recognize and understand an old dress because of its features that still have meaning, but, at the same time, you also apply your own current ideas about the dress— that it is silly, stodgy, inconvenient, heavy, hot, oppressive, or whatever. You understand the terms of the Gettysburg Address because those words live on, but at the same time, your interpretation is influenced by your own background and experience of today.

This interpretive process is paradoxical: We let the text speak to us, yet we cannot understand it apart from our own prejudices and presuppositions. Because change results from the dialogue between the prejudices of the present and the meanings of the text, prejudice is a positive force, to be acknowledged and used

---

16   Gadamer's major work is *Truth and Method* (New York: Seabury, 1975). An excellent secondary treatment can be found in Richard J. Bernstein, *Beyond Objectivism and Relativism: Science, Hermeneutics, and Praxis* (Philadelphia: University of Pennsylvania Press, 1983), pp. 107–169. See also Palmer, *Hermeneutics,* pp. 162–222; David Tracy, "Interpretation (Hermeneutics)," in *International Encyclopedia of Communications,* ed. E. Barnouw (New York: Oxford University Press, 1989), pp. 343–348.

productively in our lives. As one observer has noted, "The problem for the study of communication is not the existence of prejudices but the unawareness of their presence and subsequent inability to separate appropriate from inappropriate ones."[17]

Hermeneutics is not only a process of "questioning" the meaning of the text but also of allowing it to question us. What questions does the text itself suggest, and when we ask those questions, what answers does the text offer? What, for example, can we learn about ourselves from the Gettysburg Address?

Like Heidegger, Gadamer believes that experience is inherently linguistic. We cannot separate our experience from language. The perspectives of tradition, from which we always view the world, are in the words. Note how this conception differs from the structural view of language summarized in Chapter 4, in which language is seen as an arbitrary tool for expressing and referring to an objective reality. Gadamer's view is also different from the interactionist notion (even Schutz's), which suggests that language and meaning are created through social interaction. Gadamer's point is that language itself prefigures all experience. The world is presented to us through language. Thus, in communication, two people are not using language to interact with each other; rather, communication involves a triad of two individuals and a language.[18]

To get this idea across, Gadamer uses the analogy of the game. A game has its own existence apart from individual players. The basic structure of the game will be the same whether it is being played or not and regardless of who is playing. Poker is poker, whether played in 1920 by four old Italian men or in 1994 by a young college student and her roommates. The game lives on, only the players change.

Language and life are like games: We play them, just as we experience life, but they come to us preformed and remain intact after our particular playing is finished. One commentator explains it this way: "The world is already meaningful. That is, the world which comes to us in the only way that the human world can come to us, through language, is an already meaningful world."[19]

Gadamer brings phenomenology and hermeneutics together in one process. Phenomenology, or understanding through experience, and hermeneutics, or interpretation, are inseparable processes. Let us turn now in more detail to the field of hermeneutics.

◉ HERMENEUTICS

Hermeneutics is the study of understanding, especially that of interpreting action and text. There are several branches of hermeneutics, including interpretation of the Bible (exegesis), interpretation of literary texts (philology), and interpretation of human personal and social actions (social hermeneutics).[20]

Modern hermeneutics began in the early nineteenth century with Friedrich Schleiermacher.[21] Schleiermacher attempted to establish a system for discovering what authors meant in their writings. He used a scientific approach to text analysis, which he believed would be the key to authors' original meanings and feelings. Later in the century, Schleiermacher's biographer, Wilhelm Dilthey, was strongly influenced by these ideas.[22] For Dilthey, however, hermeneutics is the key to all of the humanities and social sciences; he believed that we come to understand all aspects of human life, not by reductionistic

---

17 Stanley Deetz, "Conceptualizing Human Understanding: Gadamer's Hermeneutics and American Communication Studies," *Communication Quarterly* 26 (1978): 14.
18 John Angus Campbell, "Hans-Georg Gadamer's Truth and Method," *Quarterly Journal of Speech* 64 (1978): 101–122.
19 Campbell, "Hans-Georg Gadamer's Truth and Method," p. 107.
20 For an analysis of different approaches to hermeneutics, see Bauman, *Hermeneutics*. See also Tracy, "Interpretation."
21 Friedrich Schleiermacher, *Hermeneutik*, ed. H. Kimmerle (Heidelberg, Germany: Carl Winter, Universitaetsverlag, 1959).
22 Wilhelm Dilthey, "The Rise of Hermeneutics," trans. F. Jameson, *New Literary History* 3 (1972): 229–244.

methods as in the natural sciences, but through subjective interpretation. For Dilthey, the human world is social and historical and requires understanding in terms of the community in which human actors live and work. Humans are not fixed and cannot be known objectively. Dilthey therefore promoted a kind of historical relativism common in the social sciences today.

Just about any interpretive activity can be labeled "hermeneutic." This means understanding another person's feelings and meanings, understanding the meaning of an episode or event, translating the actions of a group into terms understandable to outsiders, or uncovering the meaning of a written text.

For our purposes, hermeneutic scholars fall into two general groups: those who use hermeneutics to understand texts and those who use hermeneutics as a tool for interpreting actions. The first type is perhaps best termed *textual hermeneutics* and the second *social or cultural hermeneutics*.[23]

Generally speaking, *texts* are any artifacts that can be examined and interpreted.[24] Text hermeneutics, although usually applied to the written word, is not limited to it. Any kind of action can be recorded. A text is essentially a recording, whether written, electronic, photographic, or preserved by some other means. Even actions can be viewed as texts, but more often, the term designates written documents and other records.[25] The problem remains the same: How do we interpret a message that is no longer part of an actual live event?

Although little agreement exists on specific techniques of interpretation, almost all schools of thought rely on a common notion of its general process. This process is called the *hermeneutic circle*. You interpret something by going from general to specific and from specific to general. You look at a specific text in terms of a general idea of what that text may mean, then modify the general idea based on the examination of the specifics of the text. Your interpretation is ongoing, as you move back and forth between specific and general. You can look at the composite meaning of a text and then examine the specific linguistic structures of that text. Then you might return to the overall meaning, only to go back to the specifics again.

Within the circle, you always relate what is seen in the object to what you already know. You then alternate between a familiar set of concepts and the unfamiliar until the two merge in a tentative interpretation. In interpreting the actions of a foreign culture, for example, an anthropologist first tries to understand what is happening with familiar concepts; later the anthropologist discovers how the natives understand their experiences in their own way and uses this information to modify the categories initially employed. This process continues back and forth until an adequate account is generated.

So, too, with the interpretation of the Bible: The interpreter begins by relating the text to what he or she already understands, looks for strange or unaccounted-for details in the scripture, modifies the original interpretation, reexamines the text, and so on. You can see that this is really what Gadamer was talking about—a dialogue between the meanings in the text and one's own present-day assumptions.

Textual Interpretation

The interpretation of texts has long been the central problem of hermeneutics. Hermeneutics arose as a way to understand ancient texts such as the Bible that can no longer be explained by the author. The Supreme Court uses hermeneutics to interpret the Constitution. Today, virtually any text is open for interpretation, and whether the author is alive to explain what he or she

---

23   For an analysis of the different approaches to hermeneutics, see Bauman, *Hermeneutics*.

24   For a good discussion of the various senses of the term *text*, see George Cheney and Phillip K. Tompkins, "On the Facts of the Text as the Basis of Human Communication Research," in *Communication Yearbook 11*, ed. J. A. Anderson (Newbury Park, CA: Sage, 1988), pp. 455–481, and attendant commentaries (pp. 482–501).

25   Actually, the concept of *text* is complex and should not be read simply as an object, action, or writing. For an excellent brief exposition of the concept, see Cheney and Tompkins, "Facts of the Text."

meant is just not considered relevant. The text itself speaks to us; it has meanings of its own apart from what any author, speaker, or audience member might mean by it. The challenge of textual hermeneutics, then, is to ascertain the meanings of the text.

There are many prominent writers on text interpretation. Two of the best known, Paul Ricoeur and Stanley Fish, represent very different approaches to the text-interpretation problem.

Paul Ricoeur.   Ricoeur is a major interpretive theorist who relies heavily on both the phenomenological and hermeneutic traditions.[26] Although he recognizes the importance of actual speech, most important for Ricoeur is text. Once speech is recorded, it becomes divorced from the actual speaker and situation in which it was produced. Texts cannot be interpreted in the same fashion as live discourse because they exist in a permanent form. Speech is ephemeral, but texts live on. Textual interpretation is especially important when speakers and authors are not available, as is the case with historical documents. However, it need not be limited to these situations. Indeed, the text itself always speaks to us, and the job of the interpreter is to figure out what it is saying.

The separation of text from situation is *distanciation*. The text has meaning irrespective of the author's original intention. In other words, you can read a message and get meaning from it despite the fact that you were not part of the original speech event. Thus, the author's intent does not prescribe what the text can subsequently be taken to mean, nor does any reader's peculiar understanding limit what the text itself says. Once written, the text can be consumed by anybody who can read, providing a multitude of possibilities—and multiple readings (meanings) are definitely possible. For these reasons the interpretation of textual material is for Ricoeur more complex and more interesting than that of spoken discourse.

The problem is like interpreting a musical score.[27] You may not know exactly what mood and feeling Mozart had in composing and con-

ducting the Jupiter Symphony. If you are an experienced music lover, you might be able to produce a number of believable interpretations of your own, but those interpretations are not unlimited; they are constrained by the musical notation. A conductor carefully studies the elements of the text to determine what meanings are embedded in it and then proceeds to produce a musical interpretation. Orchestral versions will differ substantially in the interpretation performed, but you will always recognize the piece as the Jupiter Symphony.

Like a musical interpretation, the meaning of a text is always a pattern of the whole, never just a composite of individual elements. To account for this, Ricoeur's version of the hermeneutic circle consists of explanation and understanding. *Explanation* is empirical and analytical: It accounts for events in terms of observed patterns among parts. In studying a book of the Bible, for example, you would carefully examine the individual words of each verse and note the ways they form patterns of meaning. In the analysis of a text, an interpreter might look for recurring words and phrases, narrative themes, and theme variations. Ricoeur himself is interested in particular words that have metaphorical value, words that point to meanings hidden below the surface of the writing. None of these structural elements is meaningful in and of itself; they must be put together into a whole pattern in the understanding phase of interpretation.

Understanding is synthetic, accounting for events in terms of overall interpretation. So in continuing your study of the Bible, you would also look for a holistic, or general, meaning of the passage under consideration. In hermeneutics, one goes through both processes, breaking down a text into its parts and looking for patterns, then

---

26   Paul Ricoeur, *Interpretation Theory: Discourse and the Surplus of Meaning* (Fort Worth: Texas University Press, 1976); *Hermeneutics and the Human Sciences: Essays on Language, Action, and Interpretation,* trans. and ed. J. B. Thompson (Cambridge: Cambridge University Press, 1981); Don Ihde (ed.), *The Conflict of Interpretations: Essays in Hermeneutics* [by Paul Ricoeur] (Evanston, IL: Northwestern University Press, 1974).
27   The musical analogy of textual hermeneutics can be found in Ricoeur, *Interpretation Theory,* p. 75.

stepping back and judging subjectively the meaning of the whole. You move from understanding to explaining and back to understanding again in a continuing circle. Explanation and understanding, then, are not separate but are two poles in an interpretive spectrum.

Ricoeur agrees with Gadamer that an intimate interaction exists between text and interpreter. The text can speak to and change the interpreter. Ricoeur refers to the act of being open to the meanings of a text as *appropriation*. If you are open to the message of a text, you appropriate it, or make it your own. Thus, interpretation begins with distanciation but ends with appropriation. To interpret the sections of the Bible, you would remove your own interests from your study of the intrinsic meanings in the text, but then you would apply those meanings to your own situation.

An example of a Ricoeurian interpretation is Barbara Warnick's study of the Gettysburg Address.[28] In a careful examination of the text, Warnick looks at expressions of agent, place, and time. *Agents* include "our fathers," those who have given their lives," "we," and the people of the future. *Place* references include our nation "upon this continent" and "a great battle-field." *Time* references include the far past ("four score and seven years"), the near past, a frozen present, and a possible future. The text can transcend the immediacy of the present situation by cycling back and forth from the present to other times, from immediate agents to other agents in past and future, and from this place to other places. In so doing, the text tells a story of birth, adversity, recognition of values, rebirth, and perpetuation of the treasured values.

In an example of appropriation, Warnick notes that this story parallels that of the Christian narrative, which appeals to people so deeply in our society. Other values of American culture are deeply embedded in the text as well. Warnick shows how the details of the text and the overall understanding of it as a projection of the American ideal go hand in hand. Warnick's overall understanding of the speech, then, is that it expresses values that are part of but transcend the immediate situation, and for this reason, the text is relevant to generation after generation of Americans.

Stanley Fish. Fish is a literary critic known mostly in the fields of English and literary studies. With a keen interest in literature, much of his work centers around text interpretation and the question of where meaning resides. Taking a distinctly different turn from Riceour, Fish denies that any meaning can be found in text. For him, meaning lies strictly in the reader, which leads to the name most associated with Fish's work—*reader-response theory*.[29] The proper question is not, "What does a text mean?" but "What does a text do?"

Clearly, texts do stimulate active readership, but the readers themselves provide the meaning, not the text. If you have ever taken a nineteenth-century American literature course, you probably spent some time talking about the meaning of *Moby Dick*. You may have discovered that different students saw different things in the text. Perhaps you spent time trying to figure out what the true meaning of the text is, and you probably used hermeneutics to do it. Fish would say that *Moby Dick* as a text means nothing, but readers will take it to mean many things.

Fish is clear, however, that assigning meaning is not an individual matter. You do not arbitrarily decide what meaning to assign to a text, nor is your meaning idiosyncratic. Following a social constructionist approach (Chapter 9), Fish teaches that readers are members of *interpretive communities*, groups that interact with one another, construct common realities and meanings, and employ these in their readings. So meaning really resides in the interpretive community of readers.

---

28 Barbara Warnick, "A Ricoeurian Approach to Rhetorical Criticism," *Western Journal of Speech Communication* 51 (1987): 227–244.
29 Stanley Fish, *Is There a Text in This Class?* (Cambridge, MA: Harvard University Press, 1980). For a brief, clear secondary source, see Chris Lang, "A Brief History of Literary Theory III" (http://www.xenos.org/essays/litthry4.htm); "A Brief History of Literary Theory VII" (http://www.xenos.org/essays/litthry8.htm)

In your literature class, then, you may come to share a common reading of *Moby Dick*. This will happen because of your common identity as English students, discussions in class, sharing a common textbook, completing the same assignments, taking the same tests, and having the same professor. It is likely that the class will become an interpretive community with very similar meanings for the novel. Indeed, your class will become linked with other classes, in prior and future semesters, and because your professor reads the same journals as professors in other universities and attends conferences on nineteenth-century literature, it is very possible that you will become a member of a huge interpretive community of the American novel.

Of course, if you subscribe to Fish's theory, you will not search for a single meaning. There is no correct reading of a text. The matter is entirely dependent on the audience's interpretation. Meaning, then, is not objective, so don't look for it in the features of the text. Needless to say, this is a highly controversial idea in literary studies. Much of literary criticism looks at the intention of the author and how the author communicates that in the way the text is written.

On this point, however, Ricoeur and Fish would agree: Don't look to the author for meaning. Where they very much disagree is in the role of the text. Both Ricoeur and Fish use the hermeneutic circle, but they emphasize somewhat different things in doing so. For Ricoeur, the reader is always testing his or her interpretation by looking at features of the text so as to find the meaning that lies there. For Fish, the reader always projects his or her own meaning into features of the text and only comes up with the reader's meaning in the end. For Ricoeur, the text is like a template; for Fish it is like a Rorschach test.

Distanciation, the principle that is so important to Ricoeur, is senseless to Fish because readers can never be distanced from the text; they are always embedding their own meanings into it.

Reader-response theory has had a major impact on media studies. If literary texts always get their meaning from the reader, media depictions must also derive meaning from the interpretive community. We will take a closer look at this idea later in the chapter.

Cultural Interpretation

Cultural interpretation involves trying to understand the actions of a group or culture such as the Zulu, residents of the Castro in San Francisco, or New York City high school students.[30] This kind of hermeneutics requires observing and describing the actions of a group, just as one might examine a written text, and trying to figure out what they mean.[31] Another term for cultural interpretation is *ethnography.*

One of the leading cultural interpreters of our day is Clifford Geertz.[32] Geertz describes cultural interpretation as *thick description,* in which interpreters describe cultural practices "from the native's point of view." This level of interpretation is contrasted with *thin description,* in which people merely describe the behavioral pattern with little sense of what it means to the participants themselves.

Like all hermeneutics cultural interpretation uses a hermeneutic circle. Geertz's version of the circle involves a movement from experience-near concepts to experience-distant ones. *Experience-near concepts* are those that have meaning to the members of the culture, and *experience-distant concepts* have meaning to outsiders. The cultural interpreter essentially translates between the two, so that observers outside can have an understanding of the insider's feelings and meanings in a situation. The interpretation process, then, is one of going back and forth in a circle between what appears to be happening from outside to what insiders define as happening. Slowly, a suitable vocabulary can be developed

30   For a discussion of the role of culture in the communication field, see John H. Powers, "On the Intellectual Structure of the Human Communication Discipline," *Communication Education* 44 (1995): 191–222.
31   See Michael Agar, *Speaking of Ethnography* (Beverly Hills, CA: Sage, 1986); Paul Atkinson, *Understanding Ethnographic Texts* (Newbury Park, CA: Sage, 1992).
32   See especially his *The Interpretation of Cultures* (New York: Basic, 1973) and *Local Knowledge: Further Essays in Interpretive Anthropology* (New York: Basic, 1983).

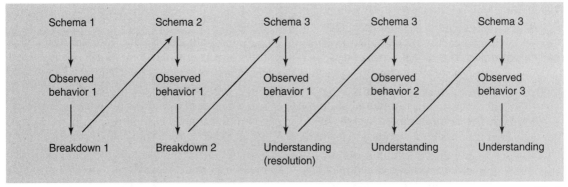

FIGURE **10.1**

Ethnographic Process of Understanding

Adapted from *Speaking of Ethnography* by Michael Agar. Copyright © 1986 by Sage Publications. Reprinted by permission of the publisher.

to explain the natives' point of view to outsiders without forsaking natives' own experience-near concepts.[33]

For example, an ethnographer might wonder about the meaning of wearing oversized pants. From an experience-distant perspective, it might appear to be a form of group conformity. If you ask several young people what it means, they would answer in a more experience-near way with something like, "Oh, it's cool, man." The ethnographer would need to investigate what it means for something to be "cool" and perhaps relate this response to statements made by others. Eventually, a vocabulary acceptable to informants and understandable to those who are not members of this group would be created.

Ethnographic problems arise when an interpreter has a lack of adequate understanding. The researcher witnesses something that cannot be understood from his or her concepts, such as wearing pants so large that you can hardly walk, and seeks to resolve the difficulty by creating an explanation. Ethnography attempts to understand things that are otherwise foreign.

How would you make sense of a cult's ceremony involving the fondling of rattlesnakes? Most of us have no frame for understanding such actions, but the ethnographer would—through careful examination, interviews, inference, and experience—create an explanation that

would make such behavior understandable.

Figure 10.1 illustrates the process.[34] The figure shows how the observer goes through a series of schemas, or ways of understanding, which become increasingly refined and useful. One's first schema may not explain much, leading to a breakdown. After a series of breakdowns, a tentative resolution is achieved. The successful schema is then applied to other acts until further breakdowns occur, forcing the development of still further refined schemas.

The interpreter, of course, does not begin an ethnography empty-handed. Previous experience always provides some kind of schema for understanding an event, but ethnography is a process in which one's understandings become increasingly more refined and accurate.

You can see that as a hermeneutic activity, ethnography is a very personal process, a process in which the researcher experiences a culture and interprets its various forms. Although ethnographers take different approaches to this process, many believe that the best approach is to live the culture firsthand. On this point, Lyall Crawford writes: "As an ethnographer, I am an expert about what only I verify—a state of affairs subject to emotional vulnerabilities, intellectual

---

33 Geertz, *Local Knowledge*, p. 57.
34 Agar, *Speaking*, pp. 28–29.

instabilities, and academic suspicion. Thought of in these terms, taking the ethnographic turn, living and writing the ethnographic life, is essentially a self-report of personal experiences."[35]

Donal Carbaugh and Sally Hastings describe ethnographic theorizing as a four-part process.[36] The first is to develop a basic orientation to the subject. Here the ethnographer assesses his or her own assumptions about culture and its manifestations. Communication ethnographers, for instance, define communication as central to culture and worthy of ethnographic study and decide to focus on various aspects of communication. They may assume further that clothing is an important expression of meaning and a form of communication.

The second phase of ethnographic theorizing defines the classes or kinds of activity that will be observed. A communication ethnographer, for example, might decide to look at the ways clothing is worn.

Next, the ethnographer theorizes about the specific culture under investigation. Here certain activities will be interpreted within the context of the culture itself. So, for example, when young people wear baggy pants, this could be taken as a sign of group conformity and acceptance.

Finally, in the fourth phase, the ethnographer moves back out to look again at the general theory of culture he or she is operating with and tests it with the specific case. The ethnographer might, for example, conclude that baggy pants are yet another instance of how clothing is used by members of a culture to establish communal bonds.

In this section we will look at three forms of cultural interpretation prominent in the communication field—the ethnography of communication, organizational culture, and interpretive media studies.

Ethnography of Communication.   The ethnography of communication is simply the application of ethnographic methods to the communication patterns of a group. Here, the interpreter attempts to make sense of the forms of communication employed by the members of the group or culture.

Gerry Philipsen isolates four assumptions of the ethnography of communication.[37] The first is that participants in a local cultural community create shared meaning. They use codes that have some degree of common understanding. Second, communicators in any cultural group must coordinate their actions. There must be some order or system to what is done in communication. Third, meanings and actions are particular to individual groups. In other words, they differ from culture to culture. Fourth, not only are patterns of behavior and codes different from group to group, but each group also has its own ways of understanding certain codes and actions.

The originator of this research tradition is anthropologist Dell Hymes.[38] Hymes suggests that formal linguistics is not sufficient by itself to uncover a complete understanding of language because it ignores the highly variable ways in which language is used in everyday communication.

Cultures communicate in different ways, but all forms of messages require a shared code, communicators who know and use the code, a channel, a setting, a message form, a topic, and an event created by transmission of the message. Anything may qualify as a message as long as it is construed as such by the natives. Is snake handling communication? How about baggy pants? Perhaps these are shared codes for expressing something among the members of the group. We cannot know until further ethnographic study is undertaken.

Another communication ethnographer, Donal Carbaugh, writes that communication ethnogra-

---

35   Lyall Crawford, "Personal Ethnography," *Communication Monographs* 63 (1996): 158.
36   Donal Carbaugh and Sally Hastings, "A Role for Communication Theory in Ethnography and Cultural Analysis," *Communication Theory* 2 (1992): 156–165.
37   Gerry Philipsen, "An Ethnographic Approach to Communication Studies," in *Rethinking Communication: Paradigm Exemplars,* eds. Brenda Dervin, Lawrence Grossberg, Barbara J. O'Keefe, and Ellen Wartella (Newbury Park, CA: Sage, 1989), pp. 258–269.
38   Dell Hymes, *Foundations in Sociolinguistics: An Ethnographic Approach* (Philadelphia: University of Pennsylvania Press, 1974).

phy addresses at least three types of problems.[39] The first is to discover the type of *shared identity* created by communication in the cultural community, be it African Americans, cheerleaders, Rotarians, Japanese businessmen, or John's Autobody Bowlers. This identity is the members' sense of who they are as a group. It is a common set of qualities with which most members of the community would identify.

The second problem is to uncover the *shared meanings of public performances* seen in the group. What constitutes communication within the culture, and what meanings do the various displays evoke? What does "playing the dozens" mean in the black youth culture? What is communicated by cheerleaders at a high school basketball game? What meaning is assigned to the "fines" at a Rotary meeting?

The third is to explore *contradictions*, or paradoxes, of the group. How are these handled through communication? How, for example, might a culture treat its members as individuals while also providing a sense of community? How might autonomy be granted while maintaining authority? How might roles be taught while instilling ideals of freedom?

In attacking these ethnographic problems, three types of questions are pursued. *Questions of norms* look for the ways communication is used to establish a set of standards and the ways notions of right and wrong affect communication patterns. *Questions of forms* look at the types of communication used within the society. What behaviors count as communication, and how are they organized? *Questions of cultural codes* draw attention to the meanings of the symbols and behaviors used as communication in the cultural community.

Although ethnography highlights aspects of group life, it can also reveal how persons see themselves as persons. In other words, our group identities give rise to our individual identities. Who you are, your identity as a person, is determined in large measure by how you communicate, with whom, and in what settings. From his own studies—of a college basketball

audience, workers in a television station, married person's names, a television talk show, and a community land-use controversy—Carbaugh concludes:

> I could not understand very well what people were saying, or communicating to me, until I explored the deeper particulars of their "sayings" in their specific social scenes. . . . I could not hear (or know) the individuals I met along the way very well until I listened within (or understood) their particular social and cultural scenes. . . . Individuals, social identities (or social classes), and cultural agents are not isolates. They are thought of and acted together in the specific scenes of particular communities.[40]

In short, culture is a powerful influence on human life in general and human lives in particular. Recognizing that cultures are richly different from one another makes generalization difficult. To meet this challenge, comparative ethnography creates categories with which one can compare cultures. Within the ethnography of communication, Hymes suggests a set of nine categories that can be used to compare different cultures.[41]

1. *Ways of speaking,* or patterns of communication familiar to the members of the group
2. *Ideal of the fluent speaker,* or what constitutes an exemplary communicator
3. *Speech community,* or the group itself and its boundaries
4. *Speech situation,* or those times when communication is considered appropriate in the community
5. *Speech event,* or what episodes are considered to be communication for the members of the group
6. *Speech act,* or a specific set of behaviors taken as an instance of communication within a speech event

---

39 Donal Carbaugh (ed.), "Culture Talking About Itself," in *Cultural Communication and Intercultural Contact* (Hillsdale, NJ: Erlbaum, 1990), pp. 1–9.
40 Donal Carbaugh, *Situating Selves: The Communication of Social Identities in American Scenes* (Albany: SUNY Press, 1996), p. 197.
41 Hymes, *Foundations,* pp. 29–66.

7. *Components of speech acts,* or what the group considers to be the elements of a communicative act

8. *The rules of speaking in the community,* or the guidelines or standards by which communicative behavior is judged

9. *The functions of speech in the community,* or what communication is believed to accomplish

This set of concepts is nothing more than a list of categories by which various cultures can be compared. Two cultures—the Apache and the Ilongot, for example—would have many different events that count as communication, varying behaviors that would be considered appropriate within those speaking events, and perhaps some distinct rules for how to communicate. On the other hand, they might have some similar types and functions of communication as well.

As an example of an ethnography of communication, consider Tamar Katriel's study on Israeli "griping."[42] Based on her own experience as a "native griper" and about fifty interviews with middle-class Israelis, Katriel explains the common communication form *kiturim*. This form of communication takes place throughout adult Israeli society, but it is most often seen among the middle class and commonly takes place at Friday night social gatherings called *mesibot kiturim,* or griping parties.

This communication form is so common that it is widely recognized by Israelis as part of their national character. Griping does not deal with personal problems but national (and sometimes local) public ones. It seems to affirm the Israeli identity as having important common national concerns. These are concerns that society could do something about theoretically but that the individual has little power to change. Thus, griping is a kind of shared venting of frustration. It is more than this, however, since Katriel's informants told her that it provides a sense of solidarity and is fun. In fact, griping and joke telling are often viewed together as the primary means of establishing cohesiveness in a social group.

Griping is ritualistic, and the content of the communication does not seem to be important. One must not mistake griping for serious problem solving on topics of concern. In fact, there is a strict prohibition against griping in the presence of non-Israelis, like tourists, because outsiders do not understand the nature of griping and may take it literally, which would be embarrassing to the Israelis.

Griping follows a predictable pattern. It usually begins with an initial gripe, followed by an acknowledgment and a gripe by another person. The pattern of a griping session can go from general societal problems to local ones, or the other way around. Katriel found two interesting variants on the griping theme. *Metagriping* is griping about griping, or complaining that Israelis gripe too much. The other form is the *antigripe:* "Stop griping, and start doing something."

This study illustrates Hymes's categories of comparative ethnography very well. The griping session is a communication event, which consists of particular types of speech acts. It has rules and meets particular functions. The example also illustrates the ethnographic problems of identity, meaning, and tension. Griping reflects a certain national identity in Israel. It is understood among Israelis according to particular meanings, and griping is a mechanism for managing the tension between such opposites as serious concern and pleasant company.

Performance Ethnography. If you were to do fieldwork in a foreign culture, you would experience many things through your senses. Most important, however, would be "seeing" what the people of the culture actually do. You would watch them and see what they do with their bodies.

The anthropologist Victor Turner is most known for bringing our attention to the fact that culture is performed.[43] So much of ethnography

---

42 Tamar Katriel, "'Griping' as a Verbal Ritual in Some Israeli Discourse," in *Cultural Communication and Intercultural Contact,* ed. Donal Carbaugh (Hillsdale, NJ: Erlbaum, 1990), pp. 99–114.
43 Victor Turner, *The Anthropology of Performance* (New York: PAJ Publications, 1987.)

focuses on what members of the culture say and not enough on what they do. Of course, saying is a kind of doing, but needs to be put into a larger frame similar to a play in the theatre. In fact, Turner sees much in common between theatre and everyday cultural life. Like actors, we say our lines as we perform with our bodies.

Cultural performance involves the manipulation of various media that may be experienced by eyes, ears, nose, tongue, and touch. And how these media are used both makes and reflects the meanings of the culture:

> different types of incense burned at different times in a performance communicate different meanings, gestures and facial expressions are assigned meanings with reference to emotions and ideas to be communicated. . . . Thus certain sensory codes are associated with each medium. The master-of-ceremonies, priest, producer, or director creates art from the ensemble of media and codes, just as a conductor in the single genre of classical music blends and opposes the sounds of the different instruments to produce an often unrepeatable effect.[44]

The public performances in a culture are like *social dramas,* in which the group works out their relationships and ideas. Such dramas are *liminal,* meaning that they mark a transition from one state to another or a border between one thing and another. A limin is like a threshold, or door between two places. Rites of passage are a good example, as they depict movement from one stage of life to another. Often rituals are liminal in the sense that they connect the sacred with the secular or symbolize the change of seasons.

Turner notes that social dramas tend to follow a certain process. The first stage is a *breach,* or some kind of violation or threat to community order. This is followed by a *crisis,* as members of the community become agitated and take various sides on the issues raised by the breach. In the third phase, *redressive or remedial procedures,* members of the culture make performances that mend the breach or in some way return to a state of acceptance. This stage of the social drama often involves the most self-examination and is the place where new meanings are created or old

ones reproduced. There is a fourth stage, *reintegration,* or restoration of peace.

The way a community responds to a threat such as an attack or a natural disaster constitutes a kind of social drama. Or, on a smaller scale, certain groups might perform rituals that symbolize its understanding of threat and response.

Not all members of a group of culture participate in these social dramas and performances. Often certain members take the lead, and others may be selected to participate. Cultural performances, like presidential elections, are ways that "stars" show an audience its own culture. By seeing how the performers work things out through breach, crisis, redressive action, and reintegration, the culture is both formed and learned.

Sporting events are a good example of social dramas. The teams come together in competition, which creates a breach, or threat to order. As the teams play and make gains against one another, a spirit of crisis arises, and fans take sides, cheer, boo, feel elated, and then disappointed. Rules, officials, time-outs, halftime, huddles, and coaching offer moments of redressive action, as the teams and fans deal with the crisis in a variety of ways. And at the end of the game, reintegration occurs, as teams shake hands, fans tear down goalposts, people leave and turn on their car radios, or even tune in to another game.

A major sporting event reproduces many aspects of the culture. It teaches us about competition, collaboration, loyalty, and a host of other values. It shows teamwork and expert coaching and play.

Performance ethnography is significant because it broadens the field beyond its traditional fixation on language and text to include *embodied practice.*[45] The performance ethnography movement is significant for the field of communication because communication itself is easily understood as performance, and indeed many

---

44 Turner, *Anthropology of Performance,* p. 23.
45 Dwight Conquergood, "Rethinking Ethnography: Toward a Critical Cultural Politics," *Communication Monographs* 58 (1991): 179–194; Dwight Conquergood, "Ethnography, Rhetoric, and Performance," *Quarterly Journal of Speech* 78 (1992): 80–97.

communication scholars are primarily interested in performance.[46] This move—from text to performance—raises a number of interesting questions.[47]

1. Is *culture* better understood as a verb rather than a noun?
2. Is ethnographic fieldwork a joint performance between the researcher and the subject?
3. How does performance impact interpretation, and can performance be considered a kind of hermeneutics?
4. How should the results of performance ethnography be published, and how should scholarly representation itself make use of performance?
5. What is the relationship between performance and power?

One of the places in which social drama is especially important is organizations. Studying organizations as cultures is a fascinating endeavor, and we turn to this subject now.

Organizational Culture.   Organizations, viewed as cultures, present opportunities for cultural interpretation.[48] An organization, which can be a way of life for its members, creates a shared reality that distinguishes it from other cultures. Gareth Morgan explains:

> Shared meaning, shared understanding, and shared sense making are all different ways of describing culture. In talking about culture we are really talking about a process of reality construction that allows people to see and understand particular events, actions, objects, utterances, or situations in distinctive ways. These patterns of understanding also provide a basis for making one's own behavior sensible and meaningful.[49]

Organizational culture is produced by interactions of the members. Task-oriented actions not only achieve immediate objectives but also create or reinforce certain ways of understanding experience. But culture is created in other ways besides the "official" task behaviors of employees,

since the most mundane everyday activities contribute to the organization's culture.

Michael Pacanowsky and Nick O'Donnell-Trujillo, leaders in the organizational culture movement, ask particular kinds of questions designed to uncover cultural patterns in an organization. Following the lead of Victor Turner, these authors note that "performances are those very actions by which members constitute and reveal their culture to themselves and others."[50] These scholars explain the difference between this approach and traditional methods in these terms:

> We believe that an intriguing thing about communication is the way in which it creates and constitutes the taken-for-granted reality of the world. Social activity, as we see it, is primarily the communicative accomplishment of interrelated actions. So whereas the underlying motive of traditional research is coming to an understanding of how to make organizations work better, the underlying motive of the organizational culture approach is coming to understand how organizational life is accomplished communicatively. To understand how organizational life is brought into being, we cannot let ourselves be limited to asking questions that require some implicit or explicit link to organizational productivity for their legitimacy.[51]

What do organizational members use to create and display their understanding of events within the organization? There are many indicators, including relevant constructs and related vocabulary, perceived facts, practices or activities, metaphors, stories, and rites and rituals. All these are "performances" because they "display"

---

46   See, for example, the journal *Text and Performance Studies.*
47   Conquergood, "Rethinking Ethnography."
48   For a brief description of this approach, see Michael Pacanowsky, "Creating and Narrating Organizational Realities," in *Rethinking Communication: Paradigm Exemplars*, eds. Brenda Dervin, Lawrence Grossberg, Barbara J. O'Keefe, and Ellen Wartella (Newbury Park, CA: Sage, 1989), pp. 250–257.
49   Gareth Morgan, *Images of Organization* (Beverly Hills, CA: Sage, 1986), p. 128.
50   Michael E. Pacanowsky and Nick O'Donnell-Trujillo, "Organizational Communication as Cultural Performance," *Communication Monographs* 50 (1983): 131. See also Victor Turner, *Dramas, Fields, and Metaphors* (Ithaca, NY: Cornell University Press, 1974).
51   Michael E. Pacanowsky and Nick O'Donnell-Trujillo, "Communication and Organizational Cultures," *Western Journal of Speech Communication* 46 (1982): 121.

the lived experience of the group. However, performances, like stage plays, are also accomplishments; they bring something about—the reality of the culture: ". . . performance brings the significance or meaning of some structural form—be it symbol, story, metaphor, ideology, or saga—into being."[52]

Pacanowsky and O'Donnell-Trujillo outline four characteristics of communication performances. First, they are interactional, more like dialogues than soliloquies. They are social actions, not solitary ones. Organizational performances are something people participate in together. Second, performances are contextual. They cannot be viewed as independent acts but are always embedded in a larger frame of activity. Context consists of the who, where, and when of the action. The performance both reflects and produces its context. Third, performances are episodes. They are events with a beginning and an end, and the performers can identify the episode and distinguish it from others. Finally, performances are improvised. There is flexibility in how a communication episode is played out, and although the same performances may be given again and again, they are never repeated exactly the same way.

The authors present a suggestive list of organizational communication performances. The first is ritual. A *ritual* is repeated regularly. It is familiar and routine, such as staff meetings or company picnics. Rituals are especially important because they constantly renew our understandings of our common experience, and they lend legitimacy to what we are thinking, feeling, and doing. Here is an example:

Each and every day, Lou Polito, owner and general manager of Lou Polito Dodge, opens all the company mail. On those occasions when he is "free," he personally delivers this mail to the appropriate divisions in the company. This is just his way of letting his people know that he is keeping in touch with what they are doing.[53]

This is an example of a *personal ritual.* Another type is a *task ritual,* which is a repeated activity that helps members do their jobs:

When a Valley View patrolman stops a driver for some traffic violation, he launches into a conversational routine that involves a question-answer sequence. "May I see your driver's license please?" "Is this your correct address?" "May I see your registration please?" "Do you know why I stopped you?" "Do you know what the speed limit is on this street?" "Do you know how fast you were going?" "Do you want to see the reading on the radar gun?" Although the officer has been taught this routine at the Police Academy as a way of being polite and professional, the Valley View police use it in order to see how the driver responds, to "size him up," and decide whether or not to give him any "breaks" in issuing a citation or warning.[54]

Social rituals are not task-related, yet they are important performances within organizations. The after-work drink is a good example: "Every Friday afternoon, the foremen from Steele Manufacturing go to the 'Pub,' one of the few places in their part of town that serves beer. The conversations are often filled with 'shop talk' but can range from sports . . . to politics."[55]

Finally, *organizational rituals* are those in which an entire work group participates with some regularity: "Each year, the department of communication has its annual picnic, highlighted by the traditional softball game which pits the graduate students against the faculty. Competition is typically fierce; but alas for the graduate nine, they have had but one win in the last five years."[56]

The second category of performances is what the authors call *passion.* Here, workers put on performances that make otherwise dull and routine duties interesting or passionate. Perhaps the most common way this is done is by *storytelling.* Almost everybody tells stories about their work, and the telling is often lively and dramatic.

---

52 Pacanowsky and O'Donnell-Trujillo, "Organizational Communication," p. 129.
53 Pacanowsky and O'Donnell-Trujillo, "Organizational Communication," p. 135.
54 Pacanowsky and O'Donnell-Trujillo, "Organizational Communication," p. 136.
55 Pacanowsky and O'Donnell-Trujillo, "Organizational Communication," p. 137.
56 Pacanowsky and O'Donnell-Trujillo, "Organizational Communication," p. 137.

Further, these stories are told over and over, and people often enjoy telling one another the same stories again and again. We tell stories about ourselves (personal stories), about other people (collegial stories), or about the organization (corporate stories).

Another way drama is created on the job is *passionate repartee*, which consists of dramatic interactions and the use of lively language: "The Valley View police, for example, do not deal with 'civilians,' but rather with 'assholes,' 'dirtbags,' 'creeps,' and 'maggots'—labels which serve as reminders that the 'negative element' is so much a part of the everyday experience of being a police officer."[57]

A third category of performance involves *sociality*, which reinforces a common sense of propriety and makes use of social rules within the organization. Courtesies and pleasantries are examples. *Sociabilities* are performances that create a group sense of identification and include things like joking, "bitching," and "talking shop." *Privacies* are sociality performances that communicate sensitivity and privacy. They include such things as confessing, consoling, and criticizing.

A fourth category of performance involves *organizational politics*. These performances, which create and reinforce notions of power and influence, may include showing personal strength, cementing allies, and bargaining.

A fifth category is *enculturation*, or processes of "teaching" the culture to organizational members. Enculturation is ongoing, but certain performances are especially vital to this process. Orientation of newcomers is an example. On a less formal scale, "learning the ropes" consists of a series of performances in which individuals teach others how things are done. Although this can be accomplished by direct instruction ("That's how we do it here"), most often this kind of learning occurs when people talk about things that happened in a way that helps other individuals learn how to interpret events.

In a police department, for example, officer Davis tells rookie Benson how to handle a rowdy drunk. Benson says he heard that Davis almost got in a fight with the drunk, and Davis replies, "Not really. I didn't give the guy a chance to get mad at me." Pacanowsky and O'Donnell-Trujillo present the following interpretation of this exchange:

> We take Davis' interaction with Benson as a unique enculturation performance, a metacommunicative commentary that instructs Benson in how he should interpret the prior performance. This metacommunication informs the rookie that the prior exchange was not an endorsement of fighting but was backstage "play." And, as the rookie observes more instances of this backstage "tough" talk, he comes to understand it as "not real," but serious nonetheless.[58]

Coming to understand the cultural meanings of organizational performances such as this exchange between the officers proceeds like any ethnography. The researcher first describes the actions of the organizational members and then constructs an interpretation of them in terms that are not only faithful from the native's point of view but are also understandable by people outside the organization. This is in every way a hermeneutic process.

Interpretive Media Studies. Traditional media studies view media as channels for transmitting information to an audience (see Chapter 15). A different, and increasingly popular, way of approaching media is to think of the audience as numerous interpretive communities, each with its own meanings for what is read, viewed, or heard.[59]

We already discussed interpretive communities earlier in this chapter in the section on Stanley Fish, who had a significant impact on interpretive media studies.[60] For Fish, interpretive communities come into being around specific media and content. A community develops around a shared pattern of consumption: common understandings of the content of what is read, heard, or viewed, and shared outcomes.

---

57   Pacanowsky and O'Donnell-Trujillo, "Organizational Communication," p. 139.
58   Pacanowsky and O'Donnell-Trujillo, "Organizational Communication," p. 145.
59   This work is part of social action media studies. See Chapter 15 and Gerard T. Schoening and James A. Anderson, "Social Action Media Studies: Foundational Arguments and Common Premises," *Communication Theory* 5 (1995): 93–116.
60   Fish, *Is There a Text in This Class?*

For example, a television audience consists of a number of "cultures," or communities of viewers, who use and perceive the medium—even individual programs—differently. Thus, if you want to discover how television affects the audience, you have to understand the cultures of these various communities.

Because the outcomes of media consumption depend on the cultural constructions of the community, this approach requires cultural interpretation.[61] James Lull refers to this type of work as the "ethnography of mass communication."[62]

For example, a program like *Sesame Street* appeals to a variety of interpretive communities. One such community might be middle-class children whose parents encourage them to watch and discuss it with them. Another community might be children who view the program on their own to kill time before dinner every evening.

Another example of an interpretive community would be people who get their news by listening to National Public Radio's *All Things Considered* in the car on the way home from work. Still another might consist of people who watch a lot of weekend football for relaxation, entertainment, and social life.

Any person may be a member of a variety of interpretive communities, and particular social groups, such as the family, may be a crossing point for a number of such communities. For example, various members of a family may enjoy television news, top-40 radio programming, sitcoms, children's programs, and biographies and are therefore members of a variety of communities.

Thomas Lindlof outlines three dimensions of an interpretive community.[63] Because interpretive communities define their own meanings for media, Lindlof refers to these elements as *genres,* or general types of media outcomes created by interaction within the interpretive community. This idea is consistent with the social phenomenology of Schutz discussed earlier in this chapter and with social constructionism discussed in Chapter 9.

The first genre that characterizes an interpretive community is *content,* which consists of the types of programs and other media consumed by the community. One group shares an interest in televised football, another in mystery novels, and still another in music videos. It is not enough that a community share an interest in one type of medium content; it must also share some common meanings for that content. A mother who thinks *Sesame Street* is a cute and harmless pastime for her children, the children who become intimately involved with the characters day after day, the teenage son who thinks it is silly, and the grandfather who loves the Muppets do not constitute an interpretive community because they see very different things in the content of that program.

Genres of *interpretation,* then, revolve around shared meaning. Members of a community interpret the content of programs and other media in similar ways. The impact on their behavior, especially what they say about the media and the language used to describe it, is similar. The Tuesday morning quarterback is a good example. Members of the Monday night football club spend a good deal of time on Tuesday morning analyzing the game.

Finally, genres of *social action* are shared sets of behaviors toward the media in question, including not only how the media content is consumed (when and where it is viewed or read) but also the ways it affects the conduct of the members of the community. How are members' relationships among themselves affected by the media? Does a particular type of content facilitate the relationship in some way? Do people talk to one another about what they have seen or heard? Do they use

---

61   See, for example, Thomas R. Lindlof and Timothy P. Meyer, "Mediated Communication as Ways of Seeing, Acting, and Constructing Culture: The Tools and Foundations of Qualitative Research," in *Natural Audiences: Qualitative Research of Media Uses and Effects,* ed. T. R. Lindlof (Norwood, NJ: Ablex, 1987), pp. 1–32; Thomas R. Lindlof, "Media Audiences as Interpretive Communities," in *Communication Yearbook 11,* ed. J. A. Anderson (Newbury Park, CA: Sage, 1988), pp. 81–107; Kevin M. Carragee, "Interpretive Media Study and Interpretive Social Science," *Critical Studies in Mass Communication* 7 (1990): 81–96; Klaus Bruhn Jensen, "When Is Meaning? Communication Theory, Pragmatism, and Mass Media Reception," in *Communication Yearbook 14,* ed. J. A. Anderson (Newbury Park, CA: Sage, 1991), pp. 3–32.
62   James Lull, "The Social Uses of Television," *Human Communication Research* 6 (1980): 197–209; see also Shaun Moores, *Interpreting Audiences: The Ethnography of Media Consumption* (London: Sage, 1993).
63   Lindlof, "Media Audiences."

relationships viewed on television as models for their own relationships?

An example of a cultural analysis of media is Linda Steiner's investigation of the "No Comment" section of *Ms.* magazine.[64] *Ms.* has regularly published a page titled "No Comment," featuring quotations and entries from other sources, sent in by readers, to illustrate the oppression of women in media. The title of the section implies that the quotation stands by itself without comment.

Items from other magazines (especially print ads), journals, newspapers, and even textbooks and manuals have found their way onto the "No Comment" page. All items were originally published with a particular meaning in mind, but the readers of *Ms.* interpret them differently. The fact that readers choose similar items again and again to make a point at odds with the original publisher's intent makes these readers an interpretive community, sharing attitudes and perceptions about the media's treatment of women.

In her analysis Steiner isolates a number of meanings for various items. For example, many depict women as the property of men. Some mock feminism as offensive. Others make use of women's bodies in ways that are exploitative. Still others promote sexual abuse and violence against women. In each case, the deliberate reading opposes that intended by the originator of the quoted item. Steiner shows how contributing to and reading the "No Comment" section solidifies a set of values and views shared by the interpretive community of *Ms.* readers.

◖ COMMENTARY AND CRITIQUE

The theories presented in this chapter are members of an extended family. Like any family, they have important differences but share a common relationship. These approaches privilege conscious human perception and experience in one form or another. In phenomenology the conscious experience of the individual provides an eye to truth. In hermeneutics the interpretation of a culture or text is a disciplined and conscious human task. We have seen several varieties of these two traditions, including classical, social, and hermeneutic phenomenology, and we have also examined theories of cultural and textual hermeneutics.

Many important theoretical questions about experience and interpretation remain. Is human experience primarily individual or social? Can reality be ascertained by careful bracketing of experience, or is reality constructed by human action? Is meaning in the text or in the reader? Or does it arise from interaction between text and reader? What is the role of history and tradition in establishing meaning?

Setting these questions aside for the moment, three serious debates surround phenomenology and hermeneutics. First, these approaches conflict with traditional structural and cognitive perspectives summarized in Chapters 6 and 7. Second, they clash also with poststructuralism and critical theory (see Chapter 11). Third, there is a tension between textual and cultural interpretation. We will now consider each of these controversies in turn.

The structuralist critique is easily anticipated from ideas presented earlier in this book. We have encountered it before in the discussions of philosophical issues in communication theory and in the critiques of structuralism, cognitivism, and constructionism. The critique begins with the opposing assumption that structures are real apart from the human experience of them and that these realities impact human experience in ways neither anticipated nor understood by communicators themselves. For the structural or cognitive theorist, these powerful outside influences must be discovered by controlled observation, and hermeneutic interpretation is inadequate for this task.[65]

---

64   Linda Steiner, "Oppositional Decoding as an Act of Resistance," *Critical Studies in Mass Communication* 5 (1988): 1–15.

65   D. W. Hamlyn, "The Concept of Social Reality," in *Explaining Human Behavior: Consciousness, Human Action, and Social Structure,* ed. Paul F. Secord (Beverly Hills, CA: Sage, 1982), p. 194.

Traditional critics believe that interpretive approaches ignore important psychological and social structures that influence human behavior. By concentrating on conscious experience, they miss the ways outside factors affect human life. Interpretive media studies are an example. As Kevin Carragee points out,

In their desire to examine audience interpretations and uses of media content, interpretive studies largely have ignored the organizational and economic factors that influence the media texts. . . . The interpretive project's failure to incorporate research examining encoding processes reduces media texts to autonomous signifying systems; they are cut off from their origin in organizational routines and procedures.[66]

According to the structural-cognitive critique, the structures that affect human life are largely unintentional and out of awareness. Cognition is a complex set of processes, many of which are hidden from the individual.[67] Although much of what we do is indeed conscious, many important structures governing social life are beyond awareness.[68]

Social structures, too, exist apart from any design or intention as people live their lives. Anthony Giddens calls these the "unintended consequences" of purposeful actions. As individuals go about their daily activities, according to Giddens, certain outcomes that may not be intended nor even conscious come about, and these have a serious impact on subsequent actions. Giddens notes the importance of such structures:

History is not an intentional project, and all intentional activity takes place in the context of institutions sedimented over long-term periods of time. The unintended consequences of action are of fundamental importance to social theory, especially insofar as they are systematically incorporated within the processes of the reproduction of institutions.[69]

This thesis flies in the face of phenomenology, which gives conscious experience great power to apprehend the structures of reality. Early phenomenologists like Husserl would probably agree that the essence of reality is not normally within the awareness of the individual when in the natural attitude, but they would suggest that what becomes conscious in reduction is that which is essential and real about an experience.

Later phenomenologists of the social and hermeneutic traditions would find the structuralist objection unacceptable in any version. For these theorists, reality is always experience as lived.

Hermeneutics is a method that grants individuals the ability to interpret actions and texts. For theorists of this tradition, there is no structural reality outside of actions or texts, and ambiguity demands interpretation. Interpretation is a necessary conscious human experience.

To the structuralist, on the other hand, people may not accurately understand, nor can they reliably report, their experience. If your intentions are elusive and important processes are hidden, what is really going on in social life is not something a perceiver can tap into experientially. Instead, scientific methods of discovery are necessary. Research on attribution theory (Chapter 7) illustrates the difficulty of explaining one's own actions.[70]

Another objection of traditional social science is that interpretive methods tend to be case-oriented and do not lend themselves to generalization and theory building. In phenomenology

---

66   Carragee, "Interpretive Media Study."
67   See, for example, Michael T. Motley, "Consciousness and Intentionality in Communication: A Preliminary Model and Methodological Approaches," *Western Journal of Speech Communication* 50 (1986): 3–23.
68   William Bailey, "Consciousness and Action/Motion Theories of Communication," *Western Journal of Speech Communication* 50 (1986): 74.
69   Anthony Giddens, "On the Relation of Sociology to Philosophy," in *Explaining Human Behavior: Consciousness, Human Action, and Social Structure*, ed. Paul F. Secord (Beverly Hills, CA: Sage, 1982), p. 180.
70   R. E. Nisbett and T. D. Wilson, "Telling More Than We Can Know: Verbal Reports on Mental Processes," *Psychological Review* 84 (1977): 231–259. See also Pamela J. Benoit and William L. Benoit, "Consciousness: The Mindlessness/Mindfulness and Verbal Report of Controversies," *Western Journal of Speech Communication* 50 (1986): 41–63. Critics of attribution theory are quick to point out that the findings in this line of research do not accurately reflect the everyday experience of people acting in context. Indeed, this criticism has been leveled against all positivistic social science research. See, for example, John Shotter, *Social Accountability and Selfhood* (New York: Blackwell, 1984), pp. 167–172; Kenneth Gergen, *Toward Transformation in Social Knowledge* (New York: Springer-Verlag, 1982), pp. 126–133.

each thing must be understood in and of itself by careful bracketing of experience. In hermeneutics one interprets a set of group actions or a text, but generalizations beyond the individual case are discouraged. Even comparative ethnography, though it may look for commonalities, is equally interested in cultural difference. What, then, can be known from this method other than the facts of the case? For some, like Schutz, the facts of the case are good enough. These thinkers eschew theory as misleading because theories espouse generalizations that are not there. For others, like Hymes, generalizations can be made after examination of several cases.

The culture approach to organizations illustrates the difficulty of generalization. If you assume that the social reality of an organization comes from the interactions among members of the organization and that organizational cultures thereby differ, you put yourself into the difficult theoretical position of being unable to make generalizations or predictions about organizational life. Each organization must be studied independently, and generalizations become difficult.

An answer, of course, is that theories should not attempt to be predictive but should capture general categories of action, which we expect to be played out differently in various cultures. For example, although every organization is different, there are categories such as rituals and stories that all organizations can be expected to have. Such middle-range theories, like that of Pacanowsky and O'Donnell-Trujillo and of Hymes, enable us to observe cultures with a sensitivity to their rich individuality and their commonalities as well.

The structural-cognitive critique can be thought of as conservative because it argues from the tradition of Western thought and social science in the twentieth century. In a sense, then, this first set of concerns is a critique from the right. There is also a critique from the left. It comes from a movement that is by definition critical of traditional social science, a movement that aims to transform the work of social science. If the critique from the right accuses interpretive theories of ignoring, bending, or breaking tradi-

tional notions of reality and structure, the critique from the left accuses them of being overly conservative and insensitive to the need for change.

As we will see in the following chapter, interpretive and critical approaches to communication theory have certain common principles. There is, however, a substantial difference between the two, which has become the source of a debate.[71] Critical theory is transformative: It not only presents a picture of society but also aims to change social structure by raising consciousness about power in society.

Critical theory accuses interpretive approaches of being conservative and of failing to recognize their own ideological character. In other words, understanding human action by itself does not go far enough. Scholars must study the ways individuals are oppressed so that people can change the circumstances of their lives. The failure of interpretive scholarship to do so merely legitimizes repressive power structures and perpetuates oppression in society. The most significant problem of phenomenology, from this vantage point, is that it denies the political nature of everyday experience.[72]

In fact, many critical scholars accuse interpretive theory of bolstering the dominant ideology. The cultural approach to organizational theory is an example. The downside to the organizational culture movement is that the empirically minded manager may come to think of culture as just another variable to be manipulated in the management of the organization. This idea can lead to the negative consequence of ideological control.[73]

The critique from the left points out that any interpreter brings an orientation, an ideology, and a set of values to the subject under investigation. This state of affairs is not merely an ob-

---

71 This debate is summarized in Brian Fay, *Social Theory and Political Practice* (London: Allen & Unwin, 1975); and Ricoeur, *Hermeneutics*.

72 This argument is made by Stanley Deetz, *Democracy in an Age of Corporate Colonization* (Albany: SUNY Press, 1992), pp. 113–144.

73 This problem is explored by Sonja A. Sackmann, "Managing Organizational Culture: Dreams and Possibilities," *Communication Yearbook 13*, ed. James A. Anderson (Newbury Park, CA: Sage, 1990), pp. 114–148.

stacle to the validity of observation, because there is no one cultural form to be validly observed in any situation. Rather, a cultural description is always a product of a perspective, because the orientation of the ethnographer determines to some degree what the interpretation will be.

Even more, the interaction between researcher and subject is fraught with power relations. This eventuality affects not only the outcome of the investigation, the interpretation presented and the way it represents persons and cultures, but also the way research subjects are treated.[74]

There have been at least four responses to this criticism. The first is to acknowledge the power of writing in the construction of an interpretation and to pay careful attention to *how* one writes up the interpretation. Here the goal is to use writing as a way to capture and express the ideology of the ethnographer.[75]

The second response, somewhat at odds with the first, is to account for the power relationship between the subject and the researcher, to acknowledge that the researcher has a source of power in defining the subject and a special responsibility to empower the subject. Interview methods, for example, can affect the political relationship between the investigator and the participant, and ethnographers need to acknowledge and describe the ways this happens.[76]

The third response is for the ethnographer to get as close as possible to the embodied performances of the native culture, to experience that culture as the natives do, to get out of one's own way of seeing things as much as possible.[77] This is precisely one of the most important objectives of the performance ethnography movement discussed in this chapter.

A fourth response is to adopt the critical stance outright and use ethnography as a means to uncover oppressive power structures within a culture. Often called critical ethnography, this approach uses cultural interpretation as a form of social critique.[78]

This critique from the left is not as unified as might be implied in the above discussion. Indeed, on the question of how much power indi-viduals and groups have to determine their fate, the voice of the left is equivocal. There are two schools of thought on this point.

The first is poststructuralism.[79] Poststructuralism denies the reality of universal structures of language and discourse, while also denying the certainty of meaning in action or text. Poststructuralists see interpretive approaches as essentially foundationalist in that they seek some sort of essential meaning in practices and texts. Phenomenologists seek the essence of experience; poststructuralists deny essence. Hermeneutic scholars are devoted to finding the center or central meaning of texts; poststructuralists deny that there is any central meaning in texts.

The version of poststructuralism most opposed to interpretation is *deconstructionism*, or the movement to obliterate meaning.[80] Interpretation reconstructs meaning; deconstruction shows that whatever meaning is derived is wrong. Since there is an unending set of possible meanings in any text, there can be no central or true meaning at all.

This postmodern critique is countered by the second school of thought, which ironically resembles the conservative structuralist objection discussed earlier. This group believes that there is certain meaning, and this is to be found in hidden oppressive social structures, expressed in discourse. These deep structural meanings determine power relations among classes and groups of people, and individuals have little or no freedom to act in the world. These structuralists believe that interpretive theories are naive in

---

74   This controversy is summarized by James T. West, "Ethnography and Ideology: The Politics of Cultural Representation," *Western Journal of Communication* 57 (1993): 209–220.
75   See, for example, Atkinson, *Understanding Ethnographic Texts.* See also, Conquergood, "Rethinking Ethnography."
76   Bette J. Kauffman, "Feminist Facts: Interview Strategies and Political Subjects in Ethnography," *Communication Theory* 2 (1992): 187–206.
77   Dwight Conquergood, "Rethinking Ethnography."
78   Jim Thomas, *Doing Critical Ethnography* (Newbury Park, CA: Sage, 1993).
79   For an excellent summary of poststructuralism, see Art Berman, *From the New Criticism to Deconstruction* (Urbana, IL: University of Chicago Press, 1988).
80   The scholar most associated with deconstruction is Jacques Derrida. See *Of Grammatology,* trans. G. Spivak (Baltimore, MD: Johns Hopkins University Press, 1976).

assuming that groups and individuals influence their worlds in any way.[81]

The above discussion implies that experiential and interpretive theories are a unified and cohesive block of ideas under attack from the outside. This is a misleading impression. In fact, substantial differences exist among the theories in this chapter. One of the most important is the difference between textual and cultural interpretation, which is a dispute about the locus of meaning.[82]

For most cultural interpretivists, meaning is found in the practices of a culture. For most textual interpretivists, meaning is found in language and text. Indeed, Ricoeur's concept of distanciation is designed to capture the separation of text from cultural practice. The culture-interpretive view is that texts are a product of social interaction, whereas the text-interpretation view holds that texts prefigure culture in important ways.

Actually, cultural interpretation and social constructionism are closely related and could easily have been put in the same chapter of this book. Both are children of social phenomenology, and both see meaning as inherent in social practice. Thus, the tension between text and practice mirrors the debate between traditional text hermeneutics and social constructionism.

This controversy can be seen in debates on media. The idea of interpretive communities assigns great power to the practices of social groups in constructing the meaning of media in their own lives. Media text theorists, on the other hand, assign great power to the content of media in the creation of culture. Carragee continues his critique of interpretive studies in this way:

Interpretive researchers need to devote far more attention to the properties and structures of media messages, to the symbolic power of texts. Characterizations of texts or indeed media as empty vessels deny the ways in which texts and media help to constitute meanings and realities for their audiences by highlighting certain meanings and values while excluding others.[83]

An important question at this juncture is whether the text-practice dispute is a true disjunction. Some important commentators believe it is not. It may be entirely possible—indeed desirable—to grant power both to text and cultural practice.

Gadamer's work is especially important because he does precisely this. For Gadamer, readers cannot be separated from their interpretive communities in the way suggested by Ricoeur. At the same time, the text itself does have inherent meaning, and readers must be open to a dialogue between the reader and the text. The text has rich meaning to convey, and the reader always approaches that text from within an interpretive tradition. The interpretive frame informs the reading of the text, whereas the text helps shape the interpretive frame itself.

In the following chapter, we continue the discussion of meaning and social power. The emphasis now switches from interpretation of text and action to their transformation.

---

81 This objection is discussed in some detail by Michael Huspek, "Dueling Structures: The Theory of Resistance in Discourse," *Communication Theory* 3 (1993): 1–25.
82 This controversy is discussed by Berman, *From the New Criticism*, pp. 281–292.
83 Carragee, "Interpretive Media Study," p. 89.

CHAPTER

11

CRITICAL
THEORIES

Criticism has a long history in the field of communication. Rhetorical criticism, for example, carefully examines and judges the quality of discourse and other communication forms.[1] Our subject in this chapter is another kind of critique—critical social science.[2]

Although there are several varieties of critical social science, all share three essential features.[3] First, critical social scientists believe it necessary to understand the lived experience of real people in context. As such, critical theories share some of the ideas and methodologies of the interpretive theories discussed in Chapter 10. What makes critical scholarship different from much of the work discussed in that chapter is that it focuses on oppression.

Second, critical approaches examine social conditions and uncover oppressive power arrangements. For this reason critical theories also borrow from structuralism (Chapter 4). Most critical theories teach that knowledge is power, for understanding the ways you are oppressed enables you to take action and overcome oppressive forces.

In the field of communication, critical scholars are particularly interested in how messages reinforce oppression in society. Although critical scholars are interested in social action, they also focus on discourse and the texts that promote particular ideologies, establish and maintain power, and subvert the interests of certain groups and classes. Critical discourse analysis looks at actual features of texts that manifest these oppressive arrangements.[4]

Third, critical social science makes a conscious attempt to fuse theory and action. Such theories are clearly normative and act to accomplish

---

1 This chapter does not cover rhetorical criticism. For more information on this topic, see, for example, Sonja K. Foss, *Rhetorical Criticism: Exploration and Practice* (Prospect Heights, IL: Waveland, 1989).
2 This is not to imply that rhetorical criticism and critical social theory are necessarily separate fields. An argument for connecting them is made by Omar Swartz, *Conducting Socially Responsible Research* (Thousand Oaks, CA: Sage, 1997).
3 Brian Fay, *Social Theory and Political Practice* (London: Allen & Unwin, 1975), p. 94.
4 See, for example, Teun van Dijk, "Discourse Semantics and Ideology," *Discourse and Society* 6 (1995): 243–289; Teun van Dijk, "Principles of Critical Discourse Analysis," *Discourse and Society* 4 (1993): 249–283.

change in the conditions that affect our lives, or as Della Pollock and Robert Cox put it, "to *read* the world with an eye towards *shaping* it."[5] Critical research aims to reveal the ways in which competing interests clash and the manner in which conflicts are resolved in favor of particular groups over other ones. Processes of domination are often hidden from view, and critical theory aims to uncover these processes.[6] Critical theories therefore frequently ally themselves with the interests of marginalized groups.

Although critical theories have traditionally focused on clashing interests within societies, they can also feature the domination of one society over another. *Postcolonial theory* is a movement that looks at the ways in which Western societies dominate Third World peoples. It focuses on the role of discourse and media in such domination. The way in which First World peoples, including scholars, write and talk about the world maintains self-serving power structures. This tendency is propelled by the domination of Western media in the world.[7]

Whether it centers on the domination of interests within a society or imperialism by one society against another, critical social science is usually economic and political in nature, and communication is usually an important ingredient. In practice, critical theorists are usually reluctant to separate communication from other factors in the overall system of oppressive forces.[8]

Critical theories as a group are nearly impossible to characterize validly. At the beginning of this chapter, it is important for us to take a closer look at the various types of critical theory.

◖● SORTING OUT CRITICAL THEORIES

Because critical theories are so broad and cast such a wide net, they are often hard to place and categorize within the overall body of communication theory. Dennis Mumby provides a simple and clear scheme that will be quite helpful to us at this point.[9]

Mumby classifies communication scholarship into two broad groups—modern and postmodern. Rather than think of this distinction as a simple dichotomy, however, he presents four "discursive positions" along a continuum from the radical modern to the radical postmodern. As we are using the term here, the first two types are not considered critical, and the second two are.

The first kind of scholarship is the *discourse of representation,* or the positivist version of modernism. Here scholars make a sharp distinction between the observer and the world. Persons can perceive reality outside themselves and represent that reality with language. Most functionalist and cognitive theories discussed in Chapter 1 fall into this group. Many of the theories we have already covered in this book, including some brands of semiotics and theories of message production and reception, are examples of this kind of discourse.

The second category is the *discourse of understanding,* or interpretive modernism. Here the line between the observer and observed is less distinct. Interpretivists, as we described them in Chapter 1, see that reality is defined by an interaction between the knower and the known, that the observer structures observation in ways that can influence what is seen. We looked at many examples of this kind of discourse in previous chapters on symbolic interaction, social construction, interpretation, and culture.

The third and fourth categories are what we are calling "critical" in this text and are primarily the subject of the current chapter. These are

---

5   Della Pollock and J. Robert Cox, "Historicizing 'Reason': Critical Theory, Practice, and Postmodernity," *Communication Monographs* 58 (1991): 171.
6   This characteristic of critical theory is discussed by Nancy Fraser, *Unruly Practices: Power, Discourse, and Gender in Contemporary Social Theory* (Minneapolis: University of Minnesota Press, 1989), p. 113.
7   Raka Shome, "Postcolonial Interventions in the Rhetorical Canon: An 'Other' View," *Communication Theory* 6 (1996): 40–59; Saba Mahmood, "Cultural Studies and Ethnic Absolutism: Comments on Stuart Hall's 'Culture, Community, and Nation,'" *Cultural Studies* 10 (1996): 1–11.
8   For a discussion of the problems associated with separating communication as a focus, see Milton Mueller, "Why Communications Policy Is Passing 'Mass Communication' By: Political Economy as the Missing Link," *Critical Studies in Mass Communication* 12 (1995): 455–472.
9   Dennis K. Mumby, "Modernism, Postmodernism, and Communication Studies: A Rereading of an Ongoing Debate," *Communication Theory* 7 (1997): 1–28.

the discourses of *suspicion,* or critical modernism, and *vulnerability,* or postmodernism. Critical modernism is in the "structural" tradition, because it is a critique of an imagined structure of social arrangements that truly exist outside human perception and endure over time. Postmodernism is "poststructural" because it denies the existence of any true enduring social arrangements.

This distinction between modern and postmodern versions marks a significant fault line within the critical tradition.[10] The modern version—often referred to as "structural"—centers on oppressive social structures. They are real and enduring, though they may be hidden from the consciousness of most people. Critical scholars in this group attempt to name and expose these oppressive arrangements.

In contrast, the postmodern version teaches that there is no reality or central meaning and that oppressive "structures" are ephemeral. There is a struggle, but it is not a struggle between monolithic ideologies. It is a struggle between fluid interests and ideas.[11]

The structural tradition in critical social science is highly "theoretical" in the sense that it presents a standing version of social life to explain how oppressive structures work. The postmodern tradition is rather "antitheoretical" because it denies the existence of any particular structure over time.

Now, labels become confusing here. Many critical approaches are marxist, but because Marx the modernist was highly structural and theoretical, postmodernists sometimes object to being called "marxist." Also, because they generally deny the validity of "theory," postmodernists sometimes are excluded from the label "critical theory."

We are treating both modernist and postmodernist approaches in this chapter as "critical" because of their shared position of opposition to traditional social science. Pollock and Cox write that although these two schools of thought have important differences, they share "a sense of failed hope and the difficulty, if not impossibility, of effecting social change. Conditioned by the atrocities of dogma and the advancing commercialization of every aspect of social life, they also similarly distrust 'centristic' thinking or 'totalizing' modes of discourse."[12]

In the remainder of the chapter, we will look at three broad traditions of critical studies—structuralism, poststructuralism, and feminism. Structuralist theories show us what the modernist tradition of critical theory looks like, and poststructuralist theories illustrate the postmodern. Both kinds of theory are present in feminist scholarship.

◖ STRUCTURAL APPROACHES

Marxist Foundations

Although critical theory has come a long way since Marx, much of it is still basically marxist. In fact, one of the most important intellectual strands of the twentieth century is marxist-based social theory. Originating with the ideas of Karl Marx and Friedrich Engels, this movement consists of a number of loosely related theories challenging the dominant order of society. Virtually all branches of social science, including communication, have been influenced by this line of thought.[13]

---

10   For more detailed discussions of these schools of thought see Mats Alvesson and Stanley Deetz, "Critical Theory and Postmodernism Approaches to Organizational Studies," in *Handbook of Organizational Studies,* eds. S. Clegg, C. Harding, and W. Nord (London: Sage, 1996), pp. 173–202; Douglas Kellner, *Media Culture: Cultural Studies, Identity and Politics Between the Modern and the Postmodern* (London: Routledge, 1995); Thomas McCarthy, *Ideals and Illusions: On Reconstruction and Deconstruction in Contemporary Critical Theory* (Cambridge, MA: MIT Press, 1993); Pollock and Cox, "Historicizing"; Donald G. Ellis, "Poststructuralism and Language: Non-Sense," *Communication Monographs* 58 (1991): 213–224; and Michael Huspek, "Taking Aim on Habermas's Critical Theory: On the Road Toward a Critical Hermeneutics," *Communication Monographs* 58 (1991): 225–233.

11   For a good description and critique of postmodern media studies, see John B. Harms and David R. Dickens, "Postmodern Media Studies: Analysis or Symptom?," *Critical Studies in Mass Communication* 13 (1996): 210–227.

12   Pollock and Cox, "Historicizing," p. 175.

13   For a brief overview of the movement, see Everett M. Rogers, *A History of Communication Study: A Biographical Approach* (New York: Free Press, 1994), pp. 102–128; Tom Bottomore and Armand Mattelart, "Marxist Theories of Communication," in *International Encyclopedia of Communications,* vol. 2, ed. E. Barnouw (New York: Oxford University Press, 1989), pp. 476–483. For coverage of a variety of Marxist-based ideas, see Cary Nelson and Lawrence Grossberg (eds.), *Marxism and the Interpretation of Culture* (Urbana: University of Illinois Press, 1988).

Marx taught that the means of production in society determines the nature of society.[14] This is the basic linear idea of Marxism, the *base-superstructure* relationship: The economy is the base of all social structure. In capitalistic systems, profit drives production and therefore dominates labor.

Working-class groups are oppressed by more powerful groups that benefit from profit. All institutions that perpetuate domination within a capitalistic society are made possible by this economic system.[15] Only when the working class rises up against dominant groups can the means of production be changed and the liberation of the worker be achieved. Such liberation furthers the natural progress of history in which forces in opposition clash in a dialectic that results in a higher social order. This classical Marxist theory is called the *critique of political economy*.

Today, marxist critical theory is thriving, although it has become diffused and multitheoretical. Not all adherents to critical theory are "Marxist," in the classical sense of Marx's teachings, but there is no question that Marx had an immense influence on this school of thought. Although few critical theorists today adopt Marx's ideas on political economy, the basic concerns of dialectical conflict, domination, and oppression remain important. For this reason critical theory today is frequently labeled "neo-marxist" or "marxist" (with a lowercase *m*).

In contrast to Marx's simple base-superstructure model, most contemporary critical theories view social processes as *overdetermined*, or caused by multiple sources. They see social structure as a system in which many things interact and affect one another (Chapter 3).

Critical theorists view their task as uncovering oppressive forces through *dialectical analysis*, which is designed to expose an underlying struggle between opposing forces.[16] The population generally perceives a kind of surface order to things, and the critical theorist's job is to point out the contradictions that exist. Only by becoming aware of the dialectic of opposing forces in a struggle for power can individuals be liberated and free to change the existing order. Otherwise, they will remain alienated from one another and co-opted into their own oppression.

Marxism places great emphasis on the means of communication in society. Communication practices are an outcome of the tension between individual creativity and the social constraints on that creativity. Only when individuals are truly free to express themselves with clarity and reason will liberation occur, and that condition cannot come about in a class-based society.

On the other hand, many critical theorists believe that contradiction, tension, and conflict are inevitable aspects of the social order and can never be eliminated. The ideal state is a social environment in which all voices can be heard so that no force dominates any other.

Language is an important constraint on individual expression, for the language of the dominant class makes it difficult for working-class groups to understand their situation and to get out of it. In other words, the dominant language defines and perpetuates the oppression of marginalized groups. It is the job of the critical theorist to create new forms of language that will enable the predominant ideology to be exposed and competing ideologies to be heard.

The term *ideology* is important in most critical theories. An ideology is a set of ideas that structure a group's reality, a system of representations or a code of meanings governing how individuals and groups see the world.[17] In classical Marxism an ideology is a false set of ideas perpetuated by the dominant political force. For the

---

14   Karl Marx's best-known works are *The Communist Manifesto* (London: Reeves, 1888) and *Capital* (Chicago: Kerr, 1909).

15   For a discussion of capitalist oppression as the basis for critical theory, see Graham Murdock, "Across the Great Divide: Cultural Analysis and the Condition of Democracy," *Critical Studies in Mass Communication* 12 (1995): 89–95.

16   See, for example, Robert Pryor, "On the Method of Critical Theory and Its Implications for a Critical Theory of Communication," in *Phenomenology in Rhetoric and Communication*, ed. S. Deetz (Washington, DC: Center for Advanced Research in Phenomenology/University Press of America, 1981), pp. 25–35; Jennifer Daryl Slack and Martin Allor, "The Political and Epistemological Constituents of Critical Communication Research," *Journal of Communication* 33 (1983): 128–218; Dallas W. Smythe and Tran Van Dinh, "On Critical and Administrative Research: A New Critical Analysis," *Journal of Communication* 33 (1983): 117–127; Everett M. Rogers, "The Empirical and the Critical Schools of Communication Research," in *Communication Yearbook 5*, ed. M. Burgoon (New Brunswick, NJ: Transaction, 1982), pp. 125–144.

17   For a brief discussion of theories of ideology, see Stuart Hall, "Ideology," in *International Encyclopedia of Communications*, vol. 2, ed. E. Barnouw (New York: Oxford University Press, 1989), pp. 307–311.

classical Marxist, science must be used to discover truth and to overcome the *false consciousness* of ideology.

More recent critical theorists tend to assert that there is no single dominant ideology but that the dominant classes in society are themselves constituted by a struggle among several. Many current thinkers reject the idea that an ideology is an isolated element in the social system; rather, it is deeply embedded in language and all other social and cultural processes.

Perhaps the best-known ideology theorist is the French Marxist Louis Althusser.[18] For Althusser, ideology is present in the structure of society itself and arises from the actual practices undertaken by institutions within society. As such, ideology actually forms the individual's consciousness and creates the person's subjective understanding of experience. In this model the superstructure (social organization) creates ideology, which in turn affects individuals' notions of reality.

For Althusser, this superstructure consists of *repressive state apparatuses* such as the police and the military and *ideological state apparatuses* such as education, religion, and mass media. The repressive mechanisms enforce an ideology when it is threatened by deviant action, and the ideological apparatuses reproduce it more subtly in everyday activities of communication by making an ideology seem normal.

We live within a real set of conditions, but we normally do not understand our relationship to actual conditions except through an ideology. The real conditions of existence can only be discovered through science, which Althusser poses in opposition to ideology. This idea has been highly controversial because it is based on a realist notion of truth, which much critical theory now opposes.

Marxist theories tend to see society as the grounds for a struggle among interests through the domination of one ideology over another. *Hegemony* is the process of domination, in which one set of ideas subverts or co-opts another. It is a process by which one group in society exerts leadership over all others. The concept was perhaps best elaborated by the Italian Marxist Antonio Gramsci.[19]

The process of hegemony can occur in many ways and in many settings. In essence, it happens when events or texts are interpreted in a way that promotes the interests of one group over those of another. This can be a subtle process of co-opting the interests of a subordinate group into supporting those of a dominant one. For example, advertisers often play into the "women's liberation" theme, making it look as though the corporation supports women's rights. What is happening here is that women's interests are being reinterpreted to promote the interests of the capital economy. Ideology plays a central role in this process because it structures the way people understand their experience, and it is therefore powerful in shaping how they interpret events.

Dennis Mumby has presented a persuasive theory of hegemony within organizations that illustrates this process very well.[20] Mumby shows how organizations are sites in which hegemonic struggles occur. Power is established within an organization by the domination of one ideology over others. We saw in the previous chapter that communication in organizations functions in part to create an organizational culture. This occurs through rituals, stories, and the like, and Mumby shows how the culture of an organization involves an inherently political process. Communication within the organization serves not only to establish meaning but also to create power and domination.

One way this happens is through storytelling, or the use of narrative. Narratives are certain kinds of texts that create and perpetuate ideologies. For example, there is a story that has been repeatedly retold at IBM. As the story goes, the chairman of the board was stopped by a

18   Louis Althusser, *For Marx*, trans. B. Brewster (New York: Vintage, 1970); *Lenin and Philosophy*, trans. B. Brewster (New York: Monthly Review Press, 1971). Althusser's work is summarized by Stuart Hall, "Signification, Representation, Ideology: Althusser and the Post-Structuralist Debates," *Critical Studies in Mass Communication* 2 (1985): 91–114; Dennis K. Mumby, *Communication and Power in Organizations: Discourse, Ideology, and Domination* (Norwood, NJ: Ablex, 1988), pp. 74–78.
19   Antonio Gramsci, *Selections from the Prison Notebooks*, trans. Q. Hoare and G. Nowell Smith (New York: International, 1971).
20   Dennis K. Mumby, "The Political Function of Narrative in Organizations," *Communication Monographs* 54 (1987): 113–127; Mumby, *Communication and Power*.

22-year-old female security guard because he did not have the appropriate badge to enter the area she was guarding. Although you might think that the boss would pull rank, he quietly secured the proper badge and got entry.[21] One reading of this story is that the chairman was a nice guy who wanted to follow the rules. But the story would not be noteworthy at all if power relations were not important. Consequently, the story reinforces the idea of power relations in this company.

The Frankfurt School and Universal Pragmatics

One of the longest and best-known Marxist traditions is the Frankfurt School. The *Frankfurt School* is such an important tradition in critical studies that it is often known simply as *Critical Theory.* These theorists originally based their ideas on Marxist thought, although it has gone far afield from that origin in the past fifty years. Communication takes a central place in this movement, and the study of mass communication has been especially important.[22]

This brand of critical theory began with the work of Max Horkheimer, Theodor Adorno, Herbert Marcuse, and their colleagues at the Frankfurt Institute for Social Research in 1923.[23] The group was originally guided by Marxist principles, although they were never members of any political party, and their work was distinctly scholarly rather than activist. With the rise of the National Socialist party in Germany in the 1930s, the Frankfurt scholars immigrated to the United States and there became intensely interested in mass communication and the media as structures of oppression in capitalistic societies.

The early Frankfurt scholars reacted strongly to the classical ideals of Marxism and the success of the Russian revolution. They saw capitalism as an evolutionary stage in the development, first, of socialism and then of communism. Their ideas at that time formed a harsh critique of capitalism and liberal democracy.

Since the early years of the Frankfurt School, however, no agreed-on unified theory characterizes its members. The best-known contemporary Frankfurt scholar is Jürgen Habermas, whose theory of universal pragmatics and the transformation of society has had considerable influence in Europe and an increasing influence in the United States. Habermas is clearly the most important spokesperson for the Frankfurt School today.[24] His theory draws from a wide range of thought and presents a coherent critical view of communication and society. We turn now to a closer look at his contribution.

Habermas teaches that society must be understood as a mix of three major interests: work, interaction, and power. All three interests are necessary. *Work,* the first major interest, consists of the efforts to create material resources. Because of its highly instrumental nature—achieving tangible tasks and accomplishing concrete objectives—work is basically a "technical interest." It involves an instrumental rationality and is represented by the empirical-analytical sciences. In other words, technology is used as an instrument to accomplish practical results and is based on scientific research. It designs computers, builds bridges, puts satellites in orbit, administers organizations, and enables wondrous medical treatments.

---

21   Mumby, "Political Function," pp. 120–125; *Communication and Power,* pp. 115–124.

22   Douglas Kellner, "Media Communications vs. Cultural Studies: Overcoming the Divide," *Communication Theory* 5 (1995): 162–177.

23   For a brief historical perspective, see Thomas B. Farrell and James A. Aune, "Critical Theory and Communication: A Selective Literature Review," *Quarterly Journal of Speech* 65 (1979): 93–120. See also Andrew Arato and Eike Gebhardt (eds.), *The Essential Frankfurt School Reader* (New York: Continuum, 1982).

24   The important works of Habermas include *Postmetaphysical Thinking: Philosophical Essays,* trans. William Mark Hohengarten (Cambridge, MA: MIT Press, 1992); *Knowledge and Human Interests,* trans. J. J. Shapiro (Boston: Beacon, 1971); *Legitimation Crisis,* trans. T. McCarthy (Boston: Beacon, 1975); *The Theory of Communicative Action, Volume 1: Reason and the Rationalization of Society,* trans. T. McCarthy (Boston: Beacon, 1984). Excellent secondary summaries can be found in Thomas B. Farrell, *Norms of Rhetorical Culture* (New Haven, CT: Yale University Press, 1993); Sonja K. Foss, Karen A. Foss, and Robert Trapp, *Contemporary Perspectives on Rhetoric* (Prospect Heights, IL: Waveland, 1991), pp. 241–272; see also Sue Curry Jansen, "Power and Knowledge: Toward a New Critical Synthesis," *Journal of Communication* 33 (1983): 342–354; Mumby, *Communication and Power,* pp. 23–54; Richard L. Lanigan, *Phenomenology of Communication: Merleau-Ponty's Thematics in Communicology and Semiology* (Pittsburgh, PA: Duquesne University Press, 1988), pp. 75–99.

TABLE **11.1**

Three Interests of Society

Type	Nature of Interest	Rationality	Associated Scholarship
Work	Technical	Instrumental	Empirical sciences
Interaction	Practical	Practical	History/hermeneutics
Power	Emancipatory	Self-reflection	Critical theory

The second major interest is *interaction,* or the use of language and other symbol systems of communication. Because social cooperation is necessary for survival, Habermas names this second item the "practical interest." It involves practical reasoning and is represented in historical scholarship and hermeneutics. The interaction interest can be seen in speeches, conferences, psychotherapy, family relations, and a host of other cooperative endeavors.

The third major interest is *power.* Social order naturally leads to the distribution of power, yet we are also interested in being freed from domination. Power leads to distorted communication, but by becoming aware of the ideologies that dominate in society, groups can themselves be empowered to transform society. Consequently, power is an "emancipatory interest." The rationality of power is self-reflection, and the branch of scholarship that deals with it is critical theory. For Habermas, the kind of work done by the critical theorists discussed thus far in this chapter is emancipatory because it can empower otherwise powerless groups. Table 11.1 summarizes the basic interests of work, interaction, and power.

As an example of these interests at work, consider the study by Steven Ealy of a Georgia State job-classification survey in the 1970s.[25] At that time Georgia was strapped with the responsibility of reclassifying 45,000 state job positions, a monumental task; according to Ealy, the result was a serious communication breakdown. The

state employed a consulting firm to conduct the necessary survey, and a plan was drafted to collect information about each position, develop job specifications, classify the positions, and then determine pay.

A strong technical interest guided the reclassification study. There was a job to be done, and the consultants developed a method to achieve this goal. They proceeded as if the task could be solved by the use of "objective" or scientific procedures—gathering data, classifying jobs, and the like.

The employees and the departments, however, did not think of the study this way. They saw the study as a practical problem, one that affected their daily work and pay. For the departments, collecting data and implementing the results should have involved a good deal of interaction and consensus building, but it did not. Immediately, then, there was a clash of interests.

Because they held the power, the organizational decision makers' technical interests prevailed, the consultants' methods were imposed, and all practical interests were eliminated. In other words, the employees were expected simply to comply with the survey without much discussion about their needs and the practical problems like operational difficulties, management problems, and moral questions that reclassification might create.

In short, the participants were unequal in power and knowledge, and the interests of workers were subverted by those of management. The study lacked the kind of open communication that Habermas says is necessary in a free society. As a result the new classification

---

25   Steven D. Ealy, *Communication, Speech, and Politics: Habermas and Political Analysis* (Washington, DC: University Press of America, 1981).

system was not accepted by employees and was implemented only partially after many delays, new studies, lawsuits, and appeals.

As this case illustrates, human life cannot be properly conducted from the perspective of only one interest—work, interaction, or power. Any activity is likely to span all three categories. Thus, all are necessary.

For example, the development of a new drug is a clear reflection of a technical interest, but it cannot be done without cooperation and communication, requiring an interaction interest as well. In a market economy, the drug is developed by a corporation to gain a competitive advantage, which is clearly a power interest, too.

No aspect of life is interest free, even science. An emancipated society is free from unnecessary domination of any one interest, and everybody has equal opportunity to participate in decision making. Habermas believes that a strong public sphere, apart from private interests, is necessary to ensure this state of affairs.

Habermas is especially concerned with the domination of the technical interest in contemporary capitalistic societies.[26] In such societies, the public and private are intertwined to the point that the public sector cannot guard against the oppression of private, technical interests. Ideally, the public and private should be balanced, and the public sector should be strong enough to provide a climate for free expression of ideas and debate. In modern society, however, that climate is stifled.

It is clear from the foregoing discussion that Habermas values communication as essential to emancipation, because language is the means by which the emancipatory interest is fulfilled. Communicative competence is therefore necessary for effective participation in decision making. Competence involves knowing how to use speech appropriately to accomplish goals, requiring compelling argument.

Habermas's approach to communication is based largely on speech-act theory, which is

summarized in Chapter 5. Habermas refers to his theory of speech acts as *universal pragmatics*, which includes the universal principles of language. He outlines three types of speech acts. *Constatives*, or assertions, are designed to get across a proposition as true. For example, if you were involved in a labor–management dispute, you might accuse the union of engaging in unfair labor practices.

Regulatives are intended to affect one's relationship with another person or party through influence. Examples are commands and promises. In the labor–management example, your statement about unfair labor practices would be regulative if it were intended to bring the union to the bargaining table. Here, your purpose is to influence the other party in some way, to regulate their behavior—specifically, to initiate negotiations.

Finally, *avowals* are designed to express the speaker's internal condition, to affirm something about oneself. In labor–management negotiations, for example, participants often express anger over the other party's activities. Notice that a message you might present could include any combination of these speech acts because you can achieve a number of intentions at once. So, for example, you might make an angry statement about unfair union practices, which is an "avowal" because it expresses your internal condition (anger), a "regulative" because it is designed to get negotiations underway, and a "constative" because you are trying to prove the truth of your statement.

Further, the type of speech act determines the kind of validity that one must meet in a statement. In a constative speech act, one must demonstrate the truth of the claim. In a regulative speech act, one must meet standards of appropriateness. And an avowal must be sincere or truthful.

Because a single speech act may fulfill any of the three types, various combinations of validity forms may also have to be met. For example, to meet all three validity requirements, your statement about union practices must be taken as true (that the union is indeed engaged in certain prac-

26   See especially Habermas, *Legitimation Crisis.*

tices), as appropriate (that under the circumstances, bargaining is proper), and as sincere (that you are truly angry over the situation).

These validity claims are not always easy to secure, since people do not always believe that one's statements are valid. In the labor–management case, you might have some difficulty proving your case, as happened in the Georgia reclassification situation. Here, the management's validity claims about the new system were severely challenged in the form of objections, lawsuits, and individual appeals.

Habermas uses the term *discourse* to describe the special kind of communication required when a speaker's statements are challenged. Unlike normal communication, "discourse" is a systematic argument that makes special appeals to demonstrate the validity of a claim.

Again, there are different kinds of discourse, depending on the type of speech act being defended. Truth claims are argued with *theoretic discourse,* which emphasizes evidence. If the union denied your allegations of improper conduct, you would be pressed to make a case by expanding your argument to include evidence showing that the union did, indeed, participate in certain activities.

When appropriateness is being argued, *practical discourse* is used. This emphasizes norms. If the union resisted your attempts to begin bargaining, you would have to create practical discourse to demonstrate the appropriateness of negotiations. Challenges to one's sincerity also require special action to demonstrate genuine concern, but this is usually direct action rather than discourse.

Of course, there is no guarantee that the union would agree with your evidence or the norms used to appeal for bargaining. Where communicators do not share the same standards or concepts for evaluating the strength of an argument, they must move to a higher level of discourse, which Habermas calls *metatheoretical discourse.* Here, communicators argue about what constitutes good evidence for a claim or what norms are indeed appropriate in the given situation. This is the kind of thing the Supreme Court does.

An even higher level of discourse is sometimes necessary—*metaethical discourse.* Here, the very nature of knowledge itself is under contention and must be argued. Such discourse is a philosophical argument about what constitutes proper knowledge, which is precisely what critical theory does, for it challenges the assumed procedures for generating knowledge in society.

Habermas believes that free speech is necessary for productive normal communication and higher levels of discourse to take place. Although impossible to achieve, Habermas describes an *ideal speech situation* on which society should be modeled. First, the ideal speech situation requires freedom of speech; there must be no constraints on what can be expressed. Second, all individuals must have equal access to speaking. In other words, all speakers and positions must be recognized as legitimate. Finally, the norms and obligations of society are not one-sided but distribute power equally to all strata in society. Only when these requirements are met can completely emancipatory communication take place.

Emancipatory communication in the form of higher levels of discourse is essential to transform society so that the needs of the individual can be met. Habermas believes that people normally live in an unquestioned *life-world,* the ordinary, daily activities of people. The life-world, however, is constrained by certain aspects of the social system such as money, bureaucracy, and corporate power. We see here shades of Althusserian ideology in Habermas's theory—the idea that the superstructure creates an ideology that affects the ordinary understanding of citizens in their everyday lives.

Habermas frames this problem as *colonization,* or the power of the system over individuals. When the life-world is colonized by the system, there is less opportunity to use language to achieve positive goals for individuals.

Here is where critical theory comes in. The primary function of critical theory is to raise questions and call attention to problems about the life-world that make critical reflection and resolution necessary. Only when we are aware of the problems of our life-world and the ways the system influences our view of life can we become emancipated from the entanglements of the system.

There is more opportunity to accomplish emancipation in modern society than in traditional society because of the relatively greater amount of conflict in modernity. In modern society we have the opportunity to hear a variety of viewpoints, but only if the system will allow free expression. Modern capitalistic societies have not yet achieved emancipation, and critical theorists have a responsibility to work toward making this possible.

◖● THE POSTSTRUCTURAL TRADITION

In this section we will look at two theories normally considered poststructural in orientation. These are cultural studies and the work of Michel Foucault. Actually, these are quite different from each other and take the poststructural tradition in quite different directions.

Cultural Studies

Cultural studies involves investigations of the ways culture is produced through a struggle among ideologies.[27] The most notable group of cultural scholars, British Cultural Studies, is associated with the Centre for Contemporary Cultural Studies at the University of Birmingham. The origins of this tradition are usually traced to the writings of Richard Hoggart and Raymond Williams in the 1950s, which examined the British working class after World War II.[28] Today, the leader of the movement is Stuart Hall.[29]

The cultural studies tradition is distinctly reformist in orientation. These scholars want to see changes in Western society, and they view their scholarship as an instrument of socialist cultural struggle.[30] They believe that such change will occur in two ways: (1) by identifying contradictions in society, the resolution of which will lead to positive, as opposed to oppressive, change;

and (2) by providing interpretations that will help people understand domination and the kinds of change that would be desirable. Samuel Becker describes their goal as "jarring both the audience and the workers in the media back from becoming too accepting of their illusions or existing practices so they will question them and their conditions."[31]

The study of mass communication is central to this work, for the media are perceived as powerful tools of the dominant ideology. In addition, media have the potential of raising the consciousness of the population about issues of class, power, and domination. We must be cautious in interpreting cultural studies in this light, however, because media are part of a much larger set of institutional forces. Media are important, but they are not the sole concern of these scholars, which is why they refer to their field as "cultural studies" rather than "media studies."

What is meant by *culture* in "cultural studies"? Two definitions have been employed. The first is the common ideas on which a society or group rests, its ideology, or the collective ways by which a group understands its experience. The second is the practices or the entire way of life of a group—what individuals do materially from day to day. These two senses of culture can-

---

27   For a readable overview, see Ben Agger, *Cultural Studies as Critical Theory* (London: Falmer, 1992). See also the review essay by Thomas Rosteck, "Cultural Studies and Rhetorical Studies," *Quarterly Journal of Speech* 81 (1995): 386–421; Kellner, "Media Communications vs. Cultural Studies."
28   Richard Hoggart, *Uses of Literacy* (London: Chatto & Windus, 1957); Raymond Williams, *The Long Revolution* (New York: Columbia University Press, 1961).
29   For a good survey of the work of Hall and others at the Centre, see Stuart Hall and others (eds.), *Culture, Media, Language* (London: Hutchinson, 1981). See also Stuart Hall, "Cultural Studies: Two Paradigms," in *Media, Culture, and Society: A Critical Reader,* ed. R. Collins (London: Sage, 1986); and Hall, "Signification." Four secondary treatments are especially helpful: Anne Makus, "Stuart Hall's Theory of Ideology: A Frame for Rhetorical Criticism," *Western Journal of Speech Communication* 54 (1990): 495–514; Ronald Lembo and Kenneth H. Tucker, "Culture, Television, and Opposition: Rethinking Cultural Studies," *Critical Studies in Mass Communication* 7 (1990): 97–116; Samuel L. Becker, "Marxist Approaches to Media Studies: The British Experience," *Critical Studies in Mass Communication* 1 (1984): 66–80; Robert White, "Mass Communication and Culture: Transition to a New Paradigm," *Journal of Communication* 33 (1983): 279–301.
30   Murdock, "Across the Great Divide."
31   Becker, "Marxist," p. 67.

not really be separated, for the ideology of a group is produced and reproduced in its practices. In fact, the general concern of cultural theorists is the link between the actions of society's institutions such as the media and the culture. Practices and ideas always occur together within a historical context.

For example, people watch television every day. The entire television industry is a cultural production because it is a means for creating, disputing, reproducing, and changing culture. The concrete or material practices involved in producing and consuming television are a crucial mechanism in the establishment of ideology, as are standing in line, eating breakfast, or driving a car.

We share a common sense about how things are. This shared understanding is an ideology determined by numerous, often subtle, influences that come together and make common experience seem real to us. In cultural studies, this process of having our realities reinforced from many sources is called *articulation.* Our shared understandings seem real because of the connection, or articulation, among several sources of verification.[32]

For example, it may seem absolutely essential to you to get a college degree. You think that a college education is good and leads to success in life. You think that you will get a good career by attending college and that you will be able to have a more meaningful life from what you learn in college. You think that a college education will make you more literate and able to participate more critically in our democratic society. These beliefs are commonly accepted by many people in our culture, but they are socially constructed ideas reinforced seemingly from every direction—from family, media, and school itself. Our acceptance of the superiority of higher education is a product of a very strong articulation.

Because of articulation, not all ideologies exist on an equal footing in society. Cultural theory posits that capitalistic societies are dominated by a particular ideology of the elite. For the workers of society, the dominant ideology is false because it does not reflect their interests. Instead, the dominant ideology is involved in a hegemony against powerless groups.

Hegemony, however, is always a fluid process, what Hall calls a temporary state in a "theatre of struggle." We must therefore "think of societies as complex formations, necessarily contradictory, always historically specific."[33] In other words, the struggle between contradictory ideologies is constantly changing.

Social institutions like education, religion, and government are interlinked in ways that support the dominant ideology, making resistance difficult. Especially important is the link between infrastructure and superstructure. *Infrastructure* is sometimes referred to as the "base," or basic economic arrangements of a society, including buildings, monetary system, capital, machinery, and so on. The *superstructure* consists of societal institutions. The exact relationship between infrastructure and superstructure is in dispute.

Early Marxist theory taught that the infrastructure (economic resource base) determined superstructure.[34] In cultural studies, however, the relationship is believed to be more complex. The forces of society are considered to be *overdetermined,* or caused by multiple sources. Infrastructure and superstructure may therefore be mutually interdependent. Because of the complexity of causation in society, no one set of conditions is required for a particular outcome to occur.

The same is true of ideology. Multiple ideologies exist next to one another in dynamic tension. Hall puts the matter this way:

> The important thing about systems of representation is that they are not singular. . . . As you enter an ideological field and pick out any one nodal representation or idea, you immediately

32   This point is explained in greater detail by Ian Angus, "The Politics of Common Sense: Articulation Theory and Critical Communication Studies," in *Communication Yearbook 15*, ed. Stanley Deetz (Newbury Park, CA: Sage, 1992): 535–570.
33   Hall, "Cultural Studies," p. 36.
34   This problem and other issues facing the cultural studies program are discussed in Stuart Hall, "Cultural Studies and the Centre: Some Problematics and Problems," in *Culture, Media, Language,* eds. Stuart Hall and others (London: Hutchinson, 1981), pp. 15–47.

trigger off a whole chain of connotative associations. Ideological representations connote—summon—one another.[35]

Communication, especially through the media, has a special role in affecting popular culture through the dissemination of information. The media are extremely important because they directly present a way of viewing reality. Even though the media portray ideology explicitly and directly, opposing voices will always be present as part of the dialectical struggle between groups in a society.

Still the media are dominated by the prevailing ideology, and they therefore treat opposing views from within the frame of the dominant ideology, which has the effect of defining opposing groups as "fringe." The irony of media, especially television, is that they present the illusion of diversity and objectivity, when in fact they are clear instruments of the dominant order.[36]

Producers control the content of media by particular ways of encoding messages. As Becker describes the process,

> Events do not signify . . . to be intelligible events must be put into symbolic form . . . the communicator has a choice of codes or sets of symbols. The one chosen affects the meaning of the events for receivers. Since every language— every symbol—coincides with an ideology, the choice of a set of symbols is, whether conscious or not, the choice of an ideology.[37]

For example, advertisers carefully design television commercials to create a certain image and thereby sell the product. Other kinds of programming such as news and comedy may seem less ideological, but they are every bit as much so.

At the same time, however, audiences may use their own categories to decode the message, and they often reinterpret media messages in ways never intended by the source.[38] As a result of alternative meanings, oppositional ideologies can and do arise in society. The intended meaning of a commercial may be completely lost on certain parts of the audience that interpret it in quite different ways. For example, an advertiser may use sex appeal for men, but feminist viewers may see the image as demeaning to women.

For Hall and his colleagues, the interpretation of media texts always occurs within a struggle of ideological control. Ronald Lembo and Kenneth Tucker describe the process as "a competitive arena where individuals or groups express opposing interests and battle for cultural power."[39] Rap music is a good example of this struggle. Does it reflect the genuine values and interests of the black youth culture, or is it a sign of the degeneration of society? The answer depends on which interpretive community is asked.

The chief aim of cultural studies, then, is to expose the ways ideologies of powerful groups are unwittingly perpetuated and the ways they can be resisted to disrupt the system of power that disfranchises certain groups.

Lawrence Grossberg's study of rock music is an especially interesting illustration of how cultural scholars work. In his essay on the subject, he discusses a sweeping range of issues related to the meaning of rock and roll in contemporary culture, the role of punk, and the place of youths in society.[40]

For Grossberg, rock and roll is an "apparatus" of culture, a movement unified by the feeling it engenders among its fans. Like any cultural text, there should be no privileged reading of it. Rock and roll of all types elicits a plethora of meanings in its various audiences and can be used for a variety of purposes. Rock music therefore has a strong potential for becoming oppositional. Grossberg points to the following evidence of rock and roll's oppositional nature:

> Rock and roll has, repeatedly and continuously, been attacked, banned, ridiculed and relegated to an insignificant cultural status. The fact that so much effort has been brought to bear in the

---

35 Hall, "Signification," p. 104.
36 This point is explored and challenged by Kevin M. Carragee, "A Critical Evaluation of the Media Hegemony Thesis," *Western Journal of Communication* 57 (1993): 330–348.
37 Becker, "Marxist," p. 72.
38 This idea is explored in more detail by Poonam Pillai, "Rereading Stuart Hall's Encoding/Decoding Model," *Communication Theory* 2 (1992): 221–233.
39 Lembo and Tucker, "Culture, Television, and Opposition," p. 100.
40 Lawrence Grossberg, "Is There Rock After Punk?" *Critical Studies in Mass Communication* 3 (1986): 50–73.

attempt to silence it, makes it reasonable to assume that some struggle is going on, some opposition is being voiced.[41]

Three characteristics demarcate rock and roll. First, it is associated with a particular group of fans, marking these individuals as somehow different from all other people. Second, the music is involved in the everyday lives of its listeners and is part of the larger context of their lives. Third, the entire rock apparatus provides intense pleasure to its fans, a pleasure of bodily sensation and emotional feeling. In short, it transforms the everyday lives of its fans: "The rock and roll apparatus is a kind of machine which, like a cookie cutter constantly changing its shape, produces or imprints a structure on the fans' desires and relations by organizing the material pieces of their lives."[42]

Rock is oppositional because it defines the youth culture as being different from "straight" and "boring." By concentrating on surface, style, and artifice, rock music opposes the predominant post–World War II hegemonic ideology of serious depth, purpose, and order. "The rock and roll apparatus not only energizes new possibilities within everyday life, it places that energy at the center of a life without meaning."[43] Grossberg identifies this primary oppositional character as the "attitude" of rock and roll.

Grossberg believes that the advent of punk had a profound effect on the role of rock music as an oppositional force. Punk itself seems to say that anything goes and that nothing matters. Punk "deconstructed" all forms, including traditional rock and roll. As such, punk itself became an oppositional force. Punk, along with a host of other social and cultural factors, has led to a deconstruction of the youth culture, which had been the chief source of meaning for rock and roll among its fans: "Punk attacked rock and roll for having grown old and fat, for having lost that which puts it in touch with its audience and outside of the hegemonic reality."[44] Grossberg is confident that youth is currently under reconstruction, but he is uncertain how.

Most of the work in critical studies has been applied to mass media of communication. The reason is clear: Media are powerful instruments of ideology in society. However, as the rock and roll case illustrates, the marxist approach need not be limited to applications in media. Indeed, any aspect of social structure can be examined in this way.

Michel Foucault

Foucault is normally thought of as a poststructuralist but is, in fact, impossible to classify neatly.[45] Although he denies a structuralist bias in his work, his writings bridge poststructural and structural traditions in critical theory.

Foucault says that each period has a distinct worldview, or conceptual structure, that determines the nature of knowledge in that period. The character of knowledge in a given epoch Foucault calls the *episteme,* or *discursive formation.* The vision of each age is exclusive and incompatible with visions from other ages, making it impossible for people in one period to think like those of another. The episteme, or way of thinking, is determined not by people but by the predominant discursive structures of the day. These discursive structures are deeply embedded ways of practicing or expressing ideas, and you cannot separate what people know from the structure of discourse used to express that knowledge. For Foucault, discourse includes written texts, but it also includes spoken language and nonverbal forms such as architecture, institutional practices, even charts and graphs.

---

41   Grossberg, "Is There Rock After Punk?" p. 53.
42   Grossberg, "Is There Rock After Punk?" p. 55.
43   Grossberg, "Is There Rock After Punk?" p. 57.
44   Grossberg, "Is There Rock After Punk?" p. 62.
45   Foucault's primary works on this subject include *The Archaeology of Knowledge,* trans. A. M. Sheridan Smith (New York: Pantheon, 1972); *The Order of Things: An Archaeology of the Human Sciences* (New York: Pantheon, 1970); and *Power/Knowledge: Selected Interviews and Other Writings 1927–1977,* trans. Colin Gordon and others, ed. Colin Gordon (New York: Pantheon, 1980). For an excellent short summary, see Foss, Foss, and Trapp, *Contemporary Perspectives on Rhetoric.* See also Carole Blair, "The Statement: Foundation of Foucault's Historical Criticism," *Western Journal of Speech Communication* 51 (1987): 364–383; Sonja K. Foss and Ann Gill, "Michel Foucault's Theory of Rhetoric as Epistemic," *Western Journal of Speech Communication* 51 (1987): 384–402; Nancy Fraser, *Unruly Practices: Power, Discourse, and Gender in Contemporary Social Theory* (Minneapolis: University of Minnesota Press, 1989), pp. 17–68.

An example of how discourse shapes knowledge is Richard Nixon's famous "Checkers" speech. Martha Cooper applied Foucault's ideas to this speech to show how the discourse made use of, indeed created, standards for responding to an accusation.[46] In the presidential campaign of 1952, vice presidential candidate Richard Nixon was accused of harboring a secret campaign fund. He responded to this accusation by denying the charge, opening his private finances to public scrutiny, and claiming that the only possible illegitimate contribution he had received was a little dog named Checkers.

This speech has been analyzed by several scholars of rhetoric, each looking at the ways this particular speaker used strategies to appeal to the national audience at that time. For Foucault, this kind of analysis is irrelevant. Cooper shows how this speech was an event that served to create and reinforce knowledge structures in our culture. In particular, the speech defined what it meant to respond to an accusation, reinforcing the rule that when accused, people should respond.

The structure of discourse is a set of inherent rules that determines the form and substance of discursive practice. Foucault's use of rules is not entirely like that of the other theories in this chapter, because for him, rules apply across the culture in a variety of types of discourse and function on a deep and powerful level. These are not merely rules for how to talk but rules that determine the very nature of our knowledge, power, and ethics. These rules control what can be talked or written about and who may talk or write (or whose talk is to be taken seriously). Such rules also prescribe the form that discourse must take. In our day, for example, "scientific authorities" are given great credibility, and in matters of "fact," most people prefer the form of "objective studies" over the form of conjecture or myth.

So in the "Checkers" speech, for instance, we see what counts as good evidence for a claim that a politician is corrupt (or not corrupt). We learn from this discourse that politicians must speak out when accused of wrongdoing, and the model of the honest, average American is created here as well.

Contrary to popular belief, according to Foucault, people are not responsible for establishing the conditions of discourse. Inversely, it is discourse that determines the place of the person in the scheme of the world. Our present discursive structure defines humans as the foundation and origin of knowledge, but people have never before achieved this status in any other period and will soon lose it. Foucault believes that the episteme will again shift, and humans will once again disappear from their central place in the world: "It is comforting . . . and a source of profound relief to think that man is only a recent invention, a figure not yet two centuries old, a new wrinkle in our knowledge, and that he will disappear again as soon as that knowledge has discovered a new form."[47]

This radical idea does not mean that humans do not produce discourse. Indeed, they do; but any number of individuals could have produced a given statement, and any speaker or writer is merely fulfilling a role in making a statement. That Nixon was the speaker of the "Checkers" address is unimportant. Nixon took the role of agent in this case, and since then any number of other politicians have done essentially the same thing. Discourse, then, does not require a knowing subject—a person who creates it, consumes it, understands it, and uses it. Rather, language itself prefigures personhood: Language creates the person. A Nixon type was created by the language in the "Checkers" speech.

In our era, persons are believed to obtain knowledge and have power, but this idea is a creation of the predominant discursive formation of our day, and the rules of expression with which we communicate establish this notion. In other times, entirely different ideas about knowledge and power emerged from the discourse in use.

Foucault's research on the penal system is a good example of this.[48] He found a dramatic

---

46   Martha Cooper, "Rhetorical Criticism and Foucault's Philosophy of Discursive Events," *Central States Speech Journal* 39 (1988): 1–17.
47   Foucault, *The Order of Things*, p. xxii.
48   Michel Foucault, *Discipline and Punish: The Birth of the Prison*, trans. A. Sheridan (New York: Vintage, 1979).

shift in the eigthteenth and nineteenth centuries away from torture and public punishment to incarceration and protection of the criminal from bodily harm. Prior to this period, convicts were publicly tortured or executed in a kind of spectacle. In the discursive formation of that day, the body was seen as the central object of political relations. It was very natural that power should be exerted against the body and that punishment should involve bodily pain. In the latter discursive formation, however, the body lost this status, as power became more a matter of the individual human psyche or soul. Thus locking people up came to be viewed as a more appropriate punishment than flogging them in public.

Foucault's work centers on analyzing discourse in a way that reveals its rules and structure. This he calls *archaeology*. Archaeology seeks to uncover, through careful description, the regularities of discourse. It displays disparities or contradictions, rather than coherence, and reveals a succession of one form of discourse after another. For this reason, Foucault places emphasis on comparative descriptions of more than one piece of discourse.

Interpretation, or establishing the meaning of a text, cannot be avoided in text analysis, but it should be minimized because interpretation does not reveal discursive structure and, in fact, may obscure it. Foucault thinks that analysts should avoid associating discourse with authors because authors are merely fulfilling the discourse's function and are not instrumental in any fundamental way in establishing the structure of the texts they produce. This is why Nixon as the speaker in the "Checkers" event is unimportant. We look to what the discourse says about knowledge, power, and ethics rather than viewing it as an instrument of one particular author.

Foucault's writings center on the subject of power. He believes that power is an inherent part of all discursive formation. As such, it is a function of discourse or knowledge and not a human or institutional property. The episteme, as expressed in language, grants power. Thus, power and knowledge cannot be divided. Power,

however, is a good, creative force that finds its zenith in "disciplinary power" or the prescription of standards of correct behavior.

☾ FEMINIST STUDIES

"Feminist studies" is a generic label for a perspective that explores the meaning of gender in society.[49] Feminist theorists have observed that many aspects of life are "gendered," meaning that they are experienced in terms of the masculine and the feminine. This includes not only biological sex but also virtually every facet of human life, including language, work, family roles, education, and socialization. The feminist critique aims to expose the powers and limits of this genderized division of the world.

Much feminist theory emphasizes the oppressive nature of gender relations under the domination of the patriarchy. As such, feminism is in many ways a study of power distribution between the sexes.

Feminist theory begins with the assumption that gender is a pervasive category of experience. Gender is a social construction that, although useful, has been dominated by a male bias and is particularly oppressive to women. Feminist theory aims to challenge the prevailing gender assumptions of society and to achieve more liberating ways for women and men to exist in the world.

---

49   Feminist theory is discussed in numerous sources. See, for example, Karen A. Foss, Sonja K. Foss, and Cindy L. Griffin, *Revisioning Rhetorics: Feminist Transformations of Rhetorical Theory* (Thousand Oaks, CA: Sage, 1998); Ramona R. Rush and Autumn Grubb-Swetman, "Feminist Approaches," in *An Integrated Approach to Communication Theory and Research*, eds. Michael B. Salwen and Don W. Stacks (Mahwah, NJ: Erlbaum, 1996), pp. 497–518; Lisa McLaughlin, "Feminist Communication Scholarship and 'The Woman Question' in the Academy," *Communication Theory* 5 (1995): 144–161; Karen A. Foss and Sonja K. Foss, "Personal Experience as Evidence in Feminist Scholarship," *Western Journal of Communication* 58 (1994): 39–43; Lana F. Rakow (ed.), *Women Making Meaning: New Feminist Directions in Communication* (New York: Routledge, 1992); Cheris Kramarae, "Feminist Theories of Communication," in *International Encyclopedia of Communications*, vol. 2, ed. E. Barnouw (New York: Oxford University Press, 1989), pp. 157–160; Brenda Dervin, "The Potential Contribution of Feminist Scholarship to the Field of Communication," *Journal of Communication* 37 (1987): 107–120.

Feminist criticism has become increasingly popular in the study of communication. Feminist communication scholars examine the ways the male language bias affects the relations between the sexes, the ways male domination has constrained communication for females, the ways women have both accommodated and resisted male patterns of speech and language, the powers of women's communication forms, and other similar concerns.

Feminist scholars point out that research and theory building, like all aspects of life, are dominated by gender biases. For the feminist scholar, traditional methods of research and male-biased theories are not only misleading but also dangerous because they mute the experience of women and hide the values of women's experience. For this reason, feminist scholarship usually focuses on women's experience as central, legitimizing the value of women's experience itself. Women's experience includes a sense of interdependence and relationship, the legitimacy of emotionality, fusion of public and private realms of experience, egalitarian values, concern for process over product, and openness to multiple ways of seeing and doing.

Feminist theorists acknowledge that the world can be understood in a variety of productive ways, and they resist the search for positive truth. They also see the feminine as a way of knowing that is distinct from the masculine, a view reflected, for example, in Carol Gilligan's well-known book *In a Different Voice,* in which she outlines the powers of the feminine values of intimacy, caring, and relationship.[50]

As a movement in which a variety of voices can be heard, feminism is not a single theory or a simple system of thought.[51] Feminist thinking has been diversified and enriched in many ways. One source of renewal has been the contribution of feminists of color. Marsha Houston, for example, has written about the different perspectives of African American and white women,[52] and Lisa A. Flores has developed a Chicana feminist view.[53]

One useful distinction is between liberal and radical feminism. *Liberal feminism,* the founda-

tion of the women's movement of the 1960s and 1970s, is based in liberal democracy, the idea that justice involves the assurance of equal rights for all individuals. Liberal feminists say that women have been oppressed as a group and that they have not had equal rights with men, as evidenced by women's lower average income, women's exclusion from centers of power and decision making, and women's lack of opportunity to advance in careers of their choice. In short, liberal feminism deals primarily with the public image and rights of women.

In contrast to the liberal school of thought, *radical feminism* believes that the oppression of women runs far deeper than public rights. For radical feminists, the problem is not just changing the law to give equal rights to women. The problem goes to the heart of our social structure, which is patriarchal. The patriarchy perpetuates a set of gender-laden meanings that promote masculine interests and subordinate feminine ones. Women are oppressed because the very fabric of society is based on a constructed reality that devalues and marginalizes women's experience. If gender is a social construction, then in our present order of things it is a man-made construction. The term *radical* is appropriate for this movement because it goes to the "root" of social structure and demands *basic redefinitions* of all facets of society.

Whereas liberal feminists want women to be able to have what men already have, radical feminists do not see this as an answer. In fact, to emulate the status of men in society only perpetuates the patriarchal definition of what is important and what is not. So, for example, women

---

50   Carol Gilligan, *In a Different Voice* (Cambridge, MA: Harvard University Press, 1982).
51   See, for example, Celeste Condit, "In Praise of Eloquent Diversity: Gender and Rhetoric as Public Persuasion," *Women's Studies in Communication* 20 (1997): in press; and Sonja K. Foss, Cindy L. Griffin, and Karen A. Foss, "Transforming Rhetoric Through Feminist Reconstruction: A Response to the Gender-Diversity Perspective," *Women's Studies in Communication* 20 (1997): in press.
52   Marsha Houston, "What Makes Scholarship about Black Women and Communication Feminist Communication Scholarship?" *Women's Studies in Communication* 10 (1988): 78–88.
53   Lisa A. Flores, "Creating Discursive Space Through a Rhetoric of Difference: Chicana Feminists Craft a Homeland," *Quarterly Journal of Speech* 82 (1996): 142–156.

not only must aspire to achieve the equal right to become physicians, but society itself must redefine the whole nature of medicine, especially in regard to how it treats the experience of women. Women not only should try to achieve equal representation among the ranks of business executives, but must strive to change the very definition of commerce and economy in society at large so that it no longer damages the welfare of women and children.

Today, many radical feminists call for women to define their own reality and their own social order, to rely on their own instincts and experience as a guide to self-definition and interpersonal relationships. In other words, the answer can only be a complete restructuring of how our society defines human experience.

Feminism presents an increasingly popular challenge to mainstream communication scholarship. Sonja Foss, Karen Foss, and Robert Trapp discuss this challenge in terms roughly equivalent to the liberal and radical schools of feminism.[54] The first type of challenge, which these authors call the *inclusion stage,* is an attempt to get more public recognition for the contributions of women.[55] It includes research on sexist language, including the ways language creates inequality between the sexes and sex differences in communication, including investigations into differences between the communication behavior of men and women.[56] This stage also includes studies of great women speakers, including research into the contributions of women to the history of public address. Studies of women's culture, including the differences between the ways men and women think and act, are also included here. In general, the inclusion stage highlights the legitimation of women's ways of knowing and being in the world.

The *revisionist stage* is consistent with radical feminism in that it challenges the very definitions used to characterize communication in society. These writings aim to revise such definitions to include women's experience. Such issues as the definition of rhetoric, what constitutes effective speech, the eloquence of ordinary women's forms of expression, the importance of

communication in private settings, the nature of social movements, and the character of persuasion and influence are questioned and reformulated in this kind of work.

The number of feminist theorists recognized in the communication field is growing. For example, in their recent book, *Re-visioning Rhetorics: Feminist Transformations of Rhetorical Theory,* Karen Foss, Sonja Foss, and Cindy Griffin present detailed summaries of the work of Gloria Anzaldúa, Paula Gunn Allen, bell hooks, Sonia Johnson, Sally Miller Gearhart, Starhawk, Mary Daly, Trinh T. Min-ha, and Cheris Kramarae.[57] Space limits our ability to include this rich body of theory. Instead, we focus here on two well-known feminist theories of communication.

The Patriarchal Universe of Discourse

One of the most highly recognized feminist communication theorists is Julia Penelope.[58] For Penelope, a linguist, language is central to all human experience and society. Our experience is always prefigured by our culture's language. It comes as no surprise, then, that language is an instrument of oppression, and Penelope's theory deals with the ways language is patriarchal and oppressive to women. (She also acknowledges its oppression of many other groups.)

For Penelope, a *universe of discourse* is a set of language conventions that reflect a particular definition of reality. Those who accept the language essentially accept its categories of truth, and the vast majority of language users do so without question. For example, Penelope was once mistaken for a "housewife" by a salesman who came to the door. On another occasion

---

54   Foss, Foss, and Trapp, *Contemporary Perspectives on Rhetoric.*
55   For example, see Foss, Foss, and Griffin, *Re-visioning Rhetorics,* chap. 1.
56   For a recent example, see Marianne LaFrance and Nancy M. Henley, "An Oppressing Hypothesis: Or Differences in Nonverbal Sensitivity Revisited," in *Power/Gender: Social Relations in Theory and Practice,* eds. H. Lorraine Radtke and Henderikus J. Stam (London: Sage, 1994), pp. 287–311.
57   Foss, Foss, and Griffin, *Re-visioning Rhetorics.*
58   Julia Penelope, *Speaking Freely: Unlearning the Lies of the Fathers' Tongues* (New York: Pergamon, 1990).

when she answered the phone, a telemarketer asked for the "lady of the house." Both of these people used common linguistic assumptions about what constitutes a household and a housewife: A household consists of a married man and woman, and any woman home during the day must therefore be a housewife. The conspicuous absence of the term *househusband* in common English reflects the same set of assumptions.

The definitions, meanings, and interpretations embedded in the patriarchal universe of discourse promote the interests of men and subordinate those of women. Most women do not question the categories of their language, so that they become co-opted into the male-dominant system. There is even a subcode used among many women in our society, the *cosmetic universe of discourse,* which signals recognition and approval of their own subordination. This female code includes such features as using the highest pitch range more often than men. It involves pausing more often than men and using a more questioning intonation than men. It includes a vocabulary of fashion, housework, and child rearing. Women also use more hedges like "well" or "sorta" than men typically use. They also tend to use more tag questions, which reflect uncertainty at the end of a statement, such as, "It's a nice day, isn't it?" Women also tend to use longer sentences than is customarily the case for men.

Penelope notes that language is a living, changing system. The problem is that most people fail to recognize that language is a human creation that is molded to meet human needs. The culprit in this misconception is *prescriptive grammar,* which is a codified set of rules that make a language seem pure and unchanging. The conventions of English—as with many other languages of the world—were established by aristocratic men, and the rules of grammar written by them promoted their own interests.

Penelope shows how many standard rules of English are arbitrary and perpetuate the interests of white men over other groups. For example, one of the most important sets of conventions for the oppression of women is grammatical gender, which she calls "an essential element of the heterosexualization of grammar."[59] Although most people think that words really are masculine or feminine, gender is "among the most contorted constructions in which misogyny and prescriptivism cooperate to befuddle and mislead us."[60]

According to Penelope the genderization of nouns goes back to ancient Greece, where Protagoras first classified nouns as masculine and feminine. Originally, the word *gender* referred to "race," "class," or "kind," but with the classification of words as masculine and feminine, this term became associated exclusively with biological sex. Penelope comments: "I do not know what motivated Protagoras to choose the adjectives *feminine* and *masculine* to describe noun classifications in Greek, and I haven't read a historian of grammars who has asked."[61]

For Penelope, classifying things into two categories based on biological sex is a distinctly male tendency. Even in English, where formal gender applies only to actual sexed animals and humans (for example, *bitch, husband, bull, daughter*), the language implicitly defines particular attitudes, actions, and objects as feminine and others as masculine. This is a quality Penelope calls *sexual dimorphism.* Thus, for example, war, money, sex, cars, and sports are most often viewed as masculine, whereas babies, cosmetics, and recipes are feminine. Another example is the association of elements of nature with women because of the male tendency to use and manipulate the environment, which Penelope believes comes from man's need to control.

Genderization is one of the most thoroughly and uncritically accepted features of language. What makes it especially insidious is that it is not just a bimodal classification system; it is a system in which the masculine is considered the "normal" point of comparison, so the semantics of the language are divided into *male* and *nonmale* (female). Masculine is normal and healthy, whereas feminine is feminine. Even *androgyny,* the sought-

---

59 Penelope, *Speaking,* p. 20.
60 Penelope, *Speaking,* p. 20.
61 Penelope, *Speaking,* p. 56.

after combination of both masculine and feminine traits, serves only to perpetuate the classification of concepts into these two categories.

To illustrate the point that masculine is normal, Penelope comments on the dictionary definitions of *manly, masculine, womanly,* and *feminine:*

> The qualities listed under *manly* and *masculine* are the "good" things an individual might wish to be: strong, brave, determined, honest, and dignified. Not a single one of the negative qualities commonly attributed to maleness is listed. . . . Look closely at the long list of characteristics in the definition for *manly* compared to the circularity of the pseudo-definition for *womanly,* "like or befitting woman." That's not a definition; it assumes that we already know the behaviors that "befit" a woman. The real definitions for *womanly* are implied as "oppositions" to "manly qualities." . . . Positive attributes commonly associated with females, nurturing, kind, and loving, have been omitted.[62]

You can see how the meanings of words have positive masculine or negative feminine connotations, but less obvious are the grammatical features of the patriarchal language. These are particularly oppressive because they enable people to use language subtly in a way that subverts the interests of women and other nondominant groups.

False deixis is an example. *Deixis* is the pointing feature of language, and deictic words point to specific objects. You might, for example, say, "Pass the salt," and everyone at the table knows exactly what you are referring to. A *false deictic* leads one to believe there is a specific object, but it fails to point it out precisely, resulting in confusion. It uses ambiguity to trick and manipulate. Penelope lists the following expressions as examples: "It's what's happening." (What is happening?) "You can't escape it." (What can't you escape?) "Don't throw it all away." (Don't throw what away?) One of the most serious problems of false deixis is that it obfuscates and hides what we don't want to talk about. It is a way to avoid being honest and direct and to subvert the interests of important groups in society, such as women.

Another example of a grammatical feature of the patriarchal universe of discourse is the *missing agent.* This is the failure to identify the person or persons responsible for an action, which is especially common in the passive voice. For example, to say, "The woman was raped," avoids identifying the agent of the act. More direct would be, "The woman was raped by five men." These types of constructions enable speakers to victimize women and other groups because they focus on the object of an act without drawing attention to the perpetrator.

The solution to the patriarchal universe of discourse is, first, to reject the assumption that the categories of language are true and invariant; second, to become conscious of the ways language oppresses; and, third, to refuse to reinforce the categories of language or to resist the rules that oppress.

Penelope capsulizes her project in these terms:

> The purpose of my analysis is to show readers how to be self-conscious about their linguistic activities. . . . I want to provide information so that women can engage in communication more consciously. Whether we are speaking or listening, writing or reading, being conscious of the functions of linguistic structures when we try to communicate or interpret someone else's utterance enables us to identify immediately and in context uses of language that are dishonest, misleading, or manipulative. . . . If we are to protect ourselves against insidious uses of English, we have to be able to identify such uses and challenge them when someone tries to coerce us linguistically.[63]

Power and Language

Cheris Kramarae is one of the most prolific scholars in the communication field and over the years has developed a strong and coherent theory of gender and power in language.[64] Her

---

62 Penelope, *Speaking,* p. 53.
63 Penelope, *Speaking,* p. xxxiii.
64 See, for example, Cheris Kramarae, *Women and Men Speaking: Frameworks for Analysis* (Rowley, MA: Newbury House, 1981), pp. 1–63; For an excellent secondary treatment, see Foss, Foss, and Griffin, *Re-visioning Rhetorics.* For a complete list of Kramarae's works, see the bibliography in Foss, Foss, and Griffin, *Re-visioning Rhetorics.*

views are entirely consistent with those of Penelope. In her many writings, she has reaffirmed that language is instrumental in constructing the world in which we live and that social power arrangements are largely embedded in language. Because language is patriarchal, it often creates an unsafe and uncomfortable world for women. Indeed, language makes a world that often silences women in profound ways.

On the latter point, Kramarae incorporates the work of anthropologists Edwin Ardener and Shirley Ardener on muted-group theory.[65] Edwin Ardener observed that anthropologists tend to characterize a culture in terms of the masculine, since ethnography seems biased toward observation of males in a culture. On closer examination, however, it appeared to Ardener that the actual language of a culture has an inherent male bias, that men created the meanings for a group, and that the feminine voice is suppressed, or "muted." This silencing of women, in Ardener's observation, leads to the inability of women to express themselves eloquently in the male parlance.

Shirley Ardener added to the theory by suggesting that the silence of women has several manifestations and is especially evident in public discourse. Women are less comfortable and less expressive in public situations than are men, and they are less comfortable in public situations than they are in private. Consequently, women monitor their own communications more intensely than do men. Women watch what they say and translate what they are feeling and thinking into male terms. When masculine and feminine meanings and expressions conflict, the masculine tends to win out because of the dominance of males in society, and the result is that women are muted.

Kramarae expands the Ardeners' work by incorporating it with the results of research on women and communication. She states that because men and women have different experiences based on the division of labor in society, they perceive the world differently. Men are politically dominant in society, and their systems of perception are therefore dominant, which prevents women's perceptions from being publicly

adopted. Further, women must translate their own ways of understanding into the terms of the male worldview in order to participate in public life. Kramarae shows the many ways that the resulting silencing of women comes out.

For one, women sometimes express themselves with more difficulty than do men. A common female experience is to lack a word for a feminine experience, apparently because men, who do not share that experience, have not developed a term for it. At the same time, however, women understand men's meanings more easily than men understand women's. This may be the case because when men fail to understand what women are talking about, they may distance themselves from it. Further, women are subjected to language experiences that men have not had, such as lacking a word for something, and men may suppress women and rationalize it on the grounds that women are not as rational or clear. Because of the power inequities in communication, women are forced to learn the male system of communication, but men in contrast do not need to learn the language of women.

And, indeed, women do have their own forms of expression, as they have created their own ways of saying things that lie outside the dominant male system. Letters, diaries, consciousness-raising groups, and alternative art forms are examples. Foss and Foss interviewed a number of women and examined their forms of communication. Their book *Women Speak: The Eloquence of Women's Lives* challenges a number of assumptions about what constitutes eloquent communication, showing that many of the forms of communication used by women have value in their own right, despite the fact that they are not viewed as significant in the masculine, public world.[66] The book makes this kind of work more

---

65   Edwin Ardener, "Some Outstanding Problems in the Analysis of Events" (paper presented at the Association of Social Anthropologists' Decennial Conference, 1973); "The 'Problem' Revisited," in *Perceiving Women*, ed. Shirley Ardener (London: Malaby, 1975); Shirley Ardener, *Defining Females: The Nature of Women in Society* (New York: Wiley, 1978). This theory is explored in some detail by Dale Spender, *Man Made Language* (London: Routledge & Kegan Paul, 1980), pp. 76–105.

66   Karen A. Foss and Sonja K. Foss, *Women Speak: The Eloquence of Women's Lives* (Prospect Heights, IL: Waveland Press, 1991).

public in an attempt to give voice to women normally muted in society.

Kramarae notes that because they are verbally muted, women rely more on nonverbal expression and use different nonverbal forms than do men. Some research has shown, for example, that facial expressions, vocal pauses, and bodily gestures are more important in women's discussions than they are in men's. Women also seem to display a wider variability of expression in their speech.

As a consequence of being silenced, women often make efforts to change the dominant rules of communication in order to get around or resist conventional rules. Advocates for women's liberation, for example, have created new words such as *Ms.* and *herstory* and have developed different communication forms that incorporate women's experiences. Consciousness-raising groups are a good example of this.

Kramarae is very interested in technology and its impact on gender relations in society. For example, the Internet seems to reproduce the same patterns of gender inequity found in society at large. As another example, she believes that female faculty and students for the most part have been excluded from technology policy making on campuses. She points to video games as yet another example of how masculine values are perpetuated in the new technologies.

Conversation is another area in which gender power relations are enacted. Kramarae says that men tend to control conversations in a variety of ways. They often dominate, interrupt, and respond only minimally to women. Men tend to withhold feelings and personal information, which gives them further control within a conversation. These patterns occur both in live conversations and on the Internet.

The ultimate exercise of power over women occurs through violence. Rape is an example of direct physical violence, but women have been the victims of communication violence as well, through electronic harassment, street harassment, and sexual harassment on the job.

Kramarae is a strong advocate of having women take control of their worlds by making communication forms that are more comfortable

and hospitable. She would like to see women make a world that is safe for the free and critical exploration of ideas. This can happen when people reject all forms of oppression, including arrogant language forms. She wants to see a world that makes connections rather than separations and a world that respects, rather than rejects, differences. She wants a world in which information is freely accessible to everyone. Along these lines, she wants cyberspace to be both accessible and comfortable to women and girls, as to all people.

How can women move toward achieving these goals? For Kramarae, this means taking control of language and becoming emancipated from patriarchal domination. She sees three ways of doing this. First, we must analyze and better understand the sometimes subtle forms of linguistic domination. Second, we must study women's communication to learn more about alternative forms. Finally, new forms must be created and used.

One thing women can do is to create new words to express their own experience. For example, a group of students was asked to create new words for aspects of their experience, which they did easily. Some of the words they created are as follows:

soul rinse—feeling after a big cry

solo wholo—describing a person not in a relationship with a significant other, not actively searching, yet not eliminating the possibility, and perfectly satisfied with the way he or she is

femipotent—female virility

silonuts—no reaction from a male; domination by silence[67]

Along the same lines, linguist Suzette Elgin has created an entire language, Láadan, to reflect women's experience.[68] Kramarae herself, along

---

67   Personal communication from Karen Foss, 1991. See also Cheris Kramarae, Paula A. Treichler, and Ann Russo, *A Feminist Dictionary* (Boston: Pandora, 1985).
68   Suzette Elgin, *A First Dictionary and Grammar of Láadan*, 2nd ed. (Madison, WI: Society for the Furtherance and Study of Fantasy and Science Fiction, 1988). See also Elgin's novel, *Native Tongue* (New York: Daw, 1984).

with colleagues Paula Treichler and Ann Russo, has written *A Feminist Dictionary*.[69] This work attempts to capture the features of a *feminist universe of discourse* by including words with special meaning for women as well as definitions that are consistent, not with men's, but with women's experience. For example, *birth name* is "a term used by feminists as a more accurate label for the name received at birth than the older term *maiden name,* which has sexual double standard implications."[70] *Birthing* is "another of the archetypal experiences exclusive to the female."[71] A *foremother* is "an ancestor."[72]

Another thing women can do is redefine terms previously used by men to perpetuate their power. This can take the form of making a previously negative term positive, such as referring to oneself proudly as a "hag." It can also take the form of making explicit the normally hidden power meanings of a word. For example, *tipping* might be defined as a means of paying less than minimum wages to women.

Women can also take control by interacting with others in new ways that break the cycle of male domination. For example, women can pay more attention and respond more to other women in conversations.

◖◗ COMMENTARY AND CRITIQUE

We have looked at three important areas of critical theory in this chapter—all explicitly displaying a set of values to raise consciousness and thereby empower people to resist dominant and oppressive ideological forces.

Feminist theory places the blame for the oppression of women on the patriarchy. Masculine values are believed to permeate society and govern all power centers, thus marginalizing the experience of women. This reasoning is not unlike that of the original Frankfurt School, which viewed capitalist society as dominated by a singular hegemonic interest, the political economy. Although the reasoning used by the Frankfurt scholars and feminists is similar, their explanatory variables are different, as the marxists would say that class, not gender, is the genesis of oppression.

The cultural studies tradition takes a more complex view. These scholars do not see any single set of ideas as perpetually dominant. Although various interests may dominate at any particular time and certain classes of people are almost always marginalized in this process, the field of ideological struggle is constantly in flux. This thesis is essentially a rejection of feminism's gender base. For the cultural scholar, gender would be just one of many elements of society in dynamic tension with all others.

Feminist theory revolves around the conceptual division of masculine and feminine, but critics question the very utility of this dualism.[73] Although the masculine–feminine distinction has been useful for critical purposes, it may have oversimplified the situation and created a conceptualization that does not accurately reflect reality. Such labeling may, in fact, reify or reinforce distinctions that feminists themselves are trying to overcome. Linda Putnam states the point in these terms: "The problem of reification, the use of feminist labels, has the double-edged effect of recognizing women while simultaneously isolating them."[74] And again, "Efforts to degenderize behaviors have the potential to liberate us from sex-role classifications that emanate from dualism."[75] The answer, according to Putnam, is not to abandon feminist theory or feminist ideals but to look at the process of communication differently. Instead of simply assuming that gender is the cause of other effects, we

---

69 Kramarae, Treichler, and Russo, *Feminist.*
70 Kramarae, Treichler, and Russo, *Feminist,* p. 72.
71 Kramarae, Treichler, and Russo, *Feminist,* p. 70.
72 Kramarae, Treichler, and Russo, *Feminist,* p. 166.
73 Linda L. Putnam, "In Search of Gender: A Critique of Communication and Sex-Roles Research," *Women's Studies in Communication* 5 (1982): 1–9.
74 Putnam, "Search," p. 4. See also Julia T. Wood and W. Barnett Pearce, "Sexists, Racists, and Other Classes of Classifiers: Form and Function of 'ist' Accusations," *Quarterly Journal of Speech* 66 (1980): 239–250.
75 Putnam, "Search," p. 7.

should also examine the ways communication patterns have led to gender distinctions themselves. If the cultural studies scholars are right, gender itself may be a construction of an ideology into which feminists themselves have been co-opted.[76]

Almost all versions of feminist and contemporary marxist theory see the answer to domination and oppression as consciousness raising and empowerment. For the feminists, when women become conscious of their own oppression, they are empowered to create a reality of their own that gives voice to their interests. For marxists, consciousness leads to the ability to create oppositional understandings that change the field of conflict in ways that promote a different, hopefully healthier, set of values in society. A common theme that seems to run through all critical theories, then, is giving voice to oppressed groups. The thesis of Habermas's work, for example, is precisely this: to create an ideal speech community in which all interests have an equal chance of being heard.

In Chapter 2 we discussed the value dimension of theory. The value issue can be stated in two ways, depending on whose perspective you take. From the perspective of traditional science, the issue is whether the theory contains value statements. From the perspective of critical theory, the issue is whether the theorist is conscious of inevitable values present in all theories.

The theories discussed in this chapter are unabashedly value laden. Critical theorists would say that all forms of research contain values, and values are only dangerous when they are not recognized or acknowledged. This belief is the basis of a critique of traditional social science. Although critical theories borrow liberally from relevant concepts of other traditions—such as system theory, structuralism, interpretation, and social construction—they also constitute an oppositional critique of many of these other traditions.

Critical theories represent a double critique, of society and of traditional social science. In a way, this is really the same critique because traditional social science is an institution within society that perpetuates its own dominant interests.

Political scientist Paul Lazarsfeld was perhaps the first to label these two theoretical camps as "administrative" and "critical."[77] *Administrative research* is designed to aid the administration of public and private programs, and *critical research* is designed to oppose and resist the administration of power in society. For critical theorists today, all research that is not critical is administrative because it automatically serves administrative interests.[78]

It is not surprising, then, to find a sharp line, even animosity, between theorists of traditional social science and those of the critical theory tradition.[79] Critical theorists accuse traditionalists of conserving centers of power, of being naively oblivious to the ways in which their work perpetuates hegemony, and of possessing a stubborn adherence to the belief in a realist epistemology.[80]

Traditional social scientists are no less harsh in their criticisms of critical theories. They accuse their critical colleagues of rationalizing ideas without data, of pushing a narrow and ill-informed agenda, and of operating on the basis of a head-in-the-clouds utopianism. Television researcher James Lull comments: "Marxist and neo-Marxist criticism in particular now sound more like an echo in the hallway than a leading theoretical perspective."[81]

---

76   Deborah Kerfoot and David Knights, "Into the Realm of the Fearful: Power, Identity, and the Gender Problematic," in *Power/ Gender: Social Relations in Theory and Practice*, eds. H. Lorraine Radtke and Henderikus J. Stam (London: Sage, 1994), pp. 67–88.
77   Paul Lazarsfeld, "Remarks on Administrative and Critical Communications Research," *Studies in Philosophy and Social Science* 9 (1941): 2–16.
78   This division is amply discussed in the special edition of *Journal of Communication* entitled "Ferment in the Field," 33 (Summer 1983).
79   Mike Allen, "Critical and Traditional Science: Implications for Communication Research," *Western Journal of Communication* 57 (1993): 200–208; Joseph F. Hanna, "Critical Theory and the Politicization of Science," *Communication Monographs* 58 (1991): 202–212.
80   See, for example, John W. Lannamann, "Interpersonal Communication Research as Ideological Practice," *Communication Theory* 1 (1991): 179–203.
81   James Lull, "The Audience as Nuisance," *Critical Studies in Mass Communication* 5 (1988): 239.

Jay Blumler summarizes the chief objections against critical theory.[82] First, even if media institutions should become more egalitarian, the critical approach does not provide sufficient guidance on how this is to be done: "But the critical paradigm, as so far enunciated, lacks a clarity of ethic and realism of political diagnosis that, when drawn on and applied, could help communication institutions to realize a vision of human beings as active, choosing, purposeful subjects."[83]

Second, the movement has a "self-defeating tendency to utopianism."[84] In other words, these theories downplay the realities of political life that require democracy, and they ignore the fact that media are required for democracy to work. Indeed, contemporary marxist approaches are inherently antidemocratic: "The critical perspective tends to slam shut, instead of prying open, doors of possible improvement in the contributions of journalism to democracy."[85]

Finally, administrative researchers deplore marxist antipathy toward behavioral and social research. The marxist claims are suspect because they are not supported by the kind of data traditional researchers find credible.

There are, of course, many differences among the various versions of feminist and contemporary marxist theory. In a way this suits critical theory because of the common belief in the existence of contradiction. Society itself is filled with contradiction, so why should critical studies be any different? In fact, one of the chief claims of critical theory is that we must be willing to acknowledge the presence of contradiction and learn to deal with it productively.

The problem for critical theory is determining where it stands in the absence of a unifying thesis. Feminism is an excellent case in point. On the one hand, feminists seem to be asking for equal rights for women, a public acknowledgment that women have the same qualities and powers as men and can perform as well in all walks of life. On the other hand, they also seem to be saying that women are different from men and that their powers and forms of expression should be valued in their own right. On one level of analysis, it may be that these are merely different brands of feminist theory. On another level these two

theses, both of which seem to have validity, form a true paradox. For women to be valued and to have equal rights, the powers of the feminine must be acknowledged, but highlighting the powers of the feminine reinforces the patriarchal view that women have their place.

There is in cultural studies, as in all critical theory, confusion about the power of groups and individuals to accomplish opposition. At times cultural studies seem to view society as a complex machine in which ideologies are constantly in conflict. At other times these theorists seem to want to give power to individuals to create oppositional readings to media texts, to take action to overcome hegemonic forces.

This is the old issue of the power of the subject. How much power do individuals have to assign meaning to messages? Are the minds of individuals shaped by social structure and language, or can individuals create their own structures and languages to meet their own ends?[86] Feminist language theories such as that of Penelope waffle on this issue. If women are oppressed by patriarchal language, how can they find the power to overcome it?

An important split in critical theory is that between the structuralists and the poststructuralists, discussed earlier in the chapter. These two schools of thought oppose each other in significant ways. For example, Habermas, representing the structural tradition, has created a rather elaborate theory of society and uses it as a template for uncovering oppression. But this theory has been criticized as being heavy-handed and ignoring the constantly changing construction of meaning that occurs in the everyday lives of individuals.[87]

82   Jay Blumler, "Communication and Democracy: The Crisis Beyond and the Ferment Within," *Journal of Communication* 33 (1983): 166–173. See also Michael Real, "The Debate on Critical Theory and the Study of Communications," *Journal of Communication* 34 (Autumn 1984): 72–80.
83   Blumler, "Communication," p. 168.
84   Blumler, "Communication," p. 168.
85   Blumler, "Communication," p. 169.
86   Sara Cobb, "A Critique of Critical Discourse Analysis: Deconstructing and Reconstructing the Role of Intention," *Communication Theory* 4 (1994): 132–152.
87   Kenneth Baynes, "Communicative Ethics, the Public Sphere and Communication Media," *Critical Studies in Mass Communication* 11 (1994): 315–326; Huspek, "Taking Aim."

This conflict is not unlike that between interpretive and critical theory. Critical theorists like Habermas accuse interpretive theorists such as Gadamer (Chapter 10) of being too conservative. Indeed, the goal of interpretation is to describe meaning structures, in texts and in social relations. Critical theory, on the other hand, is inherently radical. It aims to change the basis of society and is impatient with the conservative moves commonly found in phenomenology.

Interpretivists like Gadamer revere tradition and accuse critical theory of trying to tear down the very history from which it can never escape. Interpretivists seek ways to uncover meanings and to overcome misunderstandings so that traditions can speak to us in positive ways, and they object to critical theorists' claims that such misunderstandings are systematic distortions by powerful groups. Finally, from their position of dialogue, interpretivists object to critical theorists' call for ideal communication designed to rescue society from its iniquities.[88] Instead, they believe, language and communication as naturally given in everyday life constitute a positive voice that should be heard. Gadamer says that you cannot remove yourself from tradition, that any intellectual project is always a part of a tradition that shapes its perspectives and values.

Two related issues are suggested by Gadamer's point. First, what is the cultural tradition from which critical theory arises, and how does this influence the truth claims being made by this movement? If critical theory is a soundly Eurocentric enterprise, how relevant is it to the dynamics of cultures other than Western societies? Second, how do critical theorists get out of an ideology long enough to make judgments about ideology?

Early Marxism had an easy answer; they deferred to science as nonideological. Latter-day marxists, however, are skeptical of this solution because they do not see science as interest free. Science itself promotes particular ideologies. The most promising resolution of this dilemma is that of Hall and his colleagues, who claim that there will always be competing ideas, and the aim of cultural studies is to expose the struggle, not to suggest a permanent solution. Cultural

studies seems more interested in promoting oppositional readings of texts rather than pointing to any one ideology that should be overcome.

Paul Ricoeur crystallizes the perspectives of interpretive theory and critical theory in these terms:

> What is at stake can be expressed in terms of an alternative: either a hermeneutical consciousness or a critical consciousness. . . . In contrast to the positive assessment of hermeneutics, the theory of ideology adopts a suspicious approach, seeing tradition as merely the systematically distorted expression of communication under unacknowledged conditions of violence.[89]

Ricoeur himself argues for a "zone of intersection which . . . ought to become the point of departure for a new phase of hermeneutics."[90] Ricoeur believes that through distanciation (Chapter 10), one can understand texts in a way that reveals the limits of context. Once it is freed from situation and author, text provides insights into the problems of historical circumstances. In addition, when disembodied texts speak to us, they reveal our own limits and the limits of our own times. Such textual interpretation also opens up possibilities for new ways of being in the future. For Ricoeur then, interpretive theory and critical theory are not very far apart.

A movement that attempts to fuse the interpretive and critical traditions is critical ethnography. Critical ethnographers value the insights of both traditions. They see the need for ethnographic description, but they want to go beyond mere description to make value statements about oppressive structures observed in a culture.[91]

In many ways the answers to these questions depend on the site of meaning. How is meaning established? If meaning comes prepackaged in language, as many feminists and contemporary marxists suggest that it is, then the individual is

---

88   The primary opponents in this debate have been Gadamer and Habermas. The debate is summarized by Paul Ricoeur, *Hermeneutics and the Human Sciences: Essays on Language, Action, and Interpretation*, trans. and ed. J. B. Thompson (Cambridge: Cambridge University Press, 1981), pp. 64–80.
89   Ricoeur, *Hermeneutics*, p. 64.
90   Ricoeur, *Hermeneutics*, p. 79.
91   See, for example, Jim Thomas, *Doing Critical Ethnography* (Newbury Park, CA: Sage, 1993); Huspek, "Taking Aim."

left powerless to struggle against it. On the other hand, if meaning is constructed in social interaction, as other feminists and marxists suggest that it is, then individuals do have some power to create new realities. This issue brings us full circle back to the question of a structural versus constructional epistemology. The interest of critical theory in creating social change requires a constructionist version of society, but the need for critical theory to prove conditions requiring change requires a structuralist one. This may be the ultimate contradiction of critical theory.[92]

---

92 This conflict is discussed especially well by Michael Huspek, "Dueling Structures: The Theory of Resistance in Discourse," *Communication Theory* 3 (1993): 1–25.

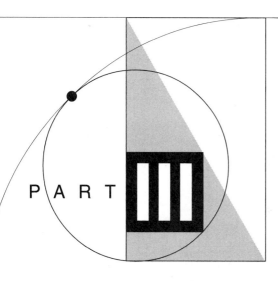

P A R T **III**

CONTEXTUAL THEMES

COMMUNICATION IN RELATIONSHIPS

With this chapter, we begin Part III of the book. Here we explore a set of important contextual themes found in communication theory—relationships, decision making, networks, and media. Each of these themes is central to one of the contexts discussed in Chapter 1: *Relationships* are at the heart of interpersonal communication, *decision making* is central to group communication, *networks* are the binding element of organizational communication, and *media* are the chief component of mass communication.

This chapter deals with relationships, which are central to the study of interpersonal communication.[1] A *relationship* is a set of expectations two people have for their behavior based on the pattern of interaction between them. This idea lies at the hub of interpersonal communication theories, and we explore it here.

The recognition that relationships are significant in interpersonal communication goes back at least to the 1960s. Although research on relationships has been done from a diversity of perspectives, most of what is referred to as "relational communication" theory is based on a core of common assumptions.[2] First, relationships are always connected to communication and cannot be separated from it. Second, the nature of the relationship is defined by the communication between its members. Third, relationships are usually defined implicitly rather than explicitly. Fourth, relationships develop over time through a negotiation process between those involved. Consequently, relationships are dynamic, not unchanging.[3] These assumptions are further explored and elaborated by the theories in this chapter.[4]

---

1 For an overview of interpersonal communication, see Mark L. Knapp and Gerald R. Miller (eds.), *Handbook of Interpersonal Communication* (Thousands Oaks, CA: Sage, 1994). For a brief history, see Charles R. Berger, "Interpersonal Communication," in *An Integrated Approach to Communication Theory and Research,* eds. Michael B. Salwen and Don W. Stacks (Mahwah, NJ: Erlbaum, 1996), pp. 277–296; Mark L. Knapp, Gerald R. Miller, and Kelly Fudge, "Background and Current Trends in the Study of Interpersonal Communication," in *Handbook of Interpersonal Communication,* eds. Mark L. Knapp and Gerald R. Miller (Thousands Oaks, CA: Sage, 1994), pp. 3–20.

2 Barbara M. Montgomery, "Communication as the Interface Between Couples and Culture," in *Communication Yearbook 15,* ed. Stanley Deetz (Newbury Park, CA: Sage, 1992), pp. 475–507.

3 Carol M. Werner and Leslie A. Baxter, "Temporal Qualities of Relationships: Organismic, Transactional, and Dialectical Views," in *Handbook of Interpersonal Communication,* eds. Mark L. Knapp and Gerald R. Miller (Thousands Oaks, CA: Sage, 1994), pp. 323–379.

4 For a discussion of the way in which relationships are made

◖ THEORETICAL FOUNDATIONS

In this section we look at two early lines of theory that gave impetus to the study of communication in relationships, beginning with the classic work of the Palo Alto Group.

The Palo Alto Group

Most relationship theorists acknowledge the importance of the work of Gregory Bateson, Paul Watzlawick, and their colleagues in the early years of the study of interpersonal communication. Bateson was briefly covered in Chapter 3, where we saw that his ideas about metacommunication have been highly formative in our field.

Bateson's early followers were known as the Palo Alto Group because they founded and worked at the Mental Research Institute based in Palo Alto, California. Their ideas are most clearly laid out in *Pragmatics of Human Communication*, now a classic.[5] In the book Paul Watzlawick, Janet Beavin, and Don Jackson present a well-known analysis of communication based on system principles (Chapter 3).

Relationships are an important part of a system. When two people communicate with each other, in addition to whatever else they may be doing, they are also defining their relationship.[6] People in a relationship are always creating a set of expectations, reinforcing old ones, or changing an existing pattern of interaction.

Relationships result from interaction. For example, if one spouse consistently exerts control over the other in a marriage, a dominant-submissive relationship will result. Communication between workers in an organization might result in a status relationship in which one person is more highly esteemed than the other. The interaction between neighbors might turn out to be an equal-and-polite relationship. Implicit rules are numerous in any ongoing relationship, be it a friendship, business partnership, love affair, family, or any other type.

Watzlawick, Beavin, and Jackson present five basic axioms about communication.[7] First, "one cannot not communicate." This axiom has been quoted again and again in textbooks on communication. Its point is important, because it emphasizes that we are always affecting others' perceptions, whether we want to or not. This axiom also emphasizes that any perceivable behavior is potentially communicative.[8] At the same time, it does not mean that every behavior is always communicative. This axiom simply means that when in the presence of another person, you must communicate something about your relationship with him or her, even if it is a "noncommunicating" relationship.[9] For example, if you are not in the mood to have a conversation on a plane, you might open a book and begin reading. This signals to the person next to you, "I am not available to talk."

The second axiom is that every conversation, no matter how brief, involves two messages—a content message and a relationship message. When two people are interacting, each is relating information to the other, and simultaneously each is also "commenting" on the information at a higher level. This simultaneous relationship talk, which often is nonverbal, is *metacommunication*.

---

in communication, see Steve Duck and Garth Pittman, "Social and Personal Relationships," in *Handbook of Interpersonal Communication*, eds. Mark L. Knapp and Gerald R. Miller (Thousand Oaks, CA: Sage, 1994), pp. 676–695. See also Steve Duck, *Meaningful Relationships: Talking, Sense, and Relating* (Thousands Oaks, CA: Sage, 1994).

5   Paul Watzlawick, Janet Beavin, and Don Jackson, *Pragmatics of Human Communication: A Study of Interactional Patterns, Pathologies, and Paradoxes* (New York: Norton, 1967).

6   Watzlawick, Beavin, and Jackson, *Pragmatics*, pp. 120–121.

7   Watzlawick, Beavin, and Jackson, *Pragmatics*.

8   This axiom has been challenged by Michael Motley, "On Whether One Can(not) Not Communicate: An Examination Via Traditional Communication Postulates," *Western Journal of Speech Communication* 54 (1990): 1–20. See also "Forum: Can One Not Communicate?" *Western Journal of Speech Communication* 54 (1990): 593–623; Peter A. Andersen, "When One Cannot Not Communicate: A Challenge to Motley's Traditional Communication Postulates," *Communication Studies* 42 (1991): 309–325; Michael T. Motley, "How One May Not Communicate: A Reply to Andersen," *Communication Studies* 42 (1991): 326–339; Theodore Clevenger, Jr., "Can One Not Communicate? A Conflict of Models," *Communication Studies* 42 (1991): 351.

9   Janet Beavin Bavelas, "Behaving and Communicating: A Reply to Motley," *Western Journal of Speech Communication* 54 (1990): 593–602.

For example, on the content level, a professor may announce an upcoming test. Many possible relationship messages could serve as meta-communication: I am the authority in this class-room; I teach, you learn; what I have lectured about is important; I need feedback on your progress; I have a need to judge you; I want you to think I am fulfilling my role as professor; and so on. Of course, the students' responses also include a relationship dimension, which might express compliance, defiance, respect, fear, equality, or any of a number of other possible metamessages. In communicating about tests and all other topics, the teacher and student con-stantly define and redefine the nature of their relationship.

Judee Burgoon and her colleagues have done research to discover the dimensions of this rela-tional level of communication.[10] They conducted a huge survey of the interpersonal communica-tion literature to find possible elements of rela-tional communication and isolated twelve com-mon aspects of relationships that seem to be communicated, labeling them the *fundamental topoi of relational communication*. These include varying levels of dominance, intimacy, affection, involvement, inclusion, trust, superficiality, emo-tional arousal, composure, similarity, formality, and orientation toward task versus social ele-ments of the relationship. These topics were fur-ther narrowed into four basic, independent di-mensions of relational communication:

1. Emotional arousal, composure, and formality
2. Intimacy and similarity
3. Immediacy (liking)
4. Dominance-submission

In announcing an examination, the professor might communicate a sense of formality (dimen-sion 1), distance from the student (dimension 2), neutrality toward individual students (dimen-sion 3), and dominance (dimension 4).

10   Judee K. Burgoon and Jerold L. Hale, "The Fundamental Topoi of Relational Communication," *Communication Monographs* 51 (1984): 193–214; Judee K. Burgoon, David B. Buller, Jerold L. Hale, and Mark A. deTurck, "Relational Messages Associated with Nonverbal Behaviors," *Human Communication Research* 10 (1984): 351–378.

A student's questions about the exam could reflect anxiety (dimension 1), distance from the professor (dimension 2), dislike of the professor (dimension 3), and acceptance of her right to ad-minister the exam (dimension 4). Another pro-fessor and student might have a very different relationship, which would be reflected in a dif-ferent set of metamessages on the same four dimensions.

Burgoon and her associates further studied the question of how nonverbal behaviors spe-cifically affect these perceptions, and some inter-esting results emerged. Four behaviors seem especially important in metacommunication. *Proximity* can be significant in communicating intimacy, attraction, trust, caring, dominance, persuasiveness, and aggressiveness. *Smiling* seems especially important in communicating emotional arousal, composure, and formality, as well as intimacy and liking. *Touching*, too, com-municates intimacy. *Eye contact* is like an excla-mation point in intensifying the effect of other nonverbal behaviors.

Watzlawick, Beavin, and Jackson's third axiom says that interaction is always organized into meaningful patterns by the communicators. This is called *punctuation*. Interaction sequences, like sentences, cannot be understood as a string of isolated elements. To make sense they must be punctuated.

An interaction may look like a string of verbal and nonverbal behaviors. Like the series of sounds in a sentence, communication is never a simple chain. Certain behaviors are perceived to be a response to other ones. Behaviors are thus grouped or punctuated into larger units, which help define the meaning of the entire set of ac-tions. This grouping is largely a matter of per-sonal perception, and there is no guarantee that the participants will punctuate their interaction the same way.

Any given string of behaviors might be punc-tuated in various ways. For example, consider a marriage involving nagging by the husband and withdrawing by the wife. This sequence can be punctuated in at least two ways. The wife's withdrawing could be seen as a response to the husband's nagging: nag-withdraw, nag-withdraw. Or the husband's nagging could be viewed as a response to the wife's withdrawal: withdraw-nag, withdraw-nag. In the first case, the punctuation of "nag-withdraw" implies an attack-retreat relationship, but the punctuation of "withdraw-nag" implies ignoring-imploring. The meaning of the interaction, then, depends on the punctuation, and in this example the husband and wife have different meanings for what is going on.

Watzlawick, Beavin, and Jackson's fourth axiom is that people use both digital and analogic codes. *Coding* was discussed in some detail in Chapter 4. As we learned there, digital coding is arbitrary, for the sign and the referent, though associated, have no intrinsic relation to each other. The relationship between the sign and the referent is strictly arbitrary. Using *bear* to designate a large black animal with claws wandering around the woods is entirely arbitrary. Further, digital signs are discrete; they are "on" or "off," uttered or not uttered. You either say *bear*, or you do not; you can't say it partially. The most common digital code in human communication is language. Sounds, words, and phrases are digital signs arranged to communicate meanings. Certain nonverbal signs, especially gestures like the victory sign or obscene gestures, are also digital.

The *analogic code* is quite different. Analogic signs are not arbitrary like digital ones. Analogic signs can actually resemble the object, as in the case of drawing a picture in the air with your hands, or they can be part of the object or condition being signified, as in the case of crying. Further, an analogue is continuous rather than discrete; it has degrees of intensity or longevity and is not just "on" or "off."

Most nonverbal signs are analogic. For example, a facial expression of surprise is not only a sign of a feeling or condition but is also actually part of the surprise itself. Its meaning is intrinsic, and the facial expression is not an either-or sign but a continuous variable between no expression and extreme facial distortion. Emotion in the voice is another analogic code with the same properties.

Although the digital and analogic codes are different from each other, they are used together and cannot be separated in ongoing communication. For instance, a word, which is digital, can be uttered in a variety of analogic ways (loud, soft; high, low; and so on). Similarly, a written message consisting of digital letters and words is presented on paper using various layouts, styles of handwriting or print, and other analogic codes.

Within the stream of behaviors in interaction, both digital and analogic coding blend, and theorists believe that they serve different functions. Digital signs, having relatively precise meanings, communicate the content dimension, whereas the analogic code, rich in feeling and connotation, is the vehicle for relationship messages. So while people are communicating content digitally, they are commenting about their relationship analogically.

Suppose a father at a playground sees his daughter fall and scrape her knee. Immediately, he says, "Don't cry. Daddy is coming." The content meaning is clear, but what is the relationship message? It depends on how the message is delivered. The father might communicate his own fear, worry, anger, boredom, or dominance. At the same time, he might communicate a number of possible perceptions, including, "You are careless," "You are an attention getter," "You are injured," and so on. When it comes to relationships, then, actions do speak louder than words.

The final axiom of communication deals with the matching or meshing of messages in an interaction. The axiom states that communicators may respond similarly to or differently from one another. When two communicators in a relationship behave similarly and differences are minimized, the relationship is said to be *symmetrical.* When communicator response differences are maximized, however, a *complementary* relationship is said to exist.

In a marriage when two partners both vie for power, they are involved in a symmetrical relationship. Similarly, co-workers are communicating symmetrically when each wants the other to tell him or her what to do. A complementary marital relationship would exist when the wife is domineering and the husband responds submissively. In the work setting, a complementary relationship would exist when the boss gives orders, and the employee is happy to follow them.

The variable most often examined in regard to complementary and symmetrical relationships is *control*. To explore this idea, let us look at the work of Edna Rogers and Frank Millar. Their work remains one of the most cogent and valuable statements about relational communication, and it provides a concrete extension of the work of the Palo Alto Group.[11] Although Millar and Rogers have discussed various dimensions of relationships, including trust and intimacy, most of their research has centered on control.

Like all relational communication, control cannot be defined by examining a single message. You must look at the pattern of messages and responses. In other words, when you make a statement, the other person's response defines a moment in the relationship. Consider a relationship you are involved in. If you make an assertive comment and your partner responds in a way that also asserts control, that response is said to be *one-up* and *domineering*. On the other hand, if your partner responds in a way that accepts your assertion of control, that message is *one-down*. If it neither asserts control nor relinquishes it, the message is *one-across*.

A complementary exchange occurs when one partner asserts a one-up message and the other responds one-down. When this kind of interaction predominates in a relationship, we can say that the relationship itself is complementary. The individual whose one-up message predominates at a given time is said to be *dominant*. Notice the difference here between "dominance" and "domineeringness." A one-up move is domineering, but it is not dominant unless the other person accepts it. A person can be domineering without being dominant if the partner does not accept the control move.

To find out the connection between dominance and domineeringness, Millar and Rogers had forty-five married couples tape-record lengthy conversations on a variety of topics.[12] Using interaction analysis, they found little cor-

relation between these two variables. It was clear from the study that, at least among these couples, a high level of domineeringness did not lead to a high level of dominance. In other words, "one-up" moves are not necessarily greeted by "one-down" moves. They also found that marital satisfaction was lower in couples in which the wife was domineering and that satisfaction was higher in cases where the husband was dominant. This pattern may have something to do with the way one-up messages were delivered and the amount of support provided by the domineering partner.

A symmetrical exchange involves both partners presenting one-up or one-down messages, and a symmetrical relationship is marked by a preponderance of such exchanges. *Competitive symmetry* is the case of two people in a power struggle, each trying to assert control over the other. Here both partners are domineering and neither dominant. A *transitional* state exists when the partners' responses are different (for instance, one-up/one-across) but not opposite. Table 12.1 illustrates nine control states generated by combinations of these types of control messages.[13]

Control consists of two dimensions in a relationship. The first variable of control is the *rigid-flexible* dimension. The more flexible the relationship, the more control passes back and forth between the two parties. *Stability-instability* relates to the predictability of the control shifts. The more consistent the pattern of control over time, the more stable the control. One couple, for

---

11   Although this work is explained in several sources, perhaps the most complete theoretical treatment is Frank E. Millar and L. Edna Rogers, "A Relational Approach to Interpersonal Communication," in *Explorations in Interpersonal Communication*, ed. G. R. Miller (Beverly Hills, CA: Sage, 1976), pp. 87–105. See also Millar and Rogers, "Power Dynamics in Marital Relationships," in *Perspectives on Marital Interaction*, eds. P. Noller and M. Fitzpatrick (Clevedon, England: Multilingual Matters, 1988), pp. 78–97; "Relational Dimensions of Interpersonal Dynamics," in *Interpersonal Processes: New Directions in Communication Research*, eds. M. E. Roloff and G. R. Miller (Newbury Park, CA: Sage, 1987), pp. 117–139.

12   L. Edna Rogers-Millar and Frank E. Millar, "Domineeringness and Dominance: A Transactional View," *Human Communication Research* 5 (1979): 238–246.

13   Millar and Rogers, "Relational Approach," p. 97.

TABLE **12.1**

Control Configurations

Control direction of speaker A's message	Control direction of speaker B's message		
	One-up (↑)	One-down (↓)	One-across (→)
One-up (↑)	1.(↑↑) Competitive symmetry	4. (↑↓) Complementarity	7. (↑→) Transition
One-down (↓)	2. (↓↑) Complementarity	5. (↓↓) Submissive symmetry	8. (↓→) Transition
One-across (→)	3. (→↑) Transition	6. (→↓) Transition	9. (→→) Neutralized symmetry

Control Pattern Examples

1. Competitive symmetry (one-up/one-up):
   A: You know I want you to keep the house picked up during the day.
   B: I want you to help sometimes.

2. Complementarity (one-down/one-up):
   A: Please help. I need you.
   B: Sure, I know how.

3. Transition (one-across/one-up):
   A: Let's compromise.
   B: No, my way is best.

4. Complementarity (one-up/one-down):
   A: Let's get out of town this weekend.
   B: Okay.

5. Submissive symmetry (one-down/one-down):
   A: I'm so tired. What should we do?
   B: I can't decide. You decide.

6. Transition (one-across/one-down):
   A: My Dad was pretty talkative tonight.
   B: You're right; he sure was.

7. Transition (one-up/one-across):
   A: I definitely think we should have more kids.
   B: Lots of people seem to be having kids these days.

8. Transition (one-down/one-across):
   A: Please help me. What can I do?
   B: I don't know.

9. Neutralized symmetry (one-across/one-across):
   A: The neighbor's house needs paint.
   B: The windows are dirty too.

example, could have a rigid relationship in which the husband is always dominant and the wife always submissive. Another couple might be flexible, so that the wife is sometimes dominant and the husband sometimes so.

Similarly, a stable relationship is one in which the husband is predictably dominant when it comes to the car, vacations, and the yard, and the wife is dominant when it comes to the house, family, and the social calendar. An unstable relationship is one in which you never know from day to day who will assert control on which issues.

Relational Perception

How a relationship is defined is largely a matter of perception. The expectations that form a relationship are the product of our perceptions of other people's behavior and of their feelings. An important foundational theory in the relational perception literature is that of psychiatrist R. D. Laing.[14] Laing's thesis is that a person's

14   Laing's works most concerned with communication include *The Politics of Experience* (New York: Pantheon, 1967); *Self and Others* (London: Tavistock, 1969); and R. D. Laing, H. Phillipson, and A. R. Lee, *Interpersonal Perception* (New York: Springer, 1966).

communicative behavior is affected by his or her perception of the relationship with the other communicator.

Laing makes a distinction between experience and behavior. *Behavior,* which involves the observable actions of another person, is public; *experience,* or internal perception and feeling, is private. If a friend waves to you, the wave itself is observable "behavior," and you "experience" it as a greeting. If a friend ignores you, the physical actions are observable "behaviors," and you "experience" these as rejection. If a friend touches you, the touch is observable "behavior," but the "experience" may be something like affection.

Although behavior can be observed, another person's experience cannot. You will infer another person's experience, but you cannot observe it directly. If you touch a friend in an affectionate way, you may perceive that he likes it, but you cannot observe that "liking" directly. Inferring the experience of another person is the basis of communication, but doing this can be difficult, as Laing points out: "I see you, and you see me. I experience you, and you experience me. I see your behavior. You see my behavior. But I do not and never have and never will see your experience of me."[15]

When you interact with another person, there are two levels of experience or perception, or *perspectives.*[16] You can observe and interpret another person's behavior in a *direct perspective.* You also experience the experience of other people when you assign meaning to what you *imagine* they are thinking and feeling. Laing calls this a *metaperspective.* Laing describes the process:

> I cannot avoid trying to understand your experience, because although I do not experience your experience, which is invisible to me (and nontastable, nontouchable, nonsmellable, and inaudible), yet I experience you as experiencing. I do not experience your experience. But I experience you experiencing. I experience myself as experienced by you. And I experience you as experiencing yourself as experienced by me. And so on.[17]

To use Laing's favorite characters, Jack perceives certain behaviors of Jill (direct perspective). He also infers or imagines Jill's perceptions (metaperspective).

A relationship then is defined by the communicator's direct perspectives and metaperspectives. Theoretically, metaperception can proceed indefinitely through higher levels: Jack loves Jill (his experience, a direct perspective); Jack thinks Jill loves him (he experiences Jill's experience, a metaperspective); Jack thinks that Jill thinks that he loves her (a meta-metaperspective); and so on. Because experience affects behavior, one often behaves in accordance with his or her metaperspectives. If Jack thinks Jill thinks he does not love her, he may try to change Jill's imagined perception.

The health of a relationship is greatly determined by perceptual accuracy, and metaperspectives may or may not be accurate. *Understanding* is the agreement or conjunction between Jack's metaperspective and Jill's direct perspective. If Jack correctly infers that Jill loves him, he "understands" her. *Being understood* is the inverse, the conjunction of Jack's meta-metaperspective and Jill's metaperspective. If Jack correctly infers that Jill believes Jack loves her, he "is understood." But being understood is not the same as *feeling understood,* or the conjunction between Jack's direct perspective and his own metaperspective. If Jack infers that Jill believes he loves her, and he does, then he "feels understood."

Because communicators attempt to behave in ways that they believe will affect others, *spirals* can develop wherein each person acts toward the other in such a way that particular metaperspectives such as mistrust become accentuated. The idea of spiral has been important for Laing as a psychiatrist because it explains various pathological relationships. For example, if Jack mistrusts Jill and does not believe she loves him, he may accuse her of having affairs. Jill, in her metaperception of Jack's mistrust, attempts to prove her love. Jack sees this attempt as covering up her lack of love and accuses her of being a liar. The spiral could continue until the relationship is destroyed.

---

15   Laing, *Politics,* p. 4.
16   Laing, Phillipson, and Lee, *Interpersonal.*
17   Laing, *Politics,* p. 5.

This is an example of a *unilateral spiral*, as Jack's mistrust of Jill becomes more and more accentuated. A *bilateral spiral* occurs when both parties move toward increasingly extreme meta-perceptions. For example, Jack believes Jill wants too much from him and thinks she is greedy. At the same time Jill sees Jack as selfish. In other words, both feel the other is withholding what he or she needs. Because both parties feel misunderstood, they retaliate, causing their meta-perceptions of greed and selfishness to increase. Such spirals need to be broken, or the relationship will be destroyed.

As behavioral patterns develop over time, expectations and perceptions develop and often change. We turn now to theories dealing with the development of relationships over time.

◐ THE DEVELOPMENT OF RELATIONSHIPS

Much has been written about relational development and dissolution, and it is clear that communication is a vital aspect in the initiation, growth, and decline of relationships. In this section we discuss a number of communication theories related to these concerns.

Development naturally implies change over time, and relationships do change in a variety of ways. Carol Werner and Leslie Baxter write about five qualities that change as relationships develop.[18] These are amplitude, salience, scale, sequence, and pace/rhythm. These qualities can be defined briefly as follows:

- *Amplitude*—the strength of feelings, behaviors, or both. For example, at certain points in the relationship, the couple may be very active or have strong feelings about what is going on.
- *Salience*—focus on past, present, or future. At some moments in the development of a relationship, partners concentrate a lot on their history (the past); at other times they are very centered on what is going on now; and at times, they think mostly about the future.

- *Scale*—how long patterns last. For example, the couple may be engaged in a certain set of rituals that they stick to for a very long time, or perhaps they do things a certain way for a much shorter period of time.
- *Sequence*—the order of events in the relationship. As a relationship changes, a variety of things may be undertaken, but they are not always organized the same way for the entire length of the relationship.
- *Pace/Rhythm*—the rapidity of events in the relationship and the interval between events. During certain periods in a relationship, events may occur in a rapid-fire way, with everything seeming to happen quickly. At other times, the pace may be much slower.

At a given time, a relationship will be characterized by some combination of these variables. Tracking the development of a relationship means watching the ways in which the profile changes over time.

According to Werner and Baxter, we can look at such changes in three different ways. The *linear* view draws attention to the pattern of change over time as the relationship moves from one state to another. The *cyclical/spiraling* view focuses on the ways in which patterns return and repeat themselves over time. Using the linear perspective is like tracing the development of the relationship along a course or line. Using the cyclical perspective is like following the movement of the relationship around the turns in a spiral.

Any of the temporal qualities outlined above can be viewed in either of these ways (except rhythm, which is strictly cyclical). So, for example, using a linear view, we would notice the order, or sequence, of events and how one leads to another over time. Using a cyclical approach, we would notice how events are repeated in patterns and how those patterns repeat themselves at various points in the history of the relationship.

Information and Disclosure in Relationships

Information is a central part of all developing relationships. We seek information about other people, and we give information about ourselves.

---

18   Werner and Baxter, "Temporal Qualities."

An important aspect of relational communication therefore involves the exchange of personal information. A number of theories address this concern.

Uncertainty Reduction Theory. The brainchild of Charles Berger and his colleagues, uncertainty reduction theory deals with the ways we gather information about other people.[19] It deals with the ways individuals monitor their social environments and come to know more about themselves and others.

The theory has two major concerns—self-awareness and knowledge of others. From research in social psychology, Berger observes that *self-awareness* varies from person to person and from situation to situation.[20] In *objective self-awareness,* the person centers on the self rather than other objects in the environment. *Subjective self-awareness,* on the other hand, puts the self in a peripheral position so that it blends into the momentary stream of experience.

When you give a speech, for example, you are conscious that the audience is watching you and you become aware of yourself as an object, which is the main reason you are nervous. On the other hand, when you are involved in a nonthreatening conversation with a good friend, your self-awareness is much more subjective and natural.

Research indicates that objective self-awareness is common because we are often required to concentrate on ourselves in various situations, but it tends to be an uncomfortable state.

Although an individual's self-awareness will vary from moment to moment, each person has a relatively enduring norm of self-awareness. Some individuals are often or always self-aware, whereas others are rarely or never so.

The enduring trait of being objectively self-aware is *self-consciousness,* and this characteristic is dominated by a tendency to *self-monitor,* or "watch yourself." High self-monitors are guarded and careful about the impression they give to others. They are highly sensitive to others' feedback and try to adapt their behaviors to suit other people. Low self-monitors tend to be less sensitive to themselves or to others and are less concerned with making impressions. Whereas high self-monitors tend to be actors, low self-monitors tend to "tell it like it is."

In these ways, then, we develop knowledge about ourselves. We also have a need in interpersonal communication to get information about the other person. When we encounter a stranger, we may have a strong desire to reduce uncertainty about that person by gaining information about them. Berger proposes that people have a difficult time with uncertainty, that they want to be able to predict behavior, and that they are therefore motivated to seek information about other people. Indeed, this kind of uncertainty reduction is one of the primary dimensions of a developing relationship.

Often, the normal behavior of the other person immediately reduces your uncertainty, greatly lessening the desire to get additional information. This is especially true when your involvement with the other person is limited to a particular situation and you have all the information you need to understand their behavior in this situation. For example, when you call a plumber, you probably feel you know all you need to know about that individual to discuss your plumbing problem.

However, under certain circumstances, your need to know more about a person is heightened. Such circumstances include abnormal behavior on the part of the other person, the expectation that you will be communicating with the other person in the future, or the prospect

19 The theory is clearly summarized in Charles R. Berger and James J. Bradac, *Language and Social Knowledge: Uncertainty in Interpersonal Relations* (London: Arnold, 1982). See also Charles R. Berger and R. J. Calabrese, "Some Explorations in Initial Interaction and Beyond: Toward a Developmental Theory of Interpersonal Communication," *Human Communication Research* 1 (1975): 99–112; Charles R. Berger, R. R. Gardner, M. R. Parks, L. Schulman, and G. R. Miller, "Interpersonal Epistemology and Interpersonal Communication," in *Explorations in Interpersonal Communication,* ed. G. R. Miller (Beverly Hills, CA: Sage, 1976), pp. 149–171; and Charles R. Berger and William Douglas, "Thought and Talk: 'Excuse Me, But Have I Been Talking to Myself?'" in *Human Communication Theory,* ed. F. E. X. Dance (New York: Harper & Row, 1982), pp. 42–60.
20 For more information on self-awareness, see, for example, S. Duval and R. A. Wicklund, *A Theory of Objective Self-Awareness* (New York: Academic, 1972).

that the encounter will be especially rewarding or costly. Under these conditions, you will probably take action to get more information about the other person. For example, if a plumber noticed that you had a "Room for Rent" sign in your window and expressed an interest in finding a new place to live, you would suddenly be motivated to get more information about the plumber.

Berger believes that uncertainty is an extremely important variable in the development of relationships. So in initial interactions, people will talk a lot to get more information, and as uncertainty is eliminated, questioning and other information-seeking strategies will decline.

How, then, do you go about getting such information about others? Berger suggests a variety of ways. *Passive strategies* are observational, whereas *active* ones require the observer to do something to get the information. *Interactive strategies* rely directly on communication with the other person.

The first passive strategy is *reactivity search.* Here the individual is observed actually doing something—reacting in some situation. For example, if you were interested in getting to know a classmate, you might observe this person discreetly for a period of time. You might watch the way he or she reacted to events in the class— questions from the instructor, class discussions, and so forth. Observers generally prefer to see how a person reacts when communicating with another person, so you might listen in on conversations this person was having with other people in class.

Disinhibition searching is another passive strategy in which people are observed in informal situations where they are less likely to be self-monitoring and are behaving in a more natural way. You might therefore be especially interested in observing your classmate outside of class in settings such as the cafeteria or residence hall.

Active strategies of information involve asking others about the target person and manipulating the environment in ways that set up the target person for observation. You might, for example, try to get assigned to a project group with this classmate.

Interactive strategies include interrogation and self-disclosure. Self-disclosure, which is discussed in more detail later, is a significant strategy for obtaining information because if you disclose something about yourself, the other person is likely to disclose in return. Once in the project group, for instance, you would probably talk to this other person, and you might ask questions and make disclosures.

To discover the ways strangers get information about one another, Charles Berger and Katherine Kellermann videotaped about fifty conversations in their laboratory.[21] The couples varied in terms of how much information they were told to get. Some participants were told to get as much information about the other person as possible, others were told to get as little as possible, and a third group was not given any instructions along these lines. Also, the dyads themselves were mixed, so that some consisted of couples in which both had been asked to get a great deal of information, some consisted of couples in which both had been asked to get little information, and some included one person from each category.

The videotaped conversations were coded by judges in a variety of ways. The researchers were interested chiefly in finding out what the communicators actually did to get or to resist getting information. Predictably, the most common strategy for getting information was to ask questions, but some other strategies were also used, such as putting the other person at ease and using self-disclosure. Even the low-information seekers used questions, but their questions tended to be innocuous inquiries into the weather and other noninformative topics.

Individuals who were trying to get a great deal of information asked significantly more questions than the low-information subjects. Those who were not given any instructions

---

21   Charles R. Berger and Katherine Ann Kellermann, "To Ask or Not to Ask: Is That a Question?" in *Communication Yearbook 7,* ed. R. Bostrom (Beverly Hills, CA: Sage, 1983), pp. 342–368.

asked about the same number of questions as those who were told to get a great deal of information, which suggests that we normally tend to ask many questions when talking with strangers. This hypothesis was supported because the low-information seekers in this experiment had a harder time than did the high-information seekers and normal subjects. As expected, high-information seekers asked more open-ended questions, requiring explanation, than did low-information seekers.

Uncertainty reduction theory has been applied by William Gudykunst to cross-cultural situations. He has found that all cultures seek to reduce uncertainty in the initial stages of a relationship, but they do so in different ways.[22] The difference can be explained by whether one is a member of a high-context culture or a low-context culture.[23] *High-context cultures* rely heavily on the overall situation to interpret events, and *low-context cultures* rely more on the explicit verbal content of messages. Members of high-context cultures such as the Japanese rely on nonverbal cues and information about a person's background to reduce uncertainty, but members of low-context cultures such as the British ask direct questions related to experience, attitudes, and beliefs.

The process of uncertainty reduction between people from different cultures is affected by additional variables as well. When you strongly identify with your own cultural group and you think the other person is typical of a different group, you will probably feel a certain amount of anxiety, and your uncertainty will be great. On the other hand, your confidence in getting to know the other person will be higher and your anxiety about doing so will be lower if you expect the results to be positive. Experience and friendships with other people from different cultures may also increase your confidence when meeting a stranger from another group. In addition, knowing the other person's language will help, as will a certain amount of tolerance for ambiguity. Also, when you are more confident and less anxious about meeting someone from a different group, you will probably do a better job of getting information and reducing uncertainty.

The work of Berger and Gudykunst demonstrates the importance of uncertainty and uncertainty reduction in relationships, especially in the initial stages. Michael Sunnafrank suggests that the chief reason we seek information is not to reduce uncertainty per se but to assess the potential outcome of the communication. His *predicted-outcome value theory* suggests that people are motivated to reduce uncertainty because they want to know whether continued communication will be positive or negative.[24] The main reason you would want to know more about your plumber, for example, is not just to reduce uncertainty but to decide whether to rent a room to this person. When you receive information that leads you to predict a rewarding outcome, you will probably be more attracted to the other person, and you will probably want to continue the association. On the other hand, if your initial information leads to a negative prediction, you will probably do all you can to decrease information and cut off the relationship.

Personal information exchange in a relationship is a two-sided coin. One side is information seeking, and the other is self-disclosure. We learned about the former from uncertainty reduction theory, and we turn now to theories related to the latter.

Self-Disclosure. Disclosure and understanding were important themes in communication theory in the 1960s and 1970s. Largely as a consequence of the humanistic school in psychology,

---

22   This work is summarized in William B. Gudykunst, "Uncertainty and Anxiety," in *Theories in Intercultural Communication*, ed. Y. Y. Kim and W. B. Gudykunst (Newbury Park, CA: Sage, 1988), pp. 123–156; and "Culture and the Development of Interpersonal Relationships," in *Communication Yearbook 12*, ed. J. A. Anderson (Newbury Park, CA: Sage, 1989), pp. 315–354.
23   This concept is developed by Edward T. Hall, *Beyond Culture* (New York: Doubleday, 1976).
24   Michael Sunnafrank, "Predicted Outcome Value During Initial Interactions," *Human Communication Research* 13 (1986): 3–33; "Predicted Outcome Value and Uncertainty Reduction Theories: A Test of Competing Perspectives," *Human Communication Research* 17 (1990): 76–103.

an ideology of "honest communication" arose, and much of our thinking about what makes good interpersonal communication was affected by this movement. Spurred by the work of Carl Rogers, the so-called Third Force in psychology teaches that the goal of communication is accurate understanding of self and others and that understanding can only happen with genuine communication.[25]

According to humanistic psychology, interpersonal understanding occurs through self-disclosure, feedback, and sensitivity to the disclosures of others. Misunderstanding and dissatisfaction in relationships are promoted by dishonesty, lack of congruence between one's actions and feelings, poor feedback, and inhibited self-disclosure.[26]

Much self-disclosure research has emerged from this humanistic movement. One theorist who has investigated this process of self-disclosure is Sidney Jourard.[27] Jourard's prescription for the human being is openness, or transparency. *Transparency* means allowing the world to disclose itself freely and disclosing oneself to others. Ideal interpersonal relationships require people to allow others to experience them fully and to be open to experiencing others fully.

Jourard developed this idea after observing that the mentally ill tended to be closed to the world. He found that they became healthy when they became more willing to disclose themselves to the therapist. Thus, Jourard equates sickness with closedness and health with transparency. Jourard sees growth—a person's moving toward new ways of behaving—as a direct result of openness to the world. The sick person is fixed and stagnant; the growing person will come to new life positions. Change, then, is the essence of personal growth.

Personal growth is tied to interpersonal communication because the world is largely social. To accept one's own change requires you to verify that you are accepted by others. Growth is difficult if others around you are not open to your own disclosures.

Humanistic psychology presents a normative theory of communication, telling us how to communicate to create better relationships. As is always the case with normative theories, however, some have questioned the wisdom of the advice embedded in the values of the theory.[28] At the same time, critics' representations of the humanistic movement may be overly simple and not always accurate. In their reinterpretation of the work of Carl Rogers, for example, Cissna and Anderson point out that Rogers's philosophy and theory are far more complex than critics have led us to believe and that he did not espouse the blatant, nonadaptive self-disclosure commonly attributed to him.[29]

This conclusion combined with more recent writings on self-disclosure shows us that self-disclosure is still important, although complex and difficult. Arthur Bochner reviewed the literature on self-disclosure and concluded that the key is thoughtful disclosure. Discriminating

---

25   For a more complete summary of these theories, see the second edition of this book, *Theories of Human Communication* (Belmont, CA: Wadsworth, 1983), pp. 193–199. See also Carl Rogers, *Client-Centered Therapy* (Boston: Houghton Mifflin, 1951); "A Theory of Therapy, Personality, and Interpersonal Relationships, as Developed in the Client-Centered Framework," in *Psychology: A Study of Science*, vol. 3, ed. S. Koch (New York: McGraw-Hill, 1959), pp. 184–256; Abraham Maslow, *The Farther Reaches of Human Nature* (New York: Viking, 1971); Joseph R. Royce and Leendert P. Mos (eds.), *Humanistic Psychology: Concepts and Criticisms* (New York: Plenum, 1981); and Joseph Luft, *Of Human Interaction* (Palo Alto, CA: National Press Books, 1969).

26   The work of Carl Rogers is summarized and interpreted by Kenneth J. Cissna and Rob Anderson, "The Contributions of Carl R. Rogers to Philosophical Praxis of Dialogue," *Western Journal of Speech Communication* 54 (1990): 125–147.

27   Sidney Jourard, *Disclosing Man to Himself* (New York: Van Nostrand, 1968); *Self-Disclosure: An Experimental Analysis of the Transparent Self* (New York: Wiley, 1971); *The Transparent Self* (New York: Van Nostrand Reinhold, 1971). For a review of early research on self-disclosure, see Shirley J. Gilbert, "Empirical and Theoretical Extensions of Self-Disclosure," in *Explorations in Interpersonal Communication*, ed. G. R. Miller (Beverly Hills, CA: Sage, 1976), pp. 197–216. See also P. W. Cozby, "Self-Disclosure: A Literature Review," *Psychological Bulletin* 79 (1973): 73–91.

28   A somewhat lengthy and penetrating critique of this ideology can be found in Malcom R. Parks, "Ideology in Interpersonal Communication: Off the Couch and into the World," in *Communication Yearbook 5*, ed. M. Burgoon (New Brunswick, NJ: Transaction, 1982), pp. 79–108. See also Daniel E. Berlyne, "Humanistic Psychology as a Protest Movement," in *Humanistic Psychology: Concepts and Criticisms*, eds. J. R. Royce and L. P. Mos (New York: Plenum, 1981), p. 261.

29   Cissna and Anderson, "Contributions."

disclosers seem more satisfied with their relationships than do those who tend to disclose indiscriminately. Bochner summarizes his overall impression from this literature:

> Self-disclosure appears to be a highly overrated activity. Perhaps the time has come to lift the fog of ideology surrounding the concept. The fact that there has been only mild, if any opposition to the thesis that openness leads to better and more satisfying relationships suggests that some investigators have been lulled into an uncritical acceptance of an untenable proposition. There is no firm empirical basis for endorsing unconditional openness. A critical evaluation of the evidence suggests at most a restrained attitude toward the efficacy of self-disclosure.[30]

Today, we understand self-disclosure as a more complex process than we did in earlier times.[31] As an example of more recent thinking on this subject, Sandra Petronio has put together a useful set of ideas about the complexity of self-disclosure in a relationship.[32] This theory is based on her own research and a survey of a great deal of other studies on the topic of relationship development and disclosure. She applies this theory to married couples in particular, but it is applicable to any kind of relationship.

According to Petronio, individuals involved in relationships are constantly managing boundaries between the public and private, between those feelings and thoughts they are willing to share with their partner and those they are not. Maintaining a closed boundary can lead to greater autonomy and safety, whereas opening the boundary can promote greater intimacy and sharing, at the cost of personal vulnerability.

This play between the need to share and the need to protect oneself is constant and requires couples to negotiate and coordinate their boundaries. When do you disclose and when do you not? And when your partner discloses personal information, how do you respond?

When a person discloses something, he or she is making a demand on the other to respond appropriately. Demands and responses need to be coordinated. When you disclose something to your partner, he or she can respond in a way that

promotes relationship quality and happiness or in a way that does not.

Boundary management, then, requires consideration and thought. People make decisions about how and when to disclose, and they make decisions about how to respond to the demands of others. A variety of direct and indirect strategies can be employed, and a persistent problem for the couple is to coordinate the kinds of disclosures and responses they use. For example, when you make a clear and direct disclosure, you usually want a clear and direct response, and when you make a soft and implicit disclosure, you may want to take more time to explore the situation, perhaps tentatively, with your partner. Petronio suggests a number of possible factors and consequences entailed in these decisions, and she enumerates a variety of research issues for further exploration.

So far, all theories discussed in this chapter show how important information is in the establishment of a relationship. We regularly monitor information provided by other people and give information about ourselves.

Politeness.   A nearly universal concern among cultures of the world is politeness, which has become an important subject of communication theory. A number of researchers have done work in this area, but the best-known theoretical treatment is that of Penelope Brown and Stephen Levinson.[33]

---

30   Arthur P. Bochner, "The Functions of Human Communicating in Interpersonal Bonding," in *Handbook of Rhetorical and Communication Theory,* eds. C. C. Arnold and J. W. Bowers (Boston: Allyn & Bacon, 1984), p. 608.
31   Duck and Pittman, "Social and Personal Relationships."
32   Sandra Petronio, "Communication Boundary Management: A Theoretical Model of Managing Disclosure of Private Information Between Marital Couples," *Communication Theory* 1 (1991): 311–335.
33   Penelope Brown and Stephen Levinson, *Politeness: Some Universals in Language Usage.* Cambridge: Cambridge University Press, 1987. See also Roger Brown, "Politeness Theory: Exemplar and Exemplary," in *The Legacy of Solomon Asch: Essays in Cognition and Social Psychology,* ed. Irvin Rock (Hillsdale, NJ: Erlbaum, 1990), pp. 23–38. For a discussion of politeness as a factor in social support, see Daena J. Goldsmith, "The Role of Facework in Supportive Communication," in *Communication of Social Support,* eds. Brant R. Burleson, Terrance L. Albrecht, and Irwin G. Sarason (Thousand Oaks, CA: Sage, 1994), pp. 29–49.

Brown and Levinson believe that politeness is a cultural universal, although different cultures have different levels of required politeness and different ways of being polite. All people have the need to be appreciated and protected, which these researchers call *face needs*.

Positive face is the desire to be appreciated and approved, to be liked and honored, and *positive politeness* is designed to meet these desires. Showing concern, complimenting, and using respectful forms of address are examples. *Negative face* is the desire to be free from imposition or intrusion, and *negative politeness* is designed to protect the other person when negative face needs are threatened. Acknowledging the imposition when making a request is a common example.

Politeness is especially important whenever we must threaten another person's face, which happens frequently in our relations with others. We commit *face-threatening acts* (FTAs) whenever we behave in a way that fails to meet positive or negative face needs. Face threatening is normal and not itself a problem, but it must be handled in certain ways to mitigate potential problems that could result. There are a wide range of ways to handle FTAs, and we do not always do it the same way. Whether we deliver an FTA, how we do so, and what forms of politeness are used depend on a variety of things.

When an FTA is possible, there are five approaches we can use. We can (1) deliver the FTA baldly, without polite action, (2) deliver the FTA along with some form of positive politeness, (3) deliver the FTA along with some form of negative politeness, (4) deliver the FTA indirectly, off the record, or (5) not deliver the FTA at all. These five choices are arranged in order from the most to the least face threatening.

Suppose that you would like to ask your professor to reconsider an exam grade. How would you do it? One approach would be to deliver the bald FTA: "I would like you to reconsider my grade," period. You probably would not choose to approach it this way because it would not be very polite.

A slightly less threatening method would be to combine the request with positive politeness,

something like this: "I would appreciate it if you could look at my grade again. Other students have said you're really nice about that." Here we have a request (FTA) combined with a compliment.

Even less threatening would be to combine the FTA with negative politeness: "I'm really sorry. I know you're very busy, but could I have a moment of your time? If you're not too busy, I would really appreciate it if you could look at my grade again." Notice that this message meets negative face needs by acknowledging and apologizing for the imposition.

Number 4 is particularly interesting and complex. An "off-record" FTA is one that is indirect and ambiguous, which enables you to deny having meant the statement as an FTA. For example, you might ask to borrow your friend's car by saying, "I wonder how I will get to town this afternoon to pick up my laundry." You hope your friend will get the hint and say, "Oh, why don't you use my car," but if he says, "Well, you can't use *my* car," you can always reply, "Oh, I wasn't asking for it."

In requesting your professor to reconsider your grade, you might say something like, "Gosh, I didn't think I had done this badly on the exam." You hope she will reply, "Well, why don't I read it again?"—but if she looks at you funny, you can always deny that you were requesting a reconsideration.

Now, what determines which of these strategies you use? Brown and Levinson say that your strategy depends on a simple formula:

$$W_x = D(S,H) + P(H,S) + R_x$$

This formula means that the amount of work (*W*) one puts into being polite depends on the social distance (*D*) between the speaker (*S*) and the hearer (*H*), plus the power (*P*) of the hearer over the speaker, plus the risk (*R*) of hurting the other person.

Let's consider two examples. Imagine that you want to ask your brother for a simple, nonthreatening favor—to drop you off at the mall, let's say. You and your brother have the same status, he does not have any special power over you, and the request is not threatening. You will probably put little work into being polite.

On the other hand, suppose you want to get a loan from your parents. Assuming that you consider your parents somewhat higher in status than you, that they have considerable power over your finances, and that a request for money is considerably more serious than asking for a candy bar, you will probably be quite polite in your request. Of course, these assumptions may not hold in your particular case, but you can probably think of other examples that would require considerable face-saving work on your part.

There are, of course, a variety of levels of politeness between these two extremes. One variable can counteract another. For example, there may be little social distance, but quite a bit of power disparity. Or perhaps the distance and power don't matter much because the FTA is so minor.

Social Penetration Theory

One of the most widely studied processes of relational development is social penetration. Briefly, this is the idea that relationships become more intimate over time when partners disclose more and more information about themselves. *Social penetration*, then, is the process of increasing disclosure and intimacy in a relationship.

Gerald Miller and his colleagues define interpersonal communication in terms of penetration.[34] The more communicators know each other as persons, the more of an interpersonal character their communication takes on. The less they know each other as persons, the more impersonal that communication. Interpersonal communication is therefore the very process of social penetration:

If the communicators continue their relationship—that is, if they are sufficiently motivated to exert the effort to continue it, and if their interpersonal skills are tuned finely enough to permit its growth—their relationship may undergo certain qualitative changes. When such changes accompany relational development,

communicative transactions become increasingly interpersonal.[35]

The best-known theory of social penetration is that of Altman and Taylor.

Original Social Penetration Theory. Irwin Altman and Dalmas Taylor coined the term *social penetration*.[36] According to their theory, as relationships develop, communication moves from relatively shallow, nonintimate levels to deeper, more personal ones. Communicators' personalities can be represented by a sphere with layers; it has both breadth and depth. Breadth is the array or variety of topics that have been incorporated into individuals' lives. Depth is the amount of information available on each topic. On the outermost shell are highly visible levels of information, like dress and speech. Inside are increasingly private details about the lives, feelings, and thoughts of the participants. As the relationship develops, the partners share more aspects of the self, providing breadth as well as depth, through an exchange of information, feelings, and activities.

Communication thus proceeds by levels. Once a certain level is reached, under the right conditions the partners share increasing breadth at that level. For example, after dating a few times a couple may begin discussing previous partners, and more and more information about previous partners will be revealed before moving to a still deeper level of disclosure such as sexual history.

Altman and Taylor's theory is based in large part on one of the most popular ideas in social

---

34   G. R. Miller and M. Steinberg, *Between People: A New Analysis of Interpersonal Communication* (Chicago: Science Research Associates, 1975); G. R. Miller and M. J. Sunnafrank, "All Is for One But One Is Not for All: A Conceptual Perspective of Interpersonal Communication," in *Human Communication Theory: Comparative Essays,* ed. F. E. X. Dance (New York: Harper & Row, 1982), pp. 220–242.

35   Miller and Sunnafrank, "All Is for One," pp. 222–223.

36   Irwin Altman and Dalmas Taylor, *Social Penetration: The Development of Interpersonal Relationships* (New York: Holt, Rinehart & Winston, 1973). For an update and summary, see Dalmas A. Taylor and Irwin Altman, "Communication in Interpersonal Relationships: Social Penetration Theory," in *Interpersonal Processes: New Directions in Communication Research,* eds. M. E. Roloff and G. R. Miller (Newbury Park, CA: Sage, 1987), pp. 257–277.

science—that relationships are sustained when they are relatively rewarding and discontinued when they are relatively costly. This process is known as *social exchange*.[37] According to Altman and Taylor, relational partners not only assess the rewards and costs of the relationship at a given moment but also use the information they have gathered to predict the rewards and costs in the future.

If the partners judge that the rewards will be relatively greater than the costs, they will risk more disclosure, which has the potential of moving the participants to a deeper level of intimacy. The greater the perceived rewards relative to cost, the faster the penetration. Altman and Taylor found that the most rapid penetration tends to occur in the early stages of development when rewards tend to outweigh costs.

There are four stages of relational development. *Orientation* consists of impersonal communication, in which one discloses only very public information about oneself. If this stage is rewarding to the participants, they will move to the next stage, the *exploratory affective exchange,* in which initial expansion of information and movement to a deeper level of disclosure takes place. The third stage, *affective exchange,* centers on evaluative and critical feelings at a deeper level. This stage will not be entered unless the partners perceive substantial rewards relative to costs in earlier stages. Finally, *stable exchange* is highly intimate and allows the partners to predict each other's actions and responses very well.

Altman and Taylor show that relational development does not involve only increasing social penetration. All too often it also involves decreased intimacy, disengagement, and dissolution. Altman and Taylor suggest that as rewards are reduced and costs increased at the more intimate levels of communication, the social penetration process will be reversed and the relationship will begin to come apart.

Modifications to Social Penetration.   Original social penetration theory was important in focusing our attention on relationship development as a communication process. There is much truth to the idea that relationships become closer as information is shared, and that development is partially a process of increasing intimacy. At the same time, the original theory was overly simple.

Many students of relationship development now believe that social penetration is a cyclical, dialectical process.[38] It is cyclical because it proceeds in back-and-forth cycles, and it is dialectical because it involves the management of the tension between opposites.

A *dialectic* is a tension between two or more contradictory elements of a system. Dialectical analysis looks at the ways the system develops or changes, how it moves, in response to these tensions; and it looks at the strategic actions taken by a system to manage contradictions.[39] Some dialectical analyses emphasize the contradictions between forces within a relationship and forces outside of it. These are called *external* contradictions. Other analyses emphasize contradictions within the relationship itself and are *internal*. Leslie Baxter puts these two together by examining three dialectical clusters. Each cluster consists of a variety of related contradictions that can occur in relationships.[40]

The first of these clusters is *integration and separation,* or the tension between coming together and moving apart. In its external form,

37   An excellent summary of this entire line of work is Michael E. Roloff, *Interpersonal Communication: The Social Exchange Approach* (Beverly Hills, CA: Sage, 1981). The best-known social exchange theory is that of John W. Thibaut and Harold H. Kelley, *The Social Psychology of Groups* (New York: Wiley, 1959); see also Harold H. Kelley and John W. Thibaut, *Interpersonal Relations: A Theory of Interdependence* (New York: Wiley, 1978). For a brief summary of the theory, see the third edition of this book, *Theories of Human Communication,* 1989, pp. 185–186.

38   This work is briefly summarized by C. Arthur VanLear, "Testing a Cyclical Model of Communicative Openness in Relationship Development: Two Longitudinal Studies," *Communication Monographs* 58 (1991): 337–361.

39   See, for example, Leslie Baxter, "A Dialectical Perspective on Communication Strategies in Relationship Development," in *Handbook of Personal Relationships,* ed. S. Duck (New York: Wiley, 1988), pp. 257–273.

40   Leslie Baxter, "The Social Side of Personal Relationships: A Dialectical Perspective," in *Social Context and Relationships: Understanding Relationship Processes,* vol. 3, Steve Duck, ed. (Newbury Park, CA: Sage, 1993), pp. 139–169; Werner and Baxter, "Temporal Qualities."

this is the tension between meeting the demands of one's partner and that of interacting with others. Do you stay home with your boyfriend or girlfriend to watch TV or go to a club meeting? If that is a hard decision, you are probably struggling with this dialectic. The internal version is the struggle between individuality and mutuality. Here we worry about such things as whether to accommodate to others or to hold our own ground.

The second cluster is *expression-nonexpression.* This is the tension between whether to reveal information or not. Again, this comes in internal and external versions, which involve tensions between revealing aspects of the relationship to others outside (external) and revealing information about yourself to your relational partner (internal). When you are trying to decide whether to tell your partner something you have been thinking about lately and feel reluctant to do so, you are probably experiencing this dialectic.

The third cluster is *stability-change,* or predictability and consistency versus spontaneity and novelty. The internal tension involves feelings about stability and change within the relationship itself, and the external tension involves feelings about whether to make constant adjustments to the demands of society. Often couples experience a quandary about whether to keep doing the same old thing or to try new things, and when this happens, they are feeling this particular tension.

In their later writings, Altman and his colleagues point out that relationships generally do not move in a single line toward greater openness. Rather, couples go back and forth between sharing and distance as they manage the tension between the need for privacy and the need for connection.[41] Relationships go back and forth between stability and change as the couple manages its contradictory needs for predictability and flexibility.

Altman and his associates now say that these dialectics are usually managed in a long-term relationship by a kind of predictability of cycles. In other words, as the relationship develops, the couple's cycle of openness and closedness pos-

sesses a certain regularity or predictable rhythm. At the same time, in more developed relationships, the cycle is larger than in a less developed one. This is because, consistent with the basic tenet of social penetration theory, developed relationships have more disclosure on the average.

Something else happens as relationships develop. Partners become more able to coordinate the cycle of disclosure. In other words, their timing and extent of disclosure are somewhat synchronized, at least in theory. The research evidence is somewhat mixed but basically supports the general idea of cycles and dialectics.

To test this idea, Arthur VanLear paired up a number of students into dyads.[42] Each couple met one-half hour per week for five weeks to talk, and their conversations were tape-recorded for analysis. The conversations were later analyzed for the amount and type of self-disclosure, and these disclosures were then examined statistically for cyclical patterns. The analysis indicated that cycles of openness did occur in these conversations and some synchronization did occur.

To compare these results with real, ongoing relationships, another group of students were asked to monitor their conversations with another person with whom they were having a relationship (such as a spouse, friend, or romantic partner) for ten weeks. After each conversation of at least fifteen minutes, they filled out a "conversation monitoring form" that asked about satisfaction and perceived openness/closedness. The results of this study mirrored those of the first study. Both studies indicated that cycles do occur, that these are complex, that the partners recognized their cycles, and that matching and synchronization often occur. Important to note, however, is the finding that the amount of synchrony is not the same for each couple, which

---

41   Irwin Altman, "Dialectics, Physical Environments, and Personal Relationships," *Communication Monographs* 60 (1993): 26–34; Irwin Altman, A. Vinsel, and B. Brown, "Dialectic Conceptions in Social Psychology: An Application to Social Penetration and Privacy Regulation," in *Advances in Experimental Social Psychology,* vol. 14, ed. L. Berkowitz (New York: Academic, 1981), pp. 76–100.
42   VanLear, "Testing a Cyclical Model."

means that there are differences between couples in their ability to coordinate self-disclosure cycles.

Relational Dissolution

For several years, Leslie Baxter and her colleagues conducted research on the disengagement process. These research results form the basis for a theory of the ways couples use communication to end relationships.[43] This program addresses three questions:

1. What communication strategies do couples use to break up a relationship?
2. Are the chosen strategies related to characteristics of the individual or the relationship?
3. What is the sequence of the disengagement process?

We will begin here with the first question. Baxter found that strategies of disengagement vary in directness and concern for the other person. *Direct strategies* involve the explicit statement of a desire to end the relationship, whereas *indirect strategies* do not. Some people choose strategies that project *concern* for the other person, in an attempt to avoid hurt, whereas others choose strategies for their *expediency,* regardless of the consequences to the other person's feelings.

In addition, endings may be *unilateral,* in which only one member wishes to terminate the relationship, or *bilateral,* in which both parties feel that the relationship should end. Both unilateral and bilateral strategies can be direct or indirect. Let's begin with indirect strategies.

The *indirect strategies of unilateral disengagement* include withdrawal, pseudoescalation, and cost escalation. *Withdrawal,* of course, is just avoiding the other person or reducing the amount of contact one has with a partner. Here is an example from one of Baxter's interviews: "I took a stand that related too much homework for an excuse to avoid her. She then initiated notes to me which contained certain things that both of us didn't like about the relationship. I never answered the notes."[44]

Pseudodeescalation is the lie that one just wishes to change the relationship to be a little less close. Here is an example: "I arranged to talk with her in a neutral location. . . . What I said basically was: 'Let's go back to being just friends' (knowing full well I meant I wanted to salvage my ego, and hers, by saying indirectly, the relationship was totally over)."

Cost escalation is behaving in a way that makes it more difficult for the other person to continue the relationship. In other words, one deliberately makes the relationship more costly to the other person so that he or she will be able to tolerate, or even initiate, a separation: "I thought I would be an 'asshole' for a while to make her like me less."

One indirect strategy of bilateral disengagement is *fading away.* Here, both parties acknowledge implicitly that the relationship is over: "My lover was a married man who was visiting overnight on his way through Portland. On the way to the airport the next day, we hardly spoke at all. When we did speak it wasn't concerning our relationship. We both knew that it was over." *Mutual pseudodeescalation* is another common indirect strategy of bilateral disengagement.

Two common forms of *direct communication in unilateral disengagement* are the *fait accompli,* or a simple direct statement that the relationship is over, and *state-of-the-relationship talk,* which is an attempt to analyze the relationship.

In *bilateral disengagement, direct communication* may take the form of attributional conflict or negotiated farewell. *Attributional conflict* is basically a fight in which each party blames the other for the breakup. *Negotiated farewell* is a mutual parting of the ways without hostility. Among these strategies, cost escalation, fait

43   The most comprehensive statement of this work is Leslie A. Baxter, "Accomplishing Relationship Disengagement," in *Understanding Personal Relationships: An Interdisciplinary Approach,* eds. S. Duck and D. Perlman (Beverly Hills, CA: Sage, 1985), pp. 243–266. See also William W. Wilmot, Donal A. Carbaugh, and Leslie A. Baxter, "Communicative Strategies Used to Terminate Romantic Relationships," *Western Journal of Speech Communication* 49 (1985): 204–216; Leslie A. Baxter, "Trajectories of Relationship Disengagement," *Journal of Social and Personal Relationships* 1 (1984): 29–48; Leslie A. Baxter, "Strategies for Ending Relationships: Two Studies," *Western Journal of Speech Communication* 46 (1982): 223–241.
44   All examples are from Baxter, "Accomplishing," p. 248.

accompli, withdrawal, and attributional conflict embody little or no concern for the other person. The other strategies include at least some attempt to smooth the waters and save face.

Baxter's second question is whether one's strategy choice is related to any personal or relational variables. Her research shows that directness is most related to both individual and relational characteristics. This finding suggests that directness itself may be the primary issue in deciding how to end a relationship.

Some interesting findings related to strategies of disengagement are as follows. First, young children have fewer strategies for disengagement than adolescents, and adults seem to have more strategies than adolescents. Preadolescents' strategies tend to be direct, whereas adolescents and adults choose more indirect strategies. At all ages, however, people seem to have a larger repertoire of communication strategies for beginning relationships than for ending them.

Baxter found no differences between men and women in her studies, but she did find that androgynous individuals, who have a balance of masculine and feminine traits, are more apt to use direct strategies than are either masculine or feminine subjects. Baxter speculates that masculine and feminine individuals have different reasons for avoiding directness. Masculine individuals may have less concern for relationships generally, and feminine persons may find direct strategies too assertive.

Communication apprehension is also related to the manner in which an individual terminates a relationship. Predictably, apprehensive individuals are less likely to use direct strategies than are nonapprehensive ones. When one is involved in a close relationship, the tendency is to use direct strategies that also embody concern for the other person. Predictably, individuals in a particularly close relationship seem to want to reduce the potential pain involved in the breakup process. Along the same line, romantic partners tend to use direct strategies more than friends do.

Baxter's third question deals with the process of disengagement itself. The dissolution of a re-

lationship seems to be more than a mere backing out or reduction in the amount of intimacy of communication, as social penetration theory suggests. Disengagement often involves repeated attempts to reduce or end the relationship in a cyclical fashion, with the use of several different strategies at different points in the process. However, no one pattern fits all relationship endings.

Baxter refers to the course of a breakup as a *trajectory*, and she notes that the specific way partners accomplish it depends on a variety of situational conditions and personal decisions. The nature of the precipitating events is a factor. Some relationships break up because of an incremental building of events, and others break up over a single critical incident. Whether the decision is one-sided or two-sided is another factor. Do both parties want to split, or is the breakup instigated by one? The trajectory is also affected by the strategies chosen. The way a partner reacts to mentioning the subject is also a concern. And finally the trajectory is affected by whether either party wants to repair the relationship.

Depending on these conditions, a large number of possible trajectories or courses of action may result. To discover which trajectories are most common, Baxter asked about a hundred volunteers who had experienced a breakup within the past year to provide information about what happened.[45] Each participant was given a stack of note cards and asked to write on separate cards each significant point in the dissolution process beginning with the problems that precipitated it. At the top of the card was to appear a single phrase that characterized the event and below was to appear a brief paragraph describing what happened at that point. Each deck of completed cards represented the story of an actual breakup. Baxter then analyzed the cards to discover what processes were employed in relational dissolution.

The most common pattern was unilateral—one person deciding he or she did not want to be in the relationship. In this pattern the initiating

---

45 Baxter, "Trajectories."

parties used indirect methods of communicating with their partners, and they had to try several times before getting through. Baxter calls this pattern *persevering indirectness.* About 30 percent of the participants experienced this trajectory.

Another trajectory type was *ambivalent indirectness.* It too was unilateral and indirect, but it did involve at least one attempt to repair the relationship before completely giving up. Eleven percent of the subjects experienced this kind of breakup. About the same number experienced *swift explicit mutuality.* Here, the termination was bilateral and direct. It did not take long, and no attempt to repair the relationship was made.

Some people—about 9 percent of Baxter's subjects—experienced *mutual ambivalence,* in which they initiated the split but were indirect about it, attempted several repairs, and took a long time getting around to the actual breakup. These four were the most common types of trajectories, although she did find others as well.

In this section, we have looked at information and disclosure in relationship development and dissolution. The following section presents theories of particular types and aspects of relationship, including friendship, marriage, and conflict.

◖◗ RELATIONSHIPS IN CONTEXT

Here we look at particular relationship types—friendships, marriages, and conflicts.

Communication in Friendships

William Rawlins's *dialectical theory of friendships* is an intriguing and sophisticated approach to this subject.[46] Rawlins believes that friendship at any stage of life presents an interesting and often

complex set of challenges. The challenges of friendship arise chiefly from the need to manage a variety of dialectical contradictions. As you will see, Rawlins's dialectics are not unlike those of Baxter reviewed earlier in the chapter.

In a friendship, for example, you may experience a tension between being an individual and being a friend. Friends respect each other as individuals, but they are also loyal to each other and meet each other's needs. How can you do both? This is an example of a dialectical tension that different friends handle in different ways.

Rawlins has done extensive research on friendships. He has surveyed the social science literature, examined reported case studies, read fictional accounts, conducted over a hundred personal interviews, and conducted in-depth case studies of his own. In his book he discusses the changing texture of friendships over the life span, including those in childhood, adolescence, young adulthood, middle adulthood, and late adulthood. Although the challenges of friendship change over the life course, all people of all ages must manage dialectical tension in one way or another. Rawlins's work applies primarily to middle-class white U.S. culture.

Rawlins suggests that two general classes of dialectics operate in friendships. The first, contextual dialectics, deals with the meaning of friendship within the broader culture. The second, interactional dialectics, deals with the ambiguities of everyday communication in any friendship.

Contextual dialectics relate to the question of the place of friendship in society at large. You cannot really characterize friendship in simple terms. Any definition must mediate two contradictions. The first contradiction is between *the public and the private.* Friendship is inherently private. By definition it is something two people work out between themselves, and yet it is simultaneously governed by social and cultural expectations. The conflict here is between what society says a friendship should be (the public realm) and what the friends themselves have worked out between themselves (the private realm). This dialectic usually involves representing one's

---

46   William K. Rawlins, *Friendship Matters: Communication, Dialectics, and the Life Course* (Hawthorne, NY: Aldine, 1992); see also William K. Rawlins, "A Dialectical Analysis of the Tensions, Functions, and Strategic Challenges of Communication in Young Adult Friendships," in *Communication Yearbook 12,* ed. J. A. Anderson (Newbury Park, CA: Sage, 1989), pp. 157–189.

friendship to the world at large in a way that is socially acceptable.[47]

An example of this tension occurs in cross-sex friendships. Because society more or less reserves such relationships for romance, love, and sex, a platonic relationship between a man and woman often has to be explained to others, and there may be a good deal of pressure by outsiders to move the relationship from a friendship to something more intimate.

The second contextual dialectic is that between *the ideal and the real.* Our culture gives us a set of ideals to achieve, and yet very few friendships meet this set of values. Friends must act in a way that accommodates this tension. For example, friends are supposed to be loyal and available to each other, yet total loyalty may diminish one's own self-integrity, individuality, and freedom.

You can see that the two contextual dialectics are related to each other because the public view of friendship is laden with ideals, whereas the private actuality is governed by real relations negotiated by the friends themselves.

The second type of tensions that affect friendships is *interactional dialectics,* involving the ambiguities and ambivalence within individual friendships. They include all conflicts that friends must endure and manage in order to sustain the friendship. Because these tensions govern communication in a friendship, Rawlins concentrates primarily on this area. He believes that four dialectical principles are used to manage the communication in friendships.

The first is to establish *the freedom to be independent and the freedom to be dependent.* People are supposed to let their friends lead their own lives, and yet they are also supposed to be available to help, counsel, and guide one another. Every time you make a decision to back off or to engage a friend, you are dealing with this contradiction. There are various ways of achieving temporary resolution of the contradiction, one of the most

common being to let the other person make his or her own choices, including the choice to ask for help.

One of Rawlins's cases is that of Lana and Darlene, 26-year-old women who had been friends since their freshman year in high school. Dependence and independence are important issues for Lana and Darlene. Over the years they have gone through several stages, and the friendship can accommodate both dependence and independence. At times either or both women desire independence, especially when their relationships with spouses and boyfriends are going well. At other times when help and support are needed, such as during Darlene's divorce, dependency is permitted.

The second principle is the dialectic of *affection and instrumentality.* Friendships often have a tension between valuing the friend as an end in itself versus using the friend as a means to some other end. This is a tension between affection and utility. Do you call a friend to help you move? You might think twice about it. Do you let a friend borrow your car? Probably so because that's what friends are for, or are they? How do people call on a friend to help them do something without the risk of having the friend feel used? Again, people work this out in different ways. Often, for example, friends have developed particular ways of asking for help or have become particularly sensitive to the timing of such requests. Friends may work hard to ensure genuine expressions of affection as well as the willingness to be of assistance.

Friendships during middle adulthood, especially between men, often arise from career contacts, entangling friendship with career advancement. Because the affection side of the tension is often unfulfilled in middle-aged men, they often feel that they have no best friend other than their wife. A male university professor, for example, said,

> I have a lot of acquaintances, a lot of people I call friends that I only see once in a while. . . . Most of these are professional. Most of those are people I come in contact with through work

47   This dialectic is also explored by Montgomery, "Communication."

and I consider friends that aren't really sharing kinds of friends. I have very, very few that I would consider true friends.[48]

Women during this period seem to balance the two sides of the dialectic more effectively and usually say they have a best friend other than their husband.

The third principle is the dialectic of *judgment and acceptance*. Friends are supposed to accept us as we are, but they are also called on to make judgments and give advice. Sometimes we criticize friends, and other times we try hard to refrain from doing so. When we criticize, we usually choose our words carefully, and we often equivocate between expressing a judgment and accepting friends as they are. Again, each set of friends works out a pattern that manages this dialectic more or less effectively.

One of Rawlins's cases is that of Carol and Brent, who by their early 20s had been close friends for seven years. The tension between judgment and acceptance is a real issue in this friendship. In their interviews they both expressed how important acceptance has been in the friendship, and for this reason they have come to be cautious about making judgments about each other. Carol, for example, most dislikes Brent when he comes off like a brother and criticizes her boyfriends.

The fourth dialectic is that between *expressiveness and protectiveness*. To what extent can you express your feelings openly with a friend? Should you protect a friend from hurtful or difficult information? In many ways this is a tension between spontaneity and strategy. It is a tension between honesty and rhetorical adaptation. You want to feel that your friends are honest with you, but at the same time you do not want to hurt your friends. A frequent response to this dialectic is to try to accomplish both horns of the dilemma at the same time, to be honest but to be careful in how that honesty is expressed. For most friends, this is a rhetorical feat.

Rawlins comments on the power of this dialectic in Darlene and Lana's friendship in these terms:

Darlene and Lana recalled numerous instances when their desire to express misgivings or hurtful information was tempered by concern for the other's feelings, and when their voiced acceptance veiled deep-seated reservations and criticisms. They cautiously chose their moments for commenting and exercised great care in broaching subjects such as family members, relationships with men, husbands, details of their sex lives, and personal appearance.[49]

Friendships constitute a unique and interesting context in which relationships are developed. Another, very different context is marriage, to which we now turn.

Communication in Marriage

A well-recognized researcher on marital communication is Mary Anne Fitzpatrick, whose extensive studies have led to a theory of marriage types.[50] Fitzpatrick's research employs a questionnaire—the Relational Dimensions Instrument—that asks individuals about various aspects of their marriages. It is based on the work of David Kantor and William Lehr, who argue that marriages can be characterized by how the partners use their space, time, and energy and the extent to which they express feelings, exert power, and share a common philosophy of marriage.[51]

Fitzpatrick administered a large number of questions on these topics to almost fifteen hundred married persons. Fitzpatrick discovered that these items measured three basic factors—ideology, interdependence, and conflict. *Ideology* is a variable involving conventional versus nonconventional notions of family. *Interdependence* is a variable reflecting dependence versus autonomy in a marriage. *Conflict* deals with the amount of disagreement or clash in the marriage.

Fitzpatrick discovered that married couples tend to cluster into three distinct groups along these dimensions—the traditionals, the indepen-

---

48   Rawlins, *Friendship*, p. 190.
49   Rawlins, *Friendship*, p. 133.
50   Mary Anne Fitzpatrick, *Between Husbands and Wives: Communication in Marriage* (Newbury Park, CA: Sage, 1988).
51   David Kantor and William Lehr, *Inside the Family* (New York: Harper & Row, 1975).

dents, and the separates. The *traditionals* tend to be conventional in their views of marriage and place more value on stability and certainty in role relations than on variety and spontaneity. They have strong interdependence and share much companionship. Although they are not assertive about disagreement, they do not avoid conflict.

A traditional wife, for example, would take her husband's name. Traditional couples would probably oppose infidelity, and they would share much time and space. They would try to work out a standard time schedule and spend as much time together as possible, and they probably would not have separate rooms for their own activities.

There is not too much conflict in a traditional marriage because power and decision making are distributed according to customary norms. Husbands, for example, may be in charge of certain kinds of decisions and wives in charge of others. Consequently, there is little need to negotiate and resolve conflict in these marriages. At the same time, there is little impetus for change and growth in the relationship. A traditional couple can be assertive with each other when necessary, but each person tends to support his or her requests with appeals to the relationship rather than by refuting each other's arguments.

Traditional couples are highly expressive and disclose both joy and frustration. The communication in this kind of family seems to encourage expression of feelings, even from men. They send many positive nonverbal cues and seem supportive of each other.

The second type of marriage is *independent.* These individuals tend to be unconventional in their views of marriage and do not rely on each other much. Although they may spend time together and share a great deal, they value their own autonomy and often have separate rooms in the house. They may also have separate interests and friends outside the family.

Because they do not rely on conventional roles, the relationship is constantly renegotiated. Because of their individuality, there is much conflict in a typical independent marriage, and they often vie for power, use a variety of persuasive techniques, and are not reluctant to refute each

other's arguments. Like the traditionals, the independents are also expressive. They respond to each other's nonverbal cues, and they usually understand each other well.

The third type of marriage is the *separates.* These individuals seem to be ambivalent about their roles and relationship. They may have a fairly conventional view of marriage, but they are not very interdependent and do not share much. For this reason, Fitzpatrick refers to separates as emotionally divorced. They have their opinions and can be contentious, but conflicts never last long because separates are quick to retreat from conflict. Actually, they do not seem able to coordinate their actions long enough to sustain a conflict. Their attempts to gain compliance rarely use relationship appeals and often mention the bad things that will happen if the spouse does not comply.

Separates have a watchful attitude. They ask many questions but offer little advice. Predictably, then, they are not very expressive, and they do not understand their partners' emotions very well.

About 60 percent of the couples Fitzpatrick has tested fall into one of these categories. In these cases the husband and wife agreed sufficiently in their answers to the questionnaires to classify them as purely traditional, independent, or separate. Obviously, spouses will not always agree, however, and a substantial number of Fitzpatrick's subjects did not. These couples are considered to be mixed, including the combinations of separate-traditional, traditional-independent, or independent-separate. The characterization of mixed types is naturally more complex.

This typology usefully classifies marriages into the pure and mixed types. Couples in different types of marriages have different patterns of interaction, and the categories reflect the way individuals in our culture think about marriage.[52]

---

52   This point is developed in Fitzpatrick, *Husbands and Wives,* pp. 255–256; Nancy A. Burrell and Mary Anne Fitzpatrick, "The Psychological Reality of Marital Conflict," in *Intimates in Conflict: A Communication Perspective,* ed. D. D. Cahn (Hillsdale, NJ: Erlbaum, 1990), pp. 167–186; and Mary Anne Fitzpatrick and L. David Ritchie, "Communication Schemata Within the Family: Multiple Perspectives on Family Interaction," *Human Communication Research* 20 (1994): 275–301.

Thus, besides being marriage types, the categories of traditional, independent, and separate are cognitive schemas with which individuals understand marriage and all that it includes. When both partners have the same schema, they share a way of understanding, and they clearly fit one of the types. When the partners do not have the same schema, they are obviously mixed in type. These schemas are used to understand your relationships with your spouse; they are used to guide your actions in relating and interacting with your husband or wife and guide how you understand your entire family system.

Depending on your point of view, you may think that one of the marriage types is better than the others. Fitzpatrick takes a strong position against this view. In her research she has discovered that there are satisfied couples in every category, and even among unsatisfied couples, you cannot judge a marriage on the basis of satisfaction alone. This means that there is no best form of marital communication. What is best depends on the needs of the couple.

The theory of marital types shows among other things that conflict is an important element of marriages. In the following section, we take a special look at this aspect of relationships.

Communication in Conflict

This section covers theories of relational conflict. Over the years many approaches to the study of conflict have emerged, and as in most theoretical areas, this work is not altogether consistent.[53] As a result defining conflict is difficult. Charles Watkins offers an analysis of the essential conditions of conflict, which form an operational definition:[54]

1. Conflict requires at least two parties capable of invoking sanctions on each other.
2. Conflicts arise due to the existence of a mutually desired but mutually unobtainable objective.
3. Each party in a conflict has four possible types of action alternatives:
   a. To obtain the mutually desired objective
   b. To end the conflict

   c. To invoke sanctions against the opponent
   d. To communicate something to the opponent
4. Parties in conflict may have different value or perceptual systems.
5. Each party has resources that may be increased or diminished by implementation of action alternatives.
6. Conflict terminates only when each party is satisfied that he or she has "won" or "lost" or believes that the probable costs of continuing the conflict outweigh the probable costs of ending the conflict.

One advantage of Watkins's definition is that it includes the possibility of communication. Ironically, many theories of conflict have neglected the communication aspect, and there are frankly few communication-based theories of relational conflict. Two have been chosen for discussion here—game theory and attribution theory.

Game Theory. Game theory was developed many years ago by John von Neumann and Oskar Morgenstern as a tool to study economic behavior and has since provided a base for popular research tools in a variety of disciplines.[55] For researchers studying the processes of decision making and goal competition, game theory provides a useful approach, and it has been used extensively to study conflict.

Game theory itself is not a relational communication theory, although it has implications for relationships. Because game research involves

53 A number of reviews are available. See, for example, Dudley D. Cahn (ed.), *Intimates in Conflict: A Communication Perspective* (Hillsdale, NJ: Erlbaum, 1990); Michael E. Roloff, "Communication and Conflict," in *Handbook of Communication Science*, eds. C. E. Berger and S. H. Chaffee (Newbury Park, CA: Sage, 1987), pp. 484–536; Alan Sillars and Judith Weisberg, "Conflict as a Social Skill," in *Interpersonal Processes: New Directions in Communication Research*, eds. M. E. Roloff and G. R. Miller (Newbury Park, CA: Sage, 1987), pp. 140–171; Joyce Frost and William Wilmot, *Interpersonal Conflict* (Dubuque, IA: Brown, 1978).
54 Charles Watkins, "An Analytic Model of Conflict," *Speech Monographs* 41 (1974): 1–5.
55 John von Neumann and Oskar Morgenstern, *The Theory of Games and Economic Behavior* (Princeton, NJ: Princeton University Press, 1944). Numerous secondary sources are also available. See, for example, Morton Davis, *Game Theory: A Non-technical Introduction* (New York: Basic, 1970).

the moves and countermoves of individuals, it is potentially useful in this area, as we will see.

Games consist of structured situations where players take turns making choices that lead to payoffs. In all games the rational decision-making process is stressed. The question is how players behave in order to gain rewards. Types of games vary in several ways, including the amount of information provided to players, the amount of communication permitted between them, and the extent of cooperation versus competition built into the payoff matrix.

Because game theory stresses rational decision making, it involves games of strategy. In such games a player makes moves (choices) that lead to rewards or punishments based on the moves of others. The object is to maximize gains and minimize losses.

For example, suppose that you and your spouse were having a disagreement about where to take your vacation; you would probably try to get your way. You might make a variety of moves, such as calling the travel agent, talking with friends, buying clothes, and discussing your preference with your partner. Each move is designed to win, to get the vacation you want. If you do, you have won, and your partner has lost.

One of the most commonly used games is the *prisoner's dilemma*.[56] This simple game is useful because it illustrates a number of salient features of games in general. Also, it is interesting as a *mixed-motive game* because players can cooperate or compete, and genuine reasons are present for doing either.

Here is the prisoner's dilemma: You and an accomplice are arrested for a crime. After being separated, each of you must choose whether to confess or not. If you confess and your accomplice does not, you will be allowed to go free, and your testimony will send the other person to prison for twenty years. If you both confess, both will be sent to prison for five years. If neither confesses, both of you will go to prison for one

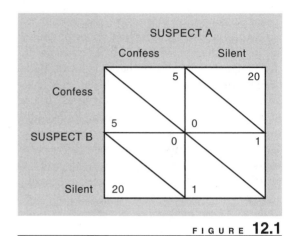

FIGURE **12.1**

Prisoner's Dilemma

year on a lesser charge. Figure 12.1 illustrates the choices.

With no communication between you and your accomplice, the two of you will not know the choice of the other. Each is in a dilemma about whether to trust and cooperate with the other prisoner by remaining silent or to compete with the other prisoner by confessing. If both of you are willing to cooperate by not confessing, the long-term payoff is maximized for both. But if one does not cooperate, the other cannot cooperate. Over several trials, most people will move ultimately toward the noncooperative strategy.

Although our earlier vacation example appears to be a win-win conflict, this kind of situation is usually not so simple; it is most often a mixed-motive conflict such as the prisoner's dilemma. You can either compete to get your way, or you can cooperate and come up with a vacation spot that suits both of you. If you compete and win, you will presumably enjoy your vacation more (although your partner will enjoy it less). If you cooperate and compromise, you will still have a good time. Will you cooperate or compete? That is the question of a mixed-motive game.

Thomas Steinfatt and Gerald Miller reviewed the literature in which games were used to investigate the process of communication in conflict.

---

56   This game is explained in Davis, *Game Theory,* pp. 93–107. This book is an excellent source of real-world analogues for many types of games.

Using games as an analogue, they list three ways parties in conflict come to assess each other's strategies. The first way is to observe the opponent's moves over several trials. In games such as the prisoner's dilemma, subjects play through a number of trials of the game. Typically, a player will observe the opponent's moves and decide what to do next. So, for example, if your partner goes out and buys beach clothes, you know that he is serious about going to the coast. So you go out and buy hiking boots to show that you are serious about going into the mountain wilderness.

The second way of assessing strategy is to observe the total conflict situation. In so doing a player makes inferences from the situation to the opponent's strategy. The player would study the game matrix and try to guess what the opponent's strategy is likely to be. Having gone on many vacations with your spouse, you try to figure out what he likes and what he will do to get to go where he wants.

The third approach is direct communication. The authors point out,

> Ideally, communication makes it possible to conduct the entire conflict at the symbolic level, with each player stating how he would respond to the stated, rather than the actual, moves of the other. . . . Besides avoiding the hostility, disruption, and subsequent losses resulting from actual moves, negotiations allow the parties to move away from a winner-take-all position toward a solution that provides some rewards for everyone.[57]

If the players in the prisoner's dilemma game could communicate and agree to cooperate, both would receive lesser sentences. Similarly, if you just sat down and talked about your vacation, you would probably realize that there is a spot that both of you would like to visit. Diplomacy in international relations is considered superior to war because the parties can try to work out their differences by talking rather than killing.

Direct communication has three advantages. The first point is that communication is symbolic and does not have the actual consequence of the real move. Thus, communication is a way to try

out an idea rather than doing something that you may later regret. Second, communication changes the probability of moves and may reduce the amount of competitiveness on the part of the conflicting parties. So, for example, if your husband tells you why he wants to go to the beach, you may be more understanding and less inclined to block his decision. Third, communication may result in changing the other person's orientations toward the problem. In other words, you may directly persuade him or her and change what he or she wants to do.

By communicating, then, the parties may reduce their own tendencies to behave chauvinistically. In fact, studies have shown that this is what tends to happen. Pregame discussions increase cooperation. The greatest effect occurs when communication exists from the beginning of the conflict. Studies also show that the fuller the communication, the more open the channels, and the greater the resultant cooperation.

An Attribution Theory of Conflict. Recall from Chapter 7 that attribution theory deals with the ways people infer the causes of behavior. The premise of this approach to conflict is that people develop their own "theories" to explain the conflicts they are involved with, and these theories are largely a product of their attributions. In other words, how you deal with a conflict depends on how you place blame. Alan Sillars has developed a theory of conflict based on this idea.[58]

According to Sillars three general strategies of conflict resolution are seen in interpersonal relationships. These include strategies designed to

---

57   Thomas Steinfatt and Gerald Miller, "Communication in Game Theoretic Models of Conflict," in *Perspectives on Communication in Conflict*, eds. G. R. Miller and H. Simons (Englewood Cliffs, NJ: Prentice-Hall, 1974), pp. 14–75.
58   Alan L. Sillars, Stephen F. Coletti, Doug Parry, and Mark A. Rogers, "Coding Verbal Conflict Tactics: Nonverbal and Perceptual Correlates of the 'Avoidance-Distributive-Integrative' Distinction," *Human Communication Research* 9 (1982): 83–95; Alan L. Sillars, "Attributions and Communication in Roommate Conflicts," *Communication Monographs* 47 (1980): 180–200; "The Sequential and Distributional Structure of Conflict Interaction as a Function of Attributions Concerning the Locus of Responsibility and Stability of Conflict," in *Communication Yearbook 4*, ed. D. Nimmo (New Brunswick, NJ: Transaction, 1980), pp. 217–236.

avoid or minimize conflict, those that aim to win in a conflict, and those that attempt to achieve mutual positive outcomes for both parties. Sillars has refined his scheme over the years and refers to these categories simply as avoidance behaviors, competitive behaviors, and cooperative behaviors.

Avoidance behaviors employ no communication or, at best, indirect communication. *Competitive behaviors* involve negative messages, and *cooperative behaviors* entail more open and positive communication. Table 12.2 illustrates a variety of strategies found by Sillars in his research.[59]

As an example of how people use these different strategies in interpersonal conflicts, consider a study by Sillars and his colleagues on conflict in marriage.[60] In this study the researchers solicited the cooperation of forty married couples. Each couple was given a kit to take home, consisting of a set of questionnaires for each spouse, a list of ten potential conflict areas, and an audiotape. Each couple was told to answer the questions separately and to seal them in an envelope before proceeding with the rest of the protocol. Then, the couple was to discuss each of the ten topics and to tape their discussions. The topics included such things as work pressures, lack of affection, how to spend leisure time, and child discipline.

The couples also completed a marital adjustment scale and Fitzpatrick's measure of marital types (discussed earlier). One objective of the study was to see how well-adjusted couples in each of Fitzpatrick's categories differed from less well-adjusted couples in their conflict communication. The tape recordings were analyzed in terms of the amount of apparent conflict and the various types of strategies used by the couple in their discussion.

The investigators discovered that in all marriage types, more satisfied couples used a more positive tone of voice than less satisfied couples. Separates tended to be avoiders: They maintained a fairly neutral tone and kept their discussions of conflict areas to a minimum. The satisfied separates tended to be even more extreme in this regard. The independents, whether satisfied with their marriage or not, tended to express negative feelings. The more satisfied members of the independent category tended to use more description and self-disclosure than did the less satisfied members of this group. Finally, there was little difference between the satisfied and nonsatisfied traditionals in the sample.

Perhaps Sillars's most important contribution is his use of attribution theory to explain conflict behavior. Recall from Chapter 7 that attributions are inferences made about the causes of behavior. One may make inferences about the causes of some effect, a disposition or trait of another person or oneself, or a predicted outcome of a situation. Whenever people try to explain an event by making inferences, attribution is involved.

Sillars believes that in at least three ways attributions are important determinants of the definition and outcome of conflicts. First, individuals' attributions in a conflict determine what sorts of strategies they will choose to deal with the conflict. This is true not only because one's reactions and feelings are colored by their attributions but also because future expectations are formed largely as a result of what has gone on in the past. If, for example, you were to see a partner as cooperative, you would probably choose a cooperative strategy, but if you saw this person as competitive, you would probably use a competitive one.

Your assessment of responsibility is also important: If you thought you were to blame, you would probably be more cooperative, but if you thought the other communicator were responsible, you would probably be more competitive. Also if you thought your partner had certain negative personality traits, you would be less likely to cooperate.

Second, biases in the attribution process discourage the use of integrative strategies. These include a tendency to see others as personally responsible for negative events and to see oneself

59   Alan L. Sillars, *Manual for Coding Interpersonal Conflict* (unpublished manuscript, Department of Communication, University of Montana, 1986).
60   Alan L. Sillars, Gary R. Pike, Tricia S. Jones, and Kathleen Redmon, "Communication and Conflict in Marriage," in *Communication Yearbook 7*, ed. R. Bostrom (Beverly Hills, CA: Sage, 1983), pp. 414–429.

TABLE **12.2**

Conflict Management Coding Scheme

Avoidance Behaviors

Denial and Equivocation

1. *Direct denial.* Person explicitly denies a conflict is present.
2. *Implicit denial.* Statements that imply denial by providing a rationale for a denial statement, although the denial is not explicit.
3. *Evasive remark.* Failure to acknowledge or deny the presence of a conflict following a statement or inquiry about the conflict by the partner.

Topic Management

4. *Topic shifts.* A break in the natural flow of discussion that directs the topic focus away from discussion of the issue as it applies to the immediate parties. Do not count topic shifts that occur after the discussion appears to have reached a natural culmination.
5. *Topic avoidance.* Statements that explicitly terminate the discussion of a conflict issue before it has been fully discussed.

Noncommittal Remarks

6. *Abstract remarks.* Abstract principles, generalizations, or hypothetical statements. Speaking about the issue on a high level of abstraction. No reference is made to the actual state of affairs between the immediate parties.
7. *Noncommittal statements.* Statements that neither affirm nor deny the presence of a conflict and that are not evasive replies or topic shifts.
8. *Noncommittal questions.* Unfocused questions or those that rephrase the questions given by the researcher.
9. *Procedural remarks.* Procedural statements that supplant discussion of the conflict.

Irreverent Remarks

10. *Joking.* Nonhostile joking that interrupts or supplements serious consideration of the issue.

Cooperative Behaviors

Analytic Remarks

1. *Description.* Nonevaluative, nonblaming, factual description of the nature and extent of the problem.
2. *Qualification.* Discussion explicitly limits the nature and extent of the problem by tying the issue to specific behavioral events.

3. *Disclosure.* Providing "nonobservable" information: i.e., information about thoughts, feelings, intentions, causes of behavior, or past experience relevant to the issue that the partner would not have the opportunity to observe.
4. *Soliciting disclosure.* Asking specifically for information concerning the other that the person himself or herself would not have the opportunity to observe (i.e., thoughts, feelings, intentions, causes of behavior, experiences).
5. *Soliciting criticism.* Nonhostile questions soliciting criticism of oneself.

Conciliatory Remarks

6. *Empathy or support.* Expressing understanding, support, or acceptance of the other person or commenting on the others' positive characteristics or shared interests, goals, and compatibilities.
7. *Concessions.* Statements that express a willingness to change, show flexibility, make concessions, or consider mutually acceptable solutions to conflict.
8. *Accepting responsibility.* Statements that attribute some causality for the problem to oneself.

Competitive Behaviors

Confrontative Remarks

1. *Personal criticism.* Stating or implying a negative evaluation of the partner.
2. *Rejection.* Rejecting the partner's opinions in a way that implies personal rejecting as well as disagreement.
3. *Hostile imperatives.* Threats, demands, arguments, or other prescriptive statements that implicitly blame the partner and seek change in the partner's behavior.
4. *Hostile questioning.* Questions that fault or blame the other person.
5. *Hostile joking or sarcasm.* Joking or teasing that is used to fault the other person.
6. *Presumptive attribution.* Attributing thoughts, feelings, intentions, and causes to the partner that the partner does not acknowledge. This code is the opposite of "soliciting disclosure."
7. *Denial of responsibility.* Statements that deny or minimize personal responsibility for the conflict.

---

as merely responding to circumstances. People tend to believe that others cause conflict because of bad intentions, lack of consideration, competitiveness, or inadequacy, but people tend to see

their own behavior as merely responding to the provocations of others.

Third, the strategy chosen affects the outcome of the conflict. Cooperative strategies encourage integrative solutions and information exchange. Competitive strategies escalate the conflict and may lead to less satisfying solutions.

We have just touched on the work related to communication and conflict, and you can see that it is an important part of the literature of relationships. Most important from the standpoint of communication theory is that communication is an integral part of the creation and management of interpersonal conflict.

◖ COMMENTARY AND CRITIQUE

In this chapter we have taken a brief look at some of the most significant theorizing in interpersonal communication. Many of the theories discussed here have been immensely popular and influential. Most focus on the interactive and relational nature of interpersonal communication. De-emphasizing individual traits and personal behavior distinguishes this body of theory from the more cognitive theories of message presentation and reception covered in Chapters 6 and 7. Cognitive theories are psychological in orientation, explaining communication differences in terms of individual variables such as traits, behaviors, or cognitive structures. Relational theories are more interactional in looking at what goes on between communicators rather than within them.

Not all theories in this chapter are strictly relational in this sense, however. For example, uncertainty reduction theory is basically psychological because it concentrates on what individuals do, albeit in response to other individuals. Even Fitzpatrick's theory of marriage types, although it appears to be relational on the surface, is based mostly on the individual perceptions of marriage partners.

There is a tendency in many individualistic theories to be overly rational. Social exchange theory and game theory, for example, see relationships as a sequence of moves motivated by personal gain. Research in game theory and so-

cial exchange theory examines the choices people make in response to different reward and cost contingencies, using points or tokens as game outcomes, but we are not at all sure whether social rewards work in this way.[61] These theories assume that people behave rationally in making decisions and that they always want to maximize positive outcomes. However, establishing exactly what outcomes people are seeking in social life is not always simple. How people behave in real social conflict depends in part on their self-concept, motives, mental health, individual life goals, and an array of other complex factors. Steinfatt and Miller crystallize this objection: "In the daily political, economic, and social conflicts we all face, mutually advantageous solutions are seldom this sharply defined, and in seeking an acceptable solution, communication serves a myriad of cognitive and affective functions."[62]

Nothing is inherently wrong with individualistic analysis, but it fails to capture important interactional dimensions of the relationship, such as conflict, control, power, mutual definition, and social meaning. Baxter expresses the difficulty of psychological theorizing in these terms:

> [Psychological] theories share the assumption that relationship dynamics can be explained adequately by understanding the individuals who comprise the relationship. Theoretical frustration with this atomistic orientation is a frequently expressed complaint in the relationship communication literature; however, the relationships field still displays a paucity of genuine relationship-level theories.[63]

The original work of the Palo Alto Group is an example of the interactionist thinking that relational theory strives to accomplish. The notion

61   John L. LaGaipa, "Interpersonal Attraction and Social Exchange," in *Theory and Practice in Interpersonal Attraction*, ed. S. Duck (New York: Academic, 1971), pp. 129–164.
62   Steinfatt and Miller, "Communication," p. 70. For an excellent debate on the value of game theory in communication research, see Robert Bostrom, "Game Theory in Communication Research," *Journal of Communication* 18 (1968): 369–388; and Thomas Beisecker, "Game Theory in Communication Research: A Rejoinder and a Re-orientation," *Journal of Communication* 20 (1970): 107–120.
63   Baxter, "Dialectical," p. 258.

that communication patterns define relationships has been and remains its central idea. This idea is what makes the research of Millar and Rogers so interesting and important; it examines not individual messages but pairs of messages in response to each other.

Most relational theories focus on face-to-face interaction patterns and the ways the relationship is shaped by these patterns. On the surface much relational communication theory may imply that interaction leads to simple and clear patterns, which in turn create discernible relationship types. Relationships are seen as complementary or symmetrical, control patterns are well defined, and marriages can be typed.

But such clarity is not always found. In her interviews, for example, Baxter found "contradictions, contingencies, nonrationalities, and multiple realities to which people gave voice in their narrative sense-making of their relational lives."[64] Relationships are, in fact, complicated, and relational partners have difficult issues to work through and balance in their lives. Rather than trying to discover types or patterns, then, perhaps it would be more productive to seek the processes by which contradictions and complexities are worked out. This is one of the advantages of the dialectical approach, followed by Baxter, Rawlins, Petronio, and others.

Another problem with a strict focus on interactionist patterns is that it distracts us from the interpretations and understandings that partners construct in their interaction. Despite all their talk about how communication is used to define the nature of a relationship within a system, original relational theorists from the Palo Alto Group and disciples like Millar and Rogers essentially ignore the definitions of the relationship held by the participants themselves, making much of this theory ironically behavioristic.[65]

The research in this tradition deals with observable behavior, and the coding is done from the perspective of the outside observer, not from within the relationship. Although interaction analysis is powerful in detecting patterns of behavior, it tells us little about what those patterns mean to the participants themselves. Here

is where the later work by researchers like Fitzpatrick, Rawlins, Baxter, and Sillars fills in a gap.

Even these researchers, however, ignore yet another aspect of relationships that could and, according to some recent thinkers, should be addressed in this literature. It is one thing to concentrate on observable behavioral patterns, as most of the theories in this chapter do, or meanings, as other theories do. It is quite another to look at the unintended and largely unconscious social outcomes of relational patterns.

A recent critique of this literature calls for a critical investigation of the power arrangements that relational patterns establish, including ideological domination.[66] The problem here is really twofold: It involves the failure to acknowledge the ideology of interpersonal relationships and that of the methods used to study them.

Like most investigators not affiliated with the critical tradition, interpersonal researchers tend to assume they are studying processes of some universality. But critics point out that the kinds of social arrangements studied by relationship theorists have not always existed and do not always appear. They are historical products, and the methods employed in the study of relationships themselves contribute to the construction of these historically based arrangements.[67] This outcome is inevitable but needs to be acknowledged, especially the power arrangements that accrue from it. This idea was explored in some detail in Chapter 11, and we will not belabor it here, except to note that the critique of communication now

---

64   Leslie A. Baxter, "Interpersonal Communication as Dialogue: A Response to the 'Social Approaches' Forum," *Communication Theory* 2 (1992): 330.

65   Edna Rogers herself discusses this problem in "Analyzing Relational Communication: Implications of a Pragmatic Approach" (paper presented at the annual conference of the Speech Communication Association, Washington, DC, November 1983).

66   John W. Lannamann, "Interpersonal Communication Research as Ideological Practice," *Communication Theory* 1 (1991): 179–203; John W. Lannamann, "Deconstructing the Person and Changing the Subject of Interpersonal Studies," *Communication Theory* 2 (1992): 139–148.

67   Kristine L. Fitch, "Culture, Ideology, and Interpersonal Communication Research," *Communication Yearbook 17*, ed. Stanley A. Deetz (Thousand Oaks, CA: Sage, 1994), pp. 104–135; Lannamann, "Interpersonal Communication"; Timothy Stephen and Teresa M. Harrison, "Interpersonal Communication, Theory, and History," *Communication Theory* 3 (1993): 163–171.

extends beyond media and organizational structures to interpersonal relationships.

Another aspect of relationships de-emphasized by certain theories are the mechanisms that provide relational continuity—processes that do not always involve face-to-face interaction. In addition to observable interaction behavior, there seems to be a kind of interaction-in-imagination that allows relationships to continue, even when the partners are absent from one another. Stuart Sigman suggests a number of ways this continuity occurs and suggests more investigation into this issue.[68]

Another difficulty in relational communication theory is conceptual confusion. The very term *communication,* for example, is fuzzy in much of this literature. Watzlawick, Beavin, and Jackson's first axiom—that you cannot not communicate—has been widely confusing.[69] There is confusion too about the report and command functions, or metacommunication.[70] One critical treatment calls the concept "muddled and confusing."[71] The problem is that the Palo Alto Group, at different points in their writing, imply as many as three different meanings for *metacommunication.* (The use of other terms, such as *command message* and *relational message,* does not help in this regard.) At points metacommunication refers to a verbal or nonverbal classification of the content message, in which one's partner guides the coding of the content. At other times metacommunication refers to nonverbal statements about the relationship itself, such as control. Or, the term sometimes refers to explicit discussion by individuals about the nature of their relationship. To make matters worse, metacommunication has been treated alternatively as strictly analogic, analogic and digital, nonverbal, and both verbal and nonverbal.

An important contribution of most of the theories in this chapter is their process-oriented, developmental focus. Development is difficult to study, and it is tempting to oversimplify the process of relational definition and development. Theories therefore often assume a single trajectory or a single set of processes without discriminating among types of relationships or variability among relationships. For example, social penetration theory's originally assumed linear trajectory is really too orderly, as several more recent theorists have pointed out.[72] Different relationships may have different processes operating, and we cannot assume that cost-reward operates in each phase of a relationship.[73]

Relational communication theory is an immensely interesting, important, and challenging field of study. We see in the theories established to date noble efforts to advance our understanding of one of the most difficult aspects of human life, and although any single theory leaves many questions unanswered, as a group they provide a great deal of insight.

---

68   Stuart J. Sigman, "Handling the Discontinuous Aspects of Continuous Social Relationships: Toward Research on the Persistence of Social Forms," *Communication Theory* 1 (1991): 106–127.
69   See Motley, "On Whether."
70   This problem is discussed by William Wilmot, "Metacommunication: A Re-examination and Extension," in *Communication Yearbook 4,* ed. D. Nimmo (New Brunswick, NJ: Transaction, 1980), pp. 61–69.
71   Arthur Bochner and Dorothy Krueger, "Interpersonal Communication Theory and Research: An Overview of Inscrutable Epistemologies and Muddled Concepts," in *Communication Yearbook 3,* ed. D. Nimmo (New Brunswick, NJ: Transaction, 1979), p. 203.
72   In addition to the earlier citations in this chapter, see James L. Applegate and Gregory B. Leichty, "Managing Interpersonal Relationships: Social Cognitive and Strategic Determinants of Competence," in *Competence in Communication: A Multi-Disciplinary Approach,* ed. R. N. Bostrom (Beverly Hills, CA: Sage, 1984), p. 39.
73   Bochner, "Functions," p. 579.

C H A P T E R **13**

COMMUNICATION IN GROUP DECISION MAKING

Small-group communication has long been a central topic of concern in the communication field.[1] By far, the most important theme associated with this subject is decision making. In this chapter we look at some of the most interesting and insightful theories related to this central motif.

Contemporary research and theory in group communication stem from a variety of early twentieth-century sources. One such source was the work of Mary Parker Follett on integrative thinking.[2] Follett wrote in 1924 that group, organizational, and community problem solving is a creative threefold process of (1) gathering information from experts, (2) testing that information in everyday experience, and (3) developing integrative solutions that meet a variety of interests rather than competing among interests. Dealing with problems and conflicts through discussion has gained general acceptance in twentieth-century American thought.

Another major influence on current theories was the group-discussion movement in the field of speech.[3] Here, students were taught how to converse productively with others, a concern still popular in high school and college speech communication curricula. A third source of current group-communication theory has been the tremendous body of group dynamics research in social psychology.[4]

1 A number of sources on small groups reflect the breadth of work in this area. See, for example, Randy Hirokawa, Abran J. Salazar, Larry Erbert, and Richard J. Ice, "Small Group Communication," in *An Integrated Approach to Communication Theory and Research*, eds. Michael B. Salwen and Don W. Stacks (Mahwah, NJ: Erlbaum, 1996), pp. 359–382; John F. Cragan and David W. Wright, "Small Group Communication Research of the 1980s: A Synthesis and Critique," *Communication Studies* 41 (1990): 212–236; Marshall Scott Poole, "Do We Have Any Theories of Group Communication?" *Communication Studies* 41 (1990): 237–247; Randy Y. Hirokawa and Marshall Scott Poole (eds.), *Communication and Group Decision-Making* (Beverly Hills, CA: Sage, 1986); Gerald M. Phillips and Julia T. Wood (eds.), *Emergent Issues in Human Decision Making* (Carbondale: Southern Illinois University Press, 1984); Dennis S. Gouran and B. Aubrey Fisher, "The Functions of Human Communication in the Formation, Maintenance, and Performance of Small Groups," in *Handbook of Rhetorical and Communication Theory*, eds. C. C. Arnold and J. W. Bowers (Boston: Allyn & Bacon, 1984), pp. 622–659; Marvin E. Shaw, *Group Dynamics: The Psychology of Small Group Behavior* (New York: McGraw-Hill, 1981).
2 Mary Parker Follett, *Creative Experience* (New York: Longmans, Green, 1924).
3 For a brief summary of this work, see Dennis S. Gouran, "The Paradigm of Unfulfilled Promise: A Critical Examination of the History of Research on Small Groups in Speech Communication," in *Speech Communication in the 20th Century*, ed. T. W. Benson (Carbondale: Southern Illinois University Press, 1985), p. 90.
4 Shaw, *Group Dynamics*.

Most of the research over the years has followed an input-process-output model.[5] This model segments the group experience into the factors that affect the group (input), the happenings within the group (process), and the results (output). For example, a study might examine the effects of heterogeneity of group members (input variable) on the amount of talking in a group and the effect of interaction patterns (process variables) on member satisfaction (output variable).

Because of its impact on group-communication theory, the input-process-output model is discussed in some detail next. Later in the chapter we discuss an alternative—the structurational approach.

◖ THE INPUT-PROCESS-OUTPUT MODEL

This section is divided into three parts. First, we present a simple descriptive model of group action. Then we look at theories of the functional tradition and two influential theories of group interaction.

A General Organizing Model

Figure 13.1 is the model of Barry Collins and Harold Guetzkow.[6] This simple model captures the major themes of research on task groups, and it illustrates the input-process-output approach very well.

This model shows that a task group is confronted with two types of problems—task and interpersonal obstacles. *Task obstacles* are the difficulties encountered by the group in tackling its assignment, such as planning an event or approving a policy. Group members deal directly with the problem. They analyze the situation, suggest possible solutions, and weigh alternatives.

Decision making in a group is different from individual problem solving because of interpersonal relations. Whenever two or more people come together to handle a problem, *interpersonal obstacles* also arise. Such obstacles include the need to make your ideas clear to others, handle conflict, manage differences, and so forth. Thus, in any group discussion, members will be dealing simultaneously with task and interpersonal obstacles.

The basic distinction between task work and interpersonal relations has been an overriding concern in the research and theory on small-group communication. Both types of behavior are important in being productive, and any analysis of group problem solving must deal with both.[7]

When task and interpersonal work is integrated effectively, an *assembly effect* occurs in which the group solution or product is superior to the individual work of even the best member. So, for example, if a club meets to plan a picnic and handles its interpersonal relations and task work well, the event should turn out to be better than if it were planned by just one person.

Group rewards can be positive or negative. Successful goal achievement is usually positively rewarding to group members. In addition, the resolution of conflict and successful communication often reap interpersonal rewards. Conversely, negative "rewards" will influence the group adversely.

A successfully planned picnic, for instance, is a task reward, and the fun involved in planning it is an interpersonal reward. If the job is well done and enjoyed by the members, their future decision making will be affected in a positive way. If the task was not well done or the mem-

---

5   This model is discussed by Marshall Scott Poole, David R. Seibold, and Robert D. McPhee, "A Structurational Approach to Theory-Building in Group Decision-Making Research," in *Communication and Group Decision-Making*, eds. R. Y. Hirokawa and M. S. Poole (Beverly Hills, CA: Sage, 1986), pp. 238–240. See also Susan Jarboe, "A Comparison of Input-Output, Process-Output, and Input-Process-Output Models of Small Group Problem-Solving Effectiveness," *Communication Monographs* 55 (1988): 121–142.

6   Barry Collins and Harold Guetzkow, *A Social Psychology of Group Processes for Decision-Making* (New York: Wiley, 1964), p. 81.

7   One proposed theory that explains leadership competence in terms of task and interpersonal variables is published in J. Kevin Barge and Randy Y. Hirokawa, "Toward a Communication Competency Model of Group Leadership," *Small Group Behavior* 20 (1989): 167–189.

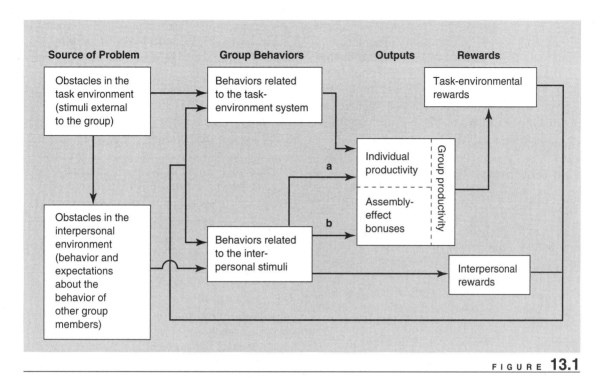

FIGURE **13.1**

A Simple Working Model of Decision-Making Groups

From *A Social Psychology of Group Processes for Decision-Making* by Barry Collins and Harold Guetzkow; John Wiley & Sons, publisher. Used by permission.

bers did not handle their differences well, negative feedback may make it more difficult next time.

Groups expend energy. Some of the effort goes to solve task obstacles, and some goes to deal with interpersonal ones. Raymond Cattell uses the term *synergy* for this group effort. The amount of energy devoted to interpersonal hassles is called *intrinsic synergy*, and the remaining energy available for the task is *effective synergy*. If effective synergy is high, the task will be accomplished effectively. If not, it will be done poorly.[8]

The level of synergy in a group results from the attitudes of the members toward one another. Conflict requires that a great deal of energy be devoted to group maintenance, leaving little for

task accomplishment. On the other hand, if individuals possess similar attitudes, there is less need for an interpersonal investment, and the effective synergy will be greater.

Suppose that you form a study group for your communication theory class. You discover that the members have varying attitudes toward the subject matter and different styles of studying. In your meetings you waste a lot of time arguing about how to organize your efforts and learn the material. This is your intrinsic synergy. Now assume that after getting your test grade back, you sense that the study group failed to achieve the goal of mutual benefit, and you withdraw to join another group or study alone. In this case the effective synergy of the group was so low that it did not accomplish more than you could have done by yourself.

But suppose that you join another group that agrees immediately on how to proceed and gets

8   Raymond Cattell, "Concepts and Methods in the Measurement of Group Syntality," *Psychological Review* 55 (1948): 48–63.

down to work. Because the interpersonal barriers are few, the group is cohesive. The effective synergy is high, and group members do better on the exam than they would have done had they studied alone.

You can see from these theories that effectiveness is important. We move now to those theories most concerned with effectiveness.

The Functional Tradition

Functional theories of group communication view the process as an instrument by which groups make decisions, emphasizing the connection between the quality of communication and the quality of the group's output.[9] Communication does a number of things, or *functions* in a number of ways, in determining group outcome. It is a means of sharing information, it is the way group members explore and identify errors in thinking, and it is a tool of persuasion.

This work has been strongly influenced by the pragmatics of teaching small-group discussion. It is based in large measure on the work of philosopher John Dewey, which, since the publication of *How We Think* in 1910, has greatly influenced twentieth-century pragmatic thought.[10]

Dewey's version of the problem-solving process has six steps: (1) expressing a difficulty, (2) defining the problem, (3) analyzing the problem, (4) suggesting solutions, (5) comparing alternatives and testing them against a set of objectives or criteria, and (6) implementing the best solution. The theories of the functional tradition address the ways communication affects each of these elements.

A General Functional Theory.   One theory of this type is that of Randy Hirokawa and his colleagues. Hirokawa's work looks at a variety of mistakes that groups can make, and it aims to identify the kinds of things groups need to take into consideration to become more effective.[11] His description of the group decision-making process essentially mirrors that of Dewey's problem-solving sequence.

Groups normally begin by *identifying and assessing a problem*, and here they deal with a variety of questions: What happened? Why? Who was involved? What harm resulted? Who was hurt? Next, the group *gathers and evaluates information* about the problem. As the group discusses possible solutions, information continues to be gathered.

Next, the group generates a variety of *alternative proposals* for handling the problem and discusses the *objectives* it wishes to accomplish in solving it. These objectives and alternative proposals are *evaluated*, with the ultimate goal of reaching consensus on a course of action. This general sequence of problem solving is depicted in Figure 13.2.[12]

The factors contributing to faulty decisions are easily inferred from this decision-making process. The first is *improper assessment* of the problem, which stems from inadequate or inaccurate analysis of the situation. The group may fail to see the problem, or it may not accurately identify the causes of the problem. The second source of error in decision making is *inappropriate goals and objectives*. The group may neglect important objectives that ought to be achieved, or it may work toward unnecessary ones. The third problem is *improper assessment of positive and negative qualities*, ignoring certain advantages, disadvantages, or both of various proposals. Or it may overestimate the positive or negative outcomes expected. Fourth, the group may develop an *inadequate in-*

---

9   This tradition is discussed by Dennis S. Gouran, Randy Y. Hirokawa, Kelly M. Julian, and Geoff B. Leatham, "The Evolution and Current Status of the Functional Perspective on Communication in Decision-Making and Problem-Solving Groups," in *Communication Yearbook 16*, ed. Stanley A. Deetz (Newbury Park, CA: Sage, 1993), pp. 573–600.
10   John Dewey, *How We Think* (Boston: Heath, 1910).
11   Randy Y. Hirokawa and Dirk R. Scheerhorn, "Communication in Faulty Group Decision-Making," in *Communication and Group Decision-Making*, eds. R. Y. Hirokawa and M. S. Poole (Beverly Hills, CA: Sage, 1986), pp. 63–80; Dennis S. Gouran and Randy Y. Hirokawa, "Counteractive Functions of Communication in Effective Group Decision-Making," in *Communication and Group Decision-Making*, eds. R. Y. Hirokawa and M. S. Poole (Beverly Hills, CA: Sage, 1986), pp. 81–92; Randy Y. Hirokawa, "Group Communication and Problem-Solving Effectiveness I: A Critical Review of Inconsistent Findings," *Communication Quarterly* 30 (1982): 134–141; Randy Y. Hirokawa, "Group Communication and Problem-Solving Effectiveness II," *Western Journal of Speech Communication* 47 (1983): 59–74; Randy Y. Hirokawa, "Group Communication and Problem-Solving Effectiveness: An Investigation of Group Phases," *Human Communication Research* 9 (1983): 291–305.
12   Hirokawa and Scheerhorn, "Faulty Group," p. 66.

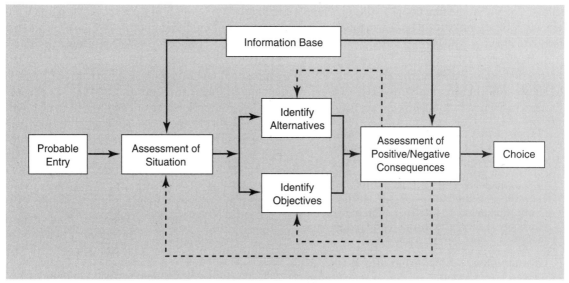

FIGURE **13.2**

General Model of the Group Decision-Making Process

formation base, which can happen in several ways. Valid information may be rejected, or invalid information may be accepted. Too little information may be collected, or too much information may cause overload and confusion. Finally, the group may be guilty of *faulty reasoning* from the information base.

Why do groups fall into these traps? Hirokawa believes that the errors most often arise from the communication in the group. The group is swayed by certain members who unwittingly mislead the group in some way, an outcome that requires someone to counteract it by influencing the group in a positive way.

As part of his investigations, Hirokawa conducted a study of four aspects of decision quality: appropriate understanding of the problem, appropriate understanding of the objectives and standards of a good decision, appropriate assessment of the positive qualities of alternatives, and appropriate assessment of the negative qualities of alternatives.[13]

In his laboratory Hirokawa formed about 40 three-person groups and had them discuss what to do about a certain plagiarism case at the university. The discussions were from seventeen to forty-seven minutes in length, and each was videotaped. Two professors experienced in student ethics cases judged the groups' decisions in terms of overall quality, and a panel of judges rated the extent to which each of the four critical elements listed above was fulfilled. Statistical analysis showed that the quality of a group's decision is definitely related to these four elements, and when the very best groups were compared to the very worst, there was a significant difference in the extent to which each was accomplished by the group. Clearly, groups that were more effective in meeting the four functions made better decisions.

Hirokawa's theory addresses the general quality of communication from a functional perspective. Let's look now at a popular theory that focuses on one particular kind of problem in group decision making.

Janis's Theory of Groupthink.   The work of Irving Janis and his colleagues has been immensely

13   Randy Y. Hirokawa, "Group Communication and Decision Making Performance: A Continued Test of the Functional Perspective," *Human Communication Research* 14 (1988): 487–515.

influential within the functional tradition.[14] Here we will look at one of his theories, most often referred to as the *groupthink hypothesis*.[15]

Janis examines in some detail the adequacy of group decisions. Emphasizing critical thinking, he shows how certain conditions can lead to high group satisfaction but ineffective output:

> I use the term groupthink as a quick and easy way to refer to a mode of thinking that people engage in when they are deeply involved in a cohesive in-group, when members' strivings for unanimity override their motivation to realistically appraise alternative courses of action. . . . Groupthink refers to a deterioration of mental efficiency, reality testing, and moral judgment that results from in-group pressures.[16]

Groupthink is a direct result of cohesiveness in groups, which was first discussed in some depth by Kurt Lewin in the 1930s and has since come to be seen as a crucial variable in group effectiveness.[17] *Cohesiveness* is the degree of mutual interest among members. In a highly cohesive group, a strong mutual identification keeps a group together.

Cohesiveness is a result of the degree to which all members perceive that their goals can be met within the group. This does not require that the members have similar attitudes but that members are interdependent and rely on one another to achieve certain mutually desired goals. The more cohesive a group, the more pressure it exerts on the members.

Cohesiveness can be a good thing because it brings the members together and enhances the group's interpersonal relationships. Although Janis does not deny the potential value of cohesiveness, he also recognizes its dangers. For one,

highly cohesive groups may invest too much energy in maintaining goodwill in the group to the detriment of decision making. Members invest much intrinsic energy in groups because of the potential rewards for doing so: friendship, prestige, and confirmation of one's self-worth. Because our self-esteem needs are high, we will sometimes devote too much energy to establishing positive bonds, and this can lead to groupthink.

Under conditions of low cohesiveness, certain factors may prevent the illusion of unanimity. The natural conflict in noncohesive groups leads to much debate and consideration of all sides of an issue. Janis found in his research that groupthink can have six negative outcomes:

1. The group limits its discussion to only a few alternatives without considering a full range of creative possibilities. The solution may seem obvious and simple to the group, and there is little exploration of other ideas.
2. The position initially favored by most members is never restudied to seek out less obvious pitfalls. In other words, the group is not very critical in examining the ramifications of the preferred solution.
3. The group fails to reexamine those alternatives originally disfavored by the majority. Minority opinions are quickly dismissed and ignored, not only by the majority but also by those who originally favored them.
4. Expert opinion is not sought. The group is satisfied with itself and may feel threatened by outsiders.
5. The group is highly selective in gathering and attending to available information. The members tend to concentrate only on the information that supports the favored plan.
6. The group is so confident in its ideas that it does not consider contingency plans. It does not foresee the possibility of failure and does not plan for failure.

All these things result from a lack of critical thinking and overconfidence in the group. Janis maintains that groupthink is marked by a number of symptoms. The first symptom is an *illusion*

---

14   See, for example, Irving Janis and Leon Mann, *Decision Making: A Psychological Analysis of Conflict, Choice, and Commitment* (New York: Free Press, 1977); Irving Janis, *Crucial Decisions: Leadership in Policy Making and Crisis Management* (New York: Free Press, 1989).
15   Irving Janis, *Groupthink: Psychological Studies of Policy Decisions and Fiascoes* (Boston: Houghton Mifflin, 1982).
16   Janis, *Groupthink*, p. 9.
17   Kurt Lewin, *Resolving Social Conflicts: Selected Papers on Group Dynamics* (New York: Harper & Row, 1948). For information on Lewin's theory of group dynamics, see Everett M. Rogers, *A History of Communication Study: A Biographical Approach* (New York: Free Press, 1994), pp. 316–355.

of invulnerability, which creates an undue air of optimism. There is a strong sense that, "We know what we are doing, so don't rock the boat." Second, the group creates collective efforts to *rationalize* the course of action decided on. It creates a story that makes its decision seem absolutely right and literally talks itself into thinking it did the right thing.

Third, the group maintains an unquestioned belief in its inherent *morality,* seeing itself as being well motivated and working for the best outcome. That leads the group to soft-pedal ethical and moral consequences. Fourth, out-group leaders are *stereotyped* as evil, weak, or stupid.

Fifth, *direct pressure* is exerted on members not to express counteropinions. Dissent is quickly squelched, which leads to the sixth symptom, the *self-censorship* of disagreement. Individual members are reluctant to state opposing opinions and silently suppress their reservations. Thus, seventh, there is a shared *illusion of unanimity* within the group. Even if the decision is not unanimous, the group rallies outwardly around a position of solidarity.

Finally, eighth, groupthink involves the emergence of self-appointed *mindguards* to protect the group and its leader from adverse opinions and unwanted information. The mindguard typically suppresses negative information by counseling participants not to make things difficult.

What is the answer to the problem of groupthink? Janis believes that decision-making groups need to recognize the dangers of groupthink and suggests steps to prevent it:

1. The leader of a policy-forming group should assign the role of critical evaluator to each member, encouraging the group to give high priority to airing objections and doubts.
2. The leaders in an organization's hierarchy, when assigning a policy-planning mission to a group, should be impartial instead of stating preferences and expectations at the outset.
3. The organization should routinely follow the administrative practice of setting up several independent policy-planning and evaluation groups to work on the same policy question, each carrying out its deliberations under a different leader.
4. Throughout the period when the feasibility and effectiveness of policy alternatives are being surveyed, the policy-making group should from time to time divide into two or more subgroups to meet separately, under different chairmen, and then come together to hammer out their differences.
5. Each member of the policy-making group should discuss periodically the group's deliberations with trusted associates in his own unit of the organization and report back their reactions.
6. One or more outside experts or qualified colleagues within the organization who are not core members of the policy-making group should be invited to each meeting on a staggered basis and should be encouraged to challenge the views of the core members.
7. At every meeting devoted to evaluating policy alternatives, at least one member should be assigned the role of devil's advocate.
8. Whenever the policy issue involves relations with a rival nation or organization, a sizable bloc [sic] of time (perhaps an entire session) should be spent surveying all warning signals from rivals and constructing alternative scenarios of the rivals' intentions.
9. After reaching a preliminary consensus about what seems to be the best policy alternative, the policy-making group should hold a "second-chance" meeting at which every member is expected to express as vividly as he can all his residual doubts and to rethink the entire issue before making a definitive choice.[18]

Janis's approach is intriguing. He uses historical data to support his theory by analyzing six national political decision-making episodes in which outcomes were either good or bad, depending on the extent of groupthink. The negative examples include the Bay of Pigs invasion,

---

18   Janis, *Groupthink,* pp. 262–271.

the Korean War, Pearl Harbor, and the escalation of the Vietnam War. Positive examples include the Cuban missile crisis and the Marshall Plan.[19]

One of Janis's cases of successful decision making is the Kennedy administration's response to the Cuban missile crisis. In October 1962, Cuba was caught building offensive nuclear weapon stations and arming them with Soviet missiles. President Kennedy had already suffered through one instance of groupthink in the Bay of Pigs invasion the year before, and he seemed to have learned what not to do in these kinds of international crises. In the missile crisis, Kennedy constantly encouraged his advisors to challenge and debate one another. He refrained from leading the group too early with his own opinion, and he set up subgroups to discuss the problem independently so as not to reinforce members' opinions. Various members, including Kennedy, talked with outsiders and experts about the problem to make sure that fresh opinions were heard. In the end Kennedy successfully invoked a military blockade and stopped the Cuban-Soviet development.

The Interactional Tradition

As we have learned, a group's outcome depends largely on the nature of interaction in the group. Theories of group interaction are especially important in this book because of their concern with communication as the core of group productivity. Here, we look at two theories of group interaction. The first, an old standard, is Robert Bales's interaction process analysis. The second modifies Bales's notion of interaction and takes it in a different direction.

Interaction Process Analysis. One of the most prominent small-group theories is Robert Bales's *interaction process analysis*.[20] Using his many years of research as a foundation, Bales created a unified and well-developed theory of small-group interaction, aiming to explain the pattern of responses in the small task group.

Figure 13.3 illustrates the categories of interactions in Bales's scheme.[21] Each is a type of statement that someone could make in a group. These twelve categories are grouped into four broader sets, as outlined at the left of the figure. In addition, the behavior types are paired, and each pair implies a particular problem area for groups, as labeled in the figure. *Gives information* is paired with *asks for information, gives opinion* is paired with *asks for opinion*, and *gives a suggestion* is paired with *asks for a suggestion*.

Bales found that one of the ways groups release tension is by telling stories, or *dramatizing*. In Chapter 8 we looked at Ernest Bormann's development of this idea in symbolic convergence theory, which has special application in small groups.[22] Bormann believes that this form of communication is crucial not only in reducing tension but also in affecting the quality of group discussion in general. Stories are often told and retold within a group. They consist of *fantasy themes*, or shared knowledge, that build a common identity in the group. Fantasy themes constitute the mechanism by which cohesiveness is developed in a group. As we know, cohesiveness can have both positive and negative effects on decision making.

There are two general classes of communication behavior. The first is *socioemotional*, represented by positive and negative actions like *seeming friendly, showing tension*, and *dramatizing*, and the second is *task behavior*, represented by *suggestions, opinions*, and *information*. (These classes are consistent with the categories of tasks and interpersonal functions found throughout the small-group literature and encountered earlier in this chapter.)

---

19   For a laboratory test of the groupthink hypothesis, see John A. Courtright, "A Laboratory Investigation of Groupthink," *Communication Monographs* 45 (1978): 229–246.

20   Robert F. Bales, *Interaction Process Analysis: A Method for the Study of Small Groups* (Reading, MA: Addison-Wesley, 1950); *Personality and Interpersonal Behavior* (New York: Holt, Rinehart & Winston, 1970); Robert F. Bales, Stephen P. Cohen, and Stephen A. Williamson, *SYMLOG: A System for the Multiple Level Observation of Groups* (London: Collier, 1979).

21   Adapted from Bales, *Personality*, p. 92.

22   Ernest Bormann, "Symbolic Convergence and Communication in Group Decision Making," in *Communication and Group Decision-Making*, eds. R. Y. Hirokawa and M. S. Poole (Beverly Hills, CA: Sage, 1986), pp. 219–236.

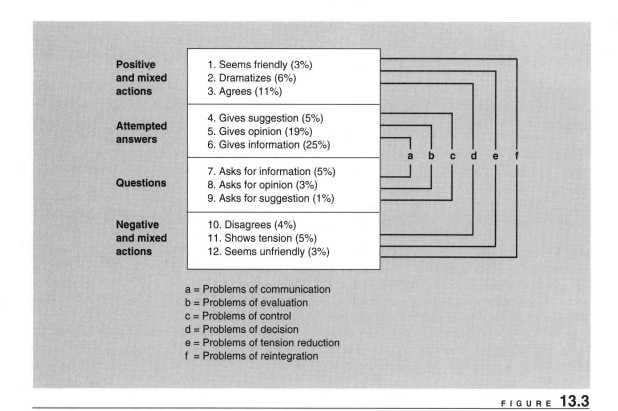

Positive and mixed actions
1. Seems friendly (3%)
2. Dramatizes (6%)
3. Agrees (11%)

Attempted answers
4. Gives suggestion (5%)
5. Gives opinion (19%)
6. Gives information (25%)

Questions
7. Asks for information (5%)
8. Asks for opinion (3%)
9. Asks for suggestion (1%)

Negative and mixed actions
10. Disagrees (4%)
11. Shows tension (5%)
12. Seems unfriendly (3%)

a = Problems of communication
b = Problems of evaluation
c = Problems of control
d = Problems of decision
e = Problems of tension reduction
f = Problems of reintegration

FIGURE **13.3**

Categories for Interaction Process Analysis

In investigating leadership, Bales has found that the same group will have two different kinds of leaders. The *task leader*, who facilitates and coordinates the task-related comments, directs energy toward getting the job done. Equally important is the *socioemotional leader,* who works for improved relations in the group, concentrating on interactions in the positive and negative sectors. Usually the task and socioemotional leaders are different people.

Bales has shown how the perception of an individual's position in a group is a function of three dimensions. These include (1) dominant versus submissive, (2) friendly versus unfriendly, and (3) instrumental versus emotional. These factors can be visualized in a three-dimensional space, with the axes of the space labeled "positive-negative," "upward-downward," and "forward-backward."

Within a particular group, any member's behavior can be placed in this three-dimensional space. An individual's position depends on the quadrant in which that individual appears (for instance, upward-positive-forward, or UPF). One's position within the quadrant is determined by the degree of each dimension represented. Thus, for example, a UPF could appear at various points in the space, depending on the degree of U, P, and F. When all group members' behavior types are plotted on the spatial graph, their relationships and networks can be seen. The larger the group, the greater the tendency for subgroups of coalitions to develop. These subgroups consist of individuals with similar value dimensions. Obviously, affinity exists among individuals who are close in value dimension and direction, whereas distant individuals are not connected.

Not only can we predict the coalitions and networks of a group from the distribution of types, but Bales also has shown that behavior type is related to the kinds of statements a person makes. The interaction that a person initiates and receives depends in part on his or her behavior type.

Fisher's Interaction Analysis.   Although Bales's theory is called "interactional," it really deals with individual acts. Aubrey Fisher and Leonard Hawes refer to this as a *human system model*. These authors believe that a more sensible approach for the study of group communication is the *interact system model*, which emphasizes associated acts, called "interacts."[23] An *interact* is the act of one person followed by the act of another. Examples are question-answer, statement-statement, greeting-greeting. Here, the unit for analysis is not an individual behavior, like making a suggestion, but a contiguous pair of acts, like making a suggestion and responding to it. Interacts can be classified along the *content* and the *relationship dimension*. For example, if someone were to ask you a question, you would probably answer it, but the manner in which you stated the answer might tip off the group that you thought it was a dumb question. Here, your answer is the content dimension and your nonverbal manner the relationship dimension.

Despite the potential utility of analyzing the relational dimension in a group discussion, Fisher has concentrated on the content dimension. Because almost all comments in a task group are related in one way or another to a decision proposal, Fisher classifies statements in terms of how they respond to a decision proposal.[24] Statements might agree or disagree with a proposal, for example.

Two essential differences exist between the theories of Bales and Fisher. First, Bales classifies a given act strictly in terms of its task or socioemotional function. Fisher assumes that any given act may fulfill either or both functions simultaneously. Second, Bales classifies only single acts, whereas Fisher classifies interacts, two acts at a time. In other words, the observer will classify each act *and* its following act, a favorable comment followed by an unfavorable one, perhaps. In this way the researcher can actually see the character and frequency of act pairs in a group discussion.

In his "theory of decision emergence," Fisher outlines four phases through which task groups tend to proceed: orientation, conflict, emergence, and reinforcement.[25] In observing the distribution of interacts across these phases, Fisher notes the ways interaction changes as the group decision formulates and solidifies.

The *orientation phase* involves getting acquainted, clarifying, and beginning to express points of view. A high level of agreement characterizes this stage, and comments are often designed to test the group. Thus, positions are both qualified and tentative. In this phase people grope for direction and understanding.

The *conflict phase* includes a great deal of dissent. People in this second phase begin to solidify their attitudes, and much polarization results. Here the interacts include more disagreement and unfavorable evaluation. Members argue and attempt to persuade, and they may form coalitions.

These coalitions tend to disappear in the third, *emergence*, phase. Here the first inklings of cooperation begin to show. People are less tenacious in defending their viewpoints. As they soften their positions and undergo attitude change, their comments become more ambiguous. The number of favorable comments increases until a group decision begins to emerge.

In the final phase, *reinforcement*, the group decision solidifies and receives reinforcement from group members. The group unifies and stands behind its solution. Comments are almost uniformly positive and favorable. The ambiguity that marked the third phase tends to disappear.

---

23   B. Aubrey Fisher and Leonard Hawes, "An Interact System Model: Generating a Grounded Theory of Small Groups," *Quarterly Journal of Speech* 57 (1971): 444–453.
24   B. Aubrey Fisher, *Small Group Decision Making: Communication and the Group Process* (New York: McGraw-Hill, 1980), p. 117.
25   B. Aubrey Fisher, "Decision Emergence: Phases in Group Decision Making," *Speech Monographs* 37 (1970): 53–60; Fisher, *Decision Making*.

To illustrate the phases of group development, Fisher presents an analysis of a mock jury deliberation in a lawsuit over an automobile-pedestrian accident.[26] In the first phase, the jury explores its responsibility. What is it supposed to do, and how is it supposed to do it? What are the possible verdicts? Much uncertainty is expressed until clarification emerges. Considerable disagreement arises in the conflict phase as the jury argues over whether the defendant is negligent and the criteria by which they should decide. Here, the interaction tends to be somewhat emotional and heated at times.

In the emergence phase, the jury begins to agree that the defendant is not negligent and that the pedestrian could have avoided the accident. This agreement is somewhat tentative, and the jurors go back and forth on the issue, but the emotionality and debate definitely subside during this period. In the final reinforcement phase, the jury is convinced, and everybody affirms their agreement in this verdict.

The phases of group decision making characterize the interaction as it changes over time. An important related topic is that of *decision modification*.[27] Fisher finds that groups typically do not introduce only one idea at a time, nor do they introduce a single proposal and continue to modify it until consensus is reached. Instead, decision modification is cyclical. Several proposals are made, each discussed briefly, and some of them reintroduced at a later time. Discussion of proposals seems to proceed in spurts of energy. Proposal A will be introduced and discussed. The group will suddenly drop this idea and move to proposal B. After discussion of this, the group may introduce and discuss other proposals. Then someone will revive proposal A, perhaps in modified form. The group finally will settle on a modified plan that was introduced earlier in the discussion in a different form.

Why does discussion usually proceed in such an erratic fashion? Probably because the interpersonal demands of discussion require "breaks" from task work. In effect, the group attention span is short because of the intense nature of group work, and "flight" behavior helps manage tension and conflict.

Fisher finds that in modifying proposals, groups tend to follow one of two patterns. If conflict is low, the group will reintroduce proposals in less abstract, more specific language. For example, in a discussion of a public health nursing conference, an original idea to begin "with a nonthreatening something" was modified to "begin with a history of the contributions which public health has made to the field of nursing."[28] A group, as it successively returns to a proposal, seems to follow the pattern of stating the problem, discussing criteria for solution, introducing an abstract solution, and moving finally to a concrete solution. Keep in mind, however, that the group most likely will not move through these four steps smoothly, but will probably do so sporadically as members depart from and return to the proposal in a stop-and-start fashion.

Another pattern is common when conflict is higher. Here, the group does not attempt to make a proposal more specific. Because disagreement exists on the basic idea, the group introduces substitute proposals of the same level of abstraction as the original. In the first pattern, which involves making proposals more specific, the group task seems to be one of mutual discovery of the best specific implementation of a general idea.

Fisher's theory is an example of a phase model of group development. Phase models predict that groups go through a series of stages in dealing with a problem or set of tasks. Because there have been many such models in the history of small-group theory, the phase approach constitutes the dominant view of group development.[29]

26   Fisher, *Decision Making*, pp. 298–306.
27   Fisher, *Decision Making*; also B. Aubrey Fisher, "The Process of Decision Modification in Small Discussion Groups," *Journal of Communication* 20 (1970): 51–64.
28   Fisher, *Decision Making*, p. 155.
29   Some of the most prominent phase models are discussed in R. F. Bales and F. L. Strodbeck, "Phases in Group Problem-Solving," *Journal of Abnormal and Social Psychology* 46 (1951): 485–495; M. A. Bell, "Phases in Group Problem-Solving," *Small Group Behavior* 13 (1982): 475–495; W. G. Bennis and H. A. Shepard, "The Theory of Group Development," *Human Relations* 9 (1956): 415–437; R. Lacoursiere, *The Life Cycle of Groups* (New York: Human Sciences, 1980); Bruce Tuckman, "Developmental Sequence in Small Groups," *Psychological Bulletin* 63 (1965): 384–399.

Recently, however, phase models have been criticized for being overly simple.[30] In the next section, we examine a theory that views group action and development in a more complex and potentially more useful way than have the preceding approaches.

● THE STRUCTURATIONAL PERSPECTIVE

The input-process-output model has contributed much to our understanding of small-group decision making, but it is limited in its approach. Recently, a group of communication researchers have proposed a new perspective—the structurational approach.[31]

Structuration Theory

Structuration theory, the brainchild of sociologist Anthony Giddens and his followers, is a general theory of social action.[32] This theory states that human action is a process of producing and reproducing various social systems. Groups act according to rules to achieve their goals and thereby create structures that come back to affect future actions. Structures like relational expectations, group roles and norms, communication networks, and societal institutions both affect and are affected by social action. These struc-

tures provide individuals with rules that guide their actions, but their actions in turn create new rules and reproduce old ones.

Giddens overcomes the debate between those who hold that human action is caused by outside forces and those who advocate the intentionality of human action. He claims that both sides in this dispute are right because social life is a two-sided coin. We do have intentions and act to accomplish these; at the same time, our actions have the unintended consequences of establishing structures that affect our future actions. When we do certain things to attain our goals, we are unaware of many of the outcomes of action and their consequent structures.

Consider how this works in group communication. A group member will bring up a topic in order to accomplish certain objectives. Because this member acts a certain way, other group members come to see this person as one who has particular ideas and who can do special kinds of things. In time, a role is created. This role, which was very much an unintended consequence of action, will become a kind of structure that constrains that individual's future behavior in the group.

For example, let's say you hate clutter and want to make sure that your group's committee room is always tidy. To accomplish this, you take the responsibility of picking things up before each meeting. Before long, the other members will expect you to do this, and you will have created the role of "custodian." Even when you don't feel like it, you may still straighten up the committee room because that is your role. Giddens believes that this kind of "structuration" saturates all social life, in ways far more profound than getting a room cleaned.

Giddens believes that structuration always involves three major modalities, or dimensions. These are (1) an interpretation or understanding, (2) a sense of morality or proper conduct, and (3) a sense of power in action. The rules we use to guide our actions, in other words, tell us how something should be understood (interpretation), what should be done (morality), and how to get things accomplished (power). In turn, our

---

30   These arguments are summarized in Marshall Scott Poole, "Decision Development in Small Groups III: A Multiple Sequence Model of Group Decision Development," *Communication Monographs* 50 (1983): 321–342.

31   Marshall Scott Poole, David R. Seibold, and Robert D. McPhee, "Group Decision-Making as a Structurational Process," *Quarterly Journal of Speech* 71 (1985): 74; Poole, Seibold, and McPhee, "Structurational Approach." See also Julie M. Billingsley, "An Evaluation of the Functional Perspective in Small Group Communication," in *Communication Yearbook 16,* ed. Stanley Deetz (Newbury Park, CA: Sage, 1993), pp. 615–622.

32   See, for example, Anthony Giddens, *New Rules of Sociological Method* (New York: Basic, 1976); *Studies in Social and Political Theory* (New York: Basic, 1977). For a brief summary of the theory, see *Profiles and Critiques in Social Theory* (Berkeley: University of California Press, 1982), pp. 8–11. See also Stephen P. Banks and Patricia Riley, "Structuration Theory as an Ontology for Communication Research," *Communication Yearbook 16,* ed. Stanley Deetz (Newbury Park, CA: Sage, 1993), pp. 167–196.

actions reinforce those very structures of interpretation, morality, and power.

Imagine a group that has created a structure in which everybody is expected to speak up on every topic. Like all structuration, this was not planned but emerged as an unintended consequence of the actions of group members over time. There may be a norm of *interpreting* in which the group is understood as egalitarian. It is considered *proper* for everyone to address every issue and not remain quiet on any subject. And *power* is granted to speech, as individuals use language to persuade one another.

In actual practice your behavior is rarely affected by a single structure such as the "cleaning-up" role or "talking-up" norm used as examples above. Rather, your acts are affected by and affect several different structural elements at the same time. Two things can happen. First, one structure can *mediate* another. In other words, the production of one structure is accomplished by producing another. For example, the group may produce a communication network, but it does so by establishing individual roles. Here, the role structure mediates the communication network.

The second way structures relate to one another is through *contradiction.* Here, the production of a structure requires the establishment of another structure that undermines the first one. This is the stuff of classical paradox. Contradictions lead to conflict, and through a dialectic or tension between the contradictory elements, system change results.

The old problem of task and socioemotional work is a good example of contradictory structure. To accomplish a task, the group has to work on its interpersonal relationships, but working on relationships detracts from accomplishing the task. The consequences of this contradiction are already well explored by some of the theories presented earlier in the chapter.

Structuration and Decision Development

Relying on the ideas of Giddens, Scott Poole and his colleagues have been working for several years on a structurational theory of group decision making.[33] This theory teaches that group decision making is a process in which group members attempt to achieve *convergence,* or agreement, on a final decision and in so doing structure their social system. Individuals express their opinions and preferences and thereby produce and reproduce certain rules by which convergence can be achieved or blocked.

In trying to achieve convergence, group members make use of Giddens's three elements of action—interpretation, morality, and power. Interpretation is made possible through language, morality is established through group norms, and power is achieved through the interpersonal power structures that have emerged in the group.

Suppose, for example, that you are interested in persuading other members of a group to endorse a particular plan. You might share an interpretation of the plan by using the terms commonly employed and understood by group members. (Some of these words might even be rather specialized and specific to the group.) By employing a particular style of speaking, then, you would be acting in a manner that is condoned by the group according to its norms. To be effective as a speaker, you would also make use of a variety of sources of power, like leadership ability or status. Your comments in the meeting may or may not accomplish your objective, but they will certainly have the unintended consequence of contributing to the shared understandings and language, norms, and power structures of the group.

This theory further recognizes that outside factors influence the group's actions. Outside factors have meaning only insofar as they are understood and interpreted by the group, and these interpretations are negotiated through interaction within the group. One of the most important

33 Poole, Seibold, and McPhee, "Group Decision-Making." For a recent overview of the entire project, see Marshall Scott Poole and Jonelle Roth, "Decision Development in Small Groups IV: A Typology of Group Decision Paths," *Human Communication Research* 15 (1989): 323–356; "Decision Development in Small Groups V: Test of a Contingency Model," *Human Communication Research* 15 (1989): 549–589.

outside factors is task type—what the group has been given to do—for the task makes certain rules appropriate and others inappropriate. For example, a study group will behave in one way when preparing for an exam and in an entirely different way when researching a group report.

Further, we act toward others in ways that reflect our views of their place in the group, and in time a "group" definition of each person and the group as a whole emerges. This group definition subsequently affects the interaction among the members of the group and is thereby reproduced again and again. This role-establishing work is *microstructuration*. Some members, for example, might become task leaders, others socioemotional leaders, others information providers, and still others conflict managers.

Poole and his associates believe that task groups are rife with contradiction, and group actions both cause and resolve these inherent tensions. For example, the group must make a good decision before a deadline, but the time pressure of the deadline is inconsistent with the need for adequate time to do a good job. A group must attend to the requirements of the task, but in so doing they must also take care of their socioemotional needs. The problem, as we saw earlier in the chapter, is that meeting socioemotional needs can detract from the quality of task work. Further, members join a group to meet individual objectives, but they can only do so by paying attention to group objectives, which may undercut their own individual needs. Convergence can only come about through agreement, yet the group is told it must disagree in order to test ideas. These are just some of the kinds of contradictions that groups must manage, and group structuration is largely a process of doing so.

One of the most interesting contributions of this theory is its version of the processes followed by groups as they make decisions. Poole and his colleagues propose that groups can follow a variety of paths in the development of a decision, depending on the *contingencies* with which they are faced. Groups sometimes follow a predictable procedure such as the one Hirokawa recommends, sometimes they are un-

systematic, and sometimes they develop their own pathway in response to unique needs.

How a group operates depends on three sets of variables. The first is *objective task characteristics*, which are the standard attributes of the task such as the degree to which the problem comes with preestablished solutions, the clarity of the problem, the kind of expertise it requires, the extent of the impact of the problem, the number and nature of values implicit in the problem, and whether the solution is a one-shot action or will have broader policy implications.

For example, you might be involved in a club that has to decide whether and how to participate in a town festival, a difficult decision involving many possible options. The potential number of values entering into the decision is fairly high, and what you decide to do this year may affect what you can do in other years. This decision may take some time, and the decision path may be complex.

On the other hand, if your group merely has to decide whether to have a taco booth, the decision is simple. The range of options is limited, the values involved in the decision are few, and the decision will have little impact outside the club. This decision will probably be made quickly and simply.

The second set of variables that affects the group's decision path is *group task characteristics*, and these will vary from group to group. They include the extent to which the group has previous experience with the problem, the extent to which an innovative solution is required as opposed to adoption of a standard course of action, and the urgency of the decision.

The third group of factors affecting the path of a group is *group structural characteristics*, including cohesiveness, power distribution, history of conflict, and group size. If your club has many members, gives the officers most of the power, and has a history of conflict, one kind of process will be used, but if it is small, cohesive, and has shared power, quite another would be predicted.

These three sets of factors will operate to influence the process adopted by the group, including whether it uses a standard or a unique path, the complexity of the decision path, the amount of organization or disorganization with which the task is handled, and the amount of time devoted to various activities.

To continue our example, your club might use a standard method of solving problems, such as Hirokawa's pattern, or it might develop a different method. The club's procedure may turn out to be simple and brief, but it could become complex and contorted; similarly, it could turn out to be organized, even though complex, or it may be completely unsystematic.

To discover various decision paths adopted by different groups, Scott Poole and Jonelle Roth studied forty-seven decisions made by 29 different groups.[34] The groups differed in their size, task complexity, urgency, cohesiveness, and conflict history. They included a medical school teaching team, an energy conservation–planning group, student term-project groups, a dormitory management committee, and a number of others. Each discussion was tape-recorded and analyzed. Each task statement in a discussion was classified by judges according to type, and these were combined into interacts similar to those of Fisher discussed earlier. Also, every thirty-second segment was classified according to a set of relationship categories. With a sophisticated method of analysis, the researchers could see the various decision paths that emerged in these interactions on both the task and relationship tracks.

Three general types of paths were discovered. Some groups followed a *standard unitary sequence,* although not always exactly the same way. Several groups followed what Poole and Roth call a *complex cyclic sequence.* Most of these were problem-solution cycles, in which the group would go back and forth in concentrated work between defining the problem and generating solution ideas, much as Fisher imagined. The third type of sequence was *solution-oriented,* in which almost no problem analysis occurred.

The decision paths taken by a group consist of three interwoven *activity tracks,* or courses along which the group develops or moves. A group may develop in different ways on each track, and the course of action taken on each track is af-

fected in part by the three contingency variables discussed above—objective task characteristics, group task characteristics, and group structural characteristics.

There are probably many possible tracks, but three are elaborated in this theory—the task-process track, the relational track, and the topic-focus track. The *task-process track* consists of activities that directly deal with the problem or task, including, for example, problem analysis, designing solutions, evaluating solutions, and getting off on tangents. The *relational track* involves activities that affect interpersonal relationships in the group, such as disagreeing and making accommodations. These two correspond neatly with the task-maintenance duality encountered in several other theories presented in this chapter. The third track, the *topic-focus track,* is a series of issues, topics, or concerns of the group over time. Figure 13.4 illustrates the activity tracks and how they work together.[35]

The multiple-sequence model imagines that the group moves along the various tracks over time, as illustrated by the time scale at the bottom of the graph. At a given moment, the group may be at a particular "spot" in the development of each track. The figure shows the three tracks divided into various activity segments. The activity segments are identified by code letters above the line. (The letters below the line are breakpoints, which will be explained later.)

In the discussion depicted in Figure 13.4, the group begins with topic 1 (T1). In discussing this topic, the group is involved in focused work (FW) in the relational track and solution development (SD) in the task-process track. As they move to another topic, the group enters problem critique (PC) on the task-process track while they are engaged in critical work (CW) on the relational track. The discussion goes on for some time through a number of phases until the end, when they go off on a tangent (NN) on the task-process track but accomplish integration (INT)

---

34   Poole and Roth, "Decision Development IV"; "Decision Development V."
35   Adapted from Poole, "Decision Development III," pp. 327, 329; Poole and Roth, "Decision Development IV," pp. 334–335.

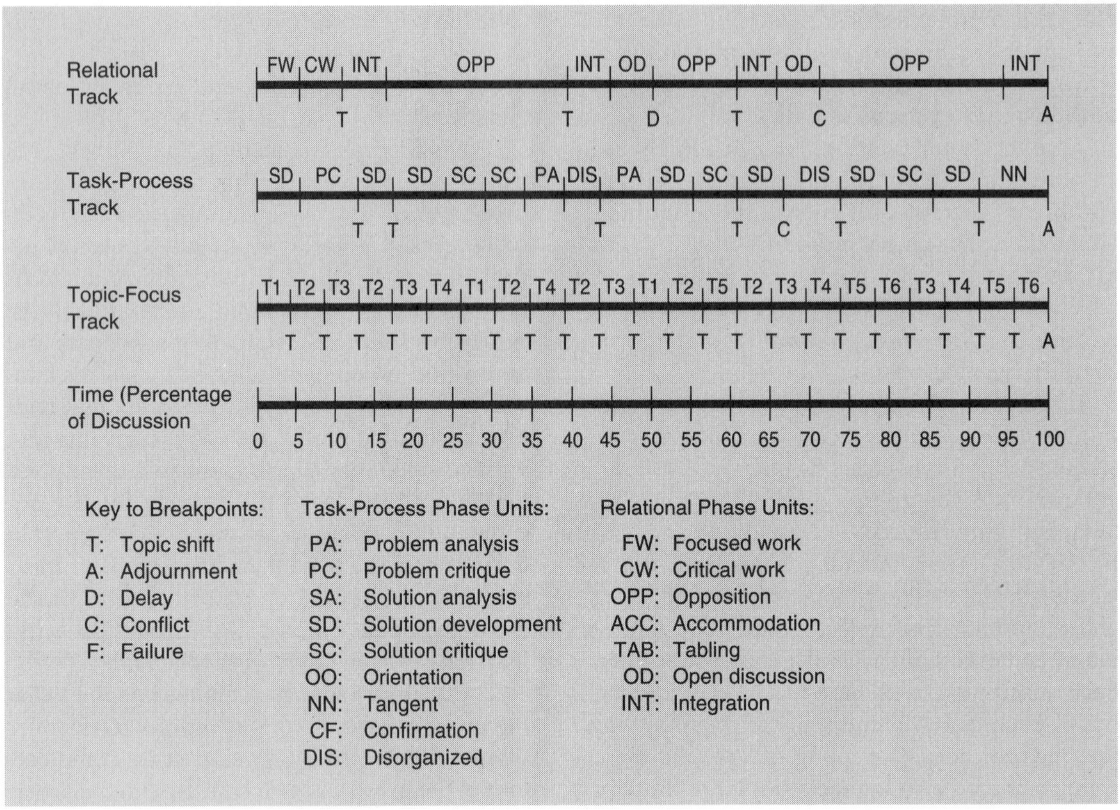
Relational Track
FW CW INT OPP INT OD OPP INT OD OPP INT
T T D T C A
Task-Process Track
SD PC SD SD SC SC PA DIS PA SD SC SD DIS SD SC SD NN
T T T T C T T A
Topic-Focus Track
T1 T2 T3 T2 T3 T4 T1 T2 T4 T2 T3 T1 T2 T5 T2 T3 T4 T5 T6 T3 T4 T5 T6
T T T T T T T T T T T T T T T T T T T T T T A
Time (Percentage of Discussion
0 5 10 15 20 25 30 35 40 45 50 55 60 65 70 75 80 85 90 95 100
Key to Breakpoints:
T: Topic shift
A: Adjournment
D: Delay
C: Conflict
F: Failure
Task-Process Phase Units:
PA: Problem analysis
PC: Problem critique
SA: Solution analysis
SD: Solution development
SC: Solution critique
OO: Orientation
NN: Tangent
CF: Confirmation
DIS: Disorganized
Relational Phase Units:
FW: Focused work
CW: Critical work
OPP: Opposition
ACC: Accommodation
TAB: Tabling
OD: Open discussion
INT: Integration

FIGURE 13.4

Sample Discussion with Activity Tracks

on the relational track. Notice that the activity segments or phases on the different tracks in the discussion depicted in this graph do not necessarily correspond to one another, which adds to the complexity of the path.

During the discussion, points of transition occur from time to time. These are *breakpoints,* or interruptions, designated by a code letter below the lines in Figure 13.4. Sometimes a breakpoint will mark a change in a single track, but often it will mark changes in several tracks. Breakpoints are important because they signal key points in the development of the group's decision-making activity.

Three types of breakpoints are apparent. *Normal breakpoints* are the expected, natural points of termination or transition. They include such things as adjournment, caucusing, or topic shifts. *Delays* are unexpected problems that cause a pause in normal group functioning. Delays often consist of rediscussion of issues necessary for the group to resolve conflicts or establish understanding. Delays may be a sign of impending difficulty, or they may be a more positive sign of careful thought or creative activity. *Disruptions* are more serious. These consist of major disagreements and group failures.

Although this is a somewhat complex and sophisticated theory, it expresses the structurational character of group decision making very well. It shows that groups do adopt particular courses of action to meet their needs but that in so doing they create structures that limit future action.

COMMENTARY AND CRITIQUE

Groups are important to individuals and society. As a person moves about in the world, cooperation becomes essential in achieving goals. People use communication to share resources in the solution of problems, and group communication thereby becomes not only an instrument for accomplishing tasks but also a means of group maintenance and cohesion.

Group communication can be viewed as a system of inputs, internal processes, and outputs. In decision making the inputs include information, group resources, and task characteristics. The process includes group interaction and decision development, and the outputs include completed tasks and decisions.

Group communication is also a form of structuration. The practices of the group create structures that limit future practices. Input-process-output models and structuration theories are not necessarily incompatible but provide two different ways of looking at group functioning. In many ways the theory of Poole and his associates is an input-process-output model because it posits a set of factors that affect processing, which in turn shapes outcomes. The difference is that this structurational model acknowledges the power of groups to shape the course of their own process to a certain extent.

Theories of small-group decision making form a distinct tradition. Their common threads and lines of influence are clear and provide a kind of coherence that binds this work. Certain basic ideas run through this history, as subsequent theories extend and develop earlier ideas.

The first basic idea is *the division of group effort into task and socioemotional factors.* It appears in almost all theories discussed in this chapter. Task energy is directed at problem solving, and socioemotional energy is directed at group maintenance and interpersonal relationships. Group effectiveness seems to depend on the balance between these two kinds of communication. Inadequate attention to these two factors can lead to dissatisfaction and poor decision making.

Perhaps the most influential theory to make the task–relationship distinction is Bales's foundational work. Bales's theory is an excellent beginning for understanding interaction in groups. His approach is highly parsimonious and internally consistent. It is built on a sensible and intuitively appealing conceptual base, from which a number of propositions about group interaction are derived.

Bales envisions the group as a body that swings between discussion of task matters and discussion of social matters, back and forth. Careful examination of groups in action, however, shows that task and socioemotional functions are thoroughly mixed. One can fulfill both task and social functions in a single statement, and in classifying group behavior, validly separating these functions is difficult. True, a given statement may be mostly task or mostly social, but to separate them completely would be a mistake.

This theory is strictly act-oriented and fails to describe true interaction. It presumes that any statement will stand on its own apart from contiguous statements by other persons. Fisher, as the second generation of interaction, looks at contiguous acts as the basic unit of analysis. Although Fisher's theory admits to the existence of the relational dimension of interaction, it makes no attempt to correlate the content and relational aspects of group discussion.

In general, Bales's and Fisher's theories share a common strength and a common weakness. The strength is that interaction analysis, of either type, allows us to look carefully at the communication behavior of groups, correlating messages with other group factors. In other words, interaction analysis provides a way to analyze group communication. Thus, these theories are both appropriate and heuristic. These advantages, however, have been gained at the price of a trade-off, which leads to their common weakness. When individual acts (or interacts) are analyzed according to a classification scheme, rich idiosyncratic meanings are glossed over. The value of understanding general group trends is bought at the price of thorough understanding of particular events in groups.

The third generation of work on task and relationship communication is represented by the research of Poole and his colleagues. It is an advance on Fisher's theory because it accounts for both tracks at the same time. It also takes a step toward capturing the idiosyncratic nature of the group experience by showing how groups can create very different patterns of decision making.

A second theme of group decision making is *group structure.* Group structure occurs in a variety of ways. Individuals differ in the kinds of statements they make in a group. Bales's research in the early 1950s classifies statements according to various categories and relates individual actions to roles. He shows how the group interaction is shaped by the types of statements made and the roles assigned to individuals from their statements. He also shows how subgroups form according to the personalities of the individuals in the group.

Fisher uses somewhat different categories, and he is interested in how statements respond to one another in interacts. Even Poole's sophisticated work begins with the classification of statements and interacts. Poole, however, goes far beyond any of his predecessors in showing how interacts combine into activity segments and how these segments combine into phases. Poole's notion of group structure is sophisticated and complex because he shows how several structures may be present in a group.

A third long-term theme in small-group research is *decision development.* Interaction differs from one time period within a discussion to another, and most theorists see this movement as a linear process of development. The precise nature of this development is unclear and in dispute, but the theorists are still looking for it. Poole's theory has great potential for revealing the complexity and individuality of group-decision development.

The fourth trend in small-group theory is its *interest in effectiveness,* as the functionalist tradition so well illustrates. Janis's theory is especially appealing because it is a highly focused and intuitively appealing explanation of effectiveness. It stems not only from laboratory research but also from field application and historical case study. It is a theory that demonstrates the utility of ideas about group dynamics for understanding actual groups at work.

As we have seen repeatedly in this book, one of the failings of most communication theories is that they are based on limited perspectives or on limited types of research. Theories such as Janis's are like a breath of fresh air in this regard. In fact, if you look at the kind of data used throughout small-group research, you see a wide spectrum of variety and real-world application. Poole's use of real decision-making groups in the field is another example.

Janis's theory is different also because of its applied nature. It is a normative, or prescriptive, theory providing guidelines for improved group functioning. However, this aspect of the theory leads to one of its weaknesses, namely, that it does not take us far in understanding or explaining how groups function. It suggests a way of guarding against one particular danger in groups, but it does not help us understand the nature of cohesiveness, conflict, roles, or communication. For this reason some scholars would be reluctant to call Janis's work a theory at all. Janis himself refers to this application merely as a hypothesis.

Hirokawa's theory is also highly normative. It is consistent with the everyday experience of groups in our society, and it seems to have practical potential in helping groups become more effective. Hirokawa's theory also limits group functioning to a kind of rational task-only process. It fails to acknowledge the ways group successes and failures are a result of socioemotional, relational, or structurational activity. In addition, the theory does not adequately integrate problems that are out of the control of the group, such as the vagaries of the situation or the pragmatic obstacles to information gathering.[36]

Small-group theory is an interesting and important part of the overall study of communica-

---

36   These problems are discussed in some detail by Cynthia Stohl and Michael E. Holmes, "A Functional Perspective for Bona Fide Groups," in *Communication Yearbook 16,* ed. Stanley Deetz (Newbury Park, CA: Sage, 1993), pp. 601–614.

tion, but it is not very popular now. This is puzzling because the work that has been done is important and sophisticated. In an article on small-group theory, Poole reflects on the status of the field.[37] He acknowledges that there were substantial theoretical advances in small group–communication theory in the 1980s, but he feels that it lacks a spark. Specifically, Poole maintains that small-group theory is missing three critical qualities.

First, it does not have the kind of imagination that will attract attention and interest, a metaphor that could inspire creative involvement. Poole would like to see more use of such images as fantasy themes, which use a dramatistic metaphor. He suggests such metaphors as the group as clan or tribe, group communication as exchange, and group work as computerlike.

Second, the area has not persuasively framed its problems as intriguing puzzles. Group theorists need to show how their work has intellectual significance. The question of whether the group really matters in decision making is a good example of the kind of puzzle of which Poole is thinking. The issue of whether group work is primarily individual or social is another example. Here, the issue is where the locus of decision making really lies, in the group or in the individual.

Third, group-communication scholars need to show that their work has important real-world implications. Clearly, groups are important, but do the theories adequately capture this quality? Are the outcome measures realistic, and do the theories catch the essence of what real groups feel like?

Poole's concerns are thought-provoking and should challenge not only small-group theorists but also scholars in all areas of the field.

---

37   Poole, "Do We Have Any Theories?"

COMMUNICATION AND ORGANIZATIONAL NETWORKS

According to sociologist Amatai Etzioni,

> Our society is an organizational society. We are born in organizations, educated in organizations, and most of us spend much of our lives working for organizations. We spend much of our leisure time playing and praying in organizations. Most of us will die in an organization, and when the time comes for burial, the largest organization of all—the state—must grant official permission.[1]

A large body of literature has been written about organizational communication.[2] Organizations can be viewed from a variety of perspectives. Gareth Morgan outlines a number of metaphors capturing their various aspects.[3] The first

metaphor is the *machine*. Organizations, like machines, have parts that produce products and services. Another metaphor is the *organism*. Like a plant or animal, the organization is born, grows, functions, and adapts to changes in the environment, and eventually it dies. Third, organizations are like *brains*: They process information, they have intelligence, they conceptualize, and they make plans. Fourth, organizations are like *cultures* because they create meaning, have values and norms, and are perpetuated by shared stories and rituals.

Next, organizations are like a *political system* in which power is distributed, influence is exerted, and decisions are made. Morgan shows also that organizations are *psychic prisons* because they can shape and limit the lives of their members, and she asserts that organizations can be understood as *flux and transformation*, because they adjust, change, and grow on the basis of information, feedback, and logical force. Finally, Morgan says that organizations are like *instruments of domination*, for they possess competing interests, some of which dominate others.

1   Amatai Etzioni, *Modern Organizations* (Englewood Cliffs, NJ: Prentice-Hall, 1964), p. 1.
2   See, for example, Myria Watkins Allen, M. Michael Gotcher, and Joy Hart Seibert, "A Decade of Organizational Communication Research: Journal Articles 1980–1991," in *Communication Yearbook 16*, ed. Stanley Deetz (Newbury Park, CA: Sage, 1993), pp. 252–330; Stacia Wert-Gray, Candy Center, Dale E. Brashers, and Renee A. Meyers, "Research Topics and Methodological Orientations in Organizational Communication: A Decade in Review," *Communication Studies* 42 (1991): 141–154.
3   Gareth Morgan, *Images of Organization* (Beverly Hills, CA: Sage, 1986).

We can add another metaphor to Morgan's list—the network—and this is the metaphor chosen to organize this chapter. *Networks* are social structures created by communication among individuals and groups.[4] As people communicate with others, contacts and links are made, and these channels become instrumental in all forms of social functioning—in organizations and in society at large. Networks, then, can touch upon virtually all aspects of organizational communication in one way or another.

Network theory tells us about the structures and functions of an organization. It addresses the means by which social reality is constructed within the organization, illustrating that networks are not only instrumental but also cultural. In addition, networks are the channels through which influence and power are exerted, not only by management in a formal way but also informally among organizational members.

◖ THE STRUCTURE OF NETWORKS

The work of Peter Monge, Eric Eisenberg, Richard Farace, and several of their colleagues constitutes an excellent overview of network concepts.[5] Their writings integrate an eclectic set of ideas in an internally consistent fashion, providing a synthesis of the network theory based on many of their own and others' research studies.

The authors define an organization as a system of at least two people (usually many more), with interdependence, input, throughput, and output. In other words, a network has all of the structural characteristics of a system, as described in Chapter 3. According to this view,

communicators cooperate to produce a product by using energy, information, and materials from the environment.

The structure of an organization consists of patterns of interaction among its members. Who talks to whom? What is the flow of information? The basic structural idea of network theory is that there are predictable pathways of communication between individuals. Individuals who communicate together form dyads, and dyads are linked together into groups. These groups are in turn linked together into the overall network.

Let's begin by looking at the *individual.* One of your major concerns as an individual in an organization is the amount of information you must process, or *load.* Load is characterized by *rate,* or the quantity of messages, and *complexity,* or the number of items that must be dealt with in processing information. In school, for example, you have times when you feel overloaded because of the amount of work you have to do, and your workload is characterized by how much you have been given to do (rate) and how difficult each assignment is (complexity). *Underload* occurs when the flow of messages falls below your processing ability, and *overload* occurs when the flow exceeds that capacity. For students, overload often occurs just before final examinations, and underload often happens at the end of vacation when boredom starts to set in.

When you communicate with another person, you form a *dyad.* Dyadic communication operates by *rules,* or expectations about what people are supposed to do (Chapters 5 and 10). Organizations have explicit and implicit rules for communicating, which govern how, when, with whom, and what to communicate. Some common rule topics include concerns about who initiates interactions, how delays are treated, what topics are discussed and who selects them, how topic changes are handled, how outside interruptions are handled, how interactions are terminated, and how frequently communication occurs. Although dyads are affected by general organizational rules, dyads also develop rules of their own. Further, the connections between members of a dyad are *links* characterized by

---

4   For a discussion of the network idea, see Peter R. Monge, "The Network Level of Analysis," in *Handbook of Communication Science,* eds. C. R. Berger and S. H. Chaffee (Newbury Park, CA: Sage, 1987), pp. 239–270.

5   Peter Monge and Eric Eisenberg, "Emergent Communication," in *Handbook of Organizational Communication: An Interdisciplinary Perspective,* eds. F. M. Jablin and others (Newbury Park, CA: Sage, 1987), pp. 304–342; Richard V. Farace, Peter R. Monge, and Hamish Russell, *Communicating and Organizing* (Reading, MA: Addison-Wesley, 1977).

symmetry, strength, reciprocity, content, and mode.

Symmetry is the degree to which a couple interacts on an equal basis. In a symmetrical relationship, the members give and take information relatively equally. An asymmetrical link goes primarily one way, with a distinct information sender and receiver. An army sergeant giving orders to a recruit is an example of an asymmetrical link, whereas two soldiers working side by side probably have a symmetrical one.

The *strength* of a link is the amount of communication between two people. Members who communicate more often have a stronger link, whereas those who communicate less often have a weaker one. Most professors probably have a pretty weak link to the dean, whereas two professors who do research together have a strong link with each other.

Reciprocity, another property of links, is the extent to which members agree about how much they communicate. If one person believes that he or she often communicates with another but the other denies it, the link is unreciprocated.

Network analysis can also look at the *content* of a link (what is talked about) and the *mode* (or what channels are used). Suppose, for example, that you are working with a partner making a training video. The two of you communicate frequently back and forth by e-mail about this project. In network terms, we would say that the two of you have a strong, reciprocated, symmetrical link. The content is the project, and the mode is e-mail.

Of course, the organization is not just a bunch of dyads. Organizational structure begins to form as dyads link together into *groups.* Network researchers define a group by four criteria: (1) More than half of the members' communication is within the group; (2) each person must be linked with all others in the group; (3) the group will not break apart with the exit of one person or the destruction of one link; (4) the group must have at least three members. The structure of the overall organization depends on these groupings.

Because people work together in different groups for different reasons, different kinds of groups exist in an organization, and a given individual simultaneously may be a member of several. You might be a member of a group working on the same project, another one that eats lunch together, a car pool, and a group of friends.

Because the members of a group are linked to one another in a particular way, groups have internal structures. Monge and colleagues outline three types of structure, including the communication pattern, or *micronetwork; power* relations, or who influences whom; and *leadership,* or role distribution.

Let's return to your video project. At some point you begin to bring more people into the project. There are employees from the multimedia department, a scriptwriter, and other members of Training and Development who will serve as actors. As you communicate with these people more and more, a group is formed. Not everyone in the group will communicate with one another equally, so some links will be stronger than others. Some members will exert more influence than others, giving the group a structure of power or influence.

Whatever their internal structure, groups are linked together into an organizational structure. This overall structure, the *macronetwork,* is the repetitive pattern of information flow among the groups in an organization. Because there are several types of groups and these may be linked to one another in different ways, so the organization consists of several structures. For example, there may be different structures for task work, power relations, social communication, or others. Perhaps the most visible is the prescribed task structure, or formal organization chart, but this is never the only one.

As the members of an organization communicate with one another, they take different network *roles,* and these roles are crucial to the structure of the network. For example, a *bridge* is a member of a group who is also a member of another group. In making your video, for example, a member of your team may be an employee of the Facilities Planning Department and is therefore able to help you get a room for shooting the video. A *liaison* connects two groups, but

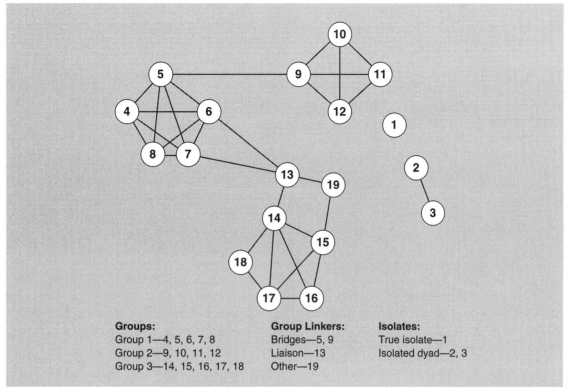

Groups:
Group 1—4, 5, 6, 7, 8
Group 2—9, 10, 11, 12
Group 3—14, 15, 16, 17, 18

Group Linkers:
Bridges—5, 9
Liaison—13
Other—19

Isolates:
True isolate—1
Isolated dyad—2, 3

FIGURE **14.1**

Illustration of Communication Network Roles

From *Communicating and Organizing* by Richard V. Farace, Peter R. Monge, and Hamish Russell (Figure 8–5). Copyright © 1977 by Addison-Wesley. Reprinted by permission of Random House, Inc.

is a member of neither. *Isolates* stand alone. Figure 14.1 illustrates how networks are formed from communication links.[6]

Organizational networks can be characterized by a number of qualities. The first is *size,* or the sheer number of people. The second is *centrality,* or the degree to which individuals have access to one another. The third quality of networks—*density,* or *connectedness*—is the ratio of actual links to possible links. Very large organizations with a sparse network would be low in connectedness, whereas a small organization with many links would be highly connected. Another characteristic of networks is *multiplexity,* or network overlap. A multiplex is a network or part of one that fulfills more than a single function. A link be-

tween two people, for example, might be both task and social. Whenever a network or portion of a network contains more than one type of content, multiplexity exists. Maybe your video partner is also your best friend, and you also share a lot of personal information and do social things together.

Because centrality is one of the most frequently studied aspects of networks, let's take a closer look at it here. Centrality has a variety of manifestations. One is the number of contacts each person has with others in the organization. A person who has a number of contacts has high *individual centrality,* and a network in which the

6   Farace, Monge, and Russell, *Communicating,* p. 192.

average number of contacts is high has high *network centrality.*

Centrality can be seen in overall closeness or "reachability." Some organizations are dispersed in such a fashion that it is difficult for any one person to make contact through the network with another individual. Other organizations are tight in the sense that one could easily reach anyone else within just a few intermediaries.

We have now discussed the individual, dyad, group, and organization. The fifth level of analysis consists of *interorganizational* or *environmental* networks, comprising linkages between people from one organization to people in others. Through the links among their individual members, organizations can become tightly intertwined with one another. Employees, for example, may have contacts with suppliers, retailers, transporters, contractors, and many other types of organizations. Interorganizational networks demonstrate that an organization never operates in isolation but is always part of an environment that affects its operation and culture.

There has been much research on almost all the features of networks described above. We do not have sufficient space here to summarize the major findings, but they are readily available elsewhere.[7]

To get an idea of how network analysis works, consider the study of Karlene Roberts and Charles O'Reilly on the network of a large Navy squadron.[8] They asked each employee three simple questions. To find the technical network, they asked: "When you need technical advice in doing your job, who are the persons you are most likely to ask?" To find the social network, they asked: "With which persons in this squadron are you most likely to have social conversations?" And to find the authority network, they asked: "If you are upset about something related to the Navy or to your job, to whom in the squadron are you most likely to express your dissatisfaction formally?"

The questionnaire was first administered when the squadron was new and again twelve months later to see how the structure of the organization had changed. Almost 500 employees responded to the first testing and 700 to the second, which constituted 80 percent of permanent personnel both times.

The data were analyzed by computer to determine every link mentioned by the respondents. About 80 percent of the employees were involved in the expertise and social networks, with about 20 percent isolates. The number of isolates increased substantially in the second testing for both networks. The number of isolates in the authority network was considerably greater at 57 percent, and that increased only slightly in the second testing.

The total number of links rose considerably from the first testing to the second, as people got to know one another better and as the kinds of problems with which they had to deal increased. There were about twenty-seven expertise groups, and that figure rose to forty-three in the second testing; there were sixteen social groups, which increased to thirty-eight; and the twelve authority groups rose to thirty during the twelve-month period. The sizes of the groups remained about the same: about ten persons per group on the average in the expertise and social networks and about seven persons in the authority networks. The average group sizes, however, are deceiving because they ranged greatly from very small to very large groups.

The role properties of the networks studied were interesting. There were sixty-two liaisons and eighty-four bridges in the expertise network at the beginning, thirty-six liaisons and thirty-eight bridges in the social network, and only three liaisons and three bridges in the authority network. The number of individuals taking these roles increased drastically in every network in the year following the first testing. In fact, the number of liaisons in the authority network rose from three to eighty-seven, and the number of bridges in this network rose from three to ninety-seven during this period!

You can see from this study that the concepts of network theory are useful in providing a pic-

7   See Monge and Eisenberg, "Emergent Communication."
8   Karlene H. Roberts and Charles A. O'Reilly, "Organizations as Communication Structures: An Empirical Approach," *Human Communication Research* 4 (1978): 283–293.

ture of the communication dynamics in an organization. These ideas provide a good beginning point for our exploration of organizational communication concepts, but much more remains to be considered.

Peter Monge and Eric Eisenberg see network theory as a way of integrating three traditions of organizational studies.[9] The first is the *positional tradition,* which is concerned with formal structure and roles in organizations. The organization in this tradition is viewed as a set of positions like administrator, teacher, and student. Each position has certain functions.

The second tradition related to networks is the *relational.* This tradition deals with the ways relationships naturally develop among participants in an organization and the manner in which networks emerge from these relationships. Here, the organization is seen as a living, changing system constantly shaped and given meaning by the interactions among members.

The third tradition is *cultural.* Here, symbols and meaning are central. The world of the organization is created by the members in stories, rituals, and task work. The real structure of the organization is not predesigned but emerges from the actions of the members informally in their daily work.

THE POSITIONAL TRADITION

The positional tradition consists of a number of theories of formal communication networks. These theories tend to examine the ways management uses formal networks to achieve its objectives. A foundational theory of this genre is Max Weber's theory of bureaucracy.

Classical Foundations: Weber

Certainly, Max Weber was one of the most prominent social theorists of all time. In his lifetime, from 1864 to 1920, he produced a great quantity of work on the nature of human institutions. One area for which he is best known is his theory of bureaucracy.[10] Weber's ideas, developed at the beginning of the century, are part of what we now refer to as "classical organizational theory."[11]

Weber defines an organization as a system of purposeful, interpersonal activity designed to coordinate tasks.[12] *Power*—the ability of a person to influence others and overcome resistance—is fundamental to most social relationships. When power is "legitimate," or authorized formally by the organization, compliance is effective and complete. Whether communications will be accepted in an organization, then, hinges on the degree to which the superior has *legitimate authority.* You tend to do what your boss says because the organization grants this person the legitimate authority to give orders.

Where does this authority come from? The most common form of authority stems from the organization's rules and regulations, which leads to *bureaucratic,* or *rational-legal, authority.* This is the kind of authority vested in supervisors and managers.

Weber sees bureaucracy as the most efficient pattern for mass administration, and it is governed by a number of well-known principles. First, bureaucracy is based on rules. Such rules allow the solution of problems, standardization, and equality in the organization. Second, bureaucracies are based on sphere of competence, in which a systematic division of labor exists. Within the sphere, each role has clearly defined rights and powers. Third, the essence of bureaucracy is hierarchy, which is seen in the formal organizational chart. Fourth, administrators are appointed on the basis of their knowledge and

9   Monge and Eisenberg, "Emergent Communication."
10   Max Weber, *The Theory of Social and Economic Organizations,* trans. A. M. Henderson and T. Parsons (New York: Oxford University Press, 1947). A lengthy interpretation and discussion of Weber's theory can be found in Parsons's introduction to the above book. For a more complete bibliography of primary and secondary sources on Weber, see S. N. Eisenstadt, *Max Weber on Charisma and Institution Building* (Chicago: University of Chicago Press, 1968).
11   The most important classical theories are those of Henri Fayol and Frederick Taylor. See Henri Fayol, *General and Industrial Management* (New York: Pitman, 1949), originally published in 1925; and Frederick W. Taylor, *Principles of Scientific Management* (New York: Harper Brothers, 1947), originally published in 1912.
12   Weber, *Social and Economic Organizations,* p. 151.

training. They are not usually elected, nor do they inherit their positions, but gain them through training, experience, and selection. Fifth, the members of the bureaucracy must not share in the ownership of the organization. Sixth, bureaucrats must be free to allocate resources within their realms of influence without fear of outside infringement. Seventh, a bureaucracy requires carefully maintained records—a principle that has led to the strong rule in most organizations to document all important transactions.

Another feature of a bureaucracy is that it is usually headed by a nonbureaucrat. Nonbureaucratic heads are often elected or inherit their positions. They include presidents, cabinets, boards of trustees, and monarchs. Bureaucrats are dispensable; they may be replaced by similarly trained individuals, but the succession of the nonbureaucratic head may well be a crisis, precipitating innovation and change.

Weber's theory is included here primarily as a general background for the theories to come and to illustrate the positional tradition. In this regard the theory serves two functions. First, it provides a "classical," or standard, picture with which the other theories can be contrasted. Second, it presents the traditional view of organizations. The theory has implicit ideas of what communication is like in organizations, but communication is not treated as an explanatory variable, nor is it seen as important. As such this is not really a communication theory. As the upcoming sections show, this failure is significant.

Likert's Four Systems

Rensis Likert is a theorist in the human relations school. Human relations, in reaction to classical theories such as Weber's, focused on the workers—their feelings and needs. It was an especially popular movement from the 1940s through the 1960s. Human relations really has a foot in both the positional and relational traditions, but most of these theories, Likert's included, look at human relations from a production, management-oriented perspective. They teach that if you care for and nurture workers, the organization's op-

erations will improve.[13] Likert's theory illustrates the positional nature of much of this theory.[14]

According to Likert, an organization can function at any point along a continuum of four systems. Under system 1, the *exploitative-authoritative system,* the executive manages with an iron hand. Decisions are made by the boss, with no use of feedback. Once step away is system 2, *benevolent-authoritative leadership.* Here, the manager is sensitive to the needs of the worker. Moving farther along the continuum, we come to system 3, the *consultative system,* in which authority figures still maintain control but seek consultation from below. At the far extreme of the spectrum, system 4, or *participative management,* allows the worker to participate fully in decision making.

The system chosen by management will cause certain outcomes to occur. In Likert's scheme, then, the system of management is a *causal* variable. In addition, certain *intervening* variables also affect the outcome, as outlined in Figure 14.2.[15]

For Likert, system 4 is clearly the best because it leads to high performance and an increased sense of responsibility and motivation. If management is authoritative, there is less group loyalty, more conflict, and consequently less mutual support. Workers have a lower attitude toward management and not much motivation to produce. The predictable result is lower sales, higher costs, and lower earnings. Consultative and participative management, on the other hand, leads to greater loyalty, higher performance goals, more mutual support, and more positive attitudes. The motivation to produce is higher, so that sales are greater, costs are less, and earnings are increased. Figure 14.3 illustrates the mechanisms of the systems.[16]

---

13 For a more detailed discussion and critique of the human relations movement, see Charles Perrow, *Complex Organizations: A Critical Essay* (Glenview, IL: Scott, Foresman, 1972).
14 Rensis Likert, *New Patterns of Management* (New York: McGraw-Hill, 1961); Rensis Likert, *The Human Organization* (New York: McGraw-Hill, 1967).
15 Rensis Likert, "New Patterns in Sales Management," in *Changing Perspectives in Marketing Management,* ed. Martin Warshaw (Ann Arbor: Bureau of Business Research, University of Michigan, 1972), p. 24.
16 Likert, *Human Organization,* p. 137.

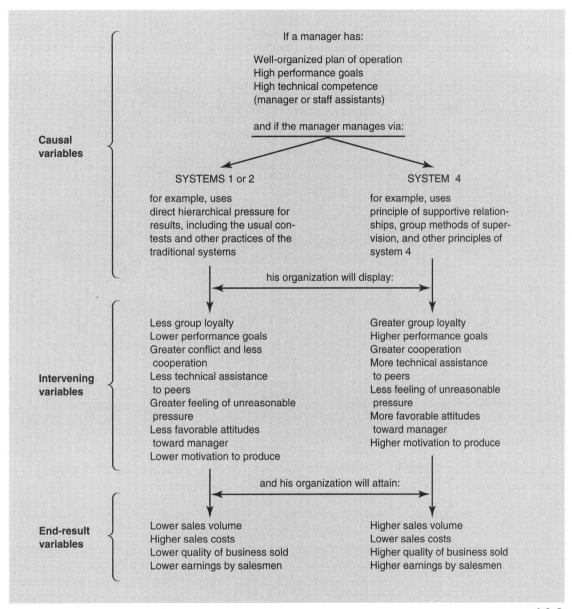

If a manager has:

Well-organized plan of operation
High performance goals
High technical competence
(manager or staff assistants)

and if the manager manages via:

SYSTEMS 1 or 2 — for example, uses direct hierarchical pressure for results, including the usual contests and other practices of the traditional systems

SYSTEM 4 — for example, uses principle of supportive relationships, group methods of supervision, and other principles of system 4

Causal variables

Intervening variables

his organization will display:

Systems 1 or 2:
Less group loyalty
Lower performance goals
Greater conflict and less cooperation
Less technical assistance to peers
Greater feeling of unreasonable pressure
Less favorable attitudes toward manager
Lower motivation to produce

System 4:
Greater group loyalty
Higher performance goals
Greater cooperation
More technical assistance to peers
Less feeling of unreasonable pressure
More favorable attitudes toward manager
Higher motivation to produce

End-result variables

and his organization will attain:

Systems 1 or 2:
Lower sales volume
Higher sales costs
Lower quality of business sold
Lower earnings by salesmen

System 4:
Higher sales volume
Lower sales costs
Higher quality of business sold
Higher earnings by salesmen

FIGURE **14.2**

Sequence of Developments in a Well-Organized Enterprise, as Affected by Use of System 1 or 2 or System 4

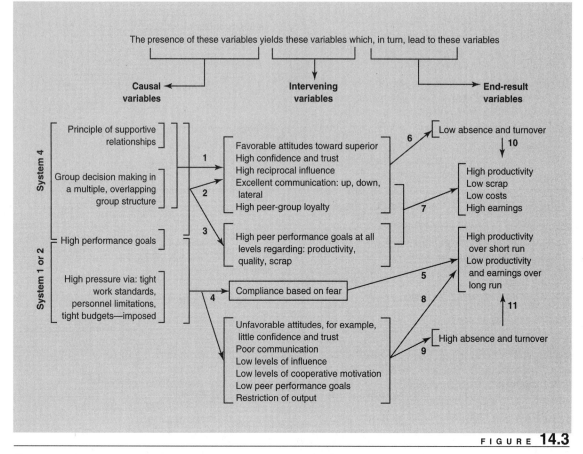

The presence of these variables yields these variables which, in turn, lead to these variables

Causal variables → Intervening variables → End-result variables

FIGURE 14.3

Simplified Diagram of Relationships among Variables for System 1 or 2 and System 4 Operations

From *The Human Organization* by Rensis Likert. Copyright © 1967 by McGraw-Hill. Reprinted by permission of the publisher.

How does communication figure in all of this? Likert treats communication as one of several intervening variables. Table 14.1 shows how communication varies across the four systems.[17] You can see that exploitative management does not think about communication very much except to express its desires clearly and forcefully to the workers. There is little upward communication, and what information that does go up the line tends to be distorted. Supervisors and subordinates are not very close to one another, and there is little accurate understanding between them.

On the other hand, participative management includes strong upward and downward communication. This communication tends to be accurate and clear. Managers and workers tend to be close and understand one another well.

Although Likert's theory and the human relations movement have been criticized for being simplistic and mechanistic, there does seem to be some truth to Likert's notion that in some organizations exploitative systems have negative results, whereas participative ones have positive ones.

Virginia Richmond and James McCroskey conducted a study of employee satisfaction

---

17   Likert, *Human Organization*, pp. 16–19.

TABLE **14.1**

Organization and Performance Characteristics of Different Management Systems Based on a Comparative Analysis

Operating Characteristics	System of Organization			
	Authoritative		Participative	
	Exploitative-Authoritative	Benevolent-Authoritative	Consultative	Participative Group
a. Amount of interaction and communication aimed at achieving organization's objectives	Very little	Little	Quite a bit	Much with both individuals and groups
b. Direction of information flow	Downward	Mostly downward	Down and up	Down, up, and with peers
c. Downward communication				
1. Where initiated	At top of organization or to implement top directive	Primarily at top or patterned on communication from top	Patterned on communication from top but with some initiative at lower levels	Initiated at all levels
2. Extent to which communications are accepted by subordinates	Viewed with great suspicion	May or may not be viewed with suspicion	Often accepted but at times viewed with suspicion. May or may not be openly questioned	Generally accepted, but if not, openly and candidly questioned
d. Upward communication				
1. Adequacy of upward communication via line organization	Very little	Limited	Some	A great deal
2. Subordinates' feeling of responsibility for initiating accurate upward communication	None at all	Relatively little, usually communicates "filtered" information but only when requested. May "yes" the boss	Some to moderate degree of responsibility to initiate accurate upward communication	Considerable responsibility felt and much initiative. Group communicates all relevant information.
3. Forces leading to accurate or distorted information	Powerful forces to distort information and deceive superiors	Occasionally forces to distort; also forces for honest communication	Some forces to distort along with many forces to communicate accurately	Virtually no forces to distort and powerful forces to communicate accurately
4. Accuracy of upward communication via line	Tends to be inaccurate	Information that boss wants to hear flows; other information is restricted and filtered	Information that boss wants to hear flows, other information may be limited or cautiously given	Accurate
5. Need for supplementary upward communication system	Need to supplement upward communication by spy system, suggestion system, or some similar devices	Upward communication often supplemented by suggestion system and similar devices	Slight need for supplementary system may be used	No need for any supplementary system
e. Sideward communication, its adequacy and accuracy	Usually poor because of competition between peers and corresponding hostility	Fairly poor because of competition between peers	Fair to good	Good to excellent
f. Psychological closeness of superiors to subordinates (that is, how well does superior know and understand problems faced by subordinates?)	Far apart	Can be moderately close if proper roles are kept	Fairly close	Usually very close
1. Accuracy of perceptions by superiors and subordinates	Often in error	Often in error on some points	Moderately accurate	Usually quite accurate

among 183 teachers in 39 school districts.[18] The teachers were given a battery of tests related to, among other things, management style, manager's tolerance for disagreement, and satisfaction. Four styles—called "tells," "sells," "consults," and "joins"—were measured in the study. These are essentially identical to Likert's systems 1, 2, 3, and 4.

The data showed a clear relationship between the perceived style of the manager and employee satisfaction. Employees who thought that their manager used a consulting or joining style were more satisfied than those who thought that a telling or selling style was used. The same relationship held for tolerance for disagreement. Employees who thought that their managers had less tolerance for disagreement were less satisfied than those who thought their managers had a higher level of disagreement tolerance.

One function of formal communication in an organization is to elicit cooperation on the part of employees. Likert suggests that this can be done by participative management. The following theory explores some of the less obvious ways in which cooperation is gained in organizations.

Unobtrusive Control and Identification

The theory of *organizational identification*, by Phillip Tompkins and George Cheney, integrates existing theory into a fresh approach to control in organizations.[19] According to this theory, control is exerted in organizations in four ways.[20] The first is *simple control*, or use of direct, open power. This is much like Likert's system 1 management, in which supervisors simply force workers to comply.

The second is *technical control*, or use of machinery. For example, if employees are given a computer and told to use it for their work, the computer itself limits what they can do and how they can do it.

The third form of control is *bureaucratic*, which involves the use of organizational procedures and formal rules, much as Weber envisioned. Employees may be given a manual that includes policies to be followed, and memos and reports are used to communicate additional expectations.

The fourth, and most interesting to Cheney and Tompkins, is *concertive control*—the use of interpersonal relationships and teamwork. This is the most subtle form of control because it relies on a shared reality and shared values:

> In the concertive organization, the explicitly written rules and regulations are largely replaced by the common understanding of values, objectives, and means of achievement, along with a deep appreciation for the organization's "mission." This we call . . . the "soul of the new organization."[21]

With its emphasis on concertive control, this theory is really in both the positional and relational traditions. Because the premises on which concertive control is based are managerial and because control is accomplished at least in part through formal channels, it is included among the positional theories in this chapter.

Although the four types of control are normally found in various combinations, there is a trend away from simple, direct control toward this more subtle and complex form. The theory of unobtrusive control deals primarily with the

---

18   Virginia P. Richmond and James C. McCroskey, "Management Communication Style, Tolerance for Disagreement, and Innovativeness as Predictors of Employee Satisfaction: A Comparison of Single-Factor, Two-Factor, and Multiple-Factor Approaches," in *Communication Yearbook 3*, ed. D. Nimmo (New Brunswick, NJ: Transaction, 1979), pp. 359–373.

19   George Cheney and Phillip K. Tompkins, "Coming to Terms with Organizational Identification and Commitment," *Central States Speech Journal* 38 (1987): 1–15; Phillip K. Tompkins and George Cheney, "Account Analysis of Organizations: Decision Making and Identification," in *Communication and Organizations: An Interpretive Approach*, eds. L. L. Putnam and M. E. Pacanowsky (Beverly Hills, CA: Sage, 1983), pp. 123–146; Phillip K. Tompkins and George Cheney, "Communication and Unobtrusive Control in Contemporary Organizations," in *Organizational Communication: Traditional Themes and New Directions*, eds. R. D. McPhee and P. K. Tompkins (Beverly Hills, CA: Sage, 1985), pp. 179–210. For a summary and extension see James S. Sass and Daniel J. Canary, "Organizational Commitment and Identification: An Examination of Conceptual and Operational Convergence," *Western Journal of Speech Communication* 55 (1991): 275–293.

20   Tompkins and Cheney base this conceptualization on the work of R. Edwards, "The Social Relations of Production at the Point of Production," in *Complex Organizations: Critical Perspectives*, eds. M. Zey-Ferrell and M. Aiken (Glenview, IL: Scott, Foresman, 1981).

21   Tompkins and Cheney, "Communication and Unobtrusive Control," p. 184.

ways control is managed within the concertive system.

Organizational control is a kind of "discipline," or force that maintains order and consistency, and power is the means by which this kind of discipline is accomplished.[22] Power can never be avoided and is always in the system. At the same time, power is not an external force but is always created by various forms of interaction within the organization. Power, then, accomplishes control, but by submitting to control, the organization itself reinforces the very sources of power.

In concertive control, discipline is accomplished by "normalizing" behaviors, making certain ways of operating normal and natural, something organizational members want to do. Many things become normalized in organizations, including power relations. So again we see that discipline reinforces the very power relations that makes discipline possible. In contemporary organizations, disciplinary control is best accomplished in four ways.

First, it involves unobtrusive methods. Discipline is not necessarily obvious or conscious but is part of the ongoing daily activity of the organization. For example, something as simple as normal work hours is a form of control, and to the extent that employees accept these hours, they are participating in their own control.

Second, discipline is collaboratively produced. Organizational members work together to make a set of practices normal, to establish a set of standards, a discipline. Meetings are a good example. In many organizations, meetings tend to start on the hour and end on the hour. Whether one, two, or three hours in length, this pattern is common. People collaborate in making this a normal state of affairs. They come on time and when the hour is up, they—following their expectations—pack up and head for the door.

Third, discipline is a part of social relations. What people say and do to one another is both governed by and produces normalized practices. The unacknowledged "rules" in an organization tell you what topics you can and cannot talk about on the job, when and where interaction

can take place, what nonverbal behaviors are appropriate or inappropriate, and who can initiate conversations.

Finally, the most effective means of control are based on the values that motivate organizational members—the very things for which they strive. This may include money, time, accomplishment, sense of teamwork, and so forth.

Following the classical work of Herbert Simon,[23] Tompkins and Cheney show how control is accomplished by shaping the decisions made by organizational members. Simon believes that organizational decision making follows a syllogistic pattern, in which decision makers reason deductively from general premises and in which choices are based on those premises. Control is exerted when workers, who accept certain general premises, reason to the conclusions desired by management.

The premises are accepted because of incentives like wages and the authority of people with legitimate power (see Weber). This acceptance does not come automatically, however, because conflict often results from differences between employees' personal beliefs and the premises of the organization. Indeed, a substantial amount of industrial strife results from such differences. How, then, do organizations achieve concertive control in the face of potential conflict? The answer lies in use of the organizational enthymeme.

Described by Aristotle over two thousand years ago, the *enthymeme* is a rhetorical device used to involve audiences in the advocate's reasoning process.[24] As such, the enthymeme is a "rhetorical syllogism." In an enthymeme, one or more premises in a reasoning chain are left out, to be supplied by the audience. The audience is then expected to imagine particular conclusions

---

22   James R. Barker and George Cheney, "The Concept and the Practices of Discipline in Contemporary Organizational Life," *Communication Monographs* 61 (1994): 19–43.
23   Herbert Simon, *Administrative Behavior* (New York: Free Press, 1976). See also Perrow, *Complex Organizations.*
24   Lane Cooper, *The Rhetoric of Aristotle* (New York: Meredith, 1932). See also Lloyd Bitzer, "Aristotle's Enthymeme Revisited," *Quarterly Journal of Speech* 45 (1959): 399–408; Jesse Delia, "The Logic Fallacy, Cognitive Theory, and the Enthymeme: A Search for the Foundations of Reasoned Discourse," *Quarterly Journal of Speech* 56 (1970): 140–148.

based on these implicit premises. Sometimes the suppressed premises are widely accepted cultural values; other times they are inculcated through persuasion.

For example, a speaker advocating the prohibition of offshore drilling might reason that (1) offshore drilling endangers the fragile coastal ecology; (2) coastal ecology is valuable and should be protected; (3) therefore, offshore drilling should be prohibited. In addressing a group of environmentalists, however, this speaker could rely on the audience's acceptance of the second premise and therefore would only need to address the first. Once the environmentalists come to believe that drilling hurts the environment, they will reason that it should be prohibited.

Tompkins and Cheney are especially interested in how enthymemes are used in organizations for unobtrusive control of decision making. These authors point out that when members display loyalty and behave "organizationally," they are essentially accepting key organizational premises. Often organizations directly sell their premises to employees through company newsletters, training programs, and the like. Other times, organizations employ a variety of incentives to induce employees to become loyal. In any case, once employees accept certain premises, their conclusions and decisions are controlled.

For example, one premise of many industrial firms is that obsolescence is positive because it maintains progress, sustains the market, and protects jobs. Once engineers buy this idea, they opt automatically for designs that include planned obsolescence because they accept the basic organizational premise.

The acceptance of organizational premises is part of a process of organizational identification.[25] Here, the theorists rely largely on the work of Kenneth Burke (Chapter 8). *Identification* occurs when individuals become aware of their common ground. We identify with individuals with whom we share something in common; and the more we share with one another, the more the potential identification between us. When

employees identify with the organization, they are more likely to accept the organization's premises and make decisions consistent with organizational objectives.

To explore organizational identification, Connie Bullis and Phillip Tompkins conducted a large study of the U.S. Forest Service.[26] These investigators interviewed fifty-five employees at Washington, DC, headquarters, three regional offices, two forest headquarters, and two ranger stations. In addition, they administered questionnaires to about seven hundred employees throughout the agency.

By comparing their findings with a study done thirty years before, they found that much more bureaucratic control is now being used and that concertive control is on the decline, as is organizational identification.[27] Some organizational identification still exists, though employees vary substantially in their commitment to the ideals of the organization. Bullis and Tompkins found that employees who had the greatest identification with the organization subscribed much more readily to organizational premises such as the Forest Service goals, multiple-use management, and the public interest than did less committed employees. Those who did not identify that much with the organization were more concerned about such things as technical correctness or special interests.

Concertive control is one of several mechanisms used by organizations to manage multiple identities. The complex organization today does not have a single image with a single set of consistent interests. Rather, it is a complex system of interacting, sometimes contradictory, identities, and organizational communication must somehow manage this multiple state of affairs. George Cheney explains the difficulty:

25   George Cheney, "The Rhetoric of Identification and the Study of Organizational Communication," *Quarterly Journal of Speech* 69 (1983): 143–158.
26   Connie A. Bullis and Phillip K. Tompkins, "The Forest Ranger Revisited: A Study of Control Practices and Identification," *Communication Monographs* 56 (1989): 287–306.
27   H. Kaufman, *The Forest Ranger: A Study in Administrative Behavior* (Baltimore, MD: Johns Hopkins University Press, 1960).

To speak of collective identity is to speak of collective or shared interests—or at least of how the interests of a collective are represented and understood. This is a fundamental concern of contemporary organizations. Large bureaucratic organizations are in the business of identity management; their controlling members must be concerned about how to (re)present the organization as a whole *and* how to connect the individual identities of many members to that embracing collective identity.[28]

Thus the organization must have a way of inducing individuals, with all their variable interests, into a common identification with the organization. A diversity of identities, even conflicting ones, can be handled if there is at least some level of overall identification with the organization as a whole. Sometimes organizations must change, which means altering an identity, but to survive, the organization must create a new identity based in part on the interests of a substantial portion of its membership.

For these reasons, unbridled pluralism and diversity cannot be tolerated by an organization, and concertive control through identification is therefore essential.

◖◗ THE RELATIONAL TRADITION

Theories in the relational tradition are concerned with the ways organization is accomplished by interaction among individuals. These theories are less concerned with the lines of communication running through the organization and more concerned with how people accomplish things together.

We looked at relational communication theory in Chapter 12. Recall that these theories are less interested in the messages that one person sends to another than they are with the effect of mutual interaction among people. This tradition has had a significant impact on the work in organizational communication as well. The chief proponent of the interactional view in organization studies is Carl Weick, and we look at his theory first.

The Process of Organizing

One of the most influential theories of the relational genre is that of Carl Weick.[29] Weick's theory of organizing is significant in the communication field because it uses communication as a basis for human organizing and provides a rationale for understanding how people organize.

The feature that distinguishes this theory from those of the positional school is that organizations are not structures made of positions and roles, but communication activities. It is more proper to speak of "organizing" than of "organizations" because organizations are something that people accomplish through a continuing process of communication. When people go through their daily interactions, their activities *create* organization. Behaviors are interlocked, since one person's behavior is contingent on another's.

In this analysis, an *act* is a statement or behavior of one individual, an *interact* involves an act followed by a response, and a *double interact* consists of an act followed by a response and then an adjustment or follow-up by the first person. Weick believes that all organizing activities are double interacts.

Consider an executive and an administrative assistant as an example. The executive asks the assistant to undertake an activity (act); the assistant then asks for clarification (interact); and the executive explains (double interact). Or the executive asks the administrative assistant a favor (act), and the administrative assistant follows through (interact), after which the executive

---

28   George Cheney, *Rhetoric in an Organizational Society: Managing Multiple Identities* (Columbia: University of South Carolina Press, 1991), p. 14.

29   Carl Weick, *The Social Psychology of Organizing*, 2nd ed. (Reading, MA: Addison-Wesley, 1979). For a recent secondary source, see James L. Everett, "Communication and Sociocultural Evolution in Organizations and Organizational Populations," *Communication Theory* 4 (1994): 93–110. See also the special section in *Communication Studies* 40 (Winter 1989): 231–265.

responds with a thank you (double interact). Simple? Yes, but these activities are exactly the kind of which Weick believes organizations are made.

Organizing activities fulfill the function of reducing the uncertainty of information received from the *environment*, or surroundings. Weick uses the term *equivocality* to mean uncertainty, or complication, ambiguity, and lack of predictability. All information from the environment, according to Weick, is equivocal to some degree, and organizing activities are designed to reduce this uncertainty.

Let's return to the example of the executive again. Suppose the executive receives a directive from the firm's president to solve a problem of plant safety. What is the nature of this problem, and how should the executive go about solving it? The answers to these questions are not clear, inasmuch as the problem can be defined and solved in a number of ways. In other words, the executive is faced with equivocal information.

Weick is saying that organizing activities, which consist of double interacts, or interlocked behaviors, are designed to make such situations clearer. Of course, the importance of information and the degree of equivocality in the information vary. Asking an administrative assistant a favor may be an insignificant act whose equivocality is low, but the example of solving safety hazards illustrates a more significant problem that has a great deal of equivocality.

This difference is not important to Weick. What is important is that organizing is accomplished through processes developed to deal with equivocal information, mild or great. The exact nature of that information is irrelevant to the fact that organizational members engage in it. Interaction serves to achieve common meanings among group members, and the meanings that individuals together assign to information provide the mechanism by which equivocality is reduced. In other words, as we interact we come to some amount of common understanding, which reduces uncertainty.

To test the relationship between equivocality and interaction, Gary Kreps studied the discussions of the faculty senate at the University of Southern California for a year.[30] He asked a sample of senate members to evaluate each of the twenty-four motions considered that year in terms of their equivocality. They filled out scales to test how complicated or uncomplicated, how predictable or unpredictable, and how ambiguous or unambiguous each motion was. Kreps then chose the five most equivocal and five least equivocal motions and counted the number of double interacts in the discussions of each of these. The difference is clear: Highly equivocal motions required much more discussion than did less equivocal ones. The average number of double interacts for less equivocal motions was seven, whereas that for highly equivocal ones was seventy-four.

We have discussed how individuals interact to deal with equivocal information from the environment, but what is the environment? Organizers are always surrounded by a mix of stimuli to which they must respond, but the "environment" has no meaning apart from what the individual makes of it. In other words, the environment is a product of the person, not something outside the person. What makes the environment salient for the individual is the person's attention to particular aspects of the stimuli. People are selective in what they attend to in any situation and what is attended to becomes the environment. Hence, like every other aspect of the organizational reality, the environment is enacted by the people in the organization. People are continually reenacting their environments, depending on their attitudes, values, and experiences of the moment.

For example, the executive of our safety example is faced with a situation in which interpretation is necessary. Immediately, he or she will attend to certain aspects of the "safety problem." In enlisting the aid of others such as the administrative assistant, the executive is beginning processes that will enable the group to treat the

---

30   Gary L. Kreps, "A Field Experimental Test and Revaluation of Weick's Model of Organizing," in *Communication Yearbook 4*, ed. D. Nimmo (New Brunswick, NJ: Transaction, 1980), pp. 389–398.

safety problem as its environment of the moment. To deal with this equivocal environment, group members make proposals (acts) to which others respond (interacts) so that the proposers can refine their initial proposals (double interacts).

The executive may ask the administrative assistant to check the files for accident records. This constitutes a proposal, an attempt to reduce the equivocality. The administrative assistant may comply, pulling the appropriate file, so that the executive can be assured that the company knows the extent of the safety problem. Here, the sequence of the double interact would be as follows: request file (act), provide file (interact), take file and review it (double interact).

Weick views organizing as an evolutionary process that relies on a series of three major processes: enactment, selection, and retention. *Enactment* is the definition of the situation, or registering equivocal information from outside. It is attention to stimuli and acknowledgment that equivocality exists. The mere acceptance of certain aspects of the environment removes some equivocality. Accepting the task of dealing with safety problems narrows the field for the executive, so that some uncertainty already is removed from the field of all possible problems that could be addressed.

The second process is *selection,* which enables the group to admit certain aspects and reject other aspects of information. It narrows the field, eliminating alternatives with which the organization does not wish to deal. This process therefore removes even more equivocality from the initial information. For example, in dealing with the safety problem, the organization may decide to consider only the aspects of safety that management can control, eliminating everything they cannot control.

The third process of organizing is *retention,* in which certain aspects of the information will be saved for future use. Retained information is integrated into the existing body of information on which the organization operates. The safety group may decide to deal with safety problems that are caused strictly by machinery, rejecting all other kinds of problems. As you can see, the

problem has become much less ambiguous; it has moved from equivocality toward clarity.

After retention occurs, organization members face a *choice point.* They must decide first whether to reenact the environment in some way. Here, they address the question, "Should we (or I) attend to some aspect of the environment that was rejected before?" The executive may decide, for example, to have the group review the rate of accidents that are not related to machinery. Then members must choose whether to modify their behavior. Here the question is, "Should I take a different action than I did before?" For instance, the executive may decide that solutions for both machinery and nonmachinery accidents should be developed.

So far this summary may lead you to believe that organizations move from one process of organizing to another in lockstep fashion: enactment, selection, retention, choice. Such is not the case. Individual subgroups in the organization are continually working on activities in all these processes for different aspects of the environment. Although certain segments of the organization may specialize in one or more of the organizing processes, nearly everybody engages in each part at one time or another.

Behavior cycles are sets of interlocked behaviors that enable the group to come to an understanding about which meanings should be included and which rejected. Thus, the safety meeting called by the executive would enable interested individuals to discuss the safety problem and decide how to proceed. Behavior cycles are a natural part of each of the three processes of organizing.

Within a behavior cycle, members' actions are governed by *assembly rules* that guide the choice of routines used to accomplish the process being conducted (enactment, selection, or retention). Rules are sets of criteria on which organizers decide what to do to reduce equivocality. The question answered by assembly rules is this: Out of all possible behavior cycles in this organization, which will we use now? For example, in the selection process the executive might invoke the assembly rule that "two heads are better than one" and on this basis call a meeting of plant engineers.

Now we have completed the basic elements of Weick's model. They are environment, equivocality, enactment, selection, retention, choice points, behavior cycles, and assembly rules, all of which contribute to the reduction of equivocality. Weick envisions these elements working together in a system, each element related to the others.

Weick's most significant contribution is the idea that organizations are made in a process of interaction between persons. This idea has been expanded by James Taylor and his colleagues in the following theory.

The Role of Conversation

As does Weick, James Taylor and his colleagues see organizing as a process of interaction.[31] As a system, the organization has a way of structuring and defining itself coherently, and this process depends on the mutual processes of conversation and interpretation. The process begins when members interact and come to interpret, or understand, what they are doing in certain ways.

This is a circular process, with interaction and interpretation each entailing the other. Taylor refers to the interaction as *conversation* and the interpretation as *text*. *Conversation* is the action itself, or how participants behave toward one another—what words they use, their demeanor, their gestures. *Text* is what is said—the content and ideas. Think of it this way: When you are talking to another person, the two of you behave in a variety of ways, back and forth, but these behaviors mean something; they have content, purpose, and effect. When you are concentrating on what is happening, you are focusing on the conversation; when you are concentrating on what is being said, you are focusing on text. Text is not the physical structure of the

interaction itself but the underlying meanings attributed by the participants.

But these two—conversation and text—cannot really be separated. The conversation is understood in terms of the text, and the text is understood in terms of the conversation. This is a process the authors call *double translation*. Here's how it works: First, behavior is translated into meaning. The language and gestures used determine what is being said. This is the first translation—from text to conversation. At the same time, however, you assign meaning to the behavior, you bracket it, or you focus on connections and make decisions about what the behavior should stand for. This is the second translation—from conversation to text. These two translations are happening simultaneously and are closely tied to each other.

Our constant interpretations of conversations give form and life to the organization. Let's say that you are a firefighter and work about forty hours a week for the city fire department. What do you do every day? You talk, give and take directions, maintain the station and equipment, give fire permits, visit schools, respond to emergency calls, and engage in many other often mundane activities. Each of these activities is done in a series of conversations, but the fire department as an organization is more than just a bunch of actions. Something results from all of this that defines and structures the organization itself. Something bigger is happening.

We turn a cluster of conversations into an organization by putting conversations together into larger units and interpreting these as something bigger than any one conversation. As a firefighter, you would speak of the fire department as if it were a thing; you give it life. But this does not happen in one fell swoop. It happens by distancing your interpretations from the initial act. This *distanciation* occurs in various *degrees of separation*, each broadening your perspective further and further from the original action of a conversation.

Specifically, Taylor and his colleagues refer to six degrees of separation. The first is when actions are interpreted as a text. Someone walks in the door and asks for a fire permit, and you un-

31   James R. Taylor, Francois Cooren, Nicole Giroux, and Daniel Robichaud, "The Communicational Basis of Organization: Between the Conversation and the Text," *Communication Theory* 6 (1996): 1–39. See also, James R. Taylor, "Shifting from a Heteronomous to an Autonomous Worldview of Organizational Communication: Communication Theory on the Cusp," *Communication Theory* 5 (1995): 1–35; James R. Taylor, *Rethinking the Theory of Organizational Communication: How to Read an Organization* (Norwood, NJ: Ablex, 1993).

derstand this as a request. The second degree of separation happens when we represent a sequence of events as a narrative or episode. You come to see the citizen's request as part of a larger fire-permit process that involves coming to the station, filling out a form, processing the form, typing up the permit, and giving it to the citizen. The third degree of separation happens when the episode gets recorded in some way. The fire-permit process is written on an instruction sheet or poster.

The fourth degree of separation happens when the organization begins to develop a special language and specialized media for handling the permit process. At fire administrators' conventions, presentations are made on the permit process using a special technical jargon far removed from the actual interaction that occurs when a citizen actually comes to get a permit.

The fifth degree of separation happens when the organization creates a physical structure associated with this type of conversation. In a large city, for example, citizens might come to a special permit office in a centralized location; permits might be stored on computer disk; and special forms might be developed. Finally, the sixth degree of separation is publication and dissemination of information about the process. For example, the local TV station might run a public service announcement on how to get a fire permit.

The initial conversation and text, asking for a fire permit, is the basis for this entire strand, but this act is understood in broader and broader ways. When you take all of the types of conversation that occur in a fire department and connect them, you develop a coherent way of understanding what a fire department is as an organization, and you can begin to talk about it as a thing, even though it is really the outcome of a complex set of conversations and texts.

If you observe people actually communicating and see their patterns of interaction and their relationships, you are noticing the *surface structure* of the organization—the daily activities of the members. But these are not random or unconnected interactions. Rather, they are generated from the *deep structure* of the organization.

The deep structure is like a grammar or structural arrangement that gives the organization its character and guides its actions. This deep structure is a complex network of rules about the patterns of interaction that are permissible in the organization, obligations of members, and expected duties and responsibilities. It is a moral order, or a sense of how things should be done.

There is a recursive relationship between the deep structure and the actual conversations of an organization. The deep structure is made by people communicating with one another, and that deep structure in turn guides the communication itself. This is a circle of influence, a reciprocal back and forth between the deep structure and the surface structure. At times this relationship is highly stable, which makes organizational life very predictable. Other times it is less stable, as the texts and conversations of the organization go through changes.

Of course all of this is not rationally planned by some master designer. Indeed, it happens incrementally and over time as real people interact with one another in their daily organizational lives. The structures that are created in the process are largely unintended, and we look more closely at how this happens in the following section.

Structuration in Organizations

In Chapter 13 we examined the theory of structuration and Scott Poole and his colleagues' application of this theory to group decision making. These researchers have also extended their theory into organizational communication.[32]

---

32 Marshall Scott Poole and Robert D. McPhee, "A Structurational Analysis of Organizational Climate," in *Communication and Organizations: An Interpretive Approach,* eds. L. L. Putnam and M. E. Pacanowsky (Beverly Hills, CA: Sage, 1983), pp. 195–220; Marshall Scott Poole, "Communication and Organizational Climates: Review, Critique, and a New Perspective," in *Organizational Communication: Traditional Themes and New Directions,* eds. R. D. McPhee and P. K. Tompkins (Beverly Hills, CA: Sage, 1985), pp. 79–108; Robert D. McPhee, "Formal Structure and Organizational Communication," in *Organizational Communication: Traditional Themes and New Directions,* eds. R. D. McPhee and P. K. Tompkins (Beverly Hills, CA: Sage, 1985), pp. 149–178. For additional commentary on structuration theory, see Stephen P. Banks and Patricia Riley, "Structuration Theory as an Ontology for Communication Research," *Communication Yearbook 16,* ed. Stanley A. Deetz (Newbury Park, CA: Sage, 1993), pp. 167–196.

Recall that the theory of structuration, attributable to sociologist Anthony Giddens, deals with the ways actions bring about unintended consequences, which in turn form social systems that affect future actions. The circle of actions and consequences is the mechanism by which sociocultural resources are produced and reproduced in all social systems.[33]

Organizations, like any other social structure, are produced through actions and interactions among individuals. As people rely on organizational resources such as roles, norms, and rules to guide their actions, they not only accomplish individual and organizational goals but also reproduce the organizational system itself, or what Weick calls enactment. Scott Poole and Robert McPhee have applied this idea to two aspects of organizational communication—structure and climate.

In an essay on the subject, McPhee recognizes the importance of organizational structure: "I would say that structure is a defining characteristic of an organization—it is what brings about or makes possible that quality of atmosphere, that sustained, routine purposiveness that distinguishes work in an organization from activities in a group, a mob, a society, and so forth."[34] Organizational structure provides the form necessary to accomplish a variety of functions. Structure is both a manifestation and a product of communication in the organization.

The formal structure of an organization as announced in employee manuals, organizational charts, and policies is really two types of communication. First, it is an indirect way of telling employees about the organization—its values, procedures, and methods. Second, it is a form of metacommunication (Chapter 12) in which the organization addresses its own communication patterns directly.

Organizational structure is created when individuals communicate with others in three metaphorical "sites," or *centers of structuration*.[35] The first includes all those episodes of organizational life in which people make decisions and choices that limit what can happen within the organization. This is the site of *conception*. A university's decision to establish a new college of creative arts, for example, will affect the lines of communication within the organization.

The second site of organizational structuration is the formal codification and announcement of decisions and choices, the site of *implementation*. Once the decision is made to establish the new college, the provost may send out a formal memorandum to the faculty and staff announcing the change. That formal announcement itself will be instrumental in shaping the structure of the organization in the future.

Finally, structuration occurs as organizational members act in accordance with the organizational decisions, which is the site of *reception*. To continue the example, after the decision is made to establish a college of arts, a dean will be recruited, certain department heads will meet with the new dean, and faculty lines of communication will change.

Although anyone in an organization may from time to time participate in communication at any or all three sites, structuration tends to be specialized. Top management usually is involved in conceptual communication, various staff personnel perform the job of implementation, and the general workforce itself participates in reception.

The communication activities at these three sites are often difficult and conflict laden. Indeed, rarely is a new college established at a university without considerable disagreement and resistance at all three stages, which is the case with major changes in any kind of organization. The communication patterns at the three sites may be complex and time-consuming, and the outcome is very much affected by the skill of the people involved.

The second area in which Poole and McPhee have applied structurational thinking is organizational climate,[36] which is one of the most

33   Anthony Giddens, *Central Problems in Social Theory* (Berkeley: University of California Press, 1979); *Profiles and Critiques in Social Theory* (Berkeley: University of California Press, 1982).
34   McPhee, "Formal Structure," p. 150.
35   Robert D. McPhee, "Organizational Communication: A Structurational Exemplar," in *Rethinking Communication: Paradigm Exemplars*, eds. Brenda Dervin, Lawrence Grossberg, Barbara J. O'Keefe, and Ellen Wartella (Beverly Hills, CA: Sage, 1989), pp. 199–212.
36   Poole, "Communication and Organizational Climates"; Poole and McPhee, "Structurational Analysis."

heavily researched topics in organizational communication.[37] Traditionally, climate has been viewed as one of the key variables affecting communication and the subsequent productivity and satisfaction of employees. For Poole and McPhee, climate is the general collective description of an organization or a part of the organization that shapes members' expectations and feelings and therefore the organization's performance. Climates are enacted by the members of the organization as they go through their daily activities, and any organization may actually have a variety of climates for different groups of people.

Poole and McPhee define climate structurationally as "a collective attitude, continually produced and reproduced by members' interaction."[38] In other words, a climate is not an objective "variable" that affects the organization, nor is it an individual's perception of the organization. Rather, climate arises out of the interaction among those who affiliate with the organization. Climate is a product of structuration: It is both a medium and an outcome of interaction.[39]

Poole sees climate as a hierarchy of three strata. The first is a set of basic terms that members use to define and describe the organization, the *concept pool.* The second is a basic, highly abstract shared conception of the atmosphere of the organization, or *kernal climate.* Finally, the groups' translations of the kernel climate into more concrete terms affecting their particular part of an organization constitutes the third element, the *particular climate.* The kernel climate permeates the entire organization, but particular climates may vary from one segment of the organization to another.

The three layers in the hierarchy are related in a linear way: (1) The concepts create an understanding of what is going on in the organization; (2) from these basic understandings, the kernel climate arises; then (3) subgroups translate these general principles into specific elements of climate that in turn affect the thinking, feeling, and behavior of the individuals.

An example of this process is found in a study of a consulting firm.[40] The firm consisted of two generations of employees—a group that had been with the firm a relatively long time and a

group of more recent employees. Though the two groups shared a common set of concepts, they seemed to experience different climates.

From these core concepts, four key elements of a kernel climate emerged in this organization:

1. "The firm has a rigid formal structure that is often constraining."
2. "Contribution to profits is very important."
3. "Creative work is valued over routine work."
4. "Commitment of employees is important."

These four elements of the kernel climate were translated differently into the particular climates of the two groups.

The first-generation employees believed that "pressure is manageable, and that there is room for growth." The second-generation employees, however, believed that "pressure hinders performance and that there is little room for growth." Figure 14.4 illustrates this example.[41]

How do the elements of climate develop in an organization? We know already from a structurational perspective that the climate is produced by the practices of organizational members; and, in turn, climate affects and constrains those practices. Thus, climate is not static but constantly in the process of development. Three interacting factors enter into this developmental process.

The first is the *structure of the organization* itself. Because structure limits the kinds of interactions and practices that can be engaged in, it limits the kind of climate that can result from these interactions and practices. For example, if the organization is highly segmented with strong differentiation among employees and departments, individuals will have a limited pool of coworkers with whom they can communicate,

---

37   This work is summarized in Poole, "Communication and Organizational Climates," pp. 79–97.
38   Poole and McPhee, "Structurational Analysis," p. 213.
39   For a contrast of the structurational approach to climate with traditional approaches, see Poole and McPhee, "Structurational Analysis."
40   This model of climate is based on a reinterpretation of a case study by H. Johnson in "A New Conceptualization of Source of Organizational Climate," *Administrative Science Quarterly* 3 (1976): 275–292.
41   Poole, "Communication and Organizational Climates," p. 98.

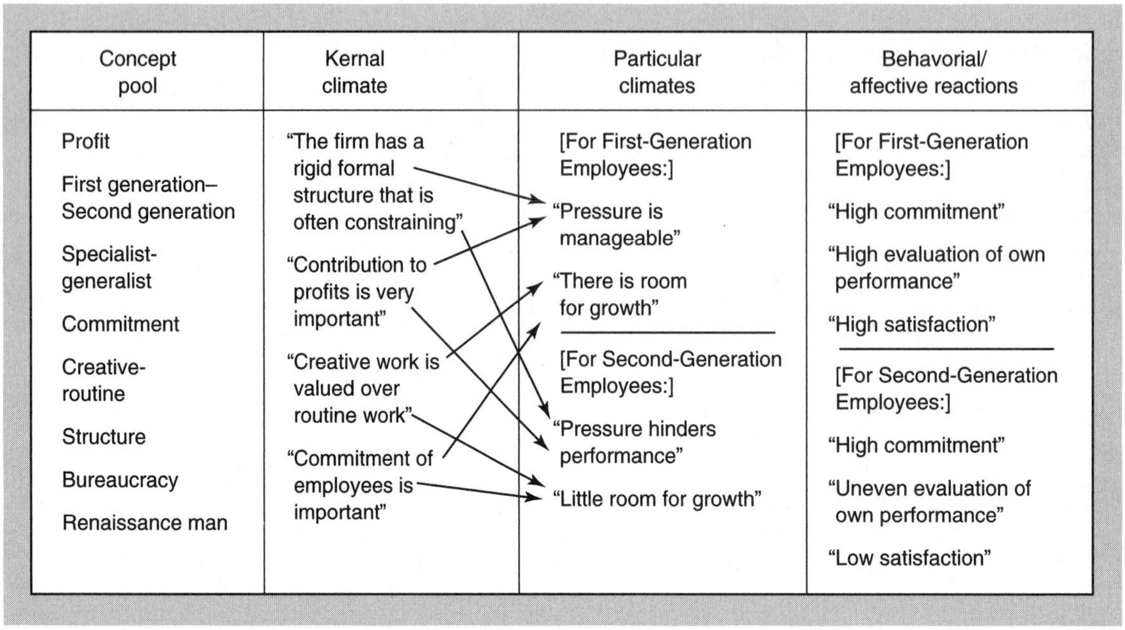

Concept pool	Kernal climate	Particular climates	Behavorial/ affective reactions
Profit	"The firm has a rigid formal structure that is often constraining"	[For First-Generation Employees:]	[For First-Generation Employees:]
First generation– Second generation		"Pressure is manageable"	"High commitment"
Specialist- generalist	"Contribution to profits is very important"	"There is room for growth"	"High evaluation of own performance"
Commitment			"High satisfaction"
Creative- routine	"Creative work is valued over routine work"	[For Second-Generation Employees:]	[For Second-Generation Employees:]
Structure		"Pressure hinders performance"	"High commitment"
Bureaucracy	"Commitment of employees is important"	"Little room for growth"	"Uneven evaluation of own performance"
Renaissance man			"Low satisfaction"

FIGURE 14.4

Schematic of Climate Structure

which increases the chance of a "restrained" climate.

The second factor affecting climate is various *climate-producing apparatuses*, or mechanisms designed to affect employee perceptions and performance, such as newsletters, training programs, and the like.

The third factor is *member characteristics*, their skills and knowledge. For example, if employees are sufficiently intelligent and reflective, they may challenge existing authority and "see through" apparatuses. Member characteristics also include the degree of agreement or coordination within work groups.

● THE CULTURAL TRADITION

The cultural tradition in organizational studies emphasizes the ways people construct an organizational reality. As the study of an organization's

way of life, this approach looks at the meanings and values of the members. It examines the way individuals use stories, rituals, symbols, and other types of activity to produce and reproduce a set of understandings.[42]

John Van Maanen and Stephen Barley outline four "domains" of organizational culture.[43] The first domain, the *ecological context*, is the physical world, including the location, the time and history, and the social context within which the organization operates. The second domain of culture consists of networks, or *differential interaction*. Then there are the common ways of interpreting events, or *collective understanding*. It is the "content" of the culture—its ideas, ideals, values,

---

42   See James A. Anderson (ed.), *Communication Yearbook 11* (Newbury Park, CA: Sage, 1988), pp. 310–405; Michael Pacanowsky, "Creating and Narrating Organizational Realities," in *Rethinking Communication: Paradigm Exemplars*, eds. Brenda Dervin, Lawrence Grossberg, Barbara J. O'Keefe, and Ellen Wartella (Newbury Park, CA: Sage, 1989), pp. 250–257.
43   John Van Maanen and Stephen R. Barley, "Cultural Organization: Fragments of a Theory," in *Organizational Culture*, eds. P. J. Frost and others (Beverly Hills, CA: Sage, 1985), pp. 31–54.

and practices. Finally, there are the practices or actions of individuals, which constitutes the *individual* domain.

Few large organizations comprise a single culture. In most cases, subcultures identified with particular groups will emerge. You can imagine an organization as a set of Venn diagrams or overlapping cultural circles.

We encountered the cultural tradition in organizational studies in Chapter 10, where we looked at Michael Pacanowsky and Nick O'Donnell-Trujillo's interpretive theory, which examines the ways the members of an organization create and perpetuate an understanding of their experience through stories, rituals, symbols, and other means.[44] For more information about organizational cultures, you may want to refer back to that chapter.

The cultural traditions in organizational communication theory mark an important shift in this field, a shift from functionalism to interpretation, from the assumption that the organization has preexisting elements that act on one another in predictable ways to the assumption that it is a constantly changing set of meanings constructed through communication.

This distinction is not limited to organizational communication but is now seen in virtually every area of the field. It was discussed in some detail earlier in the book, especially in Chapters 1, 9, and 10. Dennis Mumby believes that the increasing popularity of the interpretive approach is not trivial:

> Beginning roughly in the 70s, researchers have become increasingly concerned with examining the various ways in which communication functions dynamically, processually, and constitutively to create the collective meaning systems to which we give the name "organization." . . . This move toward a more "meaning-centered" approach to organizations has been successful in problematizing many of the terms associated with mainstream functionalist organizational research—terms such as hierarchy, message, effectiveness, and most importantly, the term "organization" itself. In effect, the shift to interpretive theory and research has created a fruitful and productive "crisis of representation" . . . in organizational

communication studies. This crisis has resulted in fundamental challenges.[45]

Mumby identifies two schools of thought in this tradition. The first, "a descriptive hermeneutic," depicts the process by which communication creates organization and presents useful interpretations of organizational events. Another branch of this work is the "hermeneutic of suspicion," in which a more critical approach is taken. Consistent with the critical theories discussed in Chapter 11, this version of hermeneutics looks at the organization as a site of domination, a place where ideology is taught and the hegemony of interests promoted.

The critical tradition in organizational communication is growing in popularity and visibility. Dennis Mumby shows that organizational cultures are not neutral, spontaneous creations but are products of ideology that promote the interests of certain groups over those of others.[46] Cultures are political, or power laden, and the language and other symbols used within the organization are products of dominant cultures and reinforce dominant interests.

Stanley Deetz adds to this analysis by writing that in contemporary democracies, the public voice is being replaced by corporate interests that dominate virtually all other aspects of society, and our lives are determined in large measure by the decisions made in the interest of managing corporate organizations, a movement called "managerialism."[47]

---

44   Michael E. Pacanowsky and Nick O'Donnell-Trujillo, "Communication and Organizational Cultures," *Western Journal of Speech Communication* 46 (1982): 115–130. See also Michael E. Pacanowsky and Nick O'Donnell-Trujillo, "Organizational Communication as Cultural Performance," *Communication Monographs* 50 (1983): 126–147.
45   Dennis K. Mumby, "Critical Organizational Communication Studies: The Next 10 Years," *Communication Monographs* 60 (1993): 18–25.
46   Dennis K. Mumby, *Communication and Power in Organizations: Discourse, Ideology, and Domination* (Norwood, NJ: Ablex, 1988).
47   Stanley Deetz, *Democracy in an Age of Corporate Colonization: Developments in Communication and the Politics of Everyday Life* (Albany: SUNY Press, 1992). See also Mats Alvesson and Stanley Deetz, "Critical Theory and Postmodernism Approaches to Organization Studies," in *Handbook of Organizational Studies*, eds. S. Clegg, C. Harding, and W. Nord (London: Sage, 1996), pp. 173–202.

The critical tradition is one of the newer additions to the growing literature on organization, and it is important. Because we devote all of Chapter 11 to critical theories, we will not go into it in more detail here.

◖ COMMENTARY AND CRITIQUE

We learn from the theories in this chapter that organizations are created through communication as people interact to accomplish their individual and joint goals. The process of communication also results in a variety of structural outcomes such as authority relations, roles, communication networks, and climate. All these structural elements are results of the interaction among individuals and groups within the organization, and all in turn affect future interactions within the organization.

The theme of networks was chosen to organize the material in this chapter because this term captures the interactive nature of organizational structure and function. Network theory is based on individual interactions among people, which build up into a macrostructure. The idea of multiple networks accommodates most of the ideas presented in this chapter, including bureaucracy, control, managerial style, culture, and structuration.

In this chapter we have looked at three traditions related to organizational networks—the positional, the relational, and the cultural. Strictly positional theories express a common structuralist mythology, but for the communication scholar, they omit a great deal. Classical theories such as Weber's reflect and may have contributed to a powerful cultural norm about how organizing should occur. These theories, however, do not provide a sense of how the interaction among members results in meaningful outcome. Indeed, one contribution of communication theory has been to provide additional insights into the importance of communication in organizations.

Likert's theory is somewhat better than earlier theories in showing the importance of communication, but even this theory fails to recognize the pervasiveness of communication as the very means by which organizing occurs. The theory is appealing because of its formalistic explanatory style. This is a strictly linear theory, however, which leaves little to the imagination of individuals other than those who establish the managerial system of the company.

Likert's theory is part of the human relations movement. The movement helped practitioners and scholars understand that people have needs and values related to organizational functioning and that communication is an important aspect of organizational life. Likert's version, like several others, though, is simplistic in its linear, causal reasoning.

Human relations was criticized almost from its beginning.[48] Its problems are primarily attributable to its extreme position and simplistic view that high morale improves productivity. The correlations that are claimed to exist between human relations factors and organizational effectiveness have, for the most part, failed the test of empirical study. We reviewed one study in which a positive correlation was found between managerial style and satisfaction, but this study does not address productivity. In many cases the correlations have not been found in research, and where they do appear, serious methodological objections have been raised.

In some ways what the human relations movement was trying to do has been more successfully accomplished by the organizational culture movement—namely to recognize and characterize the human needs within the organization. Indeed, apart from achieving task-oriented goals, organizations are also human cultures, rich with tradition, shared meaning, and ritual. What people do in organizations creates and reflects the underlying culture of the organization.

---

48   For a comprehensive critique, see Perrow, *Complex Organizations*.

The cultural approach to organizational theory is a major advance. It refocuses our attention on a set of processes that are not examined carefully in traditional management-oriented, variable-analytical studies. Traditionally, management is seen as a rational process of manipulating "things" for the benefit of the organization. The culture approach shows us that this is only partly true. In fact, a culture that is out of the conscious control of management is a major part of what characterizes an organization. The cultural approach refutes the idea that managers can somehow manipulate "objects" (like materials and machines) that are independent from the organization itself. The objects are only known through the meanings of the organizational culture, and those meanings will change from one organization, or even suborganization, to another. Organizations are not adapted to environments; rather, organizations in a real way create their own environments based on shared conceptions and interpretations.

The downside to this observation is that the empirically minded manager may think of culture as just another variable to be manipulated and that the culture can be managed.[49] This idea can lead to the negative consequence of attempted ideological control. The answer to this criticism is that all forms of management exert some kind of ideological control. Let us therefore create the most humane and productive cultures possible.

Another disadvantage of the culture approach, which is generally true of many interpretive theories of communication, is that if you assume that the social reality of an organization comes from interactions among members of the organization and that organizational cultures thereby differ, you put yourself into the very difficult theoretical position of being unable to make generalizations or predictions about organizational life. Each organization must be studied independently, and generalizations become difficult.

The answer, of course, is standard: Theories should not attempt to be predictive but should capture general categories of action, which we expect to be played out differently in various organizations. Middle-range theories like that of Pacanowsky and O'Donnell-Trujillo enable us to observe organizations with a sensitivity to their rich individuality.

Certain generalizations actually are being made within the cultural tradition, however, especially the critical version. Here theorists write that organizational cultures reflect and create power structures of domination. Although not as well developed in this field as in media studies, critical approaches to organizational communication do appear to be on the rise. Mumby alerts us to the need to address three issues in critical studies.[50] First, because the act of research is itself political, the researcher must become more aware of his or her own power over those studied and the ways research studies shape organizational relations. Second, organizational communication scholars must look at how the field itself has constructed a view of organizations that promotes certain interests over others. Finally, organizational communication has been seemingly oblivious to developments in feminist theory and should incorporate feminist insights into the critique of organization.[51]

In contrast, noncritical approaches to organizational communication examine power without drawing conclusions about hegemony. Unobtrusive control theory is an example. Although it is well integrated with important standard theories of organizational decision making, it still advances those ideas. In addition, it brings insights from rhetoric into a field that badly needs outside perspectives. This advantage not only provides significant new perspectives for organizational theory but also helps to usefully combine

49   A discussion of this possibility is presented by Sonja A. Sackmann, "Managing Organizational Culture: Dreams and Possibilities," in *Communication Yearbook 13*, ed. James Anderson (Newbury Park, CA: Sage, 1990), pp. 114–148.
50   Mumby, "Critical."
51   See, for example, Judi Marshall, "Viewing Organizational Communication from a Feminist Perspective: A Critique and Some Offerings," in *Communication Yearbook 16*, ed. Stanley Deetz (Newbury Park, CA: Sage, 1993), pp. 122–143.

divergent areas of the communication field. The theory is pragmatically helpful, while enabling interpreters and critics to uncover implicit organizational values and premises not normally available for inspection. It thereby paves the way for a necessary and significant critique of organizational communication. The theory seems to have much heuristic value and, in fact, has already generated much research.[52]

The works of Weick and Giddens are consistent with each other in capturing the structurational character of interaction. In one way these theories bring us back full circle to networks as the essence of organizing. When people communicate they establish expectations that give shape to future interactions, and as we have seen repeatedly in this chapter, this structuration process is the heart of all organizing.

---

52   Tompkins and Cheney summarize the research on the theory in "Communication and Unobtrusive Control," pp. 198–203. See also Bullis and Tompkins, "The Forest Ranger."

CHAPTER **15**

COMMUNICATION AND MEDIA

We are living in what Marshall McLuhan calls the "global village." Modern communication media make it possible for millions of people throughout the world to be in touch with nearly any spot on the globe. George Gerbner points to the importance of the media in society:

> This broad "public-making" significance of mass media of communications—the ability to create publics, define issues, provide common terms of reference, and thus to allocate attention and power—has evoked a large number of theoretical contributions.[1]

Mass communication is the process whereby media organizations produce and transmit messages to large publics and the process by which those messages are sought, used, understood, and influenced by audiences.

Central to any study of mass communication are the media.[2] Media organizations distribute messages that affect and reflect the cultures of society, and they provide information simultaneously to large heterogeneous audiences, making media part of society's institutional forces.

"Media," of course, imply "mediation" because they come between the audience and the world. Denis McQuail suggests several metaphors to capture this idea: Media are *windows* that enable us to see beyond our immediate surroundings, *interpreters* that help us make sense of experience, *platforms* or *carriers* that convey information, *interactive communication* that includes audience feedback, *signposts* that provide us with instructions and directions, *filters* that screen out parts of experience and focus on others, *mirrors* that reflect ourselves back to us, and *barriers* that block the truth.[3] Joshua Meyrowitz adds three

1   George Gerbner, "Mass Media and Human Communication Theory," in *Human Communication Theory,* ed. F. E. X. Dance (New York: Holt, Rinehart & Winston, 1967), p. 45.
2   For a recent overview and history of mass communication theory, see Bradley S. Greenberg and Michael B. Salwen, "Mass Communication Theory and Research: Concepts and Models," in *An Integrated Approach to Communication Theory and Research,* eds. Michael B. Salwen and Don W. Stacks (Mahwah, NJ: Erlbaum, 1996), pp. 63–78. Definitions of *mass communication* are discussed in Sandra J. Ball-Rokeach and Muriel G. Cantor (eds.), *Media, Audience, and Social Structure* (Beverly Hills, CA: Sage, 1986), pp. 10–11; McQuail, *Mass Communication,* pp. 29–47.
3   Denis McQuail, *Mass Communication Theory: An Introduction* (London: Sage, 1987), pp. 52–53.

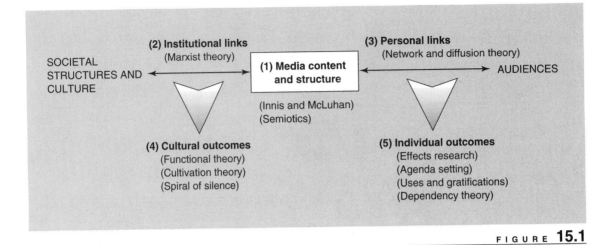

FIGURE **15.1**

An Organizing Model

additional metaphors—media as *conduits*, media as *languages*, and media as *environments*.[4] What are media, then? There is no single or simple definition.

⬤ AN ORGANIZING MODEL

Media scholars recognize two faces of mass communication.[5] One face looks from the media to the larger society and its institutions. Theorists interested in the media–society link are concerned with the ways media are embedded in society and the mutual influence between larger social structures and the media. This is the *macro* side of mass communication theory.

The second face looks toward people, as groups and individuals. This face reflects the link between the media and audiences. Theorists interested in the media–audience link focus on group and individual effects and outcomes of the media transaction. This is the *micro* side of mass communication theory.[6]

Figure 15.1 illustrates the two faces of mass communication. The model may imply that these two sides are different things, but in truth they are the same thing looked at from different perspectives. The relationship between media and institutions is possible only through the media's transaction with audiences, and the audience-media relationship is impossible to separate from the institutions of the society in which those audiences reside. Thus, the model is not a map of the mass communication process but depicts the areas of media research and theory.

The chapter is divided into five sections corresponding to the parts of the model: (1) media content and structure, (2) the media-institution link, (3) the media–audience link, (4) cultural outcomes, and (5) individual outcomes.

---

4   Joshua Meyrowitz, "Images of Media: Hidden Ferment—and Harmony—in the Field," *Journal of Communication* 43 (1993): 55–67.
5   For an excellent exploration of the links between the media and larger sociocultural structures and smaller personal and individual effects, see Karl Erik Rosengren, "Culture, Media, and Society: Agency and Structure, Continuity and Change," in *Media Effects and Beyond: Culture, Socializations, and Lifestyles,* ed. Karl Erik Rosengren (London: Routledge, 1994), pp. 3–28. See also, Veikko Pietilä, "Perspectives on Our Past: Charting the Histories of Mass Communication Studies," *Critical Studies in Mass Communication* 11 (1994): 346–361.
6   This conceptualization is adapted from a discussion of mass communication theory by McQuail, *Mass Communication Theory: An Introduction* (London: Sage, 1984), pp. 53–57.

◐ MEDIA CONTENT AND STRUCTURE

Certain theories have emphasized intrinsic structural properties of media and media messages. Of particular concern here is the "sending" side of the mass communication process, or what media producers actually produce. A useful term for this general process is *encoding*.[7] Here, we will sample two quite different theories of media content and structure.

Innis and McLuhan

Marshall McLuhan is a well-known figure in the study of popular culture, receiving attention because of his interesting and bizarre style and his startling and thought-provoking ideas. Whether one agrees with him or not, McLuhan's ideas have received too much publicity to be ignored.[8]

McLuhan's early ideas on the media are based on the work of his mentor Harold Adams Innis.[9] Innis and McLuhan treat communication media as the essence of civilization, and both see history as directed by the predominant media of each age.

Innis sees communication media as extensions of the human mind and believes that the primary interest of any historical period is a kind of bias resulting from the predominant media in use. In other words, what happens and what seems significant in a historical period are determined by the media. Heavy media such as parchment, clay, or stone are lasting and therefore *time binding*. Because they facilitate communication from one generation to another, these media are biased toward tradition. In contrast, *space-binding* media such as paper are light and easy to transport, so they facilitate communication from one location to another, fostering empire building, large bureaucracy, and the military.

Speech as a medium, because it is produced one sound at a time, encourages people to organize their experience chronologically. Speech also requires knowledge and tradition and therefore supports community and relationship. Written media, which are spatially arranged, produce a different kind of culture. The space-binding effect of writing produces interests in political authority and the growth of empires across the land.

McLuhan's most basic hypothesis is that people adapt to their environment through a certain balance or ratio of the senses, and the primary medium of the age brings out a particular sense ratio, thereby affecting perception.[10] McLuhan sees every medium as an extension of some human faculty, exaggerating the sense. "The wheel . . . is an extension of the foot. The book is an extension of the eye. . . . Clothing, an extension of the skin. . . . Electric circuitry, an extension of the central nervous system."[11]

Before printing was invented, tribal people were primarily hearing-oriented communicators, emotionally and interpersonally close. For the tribal person, "hearing was believing." But the invention of the printing press changed all that. The Gutenberg age brought a new sense ratio into being, in which sight predominated. The rise of print in Western culture forced people into a linear, logical, and categorical kind of perception. For McLuhan, the use of the alphabet "fostered

---

7   An excellent summary of the vast amount of work in this area is provided by David Barker and Bernard M. Timberg, "Encounters with the Television Image: Thirty Years of Encoding Research," in *Communication Yearbook 15*, ed. Stanley Deetz (Newbury Park, CA: Sage, 1992), pp. 209–238.
8   McLuhan's best-known works are *The Gutenberg Galaxy: The Making of Typographic Man* (Toronto: University of Toronto Press, 1962); *The Mechanical Bride* (New York: Vanguard, 1951); *Understanding Media* (New York: McGraw-Hill, 1964); Marshall McLuhan and Quentin Fiore, *The Medium Is the Massage* (New York: Bantam, 1967). Other works by McLuhan are listed in the Bibliography. I have relied on the synthesis of Bruce Gronbeck, "McLuhan as Rhetorical Theorist," *Journal of Communication* 31 (1981): 117–128.
9   J. W. Carey, "Harold Adams Innis and Marshall McLuhan," *Antioch Review* 27 (1967): 5–39. Innis's works include *The Bias of Communication* (Toronto: University of Toronto Press, 1951); *Empire and Communications,* 2nd ed. (Toronto: University of Toronto Press, 1972).
10   Good brief summaries of McLuhan's theory can be found in the following: Kenneth Boulding, "The Medium Is the Massage," in *McLuhan: Hot and Cool*, ed. G. E. Stearn (New York: Dial, 1967), pp. 56–64; Tom Wolfe, "The New Life Out There," in *McLuhan: Hot and Cool*, ed. G. E. Stearn (New York: Dial, 1967), pp. 34–56; Carey, "Innis and McLuhan."
11   McLuhan and Fiore, *Massage.*

and encouraged the habit of perceiving all environment in visual and spatial terms—particularly in terms of a space and of a time that are uniform,

c,o,n,t,i,n,u,o,u,s

and

c-o-n-n-e-c-t-e-d."[12]

We have entered a new age, according to McLuhan. Electronic technology has brought back an aural, or hearing, predominance. The Gutenberg technology created an explosion in society, separating and segmenting individual from individual, but the electronic age has created an implosion, bringing the world back together in a "global village." As a result, "it is forcing us to reconsider and reevaluate practically every thought, every action, and every institution formerly taken for granted."[13] McLuhan describes this impact:

> Electric circuitry profoundly involves men with one another. Information pours upon us, instantaneously and continuously. As soon as information is acquired, it is very rapidly replaced by still newer information. Our electrically configured world has forced us to move from the habit of data classification to the mode of pattern recognition. We can no longer build serially, block-by-block, step-by-step, because instant communication insures that all factors of the environment and of experience coexist in a state of active interplay.[14]

If McLuhan had lived long enough, what would he have said about the Internet?

McLuhan is perhaps best known for his saying "The medium is the message."[15] This curious and thought-provoking catchphrase highlights the general influence that a medium has apart from its content. Tom Wolfe puts the matter this way: "It doesn't matter if the networks show twenty hours a day of sadistic cowboys caving in people's teeth or twenty hours of Pablo Casals droning away on his cello in a pure-culture white Spanish drawing room. It doesn't matter about the content."[16] And here, of course, McLuhan parts company from most contemporary mass communication researchers, who believe that the content matters a great deal.

But McLuhan maintains that what really makes a difference in people's lives is the predominant media, not content, of the period: "They are so pervasive in their personal, political, economic, aesthetic, psychological, moral, ethical, and social consequences that they leave no part of us untouched, unaffected, unaltered."[17]

In the 1970s McLuhan's teachings changed somewhat. In his earlier works, he strongly implies that the form of media in society affects or causes certain modes of perception on the part of society's members. In his later teaching, he seems less certain of this causal link. Instead, McLuhan says that media resonate with or reflect the perceptual categories of individuals. Instead of envisioning a causal link between media and personal perception, he later sees a simultaneous outpouring of certain kinds of thought on the part of the media and the person. Media forms do not cause but bring out modes of thought that are already present in the individual. The lack of consistency between the individual's perceptual categories and the depictions of the media creates stress in society.

Semiotics

We turn now to a very different theory of media structure. Whereas McLuhan teaches that the media forms themselves create the primary impact of mass communication, semiotics makes a sharp separation between a medium and its content. For the semiotician, content matters a great deal, and content depends on the reading given to it by the producer or consumer. Semiotics focuses on the ways producers create signs and the ways audiences understand those signs. True, different media make different types of signs possible, but it is this focus on signs *in the message* that distinguishes this area of study.

12 McLuhan and Fiore, *Massage.*
13 McLuhan and Fiore, *Massage.*
14 McLuhan and Fiore, *Massage.*
15 McLuhan, *Understanding Media,* p. 7.
16 Wolfe, "New Life," p. 19.
17 McLuhan and Fiore, *Massage.*

Semiotics was discussed in Chapter 4 as part of the general topic of language and coding. Recall that semiotics has a long history of development in the twentieth century.[18] In this chapter we rely on the synthesis of Donald Fry and Virginia Fry, who apply the ideas of semiotic theorists to the study of media.[19]

Semiotics is the study of signification, or the ways signs are used to interpret events. It is, therefore, a tool for analyzing the content of media messages. Fry and Fry organize their discussion into three major postulates. First, media messages can elicit numerous meanings, so that a text can be understood in a variety of ways. Media producers do intend to convey particular meanings in their works, but audiences may or may not assign the same meanings. Consider music videos as an example:

> A music video is useful to illustrate that a particular expression can be correlated with a number of contents to produce different significations. For a teenager, video may be taken as a statement against the constraints that passing through adolescence seems to carry or as an image of the rebellious individual spurning social convention. A media researcher may study the video as a vehicle for the transmission of violent images to an audience. An executive of a record company may view the same video as an effective promotional device that is having a positive impact on sales of records. . . . In a cultural sense, the music video expression signifies different meanings for each because it is coded by each with different content planes.[20]

At the same time, audience reaction is not random. Indeed, producers go to some effort to predict the reactions of the audience and to use signs that will shape those reactions. Commercials are an excellent example. Although audience interpretations will vary, the advertiser certainly aims to elicit a predominant meaning and a particular response. Still, producers cannot and do not always predict audience response, and there will almost always be segments of the audience that assign their own strange meanings to what they read, hear, and view.

Certain "postmodern" media artists go to extremes to avoid any single meaning. Madonna is an example of an artist who works to obliterate any one predominant reading by projecting a variety of possible readings in her work. Madonna's vocal and video images vary significantly from one video to another, and even single videos often permit contradictory readings.[21]

Denotation and connotation are central concepts in semiotics. *Denotation* refers to what a sign designates. Almost all literate consumers within the culture will understand the denotation of a sign. You know without puzzling over it what the Coke logo designates.

What makes interpretations vary is not denotation but *connotation,* or the feelings, judgments, and assessments that you make about the message content. Everybody knows what Coke refers to, but people will add all sorts of different connotative meanings to it. Whereas denotations are stable, connotations vary because they are based on inferences or extensions from the denotation. Media producers try not only to present a denotation but also to affect the subsequent connotation.

An example of denotation and connotation can be seen in Farrel Corcoran's semiotic analysis of the news reporting of the crash of Korean Airlines flight 007 in 1983.[22] KAL 007, a commercial airliner that entered Soviet airspace, was shot down by a Soviet fighter, and all aboard were killed. Corcoran analyzed the reports of this event from the three major American newsmagazines, *Time, Newsweek,* and *U.S. News and World Report.* Specifically, he was interested in the meanings attached to the event, the ways the

---

18   See, for example, Wendy Leeds-Hurwitz, *Semiotics and Communication: Signs, Codes, Cultures* (Hillsdale, NJ: Erlbaum, 1993).

19   Donald L. Fry and Virginia H. Fry, "A Semiotic Model for the Study of Mass Communication," in *Communication Yearbook 9,* ed. M. L. McLaughlin (Beverly Hills, CA: Sage, 1986), pp. 443–462. For additional exploration of this topic, see Klaus Bruhn Jensen, "When Is Meaning? Communication Theory, Pragmatism, and Mass Media Reception," in *Communication Yearbook 14,* ed. James A. Anderson (Newbury Park, CA: Sage, 1991), pp. 3–32.

20   Fry and Fry, "Semiotic," p. 446.

21   See, for example, Cathy Schwichtenberg (ed.), *The Madonna Connection: Representational Politics, Subcultural Identities, and Cultural Theory* (Boulder, CO: Westview, 1993).

22   Farrel Corcoran, "KAL 007 and the Evil Empire: Mediated Disaster and Forms of Rationalization," *Critical Studies in Mass Communication* 3 (1986): 297–316.

event was used by these magazines as a symbol. The author shows how these three magazines presented an amazingly similar interpretation of the disaster and how the overriding connotation was that the Soviet Union was an evil nation.

By using "perhaps the most vitriolic language in their history," these newsmagazines made a strong link between the airline incident and the entire Soviet system. This is an example of *metonymy,* or using a part of something to symbolize the whole. Russian stereotypes were used throughout the reporting to the effect that Russians are ignorant, drab, politically insensitive, tyrannical, and barbaric. In short, the incident was used as a "condensational symbol" for the polarization between the evil Soviet Union and the rest of the world.

The first of Fry and Fry's postulates, then, is that media messages can elicit numerous meanings. The second postulate is that media messages get their meaning by the associations that audience members make. Communication is made possible by a consensus of meaning, or what Peirce (Chapter 4) calls the "final interpretant." But this is only one meaning. The audience member may also have a personal feeling associated with the content (*emotional interpretant*), an associated action such as compliance (*energic interpretant*), or a rationalization as to why a certain action is reasonable (*logical interpretant*).

In the U.S. midterm elections in 1994, the Republicans took control of Congress for the first time in over forty years. The media coverage of this event is an especially good example of various levels of meaning. The general message was that the Republicans would dominate national politics. This we might call the *final interpretant.* Many voters were elated at the prospect (an *emotional interpretant*) and could hardly wait to vote in a Republican president in the next election (an *energic interpretant*). There was also the feeling among some that fundamental changes would occur as a result of the election (*logical interpretant*).

Corcoran's study of the KAL 007 disaster shows how the final interpretant of this event in the United States was a generalized view of the Soviet Union as basically evil. The predominant emotional interpretant at that time was outrage, the energic interpretant was to speak out and act out against the Soviets for their deed, and the logical interpretant was to make overt statements about why this interpretation is reasonable while failing to consider any other possible interpretations.

Fry and Fry's third postulate is that the meaning of a message is affected by events outside the message itself. The signs used in the text do play a role in shaping meaning, but numerous nontextual influences also bear on the meaning that an individual will take from the text. The text will be influential to the extent that (1) the producer understands the kinds of content that will bring out certain meanings in the culture of the audience and (2) the actual text emphasizes certain meanings over others.

For example, a producer of a sitcom may wish to elicit a feeling of warmth and amusement from the characters. Knowing the kinds of situations that appeal to the general American audience helps writers develop situations that bring out those responses. Further, the writers and actors will concentrate on emphasizing a particular feeling for each character that will capture the attention of the audience.

The KAL 007 incident illustrates the way the media resonated with the feelings of the American public at that time. The media served as a virtual agent of the government in perpetuating an ideology of Good versus Evil in their reporting of the disaster. The newsmagazines ignored, downplayed, or dismissed alternative interpretations found commonly in the foreign press—the idea that KAL 007 was on a reconnaissance mission, for example. (This interpretation was later disproved when Russian files were opened to the world in the early 1990s.)

An objective of media is to get the attention of the audience. How is this done? One way is the use of signs to emphasize certain properties and to make other properties neutral, a process called *semantic disclosure.* Out of everything that a person could "see" in a message, some things are highlighted and others are muted, and that determines the meaning communicated. Semantic disclosure in a sitcom might be accomplished by the character's costume, use of certain expressions in dialogue, and nonverbal demeanor. In fact, stereotyping is an important kind of semantic disclosure in media messages, as can be seen in the KAL 007 reporting.

Once again, however, the audience response is not totally predictable. Indeed, many "extracodes," or outside factors, can influence meaning. *Overcoding* occurs when meanings normally attached to one kind of message or situation are used to interpret another. For example, at Christmas time Hallmark used to release Christmas card commercials that just depicted beautiful scenes without directly mentioning the product (cards). Viewers would still get that the company was trying to sell its product because of the standard interpretation given to all other commercials.

Ideological overcoding is especially important. This occurs when the viewer's ideology affects the interpretation of a message, even when the ideological interpretation is not intended. For instance, a feminist may consider certain commercials objectionable because they depict women in subordinate roles, a Marxist may view network television news as an instrument of oppression, or a union leader might read the *Wall Street Journal* as a house organ for industrial management.

Semiotics is a popular and useful way to analyze specific media messages. But there are other concerns of interest to media scholars as well. Let us look now at the macro side of media theory.

▣ MEDIA AS SOCIAL INSTITUTION

Media are more than simple mechanisms for disseminating information: They are complex organizations and an important social institution of society. McQuail presents the major media links, which are depicted in Figure 15.2.[23] Here, the media themselves are shown in the center and

include a management function, professional personnel, and a technical aspect. Media are shown in this diagram to interact with various economic, social, and political organizations; events and happenings in society at large; and the audience.

Perhaps the most important line of theory to address the institutional aspect of media is marxist critical theory. Because critical theory is discussed in Chapter 11, we will not cover it in great detail here.[24] Recall that critical theories are concerned with the distribution of power in society and the domination of certain interests over others. Clearly, the media are a major player in this ideological struggle. Dominant ideologies can be perpetuated by the media, as we saw above in the case of the news reporting on the KAL 007 disaster.

Most critical communication theories are concerned with mass media primarily because of the media's potential for disseminating dominant ideologies and their potential for expressing alternative and oppositional ones. For some critical theorists, media are part of a culture industry that literally creates symbols and images that can oppress marginalized groups.

According to McQuail there are five major branches of Marxist media theory.[25] The first is *classical Marxism.* Here, the media are seen as instruments of the dominant class and a means by which capitalists promote their profit-making interests. Media disseminate the ideology of the ruling classes in society and thereby oppress certain classes.

The second is *political-economic media theory,* which, like classical Marxism, blames media ownership for society's ills. In this school of thought, media content is a commodity to be sold in the marketplace, and the information disseminated is controlled by what the market will bear. This system leads to a conservative,

---

23 McQuail, *Mass Communication,* 1987, p. 142.
24 See the Chapter 11 section of the Bibliography for readings in this area. McQuail's *Mass Communication* (1987) discusses Marxist theories of media in some detail. See also Lawrence Grossberg, "Strategies of Marxist Cultural Interpretation," *Critical Studies in Mass Communication* 1 (1984): 392–421.
25 McQuail, *Mass Communication,* 1987, pp. 63–68.

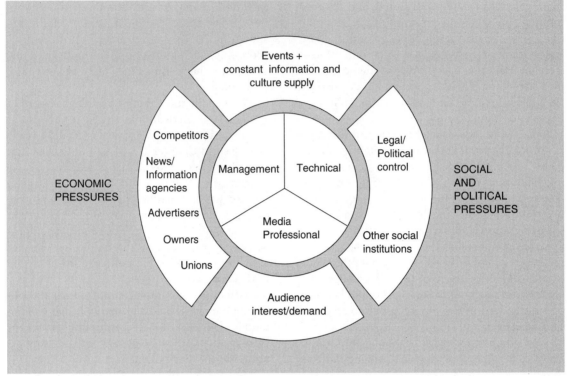

FIGURE **15.2**

The Media Organization in a Field of Social Force

non-risk-taking operation, making certain kinds of programming and certain media outlets dominant and others marginalized.

The third line of theory is the *Frankfurt School.* This school of thought, seeing media as a means of constructing culture, places more emphasis on ideas than on material goods. In this way of thinking, media lead to the domination of the ideology of the elite. This outcome is accomplished by media manipulation of images and symbols to benefit the interests of the dominant class.

The fourth school is the *hegemonic theory.* Hegemony is the domination of a false ideology or way of thinking over true conditions. Ideology is not caused by the economic system alone but is deeply embedded in all activities of society. Thus, ideology is not forced by one group on another but is pervasive and unconscious. The dominant ideology perpetuates the interests of certain classes over others, and the media obviously take a major role in this process.

The final approach to marxist media studies is the *sociocultural approach,* usually called simply "cultural studies." Relying in large measure on semiotics, this group of scholars is interested in the cultural meanings of media products, looking at the ways media content is interpreted, including both dominant and oppositional interpretations. Cultural studies sees society as a field of competing ideas in a struggle among meanings. The study by Corcoran of the news reporting of the KAL 007 disaster is very much in the cultural studies tradition. Cultural studies is becoming an increasingly popular and useful approach, and it can be used to integrate insights from a variety of schools of thought.[26]

Although critical communication theories have gained presence in North America, their real development and strength occurred in Europe and Latin America. European critical theory is perhaps more widely known, because of the larger number of sources translated into English and the greater attention paid to European traditions. In contrast, Latin American communication theory, which remains largely untranslated, has received relatively little attention in the United States. Robert Huesca and Brenda Dervin have written a good recent summary of this work.[27]

According to Huesca and Dervin, Latin American communication scholarship challenges the predominant North American approach on many fronts. In general, this work honors horizontal, artistic, democratic, and participatory communication over vertical, industrial, authoritarian, and elite forms. It tends to look more at grass roots efforts rather than top-down ones, and self-managed communication systems rather than centralized systems. Latin American communication research also concentrates on human liberation rather than information transfer, conscience building rather than domination, unity rather than fragmentation, and antiauthoritarian rather than authoritarian content.

Although these trends tend to be as dualistic as is most North American scholarship, pitting one point against another, many Latin American scholars have attempted to overcome dualism altogether. They have done this in a number of ways. For example, they have refused to dichotomize the communication source from the audience and have shown that the audience itself participates in the creation of meaning. These scholars have also emphasized global over national trends and have called for coalitions, networks, and dialogue among groups and ideas.

MEDIA AND AUDIENCE

No area in media theory has presented such quandaries and debates as studies of the audience. Media theorists are far from consensus on how to conceptualize the audience and audience effects. Disputes on the nature of the audience seem to involve two related dialectics. The first is a tension between the idea that the audience is a mass public versus the idea that it is a small community. The second is a tension between the idea that the audience is passive versus the belief that it is active. Let us consider each of these debates in turn.

Mass Society Versus Community

This controversy involves different opinions about the audience. Some see the audience as an undifferentiated mass, and some see it as a variegated set of small groups or communities. In the case of the former, audiences are viewed as a large population that can be molded by the media. In the case of the latter, audiences are viewed as discriminating members of small groups who are influenced mostly by their peers.

The theory of mass society is a concept growing out of the large, complex, bureaucratic nature of the modern state.[28] The theory envisions a malleable mass of people in which small groupings, community life, and ethnic identity are replaced by societywide depersonalized relations. This conception of society has led to widespread criticism of modern life and of the media. Critics of the mass society have suggested several propositions.

---

26   Dennis K. Davis and Thomas F. N. Puckett, "Mass Entertainment and Community: Toward a Culture-Centered Paradigm for Mass Communication Research," in *Communication Yearbook 15,* ed. Stanley Deetz (Newbury Park, CA: Sage, 1992), pp. 3–34.

27   Robert Huesca and Brenda Dervin, "Theory and Practice in Latin American Alternative Communication Research," *Journal of Communication* 44 (1994): 53–73.

28   The most prominent critics of mass society are Ortega y Gasset, Karl Mannheim, Karl Jaspers, Paul Tillich, Gabriel Marcel, and Emil Lederer. Syntheses can be found in a variety of sources. See, for example, Patrick Brantlinger, *Bread and Circuses: Theories of Mass Culture as Social Decay* (Ithaca, NY: Cornell University Press, 1983).

First, rapid developments in transportation and communication have increased human contact, and economic considerations have made people more and more interdependent. Thus, like a giant system, imbalance in one part affects everybody. Ironically, we are all more interdependent while becoming increasingly estranged from one another. Community and family ties are broken, and old values are questioned.

Second, because society is no longer believed to be led by the elite, morals, tastes, and values decline.[29] Rapid changes in society hurl men and women into multiple-role situations, causing a loss of the sense of self.[30] People become more anxious, and a charismatic leader ultimately may be required to lift society out of the abyss.

The dismal view of the theory of mass society has several implications for the mass media of communication. Critics of mass society fear that minds will be pounded and altered by propaganda through the media. As Paul Lazarsfeld and Robert Merton state: "There is the danger that these technically advanced instruments of mass communication constitute a major avenue for deterioration of aesthetic tastes and popular cultural standards."[31]

Add to this the thesis that the media are blurring social boundaries and community divisions that previously gave stability and meaning to the lives of citizens. Joshua Meyrowitz writes in his book *No Sense of Place* that television has caused us to lose our sense of boundaries, between the private and public, between the physical and social, and between social groups. People are essentially losing their "place" in the world.[32]

The theory of mass society is still popular among the general population. Although this theory is not as prevalent among scholars today as it was a few decades ago, it still has an influence. McLuhan's theory is certainly a mass society theory, as are some of the marxist theories. Certain "powerful-effects" theories, including the well-known cultivation theory discussed later in the chapter, are strongly influenced by mass society thinking.

In contrast to mass society thinking is the position that the audience cannot be characterized

as an amorphous mass, that it consists of numerous highly differentiated communities, each with its own values, ideas, and interests. Media content is interpreted within the community according to meanings that are worked out socially within the group, and individuals are influenced more by their peers than by the media.[33] We explored the idea of media-interpretive communities in Chapter 10, where we saw that the meanings of media messages are worked out interactively within groups of people who use a medium in a similar way.

Gerard Schoening and James Anderson call the community-based approach *Social Action Media Studies*, and they outline six premises of this work.[34] First, meaning is not in the message itself but is produced by an interpretive process in the audience. Different audiences will interpret or understand what they read and view in different ways. For example, talk radio programs may be taken to mean many things, depending on who is listening.

The second premise of social action media studies is that the meaning of media messages and programs is not determined passively, but produced actively. This means that audiences actually do something with what they view and read. They act as they view. Some listeners, for example, may turn on talk radio to combat bore-

29   See, for example, E. D. Hirsch, *Cultural Literacy: What Every American Needs to Know* (Boston: Houghton Mifflin, 1987); Allan Bloom, *The Closing of the American Mind* (New York: Simon & Schuster, 1987).

30   See, for example, Kenneth J. Gergen, *The Saturated Self: Dilemmas of Identity in Contemporary Life* (New York: HarperCollins, 1991).

31   Paul Lazarsfeld and Robert K. Merton, "Mass Communication, Popular Taste, and Organized Social Action," in *The Process and Effects of Mass Communication*, eds. W. Schramm and D. Roberts (Urbana: University of Illinois Press, 1971), p. 557.

32   Joshua Meyrowitz, *No Sense of Place: The Impact of Electronic Media on Social Behavior* (New York: Oxford University Press, 1985).

33   For an excellent statement of this position, see Thomas R. Lindlof, "Media Audiences as Interpretive Communities," in *Communication Yearbook 11*, ed. J. A. Anderson (Newbury Park, CA: Sage, 1988), pp. 81–107. Supportive of this position, too, is reader reception theory, which is most notably developed by John Fiske, *Introduction to Communication Studies* (New York: Methuen, 1982); *Television Culture* (New York: Methuen, 1987); *Reading the Popular* (Winchester, MA: Unwin Hyman, 1989); and *Understanding Popular Culture* (Winchester, MA: Unwin Hyman, 1989).

34   Gerard T. Schoening and James A. Anderson, "Social Action Media Studies: Foundational Arguments and Common Premises," *Communication Theory* 5 (1995): 93–116.

dom while driving, others may turn it on late in the evening as a sleep aid, and still others may listen to it actively during the day as a means of getting information about current events. What a particular talk radio program means, therefore, is a product of how listeners treat it, what they do with it.

The third premise is that the meanings of media shift constantly as the members approach the media in different ways. Sometimes the talk radio program may be strictly entertainment, sometimes serious information, and sometimes just background noise, depending on when and how it is listened to.

Fourth, the meaning of a program or message is never individually established, but communal. It is part of the tradition of a group, community, or culture. The implication of this is that when you join a community (by birth or membership), you accept the ongoing activities and meanings of that community or group. Your own behavior may influence the group or change the activities and meanings in some way, but the outcome at any given time is always sitting in the community or group.

Fifth, the actions that determine a group's meanings for media content are done in interaction among members of the group. In other words, how we act toward the media and what meanings emerge from those actions are social interactions. This does not mean that you never watch TV by yourself, but it does mean that how you watch TV and what you do with the television set are part of an ongoing interaction between yourself and others. If you listen to talk radio in the car while you commute to work, this pattern is part of a larger web of interactions with people at home and at work. It is a routine that is made possible by a huge network of interactions involving work, home, radio, boredom, cars, highways, and so on.

Finally, the sixth premise of social action media studies is that researchers join the communities they study, if only temporarily, and therefore have an ethical obligation to be open about what they are studying and share what they learn with those studied.

Active Audience Versus Passive Audience

Another controversy is the passive versus active audience. The passive-audience view suggests that people are easily influenced in a direct way by the media, whereas the active-audience view suggests that people make more active decisions about how to use the media. For the most part, mass society theories tend to subscribe to a passive conception of audience, although not all passive-audience theories can legitimately be called mass society theories. Similarly, most community theories subscribe to an active notion of audience.

These ideas about audiences are associated with various theories of media effects discussed later in the chapter. The "powerful-effects" theories tend to be based on the passive audience, whereas the "minimal-effects" theories are based more on an active one.

Frank Biocca discusses five characteristics of the active audience implied by the theories of this genre.[35] The first is *selectivity.* Active audiences are considered to be selective in the media they choose to use. The second characteristic is *utilitarianism.* Active audiences are said to use media to meet particular needs and goals. The third characteristic is *intentionality,* which implies the purposeful use of media content. The fourth characteristic is *involvement,* or effort. Here, audiences are actively attending, thinking about, and using the media. Finally, active audiences are believed to be *impervious to influence,* or not very easily persuaded by the media alone.

Many media scholars believe that the mass community and active-passive dichotomies are too simple, that they do not capture the true complexity of audiences. It may be that audiences have some elements of mass society and other elements of local communities. Audiences may be active in some ways and passive in others or

---

35   Frank A. Biocca, "Opposing Conceptions of the Audience: The Active and Passive Hemispheres of Mass Communication Theory," in *Communication Yearbook 11*, ed. J. A. Anderson (Newbury Park, CA: Sage, 1988), pp. 51–80. This article is an excellent discussion of the active-passive distinction and provides a review of the various theories on each side.

active at some times and passive at other times. Rather than ask whether audiences are easily influenced by the media, it might be better to ask when and under what conditions they are influenced and when they are not. This view changes the debate from one over what the audience really is to its meaning for people at different times and in different places.[36]

THEORIES OF CULTURAL OUTCOMES

We turn now to a study of the outcomes of media communication. Of all areas of mass communication research, outcome studies are the most prevalent, especially in the United States. An overriding question throughout the history of media theory has been the effects of media on society and individuals.[37]

Karl Erik Rosengren shows that media outcomes are complex and wide-ranging.[38] Various theories concentrate on different outcomes— short term and long term, narrow and individual, broad and cultural. He lists five examples of such differences:

- News diffusion research (hours and days)
- Agenda setting (weeks and months)
- Spiral of silence (months and years)
- Cultivation (years and decades)
- Research on public sphere (decades and centuries)

The theories included here are divided into two sections, those focusing on general cultural outcomes and those focusing on individual effects. This section deals with the former and the next section with the latter.

The Functions of Mass Communication

For many years, media theory concentrated on how media work and their effects on audiences. This was essentially a functionalist approach (see Chapter 1) that concentrated on the system of mass communication, how it works, and what it does.[39]

One of the earliest and best-known theorists in this tradition was Harold Lasswell. In his classic 1948 article, he presented the simple and often quoted model of communication:[40]

Who

Says what

In which channel

To whom

With what effect

This model outlines the basic elements of communication, the last element of which directs us to the entire outcome-research literature.

Lasswell identifies three functions of the media of communication. These are providing information about the environment, which he terms *surveillance;* presenting options for solving problems, or *correlation;* and socializing and education, referred to as *transmission.*[41]

Charles Wright has expanded Lasswell's model by developing a twelve-category model and a functional inventory, as shown in Figure 15.3 and Table 15.1.[42] Notice that Wright added a fourth function, *entertainment,* to Lasswell's list. Wright also distinguishes between functions, or positive outcomes, and dysfunctions, or negative ones.

36   This view is espoused by Martin Allor, "Relocating the Site of the Audience," *Critical Studies in Mass Communication* 5 (1988): 217–233.
37   See, for example, Pietilä, "Perspectives"; Jennings Bryant and Dolf Zillmann (eds.), *Perspectives on Media Effects* (Hillsdale, NJ: Erlbaum, 1986).
38   Rosengren, "Culture, Media, and Society."
39   For a brief history of this tradition, see Carl Patrick Burrowes, "From Functionalism to Cultural Studies: Manifest Ruptures and Latent Continuities," *Communication Theory* 6 (1996): 88–103.
40   Harold Lasswell, "The Structure and Function of Communication in Society," in *The Communication of Ideas,* ed. L. Bryson (New York: Institute for Religious and Social Studies, 1948), p. 37. For information regarding Lasswell's contribution to communication, see Everett M. Rogers, *A History of Communication Study: A Biographical Approach* (New York: Free Press, 1994), pp. 203–243.
41   Lasswell, "Structure and Function."
42   Charles R. Wright, "Functional Analysis and Mass Communication," *Public Opinion Quarterly* 24 (1960): 610–613.

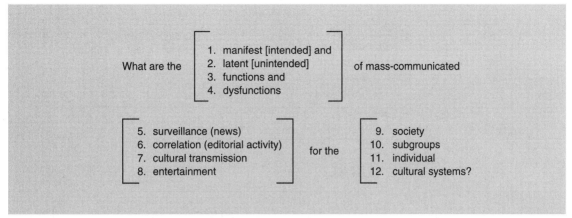

FIGURE **15.3**

Wright's Functional Model

From *Public Opinion Quarterly*, "Functional Analysis and Mass Communication," by Charles R. Wright. Copyright © 1960. Reprinted by permission of The University of Chicago Press and the author.

The Lasswell and Wright models are classic. Notice that they are essentially lists of the parts of the mass communication system and the things that mass communication accomplishes. Since this early work, many other functions have been explored. We will look at several in this chapter, beginning in the following section with the diffusion of information and influence.

The Diffusion of Information and Influence

The community view of audience discussed above was given impetus by a now-classic voting study in 1940 conducted by Lazarsfeld and his colleagues in Elmira, New York.[43] The researchers unexpectedly found that the effect of media was influenced by interpersonal communication. This effect, which came to be known as the *two-step flow hypothesis*, was startling, and it had a major impact on our understanding of the role of mass media.

This study was the beginning of a line of research on how information and influence are distributed in society. Lazarsfeld hypothesized that information flows from the mass media to certain opinion leaders in the community, who pass information on by talking to peers. He found that voters seem to be more influenced by their friends during a campaign than by the media. Since the original Elmira study, much additional data have come in, and this hypothesis has received substantial support.[44]

The two-step flow theory is best summarized in Elihu Katz and Paul Lazarsfeld's classic work *Personal Influence*.[45] These authors confirm that certain individuals known as *opinion leaders* receive information from the media and pass it to their peers.[46] Opinion leaders are in all groups: occupational, social, community, and others. These individuals are difficult to distinguish from other group members because opinion leadership is not a trait but a role taken by some individuals in certain circumstances. Opinion

43 Paul Lazarsfeld, Bernard Berelson, and H. Gaudet, *The People's Choice* (New York: Columbia University Press, 1948). See also Rogers, *A History*, pp. 244–315.
44 An excellent summary of this hypothesis is Elihu Katz, "The Two-Step Flow of Communication," *Public Opinion Quarterly* 21 (1957): 61–78.
45 Elihu Katz and Paul Lazarsfeld, *Personal Influence: The Part Played by People in the Flow of Mass Communications* (New York: Free Press, 1955).
46 Research on opinion leadership is summarized in Everett M. Rogers, *Diffusion of Innovations* (New York: Free Press, 1995), pp. 290–304.

TABLE **15.1**

Partial Functional Inventory for Mass Communications

	System under Consideration			
	Society	Individual	Specific Subgroup (e.g., political elite)	Culture
1. Mass-Communicated Activity: Surveillance (News)				
Functions (manifest and latent)	Warning: Natural dangers Attack; war Instrumental: News essential to the economy and other institutions Ethicizing	Warning Instrumental Adds prestige: Opinion leadership Status conferral	Instrumental: Information useful to power Detects: Knowledge of subversive and deviant behavior Manages public opinion: Monitors Controls Legitimizes power: Status conferral	Aids cultural contact Aids cultural growth
Dysfunctions (manifest and latent)	Threatens stability: News of "better" societies Fosters panic	Anxiety Privatization Apathy Narcotization	Threatens power: News of reality "Enemy" propaganda Exposés	Permits cultural invasion
2. Mass-Communicated Activity: Correlation (Editorial selection, Interpretation, and Prescription)				
Functions (manifest and latent)	Aids mobilization Impedes threats to social stability Impedes panic	Provides efficiency: Assimilating news Impedes: Overstimulation Anxiety Apathy Privatization	Helps preserve power	Impedes cultural invasion Maintains cultural consensus
Dysfunctions (manifest and latent)	Increases social conformism: Impedes social change if social criticism is avoided	Weakens critical faculties Increases passivity	Increases responsibility	Impedes cultural growth
3. Mass-Communicated Activity: Cultural Transmission				
Functions (manifest and latent)	Increases social cohesion: Widens base of common norms, experiences, etc. Reduces anomie Continues socialization: Reaches adults even after they have left such institutions as school	Aids integration: Exposure to common norms Reduces idiosyncrasy Reduces anomie	Extends power: Another agency for socialization	Standardizes Maintains cultural consensus
Dysfunctions (manifest and latent)	Augments "mass" society	Depersonalizes acts of socialization		Reduces variety of subcultures
4. Mass-Communicated Activity: Entertainment				
Functions (manifest and latent)	Respite for masses	Respite	Extends power: Control over another area of life	
Dysfunctions (manifest and latent)	Diverts public: Avoids social action	Increases passivity Lowers "tastes" Permits escapism		Weakens aesthetics: "Popular culture"

leadership changes from time to time and from issue to issue.

Opinion leaders may be of two kinds: those influential on one topic, or *monomorphism,* and those influential on a variety of topics, or *polymorphism.* Monomorphism becomes more predominant as systems become more modern.

Research more recent than the Lazarsfeld study has shown that the dissemination of ideas is not a simple two-step process. A *multiple-step model* is now more generally accepted.[47] This model is similar to the two-step hypothesis but admits to more possibilities. Research has shown that the ultimate number of relays between the media and final receivers is variable. In the adoption of an innovation, for example, certain individuals will hear about it directly from media sources, whereas others will be many steps removed.

The diffusion of information and innovations is now part of the interactional and network tradition discussed in some detail in Chapter 14. We saw in those chapters that interaction in networks plays an important role in relationships, small groups, and organizations. Here, we see that it plays an important role in mass communication too. The diffusion of information is one of the most significant outcomes of communication. Often distributed information promotes the adoption of innovations.

The diffusion of an innovation occurs when an idea spreads from a point of origin to surrounding geographic areas or from person to person within a single area. Several prominent American and foreign researchers in fields such as agriculture and rural studies, national development, and organizational communication have been responsible for this line of research.

The broadest and most communication-oriented theory of diffusion is that of Everett Rogers and his colleagues.[48] Rogers relates dissemination to the process of social change, which consists of invention, diffusion (or communication), and consequences. Such change can occur internally from within a group or externally through contact with outside change agents.

Contact may occur spontaneously or accidentally, or it may result from planning on the part of outside agencies.

In the diffusion of innovations, many years may be required for an idea to spread. Rogers states, in fact, that one purpose of diffusion research is to discover the means to shorten this lag. Once established, an innovation will have consequences, be they functional or dysfunctional, direct or indirect, manifest or latent. Change agents normally expect their impact to be functional, direct, and manifest, although this positive result does not always occur.

The diffusion of innovations is well illustrated by the family planning program instituted in South Korea in 1968. Mothers' clubs were established in about 12,000 villages throughout Korea for the purpose of disseminating information about family planning. Overall, the program was successful, and Korea saw a major decline in birth rate during this period. This program was built on the idea that interpersonal channels of communication would be crucial to the adoption of birth control methods. Rogers and his colleagues in 1973 studied the Korean case by interviewing about a thousand women in twenty-four villages to gather information about the networks the women used for family planning.[49]

They found that the village leaders initially received their information about family planning from the mass media and family planning worker visits, but interpersonal networks turned out to be most important in the dissemination-adoption process. Two network variables were especially important. The first was the degree to which the mothers' club leader was connected with others in the village network. The second variable was the amount of overlap between the family planning network and the general village network. Birth control adoption was greatest in

47 Rogers, *Diffusion of Innovations,* pp. 281–334.
48 Rogers, *Diffusion of Innovations.*
49 Everett M. Rogers and D. Lawrence Kincaid, *Communication Networks: Toward a New Paradigm for Research* (New York: Free Press, 1981). The Korean case is discussed throughout the book. See especially pages 258–285.

the villages in which the leader talked to many people personally and the village women talked about it among themselves. Rogers has found that people do talk about ideas, and that is how change happens. In some circumstances, however, people do not talk, and now we will look at a theory that explains why.

Public Opinion and the Spiral of Silence

As the research on Korean family planning discussed above illustrates, communication has much to do with public opinion. The topic of public opinion has been of great concern in political science, in which the concept represents opinions publicly expressed, opinions regarding public affairs, and opinions of the general public as a group rather than of smaller groups of individuals. Elisabeth Noelle-Neumann's theory of the "spiral of silence" continues this analysis by demonstrating how interpersonal communication and media operate together in the development of public opinion.[50]

As a political researcher in Germany, Noelle-Neumann observed that in elections certain views seem to get more play than others. Sometimes people mute their opinions rather than talk about them. Noelle-Neumann calls this the spiral of silence. The *spiral of silence* occurs when individuals who perceive that their opinion is popular express it, whereas those who do not think their opinion is popular remain quiet. This process occurs in a spiral, so that one side of an issue ends up with much publicity and the other side with little.

In everyday life we express our opinions in a variety of ways: We talk about them, we wear buttons, and we put bumper stickers on our cars. According to this theory, people are more apt to do these kinds of things when they perceive that others share their opinion and less apt to do so when they do not.

This thesis rests on two premises. The first is that people know which opinions are prevalent and which are not. This is called the *quasi-statistical sense* because people are not reluctant

to make educated guesses about public opinion and have a sense of the percentages of the population for and against certain positions. The second assumption is that people adjust their expressions of opinion to these perceptions.

Noelle-Neumann presents much research evidence to support these assumptions. In political elections, for example, people usually perceive quite accurately the prevailing opinion about the candidates and issues, and they are likely to express their preferences when these are shared by others.

An interesting test of the tendency to remain silent on unpopular positions is the "train test."[51] Here, respondents are asked to imagine that they were in a train compartment with a stranger for five hours and to decide whether they would be willing to discuss certain topics with this person. Respondents were told that they were to imagine that the other person mentioned his or her opinion on the subject, and were then asked, "Would you like to talk with this person so as to get to know their point of view better, or wouldn't you think that worth your while?" Topics ranged from spanking children to the government of Germany.

Interviewers presented this problem to 3,500 respondents covering numerous topics over several years. The overwhelming tendency was to freely discuss the topic when one agrees with the majority but to let it slide when one does not. People seem to not want to "make waves."

Of course, other factors enter into the decision to express one's opinion. Young people are more expressive than older people; educated individuals will speak up more than uneducated ones; men are generally more willing to disclose their opinions than women. However, the spiral of si-

---

50   Elisabeth Noelle-Neumann, *The Spiral of Silence: Public Opinion—Our Social Skin* (Chicago: University of Chicago Press, 1984). See also "The Theory of Public Opinion: The Concept of the Spiral of Silence," in *Communication Yearbook 14,* ed. J. A. Anderson (Newbury Park, CA: Sage, 1991), pp. 256–287. For a brief summary, see Charles T. Salmon and Carroll J. Glynn, "Spiral of Silence: Communication and Public Opinion as Social Control," in *An Integrated Approach to Communication Theory and Research,* eds. Michael B. Salwen and Don W. Stacks (Mahwah, NJ: Erlbaum, 1996), pp. 165–180.
51   Noelle-Neumann, *Spiral,* pp. 16–22.

lence is also a factor, and according to this research, a powerful one.

The spiral of silence seems to be caused by the fear of isolation. As Noelle-Neumann puts it, "To run with the pack is a relatively happy state of affairs; but if you can't, because you won't share publicly in what seems to be a universally acclaimed conviction, you can at least remain silent, as a second choice, so that others can put up with you."[52]

The spiral of silence is not just a matter of wanting to be on the winning side but is an attempt to avoid being isolated from one's social group. Threats of criticism from others were found to be powerful forces in silencing individuals. For example, smokers who are repeatedly criticized for advocating smokers' rights were found to remain silent rather than state their views on this subject in the presence of vocal nonsmokers.

In some cases the threat of expressing an opinion is extreme:

> Slashed tires, defaced or torn posters, help refused to a lost stranger—questions of this kind demonstrate that people can be on uncomfortable or even dangerous ground when the climate of opinion runs counter to their views. When people attempt to avoid isolation, they are not responding hypersensitively to trivialities; these are existential issues that can involve real hazards.[53]

One can easily see how the spiral of silence affects public opinion. Public opinion has been defined in numerous ways. For Noelle-Neumann, an operational definition is best: "Public opinions are attitudes or behaviors one must express in public if one is not to isolate oneself; in areas of controversy or change, public opinions are those attitudes one can express without running the danger of isolating oneself."[54] Stated differently, "public opinion is an understanding on the part of people in an ongoing community concerning some affect- or value-laden question which individuals as well as government have to respect at least by compromise in their overt behavior under the threat of being excluded or losing one's standing in society."[55]

There are, of course, exceptions to the spiral of silence. There are groups and individuals who do not fear isolation and who will express their opinions no matter what the consequences, a characteristic of innovators, change agents, and the avant-garde.

When polled, individuals usually state that they feel powerless in the face of media. Two kinds of experience accentuate this feeling of helplessness. The first is the difficulty of getting publicity for a cause or point of view. The second is being scapegoated by the media in what Noelle-Neumann calls the *pillory function* of media. In each case the individual feels powerless against the media, making the media an important part of the spiral of silence. The media publicize which opinions are prevalent and which are not.

Although public opinion is formed by both personal observation and media, individuals mix the two and confuse what is learned through the media with what is learned through interpersonal channels. This tendency is especially true for television, with which so many people have a personal relationship:

> The longer one has studied the question, the clearer it becomes that fathoming the effects of the mass media is very hard. These effects do not come into being as a result of a single stimulus; they are as a rule cumulative, following the principle that "water dripping constantly wears away stone." Further discussions among people spread the media's messages further, and before long no difference can be perceived between the point of media reception and points far removed from it. The media's effects are predominantly unconscious; people cannot provide an account of what has happened. Rather, they mix their own direct perceptions and the perceptions filtered through the eyes of the media into an indivisible whole that seems to derive from their own thoughts and experiences.[56]

It sometimes happens that journalists' opinions differ from those of the general public, so

---

52   Noelle-Neumann, *Spiral,* p. 6.
53   Noelle-Neumann, *Spiral,* p. 56.
54   Noelle-Neumann, *Spiral,* p. 178.
55   Noelle-Neumann, *Spiral,* p. 179.
56   Noelle-Neumann, *Spiral,* p. 169.

that media depictions contradict the prevailing expressions of individuals. When this occurs, a dual climate of opinion results. Here, two versions of reality operate, that of the media and that of the public. Noelle-Neumann likens this event to an unusual weather situation—interesting and seemingly bizarre.

The spiral of silence, then, is a phenomenon involving personal and media channels of communication. The media publicize public opinion, making evident which opinions predominate. Individuals express their opinions or not, depending on the predominant points of view; the media, in turn, attend to the expressed opinion, and the spiral continues.

Cultivation Analysis

Another theoretical program dealing with the sociocultural outcomes of mass communication is that of George Gerbner and his colleagues.[57] These researchers believe that because television is the great common experience of almost everyone, it has the effect of providing a shared way of viewing the world:

> Television is a centralized system of storytelling. It is part and parcel of our daily lives. Its drama, commercials, news, and other programs bring a relatively coherent world of common images and messages into every home. Television cultivates from infancy the very predispositions and preferences that used to be acquired from other primary sources. Transcending historic barriers of literacy and mobility, television has become the primary common source of socialization and everyday information (mostly in the form of entertainment) of an otherwise heterogeneous population. The repetitive pattern of television's mass-produced messages and images forms the mainstream of a common symbolic environment.[58]

Gerbner calls this effect *cultivation*, since television is believed to be a homogenizing agent in culture. Cultivation analysis is concerned with the totality of the pattern communicated cumulatively by television over a long period of exposure rather than by any particular content or specific effect. In other words, this is not a theory of individual media "effects" but instead makes a

statement about the culture as a whole. It is not concerned with what any strategy or campaign can do but with the total impact of numerous strategies and campaigns over time. Total immersion in television, not selective viewing, is important in cultivation of ways of knowing and images of reality. Indeed, subcultures may retain their separate values, but general overriding images depicted on television will cut across individual social groups and subcultures, affecting them all.

As you might imagine, the theory predicts a difference in the social reality of heavy television viewers as opposed to light viewers. Heavy viewers will believe in a reality that is consistent with that shown on television, even though television does not necessarily reflect the actual world. Gerbner's research on prime-time television, for example, has shown that there are three men to every woman on television, there are few Hispanics and those shown are typically minor characters, there are almost entirely middle-class characters, and there are three times as many law enforcement officers as blue-collar workers.

One of the most interesting aspects of cultivation is the "mean-world syndrome." Although less than 1 percent of the population are victims of violent crimes in any one-year period, "one lesson viewers derive from heavy exposure to the violence-saturated world of television is that in such a mean and dangerous world, most people 'cannot be trusted' and that most people are 'just looking out for themselves.'"[59]

Nancy Signorielli reports a study of the mean-world syndrome, in which violent acts in

57   Michael Morgan and James Shanahan, "Two Decades of Cultivation Research: An Appraisal and Meta-Analysis," *Communication Yearbook 20*, ed. Brant R. Burleson (Thousand Oaks, CA: Sage, 1997), pp. 1–45; Nancy Signorielli and Michael Morgan, "Cultivation Analysis: Research and Practice," in *An Integrated Approach to Communication Theory and Research*, eds. Michael B. Salwen and Don W. Stacks (Mahwah, NJ: Erlbaum, 1996), pp. 111–126; Nancy Signorielli and Michael Morgan (eds.), *Cultivation Analysis: New Directions in Media Effects Research*, (Newbury Park, CA: Sage, 1990).
58   George Gerbner, Larry Gross, Michael Morgan, and Nancy Signorielli, "Living with Television," in *Perspectives on Media Effects*, eds. J. Bryant and D. Zillmann (Hillsdale, NJ: Erlbaum, 1986), p. 18.
59   Gerbner and others, "Living," p. 28.

children's television programming were analyzed.[60] Over 2,000 programs, including 6,000 main characters, during prime time and weekends from 1967 to 1985 were analyzed with interesting results. About 71 percent of prime-time and 94 percent of weekend programs included acts of violence. Prime-time programs averaged almost five acts of violence each, and weekend programs averaged six. That amounts to over five acts per hour during prime time and about twenty per hour on weekends.

As part of this study, people were surveyed on five occasions between 1980 and 1986 regarding their views of the state of the world. To measure feelings of alienation and gloom, they were asked whether they agreed with three statements: (1) "Despite what some people say, the lot of the average man is getting worse, not better." (2) "It's hardly fair to bring a child into the world with the way things look for the future." (3) "Most public officials are not interested in the problems of the average man."

In addition, they were asked three questions to measure feelings about a mean world: (1) "Would you say that most of the time people try to be helpful, or are they mostly just looking out for themselves?" (2) "Do you think that most people would try to take advantage of you if they got a chance, or would they try to be fair?" (3) "Generally speaking, would you say that most people can be trusted, or you can't be too careful in dealing with people?" The findings indicate that heavy viewers tend to see the world as gloomier and meaner than do light viewers, and heavy viewers tend to mistrust people more than light viewers do.

Cultivation analysis has also found that there is a general fallout effect from television to the entire culture so that culture becomes homogenized, or *mainstreamed,* through TV. Television is not a force for change as much as it is a force for stability.

Mainstreaming can be seen in the mean-world data reviewed above. Even though heavy viewers scored higher on the mean-world index than did light viewers, a substantial number of light viewers also scored high. In fact, if you remove

people with a college education from the sample, heavy and light viewers scored about the same.

Although cultivation is a general outcome of television viewing, it is not a universal phenomenon, despite the mainstreaming effect. In fact, different groups are affected differently by cultivation. Your interaction with others affects your tendency to accept TV reality. For example, adolescents who interact with their parents about television viewing are less likely to be affected by television images than are adolescents who do not talk with their parents about television. Interestingly, people who watch more cable television tend to manifest more mainstreaming than do people who watch less.

The Agenda-Setting Function

Scholars have long known that media have the potential for structuring issues for the public.[61] One of the first writers to formalize this idea was Walter Lippman, a prominent American journalist. Lippman is known for his journalistic writing, speeches, and social commentary.[62] Lippman took the view that the public responds not to actual events in the environment but to "the pictures in our heads," which he calls the *pseudo-environment:*

> For the real environment is altogether too big, too complex, and too fleeting for direct acquaintance. We are not equipped to deal with so much subtlety, so much variety, so many permutations and combinations. And altogether we have to act in that environment, we have to reconstruct it on a simpler model before we can manage with it.[63]

60   Nancy Signorielli, "Television's Mean and Dangerous World: A Continuation of the Cultural Indicators Perspective," in *Cultivation Analysis: New Directions in Media Effects Research,* eds. N. Signorielli and M. Morgan (Newbury Park, CA: Sage, 1990), pp. 85–106.
61   For an overview, see Maxell McCombs and Tamara Bell, "The Agenda Setting Role of Mass Communication," in *An Integrated Approach to Communication Theory and Research,* eds. Michael B. Salwen and Don W. Stacks (Mahwah, NJ: Erlbaum, 1996), pp. 93–110.
62   See, for example, M. Childs and J. Reston (eds.), *Walter Lippmann and His Times* (New York: Harcourt Brace, 1959).
63   Walter Lippmann, *Public Opinion* (New York: Macmillan, 1921), p. 16.

The agenda-setting function has been described best by Donald Shaw, Maxwell McCombs, and their colleagues.[64] These authors write:

> Considerable evidence has accumulated that editors and broadcasters play an important part in shaping our social reality as they go about their day-to-day task of choosing and displaying news. . . . This impact of the mass media—the ability to effect cognitive change among individuals, to structure their thinking—has been labeled the agenda-setting function of mass communication. Here may lie the most important effect of mass communication, its ability to mentally order and organize our world for us. In short, the mass media may not be successful in telling us what to think, but they are stunningly successful in telling us what to think about.[65]

In other words, agenda setting establishes the salient issues or images in the minds of the public.

Agenda setting occurs because the press must be selective in reporting the news. The news outlets, as gatekeepers of information, make choices about what to report and how to report it. What the public knows about the state of affairs at any given time is largely a product of media gatekeeping.[66] Further, we know that how a person votes is determined mainly by what issues the individual believes to be important. For this reason some researchers have come to believe that the issues reported during a candidate's term in office may have more effect on the election than the campaign itself.

The agenda-setting function is a three-part linear process.[67] First, the priority of issues to be discussed in the media, *or media agenda*, must be set. Second, the media agenda in some way affects or interacts with what the public thinks, or the *public agenda*. Finally, the public agenda affects or interacts in some way with what policymakers consider important, or the *policy agenda*. In the theory's simplest and most direct version, then, the media agenda affects the public agenda, and the public agenda affects the policy agenda.

Although a number of studies show that the media can be powerful in affecting the public agenda, it is still not clear whether the public agenda does not itself affect the media agenda.

The relationship may be one of mutual causation rather than linear causation. Further, it appears that actual events have some impact on both the media agenda and the public agenda.

The prevailing opinion among media researchers seems to be that the media can have a powerful effect on the public agenda, but not always. The power of media depends on such factors as media credibility on particular issues at particular times, the extent of conflicting evidence as perceived by individual members of the public, the extent to which individuals share media values at certain times, and the public's need for guidance. Media most often will be powerful when media credibility is high, conflicting evidence is low, individuals share media values, and the audience has a high need for guidance.

Karen Siune and Ole Borre studied some of the complexities of agenda setting in a Danish election.[68] Because in Denmark the election campaigns last only three weeks and the number of political broadcasts are more limited than in the United States, the researchers had an excellent opportunity to study the agenda-setting process.

Three kinds of political broadcasts on radio and television were aired in this election. These included programs made by the political parties, programs in which the candidates were asked questions by a panel of journalists and citizens, and debates. All these programs were recorded

64   Donald L. Shaw and Maxwell E. McCombs, *The Emergence of American Political Issues* (St. Paul, MN: West, 1977). See also Jian-Hua Zhu and Deborah Blood, "Media Agenda-Setting Theory: Telling the Public What to Think About," in *Emerging Theories of Human Communication*, ed. Branislav Kovacic (Albany: SUNY Press, 1997), pp. 88–114. See also Everett M. Rogers and James W. Dearing, "Agenda-Setting Research: Where Has It Been, Where Is It Going?," in *Communication Yearbook 11*, ed. J. A. Anderson (Newbury Park, CA: Sage, 1988), pp. 555–593; Stephen D. Reese, "Setting the Media's Agenda: A Power Balance Perspective," in *Communication Yearbook 14*, ed. J. A. Anderson (Newbury Park, CA: Sage, 1991), pp. 309–340. See also David Protess and Maxwell McCombs, *Agenda Setting: Readings on Media, Public Opinion, and Policymaking* (Hillsdale, NJ: Erlbaum, 1991).
65   Shaw and McCombs, *Emergence*, p. 5.
66   Pamela J. Shoemaker, "Media Gatekeeping," in *An Integrated Approach to Communication Theory and Research*, eds. Michael B. Salwen and Don W. Stacks (Mahwah, NJ: Erlbaum, 1996), pp. 79–91.
67   This idea is developed by Rogers and Dearing, "Agenda-Setting Research."
68   Karen Siune and Ole Borre, "Setting the Agenda for a Danish Election," *Journal of Communication* 25 (1975): 65–73.

and analyzed by counting the number of statements made about each issue in the campaign. In addition, about 1,300 voters were interviewed at various points in the campaign to establish the public agenda. From this data the researchers could determine the media agendas of the politicians, the press, and voters.

This study suggests three kinds of agenda-setting effects. The first is the degree to which the media reflect the public agenda, called *representation*. In a representational agenda, the public influences the media. The second is the maintenance of the same agenda by the public the entire time, which is called *persistence*. In a persistent public agenda, the media may have little effect. The third occurs when the media agenda influences the public agenda, referred to as *persuasion*. This third kind of effect—media influencing the public—is exactly what classic agenda-setting theory predicts.

If you determine agendas at three points in a campaign—at the beginning (time 1), at the middle (time 2), and at the end (time 3)—you can get a sense of these three effects. A correlation between the public agenda at time 1 and the media agenda at time 2 suggests representation, or audience influencing media. A correlation between the public agenda at time 1 and at time 3 suggests persistence, or stability of the public agenda. Finally, a correlation between the media agenda at time 2 and the public agenda at time 3 suggests persuasion, or media influencing the public agenda. It is possible for any combination of these three to occur at the same time.

In their Danish study, Siune and Borre found much persistence in the public agenda, but there was also some persuasion in the sense that the broadcasts seemed to affect the public agenda somewhat. The most persuasive effects seemed to come from programs in which citizens set the media agenda. There was also a fair agenda-setting effect from the reporters and from the politicians themselves. The researchers did not find a representation effect in which the public affected the media.

A natural question is, "Who affects the media agenda in the first place?" This is a complex and difficult question. It appears that media agendas result from pressures both within media organizations and from outside sources.[69] In other words, the media agenda is established by some combination of internal programming, editorial, and managerial decisions and external influences from nonmedia sources such as socially influential individuals, government officials, commercial sponsors, and the like.

The power of media in establishing a public agenda depends in part on their relations with power centers. If the media have close relationships with the elite class in society, that class will probably affect the media agenda and the public agenda in turn. Many critical theorists believe that media can be an instrument of the dominant ideology in society, and when this happens, that dominant ideology will permeate the public agenda.

Four types of power relations between the media and outside sources can be found. The first is a high-power source and high-power media. In this kind of arrangement, if the two see eye to eye, a positive symbiotic relationship will exert great power over the public agenda. This would be the case, for example, with a powerful public official who has especially good relations with the press. On the other hand, if the powerful media and the powerful sources do not agree, a struggle may take place between them.

The second kind of arrangement is a high-power source and low-power media. Here, the external source will probably co-opt the media and use them to accomplish its own ends. This is what happens, for example, when politicians buy airtime or when a popular president such as Reagan gives the press the "privilege" of interviewing him.

In the third type of relation, a lower-power source and high-power media, the media organizations themselves will be largely responsible for their own agenda. This happens when the media marginalize certain news sources such as the student radicals in the 1960s.

---

69 Reese, "Setting the Media's Agenda."

The fourth type of relation is where both media and external sources are low in power, and the public agenda will probably be established by the events themselves rather than the media or the leaders.

As you can see, agenda setting is no simple matter, and our understanding of its complexity has come a long way since the early days of simplistic agenda-setting theory.

◗ THEORIES OF INDIVIDUAL OUTCOMES

The theories summarized in the previous section emphasize societal and cultural outcomes of mass communication. Other research has dealt with the *individual effects* of mass communication. In this section we discuss several of the theories of this individual-effects tradition.

The Effects Tradition

The theory of mass communication effects has undergone a curious evolution in this century.[70] Early on, researchers believed in the "magic bullet" theory of communication effects. Individuals were believed to be directly and heavily influenced by media messages, since media were considered to be extremely powerful in shaping public opinion.[71] According to this model, if you heard on the radio that you should try Pepsodent, you would.

Then, during the 1950s when the two-step flow hypothesis was becoming popular, media effects were considered to be minimal. It was believed that a commercial for Pepsodent would not directly influence very many people to try it. Later, in the 1960s, we came to think that the media effects were mediated by other variables and were therefore only moderate in strength. A Pepsodent commercial might or might not influence you, depending on other variables.

Now, after research in the 1970s and the 1980s, many scholars have returned to the powerful-effects model, in which the public is con-

sidered to be heavily influenced by media. This later research centers on television as the powerful medium.

Limited or Powerful Effects?

Perhaps the best-known early work on limited effects was the reinforcement approach most notably articulated by Joseph Klapper.[72] Klapper, in surveying the literature on mass communication effects, developed the thesis that mass communication is not a necessary and sufficient cause of audience effects, but that it is mediated by other variables. Thus media are only a contributing cause.

Raymond Bauer observes that audiences are difficult to persuade, and he calls them *obstinate*.[73] Bauer denies the idea that a direct hypodermic-needle effect operates between communicator and audience. Instead, many variables involved in the audience interact to shape effects in various ways.[74] Audience effects are mediated by group and interpersonal factors and by selectivity, among others. Studies have shown that audience members are selective in their exposure to information.[75] In its simplest form, the hypothesis of selective exposure predicts that people in most circumstances will select information consistent with their attitudes.

The reinforcement approach was a definite step in the right direction at the time it was in

70   This chronology is discussed by McQuail, *Mass Communication*, 1987, pp. 252–256.
71   For explorations of the history of the magic bullet or hypodermic needle theory, see J. Michael Sproule, "Progressive Propaganda Critics and the Magic Bullet Myth," *Critical Studies in Mass Communication* 6 (1989): 225–246; Jeffery L. Bineham, "A Historical Account of the Hypodermic Model in Mass Communication," *Communication Monographs* 55 (1988): 230–246.
72   Joseph T. Klapper, *The Effects of Mass Communication* (Glencoe, IL: Free Press, 1960).
73   Raymond Bauer, "The Obstinate Audience: The Influence Process from the Point of View of Social Communication," *American Psychologist* 19 (1964): 319–328.
74   Raymond Bauer, "The Audience," in *Handbook of Communication*, eds. I. de sola Pool and others (Chicago: Rand McNally, 1973), pp. 141–152.
75   Studies on selectivity are well summarized in David O. Sears and Jonathan I. Freedman, "Selective Exposure to Information: A Critical Review," in *The Process and Effects of Mass Communication*, eds. W. Schramm and D. F. Roberts (Urbana: University of Illinois Press, 1971), pp. 209–234.

vogue. Compared with the bullet theory, the re-inforcement approach viewed mass communication as more complicated than had previously been imagined. It envisioned situations ripe with mediating variables that would inhibit media effects. The research in this tradition did identify some important mediating variables, completing a more elaborate puzzle than had previously been constructed.

The problem of the limited-effects model is that it maintained a linear, cause-to-effect pattern.[76] It failed to take into account the social forces on the media or the ways that individuals might affect the media. In addition, the limited-effects model concentrated almost exclusively on attitude and opinion effects, ignoring other kinds of effects and functions such as cultivation or diffusion. Finally, true to tradition, such research focused on short-term effects of mass communication without questioning whether repeated exposure or time might affect the audience.

The work of Klapper and others on limited effects resulted in two general types of response. The first was a rejection of limited effects in favor of powerful effects, and the second was an attempt to explain limited effects in terms of the powers of audience members rather than media.

Perhaps the most vocal contemporary spokesperson in favor of powerful effects is Noelle-Neumann.[77] She believes that limited-effects theory has "distorted the interpretation of research findings over the years," and "that the 'dogma of media powerlessness' is no longer tenable."[78] Noelle-Neumann claims that the pendulum, which began swinging in the other direction after Klapper's famous work, has now reached its full extension and that most researchers believe that the media indeed have powerful effects.

Noelle-Neumann says that most limited-effects researchers were either academic journalists or people who held the media in a free society in high regard. They were interested in painting a picture of the media as disseminators of information, but not of influence. If viewed as important but not controlling, the media would continue to have the freedom to investigate and report whatever they felt to be important at a particular time, and journalists liked that. This interest led to the tendency to "see" limited rather than powerful effects in media-research results, which Noelle-Neumann calls "the media's effect on media research."

Many still believe that this reaction to limited effects is extreme and oversimple. In the following sections, we review theories that take a more moderate stand than either the limited- or powerful-effects models.

Uses, Gratifications, and Dependency

One of the most popular theories of mass communication is the uses-and-gratifications approach.[79] Here, we examine the original idea of uses and gratifications and then look at some interesting extensions.

The Original Idea. The uses-and-gratifications approach focuses on the consumer—the audience member—rather than the message.[80] Unlike the powerful-effects tradition, this approach imagines the audience member to be a discriminating user of media. The basic stance is summarized as follows:

> Compared with classical effects studies, the uses and gratifications approach takes the media consumer rather than the media message as

76   Criticism of the limited-effects approach can be found in Werner J. Severin and James W. Tankard, *Communication Theories: Origins, Methods, Use* (New York: Hastings House, 1979), p. 249.
77   Elisabeth Noelle-Neumann, "Return to the Concept of Powerful Mass Media," in *Studies of Broadcasting*, eds. H. Eguchi and K. Sata (Tokyo: Nippon Hoso Kyokii, 1973), pp. 67–112; "The Effect of Media on Media Effects Research," *Journal of Communication* 33 (1983): 157–165.
78   Noelle-Neumann, "Effect of Media," p. 157.
79   For historical overviews, J. D. Rayburn, II, "Uses and Gratifications," in *An Integrated Approach to Communication Theory and Research*, eds. Michael B. Salwen and Don W. Stacks (Mahwah, NJ: Erlbaum, 1996), pp. 145–163; Alan M. Rubin, "Audience Activity and Media Use," *Communication Monographs* 60 (1993): 98–105.
80   Elihu Katz, Jay Blumler, and Michael Gurevitch, "Uses of Mass Communication by the Individual," in *Mass Communication Research: Major Issues and Future Directions*, eds. W. P. Davidson and F. Yu (New York: Praeger, 1974), pp. 11–35. See also Jay Blumler and Elihu Katz (eds.), *The Uses of Mass Communication* (Beverly Hills, CA: Sage, 1974). See also the entire issue of *Communication Research* 6 (January 1979).

its starting point, and explores his communication behavior in terms of his direct experience with the media. It views the members of the audience as actively utilizing media contents, rather than being passively acted upon by the media. Thus, it does not assume a direct relationship between messages and effects, but postulates instead that members of the audience put messages to use, and that such usages act as intervening variables in the process of effect.[81]

Here the audience is assumed to be active and goal-directed. The audience member is largely responsible for choosing media to meet needs and knows his or her own needs and how to meet them. Media are considered to be only one way of meeting personal needs, and individuals may meet their needs through the media or in some other way. In other words, out of the options that media present, the individual chooses ways to gratify needs.

As you can see, this is an interesting idea, but it really does not tell us very much. Let's look now at some extensions that add detail.

Expectancy-Value Theory.   Acknowledging the lack of theoretical coherence in early uses-and-gratifications work, Philip Palmgreen created a theory based on his own work, that of Karl Rosengren, and others.[82] The theory is based on *expectancy-value theory,* which you read about in Chapter 7.

According to this theory, you orient yourself by your own attitudes. In Chapter 7 you learned that an attitude consists of a cluster of beliefs and evaluations, and this theory of media uses and gratifications is just an extension of this basic idea. Here your attitude toward some segment of the media is determined by your beliefs about and evaluations of it.

The gratifications you seek from media are determined by your attitudes toward the media—your beliefs about what a medium can give you and your evaluations of this material. For example, if you believe that sitcoms provide entertainment and you like to be entertained, you will seek gratification of your entertainment needs by watching sitcoms. If, on the other hand, you believe that sitcoms provide an unrealistic

view of life and you don't like this kind of thing, you will avoid viewing them.

Of course, your opinion of sitcoms consists of several beliefs and evaluations, and whether you actually watch them will be determined by several things. Your orientation to any type of program will be determined by your entire cluster of beliefs and evaluations. Palmgreen's formula for this, which mirrors the general expectancy-value formula presented in Chapter 7, is as follows:

$$GS_i = \sum_1^n b_i e_i$$

where

GS = gratification sought
b_i = belief
e_i = evaluation

The extent to which you seek gratifications in any segment of the media (a program, a program type, a particular kind of content, or an entire medium) would be determined by the same formula. As you gain experience with a part of the media, the gratifications you obtain will in turn affect your beliefs, creating a cyclical process (Figure 15.4).[83]

To test the connection between expectancy values and media gratifications, David Swanson and Austin Babrow conducted a study of the television news-viewing habits of students.[84] About three hundred students at the University of Illinois were asked to fill out a questionnaire on their news viewing. To find out whether they watched the news and how they felt about it, the students were asked how many times a week they viewed network and local news, how likely

---

81   Katz, Blumler, and Gurevitch, "Uses," p. 12.
82   Philip Palmgreen, "Uses and Gratifications: A Theoretical Perspective," in *Communication Yearbook 8,* ed. R. N. Bostrom (Beverly Hills, CA: Sage, 1984), pp. 20–55. See also K. Rosengren, L. Wenner, and P. Palmgreen (eds.), *Media Gratifications Research: Current Perspectives* (Beverly Hills, CA: Sage, 1985).
83   Palmgreen, "Uses and Gratifications," p. 36.
84   David L. Swanson and Austin S. Babrow, "Uses and Gratifications: The Influence of Gratification-Seeking and Expectancy-Value Judgments on the Viewing of Television News," in *Rethinking Communication: Paradigm Exemplars,* eds. Brenda Dervin, Lawrence Grossberg, Barbara J. O'Keefe, and Ellen Wartella (Newbury Park, CA: Sage, 1989), pp. 361–375.

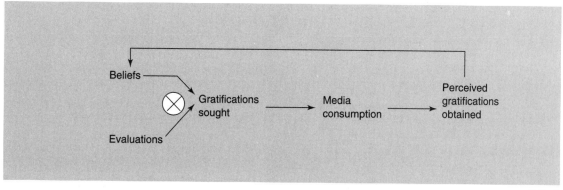

FIGURE **15.4**

Expectancy-Value Model of Gratifications Sought and Gratifications Obtained

they were to view news in an average week, and whether other people thought they should watch the news. The questionnaire also tested the students' attitudes toward the news.

To find out the extent to which the news gratified various media needs, the questionnaire asked whether each of a number of gratifications were met by watching the news. These included such items as keeping up on current events, getting entertained, and giving them things to talk about. In all, fourteen possible gratifications were included. The researchers found that the students' expectancy values (their attitudes) toward the news did relate to how much they used the news to gratify certain media needs.

Although the idea of expectancy and value is used as the basic explanatory mechanism for uses and gratifications, several other causal factors must be taken into account. Palmgreen has put together a complex model to depict the process of media use that he sees reflected in the research literature. It is clear from the model in Figure 15.5 that uses and gratifications are not a simple linear process but involve a whole network of effects.[85]

Dependency Theory.   The uses-and-gratifications approach is a limited-effects theory. In other words, it grants individuals much control over how they employ media in their lives. Although media scholars are divided on just how

powerful the media are, some scholars have argued that the limited-effects and powerful-effects models are not necessarily incompatible. Dependency theory takes a step toward showing how both may explain media effects.

Dependency theory was originally proposed by Sandra Ball-Rokeach and Melvin DeFleur.[86] Like uses-and-gratifications theory, this approach also rejects the causal assumptions of the early reinforcement hypothesis. To overcome this weakness, these authors take a broad system approach. In their model they propose an integral relationship among audiences, media, and the larger social system.

Consistent with uses-and-gratifications theory, this theory predicts that you depend on media information to meet certain needs and achieve certain goals. But you do not depend on all media equally. What determines how dependent you will become? There seem to be two factors.

First, you will become more dependent on media that meet a number of your needs than media that provide just a few. Media can serve a number of functions such as monitoring government activities and providing entertainment. For

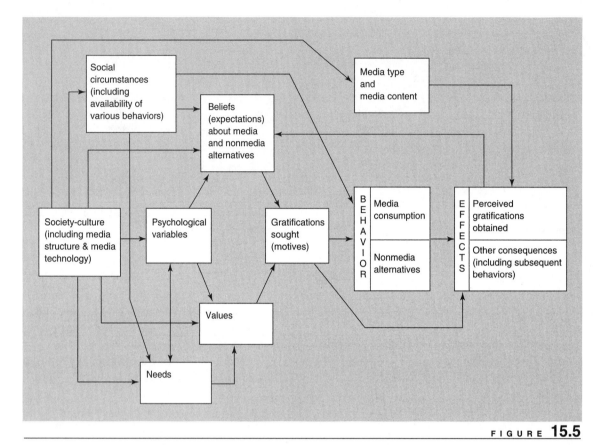

FIGURE **15.5**

Integrative Gratifications Model of Mass Media Consumption

any given group of people, some of these functions are more important than others, and your dependence on information from a medium increases when it supplies information that is more central to you. If you follow sports carefully, you will probably become quite dependent on ESPN or *Sports Illustrated.* A person who is not interested in sports will probably not even know where ESPN is on the dial, may never have looked at *Sports Illustrated,* and probably skips the entire sports section of the newspaper.

The second source of dependency is social stability. When social change and conflict are high, established institutions, beliefs, and practices are challenged, forcing you to reevaluate and make new choices. At such times your reliance on the media for information will increase. At other,

more stable times your dependency on media may go way down. During times of war, for example, people become incredibly dependent on news programming.

Figure 15.6, created by Alan Rubin and Sven Windahl, illustrates the dependency process.[87]

This model shows that social institutions and media systems interact with audiences so as to create needs, interests, and motives. These in turn influence the audience to select various media and nonmedia sources that can subsequently lead to various dependencies. Individuals who grow dependent on a particular segment of the

---

87   Alan M. Rubin and Sven Windahl, "The Uses and Dependency Model of Mass Communication," *Critical Studies in Mass Communication* 3 (1986): 188.

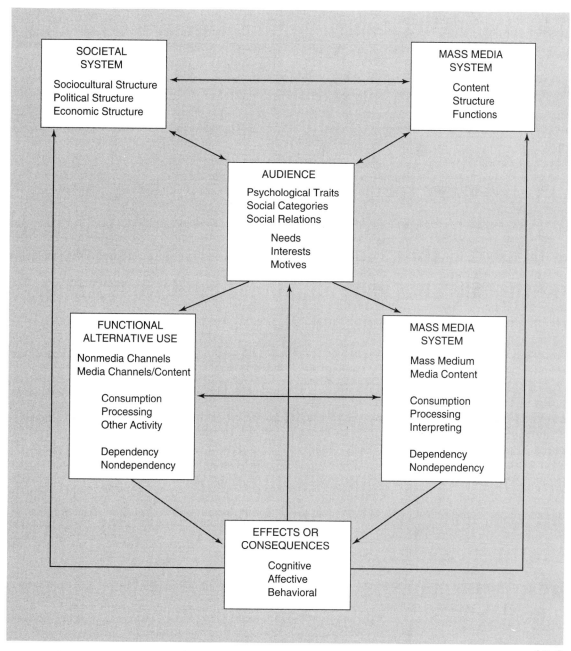

FIGURE **15.6**

The Uses and Dependency Model of Mass Communication

From *Critical Studies in Mass Communication* by Alan M. Rubin and Sven Windahl. Copyright © 1986 by the Speech Communication Association. Reprinted by permission of the author and publisher.

media will be affected cognitively, affectively, and behaviorally by that segment. Consequently, people are affected in different ways and to different degrees by the media.

Of course, one's "needs" are not always strictly personal but may be shaped by the culture or by various social conditions. In other words, individuals' needs, motives, and uses of media are contingent on outside factors that may not be in the individuals' control. These outside factors act as constraints on what and how media can be used and on the availability of other nonmedia alternatives.

For example, an elderly person who does not drive and has few friends may come to depend on television in a way that other individuals, whose life situations are different, will not. A commuter may come to rely on radio for information and news. A teenager may become dependent on music videos because of certain norms in the social group. In general, "the more readily available, the greater the perceived instrumentality, and the more socially and culturally acceptable the use of a medium is, the more probable that media use will be regarded as the most appropriate functional alternative."[88]

Furthermore, the more alternatives an individual has for gratifying needs, the less dependent he or she will become on any single medium. The number of functional alternatives, however, is not just a matter of individual choice or even of psychological traits but is limited also by factors such as availability of certain media.

◖ COMMENTARY AND CRITIQUE

Mass communication involves the dissemination of information and influence in society through media and interpersonal channels. It is an integral part of culture and is inseparable from other large-scale social institutions. Media forms like television, film, and print—as well as media content—affect our ways of thinking and seeing the world. Indeed, media participate in the very creation of culture itself, and many believe that media are instrumental in the dissemination of power and domination in society and are thereby instruments of ideology and hegemony.

Early mass communication theories concentrated on the structure and function of media. For example, Harold Lasswell's models outlined such functions as information, entertainment, and interpretation. Other functionalist theories presented additional ones such as shaping public opinion, diffusing innovations, cultivating common values, perpetuating majority views, and setting the public agenda. By the 1980s at least, this functionalist tradition was challenged vigorously by other perspectives.[89]

The extent and power of media influence is a matter of dispute. Mass communication is believed by some to reinforce attitudes and opinions, but evidence suggests that sometimes media effects are more profound than simple reinforcement. At the same time, however, people make active use of media to gratify their own needs. In fact, as people become dependent on certain types of media and content, the impact of those outlets may increase.

The controversies about media functions reflect a persistent conflict in the study of mass communication. How powerful are media in the control of culture? Some, like McLuhan, Meyrowitz, and Gerbner, argue that media are powerful forces in determining the character of culture and individual life. Other theorists claim that individuals have much control over the outcomes of media transactions in their lives. Yet a third group believes that mass media are important, but that they are only part of a complex of factors involved in social domination and that individuals are influenced by the entire system of dominating forces.

The outcome of the media-influence process is complex. In the final analysis, the outcome of mass communication may be a product of the interaction among various societal structures and individual needs, desires, and dependencies,

88 Rubin and Windahl, "Uses," p. 193.
89 Burrowes, "From Functionalism to Cultural Studies."

and it seems unlikely that this system will ever be reduced to an identifiable calculus. The theories in this chapter emphasize different aspects of this complex relationship.

McLuhan's theory is not much in favor anymore, but few would deny that his basic idea—that media forms in and of themselves do have an impact on culture—has had a major effect on our thinking about media. Media scholars today are just less glib about what those specific effects are than was McLuhan.

McLuhan's ideas are useful for stimulating a fresh look at the subject matter, but they provide little guidance on how to understand the process of mass communication. They are valuable in that they point to the importance of media forms in society, but they do not give a realistic picture of the variables involved in the effects of media forms. In sum, Kenneth Boulding points out, "It is perhaps typical of very creative minds that they hit very large nails not quite on the head."[90]

More popular today is semiotics. This field has had a major impact throughout communication studies, and it has been especially popular in media scholarship. The reasons are obvious. Semiotics provides a clear idea of what to look at when analyzing the meaning of media messages. In semiotics you look at visual, auditory, and verbal signs. Semiotics has also been useful to help explain why the media have differential effects. It is valuable, too, because it enables the observer to analyze the structure of media messages without ignoring the interpretive processes of the audience.

One of the most important lines of research on the cultural impact of media is critical theory, which maintains that media are powerful forces for dominant interests in society. The so-called media hegemony thesis maintains that media are instruments of the dominant ideology and by representing the interests of those already in power subvert the interests of marginalized groups. This thesis is hotly debated, as Kevin Carragee points out in a recent review.[91] Scholars opposing media hegemony claim that the media actually represent a diversity of values and often

speak out in opposition to the ideology of the powerful in society.

One of the obvious issues in media studies is the role of groups and interpersonal communication in the mass communication process. A whole line of research on diffusion of ideas and innovation supports the idea that interpersonal communication is a powerful part of this process. Beginning with the work of Paul Lazarsfeld, the research and theory of diffusion has been immensely successful. Dennis Davis and Stanley Baran remark of Lazarsfeld: "If one person deserves the title of founder of the field of mass communication research, that person is Paul Lazarsfeld. No one has done more to determine the way in which theory and research methods would be developed to aid our understanding of mass communication."[92]

The parsimony of diffusion theories has enabled observers to deal with a huge and complex phenomenon with relative ease. Additionally, these theories have been highly heuristic and have produced a large body of research. For many years the idea of the two-step flow (and later multiple-step flow) in the diffusion of information and innovation has been a mainstay of mass communication theory.

Traditional diffusion theory uses a linear pattern in which messages flow from person to person along a network. Some contemporary diffusion theorists now believe that this logic does not explain enough. Research has not consistently supported this notion of how diffusion occurs. At times the media appear to inform the public directly, with little interpersonal involvement; at other times different forms of diffusion are revealed. Further, the strict dichotomy between opinion leaders and followers is overly simple. In the give and take of everyday conversation, people exchange information, question it, argue about it, and come to a shared understanding.

---

90   Boulding, "The Medium," p. 68.
91   Kevin Carragee, "A Critical Evaluation of Debates Examining the Media Hegemony Thesis," *Western Journal of Communication* 57 (Summer 1993): 330–348.
92   Dennis K. Davis and Stanley J. Baran, *Mass Communication and Everyday Life: A Perspective on Theory and Effects* (Belmont, CA: Wadsworth, 1981), p. 27.

Another problem with the linear model of diffusion is that it downplays context; the actual circumstances under which diffusion occurs may have a great deal to do with the pattern of dissemination used by individuals in sharing information and innovations. Dissemination is more a matter of convergence or the achievement of shared meaning than of strict linear influence.

One of the problems of diffusion theory is to explain why information sometimes does not flow in the network. An interesting explanation is the spiral of silence. The spiral of silence exemplifies careful theory development through research. Beginning with a simple hypothesis in the early 1970s, Noelle-Neumann undertook numerous studies designed to test the basic hypothesis, its assumptions, and ramifications.

At the same time, however, the theory does not seem to apply in all societies. Hernando González, for example, in a study of public opinion in the Philippine revolution, says that the Philippine experience is not consistent with the spiral of silence. Indeed, alternative media were heard, and no spiral of silence appeared to be in favor of a dominant opinion in this society.[93]

From another corner, cultural scholars and Marxists would point to this line of research as an example of the kind of work they most distrust. First, they believe that it is false to assume that one can find an underlying structure to public opinion through surveys. Social science methods cannot be trusted to reveal any kind of reality beyond the meanings assigned by observers. Second, the failure to acknowledge the ideological nature of the public opinion is a major oversight. Third, critical scholars would point out that the spiral of silence is one possible factor in a general hegemony, in which the interests of dominant groups in society are perpetuated. Fourth, these critics would object to the suggestion that the spiral of silence is a universal phenomenon. All social life must be viewed in the context of history, and the spiral of silence, like most traditional social science findings, abstracts beyond the material world. Finally, this kind of research is truly "administrative" in the sense

that it becomes a tool in which the dominant ideology can be managed or promulgated.

Another theory of cultural media outcomes is cultivation analysis. Cultivation analysis, which is bolstered by two decades of research on cultural indicators, calls our attention to the power of television; however, the cultivation hypothesis has not been without critique.[94] In fact, television researcher Paul Hirsch has spoken out harshly against the cultivation effect. He reanalyzed Gerbner's data and failed to find evidence for cultivation. Hirsch concluded that "acceptance of the cultivation hypothesis as anything more than an interesting but unsupported speculation is premature and unwarranted at this time."[95] Gerbner and his colleagues have responded to this critique by reaffirming the validity of their findings and concluding that "Hirsch's analysis is flawed, incomplete, and tendentious."[96]

The more common tendency is to look on the cultivation effect as a possible and significant finding, but to be suspicious of the authors' precise explanation.[97] Cultivation theory is based on a simple premise: That television viewing causes individuals to accept the TV view of reality, and the more one watches television, the greater that acceptance. Critics question several things about this prediction. First, the effect may not be constant over all groups and all levels of viewing. Second, the causation may not be in the direction

---

93 Hernando González, "Mass Media and the Spiral of Silence: The Philippines from Marcos to Aquino," *Journal of Communication* 34 (1988): 33–48. For a summary of the failure of international research to confirm the theory, see Salmon and Glynn, "Spiral of Silence."

94 Morgan and Shanahan, "Two Decades of Cultivation Research."

95 Paul M. Hirsch, "The 'Scary World' of the Nonviewer and Other Anomalies: A Reanalysis of Gerbner et al.'s Findings on Cultivation Analysis," *Communication Research* 7 (1980): 404. See also Paul M. Hirsch, "On Not Learning from One's Own Mistakes: A Reanalysis of Gerbner et al.'s Findings on Cultivation Analysis, Part II," *Communication Research* 8 (1981): 3–38.

96 George Gerbner, Larry Gross, Michael Morgan, and Nancy Signorielli, "A Curious Journey into the Scary World of Paul Hirsch," *Communication Research* 8 (1981): 39.

97 A critique of this type is W. James Potter, "Cultivation Theory and Research: A Conceptual Critique," *Human Communication Research* 19 (1993): 564–601. See also John Tapper, "The Ecology of Cultivation: A Conceptual Model for Cultivation Research," *Communication Theory* 5 (1995): 36–57.

predicted; people may use TV to reinforce previously held beliefs. Third, there is some question about the strength or power of the cultivation effect among all of the other factors, such as education, that may affect our cultural beliefs. There is probably a grain of truth in cultivation theory, perhaps a very large grain, but some observers suspect that it does not tell the whole story.

Another important cultural outcome of media communication is agenda setting. Agenda-setting theory is appealing for two reasons. It returns a degree of power to the media after an era in which media effects were thought to be minimal, and its focus on cognitive effects rather than attitude and opinion change adds a badly needed dimension to effects research. The idea of issue salience as a media effect is intriguing and important.

The basic problem with this line of work is that although the theory is clear in positing a causal link between media and issue salience, the research evidence on this point is not convincing.[98] Research has uncovered a strong correlation between audience and media views on the importance of issues, but it does not always demonstrate that media choices cause audience salience. In fact, as we saw previously, some theorists argue that the emphasis given to issues in the media can be a reflection, not a cause, of audience agendas. This is a chicken-egg issue. Sometimes there may be an interaction between media and public in terms of the issue agenda, and situational factors probably always enter into how powerful the media are at any time in establishing the public agenda.

That certain studies do not support a direct causal link between media activity and audience attention does not mean that a relationship is not there. It may simply be a more complicated one. For example, there may be intervening variables or a nonlinear relationship. For example, Neuman explores the possibility that public response to an issue is aroused rather quickly at first and then levels off as a saturation point is reached.[99]

The uses-and-gratifications approach was like a breath of fresh air in media research. For the first time scholars in this tradition focused on receivers as active participants in the communication process, rather than the traditional viewpoint of the passive, unthinking audience. This approach is certainly one of the most popular frameworks for the study of mass communication, but a good deal of criticism has been leveled against it.[100]

The criticism of the uses-and-gratifications approach can be divided into three major strands.[101] The first set of objections deals with the lack of coherence and theory in the tradition. Although this objection had merit until recently, we have seen that more unified versions in the form of value-expectancy and value-dependency theories are emerging.

The second line of criticism focuses on social and political objections, which come primarily from critical theory. The problem is that uses and gratifications is so functional in orientation that it ignores the dysfunctions of media in society and culture. It is conservative at heart and sees media primarily as positive ways in which individuals meet their needs, without any attention to the overall negative cultural effects of media in society.

Finally, some critics have objected to the instrumental philosophy of uses and gratifications. Uses and gratifications makes media consumption extremely rational, behavioristic, and individualistic. Individuals are believed to control their media-consuming behavior according to conscious goals. No attention is paid to the ways media may be consumed mindlessly or ritualistically. The theory does not study the ways media content forms and reflects cultural values or

---

98   Criticism of this work can be found in Severin and Tankard, *Communication Theories*, pp. 253–254.

99   W. R. Neuman, "The Threshold of Public Opinion," *Public Opinion Quarterly* 54 (1990): 159–176.

100   See especially Philip Elliott, "Uses and Gratifications Research: A Critique and Sociological Alternative," in *The Uses of Mass Communication*, eds. J. Blumler and E. Katz (Beverly Hills, CA: Sage, 1974), pp. 249–268; and David L. Swanson, "Political Communication Research and the Uses and Gratifications Model: A Critique," *Communication Research* 6 (1979): 36–53.

101   Denis McQuail, "With the Benefits of Hindsight: Reflections on Uses and Gratifications Research," *Critical Studies in Mass Communication* 1 (1984): 177–193.

patterns of action. In other words, much of our consumption of mass media may not be easily traced to individual needs, but rather to habits of the culture. Also, individuals may not be aware of many of the factors that enter into their consumption choices. Attribution theory, which was covered in greater detail in Chapter 7, suggests that people often misjudge the causes of their own behavior; some research indicates that this principle holds true for media consumption as well.[102]

McQuail, a noted researcher of uses and gratifications, takes this third point seriously and proposes that the traditional gratifications model is only part of what happens in media use.[103] He suggests that although individuals do use media for guidance, surveillance, and information, they also have a generalized arousal need that comes from and is informed by the culture.

Dependency theory makes an attempt to reconcile some of the problems of uses and gratifications with other powerful-effects models. This theory accounts for both individual differences in responses to media and general media effects. As a system theory, it shows the complexity of the interactions among the various aspects of the media transaction. The fusion of uses-and-gratifications and dependency theories provides an even more complete integration.

Like most of the theories in this chapter, however, both dependency and uses-and-dependency theory clash with the critical theory school. This clash points out a number of stasis points in media theory: Are media powerful in influencing culture, or are effects and cultural realities the accomplishments of individuals and interpretive communities? Do individuals make real choices, and how extensive are the cultural limits on individual media choice? To what extent should theory describe and explain, and to what extent should it reform? There will always be answers to these questions, but consensus will probably never be achieved.

---

102   See, for example, Dolf Zillmann, "Attribution and Misattribution of Excitatory Reactions," in *New Directions in Attribution Research*, vol. 2, eds. J. H. Harvey, W. Ickes, and R. F. Kidd (Hillsdale, NJ: Erlbaum, 1978), pp. 335–368.
103   McQuail, "Hindsight."

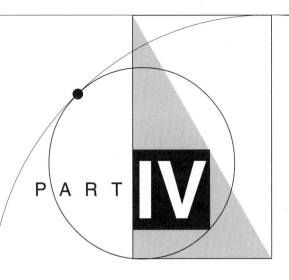

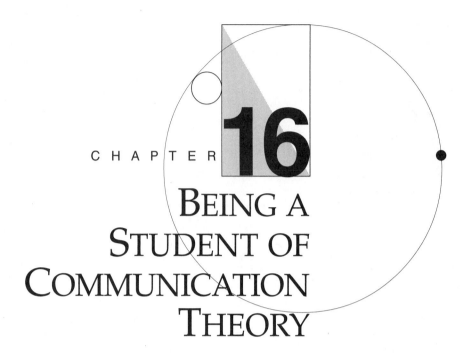

16

BEING A STUDENT OF COMMUNICATION THEORY

You are probably reading this chapter last. Perhaps it should have been the first chapter because it addresses some of your most personal concerns as a student. Coming last, however, this capstone chapter may provide an important personal context for your study of communication theory.

What does it mean to be student of communication? For the less experienced, it may only mean getting through the next assignment in each class. As you take more and more communication courses, your view will broaden and include a sense of the whole curriculum and how one course relates to another. This more sophisticated perspective may also include questions about the relative significance of various courses. On the senior and graduate levels, you begin to see the whole curriculum as an integrated experience, you may question or challenge the effectiveness of the entire program, or you may come to value your work as an important part of your personal development.

In the liberal arts tradition, the baccalaureate degree is designed to broaden perspectives and

build creative and critical thinking. The bachelor's degree includes a major focus, but it also combines numerous other perspectives ranging from nature to art, technology to humanities, science to language. Well-educated people are able to understand their experiences in numerous, productive ways; to solve problems by careful analysis and creativity; and to adjust to the vagaries of life.

Communication fits beautifully into the liberal arts tradition because it integrates focus and diversity. Communication studies include skill, art, critical thinking, history, literature and language, technology, career preparation, and more. Whether you are a communication major or minor, or whether you are just taking communication courses to meet general education requirements or electives, you will have many opportunities to learn a variety of new, interesting, and useful concepts.

You are probably reading this book as an assignment in a communication theory course. If the course has been successful, you will see things you did not consider before, you will turn events around and look at them from a variety of angles, and you will have a greater appreciation for the many intelligent ways in which human experience can be understood. If this course was successful, it will have helped you meet the goals of the liberal arts.

The communication theory course also fulfills an important function in the major. It is a place where a diversity of ideas about communication can be studied side by side, compared, evaluated, and used. A successful communication theory course provides the resources for thinking critically about the subject, for observing communication events, and for communicating in many effective ways.

As a student of communication, you have devoted considerable time to the study of human social interaction. You may have chosen this subject because of a fascination for human relationships, an appreciation for media, a love of language and symbols, or desire to obtain concrete skills. Perhaps you see that communication is a crucial aspect of contemporary social and political life. Or you may have noticed that there are many careers available in this field. Whatever your personal goals, you have recognized in some way that communication is an important topic, important enough to devote a lot of energy to.

If your communication theory course was successful, you will have an even greater appreciation for the importance of social interaction in human life. You will see that your own individuality and personhood are shaped in relationships with other people. You will consider the ways in which social categories and language affect your thinking and how you yourself put a lot of cognitive effort into planning and interpreting messages. You will have some ideas about the ways you think, the categories you use, and the symbols and language that shape your ideas.

By this point in the course, too, you will be conscious of the role of communication in determining the social, cultural, and political life of the community. You will be aware of how your own relationships are defined and negotiated,

how groups work as a unit, and how organizations are structured and how they function. You will also understand the place of media as a social and political force.

You will have a sense that there are no right and true ways of understanding communication and its connection to personal, social, cultural, and political life. Indeed, you may even be a bit mystified, maybe even amused or intrigued, by the fact that equally well-educated and intelligent scholars can come to have such different ways of thinking and working. If your communication theory course has been successful, however, you will have some tools for understanding why this is so—seeing the powers and limits of the various types of scholarship, evaluating different traditions, and making decisions about what approaches fit your own philosophy and aptitudes. You will also have a good sense of how to select different theoretical approaches when you look at communication in different ways.

There is a naive view of education that goes something like this: Smart people have studied the world and found out what it is like. Education is a process of teaching these findings to young people so that they will better understand how things are. Teachers are experts who pass this information on to younger generations. The more educated one gets, the more of this information he or she knows.

In one sense, this story is true. Within particular domains of knowledge such as medicine, physics, accounting, or history, people do obtain knowledge, become expert, and pass this knowledge on to others. In communication, scholars do know things about media, relationships, organizations, cognition, and other subjects. Communication professors often present this information as "found knowledge" to be "learned."

In another sense, however, this story is mythical. The world must always be understood from a particular perspective, and intelligent people disagree about the best one to use. Nothing is ever just learned; it is always learned from within a perspective. Every perspective has powers and limits. Every perspective is useful in some way to someone, but not in all ways to everyone.

One of the most important things you can learn from the communication theory course is this: Truth is not a set of codified facts but a sense gained by examining and reexamining things from multiple perspectives.

Imagine a different kind of communication theory course. Here the instructor determines the best theoretical perspective and proceeds to teach it. For example, the course might stress psychological and cognitive theory, social approaches, critical theory, or structuration theory. Such a course would have many benefits.

It would make use of the professor's expertise in one area. It would certainly be cohesive and much less confusing than the course you are now completing. Students in this course would probably see the materials learned as factual knowledge discovered by researchers, taught by the professor, and learned by students. They might never realize that what they learned was a perspective and one of many ways of packaging knowledge about communication. They might never come to grips with the limitations of the theory, and they would lose the opportunity to learn a variety of tools for looking at the many facets of communication. They would probably not be challenged nor given the resources to compare theoretical approaches and to evaluate them. In other words, they would become smart about communication in one way but very limited in what they know in other ways.

Because you are using this text, your communication theory course is quite different from the one described above. You have covered many theories and numerous philosophical approaches. You may feel a little confused about what you have learned, and you may wish that you had been in a course like the one described above. If the course you are in has been successful, however, you have begun to get a sense of the powers and uses of multiple perspectives.

There is an interesting paradox in all of this. The multiple-perspectives approach is itself a perspective and an approach. Like any other, it has both powers and limits, advantages and disadvantages. At this point in your career as a communication student, be challenged to think about what you gained and lost by the approach that was used here.

Being a student in any field is more than just learning information, of course. It is learning how to think in certain ways and how to act in certain ways. As a communication student, you learn to think about communication and participate in it.

There is a close relationship between thinking and doing, and education is one of the ways to shape the thinking-doing relationship. Good questions for students in any course are these:

1. How am I learning to think in this class?
2. What forms of action am I being taught?
3. How does this kind of thinking affect my behavior?
4. How does my behavior affect my thinking?

Applied to this course, these questions will lead you to consider how communication theories affect thought and action.

Thus there is a three-way relationship among theory, thought, and action. You cannot really cut these apart. Theories tell us what to think about and what categories to employ in our thinking, and theories shape the kind of action we take as communicators and scholars. Our thinking affects how we theorize and how we behave as communicators, and communicative action shapes both of the other two.

If you agree with the theory of argumentativeness (Chapter 6), you will think about communication in terms of aggression, verbal aggressiveness, assertiveness, and argumentativeness. You will see these qualities in the messages of others, and you will wonder how you as a communicator stand on the argumentativeness variable. As you talk to others, you will notice whether you tend to argue a lot and whether you enjoy doing so. Since this theory values argumentativeness and devalues aggressiveness, you will think about how to make better use of argument and how to reduce aggression. As you do these things, you will come to accept the tenets of the theory and continue to concentrate your own thinking on these concepts.

Suppose, on the other hand, that you favor the theory of symbolic interactionism (Chapter 8). This theory leads you to think about society, self, and mind as closely knit parts of an interactional process. You will see how your own self-image is shaped by how others respond to you, you'll get a sense of your "generalized other," and you'll begin to evaluate other people's behavior in terms of how it reflects their histories of interaction with significant others. Since interaction is highly influential in how people think and behave, you will be conscious of your own reactions to others and other people's reactions to you.

In a third example, consider what happens if you take a feminist perspective (Chapter 11). You will make heavy use of the concept of gender and power in your thinking. You will evaluate what happens to people largely in terms of these concepts. Since feminism is predicated on the desire to release women from oppression and give them voice in society, you will find many instances of oppression and think about how it might be overcome in those cases. In your own actions, you will work toward honoring the contributions of women, allowing women equal voice, and eliminating sex discrimination.

Are we limited to operating by a single theory? Of course not. You can and do combine a variety of theories. Some of these are highly compatible, giving you a coherent way of thinking and acting. For example, you might integrate symbolic interactionism, feminism, structuration, and cultural studies. Each provides insights that can compliment those of the others. Other combinations do not work very well. They are predicated on conflicting assumptions, and their concepts fight against one another. For example, cognitive and cultural theories are hard to use simultaneously.

We often alternate among conflicting perspectives, taking one and then another, or using one in one situation and another one elsewhere. In-

deed, we often do this without being aware of the inconsistency in how we are thinking and acting.

For example, one might join a cause for social change, believing in the power of community action, while typing the opponent with certain traits that are seen as essentially immutable. If people's behavior is determined by deeply held traits, how can we change them with community action? Living in a world of multiple perspectives can lead to these kinds of paradoxes, double binds, and dilemmas. We all employ many realities in our thinking and action; being inconsistent is entirely natural in a postmodern world.

So studying communication theory is a way of recognizing the many perspectives we may use, identifying their similarities and differences, and acknowledging the multiple realities in which we live. It provides a kit of tools for recognizing the theoretical bases of our own and others' actions, and it even gives us choices, to move in and out of different perspectives as we encounter contradictions in life. In the end, you may decide to "go multiple" or find a highly coherent set of ideas that works in your life. In any case, if this course is successful, you have some resources for making this choice rationally.

Most of the students taking this course are far enough along in college to be thinking pretty seriously about what will happen after graduation. If you are not a little worried about your career, you are probably unusual among your classmates. Let's end this book, then, by talking about communication theory and careers.

If you are really career minded, you have already done considerable reading and Web searching on careers, and you have probably visited the Career Center on your campus more than once. You have probably learned that lifetime careers are unusual nowadays, that general preparation and critical thinking are preferable to very specialized preparation, that communication is a highly ranked skill among employers, that job experience is vital, that you need to know your assets and sell yourself, and that you may have to "re-invent yourself" many times during your life.

If this course has been successful, it will have provided a step toward achieving these goals. You will be able to make connections among ideas more effectively than you did before. You will be able to think about problems in a more discriminating way than you might otherwise be able to do. You will have a larger range of responses to situations than you did earlier. You will be more in tune with social trends and think of creative ways to contribute. You will have access to more aspects of yourself and your relationships to others, and you will have a better sense of your own strengths and weaknesses. Communication theory is not a sure ticket to a good career, but it is a solid step in that direction if you think about it in this way and consciously use these insights in your daily life.

BIBLIOGRAPHY

Chapter 1
Communication Theory and Scholarship

Allen, Mike R. "Critical and Traditional Science: Implications for Communication Research." *Western Journal of Communication* 57 (1993): 200–208.

Andersen, Peter A. "When One Cannot Not Communicate: A Challenge to Motley's Traditional Communication Postulates." *Communication Studies* 42 (1991): 309–325.

Anderson, James A. *Communication Theory: Epistemological Foundations.* New York: Guilford, 1996.

Atwater, Tony. "Communication Theory and Research: The Quest for Credibility in the Social Sciences," In *An Integrated Approach to Communication Theory.* Edited by M. B. Salwen and D. W. Stacks. Mahwah, NJ: Erlbaum, 1996, pp. 539–549.

Barnlund, Dean C. *Interpersonal Communication: Survey and Studies.* New York: Houghton Mifflin, 1968.

Bavelas, Janet Beavin. "Behaving and Communicating: A Reply to Motley." *Western Journal of Speech Communication* 54 (1990): 593–602.

Beach, Wayne A. "On (Not) Observing Behavior Interactionally." *Western Journal of Speech Communication* 54 (1990): 603–612.

Berger, Charles R., and Chaffee, Steven H. "The Study of Communication as a Science." In *Handbook of Communication Science.* Edited by Charles R. Berger and Steven H. Chaffee. Newbury Park, CA: Sage, 1987, pp. 15–19.

Blalock, Hubert M. *Basic Dilemmas in the Social Sciences.* Beverly Hills, CA: Sage, 1984.

Bochner, Arthur P. "Perspectives on Inquiry: Representation, Conversation, and Reflection." In *Handbook of Interpersonal Communication.* Edited by Mark L. Knapp and Gerald R. Miller. Beverly Hills, CA: Sage, 1985, pp. 27–58.

Bormann, Ernest G. *Theory and Research in the Communicative Arts.* New York: Holt, Rinehart & Winston, 1965.

Bowers, John Waite, and Bradac, James J. "Issues in Communication Theory: A Metatheoretical Analysis." In *Communication Yearbook 5.* Edited by Michael Burgoon. New Brunswick, NJ: Transaction, 1982, pp. 1–28.

Burrell, G., and Morgan, G. *Sociological Paradigms and Organizational Analysis.* London: Heinemann, 1979.

Burrowes, Carl Patrick. "From Functionalism to Cultural Studies: Manifest Ruptures and Latent Continuities." *Communication Theory* 6 (1996): 88–103.

Cappella, Joseph N., ed. "Symposium on Mass and Interpersonal Communication." *Human Communication Research* 15 (1988): 236–318.

Clevenger, Theodore, Jr., "Can One Not Communicate? A Conflict of Models." *Communication Studies* 42 (1991): 340–353.

Craig, Robert T. "Why Are There So *Many* Communication Theories?" *Journal of Communication* 43 (1993): 26–33.

Dallmayr, Fred R. *Language and Politics.* Notre Dame, IN: University of Notre Dame Press, 1984.

Dance, Frank E. X. "The 'Concept' of Communication." *Journal of Communication* 20 (1970): 201–210.

Dance, Frank E. X., and Larson, Carl E. *The Functions of Human Communication: A Theoretical Approach.* New York: Holt, Rinehart & Winston, 1976.

Deetz, Stanley A. "Describing Differences in Approaches to Organization Science." *Organization Science* 7 (1996): 191–207.

———. "Future of the Discipline: The Challenges, the Research, and the Social Contribution." In *Communication Yearbook 17.* Edited by Stanley A. Deetz. Thousand Oaks, CA: Sage, 1994, pp. 565–600.

Delia, Jesse G. "Communication Research: A History." In *Handbook of Communication Science.* Edited by Charles R. Berger and Steven H. Chaffee. Newbury Park, CA: Sage, 1987, pp. 20–98.

de Saussure, Ferdinand. *Course in General Linguistics.* London: Peter Owen, 1960.

Diefenbeck, James A. *A Celebration of Subjective Thought.* Carbondale: Southern Illinois University Press, 1984.

Durkheim, Emile. *The Division of Labor in Society.* London: Collier-Macmillan, 1964.

Farrell, Thomas B. "Beyond Science: Humanities Contributions to Communication Theory." In *Handbook of Communication Science.* Edited by Charles R. Berger and Steven H. Chaffee. Newbury Park, CA: Sage, 1987, pp. 123–139.

Farrell, Thomas B., and Aune, James A. "Critical Theory and Communication: A Selective Review." *Quarterly Journal of Speech* 65 (1979): 93–120.

Fay, Brian. *Social Theory and Political Practice.* London: Allen & Unwin, 1975.

Fiske, Donald W., and Shweder, Richard A. "Introduction: Uneasy Social Science." In *Metatheory in Social Science: Pluralisms and Subjectivities*. Edited by Donald W. Fiske and Richard A. Schweder. Chicago: University of Chicago Press, 1986, pp. 1–18.

Foss, Karen A., and Foss, Sonja K. "Incorporating the Feminist Perspective in Communication Scholarship: A Research Commentary." In *Doing Research on Women's Communication: Alternative Perspectives in Theory and Method*. Edited by Carole Spitzack and Kathryn Carter. Norwood, NJ: Ablex, 1989, pp. 65–94.

Gergen, Kenneth J. *Toward Transformation in Social Knowledge*. New York: Springer-Verlag, 1982.

Giddens, Anthony. *Central Problems in Social Theory*. Berkeley: University of California Press, 1979.

———. *Profiles and Critiques in Social Theory*. Berkeley: University of California Press, 1983.

Glazer, Nathan. "The Social Sciences in Liberal Education." In *The Philosophy of the Curriculum*. Edited by Sidney Hook. Buffalo, NY: Prometheus, 1975, pp. 145–158.

Greene, John O. "Evaluating Cognitive Explanations of Communicative Phenomena." *Quarterly Journal of Speech* 70 (1984): 241–254.

Grossberg, Lawrence. "Does Communication Theory Need Intersubjectivity? Toward an Immanent Philosophy of Interpersonal Relations." In *Communication Yearbook 6*. Edited by Michael Burgoon. Beverly Hills, CA: Sage, 1984, pp. 171–205.

Hanson, N. R. *Patterns of Discovery*. Cambridge: Cambridge University Press, 1961.

Harper, Nancy. *Human Communication Theory: The History of a Paradigm*. Rochelle Park, NJ: Hayden, 1979.

Hawkins, Robert P., Wiemann, John M., and Pingree, Suzanne, eds. *Advancing Communication Science*. Newbury Park, CA: Sage, 1988.

Holton, Gerald. "Science, Science Teaching, and Rationality." In *The Philosophy of the Curriculum*. Edited by Sidney Hook. Buffalo, NY: Prometheus, 1975, pp. 101–108.

Jarrett, James L. *The Humanities and Humanistic Education*. Reading, MA: Addison-Wesley, 1973.

Kincaid, D. Lawrence. *Communication Theory: Eastern and Western Perspectives*. San Diego, CA: Academic, 1987.

Krippendorff, Klaus. "Conversation or Intellectual Imperialism in Comparing Communication (Theories)." *Communication Theory* 3 (1993): 252–266.

Kuhn, Thomas S. *The Structure of Scientific Revolutions*, 2nd ed. Chicago: University of Chicago Press, 1970.

Lakoff, George, and Johnson, Mark. *Metaphors We Live By*. Chicago: University of Chicago Press, 1980.

Littlejohn, Stephen W. "An Overview of the Contributions to Human Communication Theory from Other Disciplines." In *Human Communication Theory: Comparative Essays*. Edited by Frank E. X. Dance. New York: Harper & Row, 1982, pp. 243–285.

McKeon, Richard. "Gibson Winter's Elements for a Social Ethic: A Review." *Journal of Religion* 49 (1969): 77–84.

Meehl, Paul E. "What Social Scientists Don't Understand." In *Metatheory in Social Science: Pluralisms and Subjectivities*. Edited by Donald W. Fiske and Richard A. Shweder. Chicago: University of Chicago Press, 1986, pp. 317–319.

Miller, Gerald R. "On Defining Communication: Another Stab." *Journal of Communication*, 16 (1966): 92.

Miller, Gerald R., and Nicholson, Henry. *Communication Inquiry*. Reading, MA: Addison-Wesley, 1976.

Motley, Michael T. "Communication as Interaction: A Reply to Beach and Bavelas." *Western Journal of Speech Communication* 54 (1990): 613–623.

———. "How One May Not Communicate: A Reply to Andersen." *Communication Studies* 42 (1991): 326–339.

———. "On Whether One Can(not) (Not) Communicate: An Examination Via Traditional Communication Postulates." *Western Journal of Speech Communication* 54 (1990): 1–20.

Pearce, W. Barnett. *Communication and the Human Condition*. Carbondale: Southern Illinois University Press, 1989.

———. "Scientific Research Methods in Communication Studies and Their Implications for Theory and Research." In *Speech Communication in the 20th Century*. Edited by Thomas W. Benson. Carbondale: Southern Illinois University Press, 1985, pp. 255–281.

Pearce, W. Barnett, Cronen, Vernon E., and Harris, Linda M. "Methodological Considerations in Building Human Communication Theory." In *Human Communication Theory: Comparative Essays*. Edited by Frank E. X. Dance. New York: Harper & Row, 1982, pp. 1–41.

Pearce, W. Barnett, and Foss, Karen A. "The Historical Context of Communication as a Science." In *Human Communication: Theory and Research*. Edited by Gordon L. Dahnke and Glen W. Clatterbuck. Belmont, CA: Wadsworth, 1990, pp. 1–20.

Peters, John Durham. "The Gaps of Which Communication Is Made." *Critical Studies in Mass Communication* 11 (1994): 117–140.

———. "Tangled Legacies." *Journal of Communication* 46 (1996): 85–147.

Powers, John H. "On the Intellectual Structure of the Human Communication Discipline." *Communication Education* 44 (1995): 191–222.

Reardon, Kathleen K., and dePillis, Emmeline G. "Multichannel Leadership: Revisiting the False Dichotomy." In *An Integrated Approach to Communication Theory and Research*. Edited by M. B. Salwen and D. W. Stacks. Mahwah, NJ: Erlbaum, 1996, pp. 399–407.

Rogers, Everett M. *A History of Communication Study: A Biographical Approach*. New York: Free Press, 1994.

Rosengren, Karl Erik. "Culture, Media, and Society: Agency and Structure, Continuity and Change." In *Media Effects and Beyond*. Edited by Karl Erik Rosengren. London: Routledge, 1994, pp. 3–28.

———. "From Field to Frog Ponds." *Journal of Communication* 43 (1993): 6–17.

Ruesch, Jurgen. "Technology and Social Communication." In *Communication Theory and Research*. Edited by L. Thayer. Springfield, IL: Thomas, 1957, p. 462.

Semin, Gün R., and Gergen, Kenneth J. "Everyday Understanding in Science and Daily Life." In *Everyday Understanding: Social and Scientific Implications*. Edited by Gün R. Semin and Kenneth J. Gergen. London: Sage, 1990, pp. 1–18.

Sholle, David. "Resisting Disciplines: Repositioning Media Studies in the University," *Communication Theory* 5 (1995): 130–143.

Smith, Ted J., III. "Diversity and Order in Communication Theory: The Uses of Philosophical Analysis." *Communication Quarterly* 36 (1988): 28–40.

Snow, C. P. *The Two Cultures and a Second Look.* Cambridge: Cambridge University Press, 1964.

Sparks, Glen G., Potter, W. James, Cooper, Roger, and Dupagne, Michel. "Is Media Research Prescientific?" *Communication Theory* 5 (1995): 273–289.

Stacks, Don W., and Salwen, Michael B. "Integrating Theory and Research: Starting with Questions." In *An Integrated Approach to Communication Theory and Research.* Edited by M. B. Salwen and D. W. Stacks. Mahwah, NJ: Erlbaum, 1996, pp. 3–14.

Stewart, John. *Language as Articulate Contact.* Albany: SUNY Press, 1995.

———. "Speech and Human Being." *Quarterly Journal of Speech* 72 (1986): 55–73.

Streeter, Thomas. "Introduction: For the Study of Communication and Against the Discipline of Communication." *Communication Theory* 5 (1995): 117–129.

Truzzi, M. *Verstehen: Subjective Understanding in the Social Sciences.* Reading, MA: Addison-Wesley, 1974.

Winch, Peter. *The Idea of a Social Science and Its Relation to Philosophy.* London: Routledge & Kegan Paul, 1958.

Winter, Gibson. *Elements for a Social Ethic: Scientific and Ethical Perspectives on Social Process.* New York: Macmillan, 1966.

Chapter 2
Theory in the Process of Inquiry

Achinstein, P. *Laws and Explanation.* New York: Oxford University Press, 1971.

Andersen, Peter A. "The Trait Debate: A Critical Examination of the Individual Differences Paradigm in the Communication Sciences." In *Progress in Communication Sciences.* Edited by B. Dervin and M. J. Voight. Norwood, NJ: Ablex, 1986.

Anderson, James A. *Communication Theory: Epistemological Foundations.* New York: Guilford, 1996.

———. "Thinking Qualitatively." In *An Integrated Approach to Communication Theory and Research.* Edited by M. B. Salwen and D. W. Stacks. Mahwah, NJ: Erlbaum, 1996, pp. 45–59.

Beatty, Michael J. "Thinking Quantitatively." In *An Integrated Approach to Communication Theory and Research.* Edited by M. B. Salwen and D. W. Stacks. Mahwah, NJ: Erlbaum, 1996, pp. 33–44.

Berger, Charles R. "The Covering Law Perspective as a Theoretical Basis for the Study of Human Communication." *Communication Quarterly* 25 (1977): 7–18.

———. "Evidence? For What?" *Western Journal of Communication* 58 (1994): 11–19.

Berger, Peter, and Luckmann, Thomas. *The Social Construction of Reality.* Garden City, NY: Doubleday, 1966.

Black, Max. *Models and Metaphors.* Ithaca, NY: Cornell University Press, 1962.

Bormann, Ernest G. *Communication Theory.* New York: Holt, Rinehart & Winston, 1980.

Bostrom, Robert, and Donohew, Lewis. "The Case for Empiricism: Clarifying Fundamental Issues in Communi-

nication Theory." *Communication Monographs* 59 (1992): 109–129.

Bowers, John Waite, and Bradac, James J. "Issues in Communication Theory: A Metatheoretical Analysis." In *Communication Yearbook 5.* Edited by Michael Burgoon. New Brunswick, NJ: Transaction, 1982, pp. 1–28.

Brinberg, David, and McGrath, Joseph E. *Validity and the Research Process.* Beverly Hills, CA: Sage, 1985.

Bross, Irwin B. J. *Design for Decision.* New York: Macmillan, 1952.

Brummett, Barry. "Some Implications of 'Process' or 'Intersubjectivity': Postmodern Rhetoric." *Philosophy and Rhetoric* 9 (1976): 21–51.

Caley, Michael T., and Sawada, Daiyo, eds. *Mindscapes: The Epistemology of Magoroh Maruyama.* Amsterdam: Gordon and Breach, 1994.

Chaffee, Steven H. "Thinking About Theory." In *An Integrated Approach to Communication Theory and Research.* Edited by M. B. Salwen and D. W. Stacks. Mahwah, NJ: Erlbaum, 1996, pp. 15–32.

Chaffee, Steven H., and Berger, Charles R. "What Communication Scientists Do." In *Handbook of Communication Science.* Edited by Charles R. Berger and Steven H. Chaffee. Newbury Park, CA: Sage, 1987, pp. 91–122.

Coughlin, Ellen K. "Thomas Kuhn's Ideas About Science." *Chronicle of Higher Education* (Sept. 22, 1982): 21–23.

Craig, Robert T., and Tracy, Karen. "Grounded Practical Theory: The Case of Intellectual Discussion." *Communication Theory* 5 (1995): 248–272.

Cushman, Donald P. "The Rules Perspective as a Theoretical Basis for the Study of Human Communication." *Communication Quarterly* 25 (1977): 30–45.

Cushman, Donald P., and Pearce, W. Barnett. "Generality and Necessity in Three Types of Theory About Human Communication, with Special Attention to Rules Theory." *Human Communication Research* 3 (1977): 344–353.

Dance, Frank E. X., and Larson, Carl E. *The Functions of Human Communication: A Theoretical Approach.* New York: Holt, Rinehart & Winston, 1976.

Deetz, Stanley A. *Democracy in an Age of Corporate Colonization: Developments in Communication and the Politics of Everyday Life.* Albany: SUNY Press, 1992.

Dervin, Brenda, Grossberg, Lawrence, O'Keefe, Barbara, and Wartella, Ellen, eds. *Rethinking Communication: Paradigm Issues.* Newbury Park, CA: Sage, 1989.

Deutsch, Karl W. "On Communication Models in the Social Sciences." *Public Opinion Quarterly* 16 (1952): 356–380.

Fay, Brian. *Social Theory and Political Practice.* London: Allen & Unwin, 1975.

Fisher, B. Aubrey. *Perspectives on Human Communication.* New York: Macmillan, 1978.

Fiske, Donald W., and Shweder, Richard A., eds. *Metatheory in Social Science: Pluralisms and Subjectivities.* Chicago: University of Chicago Press, 1986.

Gerbner, George, ed. *Ferment in the Field.* Special issue of *Journal of Communication* 33 (Summer 1983).

Gergen, Kenneth J. "The Social Constructionist Movement in Modern Psychology." *American Psychologist* 40 (1985): 266–275.

———. *Toward Transformation in Social Knowledge.* New York: Springer-Verlag, 1982.

Gergen, Kenneth J., and Gergen, Mary M. "Explaining Human Conduct: Form and Function." In *Explaining Human Behavior: Consciousness, Human Action, and Social Structure.* Edited by Paul F. Secord. Beverly Hills, CA: Sage, 1982, pp. 127–154.

Habermas, Jürgen. *Knowledge and Human Interests.* Translated by Jeremy J. Shapiro. Boston: Beacon, 1971.

Hall, Calvin S., and Lindzey, Gardner. *Theories of Personality.* New York: Wiley, 1970.

Hamelink, Cees J. "Emancipation or Domestication: Toward a Utopian Science of Communication." *Journal of Communication* 33 (1983): 74–79.

Hanson, N. R. *Patterns of Discovery.* Cambridge, MA: Cambridge University Press, 1961.

Harré, Rom, and Secord, Paul F. *The Explanation of Social Behavior.* Totowa, NJ: Littlefield, Adams, 1979.

Hawes, Leonard. *Pragmatics of Analoguing: Theory and Model Construction in Communication.* Reading, MA: Addison-Wesley, 1975.

Houna, Joseph. "Two Ideals of Scientific Theorizing." In *Communication Yearbook 5.* Edited by Michael Burgoon. New Brunswick, NJ: Transaction, 1982, pp. 29–48.

Jacobsen, Thomas L. "Theories as Communications." *Communication Theory* 2 (1991): 145–150.

Jensen, Joli. "The Consequences of Vocabularies." *Journal of Communication* 43 (1993): 67–74.

Kaplan, Abraham. *The Conduct of Inquiry.* San Francisco: Chandler, 1964.

Kerlinger, Fred N. *Foundations of Behavioral Research.* New York: Holt, Rinehart & Winston, 1964.

Kibler, Robert J. "Basic Communication Research Considerations." In *Methods of Research in Communication.* Edited by Philip Emmert and William Brooks. Boston: Houghton Mifflin, 1970, pp. 9–50.

Krippendorff, Klaus. "Conversation or Intellectual Imperialism in Comparing Communication (Theories)." *Communication Theory* 3 (1993): 252–266.

Kuhn, Thomas S. *The Structure of Scientific Revolutions,* 2nd ed. Chicago: University of Chicago Press, 1970.

Levy, Mark R., ed. *The Future of the Field.* Special issue of *Journal of Communication* 43 (Summer 1993).

Littlejohn, Stephen W. "Communication Theory." In *Encyclopedia of Rhetoric and Composition: Communication from Ancient Times to the Information Age.* Edited by Teresa Enos. New York: Garland, 1996, pp. 117–121.

———. "An Overview of Contributions to Human Communication Theory from Other Disciplines." In *Human Communication Theory: Comparative Essays.* Edited by Frank E. X. Dance. New York: Harper & Row, 1982, pp. 243–285.

Lustig, Myron W. "Theorizing About Human Communication." *Communication Quarterly* 34 (1986): 451–459.

MacIntyre, Alasdair. "Ontology." In *The Encyclopedia of Philosophy,* vol. 5. Edited by Paul Edwards. New York: Macmillan, 1967, pp. 542–543.

Macy, Joanna. *Mutual Causality in Buddhism and General System Theory.* Albany: SUNY Press, 1991, pp. 117–137.

McNamee, Sheila. "Research as Social Intervention: A Research Methodology for the New Epistemology." Paper presented at the Fifth International Conference on Culture and Communication, Philadelphia, October 1988.

Miller, Gerald. "The Current Status of Theory and Research in Interpersonal Communication." *Human Communication Research* 4 (1978): 175.

Miller, Gerald, and Nicholson, Henry. *Communication Inquiry.* Reading, MA: Addison-Wesley, 1976.

Monge, Peter R. "The Systems Perspective as a Theoretical Basis for the Study of Human Communication." *Communication Quarterly* 25 (1977): 19–29.

Pearce, W. Barnett. "On Comparing Theories: Treating Theories as Commensurate or Incommensurate." *Communication Theory* 2 (1991): 159–164.

———. "Metatheoretical Concerns in Communication." *Communication Quarterly* 25 (1977): 3–6.

Pearce, W. Barnett, Cronen, Vernon E., and Harris, Linda M. "Methodological Considerations in Building Human Communication Theory." In *Human Communication Theory: Comparative Essays.* Edited by Frank E. X. Dance. New York: Harper & Row, 1982, pp. 1–41.

Penman, Robyn. "Good Theory and Good Practice: An Argument in Progress." *Communication Theory* 3 (1992): 234–250.

Pepper, Stephen. *World Hypotheses.* Berkeley: University of California Press, 1942.

Polanyi, Michael. *Personal Knowledge.* London: Routledge & Kegan Paul, 1958.

Rorty, Richard. *Philosophy and the Mirror of Nature.* Princeton, NJ: Princeton University Press, 1979.

Schutz, Alfred. *The Phenomenology of the Social World.* Translated by George Walsh and Frederick Lehnert. Evanston, IL: Northwestern University Press, 1967.

Secord, Paul F., ed. *Explaining Human Behavior: Consciousness, Human Action, and Social Structure.* Beverly Hills, CA: Sage, 1982.

Sigman, Stuart. "Do Social Approaches to Interpersonal Communication Constitute a Contribution to Communication Theory?" *Communication Theory* 2 (1992): 347–356.

Smith, Ted J., III. "Diversity and Order in Communication Theory: The Uses of Philosophical Analysis." *Communication Quarterly* 36 (1988): 28–40.

von Wright, Georg H. *Explanation and Understanding.* Ithaca, NY: Cornell University Press, 1971.

Wallace, Walter L. *Sociological Theory: An Introduction.* Chicago: Aldine, 1969.

Williams, Kenneth R. "Reflections on a Human Science of Communication." *Journal of Communication* 23 (1973): 239–250.

Chapter 3
System Theory

Allport, Gordon W. "The Open System in Personality Theory." In *Modern Systems Research for the Behavioral Scientist.* Edited by Walter Buckley. Chicago: Aldine, 1968, pp. 343–350.

Ashby, W. Ross. "Principles of the Self-Organizing System." In *Principles of Self-Organization.* Edited by Heinz von Foerster and George Zopf. New York: Pergamon, 1962, pp. 255–278.

Asher, Herbert B. *Causal Modeling.* Beverly Hills, CA: Sage, 1976.

Bahg, Chang-Gen. "Major Systems Theories Throughout the World." *Behavioral Science* 35 (1990): 79–107.

Bar-Hillel, Yehoshua. "Concluding Review." In *Information Theory in Psychology.* Edited by Henry Quastler. Glencoe, IL: Free Press, 1955, p. 3.

Bateson, Gregory. *Naven.* Stanford, CA: Stanford University Press, 1958.

———. *Steps to an Ecology of Mind.* New York: Ballantine, 1972.

Beach, Wayne. "Stocktaking Open-Systems Research and Theory: A Critique and Proposals for Action." Paper presented at the annual conference of the Western Speech Communication Association, Phoenix, November 1977.

Berger, Charles. "The Covering Law Perspective as a Theoretical Basis for the Study of Human Communication." *Communication Quarterly* 75 (1977): 7–18.

Bochner, Arthur P. "The Functions of Human Communication in Interpersonal Bonding." In *Handbook of Rhetorical and Communication Theory.* Edited by Carroll C. Arnold and John Waite Bowers. Boston: Allyn & Bacon, 1984, pp. 544–621.

Bochner, Arthur P., and Eisenberg, Eric M. "Family Process: System Perspectives." In *Handbook of Communication Science.* Edited by Charles R. Berger and Steven H. Chaffee. Newbury Park, CA: Sage, 1987, pp. 540–563.

Boulding, Kenneth. "General Systems Theory—The Skeleton of Science." In *Modern Systems Research for the Behavioral Scientist.* Edited by Walter Buckley. Chicago: Aldine, 1968, pp. 3–10.

Brier, Søren. "Forward." *Cybernetics and Human Knowing: A Journal of Second Order Cybernetics and Cyber-Semantics* 1 (1992). (http://www.db.dk/dbaa/sbr/vol1/v1-1for.htm)

Broadhurst, Allan R., and Darnell, Donald K. "An Introduction to Cybernetics and Information Theory." *Quarterly Journal of Speech* 51 (1965): 442–453.

Buckley, Walter. "Society as a Complex Adaptive System." In *Modern Systems Research for the Behavioral Scientist.* Edited by Walter Buckley. Chicago: Aldine, 1968, pp. 490–513.

———. *Sociology and Modern Systems Theory.* Englewood Cliffs, NJ: Prentice-Hall, 1967.

———, ed. *Modern Systems Research for the Behavioral Scientist.* Chicago: Aldine, 1968.

Caley, Michael T., and Sawada, Daiyo, eds. *Mindscapes: The Epistemology of Magoroh Maruyama.* Amsterdam: Gordon and Breach, 1994.

Cherry, Colin. *On Human Communication,* 3rd ed. Cambridge, MA: MIT Press, 1978.

Conant, Roger C. "A Vector Theory of Information." In *Communication Yearbook 3.* Edited by Dan Nimmo. New Brunswick, NJ: Transaction, 1979, pp. 177–196.

Crowley, D. J. *Understanding Communication: The Signifying Web.* New York: Gordon and Breach, 1982.

Cushman, Donald. "The Rules Perspective as a Theoretical Basis for the Study of Human Communication." *Communication Quarterly* 25 (1977): 30–45.

Delia, Jesse. "Alternative Perspectives for the Study of Human Communication: Critique and Response." *Communication Quarterly* 25 (1977): 51–52.

Deutsch, Karl. "Toward a Cybernetic Model of Man and Society." In *Modern Systems Research for the Behavioral Scientist.* Edited by Walter Buckley. Chicago: Aldine, 1968, pp. 387–400.

Donaldson, Rodney E. "Cybernetics and Human Knowing: One Possible Prolegomenon." *Cybernetics and Human Knowing* 1 (1992): 1–4.

Farace, Richard V., Monge, Peter R., and Russell, Hamish. *Communicating and Organizing.* Reading, MA: Addison-Wesley, 1977.

Fink, Edward L. "Dynamic Social Impact Theory and the Study of Human Communication." *Journal of Communication* 46 (1996): 4–77.

Fisher, B. Aubrey. *Perspectives on Human Communication.* New York: Macmillan, 1978.

———. *Small Group Decision Making: Communication and the Group Process.* New York: McGraw-Hill, 1980.

Fisher, B. Aubrey, and Hawes, Leonard C. "An Interact System Model: Generating a Grounded Theory of Small Groups." *Quarterly Journal of Speech* 57 (1971): 444–453.

Franchi, Stefano, Güzeldere, Güven, and Minch, Eric. "Interview: Heinz von Foerster." *SEHR* 4(2). (http://shr.stanford.edu/shreview/4-2/text/interviewconf.html)

Garner, Wendell R. *Uncertainty and Structure as Psychological Concepts.* New York: Wiley, 1962.

General Systems: Yearbook of the Society for General Systems Research. 1956–present (annual).

Giddens, Anthony. *Profiles and Critiques in Social Theory.* Berkeley: University of California Press, 1982.

Grene, Marjorie. *The Knower and the Known.* Berkeley: University of California Press, 1974.

Guilbaud, G. T. *What Is Cybernetics?* New York: Grove, 1959.

Hall, A. D., and Fagen, R. E. "Definition of System." In *Modern Systems Research for the Behavioral Scientist.* Edited by Walter Buckley. Chicago: Aldine, 1968, pp. 81–92.

Handy, Rollo, and Kurtz, Paul. "A Current Appraisal of the Behavioral Sciences: Information Theory." *American Behavioral Scientist* 7, 6 (1964): 99–104.

Harris, Marvin. *The Rise of Anthropological Theory.* New York: Crowell, 1968.

Kaufmann, Walter, ed. *Hegel: Texts and Commentary.* Garden City, NY: Anchor, 1966.

Kincaid, D. Lawrence. "The Convergence Theory of Communication, Self-Organization, and Cultural Evolution." In *Communication Theory: Eastern and Western Perspectives.* Edited by D. Lawrence Kincaid. San Diego, CA: Academic, 1987, pp. 11–23.

Kincaid, D. Lawrence, Yum, June Ock, and Woelfel, Joseph. "The Cultural Convergence of Korean Immigrants in Hawaii: An Empirical Test of a Mathematical Theory." *Quality and Quantity* 18 (1983): 59–78.

Koestler, Arthur. *The Ghost in the Machine.* New York: Macmillan, 1967.

Krippendorf, Klaus. "Cybernetics." In *International Encyclopedia of Communications.* Edited by Erik Barnouw et al. New York: Oxford University Press, 1989, vol. 1, pp. 443–446.

———. "Information Theory." In *Communication and Behavior.* Edited by Gerhard Hanneman and William McEwen. Reading, MA: Addison-Wesley, 1975, pp. 351–389.

Latané, Bibb. "Dynamic Social Impact: Robust Predictions from Simple Theory." In *Modelling and Simulation in the*

Social Sciences from the Philosophy of Science Point of View. Edited by R. Hegselmann, U. Mueller, and K. G. Troitzsch. Dordrecht, Netherlands: Kluwer Theory and Decision Library, 1996, pp. 287–310.

"Ludwig von Bertalanffy." *General Systems* 17 (1972): 219–228.

Macy, Joanna. *Mutual Causality in Buddhism and General System Theory.* Albany: SUNY Press, 1991.

Maruyama, Magoroh. "The Second Cybernetics: Deviation-Amplifying Mutual Causal Processes." *American Scientist* 51 (1963): 164–179. (Reprinted in *Modern Systems Research for the Behavioral Scientist.* Edited by Walter Buckley. Chicago: Aldine, 1968, pp. 304–316.)

Maturana, Humberto, and Varella, Francisco. *The Tree of Knowledge: The Biological Roots of Human Understanding.* Boston: Shambhala, 1992.

Millar, Frank E., and Rogers, L. Edna. "A Relational Approach to Interpersonal Communication." In *Explorations in Interpersonal Communication.* Edited by Gerald Miller. Beverly Hills, CA: Sage, 1976, pp. 87–203.

———. "Relational Dimensions of Interpersonal Dynamics." In *Interpersonal Processes: New Directions in Communication Research.* Edited by Michael Roloff and Gerald Miller. Newbury Park, CA: Sage, 1987.

Miller, Gerald R. "The Pervasiveness and Marvelous Complexity of Human Communication: A Note of Skepticism." Keynote address, Fourth Annual Conference on Communication, California State University, Fresno, May 1977.

Monge, Peter. "The Network Level of Analysis." In *Handbook of Communication Science.* Edited by Charles R. Berger and Steven H. Chaffee. Newbury Park, CA: Sage, 1987, pp. 239–270.

———. "The Systems Perspective as a Theoretical Basis for the Study of Human Communication." *Communication Quarterly* 25 (1977): 19–29.

Monge, Peter R., and Cappella, Joseph N. *Multivariate Techniques in Human Communication Research.* New York: Academic, 1980.

Monge, Peter R., and Eisenberg, E. M. "Emergent Networks." In *Handbook of Organizational Communication.* Edited by F. Jablin, L. Putnam, K. Roberts, and L. Porter. Newbury Park, CA: Sage, 1987.

Monge, Peter R., and Miller, Gerald R. "Communication Networks." In *The Social Science Encyclopedia.* Edited by A. Kuper and J. Kuper. London: Routledge & Kegan Paul, 1985.

Pask, Gordon. *An Approach to Cybernetics.* New York: Harper & Row, 1961.

Pressman, Todd Evan. "A Synthesis of Systems Inquiry and the Eastern Mode of Inquiry." *System Research* 9 (1992): 46–63.

Rapoport, Anatol. "Foreword." In *Modern Systems Research for the Behavioral Scientist.* Edited by Walter Buckley. Chicago: Aldine, 1968, pp. xiii–xxv.

———. "The Promises and Pitfalls of Information Theory." *Behavioral Science* 1 (1956): 303–309. (Reprinted in *Modern Systems Research for the Behavioral Scientist.* Edited by Walter Buckley. Chicago: Aldine, 1968, pp. 137–142.)

Rogers, Everett M. *Diffusion of Innovations.* New York: Free Press, 1962.

———. *A History of Communication Study: A Biographical Approach.* New York: Free Press, 1994, pp. 41–64.

Rogers, Everett M., and Adhikarya, Ronny. "Diffusion of Innovations: An Up-to-Date Review and Commentary." In *Communication Yearbook 3.* Edited by Dan Nimmo. New Brunswick, NJ: Transaction, 1979, pp. 67–82.

Rogers, Everett M., and Kincaid, D. Lawrence. *Communication Networks: Toward a New Paradigm for Research.* New York: Free Press, 1981.

Rogers, L. Edna. "Relational Communication Processes and Patterns." In *Rethinking Communication: Paradigm Exemplars.* Edited by Brenda Dervin, Lawrence Grossberg, Barbara O'Keefe, and Ellen Wartella. Newbury Park, CA: Sage, 1989, pp. 280–290.

Rosenbleuth, Arturo, Weiner, Norbert, and Bigelow, Julian. "Behavior, Purpose, and Teleology." *Philosophy of Science* 10 (1943): 18–24. (Reprinted in *Modern Systems Research for the Behavioral Scientist.* Edited by Walter Buckley. Chicago: Aldine, 1968, pp. 221–225.)

Rosengren, Karl Erik. "Substantive Theories and Formal Models—Bourdieu Confronted." *European Journal of Communication* 10 (1995): 7–39.

Ruben, Brent D., and Kim, John Y., eds. *General Systems Theory and Human Communication.* Rochelle Park, NJ: Hayden, 1975.

Ruesch, Juergen, and Bateson, Gregory. *Communication and the Social Matrix of Society.* New York: Norton, 1951.

Searight, H. Russell, and Merkel, William T. "Systems Theory and Its Discontents: Clinical and Ethical Issues." *The American Journal of Family Therapy* 19 (1991): 19–31.

Shannon, Claude, and Weaver, Warren. *The Mathematical Theory of Communication.* Urbana: University of Illinois Press, 1949.

Taschjan, Edgan. "The Entropy of Complex Dynamic Systems." *Behavioral Science* 19 (1975): 3.

Toda, Masanao, and Shuford, Emir H. "Logic of Systems: Introduction to a Formal Theory of Structure." *General Systems* 10 (1965): 3–27.

Varela, Francisco. "Heinz von Foerster, the Scientist, the Man: Prologue to the Interview." *SEHR* 4(2). (http://shr.stanford.edu/shreview/4-2/text/varella.html)

von Bertalanffy, Ludwig. "General Systems Theory: A Critical Review." *General Systems* 7 (1962): 1–20.

———. *General Systems Theory: Foundations, Development, Applications.* New York: Braziller, 1968.

von Foerster, Heinz. "Ethics and Second-Order Cybernetics," *SEHR* 4, 2:4. p. 4. (http://shr.stanford.edu/shreview/4-2/text/foerster.html)

———. *Observing Systems: Selected Papers of Heinz von Foerster.* Seaside, CA: Intersystems Publications, 1981.

Watzlawick, Paul, Beavin, Janet, and Jackson, Don. *Pragmatics of Human Communication: A Study in Interactional Patterns, Pathologies, and Paradoxes.* New York: Norton, 1967.

Weick, Carl. *The Social Psychology of Organizing.* Reading, MA: Addison-Wesley, 1969.

Wheatley, Margaret. *Leadership and the New Science: Learning About Organization from an Orderly Universe.* San Francisco: Berrett-Kochler, 1992.

Whitaker, Randall. "Overview of Autopoietic Theory."

(http://www.acm.org/signois/auto/ATReview.html#Background)

Wiener, Norbert. *Cybernetics or Control and Communication in the Animal and the Machine.* Cambridge, MA: MIT Press, 1961.

——. *The Human Use of Human Beings: Cybernetics and Society.* Boston: Houghton Mifflin, 1954.

Wilson, Donna. "Forms of Hierarchy: A Selected Bibliography." *General Systems* 14 (1969): 3–15.

Yerby, Janet. "Family Systems Theory Reconsidered: Integrating Social Construction Theory and Dialectical Process." *Communication Theory* 5 (1995): 339–365.

Yum, June Ock. "Communication Diversity and Information Acquisition Among Korean Immigrants in Hawaii." *Human Communication Research* 8 (1982): 154–169.

——. "The Communication Network Paradigm and Intercultural Communication." In *Rethinking Communication: Paradigm Exemplars.* Edited by Brenda Dervin, Lawrence Grossberg, Barbara O'Keefe, and Ellen Wartella. Newbury Park, CA: Sage, 1989, pp. 486–496.

——. "Social Network Patterns of Five Ethnic Groups in Hawaii." In *Communication Yearbook 7.* Edited by Robert Bostrom. New Brunswick, NJ: Transaction, 1983, pp. 574–591.

Chapter 4
Theories of Signs and Language

Akmajian, Adrian, Demers, Richard A., Farmer, Ann K., and Harnish, Robert M. *An Introduction to Language and Communication.* Cambridge, MA: MIT Press, 1994, pp. 123–192.

Berger, Arthur Asa. *Signs in Contemporary Culture: An Introduction to Semiotics.* Salem, WI: Sheffield, 1989.

Berman, Art. *From the New Criticism to Deconstruction.* Urbana: University of Illinois Press, 1988.

Birdwhistell, Ray. *Introduction to Kinesics.* Louisville, KY: University of Louisville Press, 1952.

——. *Kinesics and Context.* Philadelphia: University of Pennsylvania Press, 1970.

——. "A System for the Notation of Proxemic Behavior." *American Anthropologist* 65 (1963): 1003–1026.

Bloomfield, Leonard. *Language.* New York: Holt, Rinehart & Winston, 1933.

Bourdieu, Pierre. *Language and Symbol Power.* Cambridge, MA: Harvard University Press, 1991.

Burgoon, Judee K. "Nonverbal Communication Research in the 1970s: An Overview." In *Communication Yearbook 4.* Edited by Dan Nimmo. New Brunswick, NJ: Transaction, 1980, pp. 179–216.

——. "Nonverbal Signals." In *Handbook of Interpersonal Communication,* Edited by Mark L. Knapp and Gerald R. Miller. Thousand Oaks, CA: Sage, 1994, pp. 229–285.

Burgoon, Judee K., Birk, Thomas, and Pfau, Michael. "Nonverbal Behaviors, Persuasion, and Credibility." *Human Communication Research* 17 (Fall 1990): 140–169.

Burgoon, Judee K., and Saine, Thomas. *The Unspoken Dialogue: An Introduction to Nonverbal Communication.* Boston: Houghton Mifflin, 1978.

Chomsky, Noam. *The Acquisition of Syntax in Children from 5 to 10.* Cambridge, MA: MIT Press, 1969.

——. *Aspects of the Theory of Syntax.* Cambridge, MA: MIT Press, 1965.

——. *Cartesian Linguistics: A Chapter in the History of Rationalist Thought.* New York: Harper & Row, 1966.

——. *Current Issues in Linguistic Theory.* The Hague: Mouton, 1970.

——. *Essays on Form and Interpretation.* New York: North Holland, 1977.

——. *Language and Mind.* New York: Harcourt Brace Jovanovich, 1972.

——. *The Logical Structure of Linguistic Theory.* New York: Plenum, 1975.

——. *Problems of Knowledge and Freedom.* New York: Pantheon, 1971.

——. *Reflections on Language.* New York: Pantheon, 1975.

——. *Rules and Representations.* New York: Columbia University Press, 1980.

——. *The Sound Pattern of English.* New York: Harper & Row, 1968.

——. *Studies on Semantics in Generative Grammar.* The Hague: Mouton, 1972.

——. *Syntactic Structures.* The Hague: Mouton, 1957.

——. Three Models for the Description of Language." *Transactions on Information Theory* IT-2 (1956): 113–124.

——. *Topics in the Theory of Generative Grammar.* The Hague: Mouton, 1966.

Dallmayr, Fred. *Language and Politics.* Notre Dame, IN: University of Notre Dame Press, 1984.

de Saussure, Ferdinand. *Course in General Linguistics.* London: Peter Owen, 1960.

Descartes, René. *Meditations on First Philosophy.* Translated by Lawrence J. LaFleur. Indianapolis, IN: Bobbs-Merrill, 1960.

Eco, Umberto. *Semiotics and the Philosophy of Language.* Bloomington: Indiana University Press, 1984.

——. *A Theory of Semiotics.* Bloomington: Indiana University Press, 1976.

Ekman, Paul, and Friesen, Wallace. *Emotion in the Human Face: Guidelines for Research and an Integration of Findings.* New York: Pergamon, 1972.

——. "Hand Movements." *Journal of Communication* 22 (1972): 353–374.

——. "Nonverbal Behavior in Psychotherapy Research." In *Research in Psychotherapy,* vol. 3. Edited by J. Shlien. Washington, DC: American Psychological Association, 1968, pp. 179–216.

——. "The Repertoire of Nonverbal Behavior: Categories, Origins, Usage, and Coding." *Semiotica* 1 (1969): 49–98.

——. *Unmasking the Face.* Englewood Cliffs, NJ: Prentice-Hall, 1975.

Ellis, Donald G. "Fixing Communicative Meaning: A Coherentist Theory." *Communication Research* 22 (1995): 515–544.

——. "Syntactic and Pragmatic Codes in Communication." *Communication Theory* 2 (1992): 1–23.

Fisch, Max H. *Peirce, Semiotic, and Pragmatism.* Bloomington: Indiana University Press, 1986.

Fodor, J. A., Bever, T. G., and Garrett, M. F. *The Psychology of Language: An Introduction to Psycholinguistics and Generative Grammar.* New York: McGraw-Hill, 1974.

Fodor, Jerry, Jenkins, James, and Saporta, Sol. "Psycholinguistics and Communication Theory." In *Human Communication Theory*. Edited by Frank E. X. Dance. New York: Holt, Rinehart & Winston, 1967, pp. 160–201.

Fries, Charles. *The Structure of English*. New York: Harcourt, Brace & World, 1952.

Giddens, Anthony. *Central Problems in Social Theory: Action, Structure, and Contradiction in Social Analysis*. Berkeley: University of California Press, 1979.

Goudge, Thomas A. *The Thought of Peirce*. Toronto: University of Toronto Press, 1950.

Graddol, David, Cheshire, Jenny, and Swann, Joan. *Descriptive Language*. Buckingham, England: Open University Press, 1994, pp. 65–101.

Hall, Edward T. *The Hidden Dimension*. New York: Random House, 1966.

———. *The Silent Language*. Greenwich, CT: Fawcett, 1959.

Harmon, Gilbert. *On Noam Chomsky: Critical Essays*. Garden City, NY: Anchor, 1974.

Harper, Robert G., Weiss, Arthur, and Motarozzo, Joseph. *Nonverbal Communication: The State of the Art*. New York: Wiley, 1978.

Harris, Zellig. *Structural Linguistics*. Chicago: University of Chicago Press, 1951.

Harrison, Randall. "Nonverbal Communication." In *Handbook of Communication*. Edited by Ithiel de sola Pool and others. Chicago: Rand McNally, 1973.

Hodge, Robert, and Kress, Gunther. *Social Semiotics*. Ithaca, NY: Cornell University Press, 1988.

Hookway, Christopher. *Peirce*. London: Routledge & Kegan Paul, 1985.

Jacobs, Scott. "Language and Interpersonal Communication." In *Handbook of Interpersonal Communication*. Edited by Mark L. Knapp and Gerald R. Miller. Thousand Oaks, CA: Sage, 1994, pp. 199–228.

Knapp, Mark, and Hall, Judith. *Nonverbal Communication in Human Interaction*. New York: Holt, Rinehart & Winston, 1992.

Knapp, Mark, Wiemann, John, and Daly, John. "Nonverbal Communication: Issues and Appraisal." *Human Communication Research* 4 (1978): 271–280.

Langer, Susanne. *Mind: An Essay on Human Feeling*. 3 vols. Baltimore, MD: Johns Hopkins University Press, 1967, 1972, 1982.

———. *Philosophy in a New Key*. Cambridge, MA: Harvard University Press, 1942.

Leeds-Hurwitz, Wendy. *Semiotics and Communication: Signs, Codes, Cultures*. Hillsdale, NJ: Erlbaum, 1993.

Lyne, John R. "Rhetoric and Semiotic in C. S. Peirce." *Quarterly Journal of Speech* 66 (1980): 155–168.

Martyna, Wendy. "What Does 'He' Mean?" *Journal of Communication* 28 (1978): 131–138.

Mead, George H. *Mind, Self, and Society*. Chicago: University of Chicago Press, 1934.

Moriarty, Sandra E. "Abduction: A Theory of Visual Interpretation." *Communication Theory* 6 (1996): 167–187.

Morris, Charles. "Foundations in the Theory of Signs." In *International Encyclopedia of Unified Science*, vol. 1, part 1. Chicago: University of Chicago Press, 1955, p. 84.

———. *Signification and Significance*. Cambridge, MA: MIT Press, 1964.

———. *Signs, Language, and Behavior*. New York: Braziller, 1946.

Ogden, C. K., and Richards, I. A. *The Meaning of Meaning*. London: Kegan, Paul, Trench, Trubner, 1923.

Peirce, Charles Saunders. *Charles S. Peirce: Selected Writings*. Edited by P. O. Wiener. New York: Dover, 1958.

Powers, John H. "On the Intellectual Structure of the Human Communication Discipline." *Communication Education* 4 (1995): 191–222.

Redner, Harry. *A New Science of Representation: Towards an Integrated Theory of Representation in Science, Politics, and Art*. Boulder, CO: Westview, 1994.

Roskill, Mark. "'Public' and 'Private' Meanings: The Paintings of Van Gogh." *Journal of Communication* 29 (1979): 157–169.

Salus, Peter. *Linguistics*. Indianapolis, IN: Bobbs-Merrill, 1969.

Sebeok, Thomas. "The Doctrine of Sign." In *Frontiers in Semiotics*. Edited by J. Deely, B. Williams, and F. E. Kruse. Bloomington: Indiana University Press, 1986.

Silverman, Kaja. *The Subject of Semiotics*. New York: Oxford University Press, 1983.

Stewart, John. *Language as Articulate Contact: Toward a Post-Semiotic Philosophy of Communication*. Albany: SUNY Press, 1995, pp. 76–81.

———. "The Symbol Model vs. Language as Constitutive Articulate Contact." In *Beyond the Symbol Model: Reflections on the Representational Nature of Language*. Edited by John Stewart. Albany: SUNY Press, 1996, pp. 9–63.

Wasow, Thomas. "Grammar." In *International Encyclopedia of Communications*, vol. 2. Edited by Erik Barnouw, et al. New York: Oxford University Press, 1989, pp. 234–238.

Weiser, Irwin. "Linguistics." In *Encyclopedia of Rhetoric and Composition*. Edited by Theresa Enos. New York: Garland, 1996, pp. 386–391.

Chapter 5
Theories of Discourse

Austin, J. L. *How to Do Things with Words*. Cambridge, MA: Harvard University Press, 1962.

———. *Philosophy of Language*. Englewood Cliffs, NJ: Prentice-Hall, 1964.

Beach, Wayne. "Orienting to the Phenomenon." In *Communication Yearbook 13*. Edited by James A. Anderson. Newbury Park, CA: Sage, 1990, pp. 216–244.

Berger, Charles R. "The Covering Law Perspective as a Theoretical Basis for the Study of Human Communication." *Communication Quarterly* 25 (1977): 12.

Berman, Art. *From the New Criticism to Deconstruction: The Reception of Structuralism and Post-structuralism*. Urbana: University of Illinois Press, 1988.

Blair, Carole. "The Statement: Foundation of Foucault's Historical Criticism." *Western Journal of Speech Communication* 51 (1987): 364–383.

Buttny, Richard. "The Ascription of Meaning: A Wittgensteinian Perspective." *Quarterly Journal of Speech* 72 (1986): 261–273.

Button, Graham, ed. *Ethnomethodology and the Human Sciences*. Cambridge: Cambridge University Press, 1991.

Campbell, Paul N. "A Rhetorical View of Locutionary,

Illocutionary, and Perlocutionary Acts." *Quarterly Journal of Speech* 59 (1973): 284–296.

Cappella, Joseph N. "The Management of Conversations." In *Handbook of Interpersonal Communication*. Edited by Mark L. Knapp and Gerald R. Miller. Beverly Hills, CA: Sage, 1985, pp. 393–439.

Cooper, Martha. "Rhetorical Criticism and Foucault's Philosophy of Discursive Events." *Central States Speech Journal* 39 (1988): 1–17.

Craig, Robert T., and Tracy, Karen, eds. *Conversational Coherence: Form, Structure, and Strategy.* Beverly Hills, CA: Sage, 1983.

Cushman, Donald P. "The Rules Perspective as a Theoretical Basis for the Study of Human Communication." *Communication Quarterly* 25 (1977): 30–45.

———. "The Rules Approach to Communication Theory: A Philosophical and Operational Perspective." In *Communication Theory: Eastern and Western Perspectives.* Edited by D. Lawrence Kincaid. San Diego, CA: Academic, 1987, pp. 223–234.

Delia, Jesse. "Alternative Perspectives for the Study of Human Communication: Critique and Response." *Communication Quarterly* 25 (1977): 54.

Derrida, Jacques. *Of Grammatology.* Translated by Gayatri Spivak. Baltimore, MD: Johns Hopkins University Press, 1976.

Ellis, Donald. "Fixing Communicative Meaning: A Coherentist Theory." *Communication Research* 22 (1995): 515–544.

———. "Post-Structuralism and Language: Non-Sense." *Communication Monographs* 58 (1991): 213–224.

Ellis, Donald G., and Donohue, William A., eds. *Contemporary Issues in Language and Discourse Processes.* Hillsdale, NJ: Erlbaum, 1986.

Foss, Sonja K., Foss, Karen A., and Trapp, Robert. *Contemporary Perspectives on Rhetoric.* Prospect Heights, IL: Waveland, 1991.

Foss, Sonja K., and Gill, Ann. "Michel Foucault's Theory of Rhetoric as Epistemic." *Western Journal of Speech Communication* 51 (1987): 384–402.

Fraser, Nancy. *Unruly Practices: Power, Discourse, and Gender in Contemporary Social Theory.* Minneapolis: University of Minnesota Press, 1989.

Gaines, Robert. "Doing by Saying: Toward a Theory of Perlocution." *Quarterly Journal of Speech* 65 (1979): 207–217.

Ganz, Joan. *Rules: A Systematic Study.* Paris: Mouton, 1971.

Garfinkel, Harold. *Studies in Ethnomethodology.* Englewood Cliffs, NJ: Prentice-Hall, 1967.

Giddens, Anthony. *Central Problems in Social Theory: Action, Structure, and Contradiction in Social Analysis.* Berkeley: University of California Press, 1979.

Goodwin, Charles. "Turn Construction and Conversational Organization." In *Rethinking Communication: Paradigm Exemplars,* vol. 2. Edited by Brenda Dervin, Lawrence Grossberg, Barbara O'Keefe, and Ellen Wartella. Newbury Park, CA: Sage, 1989, pp. 88–102.

Grice, H. Paul. "Logic and Conversation." In *Syntax and Semantics,* vol. 3. Edited by P. Cole and J. Morgan. New York: Academic, 1975, pp. 41–58.

Hopper, Robert, Koch, Susan, and Mandelbaum, Jennifer. "Conversation Analysis Methods." In *Contemporary Issues in Language and Discourse Processes.* Edited by Donald G. Ellis and William A. Donohue. Hillsdale, NJ: Erlbaum, 1986, pp. 169–186.

Jackson, Sally, and Jacobs, Scott. "Characterizing Ordinary Argument: Substantive and Methodological Issues." *Journal of the American Forensic Association* 22 (1986): 42–57.

———. "The Collaborative Production of Proposals in Conversational Argument and Persuasion: A Study of Disagreement Regulation." *Journal of the American Forensic Association* 18 (1981): 77–90.

———. "Conversational Relevance: Three Experiments on Pragmatic Connectedness in Conversation." In *Communication Yearbook 10.* Edited by Margaret L. McLaughlin. Newbury Park, CA: Sage, 1987, pp. 323–347.

———. "Structure of Conversational Argument: Pragmatic Bases for the Enthymeme." *Quarterly Journal of Speech* 66 (1980): 251–265.

Jacobs, Scott. "Language and Interpersonal Communication." In *Handbook of Interpersonal Communication.* Edited by Mark L. Knapp and Gerald R. Miller. Thousand Oaks, CA: Sage, 1994, pp. 199–228.

———. "Recent Advances in Discourse Analysis." *Quarterly Journal of Speech* 66 (1980): 450–472.

Jacobs, Scott, and Jackson, Sally. "Argument as a Natural Category: The Routine Grounds for Arguing in Conversation." *Western Journal of Speech Communication* 45 (1981): 118–132.

———. "Building a Model of Conversational Argument." In *Rethinking Communication: Paradigm Exemplars,* vol. 2. Edited by Brenda Dervin, Lawrence Grossberg, Barbara O'Keefe, and Ellen Wartella. Newbury Park, CA: Sage, 1989, pp. 153–171.

———. "Speech Act Structure in Conversation: Rational Aspects of Pragmatic Coherence." In *Conversational Coherence: Form, Structure, and Strategy.* Edited by Robert T. Craig and Karen Tracy. Beverly Hills, CA: Sage, 1983, pp. 47–66.

———. "Strategy and Structure in Conversational Influence Attempts." *Communication Monographs* 50 (1983): 285–304.

Janik, Allan, and Toulmin, Stephen. *Wittgenstein's Vienna.* New York: Simon & Schuster, 1973.

Kellermann, Kathy, and Sleight, Carra. "Coherence: A Meaningful Adhesive for Discourse." In *Communication Yearbook 12.* Edited by James A. Anderson. Newbury Park, CA: Sage, 1989, pp. 95–129.

Lacan, Jacques. *The Four Fundamental Concepts of Psycho-Analysis.* Translated by A. Sheridan. New York: Norton, 1981.

Lyne, John. "Speech Acts in a Semiotic Frame." *Communication Quarterly* 29 (1981): 202–208.

Mandelbaum, Jenny. "Interpersonal Activities in Conversational Storytelling." *Western Journal of Speech Communication* 53 (1989): 114–126.

McLaughlin, Margaret L. *Conversation: How Talk Is Organized.* Beverly Hills, CA: Sage, 1984.

Mura, Susan Swan. "Licensing Violations: Legitimate Violations of Grice's Conversational Principle." In *Conversational Coherence: Form, Structure, and Strategy.* Edited by Robert T. Craig and Karen Tracy. Beverly Hills, CA: Sage, 1983, pp. 101–115.

Nofsinger, Robert. *Everyday Conversation.* Newbury Park, CA: Sage, 1991.

O'Keefe, Daniel J. "Two Concepts of Argument." *Journal of the American Forensic Association* 13 (1977): 121–128.

Pearce, W. Barnett. "Rules Theories of Communication: Varieties, Limitations, and Potentials." Paper presented at the annual meeting of the Speech Communication Association, New York, 1980.

Potter, Jonathan, and Wetherell, Margaret. *Discourse and Social Psychology: Beyond Attitudes and Behavior.* London: Sage, 1987.

Powers, John. "On the Intellectual Structure of the Human Communication Discipline." *Communication Education* 44 (1995): 191–222.

Psathas, George. *Conversation Analysis: The Study of Talk-in-Interaction.* Thousand Oaks, CA: Sage, 1995.

Sacks, Harvey, Schegloff, Emanuel, and Jefferson, Gail. "A Simplest Systematics for the Organization of Turn Taking for Conversation." *Language* 50 (1974): 696–735.

Searle, John. "Human Communication Theory and the Philosophy of Language: Some Remarks." In *Human Communication Theory.* Edited by Frank E. X. Dance. New York: Holt, Rinehart & Winston, 1967, pp. 116–129.

———. *Speech Acts: An Essay in the Philosophy of Language.* Cambridge: Cambridge University Press, 1969.

Shimanoff, Susan B. *Communication Rules: Theory and Research.* Beverly Hills, CA: Sage, 1980.

Sigman, Stuart J. "On Communication Rules from a Social Perspective." *Human Communication Research* 7 (1980): 37–51.

———. *A Perspective on Social Communication.* Lexington, MA: Lexington Books, 1987.

Silverman, David, and Torode, Brian. *The Material Word: Some Theories of Language and Its Limits.* London: Routledge & Kegan Paul, 1980.

Stenstrøm, Anna-Brita. *An Introduction to Spoken Interaction.* London: Longman, 1994.

Stewart, John. "Concepts of Language and Meaning: A Comparative Study." *Quarterly Journal of Speech* 58 (1972): 123–133.

Trapp, Robert. "The Role of Disagreement in Interactional Argument." *Journal of the American Forensic Association* 23 (1986): 23–41.

van Dijk, Teun A. *Communicating Racism: Ethnic Prejudice in Thought and Talk.* Newbury Park, CA: Sage, 1987.

———. "Discourse Semantics and Ideology." *Discourse and Society* 6 (1995): 243–289

———. *Macrostructures: An Interdisciplinary Study of Global Structures in Discourse, Interaction, and Cognition.* Hillsdale, NJ: Erlbaum, 1980.

———. *News as Discourse.* Hillsdale, NJ: Erlbaum, 1988.

———. "Principles of Critical Discourse Analysis." *Discourse and Society* 4 (1993): 249–283.

———. *Studies in the Pragmatics of Discourse.* The Hague: Mouton, 1981.

van Eemeren, Frans H., and Grootendorst, Rob. *Argumentation, Communication, and Fallacies: A Pragma-Dialectical Perspective.* Hillsdale, NJ: Erlbaum, 1992.

van Eemeren, Frans H., Grootendorst, Rob, Jackson, Sally, and Jacobs, Scott. *Reconstructing Argumentative Discourse.* Tuscaloosa: University of Alabama Press, 1993.

Walton, Douglas N. *Plausible Argument in Everyday Conversation.* Albany: SUNY Press, 1992.

Wittgenstein, Ludwig. *Philosophical Investigations.* Oxford: Blackwell, 1953.

———. *Tractatus Logico-Philosophicus.* London: Routledge & Kegan Paul, 1922.

Young, Robert, ed. "Post-structuralism: An Introduction." In *Untying the Text: A Post-structuralist Reader.* Boston: Routledge & Kegan Paul, 1981, pp. 1–28.

Zimmerman, Don H. "On Conversation: The Conversation Analytic Perspective." In *Communication Yearbook 11.* Edited by James A. Anderson. Newbury Park, CA: Sage, 1988, pp. 406–432.

Chapter 6
Theories of Message Production

Andersen, Peter A. "The Trait Debate: A Critical Examination of the Individual Differences Paradigm in the Communication Sciences." In *Progress in Communication Sciences.* Edited by B. Dervin and M. J. Voigt. Norwood, NJ: Ablex, 1986.

Applegate, James L. "The Impact of Construct System Development on Communication and Impression Formation in Persuasive Messages." *Communication Monographs* 49 (1982): 277–289.

Applegate, James L., and Sypher, Howard E. "A Constructivist Theory of Communication and Culture." In *Theories in Intercultural Communication.* Edited by Young Y. Kim and William B. Gudykunst. Newbury Park, CA: Sage, 1988, pp. 41–65.

Babrow, Austin. "The Advent of Multiple-Process Theories of Communication." *Journal of Communication* 43 (1993): 110–118.

Bavelas, Janet Beavin, Black, Alex, Chovil, Nicole, and Mullett, Jennifer. *Equivocal Communication.* Newbury Park, CA: Sage, 1990.

Beatty, Michael J., and McCroskey, James C. "Communication Apprehension as Temperamental Expression: Toward the Development of a Communibiological Theory of Communication Inhibition." Paper presented at the Western Communication Association, Monterey, CA, February 1997.

———. "Interpersonal Communication as Temperamental Expression." In *Personality and Communication: Trait Perspectives.* New York: Hampton, in press.

Bellah, Robert N., and others. *Habits of the Heart.* Berkeley: University of California Press, 1985.

Berger, Charles R. *Planning Strategic Interaction: Attaining Goals Through Communicative Action.* Mahwah, NJ: Erlbaum, 1997.

Berger, Charles R., Karol, Susan H., and Jordan, Jerry M. "When a Lot of Knowledge Is a Dangerous Thing: The Debilitating Effects of Plan Complexity on Verbal Fluency." *Human Communication Research* 16 (1989): 91–119.

Burgoon, Judee K., Dillman, Leesa, and Stern, Lesa A. "Adaptation in Dyadic Interaction: Defining and Operationalizing Patterns of Reciprocity and Compensation." *Communication Theory* 3 (1993): 295–316.

Burleson, Brant R. "The Constructivist Approach to Person-Centered Communication: Analysis of a Research Exemplar." In *Rethinking Communication: Paradigm Exemplars.* Edited by Brenda Dervin, Lawrence Grossberg,

Barbara O'Keefe, and Ellen Wartella. Newbury Park, CA: Sage, 1989, pp. 29–46.

Burleson, Brant R., Albrecht, Terrance L., and Sarason, Irwin C., eds. *Communication of Social Support: Messages, Interactions, Relationships, and Community*. Thousand Oaks, CA: Sage, 1994.

Cody, Michael J., and others. "Situation Perception and Message Strategy Selection." In *Communication Yearbook 9*. Edited by Margaret L. McLaughlin. Beverly Hills, CA: Sage, 1986, pp. 390–422.

Crockett, Walter H. "Cognitive Complexity and Impression Formation." In *Progress in Experimental Personality Research*, vol. 2. Edited by Brendon A. Maher. New York: Academic, 1965, pp. 47–90.

Darnell, Donald, and Brockriede, Wayne. *Persons Communicating*. Englewood Cliffs, NJ: Prentice-Hall, 1976.

Delia, Jesse G. "Interpersonal Cognition, Message Goals, and Organization of Communication: Recent Constructivist Research." In *Communication Theory: Eastern and Western Perspectives*. Edited by D. Lawrence Kincaid. San Diego, CA: Academic, 1987, pp. 255–274.

Delia, Jesse G., Kline, Susan L., and Burleson, Brant R. "The Development of Persuasive Communication Strategies in Kindergartners Through Twelfth-Graders." *Communication Monographs* 46 (1979): 241–256.

Delia, Jesse G., O'Keefe, Barbara J., and O'Keefe, Daniel J. "The Constructivist Approach to Communication." In *Human Communication Theory: Comparative Essays*. Edited by Frank E. X. Dance. New York: Harper & Row, 1982, pp. 147–191.

Devine, Patricia G., Hamilton, David L., and Ostrom, Thomas M. *Social Cognition: Impact on Social Psychology*. San Diego, CA: Academic, 1994.

Eisenberg, Eric. "Equivocal Communication." *Communication Theory* 1 (1991): 351–354.

Friedrich, Gustav, and Goss, Blaine. "Systematic Desensitization." In *Avoiding Communication: Shyness, Reticence, and Communication Apprehension*. Edited by John A. Daly and James C. McCroskey. Beverly Hills, CA: Sage, 1984, pp. 173–188.

Garko, Michael G. "Perspectives on and Conceptualizations of Compliance and Compliance-Gaining." *Communication Quarterly* 38 (1990): 138–157.

Gastil, John. "An Appraisal and Revision of the Constructivist Research Program." In *Communication Yearbook 18*. Edited by Brant Burleson. Thousand Oaks, CA: Sage, 1995, pp. 83–104.

Gergen Kenneth J., and Semin, Gün R. "Everyday Understanding in Science and Daily Life." In *Everyday Understanding: Social and Scientific Implications*. Edited by Gün R. Semin and Kenneth J. Gergen. London: Sage, 1990, pp. 1–18.

Giles, Howard, Coupland, Justine, and Coupland, Nikolas. "Accommodation Theory: Communication, Context, and Consequence." In *Contexts of Accommodation: Developments in Applied Sociolinguistics*. Edited by Howard Giles, Justine Coupland, and Nikolas Coupland. Cambridge: Cambridge University Press, 1991, pp. 1–68.

Giles, Howard, Mulac, Anthony, Bradac, James J., and Johnson, Patricia. "Speech Accommodation Theory: The First Decade and Beyond." In *Communication Yearbook 10*. Edited by Margaret L. McLaughlin. Newbury Park, CA: Sage, 1987, pp. 13–48.

Giles, Howard, and Street, Richard L., Jr. "Communicator Characteristics and Behavior." In *Handbook of Interpersonal Communication*. Edited by Mark L. Knapp and Gerald R. Miller. Thousand Oaks, CA: Sage, 1994, pp. 103–161.

Greene, John O. "Action-Assembly Theory: Metatheoretical Commitments, Theoretical Propositions, and Empirical Applications." In *Rethinking Communication: Paradigm Exemplars*. Edited by Brenda Dervin, Lawrence Grossberg, Barbara O'Keefe, and Ellen Wartella. Newbury Park, CA: Sage, 1989, pp. 117–128.

———. "A Cognitive Approach to Human Communication: An Action Assembly Theory." *Communication Monographs* 51 (1984): 289–306.

———. "Evaluating Cognitive Explanations of Communication Phenomena." *Quarterly Journal of Speech* 70 (1984): 241–254.

Greene, John O., and Geddes, Deanna. "An Action Assembly Perspective on Social Skill." *Communication Theory* 3 (1993): 26–49.

Greene, John O., and Sparks, Glenn G. "Explication and Test of a Cognitive Model of Communication Apprehension: A New Look at an Old Construct." *Human Communication Research* 9 (1983): 349–366.

Hale, Claudia. "Cognitive Complexity-Simplicity as a Determinant of Communication Effectiveness." *Communication Monographs* 47 (1980): 304–311.

Harré, Rom. "Language Games and Texts of Identity." In *Texts of Identity*. Edited by John Shotter and Kenneth J. Gergen. London: Sage, 1989, pp. 20–35.

Hart, Roderick P., and Burks, Don M. "Rhetorical Sensitivity and Social Interaction." *Speech Monographs* 39 (1972): 75–91.

Hart, Roderick P., Carlson, Robert E., and Eadie, William F. "Attitudes Toward Communication and the Assessment of Rhetorical Sensitivity." *Communication Monographs* 47 (1980): 1–22.

Hewes, Dean E., and Planalp, Sally. "The Individual's Place in Communication Science." In *Handbook of Communication Science*. Edited by Charles R. Berger and Steven H. Chaffee. Newbury Park, CA: Sage, 1987, pp. 146–183.

Hull, C. L. *Principles of Behavior: An Introduction to Behavior Theory*. New York: Appleton, 1943.

Infante, Dominic A. "Aggressiveness." In *Personality and Interpersonal Communication*. Edited by James C. McCroskey and John A. Daly. Newbury Park, CA: Sage, 1987, pp. 305–316.

———. *Arguing Constructively*. Prospect Heights, IL: Waveland, 1988.

Infante, Dominic A., Chandler, Teresa A., and Rudd, Jill E. "Test of an Argumentative Skill Deficiency Model of Interspousal Violence." *Communication Monographs* 56 (1989): 163–177.

Infante, Dominic A., and Rancer, Andrew S. "A Conceptualization and Measure of Argumentativeness." *Journal of Personality Assessment* 46 (1982): 72–80.

———. "Argumentativeness and Verbal Aggressiveness: A Review of Recent Theory and Research." In *Communication Yearbook 19*. Edited by Brant R. Burleson. Thousand Oaks, CA: Sage, 1996, pp. 319–352.

Infante, Dominic A., Rancer, Andrew S., and Womack, Deanna F. *Building Communication Theory*. Prospect Heights, IL: Waveland, 1990.

Infante, Dominic A., Trebing, J. David, Shepherd, Patricia E., and Seeds, Dale E. "The Relationship of Argumentativeness to Verbal Aggression." *Southern Speech Communication Journal* 50 (1984): 67–77.

Infante, Dominic A., and Wigley, Charles J. "Verbal Aggressiveness: An Interpersonal Model and Measure." *Communication Monographs* 53 (1986): 61–69.

Kellermann, Kathy, and Cole, Tim. "Classifying Compliance Gaining Messages: Taxonomic Disorder and Strategic Confusion." *Communication Theory* 4 (1994): 3–60.

Kelly, George. *The Psychology of Personal Constructs.* New York: North, 1955.

Kline, Susan L., and Ceropski, Janet M. "Person-Centered Communication in Medical Practice." In *Emergent Issues in Human Decision Making.* Edited by Gerald M. Phillips and Julia T. Wood. Carbondale: Southern Illinois University Press, 1984, pp. 120–141.

Kling, J. W. "Learning: Introductory Survey." In *Woodward and Schlosberg's Experimental Psychology.* Edited by J. W. Kling and Lorrin Riggs. New York: Holt, Rinehart & Winston, 1971, pp. 551–613.

Lannamann, John W. "Deconstructing the Person and Changing the Subject of Interpersonal Studies." *Communication Theory* 2 (1992): 139–148.

———. "Interpersonal Communication Research as Ideological Practice." *Communication Theory* 1 (1991): 179–203.

MacIntyre, Alistair. *After Virtue.* Notre Dame, IN: University of Notre Dame Press, 1984.

Marwell, Gerald, and Schmitt, David R. "Dimensions of Compliance-Gaining Strategies: A Dimensional Analysis." *Sociometry* 30 (1967): 350–364.

Matson, Floyd W. *The Idea of Man.* New York: Delacorte, 1976.

McCroskey, James C. "Classroom Consequences of Communication Apprehension." *Communication Education* 26 (1977): 27–33.

———. "The Communication Apprehension Perspective." In *Avoiding Communication: Shyness, Reticence, and Communication Apprehension.* Edited by John A. Daly and James C. McCroskey. Beverly Hills, CA: Sage, 1984, pp. 13–38.

———. "The Implementation of a Large-Scale Program of Systematic Desensitization for Communication Apprehension." *Speech Teacher* 21 (1971): 255–264.

McCroskey, James C., and Beatty, Michael J. "Communication Apprehension." In *Personality and Communication: Trait Perspectives.* Edited by James C. McCroskey, John A. Daly, Matthew Martin, and Michael J. Beatty. New York: Hampton, in press.

McCroskey, James C., Daly, John A., Martin, Matthew, and Beatty, Michael J., eds. *Personality and Communication: Trait Perspectives.* New York: Hampton, in press.

McCroskey, James C., Ralph, David C., and Barrick, James E. "The Effect of Systematic Desensitization on Speech Anxiety." *Speech Teacher* 19 (1970): 32–36.

Miller, Gerald R. "Persuasion." In *Handbook of Communication Science.* Edited by Charles R. Berger and Steven H. Chaffee. Newbury Park, CA: Sage, 1987, pp. 446–483.

———. "Some (Moderately) Apprehensive Thoughts on Avoiding Communication." In *Avoiding Communication: Shyness, Reticence, and Communication Apprehension.* Ed-

ited by John A. Daly and James C. McCroskey. Beverly Hills, CA: Sage, 1984, pp. 237–246.

Miller, Lynn C., Cody, Michael J., and McLaughlin, Margaret L. "Situations and Goals as Fundamental Constructs in Interpersonal Communication Research." In *Handbook of Interpersonal Communication,* 2nd ed. Edited by Mark L. Knapp. Thousand Oaks, CA: Sage, 1994, pp. 162–197.

Norton, Robert. *Communicator Style: Theory, Applications, and Measures.* Beverly Hills, CA: Sage, 1983.

O'Keefe, Barbara J. "The Logic of Message Design: Individual Differences in Reasoning About Communication." *Communication Monographs* 55 (1988): 80–103.

O'Keefe, Barbara J., and Shepherd, Gregory J. "The Pursuit of Multiple Objectives in Face-to-Face Persuasive Interactions: Effects of Construct Differentiation on Message Organization." *Communication Monographs* 54 (1987): 396–419.

O'Keefe, Daniel J. "From Strategy-based to Feature-based Analyses of Compliance Gaining Message Classification and Production." *Communication Theory* 4 (1994): 61–69.

———. *Persuasion: Theory and Research.* Newbury Park, CA: Sage, 1990.

Planalp, Sally. "Communication, Cognition, and Emotion." *Communication Monographs* 60 (1993): 3–4.

Planalp, Sally, and Hewes, Dean E. "A Cognitive Approach to Communication Theory: *Cogito Ergo Dico?*" In *Communication Yearbook 5.* Edited by Michael Burgoon. New Brunswick, NJ: Transaction, 1982, pp. 49–78.

Powers, John H. "On the Intellectual Structure of the Human Communication Discipline." *Communication Education* 44 (1995): 191–222.

Schenck-Hamlin, William J., Wiseman, Richard L., and Georgacarakos, G. N. "A Model of Properties of Compliance-Gaining Strategies." *Communication Quarterly* 30 (1982): 92–100.

Schroder, Harold M., Driver, Michael S., and Streufert, Siegfried. *Human Information Processing: Individuals and Groups Functioning in Complex Social Situations.* New York: Holt, Rinehart & Winston, 1967.

Seibold, David R., Cantrill, James G. and Meyers, Renee A. "Communication and Interpersonal Influence." In *Handbook of Interpersonal Communication,* 2nd ed. Edited by Mark L. Knapp and Gerald R. Miller. Thousand Oaks, CA: Sage, 1994, pp. 542–588.

Semin, Gün R. "Everyday Assumptions, Language, and Personality." In *Everyday Understanding: Social and Scientific Implications.* Edited by Gün R. Semin and Kenneth J. Gergen. London: Sage, 1990, pp. 151–175.

Shotter, John, and Gergen, Kenneth J. "Social Construction: Knowledge, Self, Others, and Continuing the Conversation." In *Communication Yearbook 17.* Edited by Stanley Deetz. Thousand Oaks, CA: Sage, 1994, pp. 3–33.

Skinner, B. F. *Cumulative Record: A Selection of Papers,* 3rd ed. New York: Appleton-Century-Crofts, 1972.

———. *Verbal Behavior.* New York: Appleton-Century-Crofts, 1957.

Smith, Mary John. *Persuasion and Human Action.* Belmont, CA: Wadsworth, 1982.

Stiff, James B. *Persuasive Communication.* New York: Guilford, 1994.

Waldron, Vincent R., and Cegala, Donald J. "Assessing Conversational Cognition: Levels of Cognitive Theory and Associated Methodological Requirements." *Human Communication Research* 18 (1992): 606.

Ward, Steven A., Bluman, Dale L., and Dauria, Arthur. "Rhetorical Sensitivity Recast: Theoretical Assumptions of an Informal Interpersonal Rhetoric." *Communication Quarterly* 30 (1982): 189–195.

Watson, J. B. *Psychology from the Standpoint of the Behaviorist.* Philadelphia: Lippincott, 1919.

Werner, H. "The Concept of Development from a Comparative and Organismic Point of View." In *The Concept of Development.* Edited by D. B. Harris. Minneapolis: University of Minnesota Press, 1957.

Wheeless, Lawrence R., Barraclough, Robert, and Stewart, Robert. "Compliance-Gaining and Power in Persuasion." In *Communication Yearbook 7.* Edited by Robert N. Bostrom. Beverly Hills, CA: Sage, 1983, pp. 105–145.

Wiseman, Richard L., and Schenck-Hamlin, William. "A Multidimensional Scaling Validation of an Inductively-Derived Set of Compliance-Gaining Strategies." *Communication Monographs* 48 (1981): 251–270.

Chapter 7
Theories of Message Reception and Processing

Ajzen, Icek, and Fishbein, Martin. *Understanding Attitudes and Predicting Social Behavior.* Englewood Cliffs, NJ: Prentice-Hall, 1980.

Allen, Mike, and Reynolds, Rodney. "The Elaboration Likelihood Model and the Sleeper Effect: An Assessment of Attitude Change Over Time." *Communication Theory* 8 (1993): 73–82.

Andersen, Peter A. "Nonverbal Immediacy in Interpersonal Communication." In *Multichannel Integrations of Nonverbal Behavior.* Edited by A. W. Siegman and S. Feldstein. Hillsdale, NJ: Erlbaum, 1985, pp. 1–36.

Anderson, Norman H. "Integration Theory and Attitude Change." *Psychological Review* 78 (1971): 171–206.

Aronson, Elliot. *The Social Animal.* New York: Viking, 1972.

Babrow, Austin. "Communication and Problematic Integration: Understanding Diverging Probability and Value, Ambiguity, Ambivalence, and Impossibility." *Communication Theory* 2 (1992): 95–130.

Brehm, J. W., and Cohen, A. R. *Explorations in Cognitive Dissonance.* New York: Wiley, 1962.

Brown, Roger. *Social Psychology.* New York: Free Press, 1965.

Buller, David B., and Burgoon, Judee K. "Interpersonal Deception Theory." *Communication Theory* 6 (1996): 203–242.

Burgoon, Judee K. "Communication Effects of Gaze Behavior: A Test of Two Contrasting Explanations." *Human Communication Research* 12 (1986): 495–524.

———. "Nonverbal Signals." In *Handbook of Interpersonal Communication.* Edited by Mark L. Knapp and Gerald R. Miller. Thousand Oaks, CA: Sage, 1994, pp. 253–255.

Burgoon, Judee K., and Hale, Jerold L. "Nonverbal Expectancy Violations: Model Elaboration and Application." *Communication Monographs* 55 (1988): 58–79.

Burgoon, Michael, Newton, Deborah A., and Birk, Thomas S. "A Theory of Belief, Attitude, Intention, and Be-

havior Extended to the Domain of Corrective Advertising." In *Communication Yearbook 15.* Edited by Stanley A. Deetz. Newbury Park, CA: Sage, 1992, pp. 263–286.

Burhans, David T. "The Attitude-Behavior Discrepancy Problem: Revisited." *Quarterly Journal of Speech* 57 (1971): 418–428.

Burleson, Brant R. "Attribution Schemes and Causal Inference in Natural Conversations." In *Contemporary Issues in Language and Discourse Processes.* Edited by Donald G. Ellis and William A. Donohue. Hillsdale, NJ: Erlbaum, 1986, pp. 63–86.

Cappella, Joseph N. "The Management of Conversational Interaction in Adults and Infants." In *Handbook of Interpersonal Communication.* Edited by Mark L. Knapp and Gerald R. Miller. Thousand Oaks, CA: Sage, 1994, pp. 406–407.

Cappella, Joseph N., and Greene, John O. "A Discrepancy-Arousal Explanation of Mutual Influence in Expressive Behavior for Adult-Adult and Infant-Adult Interaction." *Communication Monographs* 49 (1982): 89–114.

Chapanis, Natalia P., and Chapanis, Alphonse. "Cognitive Dissonance: Five Years Later." *Psychological Bulletin* 61 (1964): 21.

Dillard, James Price. "Persuasion Past and Present: Attitudes Aren't What They Used to Be." *Communication Monographs* 60 (1993): 90–97.

Divine, Patricia G., Hamilton, David L., and Ostrom, Thomas M., eds. *Social Cognition: Impact on Social Psychology.* San Diego, CA: Academic, 1994.

Doelger, Joel A., Hewes, Dean E., and Graham, Maudie L. "Knowing When to 'Second Guess': The Mindful Analysis of Messages." *Human Communication Research* 12 (1986): 301–338.

Donnelly, J. H., and Ivancevich, J. M. "Post-Purchase Reinforcement and Back-Out Behavior." *Journal of Marketing Research* 7 (1970): 399–400.

Festinger, Leon. *A Theory of Cognitive Dissonance.* Stanford, CA: Stanford University Press, 1957.

Festinger, Leon, and Carlsmith, James M. "Cognitive Consequences of Forced Compliance." *Journal of Abnormal and Social Psychology* 58 (1959): 203–210.

Fishbein, Martin. "A Behavior Theory Approach to the Relations Between Beliefs About an Object and the Attitude Toward the Object." In *Readings in Attitude Theory and Measurement.* Edited by Martin Fishbein. New York: Wiley, 1967, pp. 389–400.

———. "A Consideration of Beliefs and Their Role in Attitude Measurement." In *Readings in Attitude Theory and Measurement.* Edited by Martin Fishbein. New York: Wiley, 1967, pp. 257–266.

———. *Readings in Attitude Theory and Measurement.* New York: Wiley, 1967.

Fishbein, Martin, and Ajzen, Icek. *Belief, Attitude, Intention, and Behavior.* Reading, MA: Addison-Wesley, 1975.

Fishbein, Martin, and Raven, Bertram, H. "The AB Scales: An Operational Definition of Belief and Attitude." In *Readings in Attitude Theory and Measurement.* Edited by Martin Fishbein. New York: Wiley, 1967, pp. 183–189.

Gergen, Kenneth J., and Semin, Gün R. "Everyday Understanding in Science and Daily Life." In *Everyday Understanding: Social and Scientific Implications.* Edited by Gün

R. Semin and Kenneth J. Gergen. London: Sage, 1990, pp. 1–18.

Hamilton, Mark A., Hunter, John E., and Boster, Franklin J. "The Elaboration Likelihood Model as a Theory of Attitude Formation: A Mathematical Analysis." *Communication Theory* 8 (1993): 50–64.

Hample, Dale. "Argument: Public, Private, Social, and Cognitive." *Argumentation and Advocacy* 25 (1988): 13–19.

———. "The Cognitive Context of Argument." *Western Journal of Speech Communication* 45 (1981): 148–158.

———. "A Cognitive View of Argument." *Journal of the American Forensic Association* 16 (1980): 151–158.

———. "A Third Perspective on Argument." *Philosophy and Rhetoric* 18 (1985): 1–22.

Heider, Fritz. *The Psychology of Interpersonal Relations.* New York: Wiley, 1958.

Hewes, Dean E., and Graham, Maudie L. "Second-Guessing Theory: Review and Extension." In *Communication Yearbook 12.* Edited by James A. Anderson. Newbury Park, CA: Sage, 1989, pp. 213–248.

Hewes, Dean E., Graham, Maudie L., Monsour, Michael, and Doelger, Joel A. "Cognition and Social Information-Gathering Strategies: Reinterpretation Assessment in Second-Guessing." *Human Communication Research* 16 (1989): 297–321.

Hewes, Dean E., and Planalp, Sally. "The Individual's Place in Communication Science." In *Handbook of Communication Science.* Edited by Charles R. Berger and Steven H. Chaffee. Newbury Park, CA: Sage, 1987, pp. 146–183.

Hovland, Carl I., Harvey, O. J., and Sherif, Muzafer. "Assimilation and Contrast Effects in Reactions to Communication and Attitude Change." *Journal of Abnormal and Social Psychology* 55 (1957): 244–252.

Jones, Edward E., and others, eds. *Attribution: Perceiving the Causes of Behavior.* Morristown, NJ: General Learning, 1972.

Kelley, Harold H. *Attribution in Social Interaction.* Morristown, NJ: General Learning Press, 1971.

———. "Attribution in Social Interaction." In *Attribution: Perceiving the Causes of Behavior.* Edited by Edward E. Jones and others. Morristown, NJ: General Learning, 1972, pp. 1–26.

———. "Attribution Theory in Social Psychology." In *Nebraska Symposium on Motivation,* vol. 15. Edited by David Levine. Lincoln: University of Nebraska Press, 1967, pp. 192–240.

———. *Causal Schemata and the Attribution Process.* Morristown, NJ: General Learning, 1972.

———. "Causal Schemata and the Attribution Process." In *Attribution: Perceiving the Causes of Behavior.* Edited by Edward E. Jones and others. Morristown, NJ: General Learning, 1972, pp. 151–174.

———. "The Process of Causal Attribution." *American Psychologist* 28 (1973): 107–128.

Kiesler, Charles A., Collins, Barry E., and Miller, Norman. *Attitude Change: A Critical Analysis of Theoretical Approaches.* New York: Wiley, 1969.

Krippendorff, Klaus. "The Past of Communication's Hoped-For Future." *Journal of Communication* 43 (1993): 34–44.

Lannamann, John W. "Deconstructing the Person and Changing the Subject of Interpersonal Studies." *Communication Theory* 2 (1992): 139–148.

———. "Interpersonal Communication: Research as Ideological Practice." *Communication Theory* 1 (1991): 179–203.

LePoire, Beth A. "Two Contrasting Explanations of Involvement Violations: Expectancy Violations Theory Versus Discrepancy Arousal Theory." *Human Communication Research* 20 (1994): 560–591.

Martin, Leonard, and Tesser, Abraham, eds. *The Construction of Social Judgments.* Hillsdale, NJ: Erlbaum, 1992.

McGuire, William J. "A Syllogistic Analysis of Cognitive Relationships." In *Attitude Organization and Change.* Edited by M. J. Rosenberg and others. New Haven, CT: Yale University Press, 1960, pp. 65–111.

Mongeau, Paul, and Stiff, James B. "Specifying Causal Relationships in the Elaboration Likelihood Model." *Communication Theory* 8 (1993): 65–72.

O'Keefe, Daniel J. *Persuasion: Theory and Research.* Newbury Park, CA: Sage, 1990.

———. "Two Concepts of Argument." *Journal of the American Forensic Association* 13 (1977): 121–128.

Osgood, Charles. *Cross Cultural Universals of Affective Meaning.* Urbana: University of Illinois Press, 1975.

———. "The Nature and Measurement of Meaning." In *The Semantic Differential Technique.* Edited by James Snider and Charles Osgood. Chicago: Aldine, 1969, pp. 9–10.

———. "Semantic Differential Technique in the Comparative Study of Cultures." In *The Semantic Differential Technique.* Edited by James Snider and Charles Osgood. Chicago: Aldine, 1969, pp. 303–334.

———. "On Understanding and Creating Sentences." *American Psychologist* 18 (1963): 735–751.

Osgood, Charles, and Richards, Meredith. "From *Yang* and *Yin* to *and* or *but.*" *Language* 49 (1973): 380–412.

Ostrom, Thomas M., Skowronski, John J., and Nowak, Andrzej. "The Cognitive Foundation of Attitudes: It's a Wonderful Construct." In *Social Cognition: Impact on Social Psychology.* Edited by Patricia G. Devine, David L. Hamilton, and Thomas M. Ostrom. San Diego, CA: Academic, 1994, pp. 196–258.

Patterson, M. L. *Nonverbal Behavior: A Functional Perspective.* New York: Springer-Verlag, 1983.

Petty, Richard E., and Cacioppo, John T. *Communication and Persuasion: Central and Peripheral Routes to Attitude Change.* New York: Springer-Verlag, 1986.

Petty, Richard E., Cacioppo, John T., and Goldman, R. "Personal Involvement as a Determinant of Argument-Based Persuasion." *Journal of Personality and Social Psychology* 41 (1981): 847–855.

Petty, Richard E., and others. "Conceptual and Methodological Issues in the Elaboration Likelihood Model of Persuasion: A Reply to the Michigan State Critics." *Communication Theory* 3 (1993): 336–362.

Planalp, Sally, and Hewes, Dean E. "A Cognitive Approach to Communication Theory: *Cogito Ergo Dico?*" In *Communication Yearbook 5.* Edited by Michael Burgoon. New Brunswick, NJ: Transaction, 1982, pp. 49–78.

Rokeach, Milton. *Beliefs, Attitudes, and Values: A Theory of Organization and Change.* San Francisco: Jossey-Bass, 1969.

———. *The Nature of Human Values.* New York: Free Press, 1973.

Roskos-Ewoldsen, David R. "Attitude Accessibility and Persuasion: Review and a Transactive Model." In *Communication Yearbook 20.* Edited by Brant Burleson. Thousand Oaks, CA: Sage, 1997, pp. 185–225.

Seibold, David R., and Spitzberg, Brian H. "Attribution Theory and Research: Formalization, Review, and Implications for Communication." In *Progress in Communication Sciences,* vol. 3. Edited by B. Dervin and M. J. Voigt. Norwood, NJ: Ablex, 1981, pp. 85–125.

Sherif, Muzafer. *Social Interaction—Process and Products.* Chicago: Aldine, 1967.

Sherif, Muzafer, and Hovland, Carl I. *Social Judgment.* New Haven, CT: Yale University Press, 1961.

Sherif, Muzafer, Sherif, Carolyn, and Nebergall, Roger. *Attitude and Attitude Change: The Social Judgment-Involvement Approach.* Philadelphia: Saunders, 1965.

Sillars, Alan L. "Attribution and Communication." In *Social Cognition and Communication.* Edited by Michael E. Roloff and Charles R. Berger. Beverly Hills, CA: Sage, 1982, pp. 73–106.

———. "Attributions and Communication in Roommate Conflicts." *Communication Monographs* 47 (1980): 180–200.

———. "The Sequential and Distributional Structure of Conflict Interaction as a Function of Attributions Concerning the Locus of Responsibility and Stability of Conflict." In *Communication Yearbook 4.* Edited by Dan Nimmo. New Brunswick, NJ: Transaction, 1980, pp. 217–236.

Smith, Eliot R. "Social Cognition Contributions to Attribution Theory and Research." In *Social Cognition: Impact on Social Psychology.* Edited by Patricia G. Devine, David L. Hamilton, and Thomas M. Ostrom. San Diego, CA: Academic, 1994, pp. 77–108.

Smith, Mary John. *Persuasion and Human Action: A Review and Critique of Social Influence Theories.* Belmont, CA: Wadsworth, 1982.

Snider, James, and Osgood, Charles, eds. *The Semantic Differential Technique.* Chicago: Aldine, 1969.

Sperber, Dan, and Wilson, Deirdre. *Relevance: Communication and Cognition.* Cambridge, MA: Harvard University Press, 1986.

Stiff, James B. *Persuasive Communication.* New York: Guilford, 1994.

Wyer, Robert S. *Cognitive Organization and Change.* Hillsdale, NJ: Erlbaum, 1974.

Wyer, Robert S., and Goldberg, Lee. "A Probabilistic Analysis of the Relationship Between Beliefs and Attitudes." *Psychological Review* 77 (1970): 100–120.

Zajonc, Robert. "The Concepts of Balance, Congruity, and Dissonance." *Public Opinion Quarterly* 24 (1960): 280–296.

Chapter 8
Theories of Symbolic Interaction, Dramatism, and Narrative

Bales, Robert F. *Personality and Interpersonal Behavior.* New York: Holt, Rinehart & Winston, 1970.

Becker, Howard. "Becoming a Marihuana User." *American Journal of Sociology* 59 (1953): 235–242.

Blumer, Herbert. *Symbolic Interactionism: Perspective and Method.* Englewood Cliffs, NJ: Prentice-Hall, 1969.

Bormann, Ernest G. *Communication Theory.* New York: Holt, Rinehart & Winston, 1980.

———"Fantasy and Rhetorical Vision: The Rhetorical Criticism of Social Reality." *Quarterly Journal of Speech* 58 (1972): 396–407.

———. "Fantasy and Rhetorical Vision: Ten Years Later." *Quarterly Journal of Speech* 68 (1982): 288–305.

———. *The Force of Fantasy: Restoring the American Dream.* Carbondale: Southern Illinois University Press, 1985.

Bormann, Ernest G., Cragan, John F., and Shields, Donald C. "An Expansion of the Rhetorical Vision Component of the Symbolic Convergence Theory: The Cold War Paradigm Case." *Communication Monographs* 63 (1996): 1–28.

____. "In Defense of Symbolic Convergence Theory: A Look at the Theory and Its Criticisms After Two Decades." *Communication Theory* 4 (1994): 259–294.

Brock, Bernard R. "Evolution of Kenneth Burke's Criticism and Philosophy of Language." In *Kenneth Burke and Contemporary European Thought: Rhetoric in Transition.* Edited by Bernard L. Brock. Tuscaloosa: University of Alabama Press, 1995, pp. 1–33.

Burke, Kenneth. *Attitudes Toward History.* New York: New Republic, 1937.

———. *Counter-Statement.* New York: Harcourt, Brace, 1931.

———. *A Grammar of Motives.* Englewood Cliffs, NJ: Prentice-Hall, 1945.

———. *Language as Symbolic Action.* Berkeley: University of California Press, 1966.

———. *Permanence and Change.* New York: New Republic, 1935.

———. *The Philosophy of Literary Form.* Baton Rouge: Louisiana State University Press, 1941.

———. *A Rhetoric of Motives.* Englewood Cliffs, NJ: Prentice-Hall, 1950.

———. *A Rhetoric of Religion.* Boston: Beacon, 1961.

Charon, Joel M. *Symbolic Interactionism: An Introduction, an Interpretation, an Integration.* Englewood Cliffs, NJ: Prentice-Hall, 1992.

Chesebro, James. "Extending the Burkeian System: A Response to Tompkins and Cheney." *Quarterly Journal of Speech.* 80 (1994): 83–90.

Collins, Randall. "Erving Goffman and the Development of Modern Social Theory." In *The View from Goffman.* Edited by Jason Ditton. New York: St. Martin's, 1980, pp. 170–209.

Coste, Didier. *Narrative as Communication.* Minneapolis: University of Minnesota Press, 1989.

Couch, Carl J., and Hintz, Robert, eds. *Constructing Social Life.* Champaign, IL: Stipes, 1975.

Cragan, John F., and Shields, Donald C. *Applied Communication Research: A Dramatistic Approach.* Prospect Heights, IL: Waveland Press, 1981.

_____. *Symbolic Theories in Applied Communication Research: Bormann, Burke, and Fisher.* Cresskill, NJ: Hampton, 1995.

Delia, Jesse G. "Communication Research: A History." In *Handbook of Communication Science.* Edited by Charles R.

Berger and Steven H. Chaffee. Newbury Park, CA: Sage, 1987, pp. 30–37.

Denzin, Norman K. *Symbolic Interactionism and Cultural Studies: The Politics of Interpretation.* Oxford: Blackwell, 1992.

Duncan, Hugh D. "Communication in Society." *Arts in Society* 3 (1964): 105.

Fine, Gary Alan. "The Sad Demise, Mysterious Disappearance, and Glorious Triumph of Symbolic Interactionism." *Annual Review of Sociology* 19 (1993): 61–87.

Fisher, Walter R. "Clarifying the Narrative Paradigm." *Communication Monographs* 56 (1989): 55–58.

———. *Human Communication as Narration: Toward a Philosophy of Reason, Value, and Action.* Columbia: University of South Carolina Press, 1987.

———. "Narration, Reason, and Community." In *Writing the Social Text: Poetics and Politics in Social Science Discourse.* Edited by Richard Harvey Brown. New York: Aldine, 1992, pp. 199–218.

Foss, Karen A., and Littlejohn, Stephen W. "*The Day After*: Rhetorical Vision in an Ironic Frame." *Critical Studies in Mass Communication* 3 (1986): 317–336.

Foss, Sonja K., Foss, Karen A., and Trapp, Robert. *Contemporary Perspectives on Rhetoric.* Prospect Heights, IL: Waveland, 1991.

Goffman, Erving. Behavior in Public Places. New York: Free Press, 1963.

———. *Encounters: Two Studies in the Sociology of Interaction.* Indianapolis: Bobbs-Merrill, 1961.

———. *Frame Analysis: An Essay on the Organization of Experience.* Cambridge, MA: Harvard University Press, 1974.

———. *Interaction Ritual: Essays on Face-to-Face Behavior.* Garden City, NY: Doubleday, 1967.

———. *The Presentation of Self in Everyday Life.* Garden City, NY: Doubleday, 1959.

———. *Relations in Public.* New York: Basic, 1971.

Gronbeck, Bruce E. "Dramaturgical Theory and Criticism: The State of the Art (or Science?)." *Western Journal of Speech Communication* 44 (1980): 315–330.

Hall, Peter M. "Structuring Symbolic Interaction: Communication and Power." In *Communication Yearbook 4.* Edited by Dan Nimmo. New Brunswick, NJ: Transaction, 1980, pp. 49–60.

Hickman, C. A., and Kuhn, Manford. *Individuals, Groups, and Economic Behavior.* New York: Holt, Rinehart & Winston, 1956.

Johnson, C. David, and Picou, J. Stephen. "The Foundations of Symbolic Interactionism Reconsidered." In *Micro-Sociological Theory: Perspectives on Sociological Theory,* vol. 2. Edited by H. J. Helle and S. N. Eisenstadt. Beverly Hills, CA: Sage, 1985, pp. 54–70.

Kamler, Howard. *Communication: Sharing Our Stories of Experience.* Seattle: Psychological Press, 1983.

Katovich, Michael A., and Reese, William A., III. "Postmodern Thought in Symbolic Interaction: Reconstructing Social Inquiry in Light of Late-Modern Concerns." *The Sociological Quarterly* 34 (1993): 391–411.

Kuhn, Manford H. "Major Trends in Symbolic Interaction Theory in the Past Twenty-Five Years." *Sociological Quarterly* 5 (1964): 61–84.

Kuhn, Manford H., and McPartland, Thomas S. "An Empirical Investigation of Self-Attitudes." *American Sociological Review* 19 (1954): 68–76.

Lal, Barbara Ballis. "Symbolic Interaction Theories." *American Behavioral Scientist* 38 (1995): 421–441.

Leeds-Hurwitz, Wendy. "A Social Account of Symbols." In *Beyond the Symbol Model: Reflections on the Representational Nature of Language.* Edited by John Stewart. Albany: SUNY Press, 1996, pp. 257–278.

———, ed. *Social Approaches to Communication.* New York: Guilford, 1995.

———. "Social Approaches to Interpersonal Communication." *Communication Theory* 2 (1992): 131–139.

Ling, David A. "A Pentadic Analysis of Senator Edward Kennedy's Address to the People of Massachusetts July 25, 1969." *Central States Speech Journal* 21 (1970): 81–86.

Lofland, John. "Interactionist Imagery and Analytic Interruptus." In *Human Nature and Collective Behavior.* Edited by Tamotsu Shibutani. Englewood Cliffs, NJ: Prentice-Hall, 1970.

Manis, Jerome G., and Meltzer, Bernard N. "Appraisals of Symbolic Interactionism." In *Symbolic Interaction.* Edited by Jerome G. Manis and Bernard N. Meltzer. Boston: Allyn & Bacon, 1978, pp. 393–440.

———, eds. *Symbolic Interaction.* Boston: Allyn & Bacon, 1978.

McCall, Michal M., and Becker, Howard S. *Symbolic Interaction and Cultural Studies.* Chicago: University of Chicago Press, 1990.

Mead, George H. *Mind, Self, and Society.* Chicago: University of Chicago Press, 1934.

Meltzer, Bernard N. "Mead's Social Psychology." In *Symbolic Interaction.* Edited by Jerome G. Manis and Bernard N. Meltzer. Boston: Allyn & Bacon, 1972, pp. 4–22.

Meltzer, Bernard N., and Petras, John W. "The Chicago and Iowa Schools of Symbolic Interactionism." In *Human Nature and Collective Behavior.* Edited by Tamotsu Shibutani. Englewood Cliffs, NJ: Prentice-Hall, 1970.

Meltzer, Bernard N., Petras, John, and Reynolds, Larry. *Symbolic Interactionism: Genesis, Varieties, and Criticism.* London: Routledge & Kegan Paul, 1975.

Mitchell, W. J. T., ed. *On Narrative.* Chicago: University of Chicago Press, 1980.

Mohrmann, G. P. "An Essay on Fantasy Theme Criticism." *Quarterly Journal of Speech* 68 (1982): 109–132.

Morris, Charles. "George H. Mead as Social Psychologist and Social Philosopher." In *Mind, Self, and Society* (Introduction). Chicago: University of Chicago Press, 1934, pp. ix–xxxv.

Musolf, Gil Richards. "Structure, Institutions, Power, and Ideology: New Directions Within Symbolic Interactionism." *The Sociological Quarterly* 33 (1992): 171–189.

Reynolds, Larry T. *Interactionism: Exposition and Critique.* Dix Hills, NY: General Hall, 1990.

Rogers, Everett M. *A History of Communication Study: A Biographical Approach.* New York: Free Press, 1994.

Rowland, Robert C. "On Limiting the Narrative Paradigm: Three Case Studies." *Communication Monographs* 56 (1989): 39–54.

Rueckert, William, ed. *Critical Responses to Kenneth Burke.* Minneapolis: University of Minnesota Press, 1969.

Scheff, Thomas J. *Microsociology: Discourse, Emotion, and Social Structure.* Chicago: University of Chicago Press, 1990.

Sigman, Stuart J. *A Perspective on Social Communication.* Lexington, MA: Lexington, 1987.

Simons, Herbert W., and Melia, Trevor, eds. *The Legacy of Kenneth Burke.* Madison: University of Wisconsin Press, 1989.

Stewart, John. *Language as Articulate Contact.* Albany: SUNY Press, 1995.

Swartz, Omar. *Conducting Socially Responsible Research.* Thousand Oaks, CA: Sage, 1997, pp. 68–90.

Tedeschi, J. T., and Reiss, M. "Verbal Strategies in Impression Management." In *The Psychology of Ordinary Explanations of Social Behavior.* Edited by Charles Antaki. New York: Academic, 1981, pp. 271–309.

Tucker, Charles W. "Some Methodological Problems of Kuhn's Self-Theory." *Sociological Quarterly* 7 (1966): 345–358.

Verhoeven, Jef. "Goffman's Frame Analysis and Modern Micro-Sociological Paradigms." In *Micro-Sociological Theory: Perspectives on Sociological Theory,* vol. 2. Edited by H. J. Helle and S. N. Eisenstadt. Beverly Hills, CA: Sage, 1985, pp. 71–100.

Wiley, Norbert. *The Semiotic Self.* Chicago: The University of Chicago Press, 1994.

Woodward, Wayne. "Triadic Communication as Transactional Participation." *Critical Studies in Mass Communication* 13 (1996): 155–174.

Chapter 9
Theories of Social and Cultural Reality

Alvy, K. T. "The Development of Listener Adapted Communication in Grade-School Children from Different Social Class Backgrounds." *Genetic Psychology Monographs* 87 (1973): 33–104.

Averill, James. "The Acquisition of Emotions During Adulthood." In *The Social Construction of Emotions.* Edited by Rom Harré. New York: Blackwell, 1986, pp. 98–119.

———. *Anger and Aggression: An Essay on Emotion.* New York: Springer-Verlag, 1982.

———. "A Constructivist View of Emotion." In *Theories of Emotion.* Edited by K. Plutchik and H. Kellerman. New York: Academic, 1980, pp. 305–339.

———. "On the Paucity of Positive Emotions." In *Assessment and Modification of Emotional Behavior.* Edited by K. R. Blankstein, P. Pliner, and J. Polivy. New York: Plenum, 1980, pp. 7–45.

Berger, Peter L., and Luckmann, Thomas. *The Social Construction of Reality: A Treatise in the Sociology of Knowledge.* New York: Doubleday, 1966.

Bernstein, Basil. *Class, Codes, and Control: Theoretical Studies Toward a Sociology of Language.* London: Routledge & Kegan Paul, 1971.

Bostrom, Robert, and Donohew, Lewis. "The Case for Empiricism: Clarifying Fundamental Issues in Communication Theory." *Communication Monographs* 59 (1992): 109–129.

Branham, Robert J., and Pearce, W. Barnett. "Between Text and Context: Toward a Rhetoric of Contextual Reconstruction." *Quarterly Journal of Speech* 71 (1985): 19–36.

Brenders, David A. "Fallacies in the Coordinated Management of Meaning: A Philosophy of Language Critique of the Hierarchical Organization of Coherent Conversation and Related Theory." *Quarterly Journal of Speech* 73 (1987): 329–348.

Burr, Vivien. *Introduction to Social Constructionism.* London: Routledge, 1995.

Buttny, Richard. "Accounts as a Reconstruction of an Event's Context." *Communication Monographs* 52 (1985): 57–77.

———. "Sequence and Structure in Accounts Episodes." *Communication Quarterly* 35 (1987): 67–83.

Cappella, Joseph. "Remaking Communication Inquiry." In *Rethinking Communication: Paradigm Issues.* Edited by Brenda Dervin, Lawrence Grossberg, Barbara O'Keefe, and Ellen Wartella. Newbury Park, CA: Sage, 1989, p. 142.

Carroll, John B. "Introduction." In *Language, Thought, and Reality.* Edited by Benjamin L. Whorf. New York: Wiley, 1956, pp. 1–34.

Cherwitz, Richard A., and Hikins, James W. *Communication and Knowledge: An Investigation in Rhetorical Epistemology.* Columbia: University of South Carolina Press, 1986.

Cronen, Vernon E., Chen, Victoria, and Pearce, W. Barnett. "Coordinated Management of Meaning: A Critical Theory." In *Theories in Intercultural Communication.* Edited by Young Yun Kim and William B. Gudykunst. Newbury Park, CA: Sage, 1988, pp. 66–98.

Cronen, Vernon E., Johnson, Kenneth M., and Lannamann, John W. "Paradoxes, Double Binds, and Reflexive Loops: An Alternative Theoretical Perspective." *Family Process* 20 (1982): 91–112.

Cronen, Vernon, and Lang, Peter. "Language and Action: Wittgenstein and Dewey in the Practice of Therapy and Consultation." *Human Systems: The Journal of Systemic Consultation and Management* 5 (1994): 5–43.

Cronen, Vernon E., Pearce, W. Barnett, and Changsheng, Xi. "The Meaning of 'Meaning' in the CMM Analysis of Communication: A Comparison of Two Traditions." *Research on Language and Social Interaction* 23 (1989–1990): 1–40.

Cronen, Vernon, Pearce, W. Barnett, and Harris, Linda. "The Coordinated Management of Meaning." In *Comparative Human Communication Theory.* Edited by Frank E. X. Dance. New York: Harper & Row, 1982.

———. "The Logic of the Coordinated Management of Meaning." *Communication Education* 28 (1979): 22–38.

Deetz, Stanley. "Future of the Discipline: The Challenges, the Research, and the Social Contribution." In *Communication Yearbook 17.* Edited by Stanley Deetz. Thousand Oaks, CA: Sage, 1994, pp. 565–600.

Geertz, Clifford. *Local Knowledge: Further Essays in Interpretive Anthropology.* New York: Basic, 1983.

Gergen, Kenneth J. "The Social Constructionist Movement in Modern Psychology." *American Psychologist* 40 (1985): 266–275.

———. *Toward Transformation in Social Knowledge.* New York: Springer-Verlag, 1982.

Giddens, Anthony. *Profiles and Critiques in Social Theory.* Berkeley: University of California Press, 1982.

Harré, Rom. "Is There Still a Problem About the Self?" In *Communication Yearbook 17.* Edited by Stanley Deetz. Thousand Oaks, CA: Sage, 1994.

_____. "An Outline of the Social Constructionist Viewpoint." In *The Social Construction of Emotions*. Edited by Rom Harré. New York: Blackwell, 1986, pp. 2–14.

———. *Personal Being: A Theory for Individual Psychology*. Cambridge, MA: Harvard University Press, 1984.

———. *Social Being: A Theory for Social Behavior*. Totowa, NJ: Littlefield, Adams, 1979.

Harré, Rom, and Secord, Paul. *The Explanation of Social Behavior*. Totowa, NJ: Littlefield, Adams, 1972.

Krippendorff, Klaus. "The Past of Communication's Hoped-For Future." *Journal of Communication* 43 (1993): 34–44.

Leeds-Hurwitz, Wendy, ed. *Social Approaches to Communication*. New York: Guilford, 1995.

Lutz, Catherine. "Morality, Domination, and Understandings of 'Justifiable Anger' Among the Ifaluk." In *Everyday Understanding: Social and Scientific Implications*. Edited by Gün R. Semin and Kenneth J. Gergen. London: Sage, 1990, pp. 204–226.

McLaughlin, Margaret L., Cody, Michael J., and O'Hair, H. Dan. "The Management of Failure Events: Some Contextual Determinants of Accounting Behavior." *Human Communication Research* 9 (1983): 208–224.

McLaughlin, Margaret L., Cody, Michael J., and Read, Stephen, eds. *Explaining One's Self to Others: Reason-Giving in a Social Context*. Hillsdale, NJ: Erlbaum, 1992.

McLaughlin, Margaret L., Cody, Michael J., and Rosenstein, Nancy E. "Account Sequences in Conversations Between Strangers." *Communication Monographs* 50 (1983): 102–125.

Narula, Uma, and Pearce, W. Barnett. *Development as Communication: A Perspective on India*. Carbondale: Southern Illinois University Press, 1986.

Pearce, W. Barnett. "A 'Camper's Guide' to Constructionisms." *Human Systems: The Journal of Systemic Consultation and Management* 3 (1992): 139–161.

_____. *Communication and the Human Condition*. Carbondale: Southern Illinois University Press, 1989.

_____. "The Coordinated Management of Meaning: A Rules Based Theory of Interpersonal Communication." In *Explorations in Interpersonal Communication*. Edited by Gerald R. Miller. Beverly Hills, CA: Sage, 1976, pp. 17–36.

_____. "A Sailing Guide for Social Constructionists." In *Social Approaches to Communication*. Edited by Wendy Leeds-Hurwitz. New York: Guilford, 1995, pp. 88–113.

Pearce, W. Barnett, and Cronen, Vernon. *Communication, Action, and Meaning*. New York: Praeger, 1980.

Penman, Robyn. "Good Theory and Good Practice: An Argument in Progress." *Communication Theory* 2 (1992): 234–250.

Powers, John H. "On the Intellectual Structure of the Human Communication Discipline." *Communication Education* 44 (1995): 191–222.

Sankoff, Gillian. *The Social Life of Language*. Philadelphia: University of Pennsylvania Press, 1980.

Sapir, Edward. *Language: An Introduction to the Study of Speech*. New York: Harcourt, Brace & World, 1921.

Schonbach, P. A. "A Category System for Account Phases." *European Journal of Social Psychology* 10 (1980): 195–200.

Schutz, Alfred. *On Phenomenology and Social Relations*. Chicago: University of Chicago Press, 1970.

Shimanoff, Susan B. *Communication Rules: Theory and Research*. Beverly Hills, CA: Sage, 1980.

———. "Rules Governing the Verbal Expression of Emotions Between Married Couples." *Western Journal of Speech Communication* 49 (1985): 147–165.

Shotter, John. "Before Theory and After Representationalism: Understanding Meaning 'From Within' a Dialogue Process." In *Beyond the Symbol Model: Reflections on the Representational Nature of Language*. Edited by John Stewart. Albany: SUNY Press, 1996, pp. 103–134.

_____. *Social Accountability and Selfhood*. Oxford: Blackwell, 1984.

———. "Social Accountability and the Social Construction of 'You.'" In *Texts of Identity*. Edited by John Shotter and Kenneth J. Gergen. London: Sage, 1989, pp. 133–151.

Shotter, John, and Gergen, Kenneth J. "Social Construction: Knowledge, Self, Others, and Continuing the Conversation." In *Communication Yearbook 17*. Edited by Stanley Deetz. Thousand Oaks, CA: Sage, 1994, pp. 3–33.

Sigman, Stuart J. "Do Social Approaches to Interpersonal Communication Constitute a Contribution to Communication Theory?" *Communication Theory* 2 (1992): 347–356.

_____. *A Perspective on Social Communication*. Lexington, MA: Lexington, 1987.

Smith, Mary John. "Cognitive Schemata and Persuasive Communication: Toward a Contingency Rules Theory." In *Communication Yearbook 6*. Edited by Michael Burgoon. Beverly Hills, CA: Sage, 1982, pp. 330–363.

———. "Contingency Rules Theory, Context, and Compliance-Behaviors." *Human Communication Research* 10 (1984): 489–512.

Steinfatt, Thomas M. "Linguistic Relativity." In *Language, Communication, and Culture: Current Directions*. Edited by Stella Ting-Toomey and Felipe Korzenny. Newbury Park, CA: Sage, 1989, pp. 35–75.

Stewart, John. *Language as Articulate Contact: Toward a Post-Semiotic Philosophy of Communication*. Albany: SUNY Press, 1995.

———. "The Symbol Model vs. Language as Constitutive Articulate Contact." In *Beyond the Symbol Model: Reflections on the Representational Nature of Language*. Edited by John Stewart. Albany: SUNY Press, 1996, pp. 9–68.

Taylor, James R., Cooren, Francois, Giroux, Nicole, and Robichaud, Daniel. "The Communicational Basis of Organization: Between the Conversation and the Text." *Communication Theory* 6 (1996): 1–39.

Whorf, Benjamin L. "Language, Mind, and Reality." In *Language, Thought, and Reality*. Edited by John B. Carroll. New York: Wiley, 1956, pp. 246–270.

———. *Language, Thought, and Reality*. Edited by John B. Carroll. New York: Wiley, 1956.

———. "The Relation of Habitual Thought and Behavior to Language." In *Language, Thought, and Reality*. Edited by John B. Carroll. New York: Wiley, 1956, pp. 134–159.

Chapter 10
Theories of Experience and Interpretation

Agar, Michael. *Speaking of Ethnography*. Beverly Hills, CA: Sage, 1986.

Anderson, James A. *Communication Theory: Epistemological Foundations*. New York: Guilford, 1996.

Atkinson, Paul. *Understanding Ethnographic Texts.* New York: Basic, 1973.

Bailey, William. "Consciousness and Action/Motion Theories of Communication." *Western Journal of Speech Communication* 50 (1986): 74.

Bauman, Zygmunt. *Hermeneutics and Social Science.* New York: Columbia University Press, 1978.

Benoit, Pamela J., and Benoit, William L. "Consciousness: The Mindlessness/Mindfulness and Verbal Report of Controversies." *Western Journal of Speech Communication* 50 (1986): 41–63.

Berman, Art. *From the New Criticism to Deconstruction.* Urbana, IL: University of Chicago Press, 1988.

Bernstein, Richard J. *Beyond Objectivism and Relativism: Science, Hermeneutics, and Praxis.* Philadelphia: University of Pennsylvania Press, 1983.

Campbell, John Angus. "Hans-Georg Gadamer's Truth and Method." *Quarterly Journal of Speech* 64 (1978): 101–122.

Carbaugh, Donal, ed. "Culture Talking About Itself." In *Cultural Communication and Intercultural Contact.* Hillsdale, NJ: Erlbaum, 1990, pp. 1–9.

———. *Situating Selves: The Communication of Social Identities in American Scenes.* Albany: SUNY Press, 1996.

Carbaugh, Donal, and Hastings, Sally. "A Role for Communication Theory in Ethnography and Cultural Analysis." *Communication Theory* 2 (1992): 156–165.

Carragee, Kevin M. "Interpretive Media Study and Interpretive Social Science." *Critical Studies in Mass Communication* 7 (1990): 81–96.

Cheney, George, and Tompkins, Phillip K. "On the Facts of the Text as the Basis of Human Communication Research." In *Communication Yearbook 11.* Edited by James A. Anderson. Newbury Park, CA: Sage, 1988, pp. 455–501.

Conquergood, Dwight. "Ethnography, Rhetoric, and Performance." *Quarterly Journal of Speech* 78 (1992): 80–97.

———. "Rethinking Ethnography: Toward a Critical Cultural Politics." *Communication Monographs* 58 (1991): 179–194.

Crawford, Lyall. "Personal Ethnography." *Communication Monographs* 63 (1996): 158.

Deetz, Stanley. "Conceptualizing Human Understanding: Gadamer's Hermeneutics and American Communication Studies." *Communication Quarterly* 26 (1978): 14.

———. *Democracy in an Age of Corporate Colonization.* Albany: SUNY Press, 1992, pp. 113–144.

———. "Words Without Things: Toward a Social Phenomenology of Language." *Quarterly Journal of Speech* 59 (1973): 40–51.

Derrida, Jacques. *Of Grammatology.* Translated by Gayatri Spivak. Baltimore, MD: Johns Hopkins University Press, 1976.

Dilthey, Wilhelm. "The Rise of Hermeneutics." Translated by Fredric Jameson. *New Literary History* 3 (1972): 229–244.

Fay, Brian. *Social Theory and Political Practice.* London: Allen & Unwin, 1975.

Fish, Stanley. *Is There a Text in This Class?* Cambridge, MA: Harvard University Press, 1980.

Froman, Wayne. *Merleau-Ponty: Language and the Act of Speech.* Lewisburg, PA: Bucknell University Press, 1982.

Gadamer, Hans-Georg. *Truth and Method.* New York: Seabury, 1975.

———. *Wahrheit und Methode [Truth and Method].* Tuebingen, Germany: Mohr, 1960.

Geertz, Clifford. *The Interpretation of Cultures.* New York: Basic, 1973.

———. *Local Knowledge: Further Essays in Interpretive Anthropology.* New York: Basic, 1983.

Gergen, Kenneth. *Toward Transformation in Social Knowledge.* New York: Springer-Verlag, 1982, pp. 126–133.

Giddens, Anthony. "On the Relation of Sociology to Philosophy." In *Explaining Human Behavior: Consciousness, Human Action, and Social Structure.* Edited by Paul F. Secord. Beverly Hills, CA: Sage, 1982, pp. 175–188.

Giorgi, Amedeo. "Phenomenology, Psychological Science, and Common Sense." In *Everyday Understanding: Social and Scientific Implications.* Edited by Gün R. Semin and Kenneth J. Gergen. London: Sage, 1990.

Gorman, Robert A. *The Dual Vision: Alfred Schutz and the Myth of Phenomenological Social Science.* London: Routledge & Kegan Paul, 1977.

Hall, Stuart. "Encoding/Decoding." In *Culture, Media, Language.* Edited by Stuart Hall, Dorothy Hobson, Andrew Lowe, and Paul Willis. London: Hutchinson, 1980, pp. 128–138.

Hamlyn, D. W. "The Concept of Social Reality." In *Explaining Human Behavior: Consciousness, Human Action, and Social Structure.* Edited by Paul F. Secord. Beverly Hills, CA: Sage, 1982, pp. 189–210.

Heidegger, Martin. *Being and Time.* Translated by John Macquarrie and Edward Robinson. New York: Harper & Row, 1962.

———. *An Introduction to Metaphysics.* Translated by Ralph Manheim. New Haven, CT: Yale University Press, 1959.

———. *On the Way to Language.* Translated by Peter Hertz. New York: Harper & Row, 1971.

Huspek, Michael. "Dueling Structures: The Theory of Resistance in Discourse." *Communication Theory* 3 (1993): 1–25.

Husserl, Edmund. *Ideas: General Introduction to Pure Phenomenology.* Translated by W. R. Boyce Gibson. New York: Collier, 1962.

———. *Phenomenology and the Crisis of Philosophy.* Translated by Quentin Lauer. New York: Harper & Row, 1965.

Hyde, Michael J. "Transcendental Philosophy and Human Communication." In *Interpersonal Communication.* Edited by Joseph J. Pilotta. Washington, DC: Center for Advanced Research in Phenomenology, 1982, pp. 15–34.

Hymes, Dell. *Foundations in Sociolinguistics: An Ethnographic Approach.* Philadelphia: University of Pennsylvania Press, 1974.

Ihde, Don, ed. *The Conflict of Interpretations: Essays on Hermeneutics* [by Paul Ricoeur]. Evanston, IL: Northwestern University Press, 1974.

Jensen, Klaus Bruhn. "When Is Meaning? Communication Theory, Pragmatism, and Mass Media Reception." In *Communication Yearbook 14.* Edited by James A. Anderson. Newbury Park, CA: Sage, 1991, pp. 3–32.

Katriel, Tamar. "'Griping' as a Verbal Ritual in Some Israeli Discourse." In *Cultural Communication and Intercultural Contact.* Edited by Donal Carbaugh. Hillsdale, NJ: Erlbaum, 1990, pp. 99–114.

Kauffman, Bette J. "Feminist Facts: Interview Strategies and Political Subjects in Ethnography." *Communication Theory* 2 (1992): 187–206.

Kwant, Remy C. *The Phenomenological Philosophy of Merleau-Ponty.* Pittsburgh, PA: Duquesne University Press, 1963.

Lanigan, Richard L. "Life History Interviews: A Teaching and Research Model for Semiotic Phenomenology." In *Phenomenology of Communication: Merleau-Ponty's Thematics in Communicology and Semiology.* Pittsburgh, PA: Duquesne University Press, 1988, pp. 144–154.

———. *Phenomenology of Communication: Merleau-Ponty's Thematics in Communicology and Semiology.* Pittsburgh, PA: Duquesne University Press, 1988.

———. "A Treasure House of Preconstituted Types: Alfred Schutz on Communicology." In *Phenomenology of Communication: Merleau-Ponty's Thematics in Communicology and Semiology.* Pittsburgh, PA: Duquesne University Press, 1988, pp. 203–222.

Lindlof, Thomas R. "Media Audiences as Interpretive Communities." In *Communication Yearbook 11.* Edited by James A. Anderson. Newbury Park, CA: Sage, 1988, pp. 81–107.

Lindlof, Thomas R., and Meyer, Timothy P. "Mediated Communication as Ways of Seeing, Acting, and Constructing Culture: The Tools and Foundations of Qualitative Research." In *Natural Audiences: Qualitative Research of Media Uses and Effects.* Edited by Thomas R. Lindlof. Norwood, NJ: Ablex, 1987, pp. 1–32.

Lull, James. "The Social Uses of Television." *Human Communication Research* 6 (1980): 197–209.

Mallin, Samuel B. *Merleau-Ponty's Philosophy.* New Haven, CT: Yale University Press, 1979.

Merleau-Ponty, Maurice. *Phenomenology of Perception.* New York: Humanities, 1962 (original published in Paris, 1945).

———. *The Phenomenology of Perception.* Translated by Colin Smith. London: Routledge & Kegan Paul, 1974.

Moores, Shaun. *Interpreting Audiences: The Ethnography of Media Consumption.* London: Sage, 1993.

Morgan, Gareth. *Images of Organization.* Beverly Hills, CA: Sage, 1986.

Motley, Michael T. "Consciousness and Intentionality in Communication: A Preliminary Model and Methodological Approaches." *Western Journal of Speech Communication* 50 (1986): 3–23.

Nisbett, R. E., and Wilson, T. D. "Telling More Than We Can Know: Verbal Reports on Mental Processes." *Psychological Review* 84 (1977): 231–259.

Pacanowsky, Michael. "Creating and Narrating Organizational Realities." In *Rethinking Communication: Paradigm Exemplars.* Edited by Brenda Dervin, Lawrence Grossberg, Barbara O'Keefe, and Ellen Wartella. Newbury Park, CA: Sage, 1989, pp. 250–257.

Pacanowsky, Michael, and O'Donnell-Trujillo, Nick. "Communication and Organizational Cultures." *Western Journal of Speech Communication* 46 (1982): 121.

———. "Organizational Communication as Cultural Performance." *Communication Monographs* 50 (1983): 129–145.

Palmer, Richard E. *Hermeneutics: Interpretation Theory in Schleiermacher, Dilthey, Heidegger, and Gadamer.* Evanston, IL: Northwestern University Press, 1969.

Philipsen, Gerry. "An Ethnographic Approach to Communication Studies." In *Rethinking Communication: Paradigm Exemplars.* Edited by Brenda Dervin, Lawrence Grossberg, Barbara O'Keefe, and Ellen Wartella. Newbury Park, CA: Sage, 1989, pp. 258–269.

Powers, John H. "On the Intellectual Structure of the Human Communication Discipline." *Communication Education* 44 (1995): 191–222.

Ricoeur, Paul. *Hermeneutics and the Human Sciences: Essays on Language, Action and Interpretation.* Translated and edited by John B. Thompson. Cambridge: Cambridge University Press, 1981.

———. *Interpretation Theory: Discourse and the Surplus of Meaning.* Fort Worth: Texas University Press, 1976.

Sackmann, Sonja A. "Managing Organizational Culture: Dreams and Possibilities." *Communication Yearbook 13.* Edited by James A. Anderson. Newbury Park, CA: Sage, 1990, pp. 114–148.

Schleiermacher, Friedrich. *Hermeneutik.* Edited by Heinz Kimmerle. Heidelberg, Germany: Carl Winter, Universitaetsverlag, 1959.

Schoening, Gerard T., and Anderson, James A. "Social Action Media Studies: Foundational Arguments and Common Premises." *Communication Theory* 5 (1995): 93–116.

Schutz, Alfred. *The Phenomenology of the Social World.* Translated by George Walsh and Frederick Lehnert. Evanston, IL: Northwestern University Press, 1967 (original published in 1932).

Shotter, John. *Social Accountability and Selfhood.* New York: Blackwell, 1984, pp. 167–172.

Steiner, Linda. "Oppositional Decoding as an Act of Resistance." *Critical Studies in Mass Communication* 5 (1988): 1–15.

Stewart, John. "One Philosophical Dimension of Social Approaches to Interpersonal Communication." *Communication Theory* 2 (1992): 337–347.

———. "Philosophy of Qualitative Inquiry: Hermeneutic Phenomenology and Communication Research." *Quarterly Journal of Speech* 67 (1981): 110.

Thomas, Jim. *Doing Critical Ethnography.* Newbury Park, CA: Sage, 1993.

Tracy, David. "Interpretation (Hermeneutics)." In *International Encyclopedia of Communications.* Edited by Erik Barnouw. New York: Oxford University Press, 1989, pp. 343–348.

Turner, Victor. *The Anthropology of Performance.* New York: PAJ, 1987.

———. *Dramas, Fields, and Metaphors.* Ithaca, NY: Cornell University Press, 1974.

Warnick, Barbara. "A Ricoeurian Approach to Rhetorical Criticism." *Western Journal of Speech Communication* 51 (1987): 227–244.

West, James T. "Ethnography and Ideology: The Politics of Cultural Representation." *Western Journal of Communication* 57 (1993): 209–220.

Chapter 11
Critical Theories

Agger, Ben. *Cultural Studies as Critical Theory.* London: Falmer, 1992.

Allen, Mike. "Critical and Traditional Science: Implications for Communication Research." *Western Journal of Communication* 57 (1993): 200–208.

Althusser, Louis. *Lenin and Philosophy.* Translated by B. Brewster. New York: Monthly Review, 1971.

———. *For Marx.* Translated by B. Brewster. New York: Vintage, 1970.

Alvesson, Mats, and Deetz, Stanley. "Critical Theory and Postmodernism Approaches to Organizational Studies." In *Handbook of Organizational Studies.* Edited by S. Clegg, C. Harding, and W. Nord. London: Sage, 1996, pp. 173–202.

Angus, Ian. "The Politics of Common Sense: Articulation Theory and Critical Communication Studies." In *Communication Yearbook 15.* Edited by Stanley Deetz. Newbury Park, CA: Sage, 1992, pp. 535–570.

Arato, Andrew, and Gebhardt, Eike, eds. *The Essential Frankfurt School Reader.* New York: Continuum, 1982.

Ardener, Edwin. "The 'Problem' Revisited." In *Perceiving Women.* Edited by Shirley Ardener. London: Malaby, 1975.

Ardener, Shirley. *Defining Females: The Nature of Women in Society.* New York: Wiley, 1978.

Baynes, Kenneth. "Communicative Ethics, the Public Sphere and Communication Media." *Critical Studies in Mass Communication* 11 (1994): 315–326.

Becker, Samuel L. "Marxist Approaches to Media Studies: The British Experience." *Critical Studies in Mass Communication* 1 (1984): 66–80.

Blair, Carole. "The Statement: Foundation of Foucault's Historical Criticism." *Western Journal of Speech Communication* 51 (1987): 364–383.

Blumler, Jay. "Communication and Democracy: The Crisis Beyond and the Ferment Within." *Journal of Communication* 33 (1983): 166–173.

Bottomore, Tom, and Mattelart, Armand. "Marxist Theories of Communication." In *International Encyclopedia of Communications,* vol. 2. Edited by Erik Barnouw and others. New York: Oxford University Press, 1989, pp. 476–483.

Carragee, Kevin M. "A Critical Evaluation of the Media Hegemony Thesis." *Western Journal of Communication* 57 (1993): 330–348.

Cobb, Sara. "A Critique of Critical Discourse Analysis: Deconstructing and Reconstructing the Role of Intention." *Communication Theory* 4 (1994): 132–152.

Condit, Celeste. "In Praise of Eloquent Diversity: Gender and Rhetoric as Public Persuasion." *Women's Studies in Communication* 20 (1997): in press.

Cooper, Martha. "Rhetorical Criticism and Foucault's Philosophy of Discursive Events." *Central States Speech Journal* 39 (1988): 1–17.

Dervin, Brenda. "The Potential Contribution of Feminist Scholarship to the Field of Communication." *Journal of Communication* 37 (1987): 107–120.

Ealy, Steven D. *Communication, Speech, and Politics: Habermas and Political Analysis.* Washington, DC: University Press of America, 1981.

Elgin, Suzette. *A First Dictionary and Grammar of Láadan,* 2nd ed. Madison, WI: Society for the Furtherance and Study of Fantasy and Science Fiction, 1988.

Ellis, Donald G. "Poststructuralism and Language: Non-Sense." *Communication Monographs* 58 (1991): 213–224.

Farrell, Thomas B. *Norms of Rhetorical Culture.* New Haven CT: Yale University Press, 1993.

Farrell, Thomas B., and Aune, James A. "Critical Theory and Communication: A Selective Literature Review." *Quarterly Journal of Speech* 65 (1979): 93–120.

Fay, Brian. *Social Theory and Political Practice.* London: Allen & Unwin, 1975.

Flores, Lisa A. "Creating Discursive Space Through a Rhetoric of Difference: Chicana Feminists Craft a Homeland." *Quarterly Journal of Speech* 82 (1996): 142–156.

Foss, Karen A., and Foss, Sonja K. "Incorporating the Feminist Perspective in Communication Scholarship: A Research Commentary." In *Doing Research on Women's Communication: Alternative Perspectives in Theory and Method.* Edited by Carole Spitzack and Kathryn Carter. Norwood, NJ: Ablex, 1989, pp. 65–94.

Foss, Karen A., and Foss, Sonja K. "Personal Experience as Evidence in Feminist Scholarship." *Western Journal of Communication* 58 (1994): 39–43.

———. *Women Speak: The Eloquence of Women's Lives.* Prospect Heights, IL: Waveland, 1991.

Foss, Karen A., Foss, Sonja, and Griffin, Cindy L. *Revisioning Rhetorics: Feminist Transformations of Rhetorical Theory.* Thousand Oaks, CA: Sage, 1998.

Foss, Sonja K. *Rhetorical Criticism: Exploration and Practice.* Prospect Heights, IL: Waveland, 1989.

Foss, Sonja K., Foss, Karen A., and Trapp, Robert. *Contemporary Perspectives on Rhetoric.* Prospect Heights, IL: Waveland, 1991.

Foss, Sonja K., and Gill, Ann. "Michel Foucault's Theory of Rhetoric as Epistemic." *Western Journal of Speech Communication* 51 (1987): 384–402.

Foss, Sonja K., Griffin, Cindy L., and Foss, Karen A. "Transforming Rhetoric Through Feminist Reconstruction: A Response to the Gender-Diversity Perspective." *Women's Studies in Communication* 20 (1997): in press.

Foucault, Michel. *The Archaeology of Knowledge.* Translated by A. M. Sheridan Smith. New York: Pantheon, 1972.

———. *Discipline and Punish: The Birth of the Prison.* Translated by A. Sheridan. New York: Vintage, 1979.

———. *The Order of Things: An Archaeology of the Human Sciences.* New York: Pantheon, 1970.

———. *Power/Knowledge: Selected Interviews and Other Writings 1927–1977.* Translated by Colin Gordon and others. Edited by Colin Gordon. New York: Pantheon, 1980.

Fraser, Nancy. *Unruly Practices: Power, Discourse, and Gender in Contemporary Social Theory.* Minneapolis: University of Minnesota Press, 1989.

Gerbner, George, ed. "Ferment in the Field." Special issue of *Journal of Communication* 33 (Summer 1983).

Gilligan, Carol. *In a Different Voice.* Cambridge, MA: Harvard University Press, 1982.

Gramsci, Antonio. *Selections from the Prison Notebooks.* Translated by Q. Hoare and G. Nowell Smith. New York: International, 1971.

Grossberg, Lawrence. "Is There Rock After Punk?" *Critical Studies in Mass Communication* 3 (1986): 50–73.

———. "Strategies of Marxist Cultural Interpretation." *Critical Studies in Mass Communication* 1 (1984): 392–421.

Habermas, Jürgen. *Knowledge and Human Interests*. Translated by Jeremy J. Shapiro. Boston: Beacon, 1971.

———. *Legitimation Crisis*. Translated by Thomas McCarthy. Boston: Beacon, 1975.

———. *Postmetaphysical Thinking: Philosophical Essays*. Translated by William Mark Hohengarten. Cambridge, MA: MIT Press, 1992.

———. *The Theory of Communicative Action, Volume 1: Reason and the Rationalization of Society*. Translated by Thomas McCarthy. Boston: Beacon, 1984.

Hall, Stuart. "Cultural Studies and the Centre: Some Problematics and Problems." In *Culture, Media, Language*. Edited by Stuart Hall, Dorothy Hobson, Andrew Lowe, and Paul Willis. London: Hutchinson, 1981, pp. 15–47.

———. "Cultural Studies: Two Paradigms." In *Media, Culture, and Society: A Critical Reader*. Edited by R. Collins. London: Sage, 1986.

———. "Ideology." In *International Encyclopedia of Communications*, vol. 2. Edited by Erik Barnouw and others. New York: Oxford University Press, 1989, pp. 307–311.

———. "Signification, Representation, Ideology: Althusser and the Post-Structuralist Debates." *Critical Studies in Mass Communication* 2 (1985): 91–114.

Hall, Stuart, Hobson, Dorothy, Lowe, Andrew, and Willis, Paul, eds. *Culture, Media, Language*. London: Hutchinson, 1981.

Hanna, Joseph F. "Critical Theory and the Politicization of Science." *Communication Monographs* 58 (1991): 202–212.

Harms, John B., and Dickens, David R. "Postmodern Media Studies: Analysis or Symptom." *Critical Studies in Mass Communication* 13 (1996): 210–227.

Hoggart, Richard. *Uses of Literacy*. London: Chatto & Windus, 1957.

Houston, Marsha. "What Makes Scholarship About Black Women and Communication Feminist Communication Scholarship?" *Women's Studies in Communication* 10 (1988): 78–88.

Huspek, Michael. "Dueling Structures: The Theory of Resistance in Discourse." *Communication Theory* 3 (1993): 1–25.

———. "Taking Aim on Habermas's Critical Theory: On the Road Toward a Critical Hermeneutics." *Communication Monographs* 58 (1991): 225–233.

Jansen, Sue Curry. "Power and Knowledge: Toward a New Critical Synthesis." *Journal of Communication* 33 (1983): 342–354.

Johnson, Fern L. "Coming to Terms with Women's Language." *Quarterly Journal of Speech* 72 (1986): 318–352.

Kellner, Douglas. "Media Communications vs. Cultural Studies: Overcoming the Divide." *Communication Theory* 5 (1995): 162–177.

Kerfoot, Deborah, and Knights, David. "Into the Realm of the Fearful: Power, Identity, and the Gender Problematic." In *Power/Gender: Social Relations in Theory and Practice*. Edited by H. Lorraine Radtke and Henderikus J. Stam. London: Sage, 1994, pp. 67–88.

———. *Media Culture: Cultural Studies, Identity and Politics Between the Modern and the Postmodern*. London: Routledge, 1995.

Kramarae, Cheris. "Feminist Theories of Communication." In *International Encyclopedia of Communications*, vol 2. Edited by Erik Barnouw and others. New York: Oxford University Press, 1989, pp. 157–160.

———. *Women and Men Speaking: Frameworks for Analysis*. Rowley, MA: Newbury House, 1981.

Kramarae, Cheris, Treichler, Paula A., and Russo, Ann. *A Feminist Dictionary*. Boston: Pandora, 1985.

LaFrance, Marianne, and Henley, Nancy M. "An Oppressing Hypothesis: Or Differences in Nonverbal Sensitivity Revisited." In *Power/Gender: Social Relations in Theory and Practice*. Edited by H. Lorraine Radtke and Henderikus J. Stam. London: Sage, 1994, pp. 287–311.

Lanigan, Richard L. *Phenomenology of Communication: Merleau-Ponty's Thematics in Communicology and Semiology*. Pittsburgh, PA: Duquesne University Press, 1988.

Lannamann, John W. "Interpersonal Communication Research as Ideological Practice." *Communication Theory* 1 (1991): 179–203.

Lazarsfeld, Paul. "Remarks on Administrative and Critical Communications Research." *Studies in Philosophy and Social Science* 9 (1941): 2–16.

Lembo, Ronald, and Tucker, Kenneth H. "Culture, Television, and Opposition: Rethinking Cultural Studies." *Critical Studies in Mass Communication* 7 (1990): 97–116.

Lull, James. "The Audience as Nuisance." *Critical Studies in Mass Communication* 5 (1988): 239.

MacKinnon, Catharine A. "Desire and Power: A Feminist Perspective." In *Marxism and the Interpretation of Culture*. Edited by Cary Nelson and Lawrence Grossberg. Urbana: University of Illinois Press, 1988, pp. 105–122.

Mahmood, Saba. "Cultural Studies and Ethnic Absolutism: Comments on Stuart Hall's 'Culture, Community, and Nation.'" *Cultural Studies* 10 (1996): 1–11.

Makus, Anne. "Stuart Hall's Theory of Ideology: A Frame for Rhetorical Criticism." *Western Journal of Speech Communication* 54 (1990): 495–514.

Marx, Karl. *Capital*. Chicago: Kerr, 1909.

———. *The Communist Manifesto*. London: Reeves, 1888.

McCarthy, Thomas. *Ideals and Illusions: On Reconstruction and Deconstruction in Contemporary Critical Theory*. Cambridge, MA: MIT Press, 1993.

McLaughlin, Lisa. "Feminist Communication Scholarship and 'The Woman Question' in the Academy." *Communication Theory* 5 (1995): 144–161.

Mueller, Milton. "Why Communications Policy Is Passing 'Mass Communication' by: Political Economy as the Missing Link." *Critical Studies in Mass Communication* 12 (1995): 455–472.

Mumby, Dennis K. *Communication and Power in Organizations: Discourse, Ideology, and Domination*. Norwood, NJ: Ablex, 1988.

———. "Modernism, Postmodernism, and Communication Studies: A Rereading of an Ongoing Debate." *Communication Theory* 7 (1997): 1–28.

———. "The Political Function of Narrative in Organizations." *Communication Monographs* 54 (1987): 113–127.

Murdock, Graham. "Across the Great Divide: Cultural Analysis and the Condition of Democracy." *Critical Studies in Mass Communication* 12 (1995): 89–95.

Nelson, Cary, and Grossberg, Lawrence, eds. *Marxism and the Interpretation of Culture*. Urbana: University of Illinois Press, 1988.

Penelope, Julia. *Speaking Freely: Unlearning the Lies of the Fathers' Tongues.* New York: Pergamon, 1990.

Pillai, Poonam. "Rereading Stuart Hall's Encoding/Decoding Model." *Communication Theory* 2 (1992): 221–233.

Pollock, Della, and Cox, J. Robert. "Historicizing 'Reason': Critical Theory, Practice, and Postmodernity." *Communication Monographs* 58 (1991): 170–178.

Pryor, Robert. "On the Method of Critical Theory and Its Implications for a Critical Theory of Communication." In *Phenomenology in Rhetoric and Communication.* Edited by Stanley Deetz. Washington, DC: Center for Advanced Research in Phenomenology/University Press of America, 1981, pp. 25–35.

Putnam, Linda L. "In Search of Gender: A Critique of Communication and Sex-Roles Research." *Women's Studies in Communication* 5 (1982): 1–9.

Rakow, Lana F., ed. *Women Making Meaning: New Feminist Directions in Communication.* New York: Routledge, 1992.

Real, Michael. "The Debate on Critical Theory and the Study of Communications." *Journal of Communication* 34 (Autumn 1984): 72–80.

Ricoeur, Paul. *Hermeneutics and the Human Sciences: Essays on Language, Action, and Interpretation.* Translated and edited by John B. Thompson. Cambridge: Cambridge University Press, 1981.

Rogers, Everett M. "The Empirical and the Critical Schools of Communication Research." In *Communication Yearbook 5.* Edited by Michael Burgoon. New Brunswick, NJ: Transaction, 1982, pp. 125–144.

———. *A History of Communication Study: A Biographical Approach.* New York: Free Press, 1994, pp. 102–128.

Rosteck, Thomas. "Cultural Studies and Rhetorical Studies," *Quarterly Journal of Speech* 81 (1995): 386–421.

Rush, Ramona R., and Grubb-Swetman, Autumn. "Feminist Approaches." In *An Integrated Approach to Communication Theory and Research.* Edited by Michael B. Salwen and Don W. Stacks. Mahwah, NJ: Erlbaum, 1996, pp. 497–518.

Shome, Raka. "Postcolonial Interventions in the Rhetorical Canon: An 'Other' View." *Communication Theory* 6 (1996): 40–59.

Slack, Jennifer Daryl, and Allor, Martin. "The Political and Epistemological Constituents of Critical Communication Research." *Journal of Communication* 33 (1983): 128–218.

Smythe, Dallas W., and Dinh, Tran Van. "On Critical and Administrative Research: A New Critical Analysis." *Journal of Communication* 33 (1983): 117–127.

Spender, Dale. *Man Made Language.* London: Routledge & Kegan Paul, 1980, pp. 76–105.

Swartz, Omar. *Conducting Socially Responsible Research.* Thousand Oaks, CA: Sage, 1997.

Thomas, Jim. *Doing Critical Ethnography.* Newbury Park, CA: Sage, 1993.

van Dijk, Teun. "Discourse Semantics and Ideology." *Discourse and Society* 6 (1995): 243–289.

———. "Principles of Critical Discourse Analysis." *Discourse and Society* 4 (1993): 249–283.

White, Robert. "Mass Communication and Culture: Transition to a New Paradigm." *Journal of Communication* 33 (1983): 279–301.

Williams, Raymond. *The Long Revolution.* New York: Columbia University Press, 1961.

Wood, Julia T., and Pearce, W. Barnett. "Sexists, Racists, and Other Classes of Classifiers: Form and Function of 'ist' Accusations." *Quarterly Journal of Speech* 66 (1980): 239–250.

Chapter 12
Communication in Relationships

Altman, Irwin. "Dialectics, Physical Environments, and Personal Relationships." *Communication Monographs* 60 (1993): 26–34.

Altman, Irwin, and Taylor, Dalmas. *Social Penetration: The Development of Interpersonal Relationships.* New York: Holt, Rinehart & Winston, 1973.

Altman, Irwin, Vinsel, A., and Brown, B. "Dialectic Conceptions in Social Psychology: An Application to Social Penetration and Privacy Regulation." In *Advances in Experimental Social Psychology,* vol. 14. Edited by L. Berkowitz. New York: Academic, 1981, pp. 76–100.

Andersen, Peter J. "When One Cannot Not Communicate: A Challenge to Motley's Traditional Communication Postulates." *Communication Studies* 42 (1991): 326–339.

Applegate, James L., and Leichty, Gregory B. "Managing Interpersonal Relationships: Social Cognitive and Strategic Determinants of Competence." In *Competence in Communication: A Multi-Disciplinary Approach.* Edited by Robert N. Bostrom. Beverly Hills, CA: Sage, 1984.

Bavelas, Janet Beavin. "Behaving and Communicating: A Reply to Motley." *Western Journal of Speech Communication* 54 (1990): 593–602.

Baxter, Leslie A. "Accomplishing Relationship Disengagement." In *Understanding Personal Relationships: An Interdisciplinary Approach.* Edited by Steve Duck and Daniel Perlman. Beverly Hills, CA: Sage, 1985, pp. 243–266.

———. "A Dialectical Perspective on Communication Strategies in Relationship Development." In *Handbook of Personal Relationships.* Edited by Steve Duck. New York: Wiley, 1988, pp. 257–273.

———. "Interpersonal Communication as Dialogue: A Response to the 'Social Approaches' Forum." *Communication Theory* 2 (1992): 330.

———. "The Social Side of Personal Relationships: A Dialectical Perspective." In *Social Context and Relationships: Understanding Relationship Processes,* vol. 3. Edited by Steve Duck. Newbury Park, CA: Sage, 1993, pp. 139–169.

———. "Strategies for Ending Relationships: Two Studies." *Western Journal of Speech Communication* 46 (1982): 223–241.

———. "Trajectories of Relationship Disengagement." *Journal of Social and Personal Relationships* 1 (1984): 29–48.

Beisecker, Thomas. "Game Theory in Communication Research: A Rejoinder and a Re-orientation." *Journal of Communication* 20 (1970): 107–120.

Berger, Charles R. "Interpersonal Communication." In *An Integrated Approach to Communication Theory and Research.* Edited by Michael B. Salwen and Don W. Stacks. Mahwah, NJ: Erlbaum, 1996, pp. 277–296.

Berger, Charles R., and Bradac, James J. *Language and Social Knowledge: Uncertainty in Interpersonal Relations.* London: Arnold, 1982.

Berger, Charles R., and Calabrese, R. J. "Some Explorations in Initial Interaction and Beyond: Toward a Developmental Theory of Interpersonal Communication." *Human Communication Research* 1 (1975): 99–112.

Berger, Charles R., and Douglas, William. "Thought and Talk: 'Excuse Me, But Have I Been Talking to Myself?'" In *Human Communication Theory*. Edited by Frank E. X. Dance. New York: Harper & Row, 1982, pp. 42–60.

Berger, Charles R., Gardner, R. R., Parks, M. R., Schulman, L., and Miller, G. R. "Interpersonal Epistemology and Interpersonal Communication." In *Explorations in Interpersonal Communication*. Edited by Gerald R. Miller. Beverly Hills, CA: Sage, 1976, pp. 149–171.

Berger, Charles R., and Kellermann, Katherine Ann. "To Ask or Not to Ask: Is That a Question?" In *Communication Yearbook 7*. Edited by Robert Bostrom. Beverly Hills, CA: Sage, 1983, pp. 342–368.

Berlyne, Daniel E. "Humanistic Psychology as a Protest Movement." In *Humanistic Psychology: Concepts and Criticism*. Edited by Joseph Royce and Leendert P. Mos. New York: Plenum, 1981, pp. 261–293.

Bochner, Arthur P. "The Functions of Human Communicating in Interpersonal Bonding." In *Handbook of Rhetorical and Communication Theory*. Edited by Carroll C. Arnold and John Waite Bowers. Boston: Allyn & Bacon, 1984, pp. 554–621.

Bochner, Arthur, and Krueger, Dorothy. "Interpersonal Communication Theory and Research: An Overview of Inscrutable Epistemologies and Muddled Concepts." In *Communication Yearbook 3*. Edited by Dan Nimmo. New Brunswick, NJ: Transaction, 1979, pp. 197–211.

Bostrom, Robert. "Game Theory in Communication Research." *Journal of Communication* 18 (1968): 369–388.

Brown, Penelope, and Levinson, Stephen. *Politeness: Some Universals in Language Usage*. Cambridge: Cambridge University Press, 1987.

Brown, Roger. "Politeness Theory: Exemplar and Exemplary." In *The Legacy of Solomon Asch: Essays in Cognition and Social Psychology*. Edited by Irvin Rock. Hillsdale, NJ: Erlbaum, 1990, pp. 23–38.

Burgoon, Judee K., Buller, David B., Hale, Jerold L., and deTurck, Mark A. "Relational Messages Associated with Nonverbal Behaviors." *Human Communication Research* 10 (1984): 351–378.

Burgoon, Judee K., and Hale, Jerold L. "The Fundamental Topoi of Relational Communication." *Communication Monographs* 51 (1984): 193–214.

Burrell, Nancy A., and Fitzpatrick, Mary Anne. "The Psychological Reality of Marital Conflict." In *Intimates in Conflict: A Communication Perspective*. Edited by Dudley D. Cahn. Hillsdale, NJ: Erlbaum, 1990, pp. 167–186.

Cahn, Dudley D., ed. *Intimates in Conflict: A Communication Perspective*. Hillsdale, NJ: Erlbaum, 1990.

Cappella, Joseph N. "Interpersonal Communication: Definitions and Fundamental Questions." In *Handbook of Communication Science*. Edited by Charles R. Berger and Stephen H. Chaffee. Newbury Park, CA: Sage, 1987, pp. 184–238.

Cissna, Kenneth J., and Anderson, Rob. "The Contributions of Carl R. Rogers to Philosophical Praxis of Dialogue." *Western Journal of Speech Communication* 54 (1990): 125–147.

Cozby, P. W. "Self-Disclosure: A Literature Review." *Psychological Bulletin* 79 (1973): 73–91.

Cupach, William R., and Metts, Sandra. *Facework*. Thousand Oaks, CA: Sage, 1994.

Davis, Morton. *Game Theory: A Non-technical Introduction*. New York: Basic, 1970.

Duck, Steve. "How to Lose Friends Without Influencing People." In *Interpersonal Processes: New Directions in Communication Research*. Edited by Michael E. Roloff and Gerald R. Miller. Newbury Park, CA: Sage, 1987, pp. 278–298.

———. *Meaningful Relationships: Talking, Sense, and Relating*. Thousand Oaks, CA: Sage, 1994.

Duck, Steve, and Pittman, Garth. "Social and Personal Relationships." In *Handbook of Interpersonal Communication*, 2nd ed. Edited by Mark L. Knapp and Gerald R. Miller. Thousand Oaks, CA: Sage, 1994, pp. 676–695.

Duval, S., and Wicklund, R. A. *A Theory of Objective Self-Awareness*. New York: Academic, 1972.

Fitch, Christine L. "Culture, Ideology, and Interpersonal Communication Research." In *Communication Yearbook 17*. Edited by Stanley A. Deetz. Thousand Oaks, CA: Sage, 1994, pp. 104–135.

Fitzpatrick, Mary Anne. *Between Husbands and Wives: Communication in Marriage*. Newbury Park, CA: Sage, 1988.

Fitzpatrick, Mary Anne, and Ritchie, L. David. "Communication Schemata Within the Family: Multiple Perspectives on Family Interaction." *Human Communication Research* 20 (1994): 275–301.

Frost, Joyce, and Wilmot, William. *Interpersonal Conflict*. Dubuque, IA: Brown, 1978.

Gilbert, Shirley J. "Empirical and Theoretical Extensions of Self-Disclosure." In *Explorations in Interpersonal Communication*. Edited by Gerald R. Miller. Beverly Hills, CA: Sage, 1976, pp. 197–216.

Goldsmith, Daena J. "The Role of Facework in Supportive Communication." In *Communication of Social Support*. Edited by Brant R. Burleson, Terrance L. Albrecht, and Irwin G. Sarason. Thousand Oaks, CA: Sage, 1994, pp. 29–49.

Gudykunst, William B. "Culture and the Development of Interpersonal Relationships." In *Communication Yearbook 12*. Edited by James A. Anderson. Newbury Park, CA: Sage, 1989, pp. 315–354.

———. "Uncertainty and Anxiety." In *Theories in Intercultural Communication*. Edited by Young Yun Kim and William B. Gudykunst. Newbury Park, CA: Sage, 1988, pp. 123–156.

Hall, Edward T. *Beyond Culture*. New York: Doubleday, 1976.

Hofstede, G. *Cultures Consequences*. Beverly Hills, CA: Sage, 1980.

Jourard, Sidney. *Disclosing Man to Himself*. New York: Van Nostrand, 1968.

———. *Self-Disclosure: An Experimental Analysis of the Transparent Self*. New York: Wiley, 1971.

———. *The Transparent Self*. New York: Van Nostrand Reinhold, 1971.

Kantor, David, and Lehr, William. *Inside the Family*. New York: Harper & Row, 1975.

Kelley, Harold H., and Thibaut, John W. *Interpersonal Relations: A Theory of Interdependence*. New York: Wiley, 1978.

Knapp, Mark L., and Miller, Gerald R., eds. *Handbook of Interpersonal Communication.* Newbury Park, CA: Sage, 1994.

Knapp, Mark L., Miller, Gerald R., and Fudge, Kelly. "Background and Current Trends in the Study of Interpersonal Communication." In *Handbook of Interpersonal Communication.* Edited by Mark L. Knapp and Gerald R. Miller. Newbury Park, CA: Sage, 1994, pp. 3–20.

LaGaipa, John L. "Interpersonal Attraction and Social Exchange." In *Theory and Practice in Interpersonal Attraction.* Edited by Steve Duck. New York: Academic, 1971, pp. 129–164.

Laing, R. D. *The Politics of Experience.* New York: Pantheon, 1967.

———. *Self and Others.* London: Tavistock, 1969.

Laing, R. D., Phillipson, H., and Lee, A. R. *Interpersonal Perception.* New York: Springer, 1966.

Lannamann, John W. "Deconstructing the Person and Changing the Subject of Interpersonal Studies." *Communication Theory* 2 (1992): 139–148.

———. "Interpersonal Communication Research as Ideological Practice." *Communication Theory* 1 (1991): 179–203.

Luft, Joseph. *Of Human Interaction.* Palo Alto, CA: National Press, 1969.

Maslow, Abraham. *The Farther Reaches of Human Nature.* New York: Viking, 1971.

Millar, Frank E., and Rogers, L. Edna. "Power Dynamics in Marital Relationships." In *Perspectives on Marital Interaction.* Edited by P. Noller and M. Fitzpatrick. Clevedon, England: Multilingual Matters, 1988, pp. 78–97.

———. "A Relational Approach to Interpersonal Communication." In *Explorations in Interpersonal Communication.* Edited by Gerald R. Miller. Beverly Hills, CA: Sage, 1976, pp. 87–203.

———. "Relational Dimensions of Interpersonal Dynamics." In *Interpersonal Processes: New Directions in Communication Research.* Edited by Michael E. Roloff and Gerald R. Miller. Newbury Park, CA: Sage, 1987, pp. 117–139.

Miller, G. R., and Steinberg, M. *Between People: A New Analysis of Interpersonal Communication.* Chicago: Science Research Associates, 1975.

Miller, G. R., and Sunnafrank, M. J. "All Is for One But One Is Not for All: A Conceptual Perspective of Interpersonal Communication." In *Human Communication Theory: Comparative Essays.* Edited by Frank E. X. Dance. New York: Harper & Row, 1982, pp. 220–242.

Montgomery, Barbara M. "Communication as the Interface Between Couples and Culture." In *Communication Yearbook 15.* Edited by Stanley Deetz. Newbury Park, CA: Sage, 1992, pp. 475–507.

Morton, Teru L., and Douglas, Mary Ann. "Growth of Relationships." In *Personal Relationships 2: Developing Personal Relationships.* Edited by Steve Duck and Robin Gilmour. London: Academic, 1981, pp. 3–26.

Motley, Michael. "On Whether One Can(not) Not Communicate: An Examination via Traditional Communication Postulates." *Western Journal of Speech Communication* 54 (1990): 1–20.

Parks, Malcolm R. "Ideology in Interpersonal Communication: Off the Couch and into the World." In *Communication Yearbook 5.* Edited by Michael Burgoon. New Brunswick, NJ: Transaction, 1982, pp. 79–108.

Petronio, Sandra. "Communication Boundary Management: A Theoretical Model of Managing Disclosure of Private Information Between Marital Couples." *Communication Theory* 1 (1991): 311–335.

Rawlins, William K. "A Dialectical Analysis of the Tensions, Functions, and Strategic Challenges of Communication in Young Adult Friendships." In *Communication Yearbook 12.* Edited by James A. Anderson. Newbury Park, CA: Sage, 1989, pp. 157–189.

———. *Friendship Matters: Communication, Dialectics, and the Life Course.* Hawthorne, NY: Aldine, 1992.

Rogers, Carl. *Client-Centered Therapy.* Boston: Houghton Mifflin, 1951.

———. "A Theory of Therapy, Personality, and Interpersonal Relationships, as Developed in the Client-Centered Framework." In *Psychology: A Study of Science,* vol. 3. Edited by S. Koch. New York: McGraw-Hill, 1959, pp. 184–256.

Rogers, L. Edna. "Analyzing Relational Communication: Implications of a Pragmatic Approach." Paper presented at the annual meeting of the Speech Communication Association, Washington, DC, November 1983.

Rogers-Millar, L. Edna, and Millar, Frank E. "Domineeringness and Dominance: A Transactional View." *Human Communication Research* 5 (1979): 238–246.

Roloff, Michael E. "Communication and Conflict." In *Handbook of Communication Science.* Edited by Charles R. Berger and Steven H. Chaffee. Newbury Park, CA: Sage, 1987, pp. 484–536.

———. *Interpersonal Communication: The Social Exchange Approach.* Beverly Hills, CA: Sage, 1981.

Royce, Joseph R., and Mos, Leendert P., eds. *Humanistic Psychology: Concepts and Criticisms.* New York: Plenum, 1981.

Sigman, Stuart J. "Handling the Discontinuous Aspects of Continuous Social Relationships: Toward Research on the Persistence of Social Forms." *Communication Theory* 1 (1991): 106–127.

Sillars, Alan L. "Attributions and Communication in Roommate Conflicts." *Communication Monographs* 47 (1980): 180–200.

———. *Manual for Coding Interpersonal Conflict.* Unpublished manuscript, Department of Communication, University of Montana, 1986.

———. "The Sequential and Distributional Structure of Conflict Interaction as a Function of Attributions Concerning the Locus of Responsibility and Stability of Conflict." In *Communication Yearbook 4.* Edited by Dan Nimmo. New Brunswick, NJ: Transaction, 1980, pp. 217–236.

Sillars, Alan L., Coletti, Stephen F., Parry, Doug, and Rogers, Mark A. "Coding Verbal Conflict Tactics: Nonverbal and Perceptual Correlates of the 'Avoidance-Distributive-Integrative' Distinction." *Human Communication Research* 9 (1982): 83–95.

Sillars, Alan L., Pike, Gary R., Jones, Tricia S., and Redmond, Kathleen. "Communication and Conflict in Marriage." In *Communication Yearbook 7.* Edited by Robert Bostrom. Beverly Hills, CA: Sage, 1983, pp. 414–429.

Sillars, Alan, and Weisberg, Judith. "Conflict as a Social Skill." In *Interpersonal Processes: New Directions in Communication Research.* Edited by Michael E. Roloff and

Gerald R. Miller. Newbury Park, CA: Sage, 1987, pp. 140–171.

Steinfatt, Thomas, and Miller, Gerald. "Communication in Game Theoretic Models of Conflict." In *Perspectives on Communication in Conflict.* Edited by Gerald R. Miller and Herbert Simons. Englewood Cliffs, NJ: Prentice-Hall, 1974, pp. 14–75.

Stephen, Timothy, and Harrison, Teresa M. "Interpersonal Communication, Theory, and History." *Communication Theory* 3 (1993): 163–171.

Stewart, John. *Language as Articulate Contact.* Albany: SUNY Press, 1995.

Sunnafrank, Michael. "Predicted Outcome Value During Initial Interactions." *Human Communication Research* 13 (1986): 3–33.

———. "Predicted Outcome Value and Uncertainty Reduction Theories: A Test of Competing Perspectives." *Human Communication Research* 17 (1990): 76–103.

Taylor, Dalmas A., and Altman, Irwin. "Communication in Interpersonal Relationships: Social Penetration Theory." In *Interpersonal Processes: New Directions in Communication Research.* Edited by Michael E. Roloff and Gerald R. Miller. Newbury Park, CA: Sage, 1987, pp. 257–277.

Thibaut, John W., and Kelley, Harold H. *The Social Psychology of Groups.* New York: Wiley, 1959.

Trenholm, Sarah, and Jensen, Arthur. *Interpersonal Communication.* Belmont, CA: Wadsworth, 1988.

VanLear, C. Arthur. "Testing a Cyclical Model of Communicative Openness in Relationship Development: Two Longitudinal Studies." *Communication Monographs* 58 (1991): 337–361.

von Neumann, John, and Morgenstern, Oskar. *The Theory of Games and Economic Behavior.* Princeton, NJ: Princeton University Press, 1944.

Watkins, Charles. "An Analytic Model of Conflict." *Speech Monographs* 41 (1974): 1–5.

Watzlawick, Paul, Beavin, Janet, and Jackson, Don. *Pragmatics of Human Communication: A Study of Interactional Patterns, Pathologies, and Paradoxes.* New York: Norton, 1967.

Werner, Carol M., and Baxter, Leslie A. "Temporal Qualities of Relationships: Organismic, Transactional, and Dialectical Views." In *Handbook of Interpersonal Communication.* Edited by Mark L. Knapp and Gerald R. Miller. Newbury Park, CA: Sage, 1994, pp. 323–379.

Wilmot, William. "Meta-communication: A Re-examination and Extension." In *Communication Yearbook 4.* Edited by Dan Nimmo. New Brunswick, NJ: Transaction, 1980, pp. 61–69.

Wilmot, William, Carbaugh, Donal A., and Baxter, Leslie A. "Communicative Strategies Used to Terminate Romantic Relationships." *Western Journal of Speech Communication* 49 (1985): 204–216.

Chapter 13
Communication in Group Decision Making

Bales, Robert F. *Interaction Process Analysis: A Method for the Study of Small Groups.* Reading, MA: Addison-Wesley, 1950.

———. *Personality and Interpersonal Behavior.* New York: Holt, Rinehart & Winston, 1970.

Bales, Robert F., Cohen, Stephen P., and Williamson, Stephen A. *SYMLOG: A System for the Multiple Level Observation of Groups.* London: Collier, 1979.

Bales, Robert F., and Strodbeck, F. L. "Phases in Group Problem-Solving." *Journal of Abnormal and Social Psychology* 46 (1951): 485–495.

Banks, Stephen P., and Riley, Patricia. "Structuration Theory as an Ontology for Communication Research." *Communication Yearbook 16.* Edited by Stanley Deetz. Newbury Park, CA: Sage, 1993, pp. 167–196.

Barge, J. Kevin, and Hirokawa, Randy Y. "Toward a Communication Competency Model of Group Leadership." *Small Group Behavior* 20 (1989): 167–189.

Bell, M. A. "Phases in Group Problem-Solving." *Small Group Behavior* 13 (1982): 475–495.

Bennis, W. G., and Shepard, H. A. "The Theory of Group Development." *Human Relations* 9 (1956): 415–437.

Billingsley, Julie M. "An Evaluation of the Functional Perspective in Small Group Communication." In *Communication Yearbook 16.* Edited by Stanley Deetz. Newbury Park, CA: Sage, 1993, pp. 615–622.

Bormann, Ernest. "Symbolic Convergence and Communication in Group Decision Making." In *Communication and Group Decision-Making.* Edited by Randy Y. Hirokawa and Marshall Scott Poole. Beverly Hills, CA: Sage, 1986, pp. 219–236.

Cattell, Raymond. "Concepts and Methods in the Measurement of Group Syntality." *Psychological Review* 55 (1948): 48–63.

Collins, Barry, and Guetzkow, Harold. *A Social Psychology of Group Processes for Decision-Making.* New York: Wiley, 1964.

Courtright, John A. "A Laboratory Investigation of Groupthink." *Communication Monographs* 45 (1978): 229–246.

Cragan, John F., and Wright, David W. "Small Group Communication Research of the 1980s: A Synthesis and Critique." *Communication Studies* 41 (1990): 212–236.

Dewey, John. *How We Think.* Boston: Heath, 1910.

Fisher, B. Aubrey. "Decision Emergence: Phases in Group Decision Making." *Speech Monographs* 37 (1970): 53–60.

———. "The Process of Decision Modification in Small Discussion Groups." *Journal of Communication* 20 (1970): 51–64.

———. *Small Group Decision Making: Communication and the Group Process.* New York: McGraw-Hill, 1980.

Fisher, B. Aubrey, and Hawes, Leonard. "An Interact System Model: Generating a Grounded Theory of Small Groups." *Quarterly Journal of Speech* 57 (1971): 444–453.

Follett, Mary Parker. *Creative Experience.* New York: Longmans, Green, 1924.

Giddens, Anthony. *New Rules of Sociological Method.* New York: Basic, 1976.

———. *Profiles and Critiques in Social Theory.* Berkeley: University of California Press, 1982.

———. *Studies in Social and Political Theory.* New York: Basic, 1977.

Gouran, Dennis S. "The Paradigm of Unfulfilled Promise: A Critical Examination of the History of Research on Small Groups in Speech Communication." In *Speech*

Communication in the 20th Century. Edited by Thomas W. Benson. Carbondale: Southern Illinois University Press, 1985, pp. 90–108.

Gouran, Dennis S., and Fisher, B. Aubrey. "The Functions of Human Communication in the Formation, Maintenance, and Performance of Small Groups." In *Handbook of Rhetorical and Communication Theory.* Edited by Carroll C. Arnold and John Waite Bowers. Boston: Allyn & Bacon, 1984, pp. 622–659.

Gouran, Dennis S., and Hirokawa, Randy Y. "Counteractive Functions of Communication in Effective Group Decision-Making." In *Communication and Group Decision-Making.* Edited by Randy Y. Hirokawa and Marshall Scott Poole. Beverly Hills, CA: Sage, 1986, pp. 81–92.

Gouran, Dennis S., Hirokawa, Randy Y., Julian, Kelly M., and Leatham, Geoff B. "The Evolution and Current Status of the Functional Perspective on Communication in Decision-Making and Problem-Solving Groups." In *Communication Yearbook 16.* Edited by Stanley A. Deetz. Newbury Park, CA: Sage, 1993, pp. 573–600.

Hirokawa, Randy Y. "Group Communication and Decision Making Performance: A Continued Test of the Functional Perspective." *Human Communication Research* 14 (1988): 487–515.

———. "Group Communication and Problem-Solving Effectiveness I: A Critical Review of Inconsistent Findings." *Communication Quarterly* 30 (1982): 134–141.

———. "Group Communication and Problem-Solving Effectiveness: An Investigation of Group Phases." *Human Communication Research* 9 (1983): 291–305.

———. "Group Communication and Problem-Solving Effectiveness II." *Western Journal of Speech Communication* 47 (1983): 59–74.

Hirokawa, Randy Y., and Poole, Marshall Scott, eds. *Communication and Group Decision-Making.* Beverly Hills, CA: Sage, 1986.

Hirokawa, Randy Y., and Scheerhorn, Dirk R. "Communication in Faulty Group Decision-Making." In *Communication and Group Decision-Making.* Edited by Randy Y. Hirokawa and Marshall Scott Poole. Beverly Hills, CA: Sage, 1986, pp. 63–80.

Hirokawa, Randy, Salazar, Abran J., Erbert, Larry, and Ice, Richard J. "Small Group Communication." In *An Integrated Approach to Communication Theory and Research.* Edited by Michael B. Salwen and Don W. Stacks. Mahwah, NJ: Erlbaum, 1996, pp. 359–382.

Janis, Irving. *Crucial Decisions: Leadership in Policy Making and Crisis Management.* New York: Free Press, 1989.

———. *Groupthink: Psychological Studies of Policy Decisions and Fiascoes.* Boston: Houghton Mifflin, 1982.

Janis, Irving, and Mann, Leon. *Decision Making: A Psychological Analysis of Conflict, Choice, and Commitment.* New York: Free Press, 1977.

Jarboe, Susan. "A Comparison of Input-Output, Process-Output, and Input-Process-Output Models of Small Group Problem-Solving Effectiveness." *Communication Monographs* 55 (1988): 121–142.

Lacoursiere, R. *The Life Cycle of Groups.* New York: Human Sciences, 1980.

Lewin, Kurt. *Resolving Social Conflicts: Selected Papers on Group Dynamics.* New York: Harper & Row, 1948.

Phillips, Gerald M., and Wood, Julia T., eds. *Emergent Issues in Human Decision Making.* Carbondale: Southern Illinois University Press, 1984.

Poole, Marshall Scott. "Decision Development in Small Groups, III: A Multiple Sequence Model of Group Decision Development." *Communication Monographs* 50 (1983): 321–342.

———. "Do We Have Any Theories of Group Communication?" *Communication Studies* 41 (1990): 237–247.

Poole, Marshall Scott, and Roth, Jonelle. "Decision Development in Small Groups IV: A Typology of Group Decision Paths." *Human Communication Research* 15 (1989): 323–356.

———. "Decision Development in Small Groups V: Test of a Contingency Model." *Human Communication Research* 15 (1989): 549–589.

Poole, Marshall Scott, Seibold, David R., and McPhee, Robert D. "Group Decision-Making as a Structurational Process." *Quarterly Journal of Speech* 71 (1985): 74–102.

———. "A Structurational Approach to Theory-Building in Group Decision-Making Research." In *Communication and Group Decision-Making.* Edited by Randy Y. Hirokawa and Marshall Scott Poole. Beverly Hills, CA: Sage, 1986, pp. 238–240.

Rogers, Everett M. *A History of Communication Study: A Biographical Approach.* New York: Free Press, 1994.

Shaw, Marvin E. *Group Dynamics: The Psychology of Small Group Behavior.* New York: McGraw-Hill, 1981.

Stohl, Cynthia, and Holmes, Michael E. "A Functional Perspective for Bona Fide Groups." In *Communication Yearbook 16.* Edited by Stanley Deetz. Newbury Park, CA: Sage, 1993, pp. 601–614.

Tuckman, Bruce. "Developmental Sequence in Small Groups." *Psychological Bulletin* 63 (1965): 384–399.

Chapter 14
Communication and Organizational Networks

Allen, Myria Watkins, Gotcher, M. Michael, and Seibert, Joy Hart. "A Decade of Organizational Communication Research: Journal Articles 1980–1991." In *Communication Yearbook 16.* Edited by Stanley Deetz. Newbury Park, CA: Sage, 1993, pp. 252–330.

Alvesson, Mats, and Deetz, Stanley. "Critical Theory and Postmodernism Approaches to Organizational Studies." In *Handbook of Organizational Studies.* Edited by S. Clegg, C. Harding, and W. Nord. London: Sage, 1996, pp. 173–202.

Barker, James, R., and Cheney, George. "The Concept and the Practices in Contemporary Organizational Life." *Communication Monographs* 61 (1994): 19–43.

Bitzer, Lloyd. "Aristotle's Enthymeme Revisited." *Quarterly Journal of Speech* 45 (1959): 399–408.

Bullis, Connie A., and Tompkins, Phillip K. "The Forest Ranger Revisited: A Study of Control Practices and Identification." *Communication Monographs* 56 (1989): 287–306.

Cheney, George. "The Rhetoric of Identification and the Study of Organizational Communication." *Quarterly Journal of Speech* 69 (1983): 143–158.

———. *Rhetoric in an Organizational Society: Managing Multiple Identities.* Columbia: University of South Carolina Press, 1991.

Cheney, George, and Tompkins, Phillip K. "Coming to Terms with Organizational Identification and Commitment." *Central States Speech Journal* 38 (1987): 1–15.

Deetz, Stanley. *Democracy in an Age of Corporate Colonization: Developments in Communication and the Politics of Everyday Life.* Albany: SUNY Press, 1992.

Delia, Jesse. "The Logic Fallacy, Cognitive Theory, and the Enthymeme: A Search for the Foundations of Reasoned Discourse." *Quarterly Journal of Speech* 56 (1970): 140–148.

Edwards, R. "The Social Relations of Production at the Point of Production." In *Complex Organizations: Critical Perspectives.* Edited by M. Zey-Ferrell and M. Aiken. Glenview, IL: Scott, Foresman, 1981.

Eisenstadt, S. N. *Max Weber on Charisma and Institution Building.* Chicago: University of Chicago Press, 1968.

Etzioni, Amatai. *Modern Organizations.* Englewood Cliffs, NJ: Prentice-Hall, 1964.

Everett, James L. "Communication and Sociocultural Evolution in Organizations and Organizational Populations." *Communication Theory* 4 (1994): 93–110.

Farace, Richard V., Monge, Peter R., and Russell, Hamish. *Communicating and Organizing.* Reading, MA: Addison-Wesley, 1977.

Fayol, Henri. *General and Industrial Management.* New York: Pitman, 1949.

Giddens, Anthony. *Central Problems in Social Theory.* Berkeley: University of California Press, 1979.

———. *Profiles and Critiques in Social Theory.* Berkeley: University of California Press, 1982.

Johnson, H. "A New Conceptualization of Source of Organizational Climate." *Administrative Science Quarterly* 3 (1976): 275–292.

Kaufman, H. *The Forest Ranger: A Study in Administrative Behavior.* Baltimore, MD: Johns Hopkins University Press, 1960.

Kreps, Gary L. "A Field Experimental Test and Revaluation of Weick's Model of Organizing." In *Communication Yearbook 4.* Edited by Dan Nimmo. New Brunswick, NJ: Transaction, 1980, pp. 389–398.

Likert, Rensis. *The Human Organization.* New York: McGraw-Hill, 1967.

———. *New Patterns of Management.* New York: McGraw-Hill, 1961.

Marshall, Judi. "Viewing Organizational Communication from a Feminist Perspective: A Critique and Some Offerings." In *Communication Yearbook 16.* Edited by Stanley Deetz. Newbury Park, CA: Sage, 1993, pp. 122–143.

McPhee, Robert D. "Formal Structure and Organizational Communication." In *Organizational Communication: Traditional Themes and New Directions.* Edited by Robert D. McPhee and Phillip K. Tompkins. Beverly Hills, CA: Sage, 1985, pp. 149–178.

———. "Organizational Communication: A Structurational Exemplar." In *Rethinking Communication: Paradigm Exemplars.* Edited by Brenda Dervin, Lawrence Grossberg, Barbara O'Keefe, and Ellen Wartella. Beverly Hills, CA: Sage, 1989, pp. 199–212.

Monge, Peter R. "The Network Level of Analysis." In *Handbook of Communication Science.* Edited by Charles R.

Berger and Steven H. Chaffee. Newbury Park, CA: Sage, 1987, pp. 239–270.

Monge, Peter R., and Eisenberg, Eric M. "Emergent Communication Networks." In *Handbook of Organizational Communication: An Interdisciplinary Perspective.* Edited by Frederic M. Jablin, Linda L. Putnam, Karlene H. Roberts, and Lyman W. Porter. Newbury Park, CA: Sage, 1987, pp. 304–342.

Morgan, Gareth. *Images of Organization.* Beverly Hills, CA: Sage, 1986.

Mumby, Dennis K. *Communication and Power in Organizations: Discourse, Ideology, and Domination.* Norwood, NJ: Ablex, 1988.

———. "Critical Organizational Communication Studies: The Next 10 Years." *Communication Monographs* 60 (1993): 18–25.

Pacanowsky, Michael. "Creating and Narrating Organizational Realities." In *Rethinking Communication: Paradigm Exemplars.* Edited by Brenda Dervin, Lawrence Grossberg, Barbara O'Keefe, and Ellen Wartella. Newbury Park, CA: Sage, 1989, pp. 250–257.

Pacanowsky, Michael, and O'Donnell-Trujillo, Nick. "Communication and Organizational Cultures." *Western Journal of Speech Communication* 46 (1982): 115–130.

———. "Organizational Communication as Cultural Performance." *Communication Monographs* 50 (1983): 126–147.

Perrow, Charles. *Complex Organizations: A Critical Essay.* Glenview, IL: Scott, Foresman, 1972.

Poole, Marshall Scott. "Communication and Organizational Climates: Review, Critique, and a New Perspective." In *Organizational Communication: Traditional Themes and New Directions.* Edited by Robert D. McPhee and Phillip K. Tompkins. Beverly Hills, CA: Sage, 1985, pp. 79–108.

Poole, Marshall Scott, and McPhee, Robert D. "A Structurational Analysis of Organizational Climate." In *Communication and Organizations: An Interpretive Approach.* Edited by Linda L. Putnam and Michael E. Pacanowsky. Beverly Hills, CA: Sage, 1983, pp. 195–220.

Richmond, Virginia P., and McCroskey, James C. "Management Communication Style, Tolerance for Disagreement, and Innovativeness as Predictors of Employee Satisfaction: A Comparison of Single-Factor, Two-Factor, and Multiple-Factor Approaches." In *Communication Yearbook 3.* Edited by Dan Nimmo. New Brunswick, NJ: Transaction, 1979, pp. 359–373.

Roberts, Karlene H., and O'Reilly, Charles A. "Organizations as Communication Structures: An Empirical Approach." *Human Communication Research* 4 (1978): 283–293.

Sackmann, Sonja A. "Managing Organizational Culture: Dreams and Possibilities." In *Communication Yearbook 13.* Edited by James Anderson. Newbury Park, CA: Sage, 1990, pp. 114–148.

Sass, James S., and Canary, Daniel J. "Organizational Commitment and Identification: An Examination of Conceptual and Operational Convergence." *Western Journal of Speech Communication* 55 (1991): 275–293.

Simon, Herbert. *Administrative Behavior.* New York: Free Press, 1976.

Taylor, Frederick W. *Principles of Scientific Management.* New York: Harper Brothers, 1947.

Taylor, James R. *Rethinking the Theory of Organizational Communication: How to Read an Organization.* Norwood, NJ: Ablex, 1993.

———. "Shifting from a Heteronomous to an Autonomous Worldview of Organizational Communication: Communication Theory on the Cusp." *Communication Theory* 5 (1995): 1–35.

Taylor, James R., Cooren, Francois, Giroux, Nicole, and Robichaud, Daniel. "The Communicational Basis of Organization: Between the Conversation and the Text." *Communication Theory* 6 (1996): 1–39.

Tompkins, Phillip K., and Cheney, George. "Account Analysis of Organizations: Decision Making and Identification." In *Communication and Organizations: An Interpretive Approach.* Edited by Linda L. Putnam and Michael E. Pacanowsky. Beverly Hills, CA: Sage, 1983, pp. 123–146.

———. "Communication and Unobtrusive Control in Contemporary Organizations." In *Organizational Communication: Traditional Themes and New Directions.* Edited by Robert D. McPhee and Phillip K. Tompkins. Beverly Hills, CA: Sage, 1985, pp. 179–210.

Van Maanen, John, and Barley, Stephen R. "Cultural Organization: Fragments of a Theory." In *Organizational Culture.* Edited by Peter J. Frost and others. Beverly Hills, CA: Sage, 1985, pp. 31–54.

Weber, Max. *The Theory of Social and Economic Organizations.* Translated by A. M. Henderson and Talcott Parsons. New York: Oxford University Press, 1947.

Weick, Carl. *The Social Psychology of Organizing,* 2nd ed. Reading, MA: Addison-Wesley, 1979.

Wert-Gray, Stacia, Center, Candy, Brashers, Dale E., and Meyers, Renee A. "Research Topics and Methodological Orientations in Organizational Communication: A Decade in Review." *Communication Studies* 42 (1991): 141–154.

Chapter 15
Communication and Media

Allor, Martin. "Relocating the Site of the Audience." *Critical Studies in Mass Communication* 5 (1988): 217–233.

Anderson, James A. "Mass Communication Theory and Research: An Overview." In *Communication Yearbook 1.* Edited by Brent Ruben. New Brunswick, NJ: Transaction, 1977, pp. 279–290.

Ball-Rokeach, Sandra J., and Cantor, Muriel G., eds. *Media, Audience, and Social Structure.* Beverly Hills, CA: Sage, 1986.

Ball-Rokeach, Sandra J., and DeFleur, Melvin L. "A Dependency Model of Mass-Media Effects." *Communication Research* 3 (1976): 3–21.

Barker, David, and Timberg, Bernard M. "Encounters with the Television Image: Thirty Years of Encoding Research." In *Communication Yearbook 15.* Edited by Stanley Deetz. Newbury Park, CA: Sage, 1992, pp. 209–238.

Bauer, Raymond. "The Audience." In *Handbook of Communication.* Edited by Ithiel de sola Pool and others. Chicago: Rand McNally, 1973, pp. 141–152.

———. "The Obstinate Audience: The Influence Process from the Point of View of Social Communication." *American Psychologist* 19 (1964): 319–328.

Bauer, R. A., and Bauer, A. H. "America, Mass Society, and Mass Media." *Journal of Social Issues* 16 (1960): 3–66.

Bell, Daniel. "The Theory of Mass Society." *Commentary* (July 1956): 75–83.

Berger, Arthur Asa. *Signs in Contemporary Culture: An Introduction to Semiotics.* Salem, WI: Sheffield, 1989.

Bineham, Jeffery L. "A Historical Account of the Hypodermic Model in Mass Communication." *Communication Monographs* 55 (1988): 230–246.

Biocca, Frank A. "Opposing Conceptions of the Audience: The Active and Passive Hemispheres of Mass Communication Theory." In *Communication Yearbook 11.* Edited by James A. Anderson. Newbury Park, CA: Sage, 1988, pp. 51–80.

Blumler, Jay, and Katz, Elihu, eds. *The Uses of Mass Communication.* Beverly Hills, CA: Sage, 1974.

Boulding, Kenneth. "The Medium Is the Massage." In *McLuhan: Hot and Cool.* Edited by Gerald E. Stearn. New York: Dial, 1967, pp. 56–68.

Brantlinger, Patrick. *Bread and Circuses: Theories of Mass Culture as Social Decay.* Ithaca, NY: Cornell University Press, 1983.

Burrowes, Carl Patrick. "From Functionalism to Cultural Studies: Manifest Ruptures and Latent Continuities," *Communication Theory* 6 (1996): 88–103.

Bryant, Jennings, and Zillmann, Dolf, eds. *Perspectives on Media Effects.* Hillsdale, NJ: Erlbaum, 1986.

Carey, J. W. "Harold Adams Innis and Marshall McLuhan." *Antioch Review* 27 (1967): 5–39.

Carragee, Kevin. "A Critical Evaluation of Debates Examining the Media Hegemony Thesis." *Western Journal of Communication* 57 (Summer 1993): 330–348.

Childs, M., and Reston, J., eds. *Walter Lippmann and His Times.* New York: Harcourt Brace, 1959.

Corcoran, Farrel. "KAL 007 and the Evil Empire: Mediated Disaster and Forms of Rationalization." *Critical Studies in Mass Communication* 3 (1986): 297–316.

Davis, Dennis K., and Baran, Stanley J. *Mass Communication and Everyday Life: A Perspective on Theory and Effects.* Belmont, CA: Wadsworth, 1981.

Davis, Dennis K., and Puckett, Thomas F. N. "Mass Entertainment and Community: Toward a Culture-Centered Paradigm for Mass Communication Research." In *Communication Yearbook 15.* Edited by Stanley Deetz. Newbury Park, CA: Sage, 1992, pp. 3–34.

DeFleur, Melvin L., and Ball-Rokeach, Sandra J. *Theories of Mass Communication.* New York: Longman, 1982.

Eco, Umberto. *A Theory of Semiotics.* Bloomington: Indiana University Press, 1976.

Elliott, Philip. "Uses and Gratifications Research: A Critique and Sociological Alternative." In *The Uses of Mass Communication.* Edited by Jay Blumler and Elihu Katz. Beverly Hills, CA: Sage, 1974, pp. 249–268.

Eulan, Heinz. "The Maddening Methods of Harold D. Lasswell: Some Philosophical Underpinnings." In *Politics, Personality, and Social Science in the Twentieth Century: Essays in Honor of Harold D. Lasswell.* Edited by Arnold A. Rogow. Chicago: University of Chicago Press, 1969, pp. 15–40.

Fiske, John. *Introduction to Communication Studies.* New York: Methuen, 1982.

———. *Reading the Popular.* Winchester, MA: Unwin Hyman, 1989.

———. *Television Culture.* New York: Methuen, 1987.

———. *Understanding Popular Culture.* Winchester, MA: Unwin Hyman, 1989.

Foley, Joseph M. "Mass Communication Theory and Research: An Overview." In *Communication Yearbook 2.* Edited by Brent Ruben. New Brunswick, NJ: Transaction, 1978, pp. 209–214.

Friedson, Eliot. "Communications Research and the Concept of the Mass." In *The Process and Effects of Mass Communication.* Edited by Wilbur Schramm and Donald Roberts. Urbana: University of Illinois Press, 1971, pp. 197–208.

Fry, Donald L., and Fry, Virginia H. "A Semiotic Model for the Study of Mass Communication." In *Communication Yearbook 9.* Edited by Margaret L. McLaughlin. Beverly Hills, CA: Sage, 1986, pp. 443–462.

Gerbner, George. "Advancing on the Path of Righteousness (Maybe)." In *Cultivation Analysis: New Directions in Media Effects Research.* Edited by Nancy Signorielli and Michael Morgan. Newbury Park, CA: Sage, 1990, pp. 249–262.

———. "Mass Media and Human Communication Theory." In *Human Communication Theory.* Edited by Frank E. X. Dance. New York: Holt, Rinehart & Winston, 1967.

Gerbner, George, Gross, Larry, Morgan, Michael, and Signorielli, Nancy. "A Curious Journey into the Scary World of Paul Hirsch." *Communication Research* 8 (1981): 39.

———. "Living with Television: The Dynamics of the Cultivation Process." In *Perspectives on Media Effects.* Edited by Jennings Bryant and Dolf Zillmann. Hillsdale, NJ: Erlbaum, 1986, pp. 17–40.

Gergen, Kenneth J. *The Saturated Self: Dilemmas of Identity in Contemporary Life.* New York: HarperCollins, 1991.

González, Hernando. "Mass Media and the Spiral of Silence: The Philippines from Marcos to Aquino." *Journal of Communication* 34 (1988): 33–48.

Greenberg, Bradley S., and Salwen, Michael B. "Mass Communication Theory and Research: Concepts and Models." In *An Integrated Approach to Communication Theory and Research.* Edited by Michael B. Salwen and Don W. Stacks. Mahwah, NJ: Erlbaum, 1996, pp. 63–78.

Gronbeck, Bruce. "McLuhan as Rhetorical Theorist." *Journal of Communication* 31 (1981): 117–128.

Grossberg, Lawrence. "Strategies of Marxist Cultural Interpretation." *Critical Studies in Mass Communication* 1 (1984): 392–421.

Hagerstrand, Torsten. "Diffusion II: The Diffusion of Innovations." In *International Encyclopedia of the Social Sciences,* vol. 4. Edited by David Sills. New York: Macmillan, 1968.

Hirsch, Paul M. "On Not Learning from One's Own Mistakes: A Reanalysis of Gerbner et al.'s Findings on Cultivation Analysis, Part II." *Communication Research* 8 (1981): 3–38.

———. "The 'Scary World' of the Nonviewer and Other Anomalies: A Reanalysis of Gerbner et al.'s Findings on Cultivation Analysis." *Communication Research* 7 (1980): 404.

Huesca, Robert, and Dervin, Brenda. "Theory and Practice in Latin American Alternative Communication Research." *Journal of Communication* 44 (1994): 53–73.

Innis, Harold Adams. *The Bias of Communication.* Toronto: University of Toronto Press, 1951.

———. *Empire and Communications,* 2nd ed. Toronto: University of Toronto Press, 1972.

Jensen, Klaus Bruhn. "When Is Meaning? Communication Theory, Pragmatism, and Mass Media Reception." In *Communication Yearbook 14.* Edited by James A. Anderson. Newbury Park, CA: Sage, 1991, pp. 3–32.

Katz, Elihu. "The Two-Step Flow of Communication." *Public Opinion Quarterly* 21 (1957): 61–78.

Katz, Elihu, Blumler, Jay, and Gurevitch, Michael. "Uses of Mass Communication by the Individual." In *Mass Communication Research: Major Issues and Future Directions.* Edited by W. Phillips Davidson and Frederick Yu. New York: Praeger, 1974, pp. 11–35.

Katz, Elihu, and Lazarsfeld, Paul. *Personal Influence: The Part Played by People in the Flow of Mass Communications.* New York: Free Press, 1955.

Kincaid, D. Lawrence. "The Convergence Model of Communication." East-West Institute Paper No. 18, Honolulu, 1979.

Kincaid, D. Lawrence, Yum, June Ock, and Woelfel, Joseph. "The Cultural Convergence of Korean Immigrants in Hawaii: An Empirical Test of a Mathematical Theory." *Quality and Quantity* 18 (1983): 59–78.

Klapper, Joseph T. *The Effects of Mass Communication.* Glencoe, IL: Free Press, 1960.

Kornhauser, William. "Mass Society." In *International Encyclopedia of the Social Sciences,* vol. 10. New York: Macmillan, 1968, pp. 58–64.

Lasswell, Harold. "The Structure and Function of Communication in Society." In *The Communication of Ideas.* Edited by Lyman Bryson. New York: Institute for Religious and Social Studies, 1948, pp. 37–51.

Lazarsfeld, Paul, Berelson, Bernard, and Gaudet, H. *The People's Choice.* New York: Columbia University Press, 1948.

Lazarsfeld, Paul, and Merton, Robert K. "Mass Communication, Popular Taste, and Organized Social Action." In *The Process and Effects of Mass Communication.* Edited by Wilbur Schramm and Donald Roberts. Urbana: University of Illinois Press, 1971, pp. 554–578.

Lindlof, Thomas R. "Media Audiences as Interpretive Communities." In *Communication Yearbook 11.* Edited by James A. Anderson. Newbury Park, CA: Sage, 1988, pp. 81–107.

Lippmann, Walter. *Public Opinion.* New York: Macmillan, 1921.

McCombs, Maxwell, and Bell, Tamara. "The Agenda Setting Role of Mass Communication." In *An Integrated Approach to Communication Theory and Research.* Edited by Michael B. Salwen and Don W. Stacks. Mahwah, NJ: Erlbaum, 1996, pp. 93–110.

McLuhan, Marshall. "The Brain and the Media: The 'Western' Hemisphere." *Journal of Communication* 28 (1978): 54–60.

———. "Communication: McLuhan's Laws of the Media." *Technology and Culture* 16 (1975): 74–78.

———. "At the Flip Point of Time—The Point of More Return." *Journal of Communication* 25 (1975): 102–106.

———. *The Gutenberg Galaxy: The Making of Typographic Man.* Toronto: University of Toronto Press, 1962.

———. "Implications of Cultural Uniformity." In *Superculture: American Popular Culture and Europe.* Edited by C. E. E. Bigsby. Bowling Green, OH: Bowling Green University Popular Press, 1975.

———. "Laws and the Media." *Et Cetera* 34 (1977): 173–179.

———. *The Mechanical Bride.* New York: Vanguard, 1951.

———. "Misunderstanding the Media's Laws." *Technology and Culture* 17 (1976): 263.

———. "At the Moment of Sputnik the Planet Became a Global Theatre in Which There Are No Spectators But Only Actors." *Journal of Communication* 24 (1974): 48–58.

———. "The Rise and Fall of Nature." *Journal of Communication* 27 (1977): 80–81.

———. *Understanding Media.* New York: McGraw-Hill, 1964.

———. "The Violence of the Media." *Canadian Forum* (September 1976): 9–12.

McLuhan, Marshall, and Fiore, Quentin. *The Medium Is the Massage.* New York: Bantam, 1967.

McQuail, Denis. "With the Benefits of Hindsight: Reflections on Uses and Gratifications Research." *Critical Studies in Mass Communication* 1 (1984): 177–193.

———. *Mass Communication Theory: An Introduction.* London: Sage, 1987.

Meyrowitz, Joshua. "Images of Media: Hidden Ferment—and Harmony—in the Field." *Journal of Communication* 43 (1993): 55–67.

———. *No Sense of Place: The Impact of Electronic Media on Social Behavior.* New York: Oxford University Press, 1985.

Morgan, Michael, and Shanahan, James. "Two Decades of Cultivation Research: An Appraisal and Meta-Analysis." In *Communication Yearbook 20.* Edited by Brant R. Burleson. Thousand Oaks, CA: Sage, 1997, pp. 1–45.

Neuman, W. R. "The Threshold of Public Opinion." *Public Opinion Quarterly* 54 (1990): 159–176.

Noelle-Neumann, Elisabeth. "The Effect of Media on Media Effects Research." *Journal of Communication* 33 (1983): 157–165.

———. "Return to the Concept of Powerful Mass Media." In *Studies of Broadcasting.* Edited by H. Eguchi and K. Sata. Tokyo: Nippon Hoso Kyokii, 1973, pp. 67–112.

———. *The Spiral of Silence: Public Opinion—Our Social Skin.* Chicago: University of Chicago Press, 1984.

———. "The Theory of Public Opinion: The Concept of the Spiral of Silence." In *Communication Yearbook 14.* Edited by James A. Anderson. Newbury Park, CA: Sage, 1991, pp. 256–287.

Palmgreen, Philip. "Uses and Gratifications: A Theoretical Perspective." In *Communication Yearbook 8.* Edited by Robert N. Bostrom. Beverly Hills, CA: Sage, 1984, pp. 20–55.

Pietilä, Veikko. "Perspectives on Our Past: Charting the Histories of Mass Communication Studies." *Critical Studies in Mass Communication* 11 (1994): 346–361.

Potter, W. James. "Cultivation Theory and Research: A Conceptual Critique." *Human Communication Research* 19 (1993): 564–601.

Protess, David, and McCombs, Maxwell. *Agenda Setting: Readings on Media, Public Opinion, and Policymaking.* Hillsdale, NJ: Erlbaum, 1991.

Rayburn, J. D., II. "Uses and Gratifications." In *An Integrated Approach to Communication Theory and Research.* Edited by Michael B. Salwen and Don W. Stacks. Mahwah, NJ: Erlbaum, 1996, pp. 145–163.

Reese, Stephen D. "Setting the Media's Agenda: A Power Balance Perspective." In *Communication Yearbook 14.* Edited by James A. Anderson. Newbury Park, CA: Sage, 1991, pp. 309–340.

Rogers, Everett M. *Diffusion of Innovations,* 4th ed. New York: Free Press, 1995.

———. *A History of Communication Study: A Biographical Approach.* New York: Free Press, 1994, chaps. 1, 6, 7, 12.

Rogers, Everett M., and Adhikarya, Ronny. "Diffusion of Innovations: An Up-to-Date Review and Commentary." In *Communication Yearbook 3.* Edited by Dan Nimmo. New Brunswick, NJ: Transaction, 1979, pp. 67–82.

Rogers, Everett M., and Dearing, James W. "Agenda-Setting Research: Where Has It Been, Where Is It Going?" In *Communication Yearbook 11.* Edited by James A. Anderson. Newbury Park, CA: Sage, 1988, pp. 555–593.

Rogers, Everett M., and Kincaid, D. Lawrence. *Communication Networks: Toward a New Paradigm for Research.* New York: Free Press, 1981.

Rogers, Everett M., and Shoemaker, F. Floyd. *Communication of Innovations: A Cross-Cultural Approach.* New York: Free Press, 1971.

Rogow, Arnold A., ed. *Politics, Personality, and Social Science in the Twentieth Century: Essays in Honor of Harold D. Lasswell.* Chicago: University of Chicago Press, 1969.

Rosengren, Karl Erik. "Culture, Media, and Society: Agency and Structure, Continuity and Change." In *Media Effects and Beyond: Culture, Socializations, and Lifestyles.* Edited by Karl Erik Rosengren. London: Routledge, 1994, pp. 3–28.

Rosengren, K., Wenner, L., and Palmgreen, P., eds. *Media Gratifications Research: Current Perspectives.* Beverly Hills, CA: Sage, 1985.

Rubin, Alan M. "Audience Activity and Media Use." *Communication Monographs* 60 (1993): 98–105.

Rubin, Alan M., and Windahl, Sven. "The Uses and Dependency Model of Mass Communication." *Critical Studies in Mass Communication* 3 (1986): 186.

Salmon, Charles T., and Glynn, Carroll J. "Spiral of Silence: Communication and Public Opinion as Social Control." In *An Integrated Approach to Communication Theory and Research.* Edited by Michael B. Salwen and Don W. Stacks. Mahwah, NJ: Erlbaum, 1996, pp. 165–180.

Schoening, Gerard T., and Anderson, James A. "Social Action Media Studies: Foundational Arguments and Common Premises." *Communication Theory* 5 (1995): 93–116.

Schwichtenberg, Cathy, ed. *The Madonna Connection: Representational Politics, Subcultural Identities, and Cultural Theory.* Boulder, CO: Westview, 1993.

Sears, David O., and Freedman, Jonathan I. "Selective Exposure to Information: A Critical Review." In *The Process and Effects of Mass Communication.* Edited by Wilbur

Schramm and Donald F. Roberts. Urbana: University of Illinois Press, 1971, pp. 209–234.

Severin, Werner J., and Tankard, James W. *Communication Theories: Origins, Methods, Uses.* New York: Hastings House, 1979.

Shaw, Donald L., and McCombs, Maxwell E. *The Emergence of American Political Issues.* St. Paul, MN: West, 1977.

Shoemaker, Pamela J. "Media Gatekeeping." In *An Integrated Approach to Communication Theory and Research.* Edited by Michael B. Salwen and Don W. Stacks. Mahwah, NJ: Erlbaum, 1996, 79–91.

Signorielli, Nancy. "Television's Mean and Dangerous World: A Continuation of the Cultural Indicators Perspective." In *Cultivation Analysis: New Directions in Media Effects Research.* Edited by Nancy Signorielli and Michael Morgan. Newbury Park, CA: Sage, 1990, pp. 85–106.

Signorielli, Nancy, and Morgan, Michael, eds. *Cultivation Analysis: New Directions in Media Effects Research.* Newbury Park, CA: Sage, 1990.

———. "Cultivation Analysis: Research & Practice." In *An Integrated Approach to Communication Theory and Research.* Edited by Michael B. Salwen and Don W. Stacks. Mahwah, NJ: Erlbaum, 1996, pp. 111–126.

Siune, Karen, and Borre, Ole. "Setting the Agenda for a Danish Election." *Journal of Communication* 25 (1975): 65–73.

Smith, Bruce. "The Mystifying Intellectual History of Harold Lasswell." In *Politics, Personality, and Social Science in the Twentieth Century: Essays in Honor of Harold D. Lasswell.* Edited by Arnold A. Rogow. Chicago: University of Chicago Press, 1969, pp. 41–105.

Sproule, J. Michael. "Progressive Propaganda Critics and the Magic Bullet Myth." *Critical Studies in Mass Communication* 6 (1989): 225–246.

Swanson, David L. "Political Communication Research and the Uses and Gratifications Model: A Critique." *Communication Research* 6 (1979): 36–53.

Swanson, David L., and Babrow, Austin S. "Uses and Gratifications: The Influence of Gratification-Seeking and Expectancy-Value Judgments on the Viewing of Television News." In *Rethinking Communication: Paradigm Exemplars.* Edited by Brenda Dervin, Lawrence Grossberg, Barbara O'Keefe, and Ellen Wartella. Newbury Park, CA: Sage, 1989, pp. 361–375.

Tan, Alexis S. *Mass Communication Theories and Research.* Columbus, OH: Grid, 1981.

Tapper, John. "The Ecology of Cultivation: A Conceptual Model for Cultivation Research." *Communication Theory* 5 (1995): 36–57.

White, Robert. "Mass Communication and Culture: Transaction to a New Paradigm." *Journal of Communication* 33 (1983): 279–301.

Wolfe, Tom. "The New Life Out There." In *McLuhan: Hot and Cool.* Edited by Gerald E. Stearn. New York: Dial, 1967, pp. 34–56.

Wright, Charles R. "Functional Analysis and Mass Communication." *Public Opinion Quarterly* 24 (1960): 605–620.

———. "Mass Communication Rediscovered: Its Past and Future in American Sociology." In *Media, Audience, and Social Structure.* Edited by Sandra J. Ball-Rokeach and Muriel G. Cantor. Beverly Hills, CA: Sage, 1986, pp. 22–33.

Zhu, Jian-Hua, and Blood, Deborah. "Media Agenda-Setting Theory: Telling the Public What to Think About." In *Emerging Theories of Human Communication.* Edited by Branislav Kovacic. Albany: SUNY Press, 1997, pp. 88–114.

Zillmann, Dolf. "Attribution and Misattribution of Excitatory Reactions." In *New Directions in Attribution Research,* vol. 2. Edited by J. H. Harvey, W. J. Ickes, and R. F. Kidd. Hillsdale, NJ: Erlbaum, 1978, pp. 335–368.

CREDITS

AUTHOR INDEX

Subject Index